A Critical Study of Modern Scriptures

A Critical Study of Modern Scriptures

HOLY FABLE
Volume 4

Robert M. Price

PITCHSTONE PUBLISHING
DURHAM, NORTH CAROLINA

Pitchstone Publishing
Durham, NC 27705
www.pitchstonepublishing.com

ISBN 9781634312042

Library of Congress Cataloging-in-Publication Data

Names: Price, Robert M., 1954- author.
Title: A critical study of modern scriptures / Robert M. Price.
Description: Durham, North Carolina : Pitchstone Publishing, [2019] |
 Series: Holy fable ; volume 4 | Summary: "Critical commentaries on a
 wide range of scriptural works either written or rediscovered in modern
 times, including The Book of Mormon, The Gospel According to Thomas, The
 Aquarian Gospel of Jesus the Christ, The Necronomicon, and Jesus Christ
 Superstar"— Provided by publisher.
Identifiers: LCCN 2019016806 (print) | LCCN 2019980872 (ebook) | ISBN
 9781634312042 (pbk. : alk. paper) | ISBN 9781634311953 (epub) | ISBN
 9781634311977 (mobi) | ISBN 9781634311960 (pdf)
Subjects: LCSH: Jesus Christ—Biography—Apocryphal and legendary
 literature. | Christian literature—History and criticism.
Classification: LCC BT520 .P75 2019 (print) | LCC BT520 (ebook) | DDC
 229/.9—dc23
LC record available at https://lccn.loc.gov/2019016806
LC ebook record available at https://lccn.loc.gov/2019980872

For Tom Flynn, who is a Trinity of intelligence, imagination, and wit.

CONTENTS

INTRODUCTION: THE PROBLEM
OF THE CANON AND FURTHER REVELATION

The whole point of a "canon," an official list of scriptures, would seem to be to exclude any further candidates for revelation. A new prophet may come along and announce "I have a new word from God," but if those to whom he speaks have an official canon of revelations, the prophet may expect to receive pretty much the same reply as a writer getting a rejection slip from a publisher: "I'm so sorry, but we already have as many of those as we need!" A canon of scripture, for example, the twenty-seven writings of the New Testament, is rather like the doctrine of the Trinity. Trinitarianism does not so much mean that there are no less than three persons in the Godhead as it means that there can be no more than three. To choose a list of twenty-seven revealed writings is to rule out any proposed number twenty-eight. When Saint Athanasius sent out his Easter Letter in 367 A.D., listing the twenty-seven New Testament documents we still use today, he was not issuing a descriptive statement ("No one uses any others, do they?") but rather a prescriptive statement ("You'd better stop using all the others if you know what's good for you!"). The same thing had happened centuries earlier when the Jewish scribes had announced that the age of revelations had drawn to a close. It's not that no new prophets were coming forward to prophesy, you understand, but that none of them would ever again be given a hearing: "Sorry, pal, but you missed the deadline. Now hit the road!"). From now on there should be no more prophets, only scribes to interpret the old inspired writings. When the Prophet Muhammad died, that was the end of revelation. Thenceforth it would be a matter of jurists extrapolating from the Qur'an to

9

answer new questions as they should arise.

The problem of the canon versus new revelations is a perennial one throughout the history of religion. There is a cycle that repeats itself over and over again: a new prophet proclaims a new revelation. The old guard of the traditional religion refuse to accept it. The new prophet founds his own new religion, but as soon as the new prophet dies, his followers enshrine his revelations as a new canon of scripture. And when an even newer prophet arises with a new and updated revelation to share, he will be in for a rude surprise. He had expected that a new religious community, so recently started, would be open to new revelations. After all, isn't that why they started this religion in the first place? In fact, the new religion immediately becomes as rigid as the old one was, believers hugging to their breasts the new canon of scriptures, the revelation of their founder. The very revelations that had superseded the old have now become the old. The guardians of the new canon are as deaf to the new revelations as the guardians of the old canon had been. And so it starts all over again.

An early, perhaps prototypical, example of this dilemma may be found in the story of Abraham being summoned by God to sacrifice his son Isaac. The New Testament writer of the Epistle to the Hebrews sums up the situation well: "By faith Abraham, when God tested him, offered Isaac as a sacrifice. He who had received the promise was about to sacrifice his one and only son, even though God had said to him, 'Through Isaac shall your promised offspring come'" (Heb. 11:17–18). Abraham had once puzzled over the question of how God could possibly fulfill his promise to give the land of Canaan to Abraham's descendants—when Abraham had as yet no children. His wife was barren, and he himself was nearly a century old. Nonetheless, he believed God and was rewarded with the miraculous birth of a son, Isaac. So God's promise had been a real revelation, and it was corroborated when Isaac was born. That promise was, so to speak, the canon of revelation. We might imagine that, having seen this great revelation, Abraham would have stood by it and refused to listen to what purported to be a new revelation from God to the effect that he ought to go and kill his son! If the first had been true, then the second, which grossly contradicted it, could not possibly be true, could it? Why shouldn't Abraham have discarded it as a false prophecy? It would have made a lot of sense. Wouldn't that response have proven Abraham's faith? That he believed the first revelation had been of God even when what purported to be a new revelation contradicted it? This is the problem of the canon and further revelation in a nutshell.

Our problem is clearly posed in an old Muslim saying: "All other books than the Qur'an are superfluous. If a book agrees with the Qur'an, it is merely redundant; if it doesn't agree with the Qur'an, it is in error." In short, if an established canon of scripture tells you all you need to know, you do not need anything new revealed. And if a supposed new revelation must first be verified by checking it against the canon, then no new revelation can ever be accepted. It could be accepted only if everything in it was already there in the old canon—but then what new has been revealed?

This is why the Gospel of John has the scribes unable to accept Jesus as the Christ—the scriptures don't happen to anticipate any prophet coming from Galilee, and they, being "strict constructionists," don't dare go outside the letter of the law. Many centuries later, we can see the same Catch 22 creating the same mischief in the 1962 Hayward Consultation on Christianity in Africa. They had convened to consider the luxuriant growth of "Aladura" churches, indigenous African churches and denominations which felt free to mix biblical doctrines with traditional African folk belief, ancestor worship, and ritual. The Consultation branded it a "danger" for these new churches to "claim direct revelation from the Spirit not anchored in Scripture." How ironic, considering that Christianity itself began precisely by claiming such new direct revelations and flouting traditional orthodoxies.

There are, I think, certain phenomenological dynamics which help make sense of our dilemma. They will help us understand why some people, faced with the challenge of a new revelation will stick loyally to the traditional canon, whole others will stick their necks out to join with the new faith.

It is absolutely fundamental to get one thing straight: despite the fact that both the canonical scriptures and the new prophetic message are supposed to be revelations, the two have nothing in common. The resemblance is purely superficial and deceptive. This is because the same adjective, "revealed," covers a more important difference between the two that is determined not by definition but by function. The canon is a body of documents that has come to serve as a foundational charter for a particular religious community. One looks back on this revelation to legitimize the present. The revealed canon calls for faithfulness. But a new revelation is a rallying cry to start something new. It is a summons into the future, beyond the past, beyond the present, too. The new revelation calls for faith, a leap of faith into the unknown future. It is safer to stick with the canon, with the divine pedigree of the past; it is more exciting to leap into the future.

So what will happen when a new revelation is offered to the religious community? It all depends on what *kind* of a revelation it is, how much discontinuity there is between it and the traditional revelation. What we might call an *orthodox* revelation is not a revelation of anything really new. If accepted, it will serve merely to reinforce the canon and its teachings, since it is entirely within the bounds of the canonical teachings. For example, I once attended a Catholic Charismatic prayer meeting in Muskegon, Michigan in 1976. A woman arose proclaiming a word from God. In disappointingly prosaic tones she began to try to allay any doubts the group might have as to the propriety of infant baptism! Apparently some had begun to suspect that "believers' baptism" might be more consistent with the conversionistic nature of the Charismatic movement. But this prompted someone to disguise a defense of the traditional party line under the form of a new prophecy! In a similar gathering the same year in Atlantic City I heard several prophetic messages from Christ or the Virgin Mary assuring the assembled pious of God's great love for them personally. Here the point was simply to personalize the abstract doctrine of God's love for the Church. To put a new face on the old belief, pretty much the same job undertaken by a modernizing paraphrase of the Bible, making it speak its old message anew to a new generation.

An *eccentric* revelation (as I like to call them), if taken seriously, will affect only marginal details of orthodox belief. And such marginal modifications one may prudently resolve to keep to oneself. An example would be a Catholic or Fundamentalist who reads Raymond F. Moody's *Life After Life*. This is a book about visionary "near death experiences" which seem to provide proof of life after death, but in terms not very close to traditional biblical depictions of life after death. Tempted by the lure of being able to buttress one's faith with solid data, an individual may silently adjust his belief to something like Moody's, even though it requires him to take some traditional beliefs a bit less than literally. But not that much has changed in any case.

A *predictive* revelation, should the community take it seriously, will at worst cause embarrassment, since by definition it treats only of historical events, not of doctrinal truths. Radio host Harold Camping calculated the date of the return of Christ as scheduled for September of 1994. Many believed him—but were sorry they did once October 1994 rolled around. But the shock was not too severe, the damage easy to control, since Camping had not, after all, "revealed" anything like there being a fourth person in the Trinity. The failure of his "revelation" did not endanger the belief in the Second Advent of Christ; it only made Camping and his fans look pretty silly for jumping the gun. After several embarrassing attempts to predict the return of Christ, the Jehovah's Witnesses sect finally gave up and slightly revised their doctrine. They no longer claim that Christ will return soon. Now they claim only that Christ might return at any moment, so it is best always to be ready, even if it should be another thousand years.

A *really new* revelation (that is, a revelation of something genuinely and significantly new), if taken seriously, can only eventuate in the birth of a new religion from the old. Those who embrace the new revelation will have put themselves beyond the bounds of the traditional religious community, defined as it was by its canonical revelation, its charter. The acceptance of the really new revelation creates a substantially new body of soon-to-be-orthodox belief. Once enough people accepted the Book of Mormon, there had to be a Mormon Church to accommodate them and their new beliefs. Once some ministers received the revelation of the Oneness of the Godhead during an Assemblies of God spiritual retreat, a doctrine most Assemblies ministers did not much fancy, there simply had to be a new church for the new Pentecostal anti-trinitarians: The United Pentecostal Church. When Sun Myung Moon received the revelation of the Divine Principle there was no longer any question of remaining among the ranks of Korean Presbyterians and Pentecostals, and the Unification Church was born. It had to be.

Why is it that in all such cases it is only the sectarian few who will embrace the new revelation offered them, while most will remain comfortably ensconced in familiar spiritual territory? After all, wouldn't one expect even the latter to appreciate the prospect of a new revelation since they are so zealous for the old? Aren't they themselves a group of people who know the value of a revelation, since they so highly prize the old one? Actually not. What the conservatives value in their canonical scripture/creed is not the authority of revelation but the authority of tradition. A traditional revelation provides an epistemological excuse for remaining loyal to one's own religious community rather than considering another. "Oh, sure, their religion sounds reasonably nice, but ours is revealed by God!"

But isn't it a matter of importance to them that their founder did in his day challenge the established orthodoxy? Yes, but it does not lead them to venerate present or future heretics of the same kind. No, the heretical character of the founder (in other words, his transcending the bounds of the orthodoxy of religion in his day) is in retrospect considered an excuse for the founder's own opportunistic manipulation of the parent tradition and its scriptures. It was a "progressive revelation," whereby believers in the canonical revelation might extend their community's pedigree even farther into the past, co-opting the ancient challengers of their faith as well as safeguarding themselves against new challengers.

For Paul to cite the Old Testament in favor of new views no Jew had ever heard of was to co-opt the Jewish canon for his own polemical use, to undercut the traditionalists of his own day by using their own pedigree against them. Justin Martyr similarly quoted Jewish scripture in his debate with Trypho the Jew. He says he will quote "your own scriptures" to prove Christian doctrine, but then has second thoughts and corrects himself: "or rather, our scriptures, since they are not yours anymore." Thus Paul and Justin would make it appear that the old guard are themselves the innovators since they have gone off the track in rejecting the new revelation which the old scriptures had anticipated! "You search the scriptures, for in them you imagine you have eternal life. And yet it is they which testify of me, and you refuse to come to me to have eternal life" (John 5:39–40). In short, the pride taken in the radical character of their founder serves to protect the religion against the challenge of the prior, parent religion as well as the challenges of today's new rivals who seek to supersede their religion in precisely the same way theirs had superseded and co-opted the old. Of course, that is exactly what the guardians of the previous order were doing in their allegiance to the old canon of their day.

But it didn't work. It never works. New religions emerge from the old by the process of sectarian mitosis: growth by splitting. Christians still claim to have the true understanding of the Jewish scriptures, and thus to have superseded them, because their founder Jesus was a prophet like unto those who had written the old Jewish scriptures. But Christians just as keenly resist the polemical-evangelistic assaults of those newer religions which seek to supersede and co-opt Christianity in the same way Christianity superseded and co-opted Judaism (or tried to). Muslims, Moonies, Mormons, all claim possession of a new book of divine oracles which "fulfills" and thus supersedes the New Testament just as the New Testament was once said to fulfill and supersede the Old Testament.

We can, then, understand why the old, established revelation exerts a strong hold on most of its members, enabling them to spurn the invitation extended by a new prophet. We still need to explain why some few are willing to jump ship and go over to the new kid in town, the new revelation, the new religion. Now we can see why it is even more remarkable for anyone to be willing to do this, in view of the great security provided by allegiance to a religion with a venerable pedigree. A really new revelation, unlike a traditional authority, must stand on its own two feet, be accepted newly and freshly, without the solid believability of tradition, the status quo. It involves much more of a risk than it does to remain loyal to the taken-for-granted authority of tradition. What kind of person is willing to breathe the rarefied air he will find out there far beyond the safety of the tried-and-true?

There will always be within the old religious community an element that is already, like the prophet of the new revelation (who may even have emerged from their own ranks), dissatisfied with the old tradition anyway. Thus they are already in the market for something new to come along. The new prophet finds a welcome among the like-minded who had kept mum about their dissatisfactions until he appears to give them voice. Muhammad had apparently belonged to a group of seekers after a simple Abrahamic faith, who then became his first converts. The Buddha's first disciples were the ascetics among whom he had once lived in a common quest to transcend the ritualistic charades of the old Vedic system. Joseph Smith, confused, like many of his contemporaries, at the plethora of competing revivalistic churches in the Burned Over District, prays to be shown which sect to join, and the angel Moroni tells him instead to found his own sect, restoring the pristine truth of the gospel.

Other members of the established religion are not dissatisfied with it, but they will have been led by their tradition to expect a genuinely new development. Most members will no longer take such anticipations or predictions seriously, satisfied as they are with the familiar and the comfortable, but in the case of the relative few who do expect something new, the tradition has managed to work itself out of a job. It paved the way for its own suppression, at least as far as the forward-looking minority is concerned.

Jesus, for instance, gains his first adherents from the circle of John the Baptist, a Jew already preaching in anticipation of some new revelation about to dawn. The Bab (Mirza Hussein Ali) was first embraced by members of the Sheykhi sect who were already primed for the appearance of the Hidden Imam. All Shiites would have claimed to be eagerly expecting the advent of the Hidden Imam, but their violent reaction to the proclamation of the Bab showed how far they were from welcoming anything new. Sun Myung Moon, adherent of an apocalyptic Pentecostal group expecting a new Korean messiah, receives the revelation that he is to teach the Divine Principle, in order to pave the way for the new messiah, or else to become that new messiah himself.

And, again, once the new prophet establishes his own religious community, once his revelations become a new canon, it is highly unlikely that any subsequent new revelation will be accepted. After the initial formative period, the vested interests some have in preserving the new order, the new orthodoxy, will prevail and cause the whole cycle to begin again. This is why the New Prophecy of Montanus, Maximilla, and Priscilla was repudiated by the increasingly defensive hierarchy of the consolidating Catholic Church. This is why Joseph Smith, daring new prophet, felt entitled to silence the voices of even newer prophets in the fledgling Mormon community, issuing the decree that, henceforth, new revelations would come only from himself.

I saw this dynamic reenacted in the Atlantic City Catholic Charismatic conclave mentioned above. The vast convention hall was filled with delegates from countless local prayer groups, each with a prophet or two on hand for the festivities. Charismatic prophets can be expected to stand up and speak in the average Charismatic prayer session. But this one was so big, and the potential prophetic speakers such an unknown quantity, that the planners of the event had issued the regulation that anyone wishing to approach the microphone with a divine utterance had first to submit their oracle to a select magisterium seated in a bank of folding chairs called (with perfect leaden bureaucratic prose) the "Word Gifts Unit"! Paul was already beginning to rein in the spontaneity of the Spirit that bloweth where it listeth when he stipulated that each Corinthian prophet must speak in turn and then wait for the other prophets to give their reviews on his words. Prophecy is being domesticated by the establishment rule-makers in favor of their canon of established, traditional authority. It always happens.

Some subsequent prophets will try to smuggle their own revelations into the community by putting the name of some old and venerable prophet on their own new prophecy, passing off their own revelation as a neglected and rediscovered revelation from the founder. If such a prophet succeeds in this, he may actually wind up causing real change within the established religion, as did a medieval Neo-Platonic mystic posing as Dionysius the Areopagite, a biblical character and convert of the Apostle Paul (Acts 17:34). Thanks to his pious fraud, something very much like nondualist Vedanta Hinduism was able to take root in Catholic Christianity, providing a safety zone for Christian mystics who would otherwise have been recognized as departing from the orthodox norm in a heretical direction. Heresy had been smuggled into the fortress of orthodoxy in the Trojan Horse of the Pseudo-Dionysius. In precisely the same fashion, Gnostic elements had infiltrated Judaism by means of pseudepigrapha attributed to ancient patriarchs of Israel (the Apocalypse of Adam, the Revelation of the Great Seth, etc.)

But other prophets will dare to speak in their own names, believing that a real prophecy will ring true by its own authority, at least for those who have ears to hear. And since there will always be diehard loyalists to oppose the new "heresy," the hearers receptive to the new revelation will have no choice but to set up shop on their own. And thus another new religion begins. And no sooner does the community lay the first wreath on the tomb of their own founding prophet than they start work on the construction of new tombs for any future prophets who may come along to stir up trouble.

* * *

The title of this book is *A Critical Study of Modern Scriptures*. Obviously, from this one would expect *Holy Fable Volume 4* to feature discussions only of works stemming from modern times. Thus, the inclusion of the Gospel according to Thomas might seem inappropriate. Let me explain why it is not. The Gospel of Thomas, though quite ancient (first or second century C.E.) was long lost, rediscovered only in 1945 and published in translation some years later. In effect, as an additional gospel, it would seem to qualify as a modern scripture, albeit it in a slightly different sense.

The Aquarian Gospel of Jesus the Christ appeared in 1908, offered by its author, Leo ("Levi") Dowling as a channeled revelation, with him as the privileged channeler. It purported to be a new revelation appropriate to the then-dawning Age of Aquarius.

The Book of Mormon, supposedly a collection of ancient American records, was said by its "discoverer," Joseph Smith, to have been a channeled revelation by a unique means. Smith claimed the Book of Mormon was, like the Bible, a canon of ancient Judaeo-Christian writings, written by ordinary men, probably unaware of being divinely inspired. In this respect the Book of Mormon is not like, e.g., *The Urantia Book*, *A Course in Miracles*, or *The Aquarian Gospel*, which had not existed as a text before it was channeled mediumistically. The Book of Mormon (according to Joseph Smith) had existed for centuries before he himself translated it from golden plates inscribed in the "Reformed Egyptian" tongue. There is no such language, ancient or modern, from which to translate. But Smith said he had translated the golden plates by looking into his hat, focused on a "seer stone" which miraculously conveyed the meaning of the text, word by word. Thus it does come down to channeling. It all came to birth in his head. We might compare Joseph Smith's revelation with that of the Prophet Muhammad who believed he was taking dictation from the Angel Gabriel who was reading off the text from the Heavenly Book, the pre-existent Koran.

The *Necronomicon*, or *Al-Azif*, is the invention of fiction writer H.P. Lovecraft. He frequently referred to it and infrequently quoted from it in his stories, e.g., "The Dunwich Horror." It is ostensibly an Arabic work of the eighth century. Lovecraft even composed a publication history of the book. He explained that, in order to render a fiction convincing to the reader, one must employ the ingenuity required if one were actually attempting a hoax. He did his work too well, because many readers back in the 20s and 30s were in fact convinced the *Necronomicon* really existed. Despite his attempts to disabuse his fans, many of them still persist in believing there was, and is, a real *Necronomicon*. A number have written up their own versions, some passed off as the real thing, though none is. For those acolytes the *Necronomicon* is and functions as a modern scripture. But to these (mostly dreadfully silly and or boring) books I devote no attention here. Instead I have followed Lovecraft's lead and produced a tongue-in-cheek commentary on the passages composed as parts of horror tales by Lovecraft as well as subsequent writers in his tradition.

Jesus Christ Superstar makes no pretense of being either an ancient work or a revered scripture. It is instead a kind of midrash on the canonical gospels, primarily John. In this respect it represents an ancient literary genre, the exposition of a scriptural text via rewriting it. Furthermore, it has, from the rock opera's initial performance, functioned in a manner analogous to a scripture, inspiring and encouraging multitudes of eager listeners, many of them hitherto alienated from the Christian orthodoxies in which they were raised, but which had paled on them. They made the words of lyricist Tim Rice's Jesus their own: "I look for truth but find that I get damned."

1 THE AQUARIAN GOSPEL OF JESUS THE CHRIST

The Fate of the Mustard Seed

In what is probably the earliest gospel, Mark, we find a parable that has provided the focus of much scholarly scrutiny for some nineteen centuries. It is the parable of the Mustard Seed. Here it is: "And he said, 'How may we liken the kingdom of God? Or in what parable may we place it? As a grain of mustard which, when one sows it on the ground, is smaller than all the seeds on the earth, but, once it germinates, comes up and becomes greater than all the herbs and makes great branches so that the birds of the sky are able to find lodging in its shadow'" (Mark 4:30–32). One of the most influential interpretations of the parable is that it was meant to provide encouragement and comfort in the face of disappointed expectations. It presupposes that Jesus has been proclaiming, predicting, the impending end of the world as we know it, the dawn of a new world of salvation. And many have flocked to his banner, eager to leave the clinging bands of the old order behind: debts, aches and pains, political domination, etc. But it has been a while and the sky has not rolled up like a window shade. The angels have not carried the judgment throne of the Almighty to earth to convene court. Satan has not been bound and cast into the bottomless shaft. In short, despite some admittedly exciting faith healings, things continue to go on, in the same old circles as before. Disciples are beginning to wonder. Are they the avant garde of a new age, or merely one more eccentric sect? If this is the presupposed scenario, the point of the parable would seem to be to urge Jesus' followers not to give up hope. The impressive growth of the mustard plant will not occur without a preliminary period of planting the seed and waiting for it to sprout. And during that time, it seems a watched pot that will never boil. But Jesus assures his hearers that it will. The world that his sectarian followers cherish in the kingdom of their minds will break forth, inescapably, unambiguously, in due time. Rome was not built in a day, and it will take more than a day for it to fall.

The point of the parable is much like that of Nietzsche's parable of the Mad Man in *The Gay Science*. He enters the village breathlessly, announcing to a crowd of idlers and hecklers that "God is dead!" His news does not register, whereupon he concludes, "I come too soon!" Even the nova of the farthest star takes measured minutes, perhaps years, to reach the earth at the speed of light. And so even the death knell of the deity is not yet heard. The world ended this morning, yet all goes on as business as usual. The only difference is the easily-missed addition of a small flock of fanatics on the far edge of perception.

Ever since, years ago, I stumbled upon Edgar J. Goodspeed's fascinating book, *Strange New Gospels* (also called *Famous Biblical Hoaxes*), I have been intrigued with modern contributions to the gospel genre, many of them claiming to be newly discovered ancient texts deserving a place in the scriptural canon, others admitting their recent minting and billing themselves as new revelations for a new age and a new world. One wonders if their authors expected their gospels to catch fire and catalyze a new era. If so, they soon faced the same disappointment that led to the parable of the Mustard Seed. Some of these prophets might have been lucky enough to found a short-lived sect to play-act the coming of the new world in their midst, the mirror-image of those who like to invoke the past in their own circle, playing at Civil War reenactment or medieval jousting in a theme-restaurant. More likely, their books managed to sell some copies in New Age book stores, finding shelf space in the store or in the customers' homes alongside many other equivalent, cheaply-bound revelations. As a voice in a chorus, the prophet's, the evangelist's voice would be muddied and drowned, finally becoming one more disk in a spiritual record collection. As near as I can tell, this was the fate of *The Aquarian Gospel of Jesus the Christ* (1908) by Levi Dowling. It did manage to generate a sect, the Aquarian Christine Church, but many more have read (or at least bought) the book, with its interesting tales of Jesus traveling through Asia.

Levi's Truth

Leo Dowling (1844–1911) was a teen-age preacher, then a Disciples of Christ pastor, army chaplain and medical man. He "channeled" this gospel daily between 2 and 6 am, drawing, as he believed, upon the Akashic Records, an etheric deposit preserving all past events. He believed that the Father-Mother God had sent the third person of their trinity, the Son or Christ, the Manifestation of Love, to every inhabited planet at the commencement of every age. Jesus was the Christ-Manifestation for the dawn of the Piscean Age, and (he implies) Leo Dowling himself is the Christ for the Aquarian Age (7:26), bearing a new gospel fitting the more advanced spiritual sensibilities of that Age. Each individual Christ is a righteous individual prepared to serve as host to the Christ-Spirit through many reincarnations of spiritual perfecting. The result appears to approximate Nestorian "two-person" Christology.

Dowling's pseudonym, "Levi," may denote his mediatorial function, the bringer of the new gospel to the world, thus a priestly task. Specifically, his visionary journeys make the name appropriate, in light of the ancient pseudepigraphon *The Testament of Levi* in which Levi, the priestly progenitor and son of Jacob, travels to heaven and receives revelations.

Did the Age of Aquarius, once so highly touted during the Sixties, ever come? Was anyone even sure when it was *supposed* to come? We are already, in these questions, mired in an ambiguity ill-befitting the breathless revelations of Levi Dowling and his evangel. The world is not transformed, nor is it clear that universal acceptance of Dowling's gospel would have or could have transformed it. But it is a fascinating work in many ways. I doubt that *The Aquarian Gospel* ever received quite the vogue enjoyed in the 1990s by another new Jesus revelation, Helen Schucman's *A Course in Miracles*. And the disparity is astonishing given the contrast between the two books as literary objects. Schucman's alleged channelings from the ascended Son of God constitute a seemingly endless desert of turgid, numbing prose. By contrast, Dowling's *Aquarian Gospel* is an impressive work, composed in alternating iambic pentameter and hexameter, like Shakespeare. (I am presenting the longer excerpts here with appropriate line breaks.) Though this technique inevitably embellishes the wording, the *Aquarian Gospel* still manages to keep to a spare, quasi-scriptural style.

What sort of religion does the Aquarian Evangel promote as the Christian faith for the new era? The religion recommended here is that of pragmatic, rational moralism, coupled with basic New Thought. It spreads its net to include reincarnation (95:38) because of that doctrine's rationalistic calculus of debt and repayment: it is a rationalistic theodicy. According to its almost too-neat system, there is no innocent suffering, since even the infant born with AIDS may still be judged, as John Calvin did, a "little serpent in the crib," bearing the burden of sins committed in unremembered previous lives. One need not recall them or the sins committed in them, any more than the Freudian patient need remember his supposedly deep-buried hatred for his father. It is a postulate of the system. As I say, a bit *too* neat. But that counts for a great deal when one places a high premium on "pure reason" in religion.

The Aquarian Evangel, in all its populist common sense, hates liturgical pomp and finery: "When men array themselves in showy garbs to indicate that they are servants of the gods, and strut about like gaudy birds to be admired by men, because of piety or any other thing, the Holy One must surely turn away in sheer disgust" (35:9). This is a match for Fellini's hilarious "ecclesiastical fashion show" in his film *Roma*. Naturally, this antipathy is not alien to the more familiar gospels. Matthew has Jesus lambaste the Pharisees in such terms: "They widen the phylacteries across their foreheads, and they lengthen the fringes of their prayer shawls" (Matthew 23:5). Is such finery mere ostentation? Those who cultivate it see it as "the beauty of holiness." Those who do not are perhaps lower-class, anti-aristocratic, anti-artistic sectarians. And Dowling's Jesus seems to be balancing the same chip on his mighty shoulder.

We can also detect a significant interest in non-Christian faiths and a sense of being accountable for what to make of them, an anxiety not unlike that of Schleiermacher[1] and other Liberal Protestant theologians who, in their own way, were occupied with the same challenge Levi Dowling struggled with. Like Schleiermacher, Dowling can no longer simply take Christian distinctiveness for granted; he must give the other faiths a fair shake with an open mind and heart. The clearest signal that Dowling thinks we must learn from other faiths is that he depicts his Jesus learning from them. But Dowling, unlike most of his readers in our day, was no New Age syncretist. He does come quite close to identifying Jesus Christ and Gautama Buddha as co-avatars, but Dowling's Jesus remains, as for Schleiermacher and for Paul Tillich,[2] the final rule of judgment for all religions as well as Christianity. At the same time, as I read him, Dowling is motivated in this consideration by something older than the theologies of Schleiermacher and the Neo-Orthodox Tillich. Dowling is, once again, a religious rationalist of the old school, and the gospel he has his Jesus expound is the universally valid religion of the Enlightenment, a generally Kantian "religion within the limits of reason alone." Natural religionists[3] of the eighteenth century, like the Deists, held that God had created the human brain in all places and times with insight sufficient to discern right and wrong, and that only the gratuitous embellishments of self-worshipping priestcraft had obscured that moral clarity, and largely by elevating competing and ill-founded dogmas as more important than the morality all agreed on. From that poison seed spouted sectarian strife and religious warfare. Fully in accord with this commonsense stripping-down, Dowling's Jesus torpedoes establishment Christianity, subverting its doctrines, but also condemns similar sins when committed by Zoroastrians, Hindus, Buddhists, and others whom he encounters on his Asian tour. Pointedly unlike Notovitch's wandering Jesus, the Jesus of the Aquarian Gospel sought less to drink from the fountain of the Asian faiths than to purify their tainted springs. His mission was more to teach than to learn.

Giving the Aquarian Gospel Its Due

My goal is to highlight the intricate use of gospel and other biblical materials by Levi Dowling, employing the methods of the classical Higher Criticism, specifically form and redaction criticism. These tools are appropriate because, as we shall have abundant occasion to see, the evangelist Levi has very, very often rewritten the Bible. After all, it is a new version of the Jesus story he means to tell, not that of some new savior altogether, so there is going to be a great deal of overlap. At the same time, however, Dowling's book *is* supposed to be a new revelation in its own right; thus it has to have something to say. And the surest way to accomplish this goal, the telling of new truth through an old story, is to rewrite that old story to make it into a new one. And the present volume is a modest attempt to think Levi Dowling's thoughts after him, to trace his editorial, theological hand as he composes, alters, and reinscribes. This is just the way we study, say, the Gospel of Matthew, detecting through careful comparisons how and why he changed his base document, the Gospel of Mark. Having the source before us, it is not too difficult to ferret out the reasons for the changes. That is true of *The Aquarian Gospel* and its major sources, which are the four canonical gospels plus Nicholas

Notovitch's fiction (offered to the public as fact), *The Unknown Life of Jesus Christ* in which the savior traveled the length and breadth of Asia before embarking on his Galilean and Jerusalem ministries.

I feel sure that by now it will be apparent to every reader that in no way do I propose to write an expose of Levi Dowling's latter-day gospel. No, not for a moment. While I accord the text no particular authority beyond being fascinating and offering some gems worth pondering, I respect it and seek here to expound it with the methods scholars have used to illuminate the fine print of the Bible. I can think of no higher respect to pay to the text.

Christology in the Aquarian Age

A gospel is by definition a statement of some sort concerning Jesus Christ, or, as the title of this one specifies, "Jesus *the* Christ," implying that Jesus is one thing, Christ another. Jesus the Christ would mean, and be, Jesus the Anointed One. Jesus who bears a peculiar dignity and responsibility. The New Testament Christians heaped titles upon him, calling him not only the Christ, but also the Son of God, Son of Man, Lord, Savior, Logos, even God. Any such title, together with its implications, creates a Christology, a doctrine or an understanding of Jesus. And in this chapter I want to reconstruct the Aquarian understanding of Jesus as the Christ. Levi's text does not spell it out in a systematic way, but there are a number of pretty explicit statements that enable us to fill out a colorful picture. It is important first to grasp that the theology of Levi Dowling is derived from, or at least closely parallels, that of the New Thought movement which began as one of several "mind over matter" movements in the nineteenth century, born from the same womb as Christian Science, the brainchild of Phineas Parker Quimby and Mary Baker Eddy. It gave rise to religious organizations including the Unity School of Christianity and the Church of Religious Science.

At the base of all these variations was a common "Panentheistic" theology. This philosophy, one major step removed from Pantheism, posits that all is God, and one with God. Unlike Monism (non-dualism), for both Pantheism and Panentheism, the infinite variety of things, objects, and people in the world are all quite real and by no means illusions, unlike the verdict rendered by Monists, for whom all apparent diversity is illusory and serves only to mask the Divine from our unenlightened eyes. No, for Pantheists and Panentheists all things are real, but their reality is that of God. All things are not *masks obscuring* God but rather *faces revealing* him. The trick is to recognize God in all those manifestations. The difference between Pantheism (such as that of the ancient Stoics or of Spinoza) and Panentheists (such as Kabbalists, Qualified Nondualist [Visistadvaita Vedanta] Hindus, and today's Process theologians) is that, for the former, there simply is no personal deity. The Godhead is infinite and beyond definition. It cannot exist over against other realities, for there can be none. For the latter, it is not difficult to imagine that one of the many forms into which the divine essence has poured Itself is that of a personal deity over and above the world. Panentheists tend to think of God as the soul of the world and the world as the body of God.

The New Thought movement seems to teeter between Pantheism and Panentheism, and occasionally even toward Monism. This last is when they borrow an element from Christian Science, trying to be healed of disease by reminding themselves that they are really God, and God cannot be sick. That surely implies that illness symptoms are illusions incompatible with divinity. Again, often New Thought people lean in the direction of Pantheism, speaking of the cosmos as a system of spiritual and natural laws, a kind of Logos-structure, that one may manipulate in one's favor. This one may do by realizing and asserting one's own divine nature. From there on in, whether or not one is a Panentheist depends largely on whether one wishes to retain personalistic prayer and worship, keeping one foot in traditional orthodox Theism. One need not condemn all this as inconsistent. It would be better to say it is a case of a living reality (New Thought spirituality) that is too large and lively to be neatly deposited into a single box. Life is larger than the categories in which we would prefer to capture it.

As Levi Dowling depicts him, Jesus was a paradigm case of the God-man unity that exists, at least latently, in every human being. The difference between Jesus and the run of mankind is that he awakened to his divine character and began to draw upon the power to which it entitled him. The self-imposed limitations of unbelief and of low, worldly expectations stifle any expression of the inherent divinity in the rest of us. What Jesus was, we all can be, will be.

The Christological framework here is essentially that of Friedrich Schleiermacher, the father of Liberal theology, who insisted that, to have been truly incarnate, truly human, Jesus must have possessed and exercised divinity in a manner entirely compatible with his genuine humanity. Thus he cannot have owed his exceptional power and wisdom to an infusion of divinity that would have rendered him some sort of Superman. That would make him a mythical demigod, and nothing for us realistically to aspire to. Jesus "was God incarnate" in the sense that he was filled with God-consciousness,[4] ever mindful of his divine source and nature. Everyone could be this way, but all allow themselves to become preoccupied with worldly matters. In one sense Jesus was not unique: others can do what he did. In another sense, he was unique, not merely a way-shower. He became a living force, by virtue of the passing on of his gospel portrait preached in church. The preaching of Jesus as he appears in the gospel, in the atmosphere of the Christian community, enkindles in the believer an experience like that of Jesus himself, at least to some increased degree. So Jesus is the Redeemer as well as our example. It is a subtle and impressive Christology. It should be no surprise to find the same outlines in *The Aquarian Gospel* since New Thought, from which it draws, was itself inspired by Ralph Waldo Emerson and the New England Transcendentalists, and they were in turn the American children of Schleiermacher.

The Aquarian Christ admits that his power is great, but in the very next breath he diverts attention from himself to his hearers, who may reflect him as he reflects God, if only they will: "What I have done all men can do, and what I am all men shall be" (178:46). Before the cross, he announces, "What I have done all men can do. And I am now about to demonstrate the power of man to conquer death; for every man is God made flesh" (163:36–37). See also 176:19, where the Risen Jesus issues the Aquarian version of the Great Commission: "I go my way, but you shall go to all the world and preach the gospel of the omnipotence of men, the power of truth, the resurrection of the dead."

Jesus, as Jesus, deserves no worship at all. Like numerous New Testament characters, he repudiates the very idea, here in the course of a denunciation of Hindu idolatry. Chapter 26 finds the pilgrim Jesus watching the approach of one of the great ritual vehicles transporting an image of the god Krishna, or Jagganath.[5] (We derive our word "juggernaut," an unstoppable engine of destruction, from these huge-wheeled wagons, beneath the wheels of which fanatical worshippers used to throw themselves as sacrifices.)

> One day a car of Jagganath was hauled
> along by scores of frenzied men,
> and Jesus said, "Behold, a form
> without a spirit passes by;

a body with no soul;
a temple with no altar fires.
This car of Krishna is an empty thing,
for Krishna is not there.
This car is but an idol of
a people drunk on wine of carnal things.
God lives not in the noise of tongues;
there is no way to him from any idol shrine.
God's meeting place with man is in the heart,
and in a still small voice he speaks;
and he who hears is still."
And all the people said, "Teach us
to know the Holy One who speaks
within the heart, God of the still small voice."
And Jesus said, "The Holy Breath
cannot be seen with mortal eyes;
nor can men see the Spirits of
the Holy One; but in their image man
was made, and he who looks into the face
of man, looks at the image of the God
who speaks within. And when
man honors man he honors God,
And what man does for man, he does
for God. And you must bear in mind
that when man harms in thought, or word
or deed another man, he does
a wrong to God. If you would serve
the God who speaks within the heart,
just serve your near of kin, and those
that are no kin, the stranger at your gates,
the foe who seeks to do you harm;
assist the poor, and help the weak;
do harm to none, and covet not
what is not yours. Then, with your tongue
the Holy One will speak; and he
will smile behind your tears, will light
your countenance with joy, and fill
your hearts with peace."
And then the people asked.
"To whom shall we bring gifts?

Where shall we offer sacrifice?"
And Jesus said, "Our Father-God
asks not for needless waste of plant,
of grain, of dove, of lamb.
That which you burn on any shrine
you throw away. No blessings can
attend the one who takes the food
from hungry mouths to be destroyed by fire.
When you would offer sacrifice
unto our God, just take your gift
of grain, or meat and lay it on
the table of the poor. From it
an incense will arise to heaven,
which will return to you with blessedness.
Tear down your idols; they can hear you not;
turn all your sacrificial altars into fuel for flames.
Make human hearts your altars, burn
your sacrifices with the fire of love."
And all the people were entranced,
and would have worshiped Jesus as a God;
but Jesus said, "I am your brother man
just come to show the way to God;
you shall not worship man; praise God, the Holy One."

Here is a fine specimen of the same rationalist ridicule of idolatry we find in the Second Isaiah (Isaiah 44:9–20). It is, of course, a rationalism that stops short of turning its guns on religion *per se* as a superstition. In short, it is the religious rationalism of the Deists and Natural Religionists which has influenced Levi Dowling at other points, too. That Enlightenment piety shows itself as well in the disdain for wasting money on religious mummery that could have been spent for the poor, even though this point clashes with the canonical gospels (Mark 14:3–9).

Even miracles are not, as in traditional apologetics, signs pointing to the glory of Christ himself, but only to that to which Jesus himself points: "He was transfigured that the men of earth might see the possibilities of man" (129:14).

The Method and the Messiah

How did Jesus attain unto his exalted office as the revelation of divine humanity? It is important to know, for, in the nature of the case, the rest of us must do the same thing if we wish to gain the same goal.

> The greatest mystery of all times
> lies in the way that Christ lives in the heart.
> Christ cannot live in clammy dens
> of carnal things. The seven battles
> must be fought, the seven victories
> won before the carnal things,
> like fear, and self, emotions and
> desire, are put away. When this
> is done the Christ will take posses-
> sion of the soul; the work is done,
> and man and God are one. (59:10–12)

These words remind us of a similar passage from another modern gospel, perhaps the greatest of them, Nikos Kazantzakis's *The Last Temptation of Christ*:

> Struggle between the flesh and the spirit, reconciliation and submission, and finally—the supreme purpose of the struggle—union with God: this was the ascent taken by Christ, the ascent which he invites us to take as well, following in his bloody tracks. This is the Supreme Duty of the man who struggles—to set out for the lofty peak which Christ, the first-born son of salvation, attained.[6]

The Gospel speaks typically of the Christ potential in every person:

> And Jesus said,
> "I cannot show the king, unless
> you see with eyes of soul, because
> the kingdom of the king is in the soul.
> And every soul a kingdom is.
> There is a king for every man.
> This king is love, and when this love
> becomes the greatest power in life,

it is the Christ; so Christ is king.
And every one may have this Christ
dwell in his soul, as Christ dwells in
my soul." (71:4–7)

"And when he rises to the plane
of Christine consciousness, he knows
that he himself is king, is love, is Christ,
and so is son of God." (71:16)

The emphasis is off of Jesus Christ in this gospel and on the reader, since Jesus came to initiate humanity as a whole into Christhood. "Christ" means "the Anointed," but in this work it has come to mean "the Anointing." Anyone can receive it, and thus anyone can become the, or a, Christ.

Jesus comes to bring the saviour of the world to men;
Love is the saviour of the world.
And all who put their trust in Christ,
and follow Jesus as a pat-
tern and a guide, have everlasting life. (79:16–17)

Such occasional seeming demotions of Jesus from the focus of Christian worship means not to denigrate Jesus but rather to regain the focus on Jesus' desire to pass the anointing on to us. "Christ is not a man. The Christ is universal love, and Love is king" (68:11).
    Again,

"I am the lamp; Christ is the oil
of life; the Holy Breath the fire.
Behold the light! and he who follows me shall not walk in the dark,
but he shall have the light of life." (135:4)

Jesus is the bearer of the anointing, and he bears it for others. He is rather like the candle flame in the Buddhist parable which seeks to illustrate reincarnation as the sequential lighting of each candle in a series by the flame of the one before it. "I am the candle of the Lord aflame to light the way" (72:31). Jesus can even speak of himself in terms suggesting he senses the presence of the Christ as a distinct entity within him, the "sin" of the old Nestorian Christology:

> "He who believes in me and in
> the Christ whom God has sent,
> may drink the cup of life, and from
> his inner parts shall streams of li-
> ving waters flow" (134:3).

His disciple Martha already understood this, that Jesus was not identical with that which he modeled: "And Martha said, 'Lord, I believe that you are come to manifest the Christ of God'" (148:19, rewriting John 11:27).

The Aquarian Jesus is made to speak with the bitter wisdom of twentieth-century hindsight when he predicts what will happen in his name because people will have misunderstood his role as central, not as instrumental: "because of me, the earth will be baptized in human blood" (113:14b; cf. Luke 12:49). But perhaps it is not the fault of poor mankind. Perhaps it must recoil from the revelation: "Behold, the light may be so bright that men cannot see anything" (107:18).

The Aquarian Christology might be Pantheistic, given all these statements, but does it go far enough for us to be able to classify it under the rubric of New Thought? Indeed it does. We do find occasional boasts that, being one with Divine Reason and realizing it, one can move mountains at a word: "The greatest power in heaven and earth is thought" (84:22–28). Not faith, as in Mark 12:22–24, but *thought*. And there is the New Thought emphasis on wishing a thing and exercising divine power to get it, which strikes some as magical: "What he wills to gain he has the power to gain" (14:11).

If God is within us, so are heaven and hell:

> My brother, man, your thoughts are wrong;
> your heaven is not far away;
> and it is not a place of metes and bounds,
> is not a country to be reached;
> it is a state of mind.
> God never made a heav'n for man;
> he never made a hell; we are
> creators and we make our own.
> Now, cease to seek for heaven in the sky;

just open up the windows of your hearts,
and, like a flood of light, a heaven will come
and bring a boundless joy;
then toil will be no cruel task. (33:8–10)

The devil is the greatest power in
our land, and though a myth, he dan-
dles on his knee both youth and age. (56:20)

At one juncture (34:4), when Jesus is sojourning among the Buddhists, and correcting them on a point or two, an interesting question arises, seemingly inevitably: Is Jesus the Buddha come again? "The priests and all the people were astounded at his words and said, 'Is this not Buddha come again in flesh? No other one could speak with such simplicity and power'" (cf. Matthew 12:23; John 3:2). Of course, the implied answer is both yes and no. He is not Siddhartha Gautama, the Buddha of the sixth century BCE, but he is one of that one's successors, one of the pan-historical chain of Enlightened Ones. He need not be the same man reincarnated. The point is that no one individual need be the focus of Enlightenment—as if, without him coming back, we should be bereft of Enlightenment. If you or I were to give full vent to the Christ-potential we contain, we, too, should be Buddhas, at least Bodhisattvas, ourselves.

Etheric Ethics

One cannot really imagine a gospel without ethics, and, so to speak, plenty of them. After all, many people, hearing the word "gospel," probably think at once: "Sermon on the Mount" and maybe nothing more.

One thing we seldom find in the traditional gospels is metaethics, the prior thinking on the presuppositions on the basis of which we decide the morality of specific issues. We are used to referring to this lack euphemistically, as if it were a virtue for Jesus to have simply issued moral demands with no thought of an underlying system which we might propound in order to decide new questions on the same principles. By contrast, it is to the credit of our Aquarian evangelist that he has provided an important glimpse of his Jesus' moral calculus:

When men defy their consciences
and listen not to what they say,

the heart is grieved and they become
unfitted for the work of life;
and thus they sin. The conscience may
be taught. One man may do in conscience what another cannot do.
What is a sin for me to do
may not be sin for you to do.
The place you occupy upon
the way of life determines what is sin.
There is no changeless law of good;
for good and evil both are judged
by other things. One man may fast
and in his deep sincerity
of heart is blest. Another man
may fast and in the faithlessness
of such a task imposed is cursed.
You cannot make a bed to fit
the form of every man. If you
can make a bed to fit yourself
you have done well. (119:19–22)

We catch, I believe, a hint of Aristotelian-style moral relativism whereby a broader principle is ever tailored to the individual's particular abilities, needs, and options. The immediate inspiration for the passage may have been Romans chapter 14.

At the same time, there appear to be some absolutes on which Jesus Aquarius is not willing to budge. At 74:24, we are enjoined to practice the Hindu-Jainist ethic of *ahimsa*, or non-harm.

Whoever is not kind to every form of life—
to man, to beast, to bird, and creeping thing—
cannot expect the blessings of the Holy One;
for as we give, so God will give to us.

One wonders how the evangelist proposed to square this practice with the flexibility he allowed in the just-mentioned case of food. Surely it cannot be a private option whether or not to devour meat if I must already have sworn off shedding the blood of my animal cousins.

But we may in the last analysis leave such calculations to karma. Justice will be served. Good and bad karma alike shall be accrued, and the Universe itself shall know how to value each good or bad deed, doling out reward or punishment accordingly. God need not trouble his wise head figuring out who was naughty or nice and designing his list accordingly. The calculations are run unthinkingly by the innate machinery of the universe. Chapter 114 sets forth the doctrine of karma and theodicy. Poor mortals are tempted to despair of justice in the world, chafing at their own fates or those of others. We accuse God or life or the world of being unfair. Jesus laments such worm's-eye-view sentiments. How sad that only he can behold the Big Picture, the record of past incarnations passing unremembered like water under a bridge. If we could steal a glance at the scandals of the past, or the virtues, we should rest satisfied with the verdicts being meted out in this present life. For a man's life does not consist in the number of years he amasses in a single lifetime.

I believe I see in 105:28–32 a passage advocating good, honest Nietzscheanism: admit your hate rather than hiding it behind a pathetic tissue of phony forgiveness! Sin boldly! It's not the worst thing you could do!

> You men, do not deceive yourselves
> in thought; your hearts are known;
> Hypocrisy will blight a soul
> as surely as the breath of Beel-ze-bub.
> An honest evil man is more esteemed
> by guardians of the soul than a
> dishonest pious man. If you would curse
> the son of man, just curse him out aloud.
> A curse is poison to the inner man,
> and if you hold and swallow down a curse
> it never will digest; lo, it
> will poison every atom of your soul.
> And if you sin against a son of man,
> you may be pardoned and your guilt be cleansed
> by acts of kindness and of love.

Levi the evangelist seems to want to exonerate Christianity from Nietzsche's accusations that it promotes a pathetically hypocritical slave morality in which a seemingly noble willingness to forgive merely masks one's well-nursed *ressentiment*. "Oh *I'll* forgive you all right, buddy! But when the Son of Man comes, he's going to kick your butt!"

Rather than the sentimental/radical assumption that the poor are the pious saints of Yahweh, such as we find everywhere in the gospels, *The Aquarian Gospel* takes a more hard-nosed position. Poverty is no sure sign of piety.

> It is no sign that man is good
> and pure because he lives in want.
> The listless, shiftless vagabonds
> of earth are mostly poor and have to beg
> for bread. (62:18–19)

On the other hand, such squinting at the poor certainly fits this gospel's sense of karmic comeuppance. Would the casual observer not be justified in inferring that the indigent man has himself to blame, if not for being a lazy bum in this present life, then for doing something wrong in a previous life for which his present poverty is recompense?

If Jesus' (Levi's) enthusiasm for the poor is a bit restrained, he displays in no uncertain terms the classic liberal conscience based on both the fallacy of the "limited good" and on survivor guilt. "How could I seek for pleasure for myself while others are in want?" (51:16). As to the "limited good," it is the same belief that leads to the idealization of the poor. There being only so much of any good commodity to go around, the rich must have gained their goods by depriving the poor of theirs. While in ancient times this may have been true, it has long ago become a phantom and a fantasy, ever since Capitalism made it possible to expand the pie, no longer to have to cut thinner and thinner slices of it. As to survivor guilt, or "bleeding heart" liberalism, like that of Father Paneloux in Camus's *The Plague*, it stems directly from our feeling of unworthiness to have avoided the arbitrary blows which struck those to either side of us. Why did we survive when so many others became glowing shadows at Hiroshima?[7] Why are we prosperous when other nations are not? We must have exploited them. And so on. Purely as an exercise in ascetical pietism, we seek to atone for our success by renouncing it, or by feeling guilty for keeping it. We vow never to enjoy life till everyone can, oblivious of the fact that our misery, self-imposed, can never lift another out of his. We cannot get sick enough that it will heal another, poor enough that it will lift another out of poverty. It is really too bad that Jesus/Levi falls prey to this way of thinking, as it is the mirror image of the very same *ressentiment* that broods and seethes rather than acting. How so? Well, if the rich person feels guilty for being rich, he could renounce his wealth as Francis of Assisi did (though the *real* poor, those who did not choose it as a penance, would mock him as a fool). At least when the vaguely-imagined judgment struck all the rich and exalted all the poor, he would be guaranteed safety. But our hero lacks the guts to do that, just as Nietzsche's Christian coward turns the other cheek only because he lacks the courage to hate and to strike back. Likewise, the conscience-stricken liberal is content to simmer with self-hatred while continuing guiltily to enjoy what he neurotically thinks he has no right to.

In any ancient Jewish context such as an historical Jesus might be placed, the question of ethics could not have been raised without connection to the Torah of Moses. In the canonical gospels the issues of Torah-observance and Jewish customs come up constantly. We see a running battle between Jesus and the scribes over whether his followers are living in accord with the Torah. Some of these stories seem to reflect disputes among Jewish Christians who did mean to keep the Law but interpreted its stipulations differently from their critics. Others appear to stem from Hellenistic or Gentile churches which sought in Jesus license to ignore the mores of an alien (to them) culture, that of Judaism. It is hard to tell which opinion an historical Jesus might have espoused. But the issue was still alive in the age when the gospels were written. Things have changed completely by the time Levi Dowling wrote *The Aquarian Gospel*. Outside of the Seventh Day Adventist sect, no Protestants took the notion of Christians keeping Torah rules seriously enough to debate it. Most Protestant interpreters simply assumed that Jesus rejected and flouted the Torah, anticipating the Pauline polemic against it. For Jesus Aquarius, the Law of Moses, or any other, is a museum relic. "If one is full of love he does not need commands of any kind" (17:7). This saying is perhaps suggested by St. Augustine's dictum, "Love God and do as you will." But it goes farther than the pinched-faced saint could imagine, all the way to Rudolf Bultmann's pneumatic antinomianism.[8] Any fan of *The Aquarian Gospel of Jesus the Christ* would, a few decades later, have felt right at home in the pages of Joseph Fletcher's *Situation Ethics* with its dictum, "Love only is always good."[9]

Such an ethic sits loose to legal formulations and is thus very far removed from Immanuel Kant's deontological ethics, an ethics of duty and the keeping of moral absolutes. But there is a major element of Kant's approach that finds a ringing echo in the pages of our Gospel according to Levi: acting for the sake of duty and not merely in accordance with it. "And when you sow, sow seeds of right, because it is the right, and not in the way of trade, expecting rich rewards" (100:12). In this Kant would rejoice. It mirrors his distinction between mere hypothetical imperatives (prudent considerations if one wants to achieve some goal) and truly moral categorical imperatives, obeyed despite any costs, simply for the sake of one's duty, because a thing is right.

Akashic Anachronisms

For a long time, biblical scholarship has been upset by debates over the supposed "inerrancy," or factual infallibility, of the Bible. Traditionally, i.e., in a pre-critical, pre-scientific age, believers regarded the Bible as the inspired Word of God, verbally dictated by the Holy Spirit to passive writers. Even when twentieth-century apologists like Benjamin B. Warfield[10] sought to adjust this belief to the "phenomena of Scripture," including the distinguishing styles and personalities of biblical writers, the result was essentially the same: the Bible might not have been dictated verbatim to waiting stenographers, but it might as well have been. The definitive establishment of any error in the factual assertions of the Bible would bring the whole edifice down like a house of cards. The stakes were high, and apologists would mount any argument, no matter how strained, to avoid this conclusion. Since God could not lie or err, falsehoods in scripture must rule out divine authorship. The same issue arises in the case of a gospel ostensibly received by psychic mediation from the Akashic Records. If there prove to be errors, two possibilities present themselves. First, the medium, in this case Levi Dowling, has "mistranscribed" the etheric "text." He made a kind of scribal error, and we are in no position to correct it. Second, we might give up the whole premise and conclude the work is "merely" an imaginary creation by the Reverend Mr. Dowling. Take your pick, because there are errors, and it is my unhappy duty to indicate them here.

Wrong Herod

Right out of the box, we have a historical goof: "Herod Antipas" (1:1) should be "Herod the Great," father and predecessor of Antipas. Herod the Great was the king reigning (according to Matthew and Luke) when Jesus was born. Herod Antipas (= Antipatros) was the tetrarch of Galilee when Jesus was an adult. It is admittedly a challenge to keep the various Herods and

Herodiases straight. But one might have expected to find the facts in the Akashic Records, that deposit of all earthly events. One apologist[11] for *The Aquarian Gospel* maintains that Herod the Great was also called Herod Antipas I, while his son was Herod Antipas II. As far as I can tell, this is groundless surmise.

Wrong Scriptures

The Aquarian evangel pictures a young Jesus eager to learn and adept in the scriptures not only of his own religion, but those of far-flung Oriental faiths as well. But where, pray tell, would pious folks in Galilee get hold of the ritual texts of India and Persia?

> The home of Joseph was on Marmion Way in Nazareth; here Mary taught her son the lessons of Elihu and Salome. And Jesus greatly loved the Vedic hymns and the Avesta; but more than all he loved to read the Psalms of David and the pungent words of Solomon. (16:1–2)

And if Jesus did drink at the well of ecumenical wisdom, it seems doubtful whether his evangelist did, for *The Aquarian Gospel* offers (9:21–29) a cento of snippets reworked from James Legge's translation of the *Tao-te-Ching*, however misrepresenting the Tao in personalistic terms.

> In early ages of the world the dwellers in the farther East said, "Tao is the name of Universal Breath; and in the ancient books we read, 'No manifesting form has Tao Great, and yet he made and keeps the heavens and earth. No passion has our Tao Great, and yet he causes sun and moon and all the stars to rise and set. No name has Tao Great, and yet he makes all things to grow; he brings in season both the seed time and the harvest time. And Tao Great was One; the One became the Two; the Two became the Three, the Three evolved the Seven, which filled the universe with manifests. And Tao Great gives unto all, the evil and the good, the rain, the dew, the sunshine and the flowers; from his rich stores he feeds them all.' And in the same old book we read of man: 'He has a spirit knit to Tao Great; a soul which lives within the seven Breaths of Tao Great; a body of desires that springs up from the soil of flesh.'"

And what on earth is Confucianist philosopher Meng-tse (ca. 372–289 BCE) doing living in Tibet when Jesus visits there (36:3)? This is really too enormous to be a simple goof. Rather, I suspect Levi Dowling is taking for granted the Theosophist belief that various revered gurus pass the ages as Ascended Masters in a secret hideaway in the secret fastness of Tibet. Meng-tse (Mencius) must have been one of them.

It is not so easy to explain what Jesus was doing visiting Ladekh, which had not yet been established, much less an inhabited Persepolis, since Alexander the Great had destroyed that city some centuries before.

Abraham and Bramha

The Aquarian Gospel imagines that the biblical "Abraham/Abram" is derived from the Sanskrit/Hindu "Brahman," a common but false link made at the time Dowling wrote. "And in Chaldea, Brahm was known. A pious Brahm named Terah lived in Ur; his son was so devoted to the Brahmic faith that he was called A-Brahm; and he was set apart to be the father of the Hebrew race" (10:6).

Aryan Christ

Jesus is described as "a fair-haired boy, with deep blue eyes" (20:5)—Jesus the Aryan superman. It was no doubt Sunday School illustrations more than the Akashic Record that conveyed this picture of little Horst Jesu to the Reverend Dowling.

A Bit of a Pinch, but if a Camel Could Do it, Then So Could the Rich

The Aquarian Gospel reinterprets the warning that the rich will enter heaven with more difficulty than a camel squeezing through a needle's hole in a kind of super-spiritual sense. But what concerns us here is the implicit reference to the apocryphal "Needle's Eye" gate in Jerusalem, through which a camel might pass if it were unburdened and made to kneel. "The gate of this dominion is not high, and he who enters it must fall down on his knees. It is not wide, and none can carry carnal bundles through" (29:21). This quaint absurdity is first mentioned by the thirteenth-century monk Theophylact, commenting on Mark 10:25. It was a pious dodge, opening up a somewhat easier way for the (charitable) rich to be saved after all: they only needed to genuflect in repentance. No doubt Dowling had heard the same bit of homiletical lore and passed it on.

Non-Prophet

"You may have read the words of prophet Azrael" (107:20). I should say not, for he was no prophet, but the Angel of Death. If any of *his* writings survive, they would be quite the read!

Conquer by This!

Chapter 4, verse 7 presents a clever allusion to Constantine's vision at the Milvian Bridge: "Conquer by this," i.e., the sign of the cross (or the *ankh*, or the Chi-Ro sign). Here we read: "The master's cross I see upon the forehead of this child, and he will conquer by this sign." My guess is that Dowling has crossed the Constantine episode with the Simeon scene in Luke 2:34–35, which uses some of the same imagery, including that of Jesus as a battle standard, the sight of which will force all men to choose sides.

Petite!

Surely there were not yet harpsichords in Jesus' day? "God sings for us through bird, and harpsichord, and human voice; he speaks to us through wind and rain and thunder roll" (12:4; cf. 53:5). If you're looking up plain old historical records, and not those etched on imaginary ether, you'll discover that the harpsichord was invented in the late Middle Ages. At any rate, this gospel uses the instrument to make the same point as a reference to the lute in an old Buddhist analogy for the Middle Path: "The body is a harpsichord, and when its strings are too relaxed, or are too tense, the instrument is out of tune, the man is sick" (23:9; cf. 74:6–7).

Darwin Prophesied

The long history of the war between science and religion would have been a lot different had the Bible, like the contemporary Anaximander, mentioned some version of the theory of Evolution. But with *The Aquarian Gospel* we find the opposite problem: its Jesus knows too much about evolution for the time he supposedly lived. He even knows about natural selection! "Now, when the ethers reached the rate of atmosphere (and all the creatures of these planes must get their food from atmosphere) the conflict came; and then that which the finite man [Charles Darwin!] has called survival of the best, became a law. The stronger ate the bodies of the weaker manifests; and here is where the carnal law of evolution had its rise" (32:33–34).

Wrong Language

How can we tell that the conversation in John Chapter 3 between Jesus and Nicodemus cannot have taken place as reported? For the simple reason that the whole thing hinges on a play on words in the wrong language. Jesus tells Nicodemus that one must be born *anothen* in order to be saved. The Greek word can mean either "again" or "from above." Nicodemus thinks Jesus means the first, whereas Jesus goes on to explain that he means the second: people must be born from the heavenly Spirit of God up on high. The problem is, the pun only works in Greek, in which the Gospel of John is written, but which Jesus and a Jewish scribe were extremely unlikely to have been speaking in Jewish Palestine. So this conversation did not take place, at least not quite as recorded. In just the same way, we have to take a second look at *The Aquarian Gospel* 50:17. "When this short span of earthly life has all been measured out, man's bursting baubles will be buried with his bones." "Bursting baubles" is a clever pun on "bursting bubbles," equating "valuable" gem stones with pretty but evanescent soap bubbles. And it works only in English, not in the Egyptian or whatever language Jesus and the sages are imagined to be speaking here.

We come, in 24:22, upon another example of a clever phrase that is, however, dependent upon being read *in English*: the traditional pragmatism of the cliche "might makes right" gets reversed to something more acceptable morally when we read how "right is might." Clearly the reader is supposed to think of the famous original, with the same *English language* rhyme.

Jesus the Baptizer

In an anachronism almost as crude as the Book of Mormon's, Jesus himself founds the Christian (actually, in this book, "Christine") church, baptizing its first members: "And, lo, the multitudes came down, renounced their sins, confessed their faith in Christ, and were baptized" (78:16). The Book of Mormon has American frontier revivalism going full tilt in pre-Columbian America, Incas and Aztecs praying to receive Christ as personal savior in the shadow of their pyramids. As Alfred Loisy made inescapably clear, "Jesus foretold the kingdom, and it was the Church that came."[12] Yet, in order to minimize the disjuncture, to make it look in retrospect as if Jesus had planned what was to come, Matthew has Jesus already speaking of founding a "church" (Matthew 16:18; 18:17). John 4:1–2 similarly retrojects Christian baptism back into the time of Jesus in order to reinforce a side-by-side comparison to John the Baptist. Early Christians must have debated whether or not to baptize as John the Baptist's movement had done. Some, citing Mark 1:8 ("I have baptized you with water but he will baptize you with the Holy Spirit") and inferring from it that, just as John did not baptize anyone yet in the Spirit, so Jesus, the baptizer in the Spirit, would not baptize in water. Others claimed Jesus himself had emulated John's dousing, so it must be all right for Christians to continue. Who knows? The same thing had happened back in the Old Testament when the priestly author of Chronicles had rewritten the original Deuteronomic narrative of 2 Samuel. In the latter, earlier version, David is excluded from actually initiating the construction of the Temple in Jerusalem. But in the rewrite, David did all but start nailing; he had outlined and blueprinted the whole structure and litany as well as writing all the hymns. The idea was, as usual, to appropriate some ancient figure's authority for one side of a later debate.

Modernizing Jesus

Paul Tillich took a dim view of exorcism literally understood, holding that it is an abuse of the name of Christ to use it as a magic formula.[13] But he did take "the demonic" quite seriously, having witnessed first-hand the horrors of the Third Reich. For him, all Christians must heed the gospel charge of Jesus to the twelve, "Heal the sick . . . ; cast out the demons" (Matthew 10:8). This encompasses both psychological counseling and "liberating [individuals] from the social demons that have contributed to their sickness."[14] One might have expected Levi Dowling to reinterpret exorcisms in such a modernizing way, and he does indeed nod in that direction. But it is a strange, halting move, for he retells an exorcism, making it into a psychoanalysis not of the possessed man, but of the possessing demon!

> A man obsessed was brought to him.
> The wicked spirit that possessed the man
> was full of violence and lust,
> and often threw his victim to the ground.
> And Jesus spoke aloud and said,
> "Base spirit, loose your hold upon
> the vitals of this man, and go
> back to your own." And then the spir-
> it begged that he might go into
> the body of a dog that stood near by.
> But Jesus said, "Why harm the helpless dog?
> Its life is just as dear to it as mine to me.
> It is not yours to throw the burd-
> en of your sin on any living thing.
> By your own deeds and evil thoughts
> you have brought all these perils on yourself.
> You have hard problems to be solved;
> but you must solve them for yourself.
> By thus obsessing man, you make
> your own conditions doubly sad.
> Go back into your own domain;
> refrain from harming anything,
> and by and by, you will yourself be free."
> The wicked spirit left the man
> and went unto his own. The man
> looked up in thankfulness and said,
> "Praise God." (83:2–9)

How remarkable! It is no longer the man who is construed as insane and in need of therapy. No, the demonic spirit is quite real as a separate entity, and *it* is the one who is maladjusted! The demon, not the man, requires psychotherapy.

What about those afflicted with Demon Rum? Oddly, the Jesus of the traditional gospels has virtually nothing to say on the subject aside from taking for granted that drunkenness is bad (Matthew 24:49). Nor does he ever undertake to miraculously cure any drunkards, which suggests he (or the gospel writers) would not have shared the modern understanding of alcoholism as a behavioral disease. The early Christians presumably just expected drunks to repent and be done with it. So perhaps Levi's Jesus is not so far from the canonical Jesus in that, while he does minister to a drunk, he exercises no miraculous power to do it. There has been a recent fire in Bethany, Jesus directing efforts to extinguish it, though performing no miracle to that end. Now there is much reconstruction to be done, and Jesus enlists the boozer in the effort. Transferring his attention to those worse off than him helps the drunk pull himself together, and he returns to sobriety for good.

> And then the guests returned and sat
> about the board. A little child
> came in and stood by Jesus' side.
> She laid her hand on Jesus' arm
> and said, "Please, Master Jesus, hear!
> My father is a drunken man;
> my mother toils from morn till night
> and when she brings her wages home
> my father snatches them away
> and squanders every cent for drink,
> and mother and us little ones
> are hungry all the night.
> Please, Master Jesus, come with me
> and touch my father's heart.
> He is so good and kind when he
> is just himself; I know it is the wine
> that makes another man of him."
> And Jesus went out with the child;
> he found the wretched home; he spoke
> in kindness to the mother and
> the little ones, and then upon a bed
> of straw he found the drunken man.
> He took him by the hand and raised
> him up and said, "My brother, man,
> made in the image of our Father-God,

will you arise and come with me?
Your neighbors are in sore distress;
they have lost all they had in this fierce fire,
and men must build their homes again
and you and I must lead the way."
And then the man arose; the two
went arm in arm to view the wrecks.
They heard the mothers and the children crying in the streets; they saw
their wretchedness. And Jesus said,
"My friend, here's work for you to do.
Just lead the way in helpfulness;
I'm sure the men of Bethany
will furnish you the means and help."
The spark of hope that so long had
been smold'ring in the man was fanned
unto a flame. He threw his rag-
ged coat aside; he was himself again.
And then he called for help; not for
himself, but for the homeless ones;
and everybody helped. The ruined homes were built again. And then
he saw his own poor den; his heart
was stirred into its depths. The pride
of manhood filled his soul; he said,
"This wretched den shall be a home."
He worked as he had never wrought
before, and everybody helped.
And in a little while the den
became a home indeed;
the flow'ers of love bloomed everywhere.
The mother and the little ones
were filled with joy; the father never drank again. A man was saved,
and no one ever said a word
about neglect or drunkenness,
nor urged him to reform. (92:13b-28)

Picture This

There is a startling reference to photography! "They do not seem to know that every thought and wish is photographed and then preserved within the Book of Life to be revealed at any time the masters will" (109:6). There is yet another grossly anachronistic reference to "the cells of flesh" in bodily tissue. "The bread and fish and other things we eat, are simply cups to carry to the cells of flesh material for the building of the human house, and when their work is done as refuse they are cast away" (126:10). What is going on here? If we, as gospel readers, are to accept these as words of the historical Jesus, albeit coming to light only now, we must ask why Jesus did not just go the whole way and explain modern medicine, teach the wonders of modern technology, etc., for the good of the human race. If he knew about photography, cytology, and so on, he must have known the rest—or at least as much as Levi Dowling knew—or thought he knew. Of course, the answer to the question is not that Levi Dowling was revealing hitherto secret information concerning past events, but rather updating an ancient story into a new story, with more modern application. If *The Aquarian Gospel* was to be strictly analogous to Matthew, Mark, Luke, and John, it would not feature Jesus in the starring role. It would be an altogether new story for a new day. As I already suggested, Levi himself would be the Christ, the revealer for the Aquarian Age. Presumably, his modesty bade him hide behind the familiar Jesus character.

Move over Conzelmann!

But by far the clearest instance of how our evangelist has benefited from his privileged latter-day perspective is the way he deals with the prospect of the second coming of Jesus (which we must suspect he identifies with the issuing of *The Aquarian Gospel*). It is plain that the earliest Christians, in their enthusiasm, expected the End Time to arrive shortly, within the generation of Jesus and the apostles. When it did not, various excuses were offered, and the deadline adjusted. This is a strategy that numerous apocalyptic sects would utilize for centuries to follow. Scholars have shown how Matthew, for instance, has Jesus (quite implausibly) tell parables about his own return being unaccountably *delayed*, as if his hearers had already faced the disappointment he seeks to assuage. Of course, it is Matthew, not

Jesus, who would have such an occasion. It is his readers, much later than Jesus' hearers, who would need the reassurances. In like manner, Luke has rewritten various prophetic statements borrowed from Mark to inject a note of indefiniteness, opening up the possibility that Jesus had not come to herald the soon-coming end of the world but rather to inaugurate a new, possibly quite long era of Christianity. Comparatively little water had gone under the bridge by that time, but Levi writes in the twentieth century, and he lends his Jesus the benefit of his historical hindsight:

> And then he spoke to his disciples and he said,
> "The seasons of the son of man are past.
> The time will come when you will wish
> above all else to see again one of these days;
> but you can see it not. But, lo, I say,
> that many generations will have come
> and gone before the son of man shall come
> in power; but when he comes no one will say,
> 'Lo, here is Christ; lo, there.'" (145:7–8; cf. Luke 17:20–21).

Ages will pass before the End comes. This is what one would have expected had the gospel writers had any idea how long history would continue. Levi has the advantage of prophetic hindsight.

Among the Apocrypha

Often in ancient Christian apocrypha one finds bits of lore attested elsewhere in antiquity, whether in old Christian materials or those from adjacent religions. They represent, so to speak, the lens through which the ancient reader, conversant with a different set of associations than we moderns, read the prior biblical texts. One feels that, perhaps unconsciously, the apocryphal authors filled in certain gaps with what they simply assumed the original writer took for granted. Or they may have taken for granted interpretations common in their day, as when we refer to Matthew's story of the Three Wise Men, though the text gives no number. We take it for granted from a lifetime of listening to Christmas carols. Well, it is striking that Levi Dowling, a modern like us, if a century earlier, was sufficiently conversant with such lore as to build it in plausibly at just the right points. I want to call attention to a few of these "touches of authenticity," but first two points of clarification. First, I mean "authenticity" in that these touches make *The Aquarian Gospel* sound like an ancient book, not that they actually vindicate it as a true account of Jesus. Second, the occasional impression of antiquity provided by these items must be weighed against the overwhelmingly modern character of the text as a whole and cannot counterbalance it. They are not even sufficient to make us theorize that Levi might have taken them from ancient sources unknown to us, even if such were plausible on other grounds. By contrast, Rod Blackhirst[15] has shown how a document similar to *The Aquarian Gospel* in many ways, *The Gospel according to Barnabas*, though patently stemming from medieval Italy, very likely employed Ebionite and John the Baptist traditions stemming from the syncretistic Carmelite order in Palestine. But there is really no way Levi Dowling could have come by analogous materials.

Nativity Notes

Aquarian Gospel 5:17–18 (re)tells Matthew's story of the Wise Men, correctly characterizing them as Persian/Parthian Magi. These were the astrologer priests of ancient Iran whose role was briefly eclipsed by the official embrace of Zoroastrianism, but which flooded back in after a formal accommodation to the new faith. One supposes Matthew understood this, though some modern readers find it irritating that he should have been thus friendly, first, to astrology, and second, to another religion. But neither should be too surprising. After all, Isaiah (47:12–14) only denounced astrology because other Jews practiced it, so it was hardly alien to Judaism. And Matthew does not necessarily mean to issue *carte blanche* for astrology simply because he lionizes a group of astrologers. The only calculation of theirs he endorses, after all, is their recognition of the Messianic nativity. We just don't know what opinion he may have held on the subject of astrology in general. His point is rather along the lines of Titus 1:12, "One of themselves, a prophet of their own, said, 'Cretans are pathological liars, nasty brutes, shiftless gluttons.'" You quote the other guy in your own favor. (We will see an Aquarian example of the same technique in a moment.) Second, ancient Jews were by no means averse to Zoroastrianism and were happy to acknowledge their great theological debt to it. Some of their great thinkers had absorbed Zoroastrian ideas in the Persian Empire before migrating to Jerusalem at the decree of Cyrus. The Pharisees were those Jews who incorporated a number of these doctrines, earning themselves the mock-name "Parsees," i.e., "Persian

Zoroastrians." The rabbis even thought that Jeremiah's scribe Baruch was the same man as Zoroaster, the founding prophet of Zoroastrianism. At any rate, Levi Dowling makes explicit what is implicit in Matthew but is quite explicit in ancient apocrypha like the *Arabic Infancy Gospel*, which informs us that the magi set out from Iran to seek out the baby Jesus on account of an ancient prophecy of Zoroaster. Levi, of course, is much more modest than that. Operative in his case is the desire, permeating his own work, to place Christian origins in a worldwide context of religions.

What is especially interesting here is the fact that the magi are implicitly identified as the angels of Matthew's Nativity story, intuiting Herod's deception and murderous intent, and warning Joseph to flee. In Matthew, heavenly angels tell the magi, along with Joseph, of Herod's machinations. Not here.

> These magian priests could read the hearts of men;
> they read the wickedness of Herod's heart,
> and knew that he had sworn to kill the new born king.
> And so they told the secret to the parents of the child,
> and bid them flee beyond the reach of harm.

Levi has eliminated the middle "men," changing the angels into the magi. There is some indication that Matthew had already transformed an angel into a star. He was working with a story of the magi in which their observance of Jesus' natal star alerted them to the messianic birth, whereupon they journeyed, with no further supernatural guidance given or needed, to Herod's court in Jerusalem, naturally assuming it must be the birthplace of the one "born king of the Jews." They are then redirected to Bethlehem by Herod's scribes, again, with no supernatural help. How do they locate the particular house where Jesus lives with his parents? Probably Matthew read a story in which an angel appeared above it, beckoning. For some reason, he has changed this angel into a star, clumsily identifying it with the natal star, imagining that it had moved through the sky, leading the magi from Persia to Judea. The conversion was not wholly arbitrary, since in those days stars were often equated with angels (e.g., Revelation 12:4, 7). Why does Levi convert the angel into the human magi, eliminating the former and augmenting the role of the latter? It is all part of the rationalizing tendency of *The Aquarian Gospel*, which prefers natural law to miracle, divine power manifesting itself through human will power rather than emissions directly from heaven.

The Name Game

There is a natural tendency among Bible readers, scholars as well as popular devotees, to play "connect the dots" when it comes to biblical names. Was the Gaius mentioned in 3 John 1 the same man mentioned as one of Paul's converts in 1 Corinthians 1:14? It seems a bit of a stretch, but some scholars have thought so. When one has so little to work with in trying to identify any New Testament personages, it becomes quite tempting to combine all mentions of the same name, even though it implies a pretty small ancient population! Not very many Gaiuses! And that is a false impression. In fact, the confusion in the gospels over all the Marys is illuminated when you realize that over half the women in contemporary Palestine were named Mary (=Miriam, Mariamme, Maria) or Salome! Think how many Muslim men today are named Muhammad, Ali, Hussein or Hassan.

When characters sharing the same name are combined into one, some interesting stories may result. When one succumbs to the temptation and figures, e.g., all the references to "Zechariah" must be to the same man, creating a new bit of pious fiction, this is called a *scholarly legend*. It is the result not of popular imagination, but of scholarly ingenuity. Other scholarly legends, though these two do not involve the same name, include that of Lilith, first wife of Adam, and that of Matthew the converted tax collector. As for Lilith, scribes noticed that Genesis chapter one has God create men and women at the same time, while chapter 2 makes Eve Adam's wife, created only subsequently. How to harmonize the two? Originally they were features of two stories from two sources, but if one feels pressed to make them into one story, glitches like this must be ironed out. The best way to do it, some scribe thought, was to posit that Adam was the man envisioned in both stories, but that there were two different women, one replacing the other. Who could the wife before Eve have been? Well, Isaiah (34:14–15) mentioned the legendary night hag Lilith, common to Near Eastern mythology, she who caused what we call Sudden Infant Death Syndrome. She seemed a likely candidate for a reject wife, so the scribe posited that, created at the same time as Adam, she believed herself to be his equal and would not submit to him. She finally packed up and left. God then replaced her with Eve, a nice Stepford Wife. Lilith went on to become the bride of Samael (Satan).

As to Matthew as the subject of scholarly legend, one needs to realize that Matthew's story of Matthew the toll-collector leaving his booth to follow Jesus (Matthew 9:9) has been rewritten from Mark 2:14, where the converted toll-collector is named Levi, not Matthew. Mark's list of the twelve disciples (3:18) includes a man named Matthew, but nothing is said of his having worked for the Internal Revenue Service. Likewise, Mark never refers to his Levi as one of the twelve disciples. Apparently, the next evangelist (whom tradition dubbed "Matthew" on the gratuitous assumption that he was the disciple Matthew) did not like to "waste" a good discipleship story such as Levi's on a character of whom one heard no more, so he decided to enhance and embellish the character of the disciple Matthew by giving him Levi's conversion story. In Matthew's list of the twelve, Matthew shows up suddenly as "Matthew the toll-collector" (Matthew 10:3). A story is implied in this, as many sermons attest, because now we cannot help imagining the utter incongruity between Matthew, a pro-Roman stooge (toll-collectors worked for the Roman occupation) and Simon the Zealot, possibly implying a former militant, anti-Roman revolutionist. What, the preacher asks, could have brought two such disparate characters together except for the love of Christ? It is a pious, scribal legend.

And so is the story of the martyrdom of the father of John the Baptist. We read this in the apocryphal *Infancy Gospel* (or *Protevangelium*) *of James*. Hugh Schonfield hypothesized that the episode came originally from a "Lost Book of the Nativity of John" the Baptist.[16] But ultimately it comes from the gratuitous but imaginative identification of one Zechariah (the Old Testament prophet Zechariah, killed at the altar according to Matthew 23:35//Luke 11:51) with another (the Baptist's father). The *Infancy Gospel of James* 22–24 has John's father killed by the Herodian troops sent out to eliminate not only the new king of the Jews born in Bethlehem, but his rumored herald as well. Confronted by Herod's knife-wielding goons, Zechariah of course will not surrender his holy son and pays with his life. *Aquarian Gospel* 6:19 has much the same scenario. No doubt Levi Dowling borrowed it from the *Infancy Gospel of James*, available in his day, e.g., in Hone's *Apocryphal New Testament*.

Still dealing with John the Baptist's childhood, chapter 15, verse 3 speaks of "the cord that binds the human boat to earth," an image associated with John also in ancient Mandaean scripture, probably suggested by the Egyptian image of the voyaging boat of Osiris as symbolizing the progress of the life-span. It seems unlikely that Dowling was conversant with Mandaean scripture. It is probably fortuitous. After all, all John the Baptist traditions link him with a river, so boat imagery could not lie far behind.

As a boy, John the Baptist undergoes the very rite he would in later years administer to others. He is baptized by his own guru, a teacher named Matheno (a name Dowling probably derived from the Egyptian historian Manetho mentioned by Josephus in his *Against Apion*). John is eager for the experience: "John said, 'Why need I wait? May I not go at once and wash?'" (15:25). Without realizing it, I suspect, Levi has recapitulated an ancient liturgical feature of baptisms: "Do not hinder them" (Mark 10:14). "Why do you wait?" (Acts 22:16; Apuleius, *The Golden Ass*). "What hinders me?" (Acts 8:37). "Who can deny them water to be baptized?" (Acts 10:47). etc. Oscar Cullmann[17] noticed these equivalent statements and recognized them as reflecting a certain rubric in ancient baptismal services. The point would have been to move the underlying ceremony along: "So without further ado . . ." Did Levi Dowling realize this? Most likely not, but he did have a very keen eye and must have noticed that baptism stories repeated certain stock phrases. And thus he lent his version a patina of authenticity, more than he realized, as it turns out.

Pagan Witness

We saw above how the New Testament does not mind invoking outsiders, like Matthew's Zoroastrian magi, on behalf of Jesus. The same technique of co-optation underlies the Christian *Sibylline Oracles*. There were a great many ostensibly ancient prophecies ascribed to the priestess of Apollo, and late in the game, enterprising Jews and Christians got into the act, writing up new oracles, still attributed to Apollo's mouthpiece, but "predicting" biblical events (after the fact, needless to say). It was a cheap but clever way to convince pagans to jump ship and swim on over to the true faith. Acts 16:16–17 and 17:26–28 both use the same ruse. The first of these passages has a Pythoness (a possessed prophetess), despite herself, unable to keep mum about the truth as it appears to her on the astral plane. Shadowing Paul and his companions, she starts yelling, "These men are bond-slaves of El Elyon! They are preaching the way of salvation to you!" The second has Paul proof-texting Arratus and Epimenides on behalf of the Christian God, as if the Greek poets were trying their best to speak of him without knowing the full implications of what they wrote.

Likewise, *Aquarian Gospel* 45:10 depicts Apollo's Oracle at Delphi yielding to the prophetic Logos revealed in Jesus: "The gods will speak to man by man. The living Oracle now stands within these sacred groves; the Logos from on high has come."

Philonic Allegory

A really remarkable combination of texts and themes occurs at 110:15–24. It is a Philonic allegory of the Exodus, inspired, I think, by Wisdom of Solomon, in a passage that mentions the Logos in connection with the Egyptian Exodus. First *The Aquarian Gospel*:

> The sons of men have groped for ages in the darkness of Egyptian night. The Pharaohs of sense have bound them with their chains. But God has whispered through the mists of time and told them of a land of liberty and love. And he has sent his Logos forth to light the way. The Red Sea rolls between the promised land and Egypt's sands. The Red Sea is the carnal mind. Behold, the Logos reaches out his hand; the sea divides; the carnal mind is reft in twain; the sons of men walk through dry shod. The Pharaohs of sense would stay them in their flight; the waters of the sea return; the Pharaohs of sense are lost and men are free. For just a little while men tread the wilderness of Sin; the Logos leads the way; and when at last men stand upon the Jordan's brink, these waters stay, and men step forth into their own.

Philo could have written that. Now *Wisdom of Solomon* 18:5–25:

> And when they had determined to slay the babes of the saints, one child being cast forth, and saved, to reprove them, thou tookest away the multitude of their children, and destroyedst them altogether in a mighty water. Of that night were our fathers certified afore, that assuredly knowing unto what oaths they had given credence, they might afterwards be of good cheer. So of thy people was accepted both the salvation of the righteous, and destruction of the enemies. For wherewith thou didst punish our adversaries, by the same thou didst glorify us, whom thou hadst called. For the righteous children of good men did sacrifice secretly, and with one consent made a holy law, that the saints should be like partakers of the same good and evil, the fathers now singing out the songs of praise. But on the other side there sounded an ill according cry of the enemies, and a lamentable noise was carried abroad for children

that were bewailed. The master and the servant were punished after one manner; and like as the king, so suffered the common person. So they all together had innumerable dead with one kind of death; neither were the living sufficient to bury them: for in one moment the noblest off-spring of them was destroyed. For whereas they would not believe any thing by reason of the enchantments; upon the destruction of the first-born, they acknowledged this people to be the sons of God. For while all things were in quiet silence, and that night was in the midst of her swift course, Thine Almighty word leaped down from heaven out of thy royal throne, as a fierce man of war into the midst of a land of destruction, and brought thine unfeigned commandment as a sharp sword, and standing up filled all things with death; and it touched the heaven, but it stood upon the earth. Then suddenly visions of horrible dreams troubled them sore, and terrors came upon them unlooked for. And one thrown here, and another there, half dead, shewed the cause of his death. For the dreams that troubled them did foreshew this, lest they should perish, and not know why they were afflicted. Yea, the tasting of death touched the righteous also, and there was a destruction of the multitude in the wilderness: but the wrath endured not long. For then the blameless man made haste, and stood forth to defend them; and bringing the shield of his proper ministry, even prayer, and the propitiation of incense, set himself against the wrath, and so brought the calamity to an end, declaring that he was thy servant. So he overcame the destroyer, not with strength of body, nor force of arms, but with a word subdued him that punished, alleging the oaths and covenants made with the fathers. For when the dead were now fallen down by heaps one upon another, standing between, he stayed the wrath, and parted the way to the liv-ing. For in the long garment was the whole world, and in the four rows of the stones was the glory of the fathers graven, and thy Majesty upon the diadem of his head. Unto these the destroyer gave place, and was afraid of them: for it was enough that they only tasted of the wrath.

It appears that Levi Dowling took inspiration from the Exodus account in Wisdom of Solomon, a Jewish sapiential text written no doubt in Alexandria, and he then took a turn at an allegorical reinterpretation in the style of another great Alexandrian Jewish thinker, Philo. This seemed an obvious move to Dowling as a New Thought man, since allegorizing has ever been the province of New Thought, its preferred way of dealing with the Bible.

God Is My Co-Pilate

One of the oldest puzzles facing gospel historians is the strange reluctance of Pontius Pilate to rubber stamp the Sanhedrin's judgment on Jesus. They had condemned him as a troublemaker, a rabble-rouser, a revolutionist. One might think any of these charges would have been sufficient to merit Pilate's ready acquiescence. In those days, the mere fact of having a following might seem dangerously seditious in Roman eyes. And yet Pilate can be convinced to do his duty only by means of the crowd cajoling and threatening Pilate himself with the charge of disloyalty to his Roman masters. What is going on here? It now seems plain that such kid-gloved depictions of Pontius Pilate stem from second-generation attempts by Christians, after the Roman destruction of Jerusalem, to remodel once-revolutionary Zealot Christianity into a bourgeois and pacifistic movement loyal to Caesar and to Gentile mores. The ill-fated "cleansing of the temple" had been the climactic attempt of Jesus, a messianic prophet-priest, with his armed band, to seize the temple and to appropriate its treasury so to pay for armaments necessary to attack the Romans. Mark's gospel has toned the incident down to a shadow of its former self. The temple was the size of two football fields, and Jesus is said to have cleared the outer court. He must have had considerable help to turn over all the scores of tables of the livestock dealers and currency exchangers. Mark says he refused to let anyone bring sacrificial vessels back into the temple (Mark 11:16), which must mean he had secured all the entrances. And where were the armed guards who were always posted around the temple for emergencies such as this? The notorious Barabbas is later said to have killed someone in "the insurrection" (Mark 15:7). *What* insurrection? Presumably the one ignited by Jesus in the temple, a fire blazing briefly but extinguished quickly enough. To avoid further trouble, the authorities decided to arrest Jesus on the sly (Mark 14:1–2). It is already becoming evident that Mark has tried to disguise what happened by scaling it down to a scene of some fanatic overturning two or three folding tables in a church basement rummage sale. As Robert Eisler and S.G.F. Brandon[20] argued, Jesus must have been put to death as a rebel against Rome for the simple reason that he *was* one, and his latter-day followers, having learned their lesson, wanted to rewrite their history in order to render themselves unworthy of suspicion.

Part of the reason for rewriting the story was to shift the blame for Jesus' execution from the Romans, as if they had been tricked or maneuvered into it, and onto the Jews, who were vilified as acting from insane jealously as well as perverse antipathy to any message of love and compassion. This whitewash of Rome continued on until the Coptic and Ethiopian Church eventually canonized Pontius Pilate as a saint! *The Aquarian Gospel* (163, esp. vv. 18, 21–23) bows obsequiously in this direction:

> And Jesus said, "A noble prince
> has Caesar in his Pilate Pontius,
> and from the point of carnal man
> your words are seasoned with the wise
> man's salt; but from the point of Christ
> your words are foolishness. The cow-
> ard flees when danger comes; but he
> who comes to seek and save the lost
> must give his life in willing sacrifice
> for those he comes to seek and save.
> Before the pasch has been consumed,
> lo, all this nation will be cursed
> by shedding blood of innocence;
> and even now the murderers
> are at the door." And Pilate said,
> "It shall not be; the sword of Rome
> will be unsheathed to save your life."
> And Jesus said, "Nay, Pilate, nay;
> there are no armies large enough
> in all the world to save my life."
> And Jesus bade the governor farewell,
> and went his way; but Pilate sent
> a double guard with him lest he should fall
> into the hands of those who were alert to take his life.

Here Pilate is as desperate to safeguard Jesus from the violent hands of his enemies as Peter is in the canonical gospels.

Holy Hypertext

New Testament apocrypha follow a certain logic of hypertexting, whether the document is an ancient one or a modern specimen. Subsequent gospel authors tend to make the same sort of moves, fill the same sort of gaps, make the same sort of connections. Often there is a desire to provide narrative motivation for what seemed arbitrary in the original. Thus Matthew explains that Judas betrayed Jesus because he was greedy (Matthew 26:15), while Luke and John posited that he was devil-possessed (Luke 22:3; John 13:2). We are going to see some of that in Levi Dowling's gospel, both in this chapter and the next. There is also the tendency to "correct" earlier gospels, to bring them into alignment with one's own "superior" insight. Levi certainly does that, nor do I mean to criticize him for it. Later gospel writers also like to create new typological correspondences between biblical characters, so as to introduce narrative and even theological foreshadowing. Of course New Testament writers treat the Old Testament in this way, and the Koran so embellishes the Bible.

Like Grandfather, Like Son

In *Aquarian Gospel* 1:5 we learn that Mary's father Joachim already invites the down-and-out to his feasts as Jesus advises in Luke 14:12–14 (cf. *Aquarian Gospel* 141:32).

> Joachim made a feast in honor of
> the child, but he invited not the rich,
> the honored and the great; he called
> the poor, the halt, the lame, the blind,
> and to each one he gave a gift
> of raiment, food or other needful thing.

We are perhaps to understand that Jesus' advice to do just this in one's entertainment plans came to him not by unmediated divine revelation, but rather by a sterling example passed down in his family.

A Hindu Gamaliel

A Brahmin priest friendly to Jesus, one Lamaas Bramas, warns his fellow Brahmins: "If Jesus speaks the truth, if he is right, you cannot force him to desist; if he is wrong and you are right, his words will come to naught, for right is might, and in the end it will prevail" (24:22). If there was by some chance an historical Lamaas Bramas, he could never have spoken these words. This sage counsel is plainly copied from Gamaliel's speech in Acts 5:34–39.

Aw Shucks

There are New Testament echoes aplenty in *Aquarian Gospel* 4:11. Luke's prophetess Anna bows in holy adoration before the Christ infant, but she is warned away by the sudden appearance of a figure in white, not said to be an angel, but rather "a master," who tells her, "Good woman, stay; take heed to what you do; you may not worship man; this is idolatry." See also *Aquarian Gospel* 26:23–24: "And all the people were entranced, and would have worshiped Jesus as a God; but Jesus said, 'I am your brother man just come to show the way to God; you shall not worship man; praise God, the Holy One.'" Mortals are here warned not to worship Jesus, even as Peter in Acts 10:25–26 and the angel in Revelation 19:10 decline the honor. The New Testament writers conspicuously do not mind having Jesus' admirers bow before him in homage, as we see in John 9:38; Matthew 2:11; 14:33; 28:17. By contrast, in the earliest gospel, Mark, we see Jesus fending off even polite flattery that might imply he possesses divine characteristics: Mark 10:18, "Why do you call me good? No one is good, except God alone." Why does Levi Dowling revert to the more modest idiom of Mark? For a good reason. Remember, for him, the Christhood of Jesus, his divinity, lies in the anointing he bears of his own human potential, the innate divinity available to every man and woman and identical with none of them as a special individual. As Paul Tillich would say, what is divine in Jesus is not Jesus *as Jesus*, but rather Jesus *as the Christ*. [19]

I Pity the Pool

Levi's rewrite (41:1–24) of the episode of the healing shrine at Bethsaida (Bethesda/Bethzatha) in John 5:1–9 no longer contrasts the catch-as-catch-can potency of the spring with the infallible power of Jesus Christ, but rather has Jesus stand to the side and proclaim the superiority of faith to superstition. Faith ought to recognize that there is no paucity to God's power nor stinginess in his willingness to dole out blessings. Then one simply opens one's hand to receive. If Jesus were a necessary mediator, Levi clearly sees, then that would after all constitute an arbitrary constriction, a limitation on

God's willingness to serve the suppliant.

A flowing spring that people called the Healing Fount was near Persepolis. And all the people thought that at a certain time of the year their deity came down and gave a virtue to the waters of the fount, and that the sick who then would plunge into the fount and wash would be made whole. About the fount a multitude of people were in waiting for the Holy One to come and potentise the waters of the fount. The blind, the lame, the deaf, the dumb, and those obsessed were there. And Jesus, standing in the midst of them, exclaimed, "Behold the spring of life! These waters that will fail are honored as the special blessing of your God. From whence do healing virtues come? Why is your God so partial with his gifts? Why does he bless this spring today, and then tomorrow take his blessings all away? A deity of power could fill these waters full of healing virtue every day. Hear me, you sick, disconsolate: The virtue of this fount is not a special gift of God. Faith is the healing power of every drop of all the waters of this spring. He who believes with all his heart that he will be made whole by washing in this fount will be made whole when he has washed; and he may wash at any time. Let every one who has this faith in God and in himself plunge in these waters now and wash." And many of the people plunged into the crystal fount; and they were healed. And then there was a rush, for all the people were inspired with faith, and each one strove to be among the first to wash, lest all the virtue be absorbed. And Jesus saw a little child, weak, faint and helpless, sitting all alone beyond the surging crowd; and there was none to help her to the fount. And Jesus said, "My little one, why do you sit and wait? Why not arise and hasten to the fount and wash, and be made well?" The child replied, "I need not haste; the blessings of my Father in the sky are measured not in tiny cups; they never fail; their virtues are the same for evermore. When these whose faith is weak and must haste to wash for fear their faith will fail, have all been cured, these waters will be just as powerful for me. Then I can go and stay a long, long time within the blessed waters of the spring." And Jesus said, "Behold a master soul! She came to earth to teach to men the power of faith." And then he lifted up the child and said, "Why wait for anything? The very air we breathe is filled with balm of life. Breathe in this balm of life in faith and be made whole." The child breathed in the balm of life in faith, and she was well. The people marveled much at what they heard and saw; they said, "This man must surely be the god of health made flesh." And Jesus said,

"The fount of life is not a little pool; it is as wide as are the spaces of the heavens. The waters of the fount are love; the potency is faith, and he who plunges deep into the living springs, in living faith, may wash away his guilt and be made whole, and freed from sin."

As ever in New Thought, Jesus is the shower of the way, and not the center of some theological Elvis-cult.

Jesus the Prodigal Son

Then Jesus went his way, and after many days he crossed the Jordan to his native land. At once he sought his home in Nazareth. His mother's heart was filled with joy; she made a feast for him, inviting all her kindred and her friends. But Jesus' brothers were not pleased that such attention should be paid to one they deemed a sheer adventurer, and they went not in to the feast. They laughed their brother's claims to scorn; they called him indolent, ambitious, vain; a worthless fortune hunter; searcher of the world for fame, who, after many years returns to mother's home with neither gold, nor any other wealth. (43:17–20).

Jesus returns home after his Asian expeditions to find stubborn, grumbling brothers. They play the role of the brother of the returning Prodigal Son (Luke 15:29–30), with the sarcastic unbelief of Jesus' brothers borrowed from John 7:3–5. Since they thus prove themselves unworthy of his lessons gained in far quarters, Jesus tells them only to his mother and sister (43:21–22), which presumably explains why we never heard them before. Mark 16:8 used the same device to account for why no one had ever heard of the Empty Tomb story before he himself (invented and) circulated it.

The Baptist in Hot Water

In *Aquarian Gospel* 62:4, John the Baptist appears before the scribes and Pharisees who demand of him: "If you be seer and prophet, tell us plainly who has sent you here?" It represents an odd reversal of the motif of John 1:22, "They said then to him, 'Who are you? So that we may give some answer to those who sent us. What do you say about yourself?'" To this Levi has added a handy bit of similar dialogue from John 10:24, effectively combining the two scenes: "The Jews therefore gathered round him [Jesus], and were badgering him, 'How long do you intend to keep us guessing? If you are the Christ, then out with it!'"

Phantom Grapes

The water-into-wine miracle (John 2:1–11) is made to teach mind-over-matter thaumaturgy. "And Jesus said, 'Pray what is wine? It is but water with the flavoring of grapes. And what are grapes? They are but certain kinds of thought made manifest, and I can manifest that thought, and water will be wine'" (70:9–10). One wonders if Levi Dowling or any member of the Aquarian Christine Church ever managed to repeat the trick. On the other hand, demythologizing Jesus' Dionysus-miracle in this manner serves the rationalist agenda of New Thought: God manifests all power, but only according to the Logos-structure of natural laws.

Samaritan Woman, Get Away from Me

Chapter 81 gives us the Aquarian version of the Samaritan Woman dialogue from John 4, only this one restores the original point of John's Buddhist prototype: the equality and free interrelations between traditionally hostile castes.

> The Christine gate into the kingdom of the Holy One was opened up, and Jesus and the six disciples and Lamaas left the Jordan ford and turned their faces toward Galilee. Their way lay through Samaria and as they journeyed on they came to Sychar, which was near the plot of ground that Jacob gave to Joseph when a youth. And Jacob's well was there, and Jesus sat beside the well in silent thought, and his disciples went into the town to purchase bread. A woman of the town came out to fill her pitcher from the well; and Jesus was athirst, and when he asked the woman for a drink she said, "I am a woman of Samaria, and you a Jew; do you not know that there is enmity between Samaritans and Jews? They traffic not; then why ask me the favour of a drink?" And Jesus said, "Samaritans and Jews are all the children of one God, our Father-God, and they are kin. It is but prejudice born of the carnal mind that breeds this enmity and hate. While I was born a Jew, I recognise the brotherhood of life. Samaritans are

just as dear to me as Jew or Greek. And then, had you but known the blessings that our Father-God has sent to men by me, you would have asked me for a drink. And I would gladly have given you a cup of water from the Fount of Life, and you would never thirst again." The woman said, "This well is deep, and you have naught with which to draw; how could you get the water that you speak about?" And Jesus said, "The water that I speak about comes not from Jacob's well; it flows from the springs that never fail. Lo, everyone who drinks from Jacob's well will thirst again; but they who drink the water that I give will never thirst again. For they themselves become a well, and from their inner parts the sparkling waters bubble up into eternal life." The woman said, "Sir, I would drink from that rich well of life. Give me to drink, that I may thirst no more." And Jesus said, "Go call your husband from the town that he may share with you this living cup." The woman said, "I have no husband, sir." And Jesus answered her and said, "You scarcely know what husband means; you seem to be a gilded butterfly that flits from flower to flower. To you there is no sacredness in marriage ties, and you affinitise with any man. And you have lived with five of them who were esteemed as husbands by your friends." The woman said, "Do I not speak unto a prophet and a seer? Will you not condescend to tell me who you are?" And Jesus said, "I need not tell you who I am, for you have read the Law, the Prophets and the Psalms that tell of me. I am one come to break away the wall that separates the sons of men. In Holy Breath there is no Greek, no Jew, and no Samaritan; no bond, nor free; for all are one." The woman asked, "Why do you say that only in Jerusalem men ought to pray, and that they should not worship in our holy mount?" And Jesus said, "What you have said, I do not say. One place is just as sacred as another place. The hour has come when men must worship God within the temple of the heart; for God is not within Jerusalem, nor in your holy mount in any way that he is not in every heart. Our God is Spirit; they who worship him must worship him in spirit and in truth." The woman said, "We know that when Messiah comes that he will lead us in the ways of truth." And Jesus said, "Behold the Christ has come; Messiah speaks to you."

The Breathing Method

Aquarian Gospel 89:4–5 features a narrative anticipation of Pentecost a la John 20:22–23, combined with a Damascus Road-style theophany. "'The

Holy Breath will fill this place, and you will be baptized in Holy Breath.' And then they prayed; a light more brilliant than the noonday sun filled all the room, and tongues of flame from every head rose high in air."

Cloned Sayings

We find at 99:14 ("No man can serve two masters at a time no more than he can ride two asses at a time that go in different ways") a "homologous formation," a doublet of the famous "serving two masters" saying (Matthew 6:24). It is strikingly like that in the Gospel of Thomas, saying 47a: "It is impossible for a man to mount two horses or to stretch two bows, and it is impossible for a slave to serve two masters—otherwise he will honor the one and offend the other."

"The very petals of the rose he knows by name, and every one is numbered in his Book of Life" (109:23) provides a new match for the numbered hairs of the head (Luke 12:7//Matt. 10:30). It is thus another homologous formulation. Modern gospel writers tend to expand the sayings tradition the same ways ancient evangelists did.

The Baptist: Great, Not so Great?

Early Christians alternated between trying to refute rival sects and trying to assimilate them. Originally Christians competed with the John the Baptist movement but finally succeeded in assimilating them, by co-opting their famous figurehead John the Baptist. He became, in Christian hagiography, both the cousin and the forerunner of Jesus. There is a passage featured in both Matthew and Luke which seems to praise John to the skies, then suddenly to slam on the brakes and to denigrate him. "Amen, I say to you, among those born of women there has risen no one greater than John the Baptist; and yet he who ranks least in the kingdom of heaven is greater than he" (Matthew 11:11//Luke 7:28). That is a long fall from a great height! First we hear that John is the greatest human being in history, presumably greater than Jesus himself, reportedly the speaker here. And then we hear he is the merest nobody compared to the most insignificant nebbish to make it into the kingdom of heaven! Are we to imagine John as *excluded* from the kingdom? Or as *included*, but last and lowest in the pecking order? Which is more insulting? You be the judge. It is hard to believe that, as of the second half, we are looking at an acclamation of John the Baptist made by some follower of his, a member of his sect who considered him the Messiah of Israel. But that is exactly what the first half alone does sound like. The saying, originally only the positive praise half, passed over into Christian circles when some Baptist converted to the rival faith, and then Christians found it necessary to add to the text the negative reversal. How fascinating, then, that it appears in *Aquarian Gospel* 103:22 in what I am suggesting was its original version: "Among the men of earth a greater man has never lived than John." If I were otherwise inclined to view *The Aquarian Gospel* as historically authentic, I would certainly point to this verse as confirmation. But that might be a bit of a jump, since it is far more likely that Levi Dowling, at least as intelligent as your commentator, saw the same incongruity and trimmed away the secondary element.

Peter's Confession

All four canonical gospels, plus Thomas, include some version of the confession of Peter, usually at Caesarea Philippi. Each culminates with what each evangelist considers the true and normative doctrine about Jesus. For Mark (8:27–30) he is "the Christ." For Luke (9:18–22) he is "the Christ of God." For Matthew (16:13–16) Jesus is "the Christ, the Son of the Living God." John (6:66–71) makes him "the Holy One of God." In Thomas (saying 13) the answer is a secret, ineffable and unspeakable. Accordingly, Levi plugs in his own estimate of Jesus' significance, as we will see in the following (*Aquarian Gospel* 128:21–34).

> And then they journeyed on, and came into the land of Caesarea-Philippi. And as they walked and talked among themselves, the master said, "What do the people say about the son of man? Who do they think I am?" And Matthew said, "Some say that you are David come again; some say that you are Enoch, Solomon, or Seth." And Andrew said, "I heard a ruler of the synagogue exclaim, 'This man is Jeremiah, for he speaks like Jeremiah wrote.'" Nathaniel said, "The foreign masters who were with us for a time, declared that Jesus is Gautama come again." James said, "I think that most of the master Jews believe you are the reappearance of Elijah on the earth." And John spoke out and said, "When we were in Jerusalem I heard a seer exclaim, 'This Jesus is none other than Melchizedek, the king of peace, who lived about two

thousand years ago, and said that he would come again." And Thomas said, "The Tetrarch Herod thinks that you are John arisen from the dead. But then his conscience troubles him; the spirit of the murdered John looms up before him in his dreams, and haunts him as a spectre of the night." And Jesus asked, "Who do you think I am?" And Peter said, "You are the Christ, the love of God made manifest to men." And Jesus said, "Thrice blessed are you, Simon, Jonas' son. You have declared a truth that God has given you. You are a rock, and you shall be a pillar in the temple of the Lord of hosts. And your confession is the cornerstone of faith, a rock of strength, and on this rock the Church of Christ is built. Against it all the powers of hades and of death cannot prevail."

This is a fascinating, extended version of the Caesarea Philippi confession scene. The Christological punch line this time is, "You are the Christ, the love of God made manifest to men." That is just what we ought by now to expect. As for the broad outline of the scene, it is based primarily upon Matthew's version, as we can tell from the inclusion of the phrase "son of man" in Jesus' opening question, from the inclusion of Jeremiah among the candidates for Jesus' identity, and from the aftermath of the confession, in which Jesus grants Peter various prizes. Popular estimates of Jesus make him David, Enoch, Solomon, Seth, Jeremiah, Elijah, Melchizedek, and Gautama Buddha! That Herod thinks he is the ghostly Baptist (Mark 6:16) is added here. The notion of Jesus as David himself returned is unprecedented as far as I know, but he is hailed in the canonical gospels as "son of David." Once, when he has been exorcizing demons, the crowd asks, "Can this be the son of David?" the implication may be that he is Solomon returned, since, unlike David, King Solomon was remembered as a powerful wizard with all the demons beneath his heel.

Why identify Jesus as Enoch? Perhaps because Levi Dowling had noticed, in the newly rediscovered text of 1 Enoch, that the pre-Flood patriarch Enoch is hailed as "that Son of Man who is born unto righteousness" (71:14) and becomes the messiah and son of "the Lord of Spirits." That sounds an awful lot like what Christians have always said about Jesus. Besides, Enoch, like Elijah (also in this list, and in all Synoptic versions: Matthew, Mark, and Luke), was supposed to have ascended into heaven alive, making it easy, one supposes, for him to drop back down to earth.

Seth, replacement son of Adam and Eve after Cain murdered Abel, was often thought to have some vague (or esoteric) messianic role: God must have replaced Abel for *some* special reason. Accordingly, Seth became the figurehead of a whole Gnostic sect, the Sethians, who called themselves "the kingless race." Their scriptures, discovered at Nag Hammadi in 1945, identify Jesus Christ as the second coming of Seth. There is also a Gnostic text at Nag Hammadi called *Melchizedek*, in which Melchizedek is identified not only as Seth but also as a pre-incarnated Jesus. It is, needless to say, startling that Levi Dowling anticipated these discoveries as he did. Admittedly, though, the idea of identifying Melchizedek as Jesus was an old and orthodox one, hinted in Hebrews chapter 7.

That Jesus might be the return of Gautama Buddha is not far-fetched in terms of ancient Christian thinking, any more than the link between Jesus and Zoroaster, as we have already seen. The third-century Prophet Mani, who styled himself "Mani, the Apostle of Jesus Christ," claimed to be the bearer of the same Spirit that had previously visited mankind as Zoroaster, the Buddha, and Jesus. The nineteenth-century Baha'i Faith similarly claims that Zoroaster, the Buddha, Jesus, as well as Muhammad and others were "Points of Manifestation" of God on earth.

Almost incidentally, Levi combines the Roman Catholic view with the view of Justin Martyr and later Protestantism about the intended reference of "the rock" in Matthew 16:18. It is both Peter himself and the theological content of his confession.

Can the Leper Change His Spots?

Luke 17:11–19 tells the story of the ten lepers healed by Jesus. They dare not approach Jesus very closely, social taboos being what they are, but they call out to him to heal them, and he commands that they be healed. He tells them to get their cure certified by the priests, so they can return to normal life, no longer segregated for their ritual uncleanness. Apparently they are not completely healed at once. Their setting off to find a priest is an act of faith that they will have something, clear skin, to show him. And it works! They see, on the way, that they have lost their skin rash (probably what "leprosy" denotes in the gospels). How interesting that the uncleanness of the disease had hitherto sealed a fellowship of outcasts that did not survive the healing, since now other taboos fell back into place and one ex-leper, a Samaritan, could no longer associate with the others, who were all Jews. So he drops out of the group, perhaps reasoning that he dare not show himself before a Jewish priest anyway, and he returns to Jesus, thanking him profusely. Then we find that Jesus had rather expected all ten to do the same, despite his command to go to the priest. He says, so to speak, "I could have sworn there were ten! Is it only this Samaritan who comes back thankful, then?" It is a great tale. But it silently suggests a twist ending that the sharp-eyed Dowling picks up on in 133:22. The nine ungrateful lepers got their leprosy back! "You have revealed your heart and shown that you are worthy of the power; behold the nine will find again their leprous hands and feet."

Simon Cerus?

We come across an odd reference in 106:6 to "a black magician of the Simon Cerus type." I am guessing Levi has taken Mark 15:21's "Simon of Cyrene," who bore the cross of Jesus, and combined him with Simon Magus (Acts 8:9). "Cerus" equals "Cyrene" plus "Magus," splitting the difference. My suspicion is that the two were originally the same character, and that the role of Simon in Mark reflects the claim of Simon Magus (reported by Irenaeus) that he had previously suffered (or seemed to suffer) in Judea, when he was called the Son.

Family Therapy

In *Aquarian Gospel* 106:14–22 Jesus displays better manners to his interloping relatives than he does in Mark 3:20–21, 31–35, in which Jesus appears to repudiate his thick-witted family who have shown up out of nowhere as if to deprogram him from a cult. Many readers have judged Mark's Jesus to be a bit brusque in that story, including Luke (8:19–21), who tones it down, leaving Jesus' words about his *true* family ambiguous: his blood relatives might after all be included, cf. Acts 1:14. But Levi cannot leave it at that. Remember, for him, the "Christ" is divine love manifest in human form, and this means Jesus in such a scene must have looked a bit more like 1 Corinthians 13!

> As Jesus spoke a messenger approached and said to him, "Your mother and your brothers wish to speak with you." And Jesus said, "Who is my mother? And my brothers, who are they?" And then he spoke a word aside unto the foreign masters and the twelve; he said, "Behold, men recognize their mothers, fathers, sisters, brothers here in flesh;

but when the veil is rent and men walk in the realms of soul, the tender lines of love that bind the groups of fleshly kin in families will fade away. Not that the love for anyone will be the less; but men will see in all the motherhood, the fatherhood, the sisterhood, the brotherhood of man. The family groups of earth will all be lost in universal love and fellowship divine. Then to the multitudes he said, "Whoever lives the life and does the will of God is child of God and is my mother, father, sister, friend." And then he went aside to speak to mother and his other kindred in the flesh.

In just the same way, Levi softens the apparent impatience of Jesus when someone in the crowd blesses him by reference to his lucky mother: "Blessed is she whose womb bore you and whose breasts nursed you!" Jesus brushes aside the acclamation: "*Au contraire*, the blessed are those hear the command of God and obey it!" (Luke 11:27–28). *Aquarian Gospel* 108:13 has, "And Jesus said, *'Yes, blest is she*; but doubly blest are they who hear, receive and live the word of God.'" The woman's praise was aimed at Jesus, not Mary, as in the old song "Lucky Lindy" about aviator Charles Lindbergh: "This kind of a son makes a mother feel proud." And yet Jesus' reply seems to minimize Mary as if to deny her honor: mere physical kinship to Jesus means nothing. Spiritual relations are what matter. Levi smoothes it out by having Jesus accept the compliment to his mother, then go on to bless all who are faithful to God's commands.

Pouring It On

What is the "sign of the Son of Man" to be seen in the heavens, signaling the dawn of a new age (Matthew 24:30)? The evangelist Levi cleverly combines this image with that of the man carrying the pitcher (Mark 14:13) to suggest the Zodiacal sign of Aquarius the water bearer, heralding the dawn of the Aquarian Age. "And then the man who bears the pitcher will walk forth across an arc of heaven; the sign and signet of the son of man will stand forth in the eastern sky" (157:29).

Piscean Passion

The spectacle of Jesus' arrest, like that of Apollonius of Tyana (who could drop his chains any time he wished), is a charade (John 18:6; Matthew 26:53). He is merely going through the motions, condescending, even as the Bodhisattvas all did, to the script in which salvation history handed them, no matter how hackneyed. Levi gets this, and he shrewdly crosses Jesus' arrest with that of Samson in Judges 15:14, where the strongman, having allowed himself to be bound in ropes, merely flexes his mighty muscles to make the bonds disperse into dust as if they were centuries old. "'And now you try to bind me down with chains; what are these chains but links of reeds?' And then he raised his hands; the chains were broken and they fell to earth" (164:22).

Judas Goat

In *Aquarian Gospel* chapter 168 the already-apocryphal business about Pilate releasing a prisoner requested by the crowd as a Passover gesture is replaced by a Jewish human scapegoat ritual that no one ever heard of.

> A superstitious people are the Jews. They have a faith [i.e., ritual] that they have borrowed from the idol worshippers of other lands, that at the end of every year, they may heap all their sins upon the head of some man set apart to bear their sins. The man becomes a scapegoat for the multitudes; and they believe that when they drive him forth into the wilds, or into foreign lands, they are released from sin. So every Spring before the feast they choose a prisoner from the prisons of the land, and by a form their own, they fain would make him bear their sins away. Among the Jewish prisoners in Jerusalem were three who were the leaders of a vile, seditious band, who had engaged in thefts and murders and rapine, and had been sentenced to be crucified. Barabbas bar Jezia was among the men who were to die; but he was rich and he had bought of priests the boon to be the scapegoat for the people at the coming feast, and he was anxiously in waiting for his hour to come. Now, Pilate thought to turn this superstition to account to save the Lord, and so he went again before the Jews and said, "You men of Israel, according to my custom I will release to you today a prisoner who shall bear your sins away. This man you drive into the wilds or into foreign lands, and you have asked me to release Barabbas, who has been proven guilty of the murder of a score of men. Now, hear me men, Let Jesus be released and let Barabbas pay his debt upon the

cross; then you can send this Jesus to the wilds and hear no more of him." At what the ruler said the people were enraged, and they began to plot to tear the Roman palace down and drive in exile Pilate, and his household and his guards. When Pilate was assured that civil war would follow if he heeded not the wishes of the mob, he took a bowl of water, and in the presence of the multitude, he washed his hands and said, "This man whom you accuse is son of the most holy Gods, and I proclaim my innocence. If you would shed his blood, his blood is on your hands and not on mine." And then the Jews exclaimed, "And let his blood be on our hands and on our children's hands." And Pilate trembled like a leaf, in fear. Barabbas, he released, and as the Lord stood forth before the mob, the ruler said, "Behold your king! And would you put to death your king?" The Jews replied, "He is no king; we have no king but great Tiberius." Now, Pilate would not give consent that Roman soldiers should imbue their hands in blood of innocence, and so the chief priests and the Pharisees took counsel what to do with Jesus, who was called the Christ. Caiaphas said, "We cannot crucify this man; he must be stoned to death and nothing more." And then the rabble said, "Make haste! Let him be stoned." And then they led him forth toward the hill beyond the city's gates, where criminals were put to death. The rabble could not wait until they reached the place of skulls. As soon as they had passed the city's gate, they rushed upon him, smote him with their hands, they spit upon him, stoned him, and he fell upon the ground. And one, a man of God, stood forth and said, "Isaiah said, *He shall be bruised for our transgressions and by his stripes we shall be healed.*" As Jesus lay all bruised and mangled on the ground a Pharisee called out, "Stay, stay you men! behold, the guards of Herod come and they will crucify this man." And there beside the city's gate they found Barabbas's cross; and then the frenzied mob cried out, "Let him be crucified." Caiaphas and the other ruling Jews came forth and gave consent. And then they lifted Jesus from the ground, and at the point of swords they drove him on. A man named Simon, a friend of Jesus, was a-near the scene, and since the bruised and wounded Jesus could not bear his cross, they laid it on the shoulders of this man, and made him bear it on to Calvary.

The embellishing imagination runs strong here. For one thing, we have a garbled version of Barabbas' name as it appears in some Old Latin manuscripts of Matthew 27:17, where he is called "Jesus Barabbas." Barabbas is a patronymic, an epithet, meaning "son of Abbas." Jesus (Yeshua) was a common name. Levi has made Barabbas itself a personal name and made the Old Latin reading "Jesus" into a patronymic ("bar Jezia") for some reason I cannot guess. It has long been speculated that, since "Barabbas" could be taken to mean "son of the father," that the scene might have originated as a docetic crucifixion account, i.e., a story in which Jesus merely seemed to be crucified but escaped, his place taken by another. In this scenario, "Jesus, Son of the Father" would have been let go, returning to heaven, while a Jesus-substitute, "Jesus [only] *called* Christ," would have been sent to the cross. But if Levi suspected this, he has drastically altered it, reinterpreting the archaic Scapegoat ritual of Leviticus 16, in which the priest took a pair of goats, consecrating one to Yahve, the other to the desert-dwelling demon Azazel, and drove the latter over the brink of a ravine to carry away the sins of Israel. All very strange. Levi has taken this ritual, which, as John Dominic Crossan has demonstrated[20] exercised an important influence upon the gospel Passion narrative, and combined it with the old scholarly guess that Pilate's troops were playing an old Saturnalia game of "Mock King" with Jesus that they often used to play with condemned prisoners during the Roman festival. The gospels have a vaguely similar notion (unattested in any other ancient sources) that Pilate had the custom of releasing a Jewish prisoner, whomever the crowd should request, as a gesture of Roman clemency each Passover. As Levi Dowling has put it all together, the Levitical Scapegoat rite, still practiced, involved the exile of a condemned prisoner instead of executing him. Though Barabbas bears away the people's sins as the exiled scapegoat, Jesus dies, and yet does not bear sins. That anyone should pay for the sins of another Levi has already rejected as "superstition." No, Jesus' death, we have already discovered, was intended as a demonstration of the human ability to overcome death. No real atonement theology fits very well into the New Thought framework.

Judas: Misunderstanding, Misunderstood

If Levi is alert for the chance to make Pontius Pilate look good, it is no surprise that he has kind things to say concerning Judas Iscariot, too. "Now, Judas who betrayed his Lord, was with the mob; but all the time he thought that Jesus would assert his power and demonstrate the strength of God that he possessed, and strike to earth the fiendish multitudes and free himself" (169:1). Other novelists have ventured the same speculation: Judas had not meant for Jesus to die. He only wanted to force his hand to let his messianic power be shown, destroying his enemies. When this stratagem failed, Judas was accordingly horrified that he had only succeeded in delivering Jesus to his eager executioners.

Sun of God

I regard as the single most striking innovation of *The Aquarian Gospel* (though others may see little significance in it) that Levi understands Jesus' cry from the cross, "Eloi" ("My God," Mark 15:34) as not a call to Elijah (as the crowd imagines, "Elijah" meaning "my God is Yahve"), but as a summoning of **Helios**, the Greek sun god, to restore the lost daylight during the crucifixion. This is really fascinating, given that Elijah (rendered as **Elias** in Greek) is originally a sun god, too, hence his "hairy" appearance (2 Kings 1:8), suggesting the sun's rays, his scorching his enemies (2 Kings 1:10, 12), and his rising into the heaven aboard a flaming chariot (2 Kings 2:11). "And when the sun refused to shine and darkness came, the Lord exclaimed, 'Heloi! Heloi! lama sabachthani (Thou sun! thou sun! why hast thou forsaken me?)'" (171:3). One really feels Levi is onto something here, that he has somehow uncovered a genuine, very ancient secret underlying the familiar text.

Locking the Barn Before the Horse Got Out

Unlike Matthew, *The Aquarian Gospel* has the tomb guards verify that Jesus' body has not already been stolen before they seal the tomb. "Before the watch began Caiaphas sent a company of priests out to the garden of Siloam that they might be assured that Jesus' body was within the tomb. They rolled away the stone; they saw the body there, and then they placed the stone again before the door. And Pilate sent his scribe who placed upon the stone the seal of Rome, in such a way that he who moved the stone would break the seal" (172:2–4). It is nothing short of astonishing that Matthew, who seems to be the inventor of the whole guards motif, did not think to stipulate that the guards first made sure the tomb was occupied!

A Glossy Gospel

One of the major reasons people write new gospels, whether in ancient or modern times, is to clarify the text and to provide explicit answers to questions implicit in earlier gospels. Such explanations (whether correct or not) are known as "glosses." In this chapter I want to gloss Levi Dowling's glosses upon the canonical gospels. There are many, and they are among the most fascinating materials in *The Aquarian Gospel*.

Samaritan Woman, Let Me Be

Why were the disciples discomfited at the sight of Jesus talking with the Samaritan woman when they returned from food shopping in John 4:27? *The Aquarian Gospel* 82:2 suggests it was because "they thought [her] a courtesan." Of course, that is pretty close to the truth even for John, given that he says she has discarded five husbands and is now shacking up with another man without even bothering with the formality of marriage.

Aquarian Gospel 81:28–29 expands the equivocal John 4:26: "The woman said, 'We know that when Messiah comes that he will lead us in the ways of truth.' And Jesus said, 'Behold the Christ has come; Messiah speaks to you.'" This wording draws the loop closed. In John it is not Jesus himself who uses the loaded word "Messiah/Christ," but rather the woman. Even Jesus' reply, "I who speak to you am he" might equally be translated, "I am he who is speaking with you," implying it would be an evasion to shelve her question till the Messianic "answer-man" should appear "someday." Jesus has the answer she needs but fears to hear *right now*. I say, it could mean that in John, and I think it does. But *The Aquarian Gospel* is clearly trying to reinforce the traditional, orthodox reading, by which the Samaritan woman elicits from him at least an implicit messianic self-confession.

John 4:32 raised the dreaded prospect of docetism, the ancient doctrine, prevalent in some Johannine circles (1 John 4:1–3), that Jesus was an insubstantial phantom in human form. Jesus has professed himself hungry and thirsty, but when his disciples return from the marketplace, he refuses to eat, apparently fortified by his revelatory speech to the Samaritan woman. This is what Jesus refers to when he says, "I have food to eat, of which you know nothing, for my food and drink are to do the will of him who sent me" (John 4:32). But *The Aquarian Gospel* 82:12–13 explains how Jesus could get along without physical food. He didn't. He had power to conjure it up in a pinch: "Then the disciples said among themselves, 'Who could have brought him aught to eat?' They did not know that he had power to turn the very ethers into bread."

Beheading the Grain

Why does God allow his servants to come to such disgraceful, violent ends? *Aquarian Gospel* 85:13–16 tells us. "And when they asked why God permitted Herod to imprison John, he said, 'Behold yon stalk of wheat! When it has brought the grain to perfectness, it is of no more worth; it falls, becoming part of earth again from which it came. John is a stalk of golden wheat; he brought unto maturity the richest grain of all the earth; his work is done. If he had said another word it might have marred the symmetry of what is now a noble life.'" This sounds a bit cruel, but it has been suggested in our own time in the case of Dr. Martin Luther King, Jr. Suppose he had survived for decades more; who knows that he might not have tarnished his legacy by making ill-considered statements in his dotage? Of course that hardly justifies God rubbing him out to keep his mouth shut.

The Ghost Who Walks

Docetism rears its phantom head again in Luke 4:29–30, in the aftermath of Jesus' icy reception at the Nazareth synagogue. It is a classic embellishment. The Markan original (Mark 6:1–5) merely has Jesus meet with unbelief on the part of the throng. But Luke has them form a lynch mob! The pious congregation seizes Jesus and brings him to the precipice of the hill on which Nazareth was built, planning to throw him over. Instead, Luke simply says that he walked away through the crowd, unmolested. How? By sheer force of personality, cutting the nerve of their resolve at the last moment? That seems a bit contrived. Levi Dowling comes out unambiguously on the docetic side, giving the tale a better finish: "But when they thought they held him fast, he disappeared; unseen he passed among the angry men, and went his way. The people were confounded and they said, 'What manner of a man is this?' And when they came again to Nazareth, they found him teaching in the synagogue. They troubled him no more for they were sore afraid" (86:16–19). This reminds me of nothing so much as the martyrdom (July 9, 1850) of the

Bab, Ali Muhammad, founder of the Bab'i Faith. Persian troops took him from his cell and set him before a firing squad. Christian soldiers refused to fire and were replaced by eager Muslim gunmen. When the smoke cleared, there was no corpse. Searching everywhere, they found the holy man, alive and untouched, back in his cell, finishing his prayers. Then they shot him again, and it worked, but up till that point we have a pretty good parallel.

The docetism is apparently supposed to be the result of yogic discipline, through which expedient Jesus has awakened the *siddhis*, or miraculous powers, including dematerializing. He does it again in 135:37, explaining a similar puzzling escape in John 8:59, where he evades a stoning: "Again the scribes and Pharisees were in a rage; they took up stones to cast at him, but, like a phantom of the night, he disappeared; the people knew not where he went."

Full of Fish

What accounts for Peter's post-miracle shame in Luke 5:8, after he has grudgingly taken his boat out at Jesus' urging, only to find fish swamping the boat? Why not rejoice at his good fortune? But instead he kneels before the holy man and exclaims, "Depart from me, O Lord, for I am a sinful man!" The most natural reading is probably that the spectacle has lifted the veil. Fish no longer matter; they have become a sign of the inbreaking numinous: "Surely God is in this place, and I did not know it!" (Genesis 28:16). But Levi's explanation is by no means implausible. He reasons that Peter should not have been so skeptical at Jesus' suggestion. "When Peter saw the heavy catch, he was ashamed of what he said; ashamed because he had no faith, and he fell down at Jesus' feet, and said, 'Lord, I believe!'" (88:14).

He Knows Whereof He Speaks

Aquarian Gospel 89:14 explains the origin and nature of Jesus' teaching with authority, unlike the scribes (Matthew 7:28–29). "The people said, 'He teaches not as do the scribes and Pharisees; but as a man who knows, and has authority to speak.'" In other words, the scribes quite properly hedge their words, based as they are on speculation. Jesus, however, has drawn aside the veil. He has seen and *knows*.

Soul Force

97:19 explains why one ought to give the abuser more even than he asked (Matthew 5:40), seemingly an odd strategy. "Give him your coat and offer him still more and more; in time the man will rise above the brute; you will have saved him from himself." It is the strategy of *satyagraha*, "soul force," as practiced by Mahatma Gandhi and Dr. King: by turning the other cheek, one offers the abuser the clearest, because most starkly etched, portrait of ideal humanity that does not sink to the animal level. If the attacker possesses any conscience at all, it will be awakened.

Falling Sparrow Zone

99:25 adds a sequel to mitigate God's apparent nonintervention in the case of falling sparrows (Matthew 10:29): "And not a sparrow falls to earth without his care; and every one that falls shall rise again." If only it were so.

Tell Them Jesus Sent You

101:6–7 adds the magic that will cause the door always to be opened to him who asks (Matthew 7:7–8) and suggests why sometimes it doesn't open. "Just speak the Word and knock; the door will fly ajar. No one has ever asked in faith and did not have; none ever sought in vain; no one who ever knocked aright has failed to find an open door." So there are variables! The knock must be accompanied by the password, or the speakeasy remains barred. One must knock *aright*, presumably with the spiritual equivalent of the two-three or three-two rap, before one is admitted. Of course, the suggestion of such unknown quantities is not intended as help toward better results in prayer. On the contrary, the point is to mask failure. The variables remain unknown and thus cannot be eliminated. One must trust to luck.

Bloody Hands

102:8–11 explains in what sense the believing centurion reckoned himself unworthy to have Jesus come under his roof (Luke 7:6//Matthew 8:8). "Lo, Lord, it is not well that you should come unto my house; I am not worthy of the presence of a man of God. I am a man of war, my life is spent with those who oftimes take the lives of fellow men. And surely he who comes to save would be dishonored if he came beneath my roof. If you will speak the Word I know my servant will be well." The centurion is like David, who might have been allowed to construct the temple of Yahve, had his hands not been reddened by the work of war. As it was, the job had to be delegated to the uncalloused hands of his son Solomon (1 Chronicles 22:8–9).

Fickle Forerunner

103:9–11 explains how it was distress that led John the Baptist to think twice and doubt Jesus (Mathew 11:2–3). "His prison life was hard, and he was sore distressed, and he began to doubt. And to himself he said, 'I wonder if this Jesus is the Christ of whom the prophets wrote! Was I mistaken in my work? Was I, indeed, one sent from God to pave the way for him who shall redeem our people, Israel?'" This is nothing new, only the traditional orthodox harmonization of two disparate gospel episodes. How is it that John first proclaims Jesus as the Messiah (Matthew 3:14), then is shown wondering, as if for the first time, if this rumored Jesus might be the Christ (Matthew 11:2)? The "answer" (and it remains contrived) is to posit that John had grown disillusioned in captivity, perhaps from the lack of cable television in his cell. But, as David Friedrich Strauss showed,[21] the real answer is that early Christians were first satisfied to have John raise the question of Jesus' messiahship, pointedly leaving the question for the reader to answer for himself. Later Christians, however, found it advantageous to imagine that the famous John had endorsed Jesus, for the sake of attracting John's latter-day followers to the Christian camp instead.

Holy Ghost Land Mine

105:33 defines the sin against the Holy Spirit (Matthew 12:31–33): "you sin against the Holy Breath by disregarding her when she would open up the doors of life for you." As with many other guesses about the nature of the damning sin of blasphemy against the Spirit, this one reduces it to a tautology one need not worry about unduly: rather than some specific word one might say unguardedly, the sin against the Spirit is irreligion in general, refusal to repent. The goal is to salve the tortures of pious scrupulosity. "Oh no! Could

I have committed that sin? Did I blaspheme the Spirit?"

Temporary Eviction

What is the point of the parable of the sevenfold return of the demon (Luke 11:24–26//Matthew 12:43–45), he who, once ejected, finds no barrier to his soon return along with a whole gang of devils worse than himself? What did the poor possessed man do wrong so to open himself to relapse? "And so it is with you who snatch the blessings that belong to other men" (108:11). Oh.

Stand Up, Stand Up for . . . Whom?

109:28–29 resolves the question of who is the Son of Man to be confessed or denied in Mark 8:28. "Fear not to make confession of the Christ before the sons of men, and God will own you as his sons and daughters in the presence of the host of heaven. If you deny the Christ before the sons of men, then God will not receive you as his own before the hosts of heaven." "Son of Man" has become "sons of men," referring now to the audience before whom one either affirms or denies Christian (Christine) loyalty. As for whom one is denying or confessing, that is made unambiguous: it is no more the ambiguous "Son of Man," but the Christ, presumably Jesus the Christ. One can understand the anxiety that motivates the clarification. After all, it is forthright confession that is in view here, and "if the bugle call is uncertain, who will know to prepare for battle?" (1 Corinthians 14:8).

   Another ambiguity involving the Son of Man is resolved in 112:16. "Beloved, these are times when every man must be awake and at his post, for none can tell the hour nor the day when man shall be revealed." Not Jesus, but anyone, as indeed it might be anyone in a time of persecution.

What the Heck?

The idea of eternal punishment in the flames of hell is particularly difficult to swallow if one is concerned to safeguard the name of God from blasphemy and maligning as a torturing devil.[22] The Aquarian Gospel seeks to mitigate the doctrine, turning hell into Purgatory. According to Levi, hellfire (as in Luke 16:24) is purifying, not destroying. "And Philip said, 'Must men and

women suffer in the flames because they have not found the way of life?'
And Jesus said, 'The fire purifies. The chemist throws into the fire the ores
that hold all kinds of dross" (116:13–14). (Try to remember the difference
while you're screaming your brains out, why don't you?) Similarly, the
rich man found himself in *purifying* hell fire (Luke 16:24). "The rich man
also died, and he was buried in a costly tomb; but in the purifying fires he
opened up his eyes dissatisfied" (142:38). To say the least.

Legionnaires Disease

Aquarian Gospel 118:5 explains how the Gadarene demoniac came to be
infested with a whole legion of demons (Mark 5:9). "Now, spirits of the lately
dead that cannot rise to higher planes, remain about the tombs that hold the
flesh and bones of what [were] once their mortal homes." For my money, that
is quite a good explanation. Otherwise, why set the story in a cemetery in the
first place? And why are the unclean spirits averse to leaving the scene once
Jesus threatens to expel them? Their graves, their bones, are there, and they
do not want to leave them behind. They are manifestly the ghosts of the dead
buried there.

Not So Fast

119:8–9 explain why John's disciples were fasting in Mark 2:18. "A band of
John's disciples who had heard that John was dead were wearing badges for
their dead; were fasting and were praying in their hearts, which when the
Pharisees observed they came to Jesus and they said, 'Why fast? The followers
of John and your disciples do not fast.'" Apparently the Pharisees did not
recognize the nature of whatever tokens of mourning the bereaved Baptists
were sporting, unless their question is why Jesus and his disciples are not
similarly fasting; did they, too, not revere John? But that does not seem to be
the point, as what they ask is not why Jesus' men do *not* fast, but rather why
the Baptist's *do*? Or perhaps the Pharisees are pictured as utterly ignorant,
not grasping the most elementary point of fasting, merely asking an obvious
question to set Jesus up to provide a less-than-obvious answer.

No Brats

What is it about a child we ought to emulate (Mark 10:15)? The traditional gospel text leaves us guessing, and there have been many theories. *The Aquarian Gospel* clears this up for us. "The greatest is the little child, and if you would be great at all you must become as is this child in innocence, in truth, in purity in life" (131:10).

Inscribing the Scribes

What exactly did Jesus write in the dirt, while the accusers of the adulteress awaited his verdict (John 8:8)? "And Jesus stooped and made a figure on the ground and in it placed the number of a soul, and then he sat in silent thought" (134:22). Uh, whose soul did he draw? This attempt at clarification, if that is what it is supposed to be, does not help much. The original episode appears to be inspired by Plato's *Meno* dialogue, in which Socrates draws diagrams in the dirt to lead Meno's untutored slave boy through the intricacies of a geometric proof, illustrating that the knowledge is already in him, and in everyone. Traditional explanations of the story of the adulteress posit that Jesus was writing names of men in the accusing crowd whom he knew to have slept with her, prompting them to hurry away in shame.

A Lawyer Joke

136:9–11 gives us a tendentious rewrite of Luke's Good Samaritan parable. The original features two indifferent passers-by, a priest and a Levite (a kind of priestly assistant), and it does not explain their motives. It does, however, hint at them. The Lukan parable seems to be anti-sacerdotal, implying that the two temple functionaries (Luke 10:31–32) pass the injured man by because to touch a man with bleeding wounds would have rendered them temporarily "unclean" ritually and thus unable to perform the priestly service in the temple to which they were bound that day. They had a choice to make, and their priority was liturgical. After all, suppose, in the same gospel, Zecharias, the future father of John the Baptist, had found such a victim on the road before him on his way to the temple, helped him, and missed his appointment with the angel Gabriel? The Lukan original, then, compares two rival views of religion: what is more important? Temple theatrics, or helping the needy? It is the choice mandated by Isaiah and the prophets. The point in *The Aquarian Gospel* is quite different. The characters become caricatures. "A Pharisee was going down that way; he saw the wounded man; but then he had no time to lose; he passed by on the other side. A Levite came and saw the man; but he was loath to soil his sacerdotal robes, and he passed by. A lawyer on his way to Jericho observed the dying man, and then he said, 'If I could make a shekel I might help the man; but he has nothing left to give, I have no time for charity.' And he passed on.'" They are plainly wicked, hard-hearted, and the lesson is obvious, blunt.

Born Blind

Chapter 138 provides a rather tiring retelling of the story of the healing of the man born blind from John chapter 9. It features an extensive explanation of karma. Whereas in John 9, we have the disciples venture that the man may have been born blind as punishment for sins in a previous incarnation. Jesus brushes this possibility aside, replying only that such was not the case in this man's instance, but rather God had blinded him with a view to eventually revealing his glory by healing him. In *The Aquarian Gospel*, by contrast, Jesus confirms that the man was indeed suffering the effects of bad karma, whose poetic justice assured that he be punished proportionately to his past-life crime. Being born blind, he must have robbed another of his sight long ago. "An eye for an eye." Sure, there is Plan B: by the grace of God, when Jesus or the disciples heal someone, their karmic punishment has been mitigated, but only to the extent that they are to pay their original debt through atoning good works. It was such karmic bean-counting, albeit in a slightly different form, that led to the Roman Catholic penitential calculus: how many Hail Marys do you owe?

Both Gate and Gate Keeper

How can Jesus be both the shepherd and the gate of the sheepfold as in John 10:7, 9? "Christ is the gateway of the fold; I am the shepherd of the sheep, and he who follows me through Christ shall come into the fold where living waters flow, and where rich pastures are" (139:18). It is simple division of labor between the two aspects of Jesus the Christ. Jesus conducts the flock to safe (saving) pasture, but the Christ hovering over him is the spring of saving water.

Banqueting Etiquette

The heavenly banquet (Matthew 8:11) will be more of a metaphysical "Be-in" than a sensual snack. "And, lo, I say that men will come from lands afar, from east, from west, from north, from south and sit with me in consciousness of life" (141:8). Perhaps the spectacle of a Valhalla-like chow-down appeared too carnal to Levi.

In Luke 14:12–14 Jesus commands us to invite the poor, not our friends and relatives, to dinner parties. "For they consider such a courtesy loaned out, and they feel called upon to make a greater feast for you, just in the payment of a debt. But when you make a feast, invite the poor, the lame, the blind; in this a blessing waits for you, for well you know that you will get naught in return; but in the consciousness of helping those who need, you will be recompensed" (141:31–32). A this-worldly sense of satisfaction replaces the carrot of reward on resurrection day. Of course, the notion of investing the cost of a meal for hobos in order to reap a heavenly reward is scarcely less crass than inviting guests to a meal, hoping to be invited in turn.

Crossroads

In what precise sense we are to "bear the cross" (Mark 8:34)? "The paths of carnal life do not run up the mountain side towards the top; they run around the mount of life, and if you go straight to the upper gate of consciousness you cross the paths of carnal life; tread in them not. And this is how men bear the cross; no man can bear another's cross" (142:12–13). Worldly distractions result from the attempt to cut straight for the spiritual goal. Or something. The straightforward summons to martyrdom seems a lot more profound.

Full Gospel Businessmen

How exactly does God save the rich man (Mark 10:24–27//Matthew 19:23–26//Luke 18:25)? "Yea, it is easier for a camel to go through a needle's eye than for a man with hoarded wealth to find the way of life. And his disciples said, 'Who then can find the way? Who can be saved?' And Jesus said, 'The rich may give his gold away; the high may kiss the dust, and God will save'" (142:32–33). I imagine this is the intended sense of the original, not the convenient notion that the rich can be saved, while still rich, against all likelihood by the miracle-working power of God.

Welcome Back, Lazarus

I find an infelicity in the Johannine story of Lazarus' resurrection. The deed seems to strike everyone as a total surprise, yet is there not a marked hint in John 11:22 that Martha hopes Jesus may raise Lazarus now, not on the last day? Levi Dowling thought so, too: "But even now I know that you have power over death; that by the sacred Word you may cause life to rise from death" (148:14).

The gospel accounts of Jesus raising the daughter of Jairus (Mark 5:22–123, 35–43) and the son of the widow of Nain (Luke 7:11–17) are very likely not resurrection stories at all, since they match so closely various ancient Hellenistic tales in which a hero (Apollonius of Tyana, the physician Asclepiades, etc.) saves a coma victim from premature burial by discerning obscure life-signs where no one else could. After all, in the Jairus story, Jesus even says, "She is not dead." The Lazarus story is supposed to be exceptional in this regard because, even though Jesus again declares him merely to be asleep (John 11:11), John has Lazarus interred four days (John 11:17) by the time Jesus gets there, one past the cut-off time in Jewish belief for the soul to have left the body. Must not John be trying to eliminate the possibility that Lazarus had only been comatose? But this is surely circular: suppose Lazarus hadn't died and decomposed; they only surmised he must have (John 11:39). *Aquarian Gospel* 148:31 so understands the story: "And then they rolled the stone away; the flesh had not decayed; and Jesus lifted up his eyes to heaven and said . . ." (148:31).

Payback

In Luke 19:1–10 Jesus earns the ire of the crowd when he seeks the dinner company of a toll-collector named Zaccheus. Most read the story as if Jesus' offer of friendship galvanizes him to repent, whereupon he declares that he will henceforth atone for past robberies and swindles by giving half his riches to the poor outright and paying the rest back to those to whom it rightly belongs. But I wonder if we are instead to understand Zaccheus as protesting the libel of the crowd, describing his regular scrupulosity. He is no swindler but rather a philanthropist, and willing as well to pay back fourfold any amount he may have accidentally overcharged anyone. This is the way Levi Dowling tells it, too: "But Jesus did not care for what they said; he went his way with Zaccheus, who was a man of faith, and as they talked together Zaccheus said, 'Lord, I have ever tried to do the right; I give unto the poor half of my goods, and if by any means I wrong a man, I right the wrong by paying him four fold'" (148:8–9).

The Comfortress

What does it means for the Comforter to convict the world of sin, righteousness and judgment (John 16:8)? "When she has come, the Comforter, she will convince the world of sin, and of the truth of what I speak, and of the judgment of the just; and then the prince of carnal life will be cast out" (162:10). Why is the Holy Spirit female here? She is female in Jewish Christianity since Spirit (*ruach*) was grammatically feminine.

A Quick Escape

Who was the impetuous youth who fled Gethsemane at Jesus' arrest, leaving behind his linen garment in the clutches of the Romans (Mark 14:51–52)? "Now, John was last to flee; the mob laid hold of him and tore his garments all to shreds; but he escaped in nakedness" (164:31). Why John? Tradition made John a younger man than the rest of the disciples, since he was imagined to have lived to old age and written his gospel at the end of the first century.

The Jesus Nightmare

Every reader of Matthew has wished to know more about Mrs. Pilate's ominous dream (Matthew 27:19). Here is Levi's take:

> And as he mused his wife, a godly woman, chosen from among the Gauls, came in and said, "I pray you, Pilate, hearken unto me: Beware

of what you do this hour. Touch not this man from Galilee; he is a holy man. If you should scourge this man you scourge the son of God. Last night I saw it all in vision far too vivid to be set aside as idle dream. I saw this man walk on the waters of the sea; I heard him speak and calm an angry storm; I saw him flying with the wings of light; I saw Jerusalem in blood; I saw the statues of the Caesars fall; I saw a veil before the sun, and day was dark as night. The earth on which I stood was shaken like a reed before the wind. I tell you, Pilate, if you bathe your hands in this man's blood then you may dread the frowns of great Tiberius, and the curses of the senators of Rome." And then she left, and Pilate wept. (167:43–48).

The Great Explodo

It is common for Bible readers, though not scholars, to harmonize the conflicting legends of Judas' death in Matthew 27:5, where Judas hangs himself, and Acts 1:18, where he swells up and explodes. *Aquarian Gospel* 169:7–8 follows in this tradition. "Then Judas threw the silver on the floor, and, bowed with grief, he went away, and on a ledge beyond the city's walls he hanged himself and died. In time the fastenings gave way, his body fell into the Hinnom vale and after many days they found it there a shapeless mass" (169:7–8).

I'm with Stupid

In the wonderful story of the disciples on the road to Emmaus, we learn the name of one of the pair, Cleopas (Luke 24:18). Might the other disciple have been his wife? That is one inference, but Levi simply picks a name out of a hat to christen this silent character: the other Emmaus disciple (see Luke 24:18) was named Zachus. "Towards the evening of the resurrection day, two friends of Jesus, Zachus and Cleophas of Emmaus, seven miles away, were going to their home" (174:1).

A Fly on the Wall

How did the evangelists know what was said at Jesus' trial? None was present, after all. But what if the risen Christ were willing to accommodate the curiosity of the disciples on the point (cf. Philostratus, *Life of Apollonius of Tyana* VIII:12)? That is what Levi imagines him doing, making it easy for gospel writers and apologists, the only people who would have a need to know. "And Martha ran and brought the chair in which the Lord had ever loved to sit, and Jesus sat down on the chair. And for a long, long time they talked about the trial, and the scenes of Calvary and of the garden of Siloam" (175:17–18).

New Parables

Though most of the parabolic teaching of Jesus in *The Aquarian Gospel* consists of rewrites, redactions, of traditional gospel parables, Levi does venture to supply us with a trio of new parables, placed, naturally, on the lips of Jesus. It would be disappointing if he had not. The first borrows the premise of gospel parables such as the Talents and the Wicked Servants, that of the Landlord or master who has gone away, or who lives elsewhere, placing his local affairs in the hands of subordinates, in this case, sons. To choose this well-worn premise invites no charges of being derivative. It is almost irresistible in its deistic structure: God has stood aside to see what we human beings will do with his creation. In this case, the unfaithfulness consists in the division of society into various ranked and inflexible castes, such as Jesus himself has discovered in India, the fourfold caste system of the Brahmins (priests), Kshatriyas (warriors and kings), Vshaiyas (merchants and craftsmen), and Shudras (menial laborers). By contrast, the Upanishads depict the four castes as direct creations of Purusha, the Primal Man, creator, through self-immolation, of the universe. Herewith, the **Parable of the Four Sons** (25:2–21).

> A nobleman possessed a great estate;
> he had four sons, and he would have them all
> grow strong by standing forth and making use
> of all the talents they possess. And so
> he gave to each a share of his great wealth,
> and bade them go their way. The eldest son
> was full of self; he was ambitious, shrewd
> and quick of thought. He said within himself,
> "I am the oldest son, and these, my bro-
> thers, must be servants at my feet." And then

he called his brothers forth; and one he made
a puppet king; gave him a sword and charged
him to defend the whole estate. To one
he gave the use of lands and flowing wells,
and flocks and herds, and bade him till the soil,
and tend the flocks and herds and bring to him
the choicest of his gains. And to the o-
ther one he said, "You are the youngest son;
the broad estate has been assigned; you have
no part nor lot in anything that is."
[And] he took a chain and bound his brother to
a naked rock upon a desert plain,
and said to him, "You have been born a slave;
you have no rights, and you must be content-
ed with your lot, for there is no release
for you until you die and go from hence."
Now, after certain years the day of rec-
k'ning came; the nobleman called up his sons
to render their accounts. And when he knew
that one, his eldest son, had seized the whole
estate and made his brothers slaves, he seized
him, tore his priestly robes away and put
him in a prison cell, where he was forced
to stay until he had atoned for all
the wrongs that he had done. And then, as though
they were but toys, he threw in air the throne
and armor of the puppet king; he broke
his sword, and put him in a prison cell.
And then he called his farmer son and asked
him why he had not rescued from his gal-
ling chains his brother on the desert plains.
And when the son made answer not, the father took unto himself the flocks and herds,
the fields and flowing wells, and sent his farmer son to live out on the desert sands,
until he had atoned for all the wrongs
that he had done. And then the father went
and found his youngest son in cruel chains;
with his own hands he broke the chains and bade
his son to go in peace. Now, when the sons

had all paid up their debts they came again
and stood before the bar of right. They all
had learned their lessons, learned them well; and then
the father once again divided the
estate. He gave to each an equal share,
and bade them recognize the law of e-
quity and right, and live in peace.

Parable of the Vinedresser (34:5–21) teaches the vanity of ritual formalism. Perhaps suggested by John 15:1–2, the story tells us that true religion must be pruned of ritual formalism lest pomp and liturgy come to supplant and obscure true worship. Intended to facilitate worship of God, has liturgy instead become an end and object of worship in its own right? When it does, it becomes an idol to us and mere "trampling of my courts," (Isaiah 1:12) to God.

And Jesus spoke a parable; he said,
"There was a vineyard all unkept; the vines
were high, the growth of leaves and branches great.
The leaves were broad and shut the sun
light from the vines; the grapes were sour, and few,
and small. The pruner came; with his sharp knife
he cut off every branch, and not a leaf
remained; just root and stalk, and nothing more.
The busy neighbors came with one accord
and were amazed, and said to him who pruned,
"You foolish man! the vineyard is despoiled.
Such desolation!
There is no beauty left,
and when the harvest time shall come the gatherers will find no fruit." The pruner said,
"Content yourselves with what you think,
and come again at harvest time and see."
And when the harvest time came on the busy neighbors came again; they were surprised.
The naked stalks had put forth branch and leaf,
and heavy clusters of delicious grapes
weighed every branch to earth.
The gatherers rejoiced as, day by day,

they carried the rich fruitage to the press.
Behold the vineyard of the Lord!
The earth is spread with human vines.
The gorgeous forms and rites of men
are branches, and their words are leaves;
and these have grown so great
that sunlight can no longer reach the heart;
there is no fruit. Behold, the pruner comes,
and with a two-edged knife he cuts away
the branches and the leaves of words,
and naught is left but unclothed stalks
of human life.
The priests and they of pompous show,
rebuke the pruner, and would stay
him in his work. They see no beauty in
the stalks of human life; no promises of fruit.
The harvest time will come and they who scorned
the pruner will look on again and be
amazed, for they will see the human stalks
that seemed so lifeless, bending low with precious fruit.
And they will hear the harvesters rejoice,
because the harvest is so great.

The third Aquarian parable I can only call **The Limbo Supper** (153:22–26). It reads like a clumsy combination of the Great Supper with the apocryphal business from Theophylact about a Jerusalem gate called the Needle's Eye because its arch was so low to the ground that, for a camel to pass under it, the poor beast would have to be unburdened and then get down on its knees to inch through. Of course there never was such a structure. It was a homiletical invention to advise repentance: laying one's burdens down and kneeling in humility. Levi Dowling makes the gate the doorway into the Feast of Salvation.

And then he spoke a parable to them; he said, "A man once made a feast inviting all the rich and honored people of the land. But when they came, they found the door into the banquet hall was low, and they could enter not except they bowed their heads and fell down on their knees. These people would not bow their heads and fall down on their knees, and so they went away; they went not to the feast. And then the man sent forth his messengers to bid the common folks, and those of low estate, to come and feast with him. These people gladly came; they bowed their heads and fell down on their knees, and came into the banquet hall and it was full, and every one rejoiced."

New Versions of Familiar Parables

The Stalks with Broken Blades (27:25–32) is a reworking of Matthew's parable of the Wheat and Weeds/Tares (Matthew 13:24–30, 36–43) in which some rival farmer sabotages a man's wheat field by scattering darnel in it, which so resembles wheat that one can tell the difference only once both of them have neared maturity, by which time any attempt to uproot the one will take the other with it. The farmhands suggest this destructive strategy, but the farmer tells them to wait and separate the two at harvest time when the wheat has to come up anyway. The point seems to be that sectarian communities should not try to purify themselves of "sinners" in their midst, since only God knows the heart, and the judgment is not ours to make (cf. 1 Corinthians 4:5). Levi makes a related point in a simpler way.

> And Jesus spoke a parable: he said, "Behold, a farmer had great fields of ripened grain, and when he looked he saw that blades of many stalks of wheat were bent and broken down. And when he sent his reapers forth he said, 'We will not save the stalks of wheat that have the broken blades. Go forth and cut and burn the stalks with broken blades.' And after many days he went to measure up his grain, but not a kernel could he find. And then he called the harvesters and said to them, 'Where is my grain?' They answered him and said, 'We did according to your word; we gathered up and burned the stalks with broken blades, and not a stalk was left to carry to the barn.' And Jesus said, 'If God saves only those who have no broken blades, who have been perfect in his sight, who will be saved?' And the accusers hung their heads in shame; and Jesus went his way."

Levi's point is rather different: it is not so easy even for God to tell black from white if all are various shades of gray! As Paul Tillich[24] commented, this factor makes it unreasonable to imagine God saving the "righteous" and damning the "wicked." Things, and people, are much more complex.

The Gold Mine (33:13–23) appears to be a new version of Matthew 13:44, the parable of the Treasure Hidden in the Field, in which one discovers treasure in another's field, unknown to its owner, and determines to purchase the field for himself, not to use the field, but merely to get the treasure— like the time I bought a book I didn't particularly want so I could get the ten dollar bill the previous owner had used as a book mark! Levi Dowling imaginatively switches the focus to the owner ignorant of the treasure. This time he doesn't get cheated out of it.

> And Jesus spoke a parable; he said, "A certain man possessed a field; the soil was hard and poor. By constant toil he scarcely could provide enough of food to keep his family from want. One day a miner who could see beneath the soil, in passing on his way, saw this poor man and his unfruitful field. He called the weary toiler and he said, 'My brother, know you not that just below the surface of your barren field rich treasures lie concealed? You plough and sow and reap in scanty way, and day by day you tread upon a mine of gold and precious stones. This wealth lies not upon the surface of the ground; but if you will dig away the rocky soil, and delve down deep into the earth, you need no longer till the soil for naught.' The man believed. 'The miner surely knows;' he said, 'and I will find the treasures hidden in my field.' And then he dug away the rocky soil, and deep down in the earth he found a mine of gold." And Jesus said, "The sons of men are toiling hard on desert plains, and burning sands and rocky soils; are doing what their fathers did, not dreaming they can do aught else. Behold, a master comes, and tells them of a hidden wealth; that underneath the rocky soil of carnal things are treasures that no man can count; that in the heart the richest gems abound; that he who wills may open up the door and find them all."

The parable nicely balances the good news, that we have at our disposal a resource of potential we scarcely imagine, with the sobering news that we cannot gain it without great toil and discipline. So is it ignorance or laziness that keeps us in our accustomed spiritual poverty?

The Beneficent Son (36:25–35) extends the allegorical salvation history of Mark 12:1–9, adding motifs from John 14:18. Levi substitutes for the sharecropper analogues that of priests, only this is no analogue; the target of the Markan original was actually the Jewish priests. What Levi should have done, if I may say so, is to have the Santa-like son meet opposition from merchants who stand to lose money if people accept the free gifts the son offers. Thus they declare them counterfeits, their giver a swindler.

> To them he spoke a parable; he said, "A certain king so loved the people of his land that he sent forth his only son with precious gifts for all. The son went everywhere and scattered forth the gifts with lavish hand. But there were priests who ministered at shrines of foreign gods, who were not pleased because the king did not through them bestow the gifts. And so they sought to cause the people all to hate the son. They said, 'These gifts are not of any worth; they are but counterfeits.' And so the people threw the precious gems, and gold and silver in the streets. They caught the son and beat him, spat upon him, drove him from their midst. The son resented not their insults and their cruelties; but thus he prayed, 'My Father-God, forgive these creatures of thy hand; they are but slaves; they know not what they do.' And while they yet were beating him he gave them food, and blest them with a boundless love. In certain cities was the son received with joy, and he would gladly have remained to bless the homes; but he could tarry not, for he must carry gifts to every one in all the king's domain." And Jesus said, "My Father-God is king of all mankind, and he has sent me forth with all the bounties of his matchless love and boundless wealth. To all the people of all lands, lo, I must bear these gifts—this water and this bread of life. I go my way, but we will meet again; for in my Fatherland is room for all; I will prepare a place for you."

The Mighty Son (73:3–14) is a cumbersome rewrite, again, of Mark 12:1–9, the Wicked Tenants. The point of the parable is similar to that of the Four Sons, in that God stands by to see what human society will make of themselves. But instead of the caste system, it is the system of government that forms the target of this new version.

> And Jesus spoke a parable; he said, "A king had vast domains; his people all were kin, and lived in peace. Now, after many years the king said to his people, 'Take these lands and all I have; enhance their values; rule yourselves, and live in peace.' And then the people formed their states; selected governors and petty kings. But pride, ambition, selfish greed, and base ingratitude grew fast, and kings began to war. They wrote in all their statute books that might is right; and then the strong destroyed the weak, and chaos reigned through all the vast domain. A long time passed, and then the king looked out on his domain. He saw

his people in their cruel wars; he saw them sick and sore distressed; he saw the strong enslave the weak, and then he said, 'What shall I do? Shall I send forth a scourge? Shall I destroy my people all?' And then his heart was stirred with pity and he said, 'I will not send a scourge; I will send forth my only son, heir to the throne, to teach the people love, and peace, and righteousness.' He sent his son; the people scorned him and maltreated him, and nailed him to a cross. He was entombed; but death was far too weak to hold the prince, and he arose. He took a form man could not kill; and then he went again to teach the people love, and peace and righteousness. And thus God deals with men."

The Sower (115:1–9) simply retells Mark 4:3–9 in iambic pentameter.

And Jesus stood beside the sea and taught; the multitudes pressed close upon him and he went into a boat that was near by and put a little ways from shore, and then he spoke in parables; he said, "Behold, a sower took his seed and went into his field to sow. With lavish hand he scattered forth the seed and some fell in the hardened paths that men had made, and soon were crushed beneath the feet of other men; and birds came down and carried all the seeds away. Some seed fell on rocky ground where there was little soil; they grew and soon the blades appeared and promised much; but then there was no depth of soil, no chance for nourishment, and in the heat of noonday sun they withered up and died. Some seed fell where thistles grew, and found no earth in which to grow and they were lost; but other seed found lodgement in the rich and tender soil and grew apace, and in the harvest it was found that some brought forth a hundred fold, some sixty fold, some thirty fold. They who have ears to hear may hear; they who have hearts to understand may know."

In the same way, the **Parable of the Drag Net** (116:6–8) merely paraphrases Matthew 13:47–49, adding nothing. **The Sheepfold** (139:13–16) just condenses John 10:1–18. **The Little Seed** (140:38–39) adds nothing important to Matthew 13:31–32.

The Great Supper (141:33–43) adds to its Lukan prototype (Luke 14:16–24) the element that the second and final summoning to the feast of salvation will be the eschatological summoning of the angels on Judgment Day, an interesting embellishment. In Luke the second wave of invitations corresponds to the Gentile Mission.

And then he spoke a parable; he said, "A wealthy man prepared a feast; he sent his servants forth to bid his chosen ones to come; but they desired not to go, and they formed such excuses as they thought would satisfy the would-be host. One said, 'I have just bought a piece of land, and I must go and prove my title to the land; I pray to be excused.' Another said, 'I must go down and prove my ownership in sheep that I have bought; I pray to be excused.' Another said, 'I have been married but a little time and so I cannot go; I beg to be excused.' Now, when the servants came and told the man who had prepared the feast that those he had invited would not come, the man was grieved in heart; and then he sent his servants forth into the streets and alleys of the town to bring up to the feast the poor, the lame, the blind. The servants went abroad and found the poor, the lame, the blind, and brought them in; but there was room for more. The host then sent his men of arms to bring by force the people to his feast; and then the house was full. And God has made a feast for men. Long years ago he sent his servants forth unto the favored sons of men. They would not hear his call; they came not to the feast. He then sent forth his servants to the strangers and the multitudes; they came, but there is room for more. Behold, for he will send his angels forth with mighty trumpet blast, and men will be compelled to come up to the feast.

The Husbandman and the Laborers (143:7–21) is only slightly retooled from the version of Matthew 20:1–16. Apparently, Levi found Matthew's version a bit arbitrary: it's God's business how he wants to dole out his rewards and wages. Instead, Levi wants him to give everyone an "A" for effort.

The kingdom of the soul is like a man who had a vast estate. And in the morning time he went down to the market place to search for men to gather in his grain. He found three men, and he agreed to give to each a penny for his service for the day, and sent them to his field. Again he went down to the market place the third hour of the day and found five men in waiting, and he said, "Go down into my field and serve, and I will pay you what is right;" and they went down and served. He went again; it was the sixth hour of the day, and seven men were waiting at the stand; he sent them to the field to serve. And at the eleventh hour he went again; twelve men stood there in seeming idleness; he said to them, "Why stand you here in idleness all day?" They said, "Because we have no work to do; no man has hired us." And then he sent them to his field to serve. Now, when the evening came the man said to his steward, "Call the laborers from the field, and pay each for his services." And all were paid, and each received a penny for his hire. Now, when the twelve, who served but from the eleventh hour, received each one penny for his hire, the three were sore aggrieved; they said, "These twelve have served but one short hour, and now they have an equal share with us who have toiled through the scorching hours of day; should we not have at least two pennies for our hire?" The man replied, "My friends, I do no wrong to you. Did we not have a fast agreement when you went to work? Have I not paid in full? What is it unto you if I should pay these men a smaller or a larger sum? Take that which is your own and go your way, for I will give unto the twelve what I will give unto the three, the five, the seven. They did their best and you could do no more than do your best. The hire of man is based upon the intent of the heart."

The Prodigal Son (144:2–29) closely paraphrases the version of Luke 15:11–32, adding only the missing mother to the *dramatis personae*. Both parents welcome the Prodigal back. **The Importunate Widow** (145:26–30) slightly abbreviates the Lukan original (Luke 18:1–8), removing the element of eschatological vindication.

And then to teach that men should pray and never faint, he told this parable: "There was a judge who feared not God, nor yet regarded man. There was a widow who oft implored the judge to right her wrongs and to avenge her foes. At first the judge would hear her not, but after many days he said, 'I fear not God, and I regard not man, yet, lest this widow wear me out by pleading every day I will avenge her on her foes.'"

The Pharisee and the Publican (145:33–40) is practically the same as in Luke 18:9–14. **The Pounds** (149:11–26) comes right out of Luke 19:11–27, but seems more cumbersome. **The Wicked Tenants** (154:2–13) is pretty much the same as in Mark 12:1–12. **The Great Supper** and **The Guest w/o a Wedding Garment** (154:20–35) might have made a greater impact here had Levi not already borrowed some of the themes elsewhere. It is here just a paraphrase of Matthew 22:1–14. **The Unfaithful Steward** (158:9–20) adds little to its prototype, Matthew 24:45–51. **The Burglar** (158:18–20) is an iambic version of Luke 12:39–40. **The Wise and Foolish Virgins** (158:21–31) differs but microscopically from Matthew 25:1–13. **The Sheep and the Goats** (158:32–49) pretty much equals Matthew 25:31–46, except that it resolves the ambiguity in Matthew whether the "least of these my brethren" are supposed to be human beings in general or specifically the missionaries of the Matthean community. In opting for human beings in general, Levi may actually be restoring the parable to the meaning it had in a hypothetically pre-Matthean stage.[25]

2 THE BOOK OF MORMON

Prophecy and Palimpsest

Resurrected Texts

In 2 Kings chapter 22 the priest Hilkiah sends word to Josiah the King, "I have found a book." Hilkiah had been busy locating certain funds to be used to compensate the crews of workmen hired to refurbish the temple, when suddenly the shrouding dust and shadows disclosed a surprising secret, nothing less than the Book of the Covenant, or what we today refer to as the Book of Deuteronomy (or at least the core of it, chapters 4–33). The passage provides priceless information about the emergence of the Book of Deuteronomy. We only wish we had such revealing clues at other points in the history of the biblical canon. We may suppose, however, that the story of Josiah, Hilkiah, and the Book strikes deeper resonances for Latter Day Saints than for any other Christian group. This is because of the similarity to the conditions in which the Book of Mormon came to light. It, too, is said to be an ancient scripture buried in a time of religious and national crisis, only to resurface long afterward, when its forgotten message should be heard anew. Today virtually all critical scholars agree that the tale of Josiah and Hilkiah hints at the very thing it tries to hide: that the Book was not discovered and dusted off, but actually created by Hilkiah, Huldah, possibly Jeremiah, and others of the "Deuteronomic School" who thus sought to win the impressionable young king Josiah to their religious agenda. What is set forth in 2 Kings as reactionary (restoring the past) was really revolutionary (pressing on into a new future).

Again, virtually all critical scholars agree that Joseph Smith did not discover the Book of Mormon but rather created it. His goal would have been as analogous to that of Hilkiah as his methods had been: in the face of confusion over which 19th century version of Christianity to embrace, none seeming to have any particular advantage over the others, all seeming to be severely in want of something, Joseph Smith tried to make a clean break with the recent past and to go on into a new future by invoking a more distant past. And in so doing he had created something new, an imaginary Sacred Past, the way it should have been. Joseph Smith's picture of a pristine ("Nephite"[="neophyte"?]) American Christianity was his own biblically-informed ideal of what American Christianity in his own day ought to become. And, for a great many Americans, it did.

Narrative Worlds Without End

What Joseph Smith did is exactly what all ancient pseudepigraphists did, and he belongs to an illustrious company. Smith belongs among the authors of the Book of Daniel, the Book of Deuteronomy, the *Book of Zohar*;[1] the Pastoral Epistles (1 and 2 Timothy, Titus), not to mention a greater or lesser number of other epistles attributed to Paul; 1 and 2 Peter; 1, 2, and 3 Enoch; 1, 2, and 3 Baruch; the Apocalypse of Moses, Madame Blavatsky's *Book of Dzyan*,[2] and a number of "rediscovered" Tibetan Buddhist texts.[3] But is this group a company of saints or rather perhaps a rogues' gallery? Traditionally apologist and polemicist alike have equated "pseudepigraphist" with "fraud" or "liar."[4] And there is a trivial sense in which such a characterization is correct.

It is that same sense in which a fiction writer is a liar and a deceiver. That is, even though the book jacket be labeled "Fiction," the writer strives to woo the reader into that state of "temporary willing suspension of disbelief" that Coleridge called "poetic faith." For the time being, the reader of a novel, the viewer of a play, allows himself or herself to be drawn into the events of a fiction, to be moved by the fortunes and misfortunes of the characters, etc. One enters a fictive world, a narrative world, in order to feel and experience things one would never otherwise experience. We now recognize, as Aristotle did, the wholesome and edifying function of temporarily suspending disbelief. But it has not always been so. Shakespeare and others were obliged to reassure their audiences that what they were about to see or read was "The True History of Richard III," or whomever. Some were not able to understand the difference between fiction and lying. The problem was that of "bifurcation," the reduction of a complex choice to an over-simple one. One's alternatives are not either "fact or deception," "hoax or history." Were the parables of Jesus either factual or deceptive? Did he intend anyone to think he was talking about the case of a real prodigal son of whose improbable homecoming he had yesterday read in *The Galilee Gazette*? Of course not; he knew that his audience knew he was making it up as he went, as an illustration. And this is pretty much the same kind of "deception" practiced by the scriptural pseudepigraphist, whether ancient or modern.

It may help at this point to remind ourselves of the distinction between the author of a story and the narrator of the story. The author is the actual person composing and producing the text. Let Herman Melville serve as an example. The narrator, on the other hand, is one of the characters in the story, chosen by the author as the one from whose viewpoint the story is to be related to the reader. So the textual self-designation "I" refers not to the author but to the narrator. "My name is Ishmael." Does this mean that Melville is trying to deceive us as to what his name is? No, of course not. We are once again temporarily suspending disbelief, entering into a narrative world. While inside it, we are listening to the narrator, a fictive construct of the author. For the meantime, the author is forgotten in favor of the narrator. "Ishmael is certainly a tough old salt!" one reader may remark to another. But when they have both laid the finished novel aside, they will begin to speak of Melville's, not Ishmael's, strengths and weaknesses as a writer. Accordingly, we ought to realize that for Joseph Smith to be the author of the Book of Mormon, with Moroni and Mormon as narrators inside the text's narrative world, makes moot the old debates over whether Smith was a hoaxer or charlatan.

"Why Is It that You Ask My Name?"

Envision the situation that led to the production of pseudepigrapha in the ancient world and in the modern alike. It all begins with the process of the closing of the canon of scripture. Josephus informs his readers that the authority of the Jewish priests and scribes had come to substitute for that of the ancient prophets, since the voice of prophecy had long ago fallen silent. Christians reading Josephus often read him naively at this point. They cite Josephus and then point to John the Baptist as a renewal of prophecy after centuries of silence. They fail to realize that Josephus was giving a prescriptive account, not a descriptive account. The priestly and scribal establishment position had officially closed the canon of prophecy. It wasn't that new prophets were no longer forthcoming. Rather, the point was, they were no longer welcome.

In fact, the Bible makes clear that prophets had never been particularly welcome. Like Homer's Cassandra, their voices usually went unheeded and were often silenced by force. If a prophet were sufficiently popular, the authorities had to appear to take him seriously to maintain credibility with their flock (c.f., Mark 11:27–33). The first step was to silence the prophet; the second was to domesticate his inconvenient oracles by a process of official exegesis. Jesus satirized this process as adorning the tombs of the old prophets while you secretly build new ones for their present-day successors—like Jesus himself (Matt. 23:29–31). "Blessed are you when all men despise you and cast out your name as evil, for so they did to the prophets who were before you. But woe to you when all men speak well of you, for so they extolled the false prophets" (Luke 6:22, 26) of the past—and the true prophets after they killed them.

In view of this situation, what was a new visionary to do? He had a message to declare to his contemporaries, but there was no point in simply announcing it publicly, only to be carried away and executed. Then who would hear the message? So pseudepigraphy was born. Whereas the old prophets had spoken their messages, the new ones, the pseudepigraphists, wrote down their oracles and circulated them in this form as an underground *samizdat*. But they knew it was important, even when speaking in the name of the Lord, to be speaking also in the name of a famous prophet. One might have established one's own prophetic charisma by personal appearances, as Isaiah and Jeremiah had, but then personal appearances were needlessly dangerous. So, in order to gain a hearing, to have their oracles taken seriously, they wrote fictively under the names of ancient worthies such as Enoch, Moses, Daniel, Baruch, etc. Oh, the words themselves would ring with their own truth if they first managed to be read, and that was the trick. So one puts Daniel's or Moses' name on it, and then the reader soon finds himself recognizing the Word of God no matter the name of the human channel through which it may have come. Did it matter much to an ancient Jewish reader that the Word of God had come through Isaiah or through Jeremiah? No more than it does to most modern readers of either prophet. All that matters is that is one is reading the prophetic Word of God. And then it ought hardly to matter whether the real writer was Isaiah of Jerusalem or a later visionary appropriating his name (as in the cases of the Second and Third Isaiah and the *Ascension of Isaiah*).

Loose Canon

The closing of a canon is a momentous event in the history of any religion. It signals that the establishment (who caused the canon to be closed and who decided what belonged in it and what did not) has decided that the formative period of the religion is over and that the religion must be standardized and consolidated.[5] You are setting about the laborious task of building the ark of salvation, and you don't want anyone rocking the boat after you've built it. You don't want to hammer out a doctrine of the Trinity, only to find some prophet popping up who announces the revelation of a fourth person in the Godhead. So the guardians of the newly-minted orthodoxy, disdaining the doctrines taught in this or that gospel or prophet, cross these off the canonical list.[6] And they claim the prerogative of rightly interpreting the contents of what remains: "First of all, you must know this: no prophecy of scripture is a matter of one's own interpretation" (2 Pet. 1:20). Thus the long unwillingness of Roman Catholicism to open the Bible for everyone's scrutiny. Zechariah knew the situation well: "And if anyone again appears as a prophet, his father and mother who bore him will say to him, 'You shall not live, for you speak lies in the name of Yahweh' . . . On that day every prophet will be ashamed of his vision when he prophesies; he will not put on a hairy mantle [the distinctive "uniform" of prophets, as with Elijah and John the Baptist] in order to deceive, but he will say, 'I am no prophet, but I am a tiller of the soil . . .'" (Zech. 13:3–5).

In fact these very oracles are found in a section of the book that critical scholars dub Deutero-Zechariah. The original Zechariah was some sort of cultic prophet attached to the temple and its hierarchy, the very group who were trying to clamp the lid on populist prophecy. And in order still to have a chance to be heard, someone, one of those later prophets "ashamed of his vision," i.e., not daring to publish it under his own name, retreats behind the pen-name of one of the old prophets. Having discovered his imposture, though not his real name, we still call him "Deutero-Zechariah," "the Second Zechariah." But the name hardly matters; the content does, and this is why

"Deutero-Zechariah" set pen to paper. If the sharp edges of the old prophets and seers have been smoothed out by harmonizing exegesis, then it is the pseudepigraphist's aim to sharpen that edge again by introducing new and harsh words under the prophets' names. All right, the new visionary may not dare appear in public, but the authorities will not dare to condemn new, "newly rediscovered" writings by the old, canonical prophets. In this way, the newer prophets sought and managed to slip under or over the fence built around the scriptural canon.

It may seem a great irony that a religion whose leaders claim the authority of the prophetic word as their charter of authority will at the same time be so opposed to receiving any new prophecy. But it is no irony at all, for the very notion of a canon of scripture denotes that the living voice of prophecy has been choked off and replaced with scribal authority, exercised by the official exegetes who will make the old oracles ring, not with God's voice, but with their own. "I have no word from the Lord, but I give my opinion as one who by the grace of the Lord has been found trustworthy" (1 Cor 7:25; cf., 2 Tim. 1:2–3). Jesus "taught them as one who had authority, and not as the scribes" (Mark 1:22)—which is, of course, why the scribal establishment decided they had to be rid of him. It is well depicted in Dostoyevsky's Parable of the Grand Inquisitor in *The Brothers Karamazov*. Jesus reappears on earth—and the first thing the church does is to arrest him and condemn him to the stake! It has taken the Church long enough to consolidate its absolute power over the minds and consciences of the faithful, and they are not about to allow Jesus' living voice to return to stir things up. These are the battle lines: canon versus prophecy. The guardians of the canon use the fossil-prophecy of the past in order to turn back the challenge of living prophets by using their own weapon against them. "We know that God has spoken to Moses, but, as for this man, we do not even know where he comes from" (John 9: 29).

In short, both the new prophets and the establishment are trying to hide behind the names of the ancient, canonical prophets, in order to claim their authority for what each side is saying. The establishment scribes are using the corpus of the scriptural prophets as something of a ventriloquist dummy to spout their own views, but just as surely, the pseudepigraphists are impersonating the old prophets, speaking with their own voices while donning the deceptive Esau-mask of pseudepigraphy. The question is: who wears the mantle of the old prophets?

Even so, Joseph Smith, bitterly disillusioned by the strife and confusion of rival Christian sects in his own day, each claiming the authority of the Bible as the warrant for its distinctive teachings, finally decided to cut the Gordian Knot of Bible exegesis by creating a new scripture that would undercut the debating of the denominations and render them superfluous. He sought to found a new Christianity on a completely new basis: a new scripture from the old source, more Bible. A third Testament called the Book of Mormon. And just as the theologians of the Protestant sects followed the example of the scribes and Pharisees of old, resting their claims upon the scribal authority of exegeting ancient revelation writings, Joseph Smith was wise enough to adopt the old strategy of putting forth his own revelations in the outward form of an ancient manuscript, a pseudepigraph. If only writings of old prophets are to be taken seriously, then by all means let's write one! It's the only way left to gain media access.

But Joseph Smith hardly intended to reopen the gates of prophecy to all who might feel themselves inspired. His own pseudepigraph served rather as a new and ready-made canon, an authoritative pedigree to root his new community in the holy past, to give it instant venerable equality with the established Protestant sects, even superiority. Prophecy would continue, but only through his own mouth, as he soon stipulated.

Some would object that the Book of Mormon is not precisely pseudepigraphical in nature because it does not constitute an example of an unknown writer hiding behind well-known, authoritative names, since no one had ever heard of Mosiah, Almah, Moroni, and the rest before The Book of Mormon established their notoriety. Yes, but that seems to me an irrelevant distinction here, since, given the nature of the fiction, a collateral Bible representing an unknown dispensation in the Western hemisphere, you would have to use new, Bible-related characters, with new names. The story intentionally veers off the Bible's narrative trajectory. Lehi and his clan do not take Jeremiah to the Western Hemisphere with them. The Lamanites do not battle the Nephites in Palestine.

If only because the Book of Mormon must report the final slaughter of the Nephites, the narrators cannot have been portrayed as (much more ancient) Bible personalities. Grant Osborne suggests we would have real pseudepigraphy if the Book of Mormon was set forth as a dream-revelation experienced, e.g., by John of Patmos. But that would never work for the simple reason that the Book of Mormon narrative covers many centuries! Not even Rip van Winckel slept so long! In any case, Mormon, Nephi, and the rest are ancient Israelite characters. I do not think it weakens my point. It is pseudepigraphy when a nineteenth-century American writes under the names of ancient Hebrew heroes, scribes and prophets, even when he has created them and their names. If you want to deny that the Book of Mormon is a case of pseudepigraphic authorship, then you have to hold that it was really the work of historical ancient Americans named Mosiah, Nephi, etc. The exception that proves the rule, of course, is the cameo appearance of Jesus Christ, who appears, one might say, courtesy of the Bible. But as he will not be recognizable as Jesus Christ unless he repeats the teaching for which he is known in the Bible, that is (essentially) all he does in 3 Nephi.

The Same Thing

So far we have tried to indicate how, far from being a mischievous or malicious hoaxer, Joseph Smith as the author of the Book of Mormon would simply have been doing the same thing the authors of the various biblical and extra-biblical pseudepigrapha were doing. If we still wish to dismiss Smith as a hoaxer and a liar, or, to put it another way, if we feel entitled to decree that God could never sink to inspiring a pseudepigraph[7] (and if we think we are privy to the literary tastes of the Almighty, we are claiming to be prophets ourselves), then we have no option but to dismiss the biblical pseudepigraphs along with the Book of Mormon. What's good for the goose is good for the gander. What's good for the stick of Ephraim is good for the stick of Judah.

This point finds illustration in the case of literalistic biblicists of the past who tried to defend the historical genuineness of 2 and 3 Isaiah, 2 Zechariah, Deuteronomy, Daniel, the Pastoral Epistles, etc., just as zealously as they sought to debunk the Book of Mormon. A case in point would be Gordon H. Fraser,[8] author of the polemical *What Does the Book of Mormon Teach?* One can scarcely imagine him welcoming Higher Critics of Scripture to apply the same critical tools on Fraser's beloved Bible as he himself has used in vivisecting the Mormon Scripture. Such apologists/polemicists professed to see no problem in accepting the claim of the Book of Daniel to have been penned in the Babylonian and Persian periods and then sealed away to be discovered by Jews living at the time of the events predicted in the book (Dan. 12:4, 9), i.e., the period immediately preceding the ejection of the Seleucid tyranny from Judea. No matter that the "historical" descriptions nearer the ostensible of time of Daniel are filled with linguistic and historical anachronisms while the sections closer to the end are eagle-eyed in their "predictions" of Antiochus IV Epiphanies, even of his troop movements in Palestine When Gabriel directs Daniel to seal up the prophecy and stash it away for the benefit of readers hundreds of years in the future, the same alarm ought to be going off in the fundamentalist apologist's head that he hears when faced with Mormon claims that Joseph Smith "found a book" on Hill Cumorah. Of course he does not see them the same way, since Daniel is part of his Protestant canon, while Mormon is not. Thus, the latter may be safely debunked and discredited (and thus kept safely outside the charmed circle of the canon, as if by a fiery sword that turns every way), while the former must be kept safe, lest it lose its favored position within the canon and be "cast forth as an unclean thing" (Ezek. 28) from the Garden of God's Word.

But in the wake of historical criticism (which one cannot keep out as long as one resolves with Martin Luther to admit the Grammatico-Historical Method to the study of Scripture, reading Scripture as any other human writing), most theologians have come to accept that God might inspire an authoritative pseudepigraph as easily as he might inspire a parable. Thus there no longer seems anything incompatible between a book being scripturally inspired and authoritative on the one hand and being a historically spurious but fictively edifying pseudepigraph on the other. Deuteronomy and its theology are probably taken with much greater seriousness than ever before in Christian history now that its true character (and thus its intention) can be truly understood for the first time. In the same way, a new treasure house of riches may be disclosed in the pages of the Book of Mormon once one comes to recognize the skill and the goal of the theological artistry exercised by Joseph Smith as the author, not just the translator, of the Book of Mormon.

Seer or Secretary?

We have already indicated that Joseph Smith as the creator of the Book of Mormon had simply used the same strategy as many biblical writers, adopting the outward form of an ancient manuscript as a metaphor for saying that the coming of this Word was "from of old, from ancient days" (Micah 5:2). If we are going on that basis to dismiss the Book of Mormon as a spurious fake, we are showing we have the same theologically tin ear the opponents of Jesus had when they said, "How can this man say, 'I came down from heaven'?" "You are not yet fifty years old and you have seen Abraham?"

Joseph Smith even followed pretty much the same method of composition as that employed by the various biblical pseudepigraphists. Thus he looks more and more like a writer of new Scripture, not merely a discoverer or translator of ancient Scripture. But is such a role not incompatible with his own claims for himself and Latter Day Saint claims about him?

In a word, No. We have already recalled the fact that, after setting forth the Book of Mormon, Joseph Smith began to prophesy in his own voice. The Mormon canon obviously contains many such inspired speeches by the Mormon prophet. The work of a prophet is not that of a transcriber or translator. To equate the two is to deny the vast gap between Moses and the latter day scribes, the distance between the Prophet Jeremiah and his secretary Baruch, or between the Gnostic Revealer and the shepherd Muhammad 'Ali al Samman who chanced upon the Nag Hammadi texts while hiding from his enemies in an Egyptian cave. According to the traditional story of the origins of the Book of Mormon, when read the traditional way, the role of Joseph Smith was more like that of John the Baptist, hardly that of a prophetic revealer in his own right, but rather simply the herald for another (in Smith's case, Mormon and Moroni) who *would* be a prophetic revealer. And yet this picture blatantly belies the central importance of Joseph Smith as revealer, prophet, and Moses-like founder of the Latter Day Saint community. He was a living prophet whose voice was the mouthpiece for God to issue regulations for the fledgling nest of faith. So clearly Joseph Smith is supposed to be on Jeremiah's level, not Baruch's. If Smith were simply equivalent to Baruch instead of Jeremiah, then we would have a problem accounting for the full prophetic dignity subsequently ascribed to him. Would not his "new" character as a prophetic revealer have to be understood as a self-exaltation against the ostensibly sufficient revelation of Mormon and Moroni? Would not Joseph Smith actually be interposing himself between scripture and the faithful? Would it not make much better sense all around to suppose that the Book of Mormon itself was the first revelation to come by Joseph Smith, its author? Seen this way, Smith's authorship of the Book of Mormon would simplify rather than complicate, vindicate rather than discredit, his claim to prophetic inspiration.

Reformed Egyptian as Glossolalia

The clue to this as the true scenario lies in Smith's supposed use of the magical oracular glasses of the Urim and Thummim. He did not know how to read the puzzling characters in which (the story goes) the Golden Plates were written. The seer stone converted them into sense for him. The Urim and Thummim glasses constitute a metaphor exactly parallel to Paul's characterizing glossolalia not as a human language unknown to the speaker, an indefensible and absurd claim, but as the ecstatic "tongues of angels" which sing the glories "which man may not utter." While no mortal may render their meaning exactly, it is nonetheless possible, Paul says, to "interpret" them. But this is closer to interpreting omens or dreams (nonverbal) than it is to translating a text. Apollo's oracle at Delphi, overcome with volcanic sulfur fumes, would mumble on in ecstatic gibberish, which an interpreter standing by would render roughly into human conceptuality. To imagine glossolalia as a translatable language, as many Pentecostal defenders of the practice do, is to bring the practice into needless discredit, since linguistic analysis has more than once demonstrated that there is no syntactical structure among the glossolalic sounds. Pentecostal literalists fear that, if they admitted that glossolalia is simply the inspired product of the Spirit-energized glossolalist, rather than the tongues-speaker being a stenographer taking divine dictation, the divine quality they attribute to the sounds would be gone. Likewise, we fail to grasp the metaphor of the Urim and Thummim if we imagine Joseph Smith was simply using something like a translating program on a computer.

If we have ears to hear, we will recognize the Urim and Thummim tale as a metaphor for Smith looking at America through the lenses of the Bible, and at the Bible through the lenses of the American experience. The Book of Mormon was the inspired result, not an ancient text merely translated, but a creative extended metaphor. To defend the notion of a genuine ancient manuscript merely being translated from an imaginary "Reformed Egyptian" language, for fear that the Book of Mormon will otherwise forfeit its authority, is like Pentecostal literalists trying to convince themselves they are literally speaking an ancient language they never learned. Why defend a metaphor as if it were a literal fact, when factually it is manifestly false, while symbolically it may be profoundly true? Tongues-speaking is not speaking a genuine foreign language. The Book of Mormon never existed as a set of golden plates in a foreign language, either. Neither is the point. But speaking mysteries in the spirit is genuinely revelatory, and so is a book which translates the frontier heritage of America into the language of the Bible.

The promulgation of the Book of Mormon signaled that the great epic of salvation history was far from over, that it continued to unfold here and now. A powerful image for this is the discovery in one's own time of an ancient bible of American revelation. But an even more potent image for the same thing is the *writing* of a new chapter of the biblical epic in modern America. And this is just what Joseph Smith did. There are not two authorities vying for priority in Mormonism, Joseph Smith's prophecies versus the letter of the inspired text of the Book of Mormon. No, there is only one authority: the divinely inspired prophecy of Joseph Smith. And the Book of Mormon is the fundamental prophecy of Joseph Smith.

Latter Prophets and Latter Day Saints

Specifically, the Book of Mormon conforms to the genre of "the Latter Prophets" rather than that of the "Former Prophets." The difference between these two species of biblical books is that the Former Prophets are collections of prophetic oracles or speeches, gathered and recorded by their hearers and disciples (think here of the Book of Isaiah, the Book of Jeremiah, the Koran). The Latter Prophets, on the other hand, are a series of edifying (and usually semi-legendary) histories written from the moralistic standpoint of the prophets: when the people are faithful to God, God's reward follows them. But when the nation is unfaithful, they have only God's wrath to look forward to. Since the experience of the Babylonian Exile made it clear that the prophets had been quite right about all this, the exiled scribes and priests of Judah compiled what we call the Deuteronomic History (Joshua, Judges, Samuel, and Kings) according to the prophetic philosophy of history. They assembled many historical stories, sagas, and legends, welding them into one overarching unity. All victories were made into deliverances by God, all defeats and oppressions made into divine scourges. When a king goes against God's Word, he is terribly punished, while the faithful kings are honored by God. Another book of this kind in the Bible (though written too late for inclusion in the "Prophets" category) is the Chronicler's history (Ezra, Nehemiah, 1 and 2 Chronicles). It is clear that the Book of Mormon belongs with these works. It is a sort of Deuteronomic history of ancient America, illustrating its preachings with object lessons of the fates of wicked Lamanites and virtuous Nephites. It represents an artificial effort to extend the biblical histories of Israel and Judah up nearer our own day.

Biblical scholars ought to realize (as many no doubt do) that the Book of

Mormon is much the same sort of thing as the Bible they so love and ought to be accorded the same sort of respect. It is no more a hoax than Deuteronomy. Mormons ought to be more open to the possibility of the Book of Mormon having originated as a modern pseudepigraph, the work of Joseph Smith himself. As we have seen, this would only serve to enhance his prophetic dignity, not to debunk it as literal-minded critics of Mormonism have always jeered. The most important boon thus gained would be the quantum leap in interpretative possibilities. With the aid of tools like redaction and literary criticism, we may disclose theological riches in the text that, on the presupposition of literalism, have remained as buried in the text as the Golden Plates themselves were in the earth until Joseph Smith disclosed them according to the foundation myth of Mormonism.

Joseph Smith in the Book of Mormon

Did Joseph Smith write the Book of Mormon? To this over-familiar question the orthodox Latter-day Saint answer is a resounding No, because the official belief is that a series of men with quasi-biblical names wrote the book over many centuries. For some critics of Mormonism the answer is an equally emphatic No, but for a different reason. Such critics have charged that the Book of Mormon was plagiarized from Solomon Spaudling's lost novel of Israelites in ancient America, "Manuscript Found."[9] A third group, liberal Mormons and fellow travelers, tend to recognize Joseph Smith as the author of the book, inspired though he may perhaps have been by earlier works such as Ethan Smith's *View of the Hebrews*.[10] I find myself in company with this third group. Here I want to call attention to the obvious. Given that we agree on the nineteenth-century origin of the Book of Mormon, we may dismiss any theory that ascribes to it a non-Mormon, pre-Mormon origin; the Mormon origin of the scripture is clear from the simple fact that Joseph Smith and the Latter-day Saints movement, even the Book of Mormon itself, are repeatedly mentioned in its pages in an unmistakable fashion. While this observation does not preclude the possibility that some apostolic confederate of the Prophet may have written it up at his direction, the references to Joseph Smith and his church in the Book of Mormon prove that the text was not borrowed from some non-Mormon work. It is impossible that someone outside the movement wrote the book as a Bible pastiche, and that Joseph Smith subsequently decided to build a religion upon it.

Messiah ben Joseph

First there is the fact that the Book of Mormon "anticipates" the coming of a future scion of the line of Joseph the Genesis patriarch, son of Jacob. Joseph's own boyhood visions (Gen. 37:5–10) prefigured his eventual rise to the right hand of Pharaoh, to vice-regency over all mankind. Much later Jewish sectarians appear to have understood these dreams to have further prophesied the eventual advent of a Northern, Ephraimite Messiah, a Messiah ben Joseph, who, for the sake of the sins of Israel, should die in battle against the heathen in the Last Days, clearing the way for the victorious Judean Messiah ben David to emerge. As Geza Vermes has suggested,[11] this role may have been created to dignify the vanquished second-century C.E. messianic pretender Simon bar Kochba, assigning him a genuine role in the prophetic scenario, even if not that of the final deliverer. I am suggesting that, in effect, the Book of Mormon revives such a role for Joseph Smith. This is, as all acknowledge, the point of 2 Nephi, chapter 3,

> Yea, Joseph truly said: Thus saith the Lord unto me: A choice seer will I raise up out of the fruit of thy loins . . . And he shall be great like unto Moses . . . Behold, that seer will the Lord bless; and they that seek to destroy him shall be confounded . . . And his name shall be called after me; and it shall be after the name of his father. And he shall be like unto me; for the thing, which the Lord shall bring forth by his hand, by the power of the Lord shall bring my people unto salvation.

Likewise, Jacob 2:25, "I have led this people forth out of the land of Jerusalem, by the power of mine arm, that I might raise up unto me a righteous branch from the fruit of the loins of Joseph."

Did Joseph Smith ever make any claims to Jewish descent? Otherwise, we must suppose he implicitly numbered himself among that remnant of the Lost Tribes of Israel who, in the course of their migrations, splintered from the main group, henceforth to live among the Gentiles, thereby becoming a leavening influence among them, preparing the heathen nations for the coming of faith in Christ.[12] This Mormon version of the British Israel theory would seem to underlie Joseph Smith's claims to be the latter-day scion of the tribe of Joseph. In fact, one might view him as following in the footsteps of English messiah Richard Brothers (1757–1824), who esteemed himself to be the heir to the House of David, one of an imagined great legion of Jews living among the British population, oblivious of their true racial identity.[13]

Perhaps the ancient prophetic figure most closely analogous to Joseph Smith would be the Prophet Muhammad (if not the Apostle Mani, founder of Manichaeism in the third century). Muhammad, too, planted a retroactive scriptural endorsement of his own mission. In the Koran, supposedly representing the preaching of Muhammad, but at least composed by early Muslims, we read of Jesus foretelling the coming of his Arab successor: "Jesus . . . said to the Israelites: 'I am sent forth to you by Allah to confirm the Torah already revealed and to give news of an apostle that will come after me whose name is Ahmed" (61:6).

Among more recent messiahs, we may think of Pentecostal faith healer William Marrion Branham, whose followers cherished various exalted estimates of him, some deeming him the forerunner of the Second Coming, others seeing in him the Messiah himself, still others a separate incarnation of God in his own right. His own view of his mission seems humble by comparison, for he implied transparently that he was the Elijah heralding the return of Jesus Christ. And, to create his own credential for the job, Branham revealed that he who should occupy this role should have a name at least partially modeled upon "*Abraham*."[14] Similarly, the Rev. Sun Myung Moon explained how the Lord of the Second Advent, he who should fulfill the suspended mission of Jesus Christ, would have to be born in Korea, the Third Israel.[15] (Let no one infer cynicism on my part; it seems altogether fitting for such a figure to accentuate his own messianic status by creating, as it were, a scriptural door through which to walk onto the stage of history. Hugh J. Schonfield understood Jesus to have created a prophetic identity, that of the Suffering Servant, from synthesizing various scriptures, then hoisting that identity like a cross on his shoulder as he marched into destiny.)[16]

Infinite Regress

The Book of Mormon story of the Plates of Jared (Mosiah 8:5–19; 28:11–18; Ether, chapters 1–3) is an attempt to furnish a scriptural subtext to which the "discovery" of the Book of Mormon itself may be seen to correspond. The first followers of Joseph Smith will recognize themselves in an "ancient" "history" that provides the script for their own performance. Readers of the Book of Mormon are warned or reassured that model faith, such as the blessed ancients possessed, pointedly included belief in newly discovered ancient records! Like the Prophet Smith himself, King Mosiah translated these metallic records not by the exercise of linguistic skills but by use of the oracular Urim and Thummim, pictured as a pair of glasses so large that the frame encompassing the two lenses was as big as an archer's bow, hence the legacy of the antediluvian giants (mammoth Jaredites are hinted at in Ether 1:34; 13:15; 14:10; 15:26).[17] Who is sufficient unto these things? The account of the translation of the Jared text takes the opportunity, again, of magnifying the role of Joseph Smith, for whom Mosiah provides a scriptural counterpart: "a seer is greater than a prophet . . . a seer is a revelator and a prophet also; and a gift which is greater can no man have . . . a seer can know of things which are past, and also of things which are to come, and by them shall all things be revealed" (Mosiah 8:15–17).

Here is a revealing hint. When we think of a seer, literally a visionary, one who sees clairvoyantly, we do not think of him tied to written texts which may predict the future. No, we think of such texts as themselves the products of seers in the past. Likewise, for a seer to have clairvoyant access to the past ought presumably to denote something like Rudolf Steiner's claims to be able to read past history, including the hidden history of Jesus, from the Akashic Record, etheric imprints of all past events.[18] In this verse, in this claim, I think we have a candid admission of what Joseph Smith was really doing with his seer stone, gazing into the bottom of a hat, all those hours, all those days, as he sat concealed behind the blanket veil and gave dictation. He was seeing an unknown American past in his mind's eye, letting his imagination run free, much as Lord Dunsany did, dictating jeweled prose-poetic fables off the top of his head as his wife, pen in hand, sought to keep up. The result is a fictive scripture called *The Gods of Pegana*, only he never tried to get anyone to believe in the literal truth of it.[19]

We might compare the Prophet Smith's literary labors, his inspired penmanship, with that of the Roman Catholic mystic Anna Katherina Emmerich, whose *Dolorous Passion of Our Lord Jesus Christ* (1862) is still avidly read by old-school Catholics curious to know the details of the gospel stories, as well as more stories, of Jesus. Edgar Cayce, too, supplied new gospel vignettes by mining the ostensible memories of previous lives from many for whom he gave psychic readings.[20]

And again, a parallel with the Prophet Muhammad and the Koran is not far to seek. Muhammad, too, claimed, or had Allah claim, to be vouchsafing hitherto secret episodes of sacred history (3:44; 7:101; 11:49, "That which We have now revealed to you is secret history; it was unknown to you and to your people."[21] 11:121; 12:102; 20:100; 28:1), including new versions of old stories. Invariably these new versions had a way of casting light on Muhammad's own career, of paralleling it, actually of being based on it. Time and again the reader of the Koran is told that Noah, Abraham, Moses, and others suffered the same sort of opposition, even the same specific insults and cat-calls, that Muhammad is said elsewhere in the Koran to have brooked. The stories serve either to encourage the Prophet or to refute his opponents by showing how the ancient heroes faced the same conflicts and used the same polemics with their enemies as Muhammad did against the hostile Quraiysh tribe. If Muhammad's opponents mock his warnings of the final catastrophe (34:3; 79:42; 82:9), so did those of Noah and Shoaib (11:32; 29:36–37). If the unbelievers demand miracles from Muhammad (10:30; 13:27; 29:50), they did the same to Houd (11:53). If they accuse him of merely practicing "plain magic" (46:7; 74:24),[22] Jesus and Moses received the same insult (5:110; 10:77). If Muhammad be accused of subverting the religion of the fathers (34:43; 25:42), so were Moses and others (10:79; 14:10). Is Muhammad called a madman (52:29)? So was Noah (54:9). In other words, the polemics of Muhammad's day are prophetically retrojected onto the careers of the worthies of the past.

And so it was with Joseph Smith. Samuel the Lamanite refers to himself, of course, but also Joseph Smith, we cannot help but think, when he excoriates the Nephites: "if a prophet come among you [cf. Deut. 13:1–5] and declareth unto you the word of the Lord, which testifieth of your sins and iniquities, ye are angry with him, and cast him out and seek all manner of ways to destroy him; yea, you will say that he is a false prophet, and that he is a sinner, and of the devil, [cf. 1 John 3:8] because he testifieth that your deeds are evil [cf. John 3:19]" (Helaman 13:26). This is a cento of biblical phrases, a pastiche. And we see nineteenth-century polemics in 2 Nephi 28:29, "Woe be unto him that shall say: We have received the word of God, and we need no more of the word of God, for we have enough." Biblical writers never refer to scripture as "the word of God." For them the phrase always denotes a particular message, oracle, command, promise, etc., of God, not a written book. That is Protestant idiom, and the opinion expressed here is that of conventional Presbyterians, Methodists, Congregationalists, and their ilk, whether faced with a new scripture (like the Book of Mormon) or new prophetic and glossolalic utterances from the Pentecostal movement.[23] The persecutions from which King Mosiah must pass laws to shield the believers anticipate those of the Mormon faithful, while the false churches of 2 Nephi 28:3–6, which err by reason of too much fancy education, rejecting the possibility of new miracles and revelations, are plainly those stale Protestant sects of the Burned Over District with which young Joseph Smith had grown so disillusioned. Sure enough, Mormon prophetically predicts that in the days when his record is discovered, the churches will have sunk to the same lows, prizing treasure over repentance, stubbornly denying the possibility of new miracles (Mormon 8:26–33).

Finally, Joseph Smith has provided an ancient counterpart to himself in the person of Alma the church-planting high priest, the chosen vessel of the Lord (Mosiah,[24] chapters 25–26). Not coincidentally, he baptizes his many converts in the waters of Mormon (Mosiah 25:18; 26:15), as if to make them Mormons before Mormonism.

The Rest of the Story

There is, of course, much more to the Book of Mormon than the elements surveyed so cursorily here. But I venture to suggest that the rest of it exists to support these featured elements and cannot be easily separated from them. The lion's share of the Book of Mormon narrative is taken up with a fictive American pre-history parallel, not to the actual history of Israel, but to that history as rewritten by the Deuteronomic redactors of the Old Testament. Some of the seventh-century writers of Deuteronomy, and their heirs, cooling their heels by the waters of Babylon during the Exile, undertook a retrospective history of the nation, rewriting it according to the reward-and-punishment schema of the Book of Deuteronomy, namely that fidelity to the covenant should assure God's blessing, while apostasy and backsliding would call forth from God a series of wake-up calls, to put it mildly, in the form of famine, disease, and military defeats, finally issuing in deportation. The Deuteronomic historians gathered what scraps they could of tribal epic and saga, stories of local victories over Canaanite city states, the establishment of tribal independence from Amorite landlords and warlords, and on this mixed bag they superimposed, like an ill-fitting shoe, a theological framework of apostasy bringing judgment (enslavement to Canaanites) and of repentance bringing deliverance at the hands of the Judges. If not for the redactional reminders (Judg. 2:11–23; 3:7–9, 12–15; 4:1–3; 6:1–2, 6–8; 8:33–34; 10:6–16;

13:1) that the story was supposed to be tending in this direction, it would never be evident from the stories themselves. So the "karmic payback" scenario is already a foreign theological imposition on the original patriotic, nationalistic traditions.

But Christian readers of a devotional bent created an additional layer of spiritual meaning by reading the Deuteronomic History, especially Joshua, as an allegory of the Christian "victorious life," in which one might attain any desired level of victory over personal sin as long as one yielded to the leading of "Joshua" (Jesus) in one's day to day life. Besetting sins might be conquered so long as one left the battle to the grace of God instead of trusting to one's own "fleshly" efforts. The only result of self-reliance or of cherished sins held back from God could be Ai-like disasters (Josh. 7:1–13). This was the only distinctly Christian relevance such a book, with its bloody genocide and "take no prisoners" militarism, could have.

The Book of Mormon takes things further in the same direction. It in effect combines the Deuteronomic History with the Acts of the Apostles, producing an explicitly Christianized saga of the whelming of the Promised Land (America as Canaan, a familiar patriotic theme). The Book of Joshua is no more merely an allegory! The apostate Lamanites represent the forces of sin and backsliding, the constant temptation for virtuous Nephites, whose virtue, however, is as fragile as the airy currents of the Spirit upon which the "victorious Christian life" of the Revivalist Christian floats. Spiritual setbacks in the Christian life (and the life of the church) are one and the same with the political and military reversals of the Camp of the Saints. The tribes of Israel have become one with, the very same as, the apostolic churches of Acts. The twin models of evangelical piety, Joshua's host and the idyllic "Early Church," have combined, and the result is a potent paradigm of sectarian enthusiasm such as early (and many, many modern) Latter-day Saints emulated.

It is a story of a new and holy people who will not be satisfied with believing that once upon a time such things happened to some people, but rather who expect to live out such adventures—and do so. Without the elements considered above, the central role of Joseph Smith as Messiah ben Joseph, as Alma, and as Mosiah, it would all hang vaguely in space. The historical *Sitz-im-Leben* of such a book demands such a fledgling movement as that founded by Joseph Smith. The calm evening hours of leisurely writing in the study of some New England parson would not have produced such a book which resembles more than anything else a modern role-playing game scenario book: an elaborate sketch of a fantasy world into which the enthusiastic players enter as combatants in imaginary battles and dreamlike adventures of chivalry and courage. It is a script, not just a scripture, and it invites action. And the name of the drama is Mormonism. The Book of Mormon was written for that reason and purpose and no other. And it is no surprise to see that Joseph Smith assumes an important role in the play that bears such extensive traces of his creative hand.

The Nineteenth-Century Setting of 3 Nephi 1:24–25

The Book of Mormon deals many times with the role and function of the Mosaic Torah in the pre-Christian dispensation (if one can even claim there *is* a pre-Christian dispensation in the Book of Mormon!). I want to summarize some of the perspectives on the Torah, then to focus on a unique passage in which the Book of Mormon raises a fascinating point which, for all its scholastic character, is especially revealing of the historical life-setting of the Book of Mormon in the nineteenth century: given that even pre-Jesus Israelites in America knew all about the Christian plan of salvation far in advance, and given that the Torah was provided as a preparation or foreshadowing of Christ, why was it any more incumbent upon pre-Jesus Mormons to keep the Torah than it was for post-Jesus Mormons? They both knew and believed the same gospel, so why did the pre-Jesus believers have to go through the charade of "preparing" for it? The issue comes up very briefly in 3 Nephi 1:24–25.

And insofar as we acknowledge the Book of Mormon as a product of the nineteenth century, we must ask after the circumstances in that century that led to the framing and solving of the problem in 3 Nephi 1:24–25. It is fruitless to close off the matter by saying, "The Book of Mormon records that debate over scripture and its applicability simply because it arose thus in ancient America." No, as always, the sacred narrative is written to mediate the concerns of the generation in which it arose and which it addressed: in this case, the early nineteenth century.

Scripture as Credential

When new religions evolve from old ones, they have a tightrope to walk. They speak and act in the name and under the warrant of a new revelation, and so they go beyond the conventional scripture in significant ways. But few feel they can cut the umbilical cord of scripture altogether and make a leap into epistemological thin air as Buddhism did, repudiating the Vedic scriptures that came before it. Most new religions want to clutch to their breasts the old scriptures, albeit thoroughly reinterpreted. "By a remarkably creative fiat of interpretation, the Jewish scriptures (especially in Greek translation) became a book that had never existed before, the *Old* Testament, a book no longer about Israel but about Israel's hope, the Messiah, Jesus."[25]

The old scriptures function as a security blanket for the pioneers of the new faith. It makes them feel they have not sawed off the limb they were sitting upon. And the continued possession of the old scriptures makes it much easier to attract new believers, since it furnishes a point of contact. One need not abandon the old faith; one need only reinterpret it or believe in the new version of it. Anxious potential converts need to hear something like this. Thus the Jew who converts to Christianity can assure himself, when his heart tells him he has committed apostasy and severed the link binding him to countless generations of forbears, that he is instead a "completed Jew."

Christianity crossed this Rubicon in the second century when Marcion of Pontus understood the Pauline gospel to entail the total repudiation of the Jewish Scripture. He feared that as long as Christians retained the Old Testament in however vestigial-seeming a position, the influence of the old religion would insidiously permeate and "Judaize" the new faith. But most Christians did not follow him. They found they could accommodate the novelty of their new faith quite sufficiently by expanding the elbow-room allowed them by the old scripture. They found they needed only to reinterpret it.

What Gershom Scholem[26] says of Paul will be worth keeping in mind through our whole consideration here. See how well it applies to Joseph's Smith's use of the Old Testament in the Book of Mormon, and to the resulting rereading of ancient Israelite history, transplanted to America.

Paul had a mystical experience which he interpreted in such a way that it shattered the traditional authority. He could not keep it intact; but since he did not wish to forego the authority of the Holy Scriptures as such, he was forced to declare that it was limited in time and hence abrogated. A purely mystical exegesis of the old words replaced the original frame and provided the foundation of the new authority which he felt called upon to establish. This mystic's clash with religious authority was clear and sharp. In a manner of speaking, Paul read the Old Testament 'against the grain.' The incredible violence with which he did so shows not only how incompatible his experience was with the meaning of the old books, but also how determined he was to preserve, if only by purely mystical exegeses, his bond with the sacred text. The result was the paradox that never ceases to amaze us when we read the Pauline Epistles: on the one hand the Old Testament is preserved, on the other, its meaning is completely set aside. The new authority that is set up, for which the Pauline Epistles themselves serve as a holy text, is revolutionary in nature. Having found a new source, it breaks away from the authority constituted in Judaism, but continues in part to clothe itself in the images of the old authority, which has been reinterpreted in purely spiritual terms.

Evangelizing the Past

Latter-day Saint Christianity decided right from the beginning to uphold the old scripture explicitly as a foundation on which to build the new, so that the new (the Book of Mormon) might depend from the coattails of the old ("Another Testament of Jesus Christ"). In this posture they joined the Muslims who also claim to affirm the Old and New Testaments even while believing them superseded in large measure by a more recent revelation, the Koran. But here I am interested less in how early Mormons balanced off the teachings of their old and new and newer testaments than in how they understood a long-standing Christian dilemma: how Christian was the Old Testament? How Christian was ancient Israel? How fully had they, thanks to the prophets, understood the Christian plan of salvation in advance?

In order to make a thorough case that the new sect is within its rights claiming the authority of the old scripture, the new believers sooner or later tend to rewrite the whole thing retrospectively. Historical perspectives become completely reversed in a grotesque way when Christians express utter mystification that Jesus' contemporaries could not recognize him as the messiah predicted in such thorough detail by the prophets! If, as Hal Lindsey and Josh McDowell claim, over three hundred scriptural prophecies were fulfilled in the crucifixion alone, then it is easy to see where anti-Semitism almost inevitably comes from: "Those Jews couldn't have been that dense! They must have known what was going on! So they opposed our Lord out of sheer cupidity and pride!"[27]

In fact, there seem to be no overt or author-intended predictions of Jesus Christ in the Old Testament, as even a casual scrutiny of supposed proof-texts readily reveals. Every single one of them can be shown to have a different meaning, one ready to hand in the cultural and religious context of the ancient prophets. Nor is it as if the New Testament writers who appeal to Old Testament proof-texts thought they were reading them off the page. No, in concert with the Essenes and other sectarians of the day, the early Christians embraced esoteric techniques for discovering new meanings, hidden in the text long ago but quite invisible to any reader till their unexpected fulfillment should arrive.[28] When Matthew said Jesus' miraculous conception fulfilled Isaiah 7:14, he didn't imagine Isaiah had Jesus in mind. Nor did the scribe who composed the Habakkuk Pesher among the Dead Sea Scrolls imagine that the Prophet Habakkuk understood he was committing to paper a secret message about the Teacher of Righteousness. No, that message must remain locked up till centuries should pass.

But such an understanding of prophecy and prediction does not serve so well if one is trying to impress skeptics with alleged clairvoyance among the biblical writers. To really wow them and make believers of them it is more useful to imagine that biblical prophecy was like Jeanne Dixon predicting the assassination of JFK.

Everything New Is Old Again

And once you start down this road, you are headed inevitably for a startling reconceptualization of the ancient history of your religious forbears. If they knew everything you know, only before the fact, by means of predictive prophecy, then would they not already have the faith you do? And if they did, what was the occasion for God's subsequently "revealing" it anew? That is, if everybody already knew it? Well, then of course you say they must have apostatized and forgotten the truth for great periods of time.

The Koran supposes a doctrine of progressive revelation: not everything was known all at once. And yet it cannot resist the temptation to make the past seem a great deal like the present. Abraham is already the first Muslim. That is not much of a stretch, since "Muslim" means simply "one at peace with God." By itself, such a designation would not commit one to the impossible notion that five-pillar Islam as we know it today was already the faith of Abraham. But the imaginations of theologians have a way of running wild, and just a couple of years ago a Religious Studies professor in Pakistan was sentenced to death by the government because he taught that, contrary to Islamic tradition, the Prophet Muhammad's parents were not yet Muslims in the full sense of the word![29]

As Julius Wellhausen demonstrated,[30] successive generations of biblical redactors rewrote and updated Israelite history in just the same way. For instance, since the Deuteronomic Law was codified in the time of Josiah and Jeremiah (sixth century B.C.E.), the Deuteronomic Historians (who compiled and reedited Joshua, Judges, Samuel and Kings during the early Exilic period) wrote the history as if the Torah of Deuteronomy had really been promulgated by the historical Moses. This is why, for instance, the Deuteronomic Historian sneers at Solomon for importing the cults of his foreign wives. It was only wrong anachronistically, retrospectively. Solomon would have seen no problem, nor would any Nathan have warned him.

Fifty years after that, during the Exile, priests and scribes compiled the Priestly Code and prefaced it with what we call the P narrative of the Pentateuch, which recast the Moses story as if Moses had introduced the whole Priestly Code, which is why Israel is shown implausibly setting up and breaking down the cumbersome Tabernacle every day. The Priestly Code authorized sacrificial rituals that could be performed nowhere else but in the Temple, so Moses must already have had a portable one!

Again, after the Exile, once the full Pentateuch had been compiled, the Chroniclers rewrote the Deuteronomic History to make it look like Israel already had the Genesis-through-Deuteronomy Torah in front of them. The past is a holy past because it is used to sanctify and legitimize the arrangements of the present.

The New Testament writers never deal with this question ("How much like the present was the past?") in any systematic way. John 8:56 imagines Abraham had a clear view of Jesus' days, while 1 Peter 1:10–12 implies the ancient prophets only realized they were speaking of something to befall others and did not even know the name of the mysterious savior they prophesied. Hebrews 1:1–2 seems to suppose the prophets were, like Paul in 1 Corinthians 13:12, seeing vague flashes in a dim mirror, having nothing of the clarity we enjoy.

But as Christian apologetics made more and more of the "proof from prophecy," the result was that the whole Christian plan of salvation was supposed to have been clearly known in advance. People must have predicated their faith on the atonement God would one day provide through the death of Jesus Christ. Every animal sacrifice (p)reminded them of this. So the Old Testament Israelites became just what Justin Martyr had called Socrates and Plato, "Christians before Christ," though in an almost literal sense.

Progressive Revelation

In the nineteenth-and twentieth-century Protestant debates occasioned by the Modernist belief in progressive revelation in the Bible, in the unfolding history of Israel, this issue took on a whole new importance. Liberal Protestants held that the Bible begins with a more barbaric God-concept (and with a loose grip of monotheism) and ended with a clearer concept of God as a loving father, thanks to Jesus. Liberal theologians said that the evolution of human religious understanding was just the earthly side of what, from a heavenly perspective, would be called progressive revelation of God.[31]

Dispensationalist theology,[32] founded by John Nelson Darby, had a surprising sympathy for the notion of progressive revelation, since Dispensationalists, too, taught that human beings had dealt with God in very different ways in different periods ("dispensations") of revelation. Adam and Eve, much less Moses and Isaiah, had not the faintest idea that some future sacrifice of Jesus the Messiah would make their primitive mumbo-jumbo worship effective in the eyes of God. No, they were doing what God wanted them to do. God had a different plan of salvation appropriate to each dispensation. Faith in Jesus Christ as atoning savior pertained properly just to the "Dispensation of Grace," or of the Church, something not even hinted at in the Old Testament prophets.

Calvinist theology repudiated all this as a fatal compromise with Liberal theology and insisted that salvation was always the same as it is today. So ancient Israel already knew about Jesus. They *must* have! And despite all the hubbub over the coming of the Holy Spirit in Acts 1, Old Testament "believers" must already have been regenerated by the Holy Spirit. It is the same sort of anxiety that we see at work in pre-Vatican II Roman Catholicism, when they claimed with a straight face that Catholic doctrine had never changed.

Whence this anxiety? People do not like to be reminded that their cherished doctrines arrived on earth one day in the womb of a human mind. They can more comfortably believe in a Truth that has always been there. They want their religion to be a piece of Nature, not a piece of History. If it is

Nature, it is the primordial creation of God and must abide unchanged. But if it is a product of History, that implies we, or erring mortals like us, made it all up at some time in the past. Hence it is not really true after all. Or at least so we seem to fear.

(This, I suggest, is also why the historical founder of a religious community is soon deified, identified with God or some creative demiurge alongside him: he (Jesus, Moses, Muhammad, Buddha) who founded *our* world (2 Cor. 5:17) must also have founded *the* world!

Mormon's Mirror

One argument Dispensationalists could pull forth from their quiver was the sheer implausibility of the implied Calvinistic picture of ancient Bible times. When you read the stories of the Judges, the Monarchy, Elijah and Elisha, the Exile, Nehemiah, and so on—where is Jesus? Can the reader really be seriously asked to read in such knowledge on the part of all these people who must seem nearly as alien to his own Christian piety as Achilles and Agamemnon? However one might want to characterize their religion, it cannot be understood as any sort of Christianity. Fosdick puts it well: "Far from being synonymous with goodness or righteousness . . . , 'holiness,' at the first, suggested the aloofness and inviolability of the god. Even when later connotations began to appear, the earlier ones persisted, as Joshua's words reveal: 'Ye cannot serve Yahweh; for he is a holy God; he is a jealous God.' [Josh. 24:19] One does not go into one's room and shut the door to commune in secret with such a deity."[33]

The Calvinist model, with its Bronze Age Christians, entailed gross historical anachronism rivaling *The Flintstones*. But the Book of Mormon takes a somewhat different approach to the same end. With its pre-Jesus Christian believers, the Book of Mormon has in effect rewritten the Old Testament narrative of Israel the way Calvinism said it must have been. It might be taken as a *reductio ad absurdum* of the Calvinist view: if the Calvinists were right, this is what the Old Testament would look like.

It is clear that the Book of Mormon characters speak of the New Testament saving events as already in the past, as if they had already taken place. Supposedly this is the result of vivid prophetic vision, but it reflects the fact that Joseph Smith and his readers know Jesus, John the Baptist, etc., as figures from the past, as ancient Bible characters, and these figures do not lose that character even though they are ostensibly known only through clairvoyant anticipation.

Wherefore, I would that ye should remember that I have spoken unto you concerning that prophet which the Lord showed unto me, that should baptize the Lamb of God, which should take away the sins of the world. And now, if the Lamb of God, he being holy, should have need to be baptized by water, to fulfil all righteousness, O then, how much more need have we, being unholy, to be baptized, yea, even by water! And now, I would ask of you, my beloved brethren, wherein the Lamb of God did fulfil all righteousness in being baptized by water? Know ye not that he was holy? But notwithstanding he being holy, he showeth unto the children of men that, according to the flesh he humbleth himself before the Father, and witnesseth unto the Father that he would be obedient unto him in keeping his commandments. Wherefore, after he was baptized with water the Holy Ghost descended upon him in the form of a dove. And again, it showeth unto the children of men the straightness of the path, and the narrowness of the gate, by which they should enter, he having set the example before them. And he said unto the children of men: Follow thou me. Wherefore, my beloved brethren, can we follow Jesus save we shall be willing to keep the commandments of the Father? And the Father said: Repent ye, repent ye, and be baptized in the name of my Beloved Son. And also, the voice of the Son came unto me, saying: He that is baptized in my name, to him will the Father give the Holy Ghost, like unto me; wherefore, follow me, and do the things which ye have seen me do. Wherefore, my beloved brethren, I know that if ye shall follow the Son, with full purpose of heart, acting no hypocrisy and no deception before God, but with real intent, repenting of your sins, witnessing unto the Father that ye are willing to take upon you the name of Christ, by baptism—yea, by following your Lord and your Savior down into the water, according to his word, behold, then shall ye receive the Holy Ghost; yea, then cometh the baptism of fire and of the Holy Ghost; and then can ye speak with the tongue of angels, and shout praises unto the Holy One of Israel. But, behold, my beloved brethren, thus came the voice of the Son unto me, saying: After ye have repented of your sins, and witnessed unto the Father that ye are willing to keep my commandments, by the baptism of water, and have received the baptism of fire and of the Holy Ghost, and can speak with a new tongue, yea, even with the tongue of angels, and after this should deny me, it would have been better for you that ye had not known me. And I heard a voice from the Father, saying: Yea, the words of my Beloved are true and faithful. He that endureth to the end, the same shall be saved. And now, my beloved brethren, I know by this that unless a man shall endure to the end, in following the example of the Son of the living God, he cannot be saved. (2 Nephi 31:4–14)

Mosiah 16:6–7 betrays the historical self-awareness of the Book of Mormon author, as he hastens in the most artificial manner to redirect the attention of the reader to the ostensible time frame both of the action and of the narration:

And now if Christ had not come into the world, *speaking of things to come as though they had already come*, there could have been no redemption. And if Christ had not risen from the dead, or have broken the bands of death that the grave should have no victory, and that death should have no sting, there could have been no resurrection.

And if the Christian gospel is already known in such detail to the ancient pre-Jesus Americans, why not take the step and make explicit what Calvinism left implicit, that the Israelites were believing Christians, converts to Jesus Christ, repenting and believing in his name? These phrases ill-befit the Old Testament picture of Israel and Judah, where instead people are referred to in a simple and non-sectarian manner as the righteous, the wise, the upright, etc. But in the pre-Jesus Christendom of the Book of Mormon, why not import the whole apparatus of Christian conversionism lock, stock, and barrel?

And now, because of the covenant which ye have made ye shall be called the children of Christ, his sons, and his daughters; for behold, this day he hath spiritually begotten you; for ye say that your hearts are changed through faith on his name; therefore, ye are born of him and have become his sons and his daughters. And under this head ye are made free, and there is no other head whereby ye can be made free. There is no other name given whereby salvation cometh; therefore, I would that ye should take upon you the name of Christ, all you that have entered into the covenant with God that ye should be obedient unto the end of your lives. (Mosiah 5:7–8)
And now, ought ye not to tremble and repent of your sins, and remember that only in and through Christ ye can be saved? (Mosiah 17:13)

Have ye walked, keeping yourselves blameless before God? Could ye say, if ye were called to die at this time, within yourselves, that ye have been sufficiently humble? That your garments have been cleansed and made white through the blood of Christ, who will come to redeem his people from their sins? (Alma 5:27)

They are even called Christians!

For thus were all the true believers of Christ, who belonged to the church of God, called by those who did not belong to the church. And those who did belong to the church were faithful; yea, all those who were true believers in Christ took upon them, gladly, the name of Christ, or Christians as they were called, because of their belief in Christ who should come. (Alma 46:14–15)

And yet, as otherwise we might expect, these Ancient Israelites in America followed the Torah of Moses. How are they depicted as understanding the rationale for this?

Therefore, if ye teach the law of Moses, also teach that it is a shadow of those things which are to come—Teach them that redemption cometh through Christ the Lord, who is the very Eternal Father. (Mosiah 16:14–15).

Leaving aside the Patripassianism of verse 15, the rest of it comes pretty much from Colossians 2:16–17, "Therefore let no one pass judgment on you in questions of food and drink or with regard to a festival or a new moon or a Sabbath. These are only a shadow of what is to come; but the substance belongs to Christ." It is one thing to say this while the Law is ostensibly still in force, quite another to say it afterward. How much enthusiasm might one muster toward fulfilling the exacting minutiae of a legal program which one knew had no inherent importance at all? ("If the job's not worth doing, it's not worth doing well.")

Wherefore, the prophets, and the priests, and the teachers, did labor diligently, exhorting with all long-suffering the people to diligence; teaching the law of Moses, and the intent for which it was given; persuading them to look forward unto the Messiah, and believe in him to come as though he already was. (Jarom 11)

So the Torah is essentially an evangelistic tract, preaching the gospel of Jesus Christ as a *fait accompli*. But has it not done its work so well that it has effectively worked itself out of a job?

> And now ye have said that salvation cometh by the law of Moses. I say unto you that it is expedient that ye should keep the law of Moses as yet; but I say unto you, that the time shall come when it shall no more be expedient to keep the law of Moses. And moreover, I say unto you, that salvation doth not come by the law alone; and were it not for the atonement, which God himself shall make for the sins and iniquities of his people, that they must unavoidably perish, notwithstanding the law of Moses. And now I say unto you that it was expedient that there should be a law given to the children of Israel, yea, even a very strict law; for they were a stiff-necked people, quick to do iniquity, and slow to remember the Lord their God; therefore there was a law given them, yea, a law of performances and of ordinances, a law which they were to observe strictly from day to day, to keep them in remembrance of God and their duty towards him. But behold, I say unto you, that all these things were types of things to come. And now, did they understand the law? I say unto you, Nay, they did not all understand the law; and this because of the hardness of their hearts; for they understood not that there could not any man be saved except it were through the redemption of God. For behold, did not Moses prophesy unto them concerning the coming of the Messiah, and that God should redeem his people? Yea, and even all the prophets who have prophesied ever since the world began—have they not spoken more or less concerning these things? Have they not said that God himself should come down among the children of men, and take upon him the form of man, and go forth in mighty power upon the face of the earth? (Mosiah 13:27–34)

But if you know this much, what is left to be revealed?

A Wrinkle in Time

In fact, mustn't we ask if explicit prior knowledge of the Christian events of salvation (explicit enough to make Christianity a present fact among the Nephites and Lamanites, even before the American advent of Jesus) does not belie and stultify the supposed shadow-character of the Torah? What sense is there in calling it a mere adumbration of what is already fully illuminated?

The paradox could never have arisen in genuinely pre-Christian times. It only pops up as a function of the chronological contradiction of importing explicit Christianity into the pre-Jesus period, as Calvinists did implicitly and Mormons did explicitly. And this is exactly where 3 Nephi 1:24–25 comes in. It is (merely) an attempt to mediate, to harmonize this difficulty.

> And there were no contentions, save it were a few that began to preach, endeavoring to prove by the scriptures that it was no more expedient to observe the law of Moses. Now in this thing they did err, having not understood the scriptures. But it came to pass that they soon became converted, and were convinced of the error which they were in, for it was made known unto them that the law was not yet fulfilled, and that it must be fulfilled in every whit; yea, the word came unto them that it must be fulfilled; yea, that one jot or tittle should not pass away till it should all be fulfilled; therefore in this same year were they brought to a knowledge of their error and did confess their faults.

Notice that there is not much uproar over this aberrant opinion; only a few teach it, as an innocent error, and they are soon set straight without difficulty. This tells us that the Book of Mormon is not tilting at some major concern of its time, such as the business about "secret combinations" (the Masons) and worldly churches unwilling to admit of new revelations discovered upon inscribed metal plates. No, great time and energy is spent on these matters, so as to give nineteenth-century Mormons plenty of ammunition during the thick of these very disputes. I suspect that the minor mention of our subject in this manner is just a throw-away note on an idle subject from the standpoint of the nineteenth-century reader: "If pre-Jesus Mormons already practiced Christianity, and Christianity fulfills and supersedes the Torah, then why were all these people still bound to the Torah?" The question had something of the weight of those brain-teasers tossed about by modern fundamentalists almost recreationally: did Adam have to believe in Jesus to be saved? What happens to far-flung savages who never had the chance to hear the preaching of the gospel? If there are extraterrestrials out there somewhere, did Jesus die for them, too?

If the episode in 3 Nephi 1:24–25 actually reflected a once-living controversy, rather than a purely literary setting forth of a clever solution to a scriptural puzzle, we may be sure it would have appeared as a matter of far greater urgency, for it would have been in most respects parallel to the debate that so exercised Paul and the Judaizing Christians in the first century: If Christ has come to fulfill and thus suspend the Torah, why should Christians feel any obligation to keep the Torah's commands? But we have seen that the Book of Mormon's perspective is completely unhistorical, altogether reversed. There is none of the urgency of debate over the Torah issue that we read in the white-hot polemics of Galatians.

When could this issue have raged as a living controversy? It cannot have raged among early nineteenth-century Mormons, because they plainly did not find themselves in the envisioned situation, keeping the Torah before Christ's historical advent. But neither can it represent an ancient controversy, since it is strictly a product of a later author reading Christianity back anachronistically into the Torah dispensation. It is a kind of pre-echo of a future explosion! 3 Nephi 1:24–25 is nothing more than an after-the-fact attempt to iron out a few bugs in the theological system. It attempts merely to scratch an itch felt by nineteenth-century Book of Mormon readers.

3 Nephi can elsewhere have Jesus himself tell us that the Torah must pass away, has passed away, in the wake of his coming (12:17–19). But really one must recognize that complete advance knowledge of the Christian gospel in pre-Jesus Israelite America had *already* fulfilled the Torah, since absolutely nothing was left to the imagination. Unlike Paul, one does not need the pedagogy of the Torah (Gal. 3:23–26) if one has already attained maturity in Christ as Alma, Nephi, Mosiah, and all the others had.

Later and Later Day Saints

Apocalyptic Afterthought

Early Christians expected the end of the world to dawn in their own lifetime. So eager were they for the Apocalypse that some were stunned when some of their number died! Would they miss out on the Second Coming? 1 Thessalonians 4:13–18 depicts Paul attempting to set their minds at ease: all believers who die before the Parousia (the second advent) of Jesus will be raised from the dead by him when he comes. So they haven't seen the last of their pious, deceased relatives. But how can Paul have neglected to inform them of such a vital doctrine when he first preached the gospel to the Thessalonians? It seems more likely that what we have in 1 Thessalonians (as many scholars have long argued on other grounds anyway) is a pseudepigraph, attributed to the authoritative name of Paul at some later date. My guess is that the very doctrine of an end-time resurrection of the righteous (certainly already available from contemporary Judaism and Zoroastrianism) was first adopted by Christians as one of the many adjustments made necessary by the failure of the Parousia to materialize on schedule. Numerous New Testament texts make clear that the early Christians expected it to happen before the end of their generation (though they extended this period as long as they could, a "generation" being a somewhat flexible term). Martin Werner, a student of Albert Schweitzer, argued forcefully in his *The Formation of Christian Dogma* that virtually all of Christian theology as we know it developed as a set of readjustments and reinterpretations in the wake of the failure of the Parousia. Nor is this a fringe view in New Testament scholarship.

Furthermore, the same dynamics of delay and reinterpretation can be observed at work whenever any more recent apocalyptic movement has flourished, then been disappointed by the failure of its end-of-the-world deadline. Many members of a Japanese-American sect expecting the world to end on a certain October morning in the early 1990s committed suicide, unable to face the shame attached to their error. They failed it, but such a test will determine the theological creativity and adaptive staying power of a new faith. Or, from another perspective, such a trial will measure the astonishing extent to which human beings can rationalize any belief to which an intense will to believe has committed them.

Mormonism, or the Church of Jesus Christ of Latter Day Saints, as their very name announces, began as an eager apocalyptic sect sure that they lived in the last days before the end of the age. They would more than survive the eventual disappointment of their early hopes, learning to create their own new world of faith right here in the midst of the old age of fallenness. Their aggressive missionary efforts have already made them a world religion in their own right, even if one considers them separate from the parent Christian religion. How did they deal so well with their own delay of the Parousia? It may be because their founder, Joseph Smith, author ("translator") of the Book of Mormon, had already wrestled with the issue in its first-century context. His interpretation of the first time it happened may have paved the way for his church's own treatment of the problem when their turn came.

Branch (Office) of David

The Book of Mormon, fictively divided into several distinct successive accounts, as if by different ancient authors, relates the adventures of the Nephites and Lamanites, lost tribes of Jews in the New World. Eventually, following his resurrection in Jerusalem, Jesus appears in America to the faithful remnant of Nephites. In 3 Nephi 19, Jesus names the Nephite Twelve who, on the spot, fulfill the command of Jesus in Matthew's Great Commission, teaching the multitudes what Jesus has taught them, e.g., to pray to the Father in Jesus' own name. On the same occasion the Twelve are filled with the descending Holy Spirit: "And behold, they were encircled about as if it were by fire; and it came down from heaven, and the multitude did witness it, and did bear record" (19:14). Obviously this whole sequence is meant explicitly to recall and replay the New Testament events whereby the original apostles were chosen for their mission and sent forth. Those events are telescoped here, as the narrative jumps, so to speak, from Mark chapter 3 to Acts chapter 2, from the calling and numbering of the disciples to their endowment with the Spirit. There are several interesting inferences to be drawn.

First, since this sequence is a cameo of the longer Gospel-Acts sequence, what 3 Nephi 19 does is to provide a reader-response commentary by Joseph Smith on that original Gospel-Acts sequence. He has produced what he sees as the gist of the original, which is a legitimization myth for a group of leaders to mind the store in the absence of Jesus (Weber's "routinization of charisma"). The whole Mark-Acts sequence is in turn based on the Pentateuchal accounts of Moses heeding Jethro's advice to share the burden with a chosen group of seventy elders. In Exodus 18, these men are hardly chosen before they are endowed with the Holy Spirit. This pattern is broadly reproduced in Mark 3, where we can detect an underlying pre-Markan version in vv. 20–21, 31–32, 13–19, exactly paralleling Exodus 18:5–7, 13–27. Acts 2 reflects the alternate account of the same event (Num. 11:16–17, 24–30), in which these seventy assistants receive the spirit of Moses, much as elsewhere the spirit of Elijah rests on Elisha (2 Kings 2:9–11).

By chopping all the intervening material in the Gospels between the initial calling of the Twelve and their endowment with the Spirit in Acts 2, Joseph Smith has correctly recognized that both stories are functionally equivalent, both of them trying to buttress the ecclesiastical authority of the college of apostles. Joseph Smith is thus making Jesus give the American, Nephite Church, the predecessor of his own, a pedigree independent of those claimed by any other denomination, Protestant or Catholic. Likewise, the various British tales of young Jesus visiting the shores of Britain with his uncle Joseph of Arimathea,[34] and of Joseph later returning there carrying the Holy Grail with him are foundation legends for Celtic Christianity, trying to stake an apostolic claim independent of Rome. Advocates of the British Israel theory and Christian Identity sects still employ these legends for the same reason.

And Joseph Smith was doing the same sort of thing, inventing a separate origin for his own kind of American Christianity. The idea is summed up well in Galatians 1:11–12, "For I would have you know, brethren, that the gospel that was preached by me is not according to man. For I did not receive it from man, nor was I taught it, but it came through a revelation of Jesus Christ." Paul, in order to protect his own independent authority, denies he is in any way dependent on the earlier apostles or that his Christianity is derivative from theirs (and thus possibly a distortion of it, as someone seems to have been alleging). Rather, he reverses the implied accusation: since he knows his gospel came directly from God, then, if that of the Jerusalem apostles is in any important respect at variance, it is the Jerusalem apostles who must be the heretics, the revisionists. In the same way, Joseph Smith, by having Jesus Christ himself found the Nephite Church in America, is claiming to have his Christianity direct from the horse's mouth. If the Methodist, Baptist, and Congregationalist ministers choose to remain aloof from his reforms, they are only incriminating themselves as heirs of a corrupt gospel, a degenerate Christianity, "another Jesus, a different Spirit, a different gospel" (2 Corinthians 11:4). And Smith would say, with Paul, "I think that I am not in the least inferior to these superlative apostles" (2 Cor. 11:5).

So, to return to the main point, the story in 3 Nephi collapses the two-fold story of the authorization of the original Twelve into a single continuous story, directly linking the choosing of the Nephite Twelve with their Pentecost of the Spirit and fire. In the Gospels and Acts, these events in the lives of the Jerusalem Apostles are separated by many chapters because in the Gospels the original Twelve are used as object lessons or straight men during the teaching period of Jesus' ministry, often in order to warn the reader about the seductions and abuses of power in the church hierarchy (compare, e.g., Mark 9:33–35; 10:35–37, 41; 1 Cor. 1:11–12; 12:21–25). And this is inevitably the sort of argument made by those who do not currently wield power and aimed at those who do. By eliminating this material, with its frequent embarrassments to the disciples (that is, by having nothing analogous, nothing with Nephite disciples as the butt of the story), Joseph Smith gives an unambiguously positive portrait of the New Twelve. On the one hand, he has implicitly removed the Gospel's critique of power (such as Smith himself would come to wield), and on the other he has made the New World Twelve to appear superior to their Jerusalem predecessors. Mormon Christianity is thus not merely a return to or restoration of the primitive church: it is an improvement on the original, and we will presently see another sign pointing in the same direction.

If the Spirit-baptism of the Nephite Twelve recalls both the infilling of the seventy elders of Israel with the Spirit Moses had and the anointing of Elisha with the wonder-working spirit of Elijah, then we find ourselves in the position to understand the 3 Nephi motif of Jesus asking the New Twelve, just before he ascends for good, what request they would make of him (3 Nephi 28:1). We do not find such a scene in any of the Gospels, but we do find it in the analogous scene of dialogue between Elijah and Elisha just before the former ascends into heaven: "Ask what I shall do for you before I am taken from you" (2 Kings 2:9). Joseph Smith was quite sensitive to the implicit connections between the sources of the Pentecost narrative upon which he based the Spirit-baptism scene of the Nephite Twelve, and he used the various original motifs in a new combination to construct his own new episode. He based it on the choosing of the Twelve in Galilee and on the Spirit-baptism of the 120 in Jerusalem on Pentecost, seeing that these passages were in turn dependent on the two Pentateuchal accounts of the ordination of the Seventy as well as the story of the ascension of Elijah.

Joseph Smith further reinforced the greater spiritual quality of the New Twelve (= the new religion) over the old by combining the thrice-repeated Gethsemane prayer in the Synoptics with the so-called High Priestly Prayer of John chapter 17. Here (3 Nephi 19:19–35), Jesus prays in serenity, as seems becoming to the Son of God, not in the indecorous tones of an agitated death row convict as he does in the Synoptic Gethsemane. (John likewise rewrote the scene in John 12:27–30.) And yet, as in the Synoptic Gethsemane, Jesus prays at a distance from them and subsequently returns thrice to his waiting disciples. In the Synoptics Jesus finds the disciples asleep each time he returns to them, and we are to understand that they have somehow missed an opportunity to aid him, perhaps to save him from an untimely death. But in 3 Nephi, the New Twelve are made of sterner stuff than the old. Jesus finds them fervently watching and praying. Once again, the New American Christians imagine themselves superior in devotion to the original disciples and the religion represented by them. They are Elisha to mainstream American Protestantism's Elijah.

Son of Godot

We have noted the importance of the non-appearance of the awaited second advent for the back-pedaling and re-tooling of early Christianity. Let us consider briefly the three most important New Testament attempts to rationalize the failure of the promise of Jesus made in Mark 9:1, "Amen, I say to you, there are some standing here who will not taste death till they have seen the kingdom of God come with power." This was a dangerous statement, one open to clear and embarrassing disconfirmation. What happened when years went by and all those with Jesus were sound asleep in their graves, like Abraham, not having received what was promised, though espying it, as Moses did the Promised Land, from afar (Heb. 11:13)? Quite a bit of jeering, like that the Emmaus disciples no doubt expected from their neighbors once they got home! Scoffers began to mock, saying, "Where is the promise of his coming? For ever since the fathers [the first generation of disciples] fell asleep, all things continue on as they have since the beginning of time" (2 Peter [another pseudepigraph] 3:4).

Christians had their answers ready (1 Pet. 3:15), though we might wonder how convincing they sounded to anyone else. 2 Peter's answer is to say that, even though there has been a delay, it is a good thing, not a bad one, since it means God has extended the deadline for repentance (3:9). Such straw-grabbing transformations of necessity into virtue are typical among end-of-the-world movements whose deadlines pass. Mark's own attempt to sidetrack criticism aimed the failure of the promise in 9:1 was his placement, immediately following, of the Transfiguration story (9:2–8). Mark seems to want to lead the reader to accept the Transfiguration (where Jesus appears already as we imagine him in heaven, conversing with his Old Testament colleagues Moses and Elijah) as a kind of proleptic, anticipatory coming of the kingdom of God. Yet this can scarcely have been the original point of the troublesome prediction. Having forgotten the original apocalyptic meaning of the phrase "kingdom of God" as a future *time*, Mark sees the term, as centuries of subsequent Christians have done, as denoting a *place* far removed from us, but of which one might have a vision, like Moses did atop Sinai. This would explain why Jesus takes with him only Peter, James and John: Mark had to adjust the Transfiguration scene to accommodate it to Jesus having said that only "some" of those standing with him would see the vision before they died. Mark's intent was to reinterpret the promise of the second coming as referring to something secretly happening in the generation of Jesus. (Thus also: "Lord, how is it that you will manifest yourself to us, and not to the world?" John 14:22.) The event was not generally known, Mark implies, because, at the time, only a few saw it and were then sworn to secrecy (Mark 9: 9). In passing, it is worth noting that, of all the miracles 2 Peter might have attested, he chooses the Transfiguration (1:16–19) and then makes it somehow a confirmation of "the prophecy"—that of Jesus in Mark 9:1?

We find in John 21, a later appendix to that Gospel (see the original conclusion at the end of chapter 20), a related attempt to explain away the albatross promise. It appears that, by the time the Gospel of John was written, of all the Twelve, only the unnamed "Beloved Disciple" (traditionally identified with John the son of Zebedee) was left alive, but that soon after, he, too, gave up the ghost. This occasioned a crisis, as that disciple had been the last ray of hope that the second advent of Christ might come soon. With him dead, the scoffing began in earnest. The response of "the community of the Beloved Disciple" was to append a new chapter to their Gospel, containing the famous scene where Jesus tells Peter to mind his own business, that, for all he needs to know about the Beloved Disciple's eventual fate, that disciple might as well be granted to survive to the second coming. (The same point is made, i.e., to provide for the delay of the second coming, in Acts 1:6–8). The original promise as we read it in Mark 9:1 was made to "some," but in John 21 it has shrunk to apply to the only remaining disciple. (Similarly, we might wonder if Mark 13:30 preserves a still earlier version, where the whole generation was expected to behold the Parousia, and that Mark 9:1 is already a later narrowing of scope to accommodate the death of the greater part of Jesus' contemporaries.)

The far-fetched apologetical argument in John 21:23, is that, technically, Jesus didn't say that the Beloved Disciple *would* live till the Parousia, only that, *hypothetically*, he *might*. Like Matthew's attempt to disarm the scoffing of opponents on another front (Matt. 27:62–66; 28:4, 11–15), we may wonder

THE BOOK OF MORMON 135

if this rebuttal produced less skepticism or more. At any rate, we are going to find both Mark's and John's attempts to explain away the failure of the Parousia reflected in our 3 Nephi passage. There Joseph Smith has ingeniously utilized both underlying passages in the service of a radically new way of dealing with the problem, one that in the 1820s had become all the more serious.

Apocalypse and Apologia

First, in 3 Nephi 19, we find clear borrowings from the Synoptic Transfiguration narratives (there being none in John's Gospel, since there Jesus is practically transfigured from page one): "And it came to pass that Jesus blessed them as they did pray unto him; and his countenance did smile upon them, and behold they were as white as the countenance and also the garments of Jesus; and behold the whiteness thereof did exceed all the whiteness, yea, even there could be nothing upon earth so white as the whiteness thereof" (3 Nephi 19:25). In verses 31–34 we learn that Jesus went on to pray to the Father in glossolalic utterances beyond the capacity of mere humans to relate or record. It is a moment of epiphany like that of Paul, swept up to the Third Heaven in 2 Corinthians 12:1–10. The same set of elements recurs later on in the sequel to this scene, in 3 Nephi 28. Jesus, in a last dialogue with the Nephite Apostles before his final ascension, bids each one make whatever request he wishes. Nine of them make the unspectacular request that, when, as old men, their labors in the gospel are over, they may leave the world behind to join their Lord in Heaven. (What had they expected otherwise?) That artificial-sounding request reveals its point only once Jesus asks the same question of the last three disciples. They remain coyly silent until Jesus draws them out, whereupon they admit that, like the compassionate Bodhisattvas of Mahayana Buddhism who defer their own well-earned Nirvana to labor on for the good of others, they would prefer to remain alive in the flesh to spread the gospel till the end of the age. To depart and be with Christ would be good, but to continue on for the sake of the churches is better (Phil. 1:23–25).

Jesus happily grants their request, and to equip them for their long career, he transfigures them so their bodies will neither age and die nor succumb to attempts to martyr them. "Therefore, that they might not taste of death there was a change wrought upon their bodies, that they might not suffer pain nor sorrow save it were for the sins of the world" (v. 38). And then the narrator takes the reader on a proleptic survey of the vicissitudes they will endure, thanks to this divine empowerment. Most of these are derived from Paul's catalogue of apostolic sufferings in 2 Corinthians 11:23–33, a passage adjacent to that of Paul's heavenly journey, which we have seen that Joseph Smith used in composing the scene in 3 Nephi chapter 19, where Jesus speaks revelations that man may not utter. The same source is used again here in 3 Nephi 28, since the Nephite disciples are made to share the Pauline rapture and to hear the unutterable secrets spoken in the tongues of angels. In short, what happened to Jesus himself in chapter 19 now happens to them in chapter 28. When one adds the note that they will suffer, if at all, to atone for sins (!), all becomes clear: the Three Nephites are veritable vicars of Christ on earth. Second, the request of the three Nephite Bodhisattvas is also more than a little reminiscent of another revelation vouchsafed to Joseph Smith, that recorded in Chapter VI of *A Book of Commandments* (1833). Not only is the stylistic similarity of the resultant Gospel-like narrative to the text of the Book of Mormon quite revealing, implying that the Book of Mormon originated in the same fashion as the narrative of *A Book of Commandments* VI:1–3; the content forms a strikingly close parallel to the story of the Three Nephites in 3 Nephi 28: "And the Lord said unto me: 'John, my beloved [note that Smith makes explicit the traditional guess that the Beloved Disciple was John son of Zebedee], what desirest thou?' and I said 'Lord, give unto me power over death, that I may bring souls unto thee.' And the Lord said unto me: 'Verily, verily I say unto thee, because thou desirest this, thou shalt tarry till I come in my glory." And for this cause, the Lord said unto Peter: 'If I will that he tarry till I come, what is that to thee? For he desiredst of me that he might bring souls unto me; but thou desiredst that thou mightest speedily come unto me in my kingdom. I say unto thee, Peter, this was a good desire; but my beloved has undertaken a greater work. Verily I say unto you, ye shall both have according to your desires, for ye both joy in that which ye desired."

Here are all the basic elements of 3 Nephi 28: Jesus invites the disciples to make any request of him before he ascends. In verse 2's implied flashback we learn that he had already elicited and granted Peter's request, which involved ministering for Christ till he died, then going straight to the heavenly kingdom, precisely as the first nine Nephite disciples asked in 3 Nephi 28:2, "We desire . . . that we may speedily come unto thee in thy kingdom." Thus there is exactly the same contrast between Peter on the one hand and John on the other as we see in the case of the nine Nephite disciples and the last three, almost word for word.

Given the fact that John son of Zebedee is paralleled with the Three Nephites, one wonders if the Nephite trio was not perhaps suggested in the first place by John's having been one of the three Pillars (Gal. 2:9) along with James and Peter. The implied parallel becomes explicit in a subsequent redaction of the *Book of Commandments* passage two years later in *Doctrines and Covenants* 7, where Joseph Smith first seems to grant Peter's request for a speedy entrance to his kingdom, but then instead assigns him and James son of Zebedee to assist John in his age-long evangelistic mission. The fact that the first promise to Peter has not been erased and replaced, but only supplemented and retracted by means of adding new text is a classic example of what Gospel critics call a "redactional seam," a tell-tale sign of secondary embellishment. But why should Joseph Smith not simply have rewritten the text, omitting the initial granting of Peter's wish, thus avoiding the confusion that now besets the passage? Because the text of *A Book of Commandments* VI was already too familiar to a wide and eager readership for part of it to be omitted. After all, neither jot nor tittle might pass from the text of scripture! But who would complain about *more* inspired prose? Thus the strategy of doubling back.

Apparently the reason for the secondary expansion was that the Prophet Smith wanted to provide "biblical" precedent for a new administrative arrangement whereby he as the First President would be assisted by two counselors, a triumvirate pattern also replicated on the lower levels of bishopric and stake president. Not accidentally, this innovation coincided in date with the redaction of the *Book of Commandments* VI episode. So John, James, and Peter are now made, in effect, to constitute an apostolic "First Presidency" by direct order of Jesus. In all this, Joseph Smith was again following in the tradition of the biblical writers, as when the writers of Exodus 18 and Numbers 11 ascribed to Moses the pedigree for their own councils of elders.

Another fascinating development introduced in the *Doctrines and Covenants* 7 redaction of *Book of Commandments* VI, draws the parallel between John and the Three Nephites even closer. Like the Three Nephites, John is miraculously transfigured to make his superhuman longevity possible. The transfiguration is closely reminiscent of the transfiguration of the Patriarch Enoch into the fiery form of the angel Metatron, the Lesser Yahve, in the Hekhaloth apocalypse *3 Enoch*. Enoch, like John, was the especial beloved of God (Gen. 5:24). Thus the same honor is granted to both.

Surely it is no accident that in 3 Nephi 19 and 28, *Book of Commandments* VI, and *Doctrines and Covenants* 7 Joseph Smith has taken up elements from the Synoptic Transfiguration as well as from the dialogue between Jesus and Peter over the eventual fate of John, and worked them together into two parallel narratives in which John in one case and the Three Nephites in the other are transfigured to remain upon the earth till the second coming in order to preach the gospel. The effect of the singular juxtaposition and recombination of these various elements is to come up with a completely new explanation of the delay of the Parousia. You will recall that Mark's strategy was to reinterpret "seeing the kingdom of God come with power" as a reference not to the end of the age, but rather to the Transfiguration, something *else* that *could* have been seen before the death, already in the past in Mark's day, of the last of the disciples. John's strategy was quite different: he tried to escape the terrible embarrassment by saying that everyone had stupidly misinterpreted, not the character of the predicted Eschaton (the second coming of Jesus) as in Mark, but rather the role of the Beloved Disciple in that scenario. The disappointed Millerites of the nineteenth century used pretty much the Johannine rationalization (William Miller must have misinterpreted Daniel's prophecy of the judgment to come by March 21, 1844), while Jehovah's Witnesses preferred the Markan strategy when their own date for the second advent passed, reinterpreting it as something that had (invisibly) taken place.

But Smith's solution? He rejected the assumption, common to Mark and John, that the kingdom of God as predicted by Jesus was supposed to come *before the normal life spans of the disciples would have been over.* John 21:22 would never have created the crisis implied by the narrator's desperate reinterpretation unless the saying, like the promise in Mark 9:1, had been universally taken to presuppose a normal life span for the disciples. But when in Mormon Scripture Jesus grants the requests of the Three Nephites and of John for eternal life in the flesh, he supposes nothing else than the long continuance of the world beyond Apostolic times. Smith's bold version may justly be ranked as equally or more desperate than the reinterpretations of Mark 9 and John 21, but it is no less brilliant for that.

Apostles at the End of Days

Essentially Joseph Smith makes these four characters assume the role of the

Wandering Jew. This Passion legend, cut from the same pious cloth as the tales of St. Veronica and of Longinus the blind centurion at the cross, depicts a Jew in the crowd along the Via Dolorosa who reviles Jesus in his lowest moment and is cursed by Jesus to "Tarry till I come again." He walks wearily through the world seeing sorrow upon sorrow, never to be released from this tiresome penance till the trump of Gabriel should sound. Probably intended as an allegory justifying the tribulations of Jews through the centuries, the legend in all of its many forms obviously presupposes that the bitter exchange between Jesus and the Jew occurred in the *distant* past; thus, the motif cannot possibly have been an early one. Even so, Joseph Smith's application of the same motif to John and the Three Nephites reveals itself to be no tradition from the era of Jesus but rather a late apologetical attempt to root out a problem that could not otherwise be solved except by rewriting the story.

And, finally, it is perhaps not right to say Smith's version has the world continue far beyond the limits of the Apostolic Era. It would be closer to the truth to say that, by elongating the lives and apostolic ministries of John and the Three Nephites, Smith is extending the Apostolic Age up to and including our own time! The Apostles turn out to be our contemporaries in the literal sense! New chapters continue to be added to the Acts of the Apostles, so to speak, in our own day. And (need we add?) that is exactly the point of Joseph Smith producing a *new* "ancient" scripture in his own day to be added onto the canon. Joseph Smith himself was that Nephi unto whom Jesus spoke one day, saying, "Behold, other scriptures I would that ye should write, that ye have not . . . How be it that ye have not written this thing, that many saints did arise and appear unto many and did minister unto them?" (3 Nephi 23:6, 11). "And now it came to pass that Jesus commanded that it should be written; therefore it was written according as he commanded" (3 Nephi 23:13). And it was called the Book of Mormon, with none other than Joseph Smith for its author.

The Oracles of Samuel the Lamanite: A Deconstruction of Helaman 13–15

God Quoting God

In my not inconsiderable exposure to Pentecostal and Charismatic prayer meetings, I have had occasion to hear a number of spontaneous prophecies. By "spontaneous" I mean to say that there seemed no question of any prior intention to speak to the gathering, and certainly no rehearsal or composition in advance. And yet in virtually every instance the inspired utterance was a pastiche and composite of biblical phrases. If such prophecies were truly and literally the product of divine dictation, as the pious seem to believe, both speakers and hearers, why would God not modify and modernize his idiom, speak in plain and contemporary style, say something new? The answer is, of course, that these charismatic prophecies are spontaneous constructions of oral literature, a lightning-fast searching of the preconscious fund of biblical knowledge possessed by the speaker. When such individuals speak in tongues, they are tapping into what William Samarin[35] calls "pseudolanguage facility." They feel the impetus of the Spirit to speak forth in devotion, as Romans says, "with groanings which cannot be uttered" (Rom. 8:26). Intelligible prophecy is not much different, it seems to me. Shunning conscious speechifying, the speaker instead turns on a different automatic speech capability: composing centos of familiar Bible phrases and sentiments of a generally challenging and reassuring nature.

New Testament scholars have long discussed a similar written phenomenon in the case of midrashic composition of new sacred texts (in the New Testament) from the raw material of the old (in the Old Testament). This derivative relationship first became apparent in the case of apocalyptic literature where, despite overt claims to have been fed one's revelations from a dictating angel, a sweet-tasting scroll, or articulate thunderclaps, it could not be plainer that the "seers" are nothing of the kind. They are, rather, pasticheurs of previous apocalypses, and that they stick surprisingly close to their sources, as if they did not care who knew (as maybe they didn't!). One cannot read long in the Revelation of John before feeling a sense of *deja vue*. And then one has it: one has read these words before, perhaps in a slightly different version, in the Book of Daniel, or Ezekiel, or Zechariah.

More recently it has become increasingly clear that such midrashic rewriting is by no means restricted to the Apocalypse. Randel Helms, Thomas L. Brodie, John Dominic Crossan,[36] and several others have made very plausible cases for this and that New Testament narrative being a rewriting of the Old Testament (usually on the basis of the Greek Septuagint, as one might expect).

None of this denies that the writers of later books, rewriting earlier books, were acting under the influence of the Holy Spirit. It is simply to draw a line, as Thomas Aquinas did, between direct revelation and inspiration, the latter a kind of editorial skill imparted by the Spirit to make good use of previous materials.

While many biblical critics were willing to recognize the genuine inspiration of even such a Bible as criticism left them, one wonders how many of them, if familiar with the Book of Mormon, would have been equally willing to allow that its literarily derivative nature need not embarrass its own claims for divine inspiration. For it had been obvious to non-Mormon scholars for a long time that the Book of Mormon narrative was also a grand-scale pastiche. My hope is that non-LDS scripture scholars will gain new respect for the Book of Mormon in light of their more recent recognition of the character it shares with the Bible, and that LDS scholars will take heart from the critical faith of their "Gentile" counterparts and no longer see the pastiche quality of Joseph Smith's scripture as an embarrassment to be explained away. No, to lay bare the sources of the Mormon scripture and to suggest the redactional motives of its author is to illuminate the sacred text, not to debunk or disqualify it, as fundamentalist critics of LDS Christianity would have it. At least the reader may now understand the spirit in which the present inquiry is pursued and offered, for I seek to narrow the focus to the speech of Samuel the Lamanite prophet, yelled till he was hoarse, from the walls of the city of Zarahemla. I will first, examine the ways that Samuel echoes a whole host of biblical texts, and repeats once again the universal Nephite prophecy. Based on this, I will then examine how Samuel, and the rest of the Book of Mormon, predicts future events in such a way that their outcome has been predicted for centuries; with these prophecies, the event is consequently no more than the illustration of the prediction. This Nephite prophetic exercise, as we shall see, forsakes dramatic literary suspense in favor of the eternal return, in which the narrative unfolds according to ritual rather than literary logic.

Juggling the Testaments

The Book of Mormon's basic approach is to superimpose the New Testament upon the Old, so that we find ourselves reading about ancient Israelites (in American exile) who knew everything early Christians knew about Jesus and his gospel centuries before the fact. This strange perspective (though one shared implicitly with many Calvinist interpreters who seemed to suppose extensive Christian knowledge in pre-Christian times) tends to dehistoricize the gospel message into a floating myth of salvation. It shows prophets urging their contemporaries to throw their eternal destinies upon an accomplished salvation which has, however, not yet commenced. And when it *has* come to pass, nothing will be different except for switching from "B.C." to "A.D." The narrative result is a combination of the Deuteronomic History (Joshua, Judges, Samuel, Kings) and the Acts of the Apostles—a happy match, since many of the same motives guided the writers of both, albeit many centuries apart,[37] and the speech of Samuel the Lamanite is a perfect cameo of both the congruity and the incongruity. I will return to these broader issues toward the end, after a series of detailed observations on the text.

My guess is that the story with its speeches is based on two prophetic episodes in the Old Testament. First, Samuel as a foreigner to his audience, daring to make their business his (and God's), comes from the Book of Amos. Amos, emphatic that he did not belong to the professional guild of prophets, is a farmer and tree-dresser from Judah in the south (Amos 7:14). But he feels impelled by God to go to Israel in the north and deliver God's ultimatum (v. 15). Why does the job fall to him? Amaziah, chaplain of the royal shrine at Bethel, tells Amos to shut up and get packing (v. 12), back to an audience more on his level: the sheep. But Amos has no choice: the task of speaking God's word has fallen to him because all the payroll prophets of the Northern Kingdom have become mere yes-men, offering a quick imprimatur to every policy the king sends their way for ratification (cf. 1 Kings 22:1–8). They know where their bread is buttered. Just as Marcion pictured the original Twelve disciples as so thick-witted that the Risen Jesus had to outsource the apostolate to Paul, so has God resorted to a hick from rural Judah to bring his message to Israel.

Likewise, so willfully deaf have the affluent Nephites of Zarahemla grown that God must resort to a spokesman drawn from the last place one might have looked: the Lamanites (Helaman 14:10)! Can anything good come from that quarter? Apparently so.

The second book after Amos in the Bible is that of Jonah, the second inspiration for Samuel. Jonah is sent off to preach "to Nineveh, that great city, and cry against it, for their wickedness is come up before me" (1:2). This city is famous for its fortified *walls*. And as we will see, the wording of Jonah's preaching recurs in Samuel's. Samuel the Lamanite is like Jonah preaching to the walled city.

Samuel preaches the need for repentance, but at this point confusion arises. There is an implicit contradiction running through the whole discourse, beginning with the section 13:5–11. On the one hand, we recognize the Old Testament prophetic theme of the need for a wicked people to repent of its collective sins to avoid a historical overthrow by foreign powers at God's behest. Isaiah and Jeremiah are full of this sort of thing. On the other hand, we discover the New Testament urgency that individuals ought to repent of their sins, their sinful personal lives, and have saving faith in Jesus Christ, so as to avoid going to hell. Granted, even this conflation of different notions of repentance is already present in Jonah, but this is because Jonah, too, is a historical fiction. Written long, long after the time of the historical Jonah, it paints the improbable picture of the whole of Nineveh repenting from the top down, by royal command, and in a distinctly post-Exilic sense. That is, it depicts the Assyrian nation converting *en masse* from heathenism to Judaism. The Book of Mormon takes a similar long-retrospective look, as if the ancient prophets were evangelists for biblical religion.

Building Blocks of Samuel's Wall

In 13:5 we catch an early echo of Jonah's preaching to Nineveh: "four hundred years pass not away save the sword of justice falleth upon this people" seems to recall Jonah's jeremiad, "Yet forty days, and Nineveh shall be overthrown" (Jonah 3:4) plus Mark 13:30, "this generation shall not pass, till all these things be done." Again, 15:12 addresses "this great city of Zarahemla" much as God tells Jonah to address "Nineveh, that great city" (Jonah 3:2). We also think of Revelation 18:10, "Alas, alas, that great city, Babylon, that mighty city! for in one hour is thy judgment come." This passage itself may be based on Jonah's doomsaying.

In passing we may note the literary artificiality of an urgent prediction of a doom *four centuries in the future*! Since the number is merely a chronological milestone in a larger narrative, just as all readers perceive, there is no author-to-reader confusion. We must therefore attribute this to a narrator anxious to speak to the reader. But it cannot represent a historical report. Else imagine the Zarahelmites scratching their heads at this "news." What's it to them, anyway? Let tomorrow deal with its own troubles.

When God first summons Jonah, he explains the plight of the Ninevites: "cry against it, for their wickedness is come up before me" (Jonah 1:2). In a pre-theological era, when no one yet philosophized an omniscient deity, people pictured Jehovah like an Oriental despot dependant upon "the eyes of the king" reporting on his subjects, as witness Job 1:6–7. In some such way he has learned of the rumors of Sodom's disgraceful behavior and means to corroborate the reports: "Because the cry of Sodom and Gomorrah is great, and because their sin is very grievous; I will go down now, and see whether they have done altogether according to the cry of it, which is come unto me; and if not, I will know" (Gen. 18:20–21). He has heard reports, and that is also the point of Jonah 1:2, "their wickedness has come up before me," has come to my attention. My guess is that the obvious parallel between the impending fates of Nineveh and Sodom suggested the next imagery to the author, the comparison of Zarahemla to Sodom, or rather, of Zarahemla *and Gideon*, together with the adjacent cities, to Sodom *and Gomorrah* and their surrounding cities. We read,

> for behold, it is because of those who are righteous that it is saved; yea, woe unto this great city, for I perceive, saith the Lord, that there are many, yea, even the more part of this great city, that will harden their hearts against me, saith the Lord. But blessed are they who will repent, for them will I spare. But behold, if it were not for the righteous who are in this great city, behold, I would cause that fire should come down out of heaven and destroy it. But behold, it is for the righteous' sake that it is spared. But behold, the time cometh, saith the Lord, that when ye shall cast out the righteous from among you, then shall ye be ripe for destruction; yea, woe be unto this great city, because of the wickedness and abominations which are in her. Yea, and woe be unto the city of Gideon, for the wickedness and abominations which are in her. Yea, and woe be unto all the cities which are in the land round about, which are possessed by the Nephites, because of the wickedness and abominations which are in them. (vv. 12–16)

Zarahemla will stand as long as she does not expel the few righteous within her—just as Sodom falls as soon as Lot and his daughters are safely away. And the destruction of both metropolitan areas will be by fire falling from heaven.

The basic philosophy of history dictating the flow of events in the Book of Mormon is that of the Deuteronomic School: obedience to the covenant and commandments of God results in blessing, victory, prosperity, while apostasy and backsliding presage conquest, illness, famine and poverty. See

Deuteronomy chapters 11 and 28. "But it shall come to pass, if thou wilt not hearken to the voice of the LORD thy God, to observe to do all his commandments and his statutes which I command thee this day; that all these curses shall come upon thee, and overtake thee" (Deut. 28:15). "Cursed shall be . . . the fruit of thy land" (Ibid., 28:18). That understanding is summed up succinctly in Helaman 13:17, "And behold, a curse shall come upon the land, saith the Lord of Hosts, because of the people's sake who are upon the land, yea, because of their wickedness and their abominations." Also lurking in the background, unless I miss my guess, is Malachi 4:6, the very last verse of the Old Testament: "lest I come and smite the earth with a curse."

Helaman 13:18–23 echoes Deuteronomy's warning against imagined self-sufficiency, patting oneself on the back for one's prosperity: "And thou say in thine heart, My power and the might of mine hand hath gotten me this wealth. But thou shalt remember the LORD thy God; for it is he that giveth thee power to get wealth, etc" (Deut. 8:17–20). Samuel the Lamanite's version:

> And it shall come to pass, saith the Lord of Hosts, yea, our great and true God, that whoso shall hide up treasures in the earth shall find them again no more, because of the great curse of the land, save he be a righteous man and shall hide it up unto the Lord. For I will, saith the Lord, that they shall hide up their treasures unto me; and cursed be they who hide not up their treasures unto me; for none hideth up their treasures unto me save it be the righteous; and he that hideth not up his treasures unto me, cursed is he, and also the treasure, and none shall redeem it because of the curse of the land. And the day shall come that they shall hide up their treasures, because they have set their hearts upon riches; and because they have set their hearts upon their riches, and will hide up their treasures when they shall flee before their enemies; because they will not hide them up unto me, cursed be they and also their treasures; and in that day shall they be smitten, saith the Lord. Behold ye, the people of this great city, and hearken unto my words; yea, hearken unto the words which the Lord saith; for behold, he saith that ye are cursed because of your riches, and also are your riches cursed because ye have set your hearts upon them, and have not hearkened unto the words of him who gave them unto you. Ye do not remember the Lord your God in the things with which he hath blessed you, but ye do always remember your riches, not to thank the Lord your God for them; yea, your hearts are not drawn out unto the

Lord, but they do swell with great pride, unto boasting, and unto great swelling, envyings, strifes, malice, persecutions and murders, and all manner of iniquities. For this cause hath the Lord God caused that a curse should come upon the land, and also upon your riches, and this because of your iniquities.

In Helaman 13:24–25 ("Yea, wo unto this people, because of this time which has arrived, that ye do cast out the prophets, and do mock them, and cast stones at them, and do slay them, and do all manner of iniquity unto them, even as they did of old time. And now when ye talk, ye say: If our days had been in the days of our fathers of old, we would not have slain the prophets; we would not have stoned them, and cast them out.") it is hard to miss the influence of Matthew 23:29–34:

Woe unto you, scribes and Pharisees, hypocrites! Because ye build the tombs of the prophets, and garnish the sepulchers of the righteous, and say, If we had been in the days of our fathers, we would not have been partakers with them in the blood of the prophets. Wherefore ye be witness unto yourselves, that ye are the children of them which killed the prophets. Fill up ye then the measure of your fathers . . . Wherefore, behold, I send unto you prophets, and wise men, and scribes; and some of them ye shall kill and crucify; and some of them shall ye scourge in your synagogues, and persecute them from city to city.

The Book of Mormon narrator has merely reversed the two major sections of the Matthew passage, summarizing the second.

Next Samuel warns against false prophets:

Behold ye are worse than they; for as the Lord liveth, if a prophet come among you and declareth unto you the word of the Lord, which testifieth of your sins and iniquities, ye are angry with him, and cast him out and seek all manner of ways to destroy him; yea, you will say that he is a false prophet, and that he is a sinner, and of the devil, because he testifieth that your deeds are evil. But behold, if a man shall come among you and shall say: Do this, and there is no iniquity; do that and ye shall not suffer; yea, he will say: Walk after the pride of your own hearts; yea, walk after the pride of your eyes, and do whatsoever your heart desireth—and if a man shall come among you and say this, ye will receive him, and say that he is a prophet. Yea, ye will lift him up, and ye will give unto him of your substance; ye will give unto him of your gold, and of your silver, and ye will clothe him with costly apparel; and because he speaketh flattering words unto you, and he saith that all is well, then ye will not find fault with him. (Helaman 13:26–28).

For the basis of this preachment we need look no farther than Deuteronomy 13:1–5 ("If there arise among you a prophet . . . and giveth thee a sign or a wonder, and the sign or wonder come to pass, whereof he spake unto thee, saying, Let us go after other gods, which thou hast not known, and let us serve them," etc.) and 2 Corinthians 11:4, "For if he that cometh preacheth another Jesus, whom we have not preached, or if ye receive another spirit, which ye have not received, or another gospel, which ye have not accepted, ye might well bear with him." (See also vv. 19–20).

Helaman 13:29b ("Yea, how long will ye suffer yourselves to be led by foolish and blind guides? Yea, how long will ye choose darkness rather than light?") seems to owe a great debt to Matthew 23:16, "Woe unto you, ye blind guides, etc." (or 23:24, "Ye blind guides, which strain at a gnat, and swallow a camel") and John 3:19b, "men loved darkness rather than light, because their deeds were evil."

James 5:1–6 features an Isaiah-like tirade against the wicked rich:

Go to now [Come now], ye rich men, *weep and howl* for *your miseries that shall come upon you. Your riches are corrupted*, and your garments are moth-eaten. Your gold and silver is cankered; and the rust of them shall be a witness against you, and shall eat your flesh as it were fire. Ye have heaped treasure together for the last days. Behold, the hire of the labourers who have reaped down your fields, which is of you kept back by fraud, crieth; and the cries of them which have reaped are entered into the ears of the Lord of sabaoth. Ye have lived in pleasure on the earth, and been wanton; ye have nourished your hearts, as in a day of slaughter. Ye have condemned and killed the just; and he doth not resist you.

Surely this passage forms the basis of the more prolix Helaman 13:30–36:

Yea, behold, the anger of the Lord is already kindled against you; behold, he hath cursed the land because of your iniquity. And behold, the time cometh that he curseth *your riches, that they become slippery*, that ye cannot hold them; and in the days of your poverty ye cannot retain them. And in the days of your poverty ye shall cry unto the Lord; and in vain shall ye cry, for *your desolation is already come upon you*, and your destruction is made sure; and then shall ye *weep and howl* in that day, saith the Lord of Hosts. And then shall ye lament, and say: O that I had repented, and had not killed the prophets, and stoned them, and cast them out. Yea, in that day ye shall say: O that we had remembered the Lord our God in the day that he gave us our riches, and then they would not have become slippery that we should lose them; for behold, our riches are gone from us.

The familiar refrain about killing the prophets was suggested by James 5:6, "Ye have condemned and killed the just."

The image of one's riches, tools, and weapons having gone all "slippery" must strike us first as an apt and picturesque metaphor for our inability to find security in possessions or to be sure of keeping them against the day we will need them. That much is clear. But it should really have stopped right there. Played out farther in verses 34–36, the "slippery" business seems to become some kind of literal description, though it is hard to envision exactly what the writer has in mind:

Behold, we lay a tool here and on the morrow it is gone; and behold, our swords are taken from us in the day we have sought them for battle. Yea, we have hid up our treasures and they have slipped away from us, because of the curse of the land. O that we had repented in the day that the word of the Lord came unto us; for behold the land is cursed, and all things are become slippery, and we cannot hold them.

We might think of a scene in *Monty Python's Life of Brian (of Nazareth)*, when we overhear the speech of one of the street-corner prophets, whom the script denominates the Boring Prophet:

And there shall in that time be rumours of things going astray, and there will be a great confusion as to where things really are, and nobody will really know where lieth those little things with the sort of raffia work base, that has an attachment; they will not be there. At this time a friend shall lose his friend's hammer and the young shall not know where lieth the things possessed by their fathers that their fathers put there only just the night before . . .[38]

Here's something odd. At the close of this oration, the narrator seems to be easing Samuel off the podium with this colophon (14:1), "And now it came to pass that Samuel, the Lamanite, did prophesy a great many more things which cannot be written." And yet he starts right up again with more from Samuel! Apparently he just took a break for a glass of water, or a cup of coffee-near. And the loquacious Lamanite gusts on for another two chapters. But then again, perhaps it is not so strange after all. For 14:1 is obviously based upon John 20:30, "And many other signs truly did Jesus in the presence of his disciples, which are not written in this book." That was the original closer to the gospel. But someone came along with more to add, so he appended chapter 21 with its resurrection appearance by the Sea of Tiberias, etc., and felt bound to paraphrase the original conclusion so that the book might end on pretty much the note its original author had intended. This new copy-conclusion was 21:25: "And there are also many other things which Jesus did, the which, if they should be written every one, I suppose that even the world itself could not contain the books that should be written."

That tells us, incidentally, that the author of the Johannine Appendix (chapter 21) had not made a new copy concluding with his annex. Had he done that, he would have simply used the original conclusion, waiting to copy it until he had added his new material. As it now reads, it is clear that instead he just started writing on the leftover space on a scroll already containing the text of chapters 1–20. Thus he had to leave the original conclusion intact and then paraphrase it once he finished his new chapter. At any rate, the Book of Mormon narrator knew the text of John only in its canonical form, in which what seems to be a conclusion (20:30) issues in another chapter. Odd as it might seem, there it was in the Bible, and if it was good enough for the Bible, it was good enough for the Book of Mormon. When Samuel (14:2) predicts the birth of Jesus Christ ("And behold, he said unto them: Behold, I give unto you a sign; for five years more cometh, and behold, then cometh the Son of God to redeem all those who shall believe on his name.") what we have is what Christians, all the way back to Matthew the evangelist, wished they had in Isaiah 7:14 ("Therefore the Lord himself shall give you a sign; Behold, a virgin shall conceive, and bear a son, and shall call his name Immanuel."), an explicit prediction of the nativity. Helaman 14:2 is, then, a prime example of how the Book of Mormon superimposes the New Testament upon the Old in the manner of ancient Christian pseudepigrapha like *The Ascension of Isaiah*.

The Book of Mormon makes a surprising departure from canonical biblical history when it posits two days without an intervening night to mark the birth of Jesus.

> And behold, this will I give unto you for a sign at the time of his com-
> ing; for behold, there shall be great lights in heaven, insomuch that in
> the night before he cometh there shall be no darkness, insomuch that
> it shall appear unto man as if it was day. Therefore, there shall be one
> day and a night and a day, as if it were one day and there were no night;
> and this shall be unto you for a sign; for ye shall know of the rising of
> the sun and also of its setting; therefore they shall know of a surety that
> there shall be two days and a night; nevertheless the night shall not be
> darkened; and it shall be the night before he is born. (Helaman 14:3–4).

Can this anomaly have been suggested by the long day of Joshua (Josh. 10:13)? Joshua, is of course, the Old Testament Hebrew counterpart to "Jesus." As for the "great lights in heaven," surely this phrase comes straight from Genesis 1:14–16, "And God said, Let there be *lights in* the firmament of *the heaven* to divide the day from the night; and let them be for signs, and for seasons, and for days, and years . . . And God made two *great lights*; the greater light to rule the day, and the lesser light to rule the night." In Genesis, the reference is not to any apocalyptic enormity, but rather to the changeless sun and moon. Perhaps the Book of Mormon narrator associated them with a day of heavenly portents because of the note in the Olivet Discourse that "in those days, after that tribulation, the sun shall be darkened, and the moon shall not give her light, and the stars of heaven shall fall, and the powers that are in heaven shall be shaken" (Mark 13:24–25).

More prediction of Jesus' birth follows in Helaman 14:5, where we read: "And behold, there shall a new star arise, such an one as ye never have beheld; and this also shall be a sign unto you." This announcement combines Matthew's natal star and the angelic words to the shepherds in Luke 2:12. "And this shall be a sign unto you; Ye shall find the babe wrapped in swaddling clothes, lying in a manger."

Helaman 14:8 provides another case of explicit "pre"-Christian prophecy of Jesus: "And it shall come to pass that whosoever shall believe on the Son of God, the same shall have everlasting life." And it does so with the help of Joel 2:32a as quoted in Acts 2:21, "And it shall come to pass, that whosoever shall call on the name of the Lord shall be saved," plus the familiar John 3:16.

Samuel the Lamanite beats John the Baptist to the punch in verse 9: "And behold, thus hath the Lord commanded me, by his angel, that I should come and tell this thing unto you; yea, he hath commanded that I should prophesy these things unto you; yea, he hath said unto me: Cry unto this people, repent and prepare the way of the Lord." Of course Mark the evangelist applies the same passage, Isaiah 40:3 ("The voice of him that crieth in the wilderness, Prepare ye the way of the LORD, make straight in the desert a highway for our God.") to the Baptizer. And this is surely where our author derived it.

We find a half-assimilated piece of atonement theology in Helaman 14:13. "And if ye believe on his name ye will repent of all your sins, that thereby ye may have a remission of them through his merits." The language is derived from Mark 1:4, "John did baptize in the wilderness, and preach the baptism of repentance for the remission of sins," a passage cheek by jowl with the Mark 1:3 quotation of Isaiah 40:3, just above. It is no wonder that the two paraphrases should appear so close together. But the notion of Christ atoning through "his merits" seems to be the tip of a much larger soteriological iceberg taken for granted on the part of the intended Christian readers, who can be safely assumed to be thoroughly familiar with the oft-preached theology of the cross. The death of Jesus Christ is never explained in such detail in the Book of Mormon to justify a glancing reference such as this, it simply demands that readers are already familiar with Christian soteriology. What on earth could the audience of a historical Samuel have thought he was talking about?

The same might be said of verse 15, "For behold, he surely must die that salvation may come; yea, it behooveth him and becometh expedient that he dieth, to bring to pass the resurrection of the dead, that thereby men may be brought into the presence of the Lord." This material comes directly from John 11:50: "it is expedient for us, that one man should die for the people, and that the whole nation perish not." John writes with irony: the unbelieving priest spoke more truly than he knew—precisely because he knew nothing of Christian doctrine! But the readers of Helaman know, because they are catechized Christians.

By contrast, verse 16 provides a piece of harmonizing theology typical of the sort of fundamentalist biblicism familiar today. Why does God predict that Adam and Eve will not outlive the day on which they eat the forbidden fruit (Gen. 2:17; 3:3), and yet they do not die? As the ancient Gnostics saw, the Genesis narrative has no problem with Jehovah lying to keep the fledgling humans' mitts off his own preferred groceries. The Serpent lets them in on the secret when he debunks Jehovah's priestcraft: "Ye shall not surely die: For God knoweth that in the day ye eat thereof, then your eyes shall be opened, and ye shall be as gods, knowing good and evil" (Gen. 3:4–5), his own prerogative. The ancient story is parallel to that of Prometheus, bringer of knowledge to mankind against the will of God. But such an answer was not open to fundamentalists, for whom God cannot err, much less lie. And so pious readers resorted to equivocation, much as Obi-wan Kenobi does in *Star Wars*, telling Luke that his father was "betrayed and murdered by a young Jedi named Darth Vader," when it turns out that Luke's father is none other than Darth Vader himself. What gives? Well, Obi-wan later explains, since Luke's dad did apostatize from the Light Side of the Force to the Dark Side, it was sort of true, in a sense, that he had betrayed and murdered the man he had previously been. We observe the same fancy footwork, redefining "death," in Helaman 14:16: "Yea, behold, this death bringeth to pass the resurrection, and redeemeth all mankind from the first death—that spiritual death; for all mankind, by the fall of Adam being cut off from the presence of the Lord, are considered as dead, both as to things temporal and to things spiritual."

We find more of the same in verse 18: "Yea, and it bringeth to pass the condition of repentance, that whosoever repenteth the same is not hewn down and cast into the fire; but whosoever repenteth not is hewn down and cast into the fire; and there cometh upon them again a spiritual death, yea, a second death, for they are cut off again as to things pertaining to righteousness." And this verse has two New Testament prototypes, Matthew 3:10 ("And now also the axe is laid unto the root of the trees: therefore every tree which bringeth not forth good fruit is hewn down and cast into the fire.") and Revelation 20:14 ("And death and hell were cast into the lake of fire. This is the second death."), the two texts being linked in the authors's mind by their common reference to being "cast into the fire."

> But behold, as I said unto you concerning another sign, a sign of his death, behold, in that day that he shall suffer death the sun shall be darkened and refuse to give his light unto you; and also the moon and the stars; and there shall be no light upon the face of this land, even from the time that he shall suffer death, for the space of three days, to the time that he shall rise again from the dead" (Helaman 14:20).

Again (as in Helaman 14:3–4 above), the reference is to Mark 13:24–25, and our redactor has transferred the signs heralding the end of the age to the time of the death of Jesus. In so doing, he was only carrying further a tendency evident in the gospel crucifixion accounts themselves, especially Matthew, where the apocalypse seems to begin in earnest already on Good Friday, as we will shortly see.

Samuel's prophecy inverses 21–22 ("Yea, at the time that he shall yield up the ghost there shall be thunderings and lightnings for the space of many hours, and the earth shall shake and tremble; and the rocks which are upon the face of this earth, which are both above the earth and beneath, which ye know at this time are solid, or the more part of it is one solid mass, shall be broken up; yea, they shall be rent in twain, and shall ever after be found in seams and in cracks, and in broken fragments upon the face of the whole earth, yea, both above the earth and beneath.") is plainly a heightening of Matthew 27:50–51: "Jesus, when he had cried again with a loud voice, yielded up the ghost . . . and the earth did quake, and the rocks rent." The pedantic details of fractured rocks and their scattering is typical of the apocryphal embellishment of writers who want to have more Bible yet cannot think of anything good to add.

Samuel returns in verse 23 to Isaiah 40. Having used, with Mark, the contents of verse 3, the voice crying in the wilderness, the narrative returns to pluck verse 4, literalizing it in a manner the Second Isaiah (for it is his work) never imagined: "And behold, there shall be great tempests, and there shall be many mountains laid low, like unto a valley, and there shall be many places which are now called valleys which shall become mountains, whose height is great." The original was obviously metaphorical hyperbole: "Every valley shall be exalted, and every mountain and hill shall be made low: and the crooked shall be made straight, and the rough places a plain."

The next verse, 24, "And many highways shall be broken up, and many cities shall become desolate," perhaps borrows from Isaiah 6:11, "Until the cities be wasted without inhabitant."

Matthean Passion apocalyptic again forms the basis of verse 25: "And many graves shall be opened, and shall yield up many of their dead; and many saints shall appear unto many." The source is Matthew 27:52–53. "And the graves were opened; and many bodies of the saints which slept arose, and came out of the graves after his resurrection, and went into the holy city, and appeared unto many." Paul spoke of the resurrection of Jesus as the beginning of the process of the resurrection of all the dead, a process which therefore must be hastening to its fulfillment in his own day (1 Cor. 15:22–23). But as time went by, with no collective resurrection of the dead manifesting itself, it became necessary in the minds of some to preserve the connection, now deemed mysterious, between the resurrection of Jesus and the end time events by depicting an anticipatory run-through of the eschatological events in direct connection with Golgotha and Easter. Thus Matthew has not only earthquakes and the apocalyptic darkening of the sun, but even the opening of the tombs and the resurrection of the righteous! Of course this "solution" to an ancient enigma has created a much worse headache for subsequent exegetes. What happened to these people? Did Matthew think they were still alive in his day? Are they supposed to be alive today? Are they the three Nephites?

The mention of thunder and lightning in verse 22 put our redactor/author in mind of another biblical passage in which they occur, one with much apocalyptic import, Revelation 8:1, 5 "And when he had opened the seventh seal, there was silence in heaven about the space of half an hour." "And the angel took the censer, and filled it with fire of the altar, and cast it into the earth; and there were voices, and thunderings, and lightnings, and an earthquake." From these texts he produced a new one with details of both: "And behold, thus hath the angel spoken unto me; for he said unto me that there should be thunderings and lightnings for the space of many hours" (Helaman 14:26).

Now the angel which sent Samuel on his way preaching has become a full-fledged interpreting angel typical in apocalypses, like the series of them that interrogate and inform John the Revelator: "And he said unto me that while the thunder and the lightning lasted, and the tempest, that these things should be, and that darkness should cover the face of the whole earth for the space of three days" (Helaman 14:27). Note again that our author has adjusted the biblical time line, expanding the three hours of darkness that fell on the world or the land during Jesus' crucifixion to a whole three days, so that the emergence of Jesus from the tomb thereafter should assume the dimensions of a sunrise in more than a metaphorical sense (Mal. 4:2, "But unto you that fear my name shall the sun of righteousness arise with healing in his wings").

"And the angel said unto me that many shall see greater things than these, to the intent that they might believe that these signs and these wonders should come to pass upon all the face of this land, to the intent that there should be no cause for unbelief among the children of men" (Helaman 14:28). Verily he quoteth John 1:50, "Jesus answered and said unto him, Because I said unto thee, I saw thee under the fig tree, believest thou? Thou shalt see greater things than these."

Christians, despite the nonsense it makes of any plain reading of the Old Testament, continue to speak as if the whole Bible were one big evangelistic tract, as if the whole message of it were to persuade the reader to accept Jesus as his or her personal savior (a notion foreign to the Bible as far as I can see, read into it from the devotional theology of German Pietism). Non-pietists still say the whole canon witnesses to Jesus Christ. But on any straightforward reading, we have suggested, it certainly does not. And this is, again, one of those places where the Book of Mormon attempts to improve on the Bible. It actually does have Old Testament prophets give Christian evangelistic sermons. Samuel the Lamanite is certainly shown doing that here: "And this to the intent that whosoever will believe might be saved, and that whosoever will not believe, a righteous judgment might come upon them; and also if they are condemned they bring upon themselves their own condemnation" (Helaman 14:29). It is based upon Mark 16:16 ("He that believeth and is baptized shall be saved; but he that believeth not shall be damned") and perhaps also 1 Corinthians 11:29, "For he that eateth and drinketh unworthily, eateth and drinketh damnation to himself, etc."

Helaman 14:30 ("And now remember, remember, my brethren, that whosoever perisheth, perisheth unto himself; and whosoever doeth iniquity, doeth it unto himself; for behold, ye are free; ye are permitted to act for yourselves; for behold, God hath given unto you a knowledge and he hath made you free.") combines two Pauline texts, Romans 14:7 ("For none of us liveth to himself, and no man dieth to himself.") and Galatians 5:1a ("Stand fast therefore in the liberty wherewith Christ hath made us free."). The Galatians quote may not seem to register very strongly here, but the plain fact of its use below implies the redactor had it in mind here, too.

Above, we noticed how the Book of Mormon narrator employed a traditional bit of harmonization used to get God off the hook for lying in the Garden of Eden. And yet in Helaman 14:31, he seems to have embraced a Gnostic glorification of Eve as a salvific bringer of knowledge: "He hath given unto you that ye might know good from evil." Is not this the perspective of the Serpent in Genesis 3:5, "For God doth know that in the day ye eat thereof, then your eyes shall be opened, and ye shall be as gods, knowing good and evil"?

The same verse goes on ("and he hath given unto you that ye might choose life or death; and ye can do good and be restored unto that which is good, or have that which is good restored unto you; or ye can do evil, and have that which is evil restored unto you.") to borrow from Deuteronomy 30:19, "I call heaven and earth to record this day against you, that I have set before you life and death, blessing and cursing: therefore choose life, that both thou and thy seed may live."

Helaman 15:1 ("And now, my beloved brethren, behold, I declare unto you that except ye shall repent your houses shall be left unto you desolate.") plainly derives from Matthew 23:38 ("Behold, your house is left unto you desolate.").

Back to the Olivet Discourse, the Synoptic Apocalypse, in its Lukan redaction, for Helaman 15:2, "Yea, except ye repent, your women shall have great cause to mourn in the day that they shall *give suck*; for ye shall attempt to flee and there shall be no place for refuge; yea, and wo unto them which are *with child*, for they shall be heavy and cannot flee; therefore, they shall be *trodden down* and shall be left to perish." No one can miss the echoes of Luke 21:23–24, "But woe unto them that are *with child*, and to them that *give suck*, in those days! For there shall be great distress in the land, and wrath upon this people. And they shall fall by the edge of the sword, and shall be led away captive into all nations: and Jerusalem shall be *trodden down* of the Gentiles, until the times of the Gentiles be fulfilled."

Samuel's attempt to soften the blow of his words somewhat (verse 3: "Yea, wo unto this people who are called the people of Nephi except they shall repent, when they shall see all these signs and wonders which shall be showed unto them; for behold, they have been a chosen people of the Lord; yea, the people of Nephi hath he loved, and also hath he chastened them; yea, in the days of their iniquities hath he chastened them because he loveth them.") stem directly from Hebrews 12:6, "For whom the Lord loveth he chasteneth, and scourgeth every son whom he receiveth." Hebrews itself is quoting from Proverbs 3:12 at this point, but the Helaman text is closer to Hebrews.

Samuel recalls the strike against his own heritage when he says (verse 4), "But behold my brethren, the Lamanites hath he hated because their deeds have been evil continually, and this because of the iniquity of the tradition of their fathers. But behold, salvation hath come unto them through the preaching of the Nephites; and for this intent hath the Lord prolonged their days." This comes from Romans 9:13, "As it is written, Jacob have I loved, Esau I have hated." However, our redactor has rejected the apparent predestinarianism of Romans, where God had decided whom he loved and whom he hated before and regardless of any deed either might commit. We can also see the influence of Genesis 6:5, "And GOD saw that the wickedness of man was great in the earth, and that every imagination of the thoughts of his heart was only evil continually." And the phrase "salvation is come unto the Gentiles" comes from Romans 11:11.

The Lamanite prophet fears to paint with too broad a brush, so he admits that most of the Nephites share neither the sin nor the destiny of the backsliders of Zarahemla. "And I would that ye should behold that the more part of them are in the path of their duty, and they do walk circumspectly before God, and they do observe to keep his commandments and his statutes and his judgments according to the law of Moses" (Helaman 15:5). The operative phrase appears to come from Deuteronomy 28:15, "to observe to do all his commandments and his statutes which I command thee this day."

In verse 6, Samuel switches back (forward?) to the New Testament again. "Yea, I say unto you, that the more part of them are doing this, and they are striving with unwearied diligence that they may bring the remainder of their brethren to the knowledge of the truth; therefore there are many who do add to their numbers daily." 1 Timothy 2:4; 2 Timothy 3:7; and Hebrews 10:26 all share the phrase "the knowledge of the truth." Acts 2:47b has provided the phraseology of church growth: "And the Lord added to the church daily such as should be saved."

Verse 8, "Therefore, as many as have come to this, ye know of yourselves are firm and steadfast in the faith, and in the thing wherewith they have been made free," is clearer evidence of the use of Galatians 5:1a, "Stand fast therefore in the liberty wherewith Christ hath made us free."

Helaman 15:11 ("Yea, even if they should dwindle in unbelief the Lord shall prolong their days, until the time shall come which hath been spoken of by our fathers, and also by the prophet Zenos, and many other prophets, concerning the restoration of our brethren, the Lamanites, again to the knowledge of the truth.") resembles in both basic structure and specific phrases Acts 3:21 ("Whom the heaven must receive until the times of restitution of all things, which God hath spoken by the mouth of all his holy prophets since the world began.").

The Good Shepherd discourse of John 10:1–18 makes its influence known in Helaman 15:13: "And this is according to the prophecy, that they shall again be brought to the true knowledge, which is knowledge of their Redeemer, and their great and true shepherd, and be numbered among his sheep." And again the apparent Johannine predestinarian doctrine ("ye believe not, because ye are not of my sheep," John 10:26) is conspicuous by its absence.

Matthew 11:21–24 shows Jesus lambasting towns where no one showed up for his rallies. To him they seem more reprehensible than the legendary necropoli:

> Woe unto thee, Chorazin! Woe unto thee, Bethsaida! For if the mighty works which were done in you, had been done in Tyre and Sidon, they would have repented long ago in sackcloth and ashes. But I say unto you, It shall be more tolerable for Tyre and Sidon at the day of judgment, than for you. And thou, Capernaum, which art exalted unto heaven, shall be brought down to hell: for if the mighty works, which have been done in thee, had been done in Sodom, it would have remained until this day. But I say unto you, That it shall be more tolerable for the land of Sodom in the day of judgment, than for thee.

We find a weak but definite echo of these thunderings in Helaman 15:14–15,

> Therefore I say unto you, it shall be better for them than for you except ye repent. For behold, had the mighty works been shown unto them which have been shown unto you, yea, unto them who have dwindled in unbelief because of the traditions of their fathers, ye can see of your-selves that they never would again have dwindled in unbelief.

Since I do not believe in the historicity of the Book of Mormon, I see of course that all of this biblical redaction and narrator allusion is quite naturally the result of Joseph Smith acting much like Pentecostal pasticheurs and biblical writers borrowing from earlier scripture. I will leave it to FARMS and other Mormon groups to sort out how (either by ahistorical spiritual whisperinsgs or lost pre-Christian texts) the Book of Mormon could be so close in its wording and theology to so many New Testament passages. But there is something more going on here than mere biblical allusion and quotation.

Helaman's Hall of Mirrors

I would suggest that the Book of Mormon, like *The Quest of the Holy Grail*, "is built on the tension between . . . two kinds of logic: narrative and ritual, or, one might say, the profane and the religious." I must beg the reader's indulgence for stepping aside and yielding to the expert, Tzvetan Todorov (*The Poetics of Prose*).

The articulation of these two kinds of logic derives from two contrary conceptions of time (neither of which coincides with the one most habitual to us). Narrative logic implies, ideally, a temporality we might call the 'perpetual present.' Time here is constituted by the concatenation of countless instances of discourse; it is these latter which define the very idea of the present. We speak of the event occurring during the very act of speech; there is a perfect parallelism between the series of events one speaks of and the series of the instances of discourse. Discourse is never behind and never ahead of what it evokes. The characters, too, live in the present alone; the succession of events is governed by a logic proper to it, and is influenced by no external factor.

On the other hand, ritual logic is based on a conception of time which is that of the 'eternal return.' Here no event happens for the first or the last time. Everything has already been foretold, and now one foretells what will follow. The origin of the rite is lost in the origin of time; what matters is that the rite constitutes a rule which is already present, already there. Contrary to the preceding case, the 'pure' or 'authentic' present, experienced fully as such, does not exist. In both cases, time is suspended, but conversely: in the first instance by the hypertrophy of the present, in the second by its disappearance.

The Quest of the Holy Grail [or the Book of Mormon] acknowledges, like any narrative, both kinds of logic—when an ordeal occurs and we do not know how it will end; when we experience it with the hero moment by moment and the discourse remains glued to the event, the tale is obviously obeying narrative logic, and we inhabit the perpetual present. When, on the contrary, the ordeal begins and it is stated that its outcome has been predicted for centuries, that it is consequently no more than the illustration of the prediction, we are in the eternal return, and the narrative unfolds according to ritual logic. This second logic, as well as the temporality of the 'eternal return' type, here emerges in the conflict between the two.

Everything has been foretold. At the moment the adventure occurs, the hero learns he is merely fulfilling a prediction . . . There was no accident, nor even any adventure; Galahad [or Nephi or Samuel or Jesus] has simply played his part in a pre-established rite . . .

This retrospective future, reestablished at the moment a prediction is fulfilled, is completed by the prospective future, in which we are confronted with the prediction itself. The denouement of the plot is recounted, from the very first pages, with all the necessary details. . . What could be clearer and more definitive? And just so that we do not forget the prediction, it is constantly repeated for us . . .

The reader's interest . . . does not come, as we see, from the question which [ordinarily] provokes such interest: what happens next? We know, from the beginning, what will happen . . . The interest is generated by a very different question: what is the Grail [or what will it be like when Jesus finally appears?] These are two different kinds of interest, and also two kinds of narrative. One unfolds on a horizontal line: we want to know what each event provokes, what it *does*. The other represents a series of variations which stack up along a vertical line: what we look for in each event is what it *is*. The first is a narrative of contiguity, the second a narrative of substitutions. In our case, we know from the start that Galahad will complete the quest victoriously; the narrative of contiguity is without interest. But we do not know precisely what the Grail is, so that there is occasion for an enthralling narrative of substitutions, in which we slowly arrive at comprehension of what was given at the beginning.[39]

In just this way, we can readily recognize the negligibility of the various seeming historical developments recounted, or should we say "rehearsed" (to highlight their secondary, merely dramatic, "filler" character) along the contiguous trajectory of the Book of Mormon. It really does not matter which patriarch, which king, which prophet or false prophet passes on stage before us at a given moment, on a given page, despite the careful timeline notes on each page of printed editions. What we are interested in is this gospel that is foretold, really fore-*preached* "in advance" as if it has already happened—which it *has*. The whole thing is, as Todorov says, a ritual. And the ritual unveiling (narrative disclosure) of which we have been ever and again reminded by its pre-intrusion into the narrative is *the American advent of Jesus Christ*. The endlessly reiterated predictions of the biblical coming of Christ to Jewry in Palestine reminds us of the part of the Christian belief in the Incarnation we already knew. The Book of Mormon succinctly states this ritual process among the Nephite prophets: "Wherefore, I speak the same words unto one nation like unto another" (2 Nephi 29:8). But the immediate aftermath, unhinted in the Bible, is that Jesus made a second stop in the Western hemisphere! That is the punch of LDS Christianity and of the Book of Mormon.

And what did the resurrected Savior do when he got here (besides posing for those unique LDS statues and paintings!)? He repeats his best lines, from the Sermon on the Mount and the Gospel of John. Now from one point of view one wonders why on earth the Book of Mormon did not take this choice opportunity, as many writers, both ancient and modern, did, to put his own teachings on the lips of Jesus. Why not something radically new? Simply because it is most important that the ritual, the "theology of recital" (Gerhard von Rad), be enacted again, but this time on American soil. The idea is what modern missiologists call theological indigenization. Prophets of Cargo Cults and other Revitalization movements often learn about Christianity from Western missionaries and then create their own version according to which Jesus and/or the Bible were originally part of their non-Western culture, but that he/it was stolen by the colonial powers like they stole everything else.[40] Jesus may be redrawn as a tribal ancestor, or he may be imagined as having returned in the person of one of the movement's leaders, like Andre "Jesus" Matswa.[41] Something new would defeat the crucial point: the same thing that happened before (the much-predicted biblical advent of Jesus) must happen again the same way (the return of the sacred time) for us, on our soil. Thus if the Book of Mormon's Jesus is to say anything, he must say what we expect him to say and remember him to have said. Otherwise it will not be the real Jesus, the one we know from the Bible. (Again, if prophecies don't sound like Bible passages, they don't sound like prophecies!)

The Book of Mormon is the perfect example of the pattern Todorov discusses. What forward narrative progress there is, is all a charade, dictated in advance. To a degree, as Structuralist critics contend,[42] all narrative possesses simultaneity: it is all set out as a highway grid which, in the reading, we traverse foot by foot, inch by inch, creating an illusion of temporal movement. But what Todorov calls narrative logic tries to conceal this trick precisely by keeping your nose to the ground, keeping the reader in close, moment-by-moment connection with the narration. This is a species of misdirection like that employed by a stage magician. The narrator is trying to distract you from the simultaneous structure that would otherwise be present. Otherwise you will know too soon that the butler did it. Too many clues are for this reason not provided all at once. But ritual logic is just the opposite: the cat is let out of the bag again and again, because there is no suspense. You are just moving from one shrine to another in the same cathedral, from one station of the cross to the next. You are never surprised when you come to the last one.

The gospels certainly sacrifice narrative logic to ritual logic. On the one hand, the arrest and crucifixion of Jesus are foretold at least four or five times (depending on how explicit you want to get) in Mark's narrative, with Jesus speaking to the disciples, and yet they are surprised when it happens. This is because the ritual logic has trounced the narrative logic. As Robert M. Fowler points out,[43] this is also because ritual logic speaks over the heads of the characters, so that they do not hear what the reader hears. Monika Hellwig calls this approach to the gospels an "iconic" technique, observing that the Nativity, Transfiguration, and Resurrection stories are all depicting the same thing, the divine sonship of Jesus Christ, in various ways, in the fashion of a series of icons.[44] The gospels do not depict any Christological development (unlike, say, the transition in the Disney cartoon *Hercules* of the protagonist "from zero to hero"). No, they are precisely *narratives of substitutions*. And so is the Book of Mormon.

The speech of Samuel the Lamanite is a particularly apt instance of this tendency, for as we have seen, it turns out to be little more than a web of quotations from the Old and New Testaments. This is not a matter of a plagiarist's lack of imagination. On the contrary, it is a question of someone with a great creative imagination unraveling and reweaving the ancient tapestry into a new one. Every biblical phrase or even cliché we read in Samuel's speech is a micro-substitution, a re-presentation of the salvation epic of scripture, a theology of recital. Borrowing as it does from Genesis on through Deuteronomy, Isaiah, Amos, Jonah, Matthew, Luke, John, Acts, Romans, 2 Corinthians, Galatians, and Revelation, the text of Helaman 13–15 is practically a miniature Bible in its own right. Even the incarnate Son of God is present in it because his "future" coming, as elsewhere in the Book of Mormon, is treated as a *fait accompli*. Traditional Christian theologians have, through the devices of typology and allegory, attempted to read the whole biblical canon as one book in which every part is basically equivalent to each other part, all setting forth the gospel of Christ, *as long as one knows how to read it*. But in the Book of Mormon no exegetical subterfuges are required. In the Book of Mormon, the "pre-Jesus" prophets actually do predict Jesus, and the exegete need not try to induce water from the rock by resorting to kabbalistic ventriloquism.

King Benjamin's Farewell Speech (Mosiah 1–5)

King Benjamin's famous last words as he abdicated his throne in favor of his heir Mosiah II have of late been the occasion for much analytical prose, little of it as prolix, but much of it as pedantic, as the speech itself. The text is one of those which, like a dead body, may prove more interesting during the autopsy than in life. I venture to apply my scalpel, then, to a literary cadaver that has already suffered more than enough critical indignity from buzzards like myself. The speech, though it makes ample use of many biblical source texts, seems primarily based upon Paul's farewell speech to the Ephesian bishops at Miletus in Acts 20:17–38, plus other echoes of Acts as well. I would hazard the guess that the long-winded king's creator assigned him the name "Benjamin" based on the parallel with Paul, a son of the tribe of Benjamin. The name is all the more appropriate given the near certainty of many in the audience succumbing to sleep before his sermon was complete, though, given their being in tents, it is a safe bet none of them fell to their deaths like poor Eutychus (Acts 20:9).

Actually King Benjamin combines elements of two prophetic heroes. He is Paul at Miletus, for sure, but our author has split the Paul character from Acts between King Benjamin and the converted Alma the Apostle, whose conversion story in Alma 27:9–19 exactly matches Paul's in Acts, save that Alma goes mute instead of blind for a time after his theophanic encounter.[45] So King Benjamin is half *Paul*. He is also half *Joseph Smith*, entertainer of angels (Mosiah 3:2ff), also like Nephi, another Joseph analogue, and champion of the inscribed metal plates of scripture. Benjamin also plays the role of Moses in Exodus and Deuteronomy, so maybe we ought to divide him into thirds.

Verses versus Verses

Like most of the Book of Mormon, Mosiah chapters 1–5 are analogous to a ransom note in an old gangster movie. Just as the kidnapper's note appears to have been pasted together from isolated bits of typed pages and magazine ads, the Book of Mormon is a pasting together, a "sampling," of biblical texts split and spliced in new combinations. The speech of Benjamin obeys this axiom.[46] Let's pull the plant up by the roots and see what we find.

Benjamin's Polonius-like admonitions to his son Mosiah II (Mosiah 1:3–7) provide an intradiegetic "fore-"shadowing of Joseph Smith's advocacy of the Book of Mormon itself, just as the Koran frequently indulges in the anachronism of having the ostensibly not-yet-compiled book refer to itself as "this Koran."

Verse 8 cuts off the mike, pretending the preceding verses were the tip of a largely hidden iceberg: "And many more things did king Benjamin teach his sons, which are not written in this book." The sentence comes bodily from John 20:30, "Now Jesus did many other signs in the presence of his disciples, which are not written in this book." That is, he *must* have.

The very next verse, Mosiah 1:9 ("And it came to pass that after king Benjamin had made an end of teaching his sons . . ."), virtually repeated in 1:15; 4:1; 5:1; 6:1, borrows a similar wrap-up transitional phrase appearing five times in Matthew, concluding each of the great "pentateuchal" blocs of Jesus' teaching (Matt. 7:28; 11:1; 13:53; 19:1; 26:1): "And when Jesus finished these sayings;" "And when Jesus had finished instructing his twelve disciples," etc.

The same verse says, "he waxed old, and he saw that he must very soon go the way of all the earth." The phrase comes right from Joshua 23:14, where it similarly introduces a wrapping up of final arrangements.

Benjamin makes the first of several withdrawals from the Revelation of John in Mosiah 1:11, "I shall give this people a name . . ." My guess is that this promise comes from Revelation 2:17, where the Risen One promises to grant a new, unknown name to his overcomers, implicitly his own (cf. 19:12–13), just as Benjamin bequeaths the name "Christ." The very next verse (Mosiah 1:12), "And I give unto them a name that never shall be blotted out, except it be through transgression," jumps a little farther down the page in Revelation 3:5. In fact, to me it looks like a succinct attempt to settle a theological-exegetical debate that has longed vexed contentious Protestants, that of the "eternal security of the believer." If one embraced a full or half-Calvinist theology whereby the believer is "once saved, always saved," what does one make of the veiled threat in Revelation 3:5 that one's name, having once been inscribed in the Mother of the Book, might subsequently be blotted, erased? Our redactor has paused to settle the debate, providing an explicit scriptural decision in favor of Arminians.

The rest of the chapter provides a Cliff Notes summary of salvation history rather in the manner of Deuteronomy chapters 1–3, which similarly function as a historical preface to the lengthy oration of Moses. The description (Mosiah 2:5–6) of the camp meeting of the people, tent flaps facing the tower platform, plainly derives from the arrangement of the tent-dwelling audience ringing the Tent of Meeting in Exodus 33:7–10, from which new Mosaic revelations were eagerly expected. The preceding description of the journey of the people comes from Pentateuchal directions for Israel to report ("go up") to the Jerusalem Temple for sacrificial feasts and does not quite seem to fit here.

The scene may owe something to Ezra's reading of the newly-compiled Torah to the people. Both stories envision too great a multitude to be capacitated without loudspeakers. In Ezra, they adopt the expedient of positioning more simultaneous readers and interpreters throughout the crowd. This presupposes, obviously, a prepared text. But King Benjamin seems to be speaking extemporaneously, despite what John W. Welch reads as ample evidence of careful prior composition.[47] For he seems to have hand-copied transcripts distributed only subsequently, once he beheld the enormity of the crowd. If he had composed the speech in advance, he might have obviated the problem by providing copies to a small number of other readers stationed among the crowds as Ezra did. It would have saved a lot of paper, ink, and scribal man-hours. In any case, whether such a mass-production of written texts would have been practicable in the ancient circumstances, I leave for others to decide.

Prophecy and Prolixity

Just as ancient rhetoric had the orator repudiate all attempts at eloquence before undertaking them (!), so the verbose Benjamin warns his hearers that he will not "trifle with words" (2:9). And thus does he pull his finger from the exploding dyke: "that you should hearken unto me, *and* open your ears that ye may hear, *and* your hearts that ye may understand, *and* your minds that the mysteries of God may be unfolded to your view." I can't help thinking of an old parody of Hubert Humphrey's speechifying style: "My fellow Americans, I shall be brief. Yes, I shall be brief. Also terse, succinct, and economical of both word and phrase and sentence and paragraph!" "Synonymous parallelism" be damned; this is sheer prolixity that makes the Priestly Writer of the Pentateuch seem taciturn by comparison.

We are told how God does not favor worshippers who imagine they will be heard for their "much speaking," but in case it is possible people may take the same trait as evidence of divinity, King Benjamin reassures the crowd: "I have not commanded you to come up hither that ye should fear me, or that ye should think that I of myself am more than a mortal man. But I am like as yourselves, subject to all manner of infirmities in body and mind" (2:10–11a). He does not want to make the same mistake as his future counterpart Herod Agrippa I in Acts 12:20–23.

We jump ahead to Acts 20:33 in Mosiah 2:12, "I say unto you that as I have been suffered to spend my days in your service, even up to this time, and have not sought gold nor silver nor any manner of riches of you." Neither did Paul: "I coveted no one's silver or gold." Benjamin clairvoyantly quotes his literary prototypes, and from the same discourse (Acts 20:34) in Mosiah 2:14: "And even I, myself, have labored with mine own hands that I might serve you." Paul: "You yourselves know that these hands ministered to my needs, and those of my colleagues." Benjamin's self-exoneration ("I tell you these things that ye may know that I can answer a clear conscience before God this day" 2:15) recalls the protestations of both Paul (Acts 20:26; 1 Cor. 4:4) and the Writer to the Hebrews (13:18).

"And behold, I tell you these things that ye may learn wisdom; that ye may learn that when ye are in the service of your fellow beings ye are only in the service of your God" (v. 17). These fine sentiments seem to me rooted in Matthew's judgment scene of the sheep and the goats (Matt. 25:40, 44), to which further reference will be made below. An adjacent exhortation ("Behold, ye have called me your king; and if I, whom ye call your king, do labor to serve you, then ought not ye to labor to serve one another?" 2:18) jumps to the Gospel of John, whence it has unmistakably borrowed and paraphrased John 13:13–14. A few verses of homiletical ballast follow, leading us at length to Benjamin's version ("I say, if ye should serve him with all your whole souls yet ye would be unprofitable servants.") of Luke 17:10, an excellent, virtually Kantian, repudiation of any notion that righteous acts merit a reward.

Mosiah 2:22 ("And behold, all that he requires of you is to keep his commandments; and he has promised you that if ye would keep his commandments ye should prosper in the land; and he never doth vary from that which he hath said; therefore, if ye do keep his commandments he doth bless you and prosper you.") elaborates the similarly "Kantian" rational religion of Micah 6:8 ("He has shown you, O man, what is good; and what does the LORD require of you but to do justice, and to love kindness, and to walk humbly with your God?") in such a way as to restore the very legalism the prophet sought to trim away!

We are back to Paul's farewell apologia, Acts 20:26 ("Therefore I testify to you this day that I am free of the blood of all of you.") in Mosiah 2:27, "Therefore, as I said unto you that I had served you, walking with a clear conscience before God, even so I at this time have caused that ye should assemble yourselves together, that I might be found blameless, and that your blood should not come upon me, when I shall stand to be judged of God of the things whereof he hath commanded me concerning you." We pick it up again in Mosiah 2:32: "But, O my people, beware lest there shall arise contentions among you, and ye list to obey the evil spirit, which was spoken of by my father Mosiah." This comes from Paul's "prescient" warning of sectarianism to erupt in the time of the writer of Acts, for which that writer does not want Paul to be blamed: "I know that after my departure, fierce wolves will infiltrate you, ravaging the flock; men will arise from your own number speaking perverse things to draw away disciples after them" (Acts 20:29–30). As Benjamin refers back to his father's prediction, so does the writer of Acts refer back to a (retrojected) prediction ascribed to his own predecessor, Paul.

The image of perdition as poisoning oneself, "drinking damnation to his own soul" (2:33; 3:18) comes from 1 Corinthians 11:29, "He drinks judgment unto himself/his soul."

Benjamin addresses all age groups in words borrowed from 1 John 2:12–14. His paraphrase: "O, all ye old men, and also ye young men, and you little children" (Mosiah 2:40).

The faithful are admonished: "if they hold out faithful to the end they are received into heaven, that thereby they may dwell with God in a state of never-ending happiness" (Mosiah 2:41). These words provide a pedantic commentary upon the apocalyptic warning of Mark 13:13b, "But he who endures will be saved." Even today one hears Bible students deliberating over whether "saved" in this verse means "escape the persecution" or "find eternal life in heaven." The Book of Mormon hereby settles another exegetical tempest in a teapot.

The greeting of the angel in Mosiah 3:3 ("I am come to declare unto you the glad tidings of great joy") come right from the text of Luke 2:10, while the next bit ("For the Lord hath heard thy prayers, and hath judged of thy righteousness, and hath sent me to declare unto thee that thou mayest rejoice") comes directly from the twice-told tale of an angel appearing to Cornelius in answer to his prayers in Acts 10:4, 31. He predicts the incarnation of God in "a tabernacle of clay," recalling 2 Corinthians 5:1. Christ's trials are to include the bloody sweat of Luke 22:44, which, though present in the Byzantine text underlying the King James Version, is at least textually dubious.

Mosiah 3:9–11 provides a summary of Pauline soteriology from Romans, reflecting the theological anachronism widespread among fundamentalist Bible readers today, that Old Testament Israelites understood all about Protestant Reformation theology in advance. The Christian-era viewpoint of the author is clearly evident in Mosiah 3:13–15 (borrowed from Hebrews 1:1), where King Benjamin is made to speak of Old Testament prophecy and typology as relics of a pre-Christian past. Of course the Book of Mormon strives everywhere to maintain the anachronistic illusion that there *was* no "pre-Christian past."

Mosiah 3:16–18 pulls rank to settle another widespread matter of theological debate in the eighteenth and nineteenth centuries: the damnation of infants. It reminds me of a labored prophecy at a Catholic charismatic prayer meeting I attended in the summer of 1976 in which one woman arose and set the crowd straight, in the name of the Holy Spirit, that they should not flirt with Protestant doctrines of adult baptism!

Acts 4:12 ("And there is salvation in no one else, for there is no other name under heaven given among men whereby we must be saved.") is the basis for Mosiah 3:17, "And moreover, I say unto you, that there shall be no other name given nor any other way nor means whereby salvation can come unto the children of men, only in and through the name of Christ, the Lord Omnipotent." Mosiah 5:8 paraphrases it pretty closely, too: "And this is the means whereby salvation cometh. And there is none other salvation save this which hath been spoken of; neither are there any conditions whereby man can be saved except the conditions which I have told you."

The Urim and Thummim of Hindsight

As is well known, the Book of Mormon is supposed to clarify the Old and New Testaments. Though precious little of developed Mormon doctrine is to be found in the pages of the Mormon Testament, it is certainly true that at numerous points the book does raise issues of theological debate and scriptural ambiguity, seeking to clarify them for its readers. We have already seen some examples and will have occasion to mention more.

To avail oneself of Christ's salvation, men must "humble themselves and become as little children" (Mosiah 3:18), precisely as in Matthew 18:34, whence the very wording is borrowed. There is still a lively debate as to what "becoming children" means. Mosiah 3:19 answers this perennial question by detailed exegesis of Matthew 18:34: the convert "becometh as a child, submissive, meek, humble, patient, full of love, willing to submit to all things which the Lord seeth fit to inflict upon him, even as a child doth submit to his father." He is no longer a "natural man," a term borrowed from 1 Corinthians 2:14.

The believer in the atonement can face the judgment with some confidence "at the judgment day; whereof they shall be judged, every man according to his works, whether they be good, or whether they be evil." This comes from Mosiah 3:24, based on Revelation 20:12. The descriptions of damnation ("And their torment is as a lake of fire and brimstone, whose flames are unquenchable, and whose smoke ascendeth up forever and ever," Mosiah 3:27) and as drinking from "the cup of the wrath of God" (3:26) come from Revelation 14:11 and 16:19 respectively.

Mosiah 2:38 already brought up the eschatological torment of the Lake of Fire.

> Therefore if that man repenteth not, and remaineth and dieth an enemy to God, the demands of divine justice do awaken his immortal soul to a lively sense of his own guilt, which doth cause him to shrink from the presence of the Lord, and doth fill his breast with guilt, and pain, and anguish, which is like an unquenchable fire, whose flame ascendeth up forever and ever.

The nature and pains of Hell formed a lively topic of theological dispute in the seventeenth through the nineteenth centuries, and the Book of Mormon elsewhere locks horns with Universalism. Here in Mosiah 2:38 we see an attempt to mitigate the barbarism of traditional Hell belief. The sufferings of the Inferno are not to be understood as torture imposed by a vengeful deity, but rather the psychological pangs of remorse that sinners will supposedly feel after death, once they recognize they are forever shut out from God. It is a rationalization still popular today among evangelicals who feel they must continue to maintain the appearance of a belief in Hell though their conscience tells them otherwise.

1 Peter 1:19–20 speaks of Christ's blood atonement as somehow existing "from the foundation of the world," implying not a historical, world-changing event, as usual in the New Testament, but rather a static, eternal condition of atonement symbolically manifested on the cross. And that is certainly how the Mormon prophets see it, as it already exists and may be applied to the hearts of people about a century and a half before the (superfluous) historical crucifixion. That 1 Peter 1:19–20 is the potent source of the whole idea is evident from the near-quotation of the passage in Mosiah 4:6–7, "I say unto you, if ye have come to a knowledge of the goodness of God, and his matchless power, and his wisdom, and his patience, and his long-suffering towards the children of men; and also, the atonement which has been prepared from the foundation of the world, that thereby salvation might come to him that should put his trust in the Lord, and should be diligent in keeping his commandments, and continue in the faith even unto the end of his life, I mean the life of the mortal body—I say, that this is the man who receiveth salvation, through the atonement which was prepared from the foundation of the world for all mankind, which ever were since the fall of Adam, or who are, or who ever shall be, even unto the end of the world."

Benjamin returns home to Acts 20, this time verse 35, in Mosiah 4:16–24, which expounds at considerable length on the Christian's duty to aid the poor. One suspects that these words reflect considerable discussion within the fledgling LDS movement over how to deal with its disadvantaged. If so, we can see how these seeds have grown into the mighty oak of the mutual assistance network among LDS Christians.

We have seen how frequently our author in this passage bounces around between Acts, Revelation, Matthew, and 1 Corinthians, and he borrows the tail-end of Mosiah 4:27 ("all things must be done in order") from 1 Corinthians 14:40.

"Yes, We've All Got to Think for Ourselves!"

One mark of the non-historical, non-reportorial character of biblical narrative is the frequent mention of a whole crowd, or indeed, even the whole nation of Israel, speaking in unison. It is a fine technique exactly equivalent to the Greek Chorus. We find another case of it here in Mosiah 5:2–5, a rather long one: "And they all cried with one voice, saying: Yea, we believe all the words which thou hast spoken unto us; and also, we know of their surety and truth, because of the Spirit of the Lord Omnipotent, which has wrought a mighty change in us, or in our hearts, that we have no more disposition to do evil, but to do good continually. And we, ourselves, also, through the infinite goodness of God, and the manifestations of his Spirit, have great views of that which is to come; and were it expedient, we could prophesy of all things. And it is the faith which we have had on the things which our king has spoken unto us that has brought us to this great knowledge, whereby we do rejoice with such exceedingly great joy. And we are willing to enter into a covenant with our God to do his will, and to be obedient to his commandments in all things that he shall command us, all the remainder of our days, that we may not bring upon ourselves a never-ending torment, as has been spoken by the angel, that we may not drink out of the cup of the wrath of God."

We are supposed to think here of the people's dramatic, collective response to Moses in Exodus 24:3, 7: "All the words which the LORD has spoken, we will do." The response of the people to Joshua in Joshua 24:16–18 is longer, and more obviously artificial. To vindicate the historical accuracy of all these scenes, especially Mosiah 5:2–5, some have appealed to the fact that in ancient times royal and religious "cheer-leaders" would coach the crowd to chant some prescribed formula on a public occasion. But neither the Exodus nor the Joshua passage hints that the people are merely parroting a scripted responsive reading. Surely, in the context, we are to understand what they (collectively) say as the spontaneous reply of the group. Moses and Joshua need to know where they stand. In the Mosiah scene, the idea of sacred cheer-leading really becomes grotesque: "And now, these are the words which King Benjamin desired of them; and therefore he said unto them: Ye have spoken the words that I desired"—no wonder, if he had coaches in the audience with cue-cards telling them what to say! Better just to admit the fictitious character of the whole thing.

How striking that the people's reply contains a clear affirmation of the Wesleyan doctrine of "entire sanctification" or "Christian perfection." "The Spirit of the Lord Omnipotent . . . has wrought a mighty change in us, or in our hearts, that we have no more disposition to do evil, but to do good continually." The sin nature has been extinguished, and only a desire to do good remains.

These people were apparently already pious Christians before King

Benjamin addressed them. Their tearful conversion here attests to the Arminian, Revivalistic circumstances in which the Book of Mormon was written. Benjamin makes this conversion or rededication or whatever it was tantamount to a new birth, appropriating the ancient Judean coronation protocol of Psalm 2:7, "Thou art my son; this day have I begotten thee." Of course, at this time no one even realized this was the import of the Psalm. It was (mis)understood as a prophecy of Jesus. At any rate, it is democratized, applied to all the people in Mosiah 5:7, "And now, because of the covenant which ye have made ye shall be called the children of Christ, his sons, and his daughters; for behold, this day he hath spiritually begotten you; for ye say that your hearts are changed through faith on his name; therefore, ye are born of him and have become his sons and his daughters."

And yet the saved are not out of the woods till Judgment Day, the outcome of which remains up for grabs: "And it shall come to pass that whosoever doeth this shall be found at the right hand of God, for he shall know the name by which he is called; for he shall be called by the name of Christ. And now it shall come to pass, that whosoever shall not take upon him the name of Christ must be called by some other name; therefore, he findeth himself on the left hand of God" (Mosiah 5:9–10). This plainly depends on Matthew 25:33, the eschatological placement of the sheep to the right and the goats to the left of the reigning Son of Man. The shepherd/sheep imagery from that passage has suggested to our writer that he might do well to hop over (in Mosiah 5:12–14) to John 10:3, 27, where Jesus is the Good Shepherd who calls his flock by name.

The King concludes ("Therefore, I would that ye should be steadfast and immovable, always abounding in good works," Mosiah 5:15) with a quotation of 1 Corinthians 15:58.

Myth and Ritual in the Book of Mormon?

To my mind the most powerful argument for the ancient date of the Book of Mormon, focusing on King Benjamin's speech, is the attempted demonstration that the topics of the oration seem to match the chief images and ritual moments of the ancient pan-Near Eastern annual rite of Kingship Renewal.[48] As many scholars have argued, there is much reason to think that ancient Judah practiced the same sort of rite as we have explicitly documented in neighboring Babylon and other kingdoms. The myth of the underlying royal ideology was that the earthly king owed his mandate to his heavenly counterpart. The earthly kingdom was the microcosm of the heavenly kingdom. A virile warrior god (Marduk, Baal, Yahweh, even Zeus and Indra) had ventured to slay a dragon (Tiamat, Lotan, Leviathan/Rahab, Typhon, Vritra) too fearful for the older deities to fight. He was initially killed in battle but rose from the dead, disgorged by the dragon, whereupon he disemboweled the monster, creating the heavens, the earth, the firmament, and the upper and lower oceans from its carcass. His victory won, he became king of gods and mortals and ruled the new-made world. A ritual mock-combat portrayed and mystically repeated the victory/creation each year. The king played the role of his heavenly patron, and his rule was secured for another year, his kingdom renewed along with the world. To portray the god's temporary defeat, the king allowed himself to be tweaked and slapped by the high priest, who would also deprive him of his crown. The king would confess his innocence and his service to the people, then regain the emblems of his office.

Apologists, having studied these rituals in great detail, point out a fascinating series of correspondences with King Benjamin's speech, leading them to believe that it enshrines the memory of just such a Nephite New Year ritual of Kingship Renewal. Granted, Benjamin is abdicating the throne, but he is ushering in the reign of his heir, so that is something of a Kingship Renewal, and Psalm 2 was certainly used at such occasions, too. Benjamin freely confesses his ordinary human mortality and his common fate with his hearers, all doomed to return to the dust. In this we are to see the language of the royal resurrection mythology, since the king would be said to rise again from the dust of death. (This would even apply to the dooming of Adam to return to the dust, as the Eden myth may be based on an older version in which Adam is the primordial king of the world, and his death mirrors that of the world in winter.) The pitching of tents for the people of Zarahemla might be understood as implying the speech took place at the Feast of Tabernacles, originally the time of the Kingship Renewal. Connected with renewal of the government might be the renewal of the covenant between God and Israel, and, sure enough, there is much talk in Benjamin's speech of making a covenant with God.

It is impressive, but I have my doubts. There are no references in Benjamin's speech to the central myth of destroying the monster and creating the world, though the dependence of the creation upon its kind

Creator is stressed. But the lack of the dragon myth, as well as of the ritual reenactment of the battle, seems a major omission. And, while the king is humble, he is not ritually humiliated. His protestations of innocence are not presented, either, as part of a scripted rite. (If it were, that would contradict all the usual lionizing hagiography of Benjamin.) The talk of returning to the dust does not eventuate in any talk of resurrection, though Christian salvation is offered to all. As mentioned above, the royal decree of divine sonship is used, but *not of the king*, as if the original context and meaning have been totally lost sight of. And King Benjamin pointedly and repeatedly denies any divinity, which seems to me the very opposite of the point of the Kingship myth and ritual. If the redactor or author had ever heard of the rituals and myths apologists find beneath the story and the speech, he has not embodied them there but rather *hidden* them there. Contrast the speech of King Benjamin with texts like Psalm 74:12–17 and Psalm 89. I dare say that the modern reader stumbles over these Psalms because the imagery seems to make little sense, the references to gods and monsters are theologically offensive, and the major topics appear almost randomly juxtaposed. What does the business about creation, the mountains, the seasons, etc., have to do with God's throne, or with his covenant with the king? And what is the multi-headed dragon doing there? What on earth is going on? The average, pious reader has no way of knowing, and just cruises through the text till something edifying pops up. I suggest that such texts make any kind of sense only once one plugs in the royal ideology, the enthronement liturgy, etc. Then the association of God's victory over the dragon, the establishment of his throne, his rule over the creation, and his covenant with the King of Judah (now seen to be his earthly vicar, just as in Babylon) make complete sense, for the first time, of the beloved lyrics. By contrast, King Benjamin's speech makes perfect sense, better sense, with no reference to any of these ancient Near-Eastern mythologoumena. To read into Mosiah 1–5 these fossils of ancient liturgy and myth is to dismantle an already coherent narrative in which an old king makes a farewell address to his people, introduces his successor, and preaches a Revivalist gospel. If there is a Kingship Renewal rite behind this story, it has been completely distorted, concealing the very different import of the hypothesized original.

Again, the case is parallel to apologetical attempts to vindicate Matthew's story of the Wise Men and the Star by suggesting they saw a planetary alignment or a supernova. If either of these things happened, Matthew's story is *wrong*, since he has the star as a small object moving in the sky and hovering over a particular hovel in a small village. Planetary alignments and novas don't behave that way. In like manner, if the kingship parallels are real, then the story as we read it is completely inaccurate and hides the original events.

3 THE GOSPEL ACCORDING TO THOMAS

Gospel Sources

Anyone who has read the four canonical gospels has no doubt noticed a large degree of overlap, even of verbal repetition, between Matthew, Mark, and Luke. Most scholars adopt the following explanation of this phenomenon.[1] It seems that the two earliest surviving sources of information about Jesus, collections of his sayings and stories about him, were the Gospel of Mark written in Greek some time after 70 CE (I would date it some three decades later), and a list of sayings that scholars have dubbed "Q," for the German *Quelle*, "source." It was compiled and written in Aramaic, perhaps in more than one draft, around 50 CE as some think[2] (I would place it contemporary with Mark, maybe a bit earlier if we think he used it in a few instances).[3] Some years or decades later, Matthew, a catechist in the bi-lingual, bi-ethnic church at Antioch, decided to prepare his own expanded, clarified, and corrected edition of Mark. Since he was striving for a definitive book about Jesus he decided to use most of the sayings of Jesus recorded in Q, which he translated and interspersed at various points in Mark's narrative. He used some other material from a third source, which we call "M," denoting "special Matthean material" found nowhere else. This M material may have come from oral tradition (what people were repeating, rightly or wrongly, as sayings of Jesus, or from other documents unknown to us—or, as I think most likely, from Matthew's own sanctified imagination).

Independently of Matthew, Luke also decided to improve on Mark. Though he used somewhat less of Mark's text than Matthew did (about 65% compared to Matthew's 95%), he, too, used Mark as the basis for his enlarged version. He also used his own (or at least a different) translation of Q. He, too, had special material which we denominate as "L." Again, some or all of the L material seems to come from Luke's own creative pen, but some may have come from floating oral tradition. Things are probably a bit more complicated than this with Luke. There is some reason to think he may have written a first, now lost, edition ("Proto-Luke")[4] that supplemented Q with L. Then someone showed Luke a copy of Mark's gospel, and he decided it was too good to ignore, so he went back to the drawing board, combining Proto-Luke with Mark to create our canonical Gospel of Luke. Others think this gospel began with what is called "Ur-Lukas," the Gospel of Marcion. This theory eliminates Q and holds that this evangelist compiled something answering more or less to Proto-Luke but with some so-called "M" material to boot. According to this theory,[5] Matthew used both Mark and the Ur-Lukas. So did "Luke," the redactor (editor) of our canonical Third Gospel. In fact, there is good reason for thinking this Lukan redactor was Polycarp of Smyrna.[6] He would have omitted some of the Ur-Lukas material that Matthew did include, and he would have added a good deal more material, including the Nativity story we find in Luke 1–2. And there are other theories besides, but they will not concern us here.

How is the reader to determine which sayings and stories in Matthew and Luke come from Q, Mark, M, or L? Of course we can compare the two finished gospels Luke and Mathew with Mark, but no copy of Q survives (if there *was* a Q!). Yet we are not left with a great mystery. Whatever material is found in both Matthew and Luke *but not in Mark* represents the other common source of Matthew and Luke: Q. And obviously whatever is only in Luke is L material. If it is only in Matthew it is by definition M material.

The fourth gospel, John, written, as most think, about 100 CE (I say fifty years later), looks quite different from the other three. The others, because of the shared perspective, are called the Synoptic ("seeing together") gospels. Many scholars (me included) think John had read the Synoptics but did not copy material directly out of the texts as Matthew and Luke did from Mark. Others, like C.H. Dodd, make a good case that John had never laid eyes on the Synoptics. Rather, he would have made his own fresh selection from the Jesus-traditions current in his own circles, perhaps in Asia Minor. He would have filtered this material through his own theological lens, much of it in his own words, or the distinctive lingo of his sect.[7]

The issue at stake in John meets us everywhere in the critical study of the gospels: the evangelists were not reporters. Most likely, none was an eye-witness of the ministry of Jesus (much less of his nativity or the temptation!), and there is really no telling whether Jesus actually did or said what any gospel ascribes to him at any point. The gospel writers (evangelists) seem to have attributed their own ideas to Jesus, "updating" him for new generations of disciples, so to speak. And the long chain of unknowns who transmitted the oral tradition (whether under the watchful eye of the apostles or completely outside their jurisdiction) may have, must have, made their own contributions. There must have been prophets who felt impelled to speak with the voice of the risen Christ ("Verily I say unto you . . . !").[8] What in the gospel, then, did Jesus say or do? For faith this ought to be irrelevant: all the stories and sayings (if you'll forgive a subjective judgment) seem to breathe much the same prophetic spirit even when they contradict one another or feature anachronisms. Nonetheless, contradictions and anachronisms do pose puzzles for the historian to solve, and we might as well try to solve them. But why should the post-Jesus authorship of any Jesus saying make it any less worthy? Do we discount the teaching of the epistles because Jesus didn't write them?

Where, you may be asking, does Thomas fit into all of this? Some scholars maintain that the Gospel of Thomas drew on two or more of the Synoptics,[9] but many others think Thomas is like Q, an independent collection of oral tradition[10] (though not necessarily without new creations by the evangelist). Where Thomas' sayings parallel or overlap with canonical sayings, these scholars deem Thomas' more primitive (original) in form.[11] I believe that Thomas would not read as it does if its evangelist/redactor were simply working from copies of Matthew and Luke, etc. Yet I also believe I detect stubborn instances where Thomas does seem to reflect either a harmonization of two canonical gospels' versions of a saying or the unique redactional perspective of one of the canonical evangelists.

These factors lead me to propose a compromise solution: I suggest that Thomas does indeed draw independently on oral tradition, hence this gospel's possible occasional preservation of earlier, simpler versions of sayings also found in the canonical gospels. But Thomas also compiled his gospel after the canonical gospels (at least after the Synoptics) yet without direct access to them. Matthew and Luke each had copies of Mark to work from, open on his scriptorium. Thomas did not. He remembered sayings as best he could from having heard them read in church; or else, other people quoting the gospel texts without direct access to them caused the sayings to re-enter the stream of oral tradition after pausing in stable, written form for a while. Memory quotations of the gospels have fed back into the oral tradition, as if a stream should branch off a river for a while, gather fertile silt along the way, and then later rejoin the river downstream. Thus Thomas presents some sayings which had survived in oral tradition independent of their written canonical versions, alongside others which preserve Matthew or Luke's redactional coloring, though not word for word, because they had come to circulate orally anew, quoted from memory from hearing them in church.[12]

Another reason I think it less likely that, e.g., the parable of the Rich Fool or of the Wheat and the Tares survives independently in Thomas is that, for various reasons, the L and M versions seem to be cut from the redactional cloth of each evangelist. In other words, from studying them in the contexts of Mathew and Luke, I think they make good sense as redactional creations originating in these gospels. I think most of the M and L material had no pre-textual existence in oral tradition at all. Or, they first entered the stream of oral tradition once people began loosely repeating them by word of mouth with no direct availability of the texts from which they were derived.

The most exciting thing about the discovery of the Gospel of Thomas is the possibility that it contains hitherto-unknown (or, better, hitherto-forgotten) sayings of the historical Jesus. Does it? My comments on individual sayings will treat the question of historical genuineness, but at the outset I may say that Thomas' case is little different from those of Matthew, Luke, or John. That is, we can often detect material created by the evangelist himself by its stylistic or theological distinctiveness. If a particular saying, story, parable, etc., features style, vocabulary, ideas, unique (or nearly so) to a particular gospel, we have to assume it is that evangelist's own creation. Of course it is always possible a gospel writer happened to hear and include some Jesus saying that none of the others recalled or thought worth mentioning, but if the style of the saying is characteristically Lukan, Matthean, or Johannine (and very many *are*), we not only may but *must* doubt its authenticity.[13] (I'm leaving Mark out of this simply because the only reason there are any uniquely Markan sayings (very few) is that Matthew and Luke didn't pick them up.) In just this way, a number of sayings unique to Thomas seem to share a common theology and style and so must be considered that evangelist's own creations. Some, however, of the uniquely Thomasine sayings show no such characteristics. They remain in contention, though there may turn out to be other reasons to doubt them.

Wisdom's Twin

If we can, as I have just suggested, recognize certain stylistic or theological markers of the compiler of the Gospel of Thomas, is remains no easy task to know precisely who he was. It is most likely we will never know, and if by some fluke his real name did come to light, it would almost certainly mean nothing to us anyway. But "Thomas" is either a pseudonym or a title supplied by a scribe for an anonymous work. It seems that it was Polycarp of Smyrna[14] who first chose and edited the canonical four gospels, none of them hitherto bearing any titles, but simply known, each in a different region or church, as "the gospel." He chose apostolic names for two of them, "Matthew" functioning as a pun for *mathetes*, "disciple," a prominent theme in the book, and "John" in order to counter the suspicions that the originally Gnostic work (which Polycarp edited, censored, and padded) was the heretical screed of Cerinthus. (Why take the trouble? "John" was the only gospel on hand that provided the basis for the Eastern churches' practice of observing Easter according to the Passover calendar of the Jews, and Polycarp wanted to mollify this wing of the church.) Mark and Luke were given their sub-apostolic names because, though adjusted to Catholic orthodoxy, they were deemed inferior or disturbingly different from the other two, hence were supplied secondary (fictive) links to the apostles Peter (for Mark) and Paul (for Luke). This was also a way of reinforcing the unity Polycarp was concerned to build between Catholicism (whose figurehead was Peter) and Marcionites (who venerated Paul). Polycarp had, as already mentioned, to fumigate the Marcionite Ur-Lukas in order to make it our "Luke." He may have similarly had to launder some Carpocratian Gnostic teaching from what we today call Secret Mark to make it palatable as our "Mark."[15]

So "Thomas," while intended to be the famous apostle "Doubting Thomas," merely masks some unknown compiler. There is, however, a further point to it. The choice was not arbitrary. Ancient tradition preserved this apostle's full name as "Judas Thomas." The Aramaic "Thomas," like its Greek counterpart "Didymus," means "twin." It is a nickname, not a name in its own right as it has become today, so its bearer must have been named "*Something* Thomas," "*Someone* the Twin." Whose twin *was* this Judas? Early Christians were not slow to notice that Jesus had a brother named Judas (Mark 6:3). Could Judas Thomas have been the twin brother of Jesus Christ? Though it may seem far-fetched to us, many in the early church accepted the identification (never mind what a monkey-wrench it cast into the developing doctrine of the perpetual virginity of Mary!). I think the editor of our gospel knows of this identification and employs it metaphorically, whatever he may have thought of it as biographical fact. His point is that, as his gospel eventually reveals (saying 13), *whoever* understands the teaching of Jesus becomes exactly like him, his spiritual twin. A "Thomas" in his own right. Thus "Thomas" is both the (pen) name of the fifth evangelist *and* of any reader who grasps the meaning of his gospel's sayings.

We start to read references to the Gospel according to Thomas early in the third century, and our Nag Hammadi copy was written down in the mid-fourth century. The first surviving mention is by the schismatic (but not heretical) Roman bishop Hippolytus about 230. There was also an Infancy Gospel of Thomas floating around, but we know Hippolytus was referring to ours because he quotes from it and calls it a Naassene Gnostic scripture. About the same time, estimated at 233, the Alexandrian theologian and Bible scholar Origen mentions it as suspiciously heterodox. A few centuries later, Thomas is sneered at as a Manichaean gospel. We know the Manichaeans did use it, because its distinctive language colors their liturgical texts. The Acts of Thomas (ca. 200) and the Nag Hammadi text, the Book of Thomas the Contender (also early third century, we think) show knowledge of the Gospel of Thomas, as does the Gospel of Mary.

Not surprisingly, a gospel that circulated so widely and amid different faith communities eventually came to exist in several versions. Scribes who copied and recopied it over the generations occasionally added, deleted or paraphrased it in accord with their own beliefs. We have quotations from rather different Naassene and Manichaean versions, as well as fragments of three different Greek copies discovered among the Oxyrhynchus Papyri in Egypt in 1897 and 1904. Our only complete copy is the Coptic translation found in Chenoboskion (Nag Hammadi), Egypt in 1945. Comparing what remains of the various versions will sometimes help us arrive at the original reading of the text. Or so we may hope. (Of course, each version has its own integrity as a redacted text, but it will be interesting to see if we can trace how the document has evolved.) Davies argues that the text was composed in Egypt, but most scholars think it is a product of Syria, where there was great veneration of Thomas as well as literary productivity in his name (the Acts of Thomas, Apocalypse of Thomas, etc.). Most believe Thomas to have been composed originally in Greek, though Nicholas Perrin makes an impressive case for a Syriac origin.[16]

If early third-century writings refer to "the Thomas gospel" (as Joseph Campbell used to refer to it), then it cannot be dated later than the mid- to late second century, and I for one do not place it earlier. (And remember, I date the canonical gospels in the second century, too.) As I have said, a number of scholars such as Helmut Koester, Stevan L. Davies, and Stephen J. Patterson argue for a first-century date for Thomas.[17] Their arguments are powerful. First, they note that Thomas is basically a collection of sayings with no real narrative framework. The Q source would have been just such a collection, but it seems this kind of gospel subgenre was quickly superseded by narrative gospels like the Synoptics and John. Thomas was either a strange throwback or comes from more or less the same period as the Q source.

A second consideration is that, while all New Testament writings abound in various titles heaped upon Jesus (Lord, Christ, Son of God, Logos, Son of Man, etc.), *not one of these titles ever occurs in Thomas.* Can it be that Thomas is a collection of sayings compiled in the very early days before Jesus' followers had decided what to make of him, what to call him?[18] This is quite possible, though it seems at least as likely to me that Thomas knows these Christological titles and rejects them in principle (see saying 89).

A third reason for making Thomas a very early gospel is the non- or anti-apocalyptic stance it seems to take. Many scholars (including the published consensus of the Jesus Seminar) believe the historical Jesus was by no means an apocalyptic prophet or eschatological preacher (which is pretty much the same thing, only it sounds less fanatical). They see him instead as an itinerant sage like Diogenes of Sinope, the Cynic philosopher. They calculate, not without reason, that the apocalyptic ("Here comes the kingdom of God!") business was an importation into the Jesus tradition as of the eve of the Jewish war with Rome (66–73 CE). Thus it might make sense to place the non-eschatological teaching of Thomas closer to Jesus, farther from the Jewish War.[19] But I think Thomas (which certainly retains some pretty colorful apocalyptic vestiges) is not innocent of eschatology; rather, it repudiates it as a big mistake. James D.G. Dunn is right on the money: "The Thomas material just mentioned in these logia [1, 3, 10, 11, 18, 19, 35, 37, 46, 51, 59, 111, 113] looks much more like *de-eschatologized* tradition rather than pre-apocalyptic tradition."[20] This was one way of dealing with the utter failure of the early Christian hope of Jesus' return to materialize. So I take the rejection of apocalyptic, as in John, to denote a *later* date.

Different Gospels, Different Churches

Why are there several different gospels in the first place? And why do they differ from one another? The several gospels originated in quite different early Christian contexts. This brings us to the question of the composition of the early Christian movement itself. One often hears that "the early church" was pristine, pure, and harmonious (providing a ruler for preachers to wield to smack their flocks on the knuckles). But even a cursory reading of the New Testament ought to be enough to dispel that illusion like a cloud of mist. Virtually from Day One there was acrimony even over essential matters.[21] I will briefly sketch out four important early Christian viewpoints or factions, or camps, or families. They all bear on the Gospel according to Thomas.

First there were the so-called Jewish Christians,[22] who would never have used that name. Though Jews belonged to all four categories, and though the categories themselves are more coordinates than containers, the term "Jewish Christians" here refers to those who maximized the connection between Christianity and its parent religion. For Jewish Christians, all believers in Jesus Christ (Messiah Jesus, Yeshua ha-Mashiach) had to agree to circumcision for themselves and their children and henceforth keep the moral and ritual laws of Moses. This seemed fairly obvious: had Jesus himself not been a Jew, and was his office not distinctly Jewish, more than any other? Who could ever imagine, then, that his followers should do anything but keep the Jewish Torah?

Such Christians did not at first envision any evangelistic mission to Gentiles; instead they apparently believed that in the Last Days (albeit set to arrive soon), the nations would gather in Jerusalem to learn the true faith of Israel, scoffing at it no more once it became evident who had been right all along (Micah 4:1–3; Isaiah 2:2–4).[23] But as history lingered and Gentiles here and there joined the Christian fold, the Jewish Christians were faced with a dilemma: was faith in Jesus, with baptism in his name, sufficient unto salvation? Or mustn't one embrace Messiah's own religion along with the Messiah himself? They decided on the latter course and held that Gentile converts, in order to become Christians, must become Jews because there really wasn't any difference. (True, many Jews would not get on board, but that was a different issue.)

Jean Danielou divides Jewish Christians into two groups.[24] The first is *Nazarene Christianity*. This group's beliefs were little different from those of other Christians on most matters, their main distinctive being to insist on Jewish and Gentile Christians keeping the Law of Moses. I believe the Gospel of Matthew and the Epistle of James issued from Nazarene Christianity. I think this was the Christianity of "the circumcision party" at Galatia.

The second group was the Ebionites ("the poor"). They were a secretive, esoteric sect sharing much in common with the Essenes. Ebionites rejected the doctrine of the virgin birth of Jesus, believing instead that he had been adopted as God's son (= the Messiah, as in Psalm 2, an ancient coronation liturgy whereby each new king of Judah was made God's son). This took place at some point subsequent to his natural birth as the son of Mary and Joseph, perhaps at his baptism or at his resurrection. According to their esoteric doctrine, Jesus was also the reincarnation of Adam (hence "the son of Man"), himself the first incarnation of a heavenly revealer whom they called "the True Prophet." He had long ago spoken through the biblical prophets over many centuries but had now come to rest in his fullness in Jesus, his chosen vessel. His mission on earth was to abolish animal sacrifice and meat-eating, calling humanity back to the pristine vegetarianism of the creation (Genesis 1:29–30).[25] To this end he taught his followers to recognize certain "false pericopes (passages)" in scripture (namely the laws mandating animal sacrifices) as spurious interpolations, scribal corruptions. Jeremiah had made the same charge centuries earlier (Jeremiah 7:21–23; 8:8). Having thus purified the Torah, the Ebionite Messiah reaffirmed its validity for Jews but opened the way of faith for the Gentiles, creating an equally valid Jesus-covenant for Gentiles, parallel to the Moses covenant for Jews.[26]

I would add a third group of Jewish Christians, the followers of Cerinthus. He is usually classified as a Gnostic, but that only shows how the categories are not air-tight. Cerinthus was a kind of adoptionist, like the Ebionites, but like the Gnostic Basilides, he understood the fleshly Jesus as a channeler for the Christ-spirit that descended into him at his baptism, remaining with him during his ministry until, at the crucifixion, it was time to go, whereupon Jesus cried out, "My God, my God, why did you forsake me?" Like Marcion and the Gnostics, Cerinthus believed God had not created the world; rather the angels did the job. He expected a future millennium of sensual delights and believed that Jesus had not yet risen from the dead but would do so at the general resurrection at the end of the age.

Jewish Christians divided their loyalty between at least two leadership factions. The first was the Twelve apostles, whose very number implies (as did the Qumran council of twelve elders) a renewed twelve tribes of Israel (Matthew 19:28; Luke 22:29–30), but not Gentiles (Galatians 2:9). The other group was the Heirs, the blood dynasty of Jesus. His brother James the Just succeeded him as caliph in Jerusalem and was in turn succeeded by another brother, Simeon (both are listed in Mark 6:3). James eclipses Peter as leader of the Jerusalem church already in Acts. Other scriptures emanating from Jewish Christianity include 3 Peter (the Letter from Peter to James), the Gospel according to the Hebrews, the Gospel according to the Ebionites, and the Gospel according to the Nazarenes.

The second major branch of early Christianity was Hellenistic Christianity.[27] Its first adherents were Greek-speaking Diaspora Jews or their children who had moved back to the Holy Land. These would have been the "Hellenists" of the Jerusalem Church (Acts 6:1), overlapping the Synagogue of the Freedmen in Acts 6:9. The great danger for Diaspora Jews was assimilation into the Gentile cultures amid which they lived. Some reacted by buttressing the walls that separated them, taking Jewish customs more seriously than ever. Others relaxed their traditional observance and mixed Jewish with pagan beliefs so as to fit in better with their Gentile friends and neighbors—and because they liked the breadth of Hellenistic culture. Hellenistic Christianity was perfect for them: a kind of Jewish religiosity that dropped the cultural identity markers like circumcision, kosher laws, and the observance of the holy days.[28] Many Gentiles admired Judaism and attended Jewish synagogue service, listening avidly to the scripture readings, but they did not want the social stigma of being Jews, even though Judaism and its exalted morality appealed to them. Christianity of this type looked like the best of both worlds. Eventually, once they started recruiting Gentile converts, they began to think that Jesus' martyr death atoned for the sins (really, the chronic ritual uncleanness) of the Gentiles. His sacrifice washed them clean of their worldly taint and grafted them into the heavenly and theocratic Judaism).[29] Jesus' death had obliterated the barrier hitherto separating Jews from heathendom. If Gentile converts need not trouble themselves to keep the Torah, how much could it matter for Jews, either? Soon the Torah of Moses had been relegated to the sacred museum of the past. This was so whether, like the Catholic Church, one gave lip-service to the Old Testament or, like Gnostics and Marcionites, one overtly rejected it as the Buddha rejected the Vedas. It was not long before Gentile Christians vastly outnumbered their Jewish brethren.

Many Hellenistic Christians held the familiar doctrine of Jesus "Christ" (which they quickly came to regard as Jesus' last name, since one could hardly expect them to be much interested in Palestinian politics, and "Messiah" meant pretty much the same as "king of the Jews"), believing him to be the Son of God on earth. This belief may have evolved from the greater emphasis Greek-speaking Jews and Gentiles placed upon the biblical Wisdom Literature (Proverbs, Ecclesiastes, Job, Wisdom of Solomon, Sirach) than on the largely irrelevant legal portions of the Torah (Leviticus, Numbers, etc.). The Wisdom Literature was more universalistic, more cosmopolitan in character, less specifically Jewish, and the ethical approach to religion linked Greek-speaking Jews to their "noble pagan" neighbors more readily than the arcane and parochial laws of sacrifice and diet. Thus it is no accident that the Greek translation of the Hebrew Bible, called the Septuagint (LXX), contained additional sapiential books like Wisdom of Solomon and Sirach. In some of these works we find God's wisdom personified as a kind of co-Creator and teacher of humanity, who, having worked alongside God in designing the universe, appears in human society, urging the human race to forsake foolishness and to embrace wisdom (Proverbs 8:1–9:6). Wisdom, however, gets an indifferent if not outright hostile response and finally abandons men to their sins and returns to heaven, where she knows she will be appreciated. Philo of Alexandria thought it more seemly to switch genders and to regard Wisdom (grammatically and dramatically female) as a male, the Logos. It was not hard to see in this metaphorical story a reflection of the ministry, rejection and ascension of Jesus Christ, so Christian readers concluded that Wisdom or the Word had literally descended to the earth, taught, been rejected and returned to God. The result was a "wisdom Christology" attested here and there in the New Testament: John 1:1–3, 9–11, 14; 1 Corinthians1:23–24; Colossians 1:15–17; Hebrews 1:1–13. We will see an enormous amount of this in Thomas, surely the greatest repository of Wisdom Christology.

Major leaders of the first generation of Hellenistic Christians were the Greek-speaking Jews Stephen (unless he is a fictive twin of James the Just),[30] Philip the evangelist, Prochorus, Nicanor, Parmenas, Timon, Nicolaus, Nicanor, Apollos, Barnabas, Priscilla, Aquila, Andronius, Junia, and Paul.

New Testament documents stemming from this type of Christianity include (obviously) the Pauline Epistles, Hebrews, Mark, Luke, and John.

The third great family of early Christian movements was Gnostic Christianity.[31] This category embraces a wide variety of sects and mystical societies. Here we can only mention a few ideas common to all Gnostics. By our humanistic, compromising standards, Gnosticism would be considered "super-spiritual." Only spirit is good; it is light. Matter and flesh are sinful and darkness. As such it can scarcely have been the creation of a wise and righteous Deity. The Hebrew Scriptures depict God as being petty (he jealously guards his privileges of knowledge and eternal life, lying to protect them if he has to), ignorant (he must ask where Adam and Eve are hiding), and vengeful. He assigns pointless and disgusting laws to his people. This, the God of conventional Judaism and Catholic Christianity, cannot be the pure Spirit that is alone worthy of worship. That Deity, by contrast, exists in blissful repose in the *Pleroma* (divine "fullness") of light, in glorious harmony with the *aions*, personified extensions of his own essence, spiritual entities emanated from himself. How are the two deities connected? *Sophia* ("Wisdom") was the latest and the least of the emanated *aions*. Whereas the others were emanated in pairs (*Syzygies*), each pair begetting the next pair, she was at a loss. She wanted to "conceive," i.e., to have her own offspring and to understand the secrets at the heart of the Godhead, from which she stood at the extreme distance, on the border, the Limit. At this distance the divine glory had grown pale and weak. She did bring forth a son, a malevolent, bungling megalomaniac. He was Jehovah, the Creator God! This Creator (*"Demiurge"*) constructed the disgusting material world and rules it with his created angelic henchmen, the *archons* ("rulers"), who are the old elemental spirits, or angels in charge of nature, as well as the Babylonian planetary deities. But the world as created is inert. In order to vivify it, the *archons* manage to steal sparks of the divine light from the Pleroma. This they do, according to some versions of the myth, by trapping and dismembering one of the *aions*, the Primal Man who henceforth sleeps as dormant sparks of light within the elite of humanity (the Gnostics and those whom they hope to recruit). In another version, they steal the reflected light of Sophia as she stoops down to look into the swamp of the earth.

By Gnostic reckoning, most humans were unworthy *hylics* ("wooden heads") bereft of any real spirit. Others were psychical ("soulish ones"). Only the elite possessed one of the original divine pleromatic sparks, i.e., a soul.

These were the pneumatics, or "spiritual ones." They believed that Christ had appeared in the world for their sake, but he had not exactly been incarnated (though some Gnostics pictured him with a body of flesh, e.g., The Hymn of the Pearl). Most believed the Christ-*aion* (somehow identical with the slumbering Primal Man) had temporarily joined with the human Jesus (as Cerinthus and Basilides taught). Some believed the Christ only appeared (*dokeo*) to have a fleshly body, an illusion to make communication with humans easier. The poor disciples had enough trouble coping with a visible Christ: imagine them following a disembodied voice! This is the doctrine of "docetism," and it was independently evolved by Mahasangika Buddhists and applied to Gotama Buddha,[32] as well as by Alawi Muslims who believe Ali the Imam was Allah incarnate and only feigned humanity.[33] In all these cases, believers just could not imagine their savior sullying himself by truly taking on our lot.

Gnostics claimed to have their doctrines from certain disciples of Jesus whom he deemed worthy of his inner teachings. Some Gnostics made Thomas, Philip, James, Peter, Mary Magdalene, and Matthias (or Matthew, it's hard to tell) the channels of transmission of the *gnosis* (secret knowledge). Peter had taught his secretary Glaukias who passed it on to Basilides, while Paul had taught the esoterica to his disciple Theudas, who taught Valentinus. After all, had not Paul admitted that "among the perfect we do impart wisdom, a secret and hidden wisdom of God" (1 Corinthians 2:6, 7)?

Important early Gnostic leaders include Simon Magus and others just mentioned. They credited Paul as the great fountainhead of their doctrine, while Church Fathers traced all Gnosticism back to Simon Magus. And in fact Simon Magus and Paul are connected, perhaps even identical, one a fictive counterpart of the other.[34] The New Testament canon contains, by my reckoning, just a few Gnostic texts, some of them bowdlerized: Colossians, John, and Ephesians. On the other hand, we do have plenty of Gnostic scriptures including most of the Nag Hammadi texts discovered along with the Gospel of Thomas, plus the Pistis Sophia, the two Books of Jeu, the Acts of Thomas, and the Acts of John.

The fourth type of early Christianity was Encratism, from the Greek word *encrateia*, literally "self-control" but specifically implying sexual continence.[35] Though there was a particular sect called the Encratites, founded by Tatian (ostensible author of the Diatessaron) in the second century, the term is sometimes used (as I do) to refer to a much broader ascetical movement that cut a wide swath through all parties of early Christians. Encratites were socially, ethically, and theologically radical. They sought to preserve certain elements from the ministry of Jesus and the early church that were otherwise in danger of slipping away. Just as Jesus was remembered as preaching the imminent end of the world, encratites expected the kingdom of God to appear in their day. They renounced family ties and family structure, just as Jesus had directed his followers to abandon home and kin (Mark 10:29; Luke 14:26). They were disdainful of both secular authority and that of the bishops of the church. Ecclesiastical office meant nothing to them since they were prophets and prophetesses, beneficiaries of the End-Time outpouring of the Holy Spirit.[36] To make ready for the kingdom they sought the lost purity of Eden. They eschewed all meat and wine, which were innovations introduced after the Fall, after the Flood, in Noah's time (Genesis 9:3). Most important, they swore off sex, which they believed had been the original sin of the virginal Adam and Eve. Once Sin had thus blazed a path into the world, Death followed it into the world, just as Sin had followed Sex (if there was any distinction to be drawn). Had our remote ancestors never poached the fruit of Carnal Knowledge, God would never have condemned the human race to death. Had Adam never been split down the middle, like conjoined twins being separated, there never would have been races of men and women to repeat and confound the sin *ad nauseam*. As Wayne A. Meeks[37] has shown, early Christian baptismal theology seems to have assumed an understanding much like this. The language of Galatians 3:27–28 ("For as many of you as have been baptized into Christ have donned Christ. There is no more Jew versus Greek, no longer slave versus free; no male-female division.") seems to presuppose that all worldly distinctions are obliterated in baptism because baptism marks the return to the Edenic state, before the splitting of the primordial Adam into races, classes, and genders. Jesus Christ is the second Adam (1 Corinthians 15:45), a restored Adam, and baptism joins the baptized to him, as members of his cosmic Light-body, a re-merging of Adam and his many "ribs." On the basis of such a theology, encratite Christians rejected all worldly role distinctions, including sex and family roles, roles of ruler and ruled, and male or female function or privilege. Either sex could prophesy since prophecy by definition comes from the divine Spirit, the gender of its channel being as irrelevant as its height or hair color. The Revelation of John seems to be an encratite document, as it extols the 144, 000 "who have not defiled themselves with women" (Revelation 14:4), which is to compare them to the angels who did not fraternize with mortal women (Genesis 6:1–4).[38]

The Death of the Dinosaurs

What became of the diverse kinds of Christians that flourished during this period of ferment? The four parties did not merely grow closer and eventually merge. Jewish Christian sects became more and more isolated: Gentiles found Law-free Hellenistic Christianity more attractive, while Jews accordingly came to see Christianity as a new Gentile (pagan) religion. Sure it had biblical roots, but what about this new god Jesus? It must have looked to Jews like Mormonism looks to conservative Christians today, with Jesus like Joseph Smith, becoming a new center displacing the original object of worship. Jews would have drawn no distinction between types of Christianity, and a "Jewish Christianity" sounded like a contradiction in terms. A Jew might rebuff a Jewish Christian, saying, "Oh yes! You worship that false god Yeshua, don't you? Like those Goyim!" He might reply, "But we're not like those Gentiles who make an idol of Yeshua! We keep the Torah!" But they got the cold shoulder, being guilty by association. Jewish Christianity attracted some Gentiles to its own ranks, but obviously most Gentiles preferred Hellenistic Christianity as requiring less of a wrenching change. Jewish Christians were too Jewish to appeal to Gentiles, not Jewish enough to succeed with other Jews. Sometime in the fourth century Jewish Christianity seems to have largely died on the vine.

Gnostics eventually found themselves persecuted, once the Christian emperor gave Catholic/Orthodox bishops the power to do so. Their scriptures were burned and heretics were put to death. Other Christians had always found Gnostic tenets blasphemous, but now they were able to give teeth to their threats. Valentinians and other Gnostics had always maintained a shadow existence as secretive subgroups in larger Catholic congregations, much, I imagine, like Catholic Charismatic prayer groups within local parishes, going to mass on Sunday but holding their own meetings Tuesday nights.[39] Marcionites (theological cousins to Gnostics) had their own congregations (called synagogues) all over the Empire and beyond, and this made them easy targets once persecution began. Still, beyond Rome's reach, Marcionites and the third-century Manichaeans lasted for centuries. The latter became a world religion that lasted a millennium until it succumbed to the persecutions of Zoroastrians and Muslims. Islam, however, has many characteristics of Gnostic and Jewish Christians, no doubt the result of converts from these faiths contributing their cherished beliefs to their new religion.

Encratites had an easier time of it, at least those who were not already under a cloud for also being Gnostics. Their notion of the sexual character of the Fall was quite attractive to many Hellenistic Christians, those whose churches would become Catholic Orthodoxy (these two communions did not split into Eastern Orthodoxy and Roman Catholicism until the eleventh century). Augustine hardly stops short of it. Encratism was eventually folded into Catholicism in the form of monasticism and celibate clergy. The only real adjustment was to take what for encratites had been the way of salvation for all and to restrict it to a higher path ("counsels of perfection") for an elite, i.e., priests, bishops, monks, and nuns.[40] Yes, the rank and file of Christians, legally fornicating, were wallowing in lasciviousness, even within marriage, but they could be forgiven and their souls were always mortgaged to the clergy who could still issue passes to heaven for those who obeyed and took the sacraments.

The Jewish Christian legacy was the survival of the Old Testament into Christianity where it has never really fit naturally theologically. Gnosticism bequeathed some aspects of their speculative theology that Catholics retained, for instance the idea of plural hypostases in the Godhead and the notion that the historical Jesus was but a temporary manifestation of an invisible, eternal heavenly being, and the requirement of a stipulated set of beliefs (saving *gnosis* in the form of creeds) for salvation. Encratism contributed its stern view of sex and sin. The Catholic/Orthodox sacraments came from the Mystery Religions, closely related to Gnosticism.

Where exactly does Thomas fit into this Mosaic of early Christianity? Since Thomas was discovered among a collection of largely Gnostic documents, many scholars simply assumed it, too, was Gnostic in origin and orientation. Their commentaries proceed to explain what Thomas' sayings would have meant to Gnostic readers.[41] But did Thomas come from a Gnostic *writer*? Some scholars have now given a negative answer to this question.[42] As a collection of isolated sayings, Thomas seems to draw on various streams of oral tradition, including the Jewish Christian stream, but the great tendency of Thomas seems to me clearly encratite, with a healthy dose of Gnostic material as well.

* * *

I have purposely kept this commentary short and to the point. There are, fortunately, several commentaries on Thomas available, but in my opinion, many of these either recruit Thomas in the service of metaphysical New Age notions alien to the book or they labor mightily, setting forth the huge, clanking machinery of their methodology, and bring forth a mouse as far as understanding the text is concerned.[43]

One last thing: I am keenly aware of the warning of Jonathan Culler[44] not to "naturalize" a strange-sounding text, lest we miss the strange and needful messages they would teach us. We are too eager to domesticate an odd-sounding saying or story so it will not seem so alien to us. But then we run the danger of whittling the real challenge of the text away, cutting it down to size. It will no longer challenge us or provide a higher bar to leap. But if a text is manifestly a puzzle, I think it proper to pick up the thrown gauntlet and see what I can make of it, if I can finally make sense of it. Looking at it dumbly doesn't help much either.[45]

The Gospel according to Thomas

Introduction to the Collection

These are the secret words which the Risen Jesus spoke and Didymus Judas Thomas wrote.

"Secret words" implies esoteric instruction, but as the next line implies, it is not the *sayings themselves* that were secret (e.g., held back from the masses), but rather a special interpretation of them (an interpretation not provided in the text, hence the promise). This accords well with the fact that many of these sayings are presented in the canonical gospels as public teachings of Jesus, e.g., parables. Such sayings are plain enough on a surface level, but they both conceal and reveal a deeper truth to the one who "has ears to hear."

Literally, the Coptic text has "the living Jesus," a phrase which appears twice in the New Testament, Luke 24:5 ("Why do you seek the living one among the dead?") and Revelation 1:18 ("I am the first and the last and the living one."). In both cases it characterizes Jesus as the risen one, the resurrected one. I think it means the same thing here, especially since otherwise there seems little point in using the adjective. *Of course* he said these things while alive. Corpses tend not to say much. The only way it is worth pointing out is if he is living *once more*. Granted, sometimes Thomas seems to refer to the divine Father as "the Living One," but that epithet has a long history in the Old Testament, marking out "the living God" from his stone-cold rivals, heathen idols.

With Jesus understood as teaching after his resurrection, the Gospel according to Thomas becomes recognizable as a primitive example of a Gnostic "Resurrection Dialogue" like the Epistle of the Apostles, the Dialogue of the Savior, the Apocryphon of James, Pistis Sophia, a kind of Easter news conference.[46] But there is one important difference: whereas the whole point of the genre is to portray Jesus at last dropping his maddening figures and ciphers to speak his revelations plainly (this point comes in John 16:25, 29–30, which has been pushed back before the crucifixion as a result of the conflation of the originally distinct Discourse Source and Passion Narrative in John),[47] Thomas, by contrast, has the risen Jesus speaking still in metaphor and riddle. This is equally natural in its own way, since, even if we share the conventional assumption of an historical Jesus, virtually all of the teachings attributed to him in the gospels, as if delivered during his public ministry, seem actually to stem from Christian prophets or channelers in the early church (when they have not merely been borrowed from the common fund of Jewish and Hellenistic lore).

As for the apostolic name, the Greek Oxyrhynchus version has "Didymos Judas who is also Thomas." This form of the name, not just Thomas but *Judas* Thomas, implies a Syrian origin for the Gospel of Thomas, as other Syrian sources call the character Judas Thomas. These include the Acts of Thomas and some Syriac manuscripts of John 14:22 which replace "Judas not Iscariot" with "Judas Thomas."[48] "Didymus" is just the Greek equivalent to "Thomas," both meaning "twin." ("Didymus" is the origin for "ditto.") Whose twin was this Judas? He is the twin, or the earthly double, of Jesus himself. Mark lists a Judas among the brothers of Jesus (6:3) as well as a Thomas among the disciples (3:18). The Gospel of Thomas makes no reference to Judas Thomas being Jesus' twin brother in a natural sense but speaks instead of a spiritual brotherhood between the two, the one having become a spiritual double of the other (sayings 13, 108). This prospect it implicitly offers to any and all readers.

1 And he says, "Whoever discovers the interpretation of these words will not taste death."

There is no magic promised here, as if eternal life were the reward, the Golden Fleece, extrinsic in nature, the prize awarded for contriving to penetrate the code. No, the idea is that, as in the New Testament, Jesus' sayings are "the words of life" (John 6:68). To understand them is to understand the way of salvation. What that way *is* will become apparent. But it is not the "good works" of puzzle-solving per se.[49]

The Old Testament already says the same for wisdom's teaching. "I love those who love me, and those who seek me diligently find me . . . for he who finds me finds life" (Proverbs 8:17, 35a). The seeker of wisdom "preserves the sayings of famous men and penetrates the intricacies of parables. He investigates the hidden meaning of proverbs and knows his way among riddles" (Sirach 39:2–3). The point, again, is exactly the same as Jesus' saying in John 8:51, 52: "If anyone keeps my word he will never see death . . . If anyone keeps my word he will never taste death."[50]

2 Jesus says, "Let the seeker not give up seeking until he finds, and when he finds, he will be perplexed, and once perplexed, he shall marvel, and he shall rule over all things."

The original Greek version from the Oxyrhynchus Papyri reads: "Let not him who seeks cease till he finds, and when he finds he will be astonished; astonished, he will attain the Kingdom, and having attained the Kingdom, he will rest." Clement of Alexandria (*Stromateis* 2:9; 45:5) quotes part of the same saying, or else a shorter version of it: "He that marvels shall reign, and he that has reigned shall rest." Clement ascribes the saying to the Gospel according to the Hebrews. Whence the differences? I would judge that the Coptic translator has simply expanded thaumazo ("marvel," "be astonished"), adding "be troubled." Perhaps "be troubled" reflects the temporary disorientation and dismay of the initiate who mourns the death of his accustomed, childish faith. He sees he must admit that what he had long cherished as the true meaning of the gospel was only the surface meaning. But if the translator added it, that would mean this distinction between "being troubled" and "marveling" was not present in the original text, for whatever that is worth. In fact, as we now read it in Coptic Thomas, Nag Hammadi Thomas, we do have a perfect description of the trial of the initiate. It is because of such "putting away of childish things" that outsiders condemned the Christian Gnostics, the Advaita Vedantists (like Shankara), and the Ismail'i ("Sevener") Shi'ites of concealing irreligion and nihilism beneath the deceptive cloak of piety.[51]

It may be, however, that the whole saying is an expansion of the saying in Matthew 7:7b, "Seek and you will find," which refers to seeking boons of God in prayer, not the seeking of higher knowledge. But in the Thomasine context, we have to ask, what will the persistent seeker find himself marveling *at*? He will marvel at the greatness of what he has found, as the man rejoices at the treasure he has discovered in the field in Matthew 13:44.

That he will "reign" is a good New Testament idea; see Luke 22:30; 2 Timothy 2:12; Revelation 20:4, where the idea is reigning with Christ, belonging to his junta, in the end-time Messianic Kingdom. That was the fanatical day-dream of the sons of Zebedee in Mark 10:37. It is easy to dismiss such expectation (indeed we must) as so much Cargo Cult fantasy, but the New Testament Christians had already begun to demythologize it, perhaps no less fanatically. 1 Corinthians 4:8 rejects this "realized eschatology" taken to some kind of triumphalistic extremes: "Already you are filled! [Contrast Matthew 5:6; Luke 6:21] Already you have become rich! Without us you have become kings! And would that you did reign, that we might share the throne with you!"

The idea of reigning in Thomas saying 2 seems to be that in the midst of this present age we can already rule with Christ, as Ephesians 2:6 says: God "raised us up with him [Christ] and made us sit with him in the heavenly places in Christ Jesus," i.e., sharing in his exalted session at the right hand of the Father. Thomas' seeker, too, will reign with God in the here and now. This might imply freedom from old, besetting sins or (Gnostic-style) freedom from the strictures of the Torah.

I'll bet "he shall rest" (present in the Greek original) originally stood in the Coptic text, too, but was accidentally omitted by a scribe somewhere along the way. Thomas often mentions "rest" or "repose." It seems unlikely our translator would have omitted it here for theological reasons. Hebrews, too, speaks of a "sabbath rest for the people of God" (3:11–4:11), and Barnabas makes much of the coming cosmic Sabbath day of the Millennium (chapter 15). Again, we recognize an Old Testament Wisdom Literature frame of reference: the one who has tirelessly sought after wisdom, having at last found her, finds rest (Wisdom of Solomon 8:13, 16; Sirach 51:26–27:

"Put your neck under her yoke, let your souls receive instruction, she is near, within your reach. See for yourselves: how slight my efforts have been to win so much rest."), with which compare Matthew 11:29–30 and Thomas 90.[52]

This rest corresponds to the "ceasing" from seeking at the beginning of the saying. The idea is that, once you have reigned, *and only then*, it is time to cease seeking.

> **3a Jesus says, "If your leaders tell you, 'Behold, the kingdom is in the sky,' then the birds of the sky will have the advantage over you. If they say to you, 'Behold, the kingdom is in the sea,' then the fish will have the advantage over you. But the kingdom is inside you, and it is outside you.**

Here is an elaboration of the saying in Luke 17:20–21: "Being asked by the Pharisees when the kingdom of God was coming, he answered them, 'The kingdom of God is not coming with signs to be observed; nor will they say, "Lo! Here it is!" Or "There!" for, behold, the kingdom of God is within you.'" There, the contrast is either a *temporal* one between a calculable *futurity* of the kingdom's coming and an unsuspected *presence* of it in their midst, or else a *spatial* contrast between *exteriority* and *interiority*. The latter would also imply a contrast between *literal* and *metaphorical*. In Thomas' version, the second option is taken, and to it is added a sarcastic taunt, coming up next: a literally *heavenly* kingdom would already be the property of the birds. This hints at Aristophanes' comedy *The Birds*, in which the birds decide to establish toll booths in the sky, waylaying the rising sacrificial smoke before it can arrive at Olympus to feed the gods. The gods, their stomachs groaning, eventually come to terms. Aristophanes in this way poked fun at the primitive notion that the gods required sacrifice to maintain strength enough to answer prayers. Likewise, Thomas ridicules the very idea of a divine realm up there in Cloud-Cuckoo Land. What matters is the reign of God in the individual heart.

Likewise, a kingdom in the sea, weed-throttled Atlantis, would be populated only by oblivious fish. But how could the kingdom be said to be "hidden in the sea"? Perhaps the reference is to the succession of pagan world empires, preliminary to the kingdom of the saints of the Most High (Daniel 7:2–3ff); they are described in a visionary allegory as arising, like the primordial chaos monsters, from the sea. The seer of 4 Ezra extended the metaphor, perhaps confusedly, to include the Man (Daniel's "one like a son of man") who vanquishes these beasts/empires. Now he, like them, arises from concealment in the depths (4 Ezra 13:1ff.). So conceivably someone pictured the kingdom arising from the sea.

Does not the text backtrack, restoring an external reference, when it adds, "and it is outside you"? Not really. My guess is that a scribe, or our Coptic translator (the phrase does not occur in the Oxyrhynchus Greek), has added "and it is outside you" to elaborate the saying in the direction of saying 113: the kingdom is not a special province of the physical world but rather permeates it completely if only one's eyes are open to seeing it. The insight is akin to that of Mahayana Buddhism. Where is Nirvana? Why, it is coincident with Samsara if one learns how to look through the one to behold the other. Samsara is only the realm of illusion insofar as we expect it to be reality in its own right. Once we recognize it as a veil of illusion, it is not to be despised but becomes transparent to the divinity close beneath it.

In any case, Stevan L. Davies[53] is doubtless correct tracing the imagery of the saying back to Deuteronomy 30:11–14:

> For this commandment I command you this day is not too hard for you, neither is it far off. It is not in heaven, that you should say, "Who will go up for us to heaven, and bring it to us that we may hear it and do it?" Neither is it beyond the sea, that you should say, "Who will go over the sea for us, and bring it to us, that we may hear it and do it?" But the word is very near you; it is in your mouth and in your heart, so that you can do it.

This important text had been reapplied by Jewish writers (scribes, philosophers) who made it refer to the divine wisdom. For example, Job 28:12–14, 20–28 has:

> Man does not know the way to it, and it is not found in the land of the living. The deep says, "It is not in me," and the sea says, "It is not with me." . . . Whence, then, comes wisdom? And where is the place of understanding? It is hid from the eyes of all living, and concealed from the birds of the air . . . God understands the way to it . . . "Behold, the fear of the Lord, that is wisdom; and to depart from evil is understanding."

Baruch 3:29–30 also applies the Deuteronomy text to Wisdom: "Who has gone up into heaven and taken her, and brought her down from the clouds?

Who has gone over the sea and found her and will buy her for pure gold?" Romans 10:6–8 uses the same text on behalf of the gospel of grace: "But the righteousness based on faith says, 'Do not say in your heart, "Who will ascend into heaven?" (that is, to bring Christ down) or "Who will descend into the abyss?" (that is, to bring Christ up from the dead).' But what does it say? 'The word is near you, on your lips and in your heart' (that is, the word of faith which we preach)." Thomas 3a represents the continuation of this exegetical tradition, applying it to the kingdom of God by conflating it with Luke 17:20–21.

> **3b If you will only know yourselves, then you will be known, and you will know that you are the sons of the Living Father. But if you do not know yourselves, then you are mired in poverty, and you are that poverty."**

The parallel with Romans 10:6–8 in the previous saying opens up an interesting possible parallel between Thomas 3b and the argument in Galatians 4:1–10.[54] In arguing against the Torah-gospel of Jewish Christianity, Paul says that baptized Christians should recognize themselves as *mature sons of the Father* who do not need to keep the laws that were regulative only for children. If they fail to recognize their true sonship to the Father they will be in bondage to "beggarly" elemental spirits, or, in Thomas' idiom, "in poverty." The alternative to beggarly slavery/poverty in both Paul and Thomas is to know oneself a son of the Father and thus to be "known by God."

Was the intent of the Coptic redactor, then, as with Paul, to argue specifically against Jewish-Christian legalism as bondage to poverty? We can't say for sure, but there certainly are other Thomas sayings inimical to Torah observance (especially circumcision, also a special target of Paul in Galatians), as we will see in due course. Pauline teaching understands the Torah to be a spurious imposition by the *archons*, or elemental spirits (Galatians 3:19–20) to redirect worship due God to themselves instead, since it is their commandments their hapless human protégés are obeying (Colossians 2:16–18), not God's, since he has issued none. In an important sense, these laws are not arbitrary; they do properly pertain to life in the flesh, the creation of the Demiurge and the realm ruled by his lieutenants, the *archons*. But the goal of salvation is liberation from the prison of the flesh and the laws governing it. That incarnation/incarceration in the flesh is the poverty (2 Corinthians 8:9), the slavery (Philippians 2:7), from which the revelation of self-knowledge brings freedom.

One might demythologize this, if one fears over-theologizing, and make it equivalent to Harnack's summation of Jesus' message of "God the Father and the infinite value of the human soul."[55] One is mired in terrible poverty as long as he does not know the value God sees in him, as in the Gospel of Philip 48: "When the pearl is cast down in the mud it does not become dishonored the more, nor if it is anointed with balsam oil will it become more precious. But it has its worth in the eye of its owner at all times. So with the sons of God wherever they may be. For they have the value in the eyes of their Father."

Why the preference for "the Father" and not "God," as in the repeated "kingdom of the Father"? It might reflect the super-piety of Judaism which caused Jews to observe a moratorium on vocalizing the divine name Yahve, speaking of "Adonai" (Lord) instead, then eventually, of the more generic "God," then of "ha Shem" (the Name) or "the Holy One." Remember the interchange between Jesus and the High Priest: "Are you the Christ, the son of *the Blessed*?" "I am, and you shall see the son of man seated at the right hand of *Power*." In the same way, Matthew has almost always changed Mark's "kingdom of God" references to "kingdom of heaven." Matthew once uses Thomas' favorite term in 13:43: "the kingdom of their Father," implying the phrase was current in Jewish-Christian circles.

On the other hand, the usage might reflect the Gnostic relegation of the title "God" to the Demiurge (the inferior Creator and law-giving deity). In Thomas 100 "God" certainly seems to mean the Demiurge. In saying 30, the Coptic redactor has altered "God" (attested in the Greek) to "gods."

> **4 Jesus says, "The man ancient of days will not hesitate to ask a little child of seven days concerning the place of Life, and he will live. For many who are first in rank shall become last, and they shall become identical."**

Hippolytus (ca. 200, schismatic bishop of Rome) quotes from a Naassene copy of the Gospel of Thomas a strikingly different version of this saying: "He who seeks me will find me in children from seven years, for there in the fourteenth age/*aion*, having been hidden, I shall be manifest." Though I have trouble imagining why anyone would have done it, this version almost sounds like an amalgamation of the Coptic version with a saying found in the Infancy Gospel of Matthew, a text dependent upon the infancy Gospel of Thomas: "I have been among you with the children, and ye have not recognized me. I have spoken with you as with people of understanding, and ye have not recognized my voice" (chapter 30).

There also seems to be a reference here to a Hippocratic theory preserved by the Stoics (Zeno, Cleanthes, Diogenes of Babylon): up to the seventh year, when one loses the baby teeth (or milk teeth), a child has neither understanding nor *logos* (reason). *Logos* develops between ages seven and fourteen, and the process is complete by puberty. According to Hippolytus' version of Thomas 4, then, in the fourteenth year the divine *Logos* replaces human reason, and in this manner the presence of Christ is made manifest.

The Coptic *Manichaean Psalm Book* provides another variant, perhaps a direct transcript from their copy of Thomas (various Church Fathers mention that the Manichaeans used Thomas): "The gray-haired old men: the little children instruct them. They that are six years old instruct them that are sixty years old." Both Manichaean and Naassene versions agree against both the Nag Hammadi and Oxyrhynchus versions in making the wise child years, not mere days, old. Which is the original? It is impossible to say since the former (years old) may only reflect a scribal "correction" of a troublesome original that had "days." It is certainly difficult to imagine a scribe finding the more reasonable "years" and changing it to "days"! But maybe he still had the word "days" fresh on his mind from the line he had just copied containing "ancient of days."

Then again, Davies[56] makes a valuable suggestion when he observes the Jewish baptism of adult converts took place on the seventh day after circumcision. If it is intended as baptismal language here, stemming from "the circumcision party" (Galatians 2:12), the point would be to stress the superiority of even the Christian neophyte/neonate to anyone outside the fold, no matter how erudite.

At any rate, the notion of abolishing age distinctions is a biblical one, found in Isaiah 11:6 and Joel 2:28, both of which had become associated with the Last Days. On the other hand, the somewhat different idea of children surpassing their elders already during this present age is found in Psalm 119:19, "I have more understanding than all my teachers, for thy testimonies are my meditations." This is precisely the point of the scene depicting young Jesus respectfully trading halakhic opinions with the temple elders in Luke 2:46–47. Again we are reminded of various Infancy Gospel traditions where Jesus himself is the child of few years who instructs the old men. Perhaps the point is to congratulate the "newborn" initiates, the newly baptized, those who have "become children" to enter the kingdom and as a result know the way of salvation better than the old who, for all their learning, have not put it on the shelf and submitted to baptism. The point would be precisely the same as Matthew 11:25, "You have hidden these things from the wise and understanding and revealed them unto babes."

The conclusion, "Many that are first shall become last and they shall become a single one" (which I have rendered "identical"), implies an overcoming of differences, a reconciliation. What exactly is a "single one"? A "solitary"? The Greek word here is *monachos*, from which the word "monk" derives. Remember that the Nag Hammadi copy of Thomas was recovered from a monastery. That is no accident. The monkish ideal of a solitary contemplative life, isolated from worldly distractions, is a direct embodiment of the *monachos* teaching of this gospel. This word covers a complex of associations throughout the gospel. On the one hand, "single" seems to entail a combination of *celibate* (cf. our "married versus single") and, especially "single-minded," a combination attested in Paul (1 Corinthians 7:32–34, where marriage is said to distract one from Christ and results in "divided" devotion, i.e., prevents a spouse from being a "single one").

Also implicit in the "single one" ideal is the overcoming of inner divisions, as of mixed loyalties. The single one no longer tries to serve two masters. He serves his Lord with heart, soul, mind, and strength.

On the other hand, the celibacy aspect is most important; we must not leave it aside in a rush to "psychologize" the text and make it amenable to twenty-first century healthy-mindedness. The *monachos* business no doubt reflects the widespread encratite doctrine that permeated the Apocryphal Acts of the Apostles,[57] Gnosticism, Marcionism, and Encratism proper (the sect of Tatian). The belief here was that God had never intended for Adam and Eve to beget the human race. He wanted a single man to tend his garden, an easy job tending to boredom, so he made a second human from this one's body to keep him company. Thanks to the Serpent, the pair learned the divine secret of procreation, issuing in a human race sundered at once by strife and alienation. Eventually this cockroach-like multiplication of men and women resulted in domestic slavery for wives, hatred between tongues and nations and peoples, between Jew and Greek, slave and free, male and female. Salvation lay in a return to the unity and innocence of Eden. Through baptism into Christ, the Last Adam, one reversed the Fall, renounced the original sin, sexuality, and henceforth enjoyed (at least within the encratite Christian communities) an egalitarian, communistic, vegetarian, apocalyptic, anarchistic, pacifistic life in a kingdom not of this world. Such Christians shall stand "as a single one."

5 Jesus says, "Recognize what is right in front of you, and what is concealed from you will suddenly be revealed to you. For there is nothing hidden that will not be brought to light [and buried that will not be raised up]."

The last, bracketed clause is supplied from one of the Greek fragments from Oxyrhynchus. It does not occur in the Coptic, but my guess is that it has been omitted accidentally. The "burial" half-saying appears as a separate saying in other ancient sources, including a strip of burial gauze in the Oxyrhynchus tombs!

We seem to have here a conflation of two originally separate sayings, joined by the catchwords "hidden—revealed." The first half is roughly paralleled in John 3:12, "If I have told you of earthly things and you do not believe, how will you believe if I tell you of heavenly matters?" Closer still may be Matthew 16:3, "How is it you know how to discern the face of the heavens, but you cannot discern the signs of this present time?" The larger thought seems to be: Take off your blinders, and then you will easily see what seems so obscure a mystery now. The problem is not that it is invisible; the problem is that you are blind. But you can correct that! Is it an unwillingness to obey your conscience that produces a neurotic confusion?

Does Thomas provide any clue as to what the unseen spectacle might be? Elsewhere, as we have already seen, he speaks of the ubiquitous kingdom of the Father which men have not allowed themselves to recognize, for all that it should be self-evident.

"For there is nothing hidden that will not be brought to light" appears as a separate saying in (Mark 4:22; Luke 8:17). Another version appears in Q ("Nothing is covered up that will not be revealed or hidden that will not be known." In Matthew 10:26 it is used as a parable instructing the disciples/ missionaries one day to broadcast what Jesus has told them privately. Luke 12:2 uses it as a warning about idle words, parallel to Matthew 12:36: "Men shall account for every idle word they speak; by your words you shall be acquitted and by your words you shall be condemned." But Mark 4:22 is either an independent version, or as some think, a rewrite of the Q version. It says, "There is nothing hid except to be made manifest; nor is anything secret except to come to light." This time it seems to be about secret teaching. We catch a whiff of the Markan Messianic Secret motif: Mark 4:12 might be an apologetic trying to explain how it is that certain latter-day teachings "really" go back to Jesus even though most Christians never heard of them till just recently. In such a way the gap was bridged between the teaching *of* Jesus and the teaching *about* Jesus. Other examples of retro-fitting later teachings include Mark 8:30; 9:9; 16:8. Finally, Luke combines the Q and Mark versions: "For nothing is hid that shall not be made manifest, nor anything secret that shall not be known and come to light."

Thomas' "and nothing buried that shall not be raised" seems just to be a variant of "nothing is *covered* that shall not come to light." An example would the talent that the fearful slave buried in the ground, hesitant to risk losing it by investing. He knew the day would come to dig up the money and return it to his Lord. See Matthew 25:14 ff. But in Egypt the saying had come to be applied to the resurrection, as its inscription on a burial shroud attests. This would explain why the Coptic redactor cut this portion of the saying: as a Gnostic he could not countenance the resurrection of the body.

> **6 His disciples ask him, saying to him, "Do you want us to fast? And how should we pray? Should we give alms? And what diet should we keep?" Jesus says, "Do not lie, and do not do what you hate, for everything is observed from heaven. For there is nothing hidden that shall not finally be revealed, and there is nothing covered up that shall remain unexposed."**

Different Jewish sects followed different practices of piety. Note how Jesus taught his disciples not to fast and thus was out of step with both the Pharisees and John the Baptist's followers (Mark 2:2:18). Here Jesus' disciples ask what rules are entailed in discipleship to him? As Bultmann showed, any time the disciples instead of Jesus himself are in view, we may be sure we have a creation of the early church, trying to supply (as by a spurious hadith) some guidance Jesus had neglected to give.

Fasting, prayer (at certain designated hours three times daily), and almsgiving were the three trademark practices of the Pharisee sect. Matthew 6:1–18 has Jesus lampoon the hypocrisy bred by the conspicuous public observance of these disciplines. (Pharisees, naturally, viewed them as no more ostentatious or self-aggrandizing than we would think of rising to salute the flag, but Matthew was eager to believe the worst about fellow Jews with whom he was in competition.) Thomas' opinion of these same three practices goes considerably farther, at least as the text must once have read, for the original reply of Jesus has been displaced to saying 14. For the moment, suffice it to say Jesus, in a nihilistically Gnostic fashion, roundly condemns all three customs as positively harmful, even lethal, to the soul! Some redactor somewhere along the way could not credit that, and, though he left the original saying intact elsewhere, here he has Jesus give a very different response, one altogether in line with the Hebrew prophets' no-nonsense approach: "Do not lie, and do not do what you hate, for everything is observed from heaven. For there is nothing hidden that shall not finally be revealed, and there is nothing covered up that shall remain unexposed." The contrast is only implicit, but the point seems to be that niceties of devotional piety pale in comparison to simple honesty and avoidance of hypocrisy. The saying may have been derived from Tobit chapter 4: "If you do what is true, your ways will prosper through your deeds" (verse 6) and "And what you hate, do not do to anyone" (verse 15). We might also think of the Third Isaiah: "Is not this the fast that I choose: to loose the bonds of wickedness, to undo the thongs of the yoke, to let the oppressed go free, and to break every yoke? Is it not to share your bread with the hungry, and bring the homeless poor into your house; when you see the naked, to cover him, and not to hide yourself from your own needy kinfolk?" (Isaiah 58:6–7).

The last sentence of this Thomas saying, repeated from the previous saying (unless perchance a scribe accidentally miscopied it from here to there!), occurs here with what I suggested was its original meaning: "Be sure your sin will find you out" (Numbers 32:23); "Thou, God, seest me" (Genesis 16:13).

7 Jesus says, "Blessed is the lion eaten by the man and the lion will become man; and cursed is that man whom the lion eats for the lion will become man."

This may take the cake as the most difficult saying for the modern reader, so much so that some scholars resort to the desperate expedient of "surgical exegesis," or conjectural emendation, reconstructing the last line as "and the man shall become lion."[58] There are indeed copyist errors elsewhere in the Coptic manuscript, so this might be another—but how would it have happened? Some suggest that the copyist just zoned out and repeated the second line, but as Howard M. Jackson[59] points out, the two are not worded quite the same. The tenses are not the same. And, yes, the scribe might possibly have simply reversed "lion" and "man," but usually you err by absently writing what you expect to appear next, and who could *not* expect the order to be opposite that in line 2? An odd mistake to make! So let's see if we can make sense of the text as it stands. There seem to be three viable possibilities.

The first half of the saying may refer to an idea we find elsewhere in the gospel, that the physical body subsists on "dead things," dead meat, which then, being assimilated into the body of the eater, *becomes* the eater. Thus consumed animal life is blessed because it is moving up the scale when eaten by a human. In this case, the second half might simply be telling us the converse: that since a human being is not simply flesh, but has a spirit/soul, then that spirit is degraded, and the lion simultaneously ennobled, since the human soul passes on into the lion. This would be an interesting curiosity, but little more, unless the point were to highlight the difference between human and animal life, a contrast drawn elsewhere in Thomas.

Or the lion may symbolize the passion against which the encratite struggles. The imagery would be drawn from Socrates' parable of the struggle of the elements within a human being. The parable appears in Plato's *Republic*, in a section which occurs among the Nag Hammadi collection, a pretty good hint! Reason is symbolized by a man; courage (or spirit) is represented by a lion; and the appetites appear under the form of a many-headed beast like the chimera. It may be that the man can dominate the lion, gaining a necessary ally against the chimera. But should the man fail to tame the lion, it and the chimera will devour one another (as well as the man?). Perhaps for the lion to become man would signify that the lion usurps the once-exalted position of the man or dominates him. "Cursed" in Coptic is the word used for something sexually shameful, not merely, "Woe to the man." So if it refers to the rational man going down before the flood of appetites, the "shame" element would be natural. The point of the saying, read in this fashion, would be that the will allied with the reason is blessed, but the reason submerged in the passions is shameful and reprobate.

Or the saying may belong in a full-blown Gnostic frame of reference. In Pistis Sophia, a major Gnostic Revelation dialogue, we read that the evil Demiurge had stolen Pleromatic light to give order and life to his material creation (a kind of cosmic Golem). In some versions of the myth the light comes from the Primal Man, one of the *aion*s captured and dismembered by the *archon*s, henchmen of the Demiurge. In other versions, it is the reflected image of Sophia which provides the strategic photons. Pistis Sophia says Sophia (Wisdom) descended to the material world her misbegotten son created. She wanted to erase her mistake and devour her son, the Demiurge— who is described as *lion-headed*. ("Blessed is the lion devoured by man.") But as she descends, *she* is devoured *by* the Demiurge! He thereby captures her light to provide self-replicating order for his mud-ball of a world. ("Shame on the man devoured by the lion."). Having absorbed this divine substance, the creatures, specifically human beings, rise to the level of Sophia (or the Primal Man) whose photons they now contain ("The lion becomes man.").[60]

One oddity that might mean something is the fact that, while lions are happy enough to eat humans, humans do not eat lion meat. And there is also the undeveloped possibility that the saying intends a reference to reincarnation: would a man-eater get a head start on reincarnating his way up the ladder to humanity?

8 And he says, "The man is like a shrewd fisherman who cast his net into the sea. He pulled it up from the sea full of small fish. He found among them a large, good fish. That shrewd fisherman threw all the small fish back into the sea. He chose the large fish without a second thought. Whoever has ears to hear, let him hear!"

There seems to be some sort of relation between this parable and Matthew's parable of the Net in Matthew 13:47–48 (verses 49–50 are clearly Matthean redaction). There are three possibilities.

First, Matthew's version, at least of verses 47–48, is original, and Thomas' is a later version of it, assimilating it to the directly adjacent parables of the Treasure in the Field (Matthew 13:44) and the Pearl Merchant (Matthew 13:45–46). Second, Thomas' version may be the original, forming a third in a series with the Treasure and Pearl parables. All three would convey the image of someone (whom the hearer/reader is to emulate) smart enough to choose one great prize even at the cost of everything else. In this case, Matthew will have altered the version more faithfully preserved in Thomas in order to make it into a glimpse of the final judgment, a recurring motif in uniquely Matthean material (13:40, 49; 22:2, 11–14; 25:31–46). Third, they might just be two separate parables, making different points both using the fishing metaphor.

Why does the parable open with "The man is like . . ." rather than, say, "The kingdom is like . . ."? Perhaps it is simply shorthand for "I will show you whom the wise man is like." Or maybe it is a scribal error, copying "the man" from the last line of saying 7: "the lion will become man." That, in turn, is evidence that the text our scribe was copying from already had the reading in saying 7 that we do, instead of the hypothetical original discussed above, that it first read: "the man shall become lion."

James Breech[61] makes the interesting suggestion that here alone we find preserved the sort of opening all Jesus' parables had, and that it somehow escaped having a new introduction imposed: "The kingdom of God/heaven/ the Father is like . . ." All such introductions, Breech argues, are secondary. That would certainly comport nicely with the theory that eschatology was a secondary layer added to the teachings of Jesus only during the run-up to the Roman War.

What is the point of the parable? Ray Summers[62] and others suggest that the parable is Gnostic in character. On this reading, we ought to see the fisherman as God or Christ rejoicing to find a valuable Gnostic among the worthless mass of worldly small-fry. But this seems an over-interpretation. Why not take the fisherman the same way we do the protagonists in the parables of the Treasure and the Pearl: a human being astute enough to recognize the opportunity before him, and to seize it at any cost, since it is worth more than the rest put together?

> **9 Jesus says, "Behold, the sower went out. He filled his hand with seed and threw. Some seeds fell on the road where the birds lit and gathered them. Others fell on the rock and did not strike root in the earth and did not produce ears. And others fell on the thorns, which choked the seed and the worm ate them. And others fell on good soil, and it yielded good fruit, bearing sixty per measure and one hundred twenty per measure."**

This is another version of the Markan parable of the Sower (Mark 4:3–9; Matthew 13:3–9; Luke 8:5–8). It shows only the same sort of minor embellishments we find in Matthew and Luke: variations in number and detail. As Luke has the seed "trod underfoot," Thomas has it "eaten by a worm." Such are the vagaries of oral transmission. The main difference is that Thomas lacks the subsequent interpretation supplied by Mark and repeated by Matthew and Luke. This may be, as many critics think, because Thomas has taken the parable from oral tradition at a stage before the interpretation was added. Or it may be that someone had heard the parable read and remembered only part of it, not the pedantic interpretation.

As for the Markan interpretation, the focus falls on the variety of soils, making them represent different typical responses to the preaching of the gospel. One may assess himself to determine which category of soil his heart reveals him to be. But it is all a device to prompt the reader (any readers, all readers) to secure one's election by resolving to be or become the good, fertile soil.

But if we approach the parable as it stands, the point may rather be the same as we read in Galatians 6:9: "Let us not grow weary in doing good, for in due season we shall reap, so long as we do not lose heart." Yes, it may seem as if most of your efforts at evangelism may appear a fruitless waste of time, producing only ridicule and indifference, but when your preaching hits pay-dirt, the pay-off is vastly disproportionate to the trouble you put into it. The loss of most of the original seed is afterward seen to be no real waste at all. One must wonder if perhaps the parable is itself an elaboration of Galatians 6:9, later attributed to Jesus.

10 Jesus says, "I have let loose fire upon the world, and behold, I tend it until the world is consumed."

Here is another version of a saying found in Luke 12:49, "I have come to cast fire upon the earth, and would that it were already kindled!" The fire is apparently that of the end-time conflagration, preceded by unnatural strife between family members and friends, a notion found in many apocalyptic works (see saying 16). Jesus is here said already to have kindled the flame rather than anxiously to await it as in Luke's version. The eschatology has been "realized," fulfilled already, at least by way of anticipation or inauguration, in the present. The eschatological fire merely smolders now and in fact must be carefully tended lest it go out, but soon it must burst into full blaze, as envisaged in the next saying. The idea is parallel to that in the parables of the Mustard Seed (Mark 4:30–32) and the Leaven (Matthew 13:33): the kingdom of God is already present in the affairs of men, yet not manifest, all the while silently and subtly at work. One day it will burst forth so no one can miss it, and then people will wonder where it came from.

11 Jesus says, "This heaven shall pass away, and the one above it shall pass away. And the dead are not alive, and the living shall not die. In the days when you consumed the dead meat, you made it alive. When you consume what is living, what will you do? You will come into the light. On the day when you were one, you became two. But when you have become two, what will you do?"

This is a series of separate apocalyptic sayings strung together. The first describes the burning away of the two lower concentric heavens (cf. 2 Peter 3:12, In "the day of God, . . . the heavens will be kindled and dissolve, and the elements will melt with fire."): the blue sky and the black veil of stars, leaving exposed the highest heaven where God dwells above the flood, as in ancient cosmology, and no one will be able to flee his scrutiny. Thomas' compiler sees this fire as that Jesus is soon to kindle, since he has placed this saying immediately after that one.

"The dead are not alive, and the living shall not die" looks like a separate saying denying the resurrection of the fleshly body in the interest of Gnosticism. The body is *already* a corpse and thus will never enter the true, spiritual life that is alien to it. And it is absurd to speak of a "resurrection" of something not susceptible to death anyway (the soul).

The next sentence reads, more literally, "In the days when you ate the dead, you made it living." It is not living but can be *made* living. (Recall how the lion may become man.) I am taking the Naassene version of the text, quoted by Hippolytus, as the original, and then we get this result: "The living will not die," so "when you eat living things what will you do?" That is, what will result? You will not make them dead, since what is living cannot die. (Hence, when the lion eats the man, the man does *not* become lion, because that would entail the living becoming dead.) Stevan L. Davies suggests that "you will come to dwell in the light" is a scribal gloss attempting to answer what was really a rhetorical question, "What will you do?" The gloss was then copied into the text by a subsequent scribe where he supposed it had originally belonged.[63]

What does it mean to "eat dead things"? Eating meat, of which the encratites bitterly disapproved. To eat living things as opposed to dead things seems to denote spiritual nourishment (cf. John 4:31–34; 1 Corinthians 10:3–4), the favored menu item of abstemious ascetics everywhere. "When you were one, you became two." This is certainly a reference to the division of the Primal Adam into male and female, upon which the Fall ensued. "When you become two, what will you do?" You will, or must, become one, a "single one" (*monachos*) in Christ, the Second Adam, This is good encratite soteriology: the return to Edenic innocence and immortality.

12 The disciples say to Jesus, "We know that you will depart from us. Who is it who will be great over us?" Jesus says to them, "Wherever you have come from, you will go report to James the Just, for whom heaven and earth were prepared."

The phrase "for whom heaven and earth were prepared" is a rabbinical honorific used also of the Torah, King David, the Messiah, Israel, Abraham, Aaron, and (by Christians) Jesus Christ (Colossians 1:16). It usually does not imply literal pre-existence in some heavenly realm. Rather, the idea is that God had the brilliant idea of creating So-and-so, and of course that meant he would need a world to *put* him/it in. Why was such prominence accorded to James the Just? It is not hard to figure out if one accepts his epithet "brother of the Lord" as implying he was literally a sibling of an historical Jesus. Then it would have been on this basis, with this clout, that he rose to the leadership of the Jerusalem church (Acts chapters 15 and 21; Galatians 2:12). Thomas 12 is a credential (after the fact, on his behalf) to reinforce his authority, counterbalancing other gospel texts that seek to discredit him and/or his successors (Mark 3:19b-21, 31–35; John 7:5) in favor of other leadership factions. The otherwise puzzling phrase "wherever you have come from" seems to suggest the duty of apostolic missionaries, upon conclusion of a preaching mission, to go report to James, as we read in 3 Peter (the Letter of Peter to James), which even Paul does in Acts 15 and 21.

Especially in light of the Jewish character of the language, the saying may come from the Jewish quarter of early Christianity, but it may as easily have emanated from Gnostic circles, since many of them also honored James as a preeminent revealer. The Apocryphon (Secret Book) of James as well as 1 and 2 Apocalypse of James attest his importance as a mediator of *gnosis*.

13 Jesus says to his disciples, "Compare me and tell me what I am like." Simon Peter says to him, "You are like a righteous an-gel." Matthew says to him, "You are like a philosopher possessed of understanding." Thomas says to him, "Master, my mouth can scarcely frame the words of what you are like!" Jesus says, "I am not your master, because you have drunk, you have become filled,

from the bubbling spring which I have measured out." He took him aside privately and said three things to him. So when Thomas rejoined his companions, they pressed him, saying, "What did Jesus say to you?" Thomas said to them, "If I tell you even one of the things he said to me, you will pick up stones and hurl them at me—and fire will erupt from the stones and consume you!"

Of course, this is Thomas' version of the famous Confession of Peter story. I believe it will be quite instructive to trace the trajectory of the story through the gospels. We begin, most pointedly, *not* with some imagined oral tradition, but with literary invention by the evangelist Mark, who, as Gerd Theissen[64] has shown, created the episode from whole cloth. First comes Mark 6:14–16: "King Herod heard of it, for his name had become well known. Some said, 'John the baptizer has been raised from the dead; that explains why miraculous powers are at work in this person.' But others said, 'It is Elijah.' And others said, 'It is a prophet, like one of the ancient prophets.' But when Herod heard of it he said, 'John, whom I decapitated, has been raised.'" We cannot imagine any *Sitz-im-Leben* for this scene as a piece of kerygmatic preaching or catechetical instruction. It is a dramatic transitional scene created by Mark, "meanwhile back at the ranch." How, pray tell, would Mark be privy to the guilty reflections of Herod Antipas, brooding over the newspaper and his morning coffee? He knew of it the same way he knew of Jesus' private prayers in Gethsemane: he made it all up.

And then he made up the scene in Mark 9:27–33:

And Jesus went on with his disciples, to the villages of Caesarea Philippi; and on the way he asked his disciples, "Who do men say that I am?" And they told him, "John the Baptist; and others say, Elijah; and others one of the prophets." And he asked them, "But who do you say that I am?" Peter answered him, "You are the Christ." And he charged them to tell no one about him. And he began to teach them that the Son of man must suffer many things, and be rejected by the elders and the chief priests and the scribes, and be killed, and after three days rise again. And he said this plainly. And Peter took him, and began to rebuke him. But turning and seeing his disciples, he rebuked Peter, and said, "Get behind me, Satan! For you are not on the side of God, but of men."

How do we know Mark created the scene? In the Herod scene, the same three options for the identity of Jesus are raised, but there they occur in direct discourse, direct quotes, and the nominative case is used for all three answers, introduced quite properly by the conjunction *oti*. In the Caesarea Philippi scene, however, the three options are given in indirect discourse, summarized at second hand, which properly takes the accusative case, but only the first two (John the Baptist and Elijah) are in the accusative, while the third appears, incorrectly, with the nominative. Also, though *oti* cannot introduce the accusative, it is made to do so here. In short, Mark has hastily and clumsily patched in a section of his own previous text, failing to make all the needful grammatical changes. This passage is based on that passage. It is fiction. This is important for us here for the simple reason that it means Thomas could not have independently derived the story from free-floating oral tradition. Thomas used Mark, though he had to rely on his memory as to what it said.

Luke 9:18–22 is based on Mark, too.

Now it happened that as he was praying silently the disciples were with him; and he asked them, "Who do the people say that I am?" And they answered, "John the Baptist; but others say, Elijah; and others, that one of the old prophets has risen." And he said to them, "But who do you say that I am?" And Peter answered, "The Christ of God." But he charged and commanded them to tell this to no one.

The scene's location is omitted. The three identity options are the same, except that in Luke Jesus is identified not as a prophet of the old school, but rather as another *of* the ancient prophets come back again, just like Elijah, but one of his colleagues. Peter's answer is essentially the same, only a bit elaborated: "You are the Christ *of God*." Luke omits the Satan rebuke because he does not accept Mark's Marcionite distaste for the twelve, Peter in particular.

Matthew 16:13–22, also based on Mark, has Caesarea Philippi and the same three options. But like Luke, he has someone in the crowd posit that Jesus is a particular Old Testament prophet, besides Elijah, and Matthew specifies Jeremiah. Here it looks as if Matthew has sharpened Luke, implying that he knew Luke's gospel as well as Mark. This is to crack open the door to source-critical debates that are not our topic here, but it is worth noting. Even a casual reading reveals major modifications of the Markan original.

> Now when Jesus came into the district of Caesarea Philippi, he asked his disciples, "Who do men say that the Son of man is?" And they said, "Some say John the Baptist, others say Elijah, and others Jeremiah or one of the prophets." He said to them, "But who do you say that I am?" Simon Peter replied, "You are the Christ, the Son of the living God." And Jesus answered him, "Blessed are you, Simon Bar-Jona! For flesh and blood has not revealed this to you, but my Father who is in heaven. And I tell you, you are Peter, and on this rock I will build my church, and the gates of hell shall not withstand its assault. I will give you the keys of the kingdom of heaven, and whatever you bind on earth shall be bound in heaven, and whatever you loose on earth shall be loosed in heaven." Then he strictly charged the disciples to tell no one that he was the Christ. From that time Jesus began to show his disciples that he must go to Jerusalem and suffer many things from the elders and chief priests and scribes, and be killed, and on the third day be raised. And Peter took him and began to rebuke him, saying, "God forbid, Lord! This shall never happen to you." But he turned and said to Peter, "Get behind me, Satan! You are a hindrance to me; for you are not on the side of God, but of men."

Instead of asking, "Who do people say I am?" the Matthean Jesus asks, "Who do men say *the son of man* is?" Technically, there ought not to be any difference in meaning, since "son of man" was usually a humble way of referring to oneself: "this man." But here, in view of the Christological focus, one almost feels Matthew must be slipping the answer into the question, as if to reassure the reader that Jesus already knows the correct answer: the Son of Man from Daniel 7. Who knows?

As for Peter, he again breaks from the pack, contradicting the clueless crowd: "You are the Christ, *the Son of the living God*." He has augmented the true Christological confession as Mark stipulated it, but it looks again as if Luke's version stands at a point intermediate to Mark and Matthew, as Luke had added "of God," and Matthew, seeing that, decided to up the voltage and add "the Son of the living." Why use the Deuteronomic term "the living God"? My guess is that he was aware of the pagan ring of the phrase "son of God" in the ears of some and thought to Judaize it by specifying "the living God," not the idols of the heathen. Pythagoras was called the son of Apollo, but Apollo was just a statue, Pythagoras just a banjo-playing math teacher.

Jesus heaps the blessings on Peter, rewarding him for his bright answer like a game show host listing the terrific prizes a lucky contestant has won:

He gets a new name, "Peter" (the Rock), denoting that he is the bedrock of the "church" (an obvious anachronism—Jesus might as well call him the Pope!). He gets to command a strike force that will storm the gates of Sheol to rescue the Old Testament saints long languishing there like John the Baptist in Herod's dungeon. He is granted the rabbinical keys to bind and loose halakhic duties for faithful Jews, lengthening the allowable range of a Sabbath day's journey, suspending kosher laws for evangelism's sake, allowing Gentiles to be baptized—it will all be up to him, with heaven's (i.e., God's) imprimatur. And not because of any superior insight on his part; rather he has been the passive recipient of revelation from on high: flesh and blood has not revealed the secret to him. This is a "me-too" claim made on Peter's behalf to meet the challenge of Paul who insisted his gospel was no human doctrine nor revealed to him by any human source (Galatians 1:1,11–12). Here we are no doubt reading ecclesiastical politics: to enhance the picture of Peter is to enhance the position of those who claim succession from him. The use made of this text by the Roman Catholic Church is only slightly off-target: originally it was aimed at securing the prestige of the bishop(s) of Antioch, not Rome.

Astonishingly, after all this shower of blessings, the text goes on to have Peter rebuke Jesus as he did in Mark, only more explicitly, whereupon Jesus again lowers the boom. I am sure Arlo J. Nau[65] is correct that at a previous stage of redaction of Mark on its way to becoming canonical Matthew, a redactor had entirely reversed Mark's systematic denigration of Peter, e.g., having him given plenipotentiary authority as we have just seen, having him successfully walk on the water to Jesus' side (Matthew 14:28–25), and having Jesus bless him at Caesarea Philippi, not curse him. But then a second redactor, less enamored of Peter for some other apostle's sake, changed the text, e.g., diluting Peter's authority and redistributing it to the twelve collectively (Matthew 18:18–20); having him sink into the drink for lack of faith (Matthew 14:26–27); and restoring the Markan Satan rebuke.

John, too, has a version of the Confession episode, found in John 6:66–71. It is significantly different from the Synoptics, but it is nonetheless recognizable as a variant version of the same episode.

> After this many of his disciples drew back and no longer went about with him. Jesus said to the twelve, "Do you also wish to go away?" Simon Peter answered him, "Lord, to whom shall we go? You have the words of eternal life. And we have believed, and have come to know, that you

are the Holy One of God." Jesus answered them, "Did I not choose you, the twelve, and one of you is a devil?" He spoke of Judas the son of Simon Iscariot, for he, one of the twelve, was to betray him.

The setting has been changed to Capernaum. The three identity options have been traded off with John the Baptist over in John 1:19–21, where envoys of the priests interrogate John: Are you Elijah? No. The Prophet like Moses? No. The Christ? No. Obviously they are not going to ask John if he is John. The three guesses have be wrong, as at Caesarea Philippi, so John must be asked if he is the Christ, just as Christ is taken for John. And, as in the Synoptics, Peter speaks for the twelve over against the ignorance of the crowd (whose opinions are not reported, but who are drifting away in confusion): "You are the Holy One of God." And this time it is the betrayer (Judas), not the denier (Peter) who is made the devil. Or at least John so applies the accusation; he does not actually have Jesus say whom he means.

Finally, in Thomas saying 13 we have, as in Luke, no geographical reference. Strikingly, there is no contrast between some outside group and the twelve insiders. This time the line is drawn *within* the group of apostles. The contrast is now pointedly between Thomas and the other disciples. Peter, extolled in the other gospels, is rudely shoved aside in favor of Thomas. Why? Peter has come to be identified with the institutional church, almost overtly in Matthew. Peter stands for the bishops here, too. Matthew is lampooned, too, because it is his gospel's version of the story that makes the most of Peter. Thomas, on the other hand, plainly stands for the beleaguered Gnostic communities. We need not think of the ecclesiastical persecutions of Constantine's time. The investigations of Irenaeus, trying to smoke out the closet Gnostics in his churches, are enough to provide the type of situation Thomas 13 presupposes. Just as Thomas declines to tell his esoteric revelation to the insistent disciples lest they hear it as blasphemy and persecute him, so the Gnostic initiates within the local congregations had to keep their doctrine, even their allegiance, secret from their unenlightened fellow parishioners. Sufis, Druzes, and other possessors of higher knowledge throughout history have had to learn this lesson the hard way. The Sufi al-Hallaj went about declaring the revelations of his mystic trances: "I am the Truth!" For thus seeming to blaspheme he was crucified and bludgeoned to death. His colleagues blamed him, not his persecutors: al-Hallaj should have known better; as it was, he had goaded the unenlightened to their too-predictable act of murder. Better to feign ignorance and unbelief so as to protect the truth from those not ready for it, and vice versa! Surely this is the point of the saying, "Do not give dogs what is holy; and do not throw your pearls before swine, lest they trample them under foot and turn to attack you" (Matthew 7:6).

Thomas has proved ready for a higher, secret revelation because he has already come to a higher knowledge unaided. He is already enlightened by having drunk, and having had his consciousness altered by, the spring of water Jesus dispenses. Where were the others when he was dipping out revelation to the thirsty? They were right there alongside Thomas, but the difference was, they *did not thirst*. Thomas, by contrast, was like the Rich Young Ruler, already doing all that righteousness required, yet able to sense there was something *more*, something he still lacked. And he found it, silently coming to the knowledge that this Jesus signified more than his fellows said, indeed more than a mortal man might put into words (2 Corinthians 12:4). And so he shows himself to be ready for more. In Mark the same structure exists: once Peter shows he has grasped the first fundamental, Jesus' messiahship, Jesus is free to explain the next step: the necessity of his impending Passion. But in Thomas, it is the eponymous disciple alone who clears the hurdle and receives the laurel wreath of higher revelation.

Mark deemed "You are he Christ" an adequate Christology. Luke thought "the Christ of God" a better one. And Matthew improved it to "the Christ, the Son of the living God." John had Martha say such things (John 11:27), but for Peter he thought "the Holy One of God" the right confession. Now Thomas rejects all words to convey his Christ. None are adequate; as soon as he might distill his faith into a title, it would, being inevitably inadequate, become an idol. And thus he graduates; Jesus tells him no longer to consider himself Jesus' student. The two are now on the same level, which is why he can vouchsafe special knowledge to him alone among the twelve. This is why this gospel is named for Thomas: it is a guide for the reader whereby he himself may come to share the identity of Jesus, a mere disciple no longer, but a "Thomas," a twin of Jesus, in his own right. The same promise is made in saying 108. We read something like it in John 15:14–15, "You are my friends if you do what I command you. No longer do I call you servants, for a servant does not know what his master is doing; but I have called you friends, for all I have heard from my Father I have made known to you."

But we must ask what the disciples asked Thomas: "What did he tell you?" It might not have been three literal words, but sayings, "he said three things." The word could denote either of these possibilities. And there have been theories. Some suggest a parallel with Pistis Sophia chapter 136, where "Jesus cried out, being with the disciples who were dressed in linen clothes; he turned to the four quarters of the world and said: '*Iao! Iao! Iao!*' Its interpretation is: *Iota*, because the All has proceeded [cf. Thomas 77]; *Alpha*, because it shall return [cf. Ephesians 1:9–10; Colossians 1:16, 20]; *Omega*, because the consummation of all consummations shall take place." Iao was also a divine name or part of one, as in the name of the Demiurge, Ialdabaoth, i.e., Yahve Sabaoth.

Bertil Gärtner, Marco Frenschkowski, and others[66] suggest that Jesus uttered the divine name, the Tetragrammaton, in the form God declared it to Moses at the burning bush: "I-am That I-am," three words in Hebrew. But this is drastically incompatible with the seeming Gnostic character of the rest of the saying. Gnostics, as just noted, despised the Old Testament Jehovah/ Yahve as the bungling and malicious Demiurge. Jesus would scarcely be claiming identity with *him*.

The ancient Naassene Gnostics, devout students of Thomas, hypothesized that the enigmatic three words were *kaulakau*, *saulasau*, and *zeesar*. The first denoted the Primal Man or Heavenly Adam. The second referred to the earthly Adam. The third somehow signified "the Jordan which flows upward," further suggesting the reversal of sexual passion.[67] This last hints at an astonishing parallel with Hindu-Buddhist Tantric mysticism.[68] Just as encratism required celibacy for salvation, Tantra involved ritual sexual intercourse with a partner other than one's spouse. In an exercise maintaining a state of yogic "mere witness" of one's own sexual arousal, the yogi allows the orgasm to bloom up to the very point of ejaculation, only to slam on the brakes at the last second, initiating a shock propelling one into a non-dual state of unitive consciousness. Tantra presupposes a non-dualist cosmology whereby all multiplicity is an illusion. The only reality is Lord Siva, the Impersonal Absolute. Mythically they speak of him sexually uniting with his bride, Shakti (Kali), the coupling producing the vast cosmos of *maya* in which we find ourselves. The goal of the yogi is to attain an experience of the divine Oneness as it was (and still *is*, behind the illusion) before the primordial coupling. The parallel with encratite mythology/soteriology is striking. Encratites, too, traced the woes of life back to a diversity born of the primeval coupling of Adam and Eve and hoped to find salvation by reversing that event in their own cases, being baptized into Christ, the Son of Man, the undivided Adam, and then eschewing sex and all the inequities and iniquities it introduced.

The three words, from which the Naassenes pressed out so much theology, came from Isaiah 28:9–13. They represent the nonsense words (in verses 10 and 13) the prophet attributes to the foreign conquerors to come.

"Whom will he teach knowledge, and to whom will he explain the message? Those who are weaned from the milk, those taken from the breast? For it is *precept upon precept* [*kaulakau*], precept upon precept, *line upon line* [*saulasau*], line upon line, *here a little, there a little* [*zeesar*]." Nay, but by men of strange lips and with an alien tongue the LORD will speak to this people, to whom he has said, "This is rest; give rest to the weary; and this is repose"; yet they would not hear. Therefore the word of the LORD will be to them precept upon precept, precept upon precept, line upon line, line upon line, here a little, there a little; that they may go, and fall backward, and be broken, and snared, and taken.

What attracted Naassene exegetes to this peculiar text? All becomes clear with a glance at verse 9, just before the verse containing the three bits of gibberish: "Whom will he teach knowledge, and to whom will he explain the message?" In this question the Naassenes recognized Jesus entrusting the secret to Thomas. The verse continues: "Those who are weaned from the milk, those taken from the breast." Here the interpreter recognized the newly reborn initiate of Thomas 4, "the young child of seven days." Verse 10, then, is seen to yield the three words themselves. Verse 11 announces that "by men of strange lips and with an alien tongue," i.e., those who know and speak the three glossolalic words themselves, "the Lord will speak to his people, to whom he said, 'This is rest, give rest to the weary, and this is repose." Of course, "rest" and "repose" are major terms in Thomas for the state of salvation and blessedness.

14 Jesus says to them, "If you fast, you will only engender sin for yourselves. And if you pray, you will be damned. And if you give alms, you will only do your spirit harm. And if you journey to any land and travel about the region, if they welcome you, eat whatever they set before you. Cure their sick. For what goes into your

**mouth will not render you profane. Rather, what comes out of your
mouth, that is what will render you profane."**

Here is the original reply of Jesus to the question of the disciples back
in saying 6. The question is artificial, an implicit attempt to set parameters
for the ensuing text as an answer to something. An answer to what? The
question preinterprets it. This happens frequently in the other gospels, too, as
when Luke takes a Q saying of John the Baptist about the Coming One being
greater than himself, and refocuses it with the set-up: "The crowd wondered
in their hearts whether John might be the Christ," a view in fact held by
many of Luke's intended readers, whom he seeks to convert. With this loaded
question, the saying is given a whole new polemical point. The same is true
here in Thomas 6 and 14. As if in a vacuum, the disciples ask Jesus to stipulate
Christian practices of piety. Should they follow the example of the Pharisees?
The whole thing may be a radicalized version of Mark 2:18, where outsiders
ask why Jesus' sect does not follow conventional duties of piety. There, in a
composite of two earlier pericopes (there is a time for feasting and for fasting;
new wineskins for new wine), Jesus appears to abolish fasting as obsolete,
as it is by nature penitential and preparatory to eschatological fulfillment,
which has now arrived, or at least begun.

The question presents, for evaluation, the slate of all three pious practices
(prayer, fasting, almsgiving) and then asks about *kashrut* (kosher laws). In
order to supply a tailor-made answer, Thomas has had to cobble together
disparate bits and pieces. As for kosher rules, namely abolishing them, he
adds a pinch of Mark 7:16 ("There is nothing outside a man, which by going
into him can defile him; but the things which come out of a man are what
defile him.") and a bit of Luke 10:8, part of Luke's version of the Synoptic
Mission Charge: "Whenever you enter a town and they welcome you, eat
what they set before you." Luke 10:8 is a capsule summary of Acts 10, where
disregarding kosher laws is the key to the Gentile Mission. If a Jew is going to
go door to door preaching in Gentile territory, supported by contributions,
well, beggars can't be choosers. "I'm sorry, ma'am, but do you have anything
kosher?" Not likely. You can see the artificiality of the reply Thomas compiles
for Jesus in this scene.

"If you fast, you will only engender sin for yourselves. And if you pray,
you will be damned. And if you give alms, you will only do your spirit
harm." I can see two possible meaning-contexts for these shocking sayings.

First, Jesus may be pictured like Shankara and other mystics who altogether transcended conventional religiosity in favor of an unmediated experience of the Divine. In a flash of Satori, Jesus would have come to realize that these practices which supposedly bring us to God, have come instead to function as ends in themselves, cutting us off from God. We can think of the Buddhist parable of the Raft:[69] once the Dharma has brought you to the farther shore of salvation, why carry it around with you like a turtle shell? It was intended to carry you across, and now, precisely in having fulfilled its purpose, it is obsolete and must be discarded. If one fails to do that, one will find oneself sliding backwards into the stream which one had crossed over! You will, as Thomas warns us elsewhere, miss the presence of the kingdom because you are mistakenly still only *expecting* it.

This makes a good deal of sense, but there is another explanation ready to hand. Just as Luke 10:8 has been taken out of its original context, it may be that saying 14 has been excerpted from some longer discourse in which Jesus upbraided his audience for pious hypocrisy (something Jesus does often enough in the gospels!). His warning is that not only does their unconfessed immorality cause God to ignore their supplications, but their very acts of piety and devotion to God have the opposite of their intended effect in view of their hypocrisy. Here is an example of such fiery discourse from the Third Isaiah: "He who slaughters an ox is like him who kills a man; he who sacrifices a lamb, like him who breaks a dog's neck; he who presents a cereal offering, like him who offers swine's blood; he who makes a memorial offering of frankincense, like him who blesses an idol. These have chosen their own ways, and their soul delights in their abominations" (Isaiah 66:3). Similarly, Thomas 14 may have intended to say, "Because of your hypocrisy, any fasting, prayer, and almsgiving will only get you in deeper! Don't do these things as long as you are making them into an ugly farce!"

15 Jesus says, "When you see him who was not born from woman, fall on your face before him! He is your father!"

Compare saying 50, where we read of "the Light [which] has originated through itself" and which is paralleled with "the living Father," implying that your father" is the heavenly Father, a being of uncreated light. But what is the point of observing that it is he before whom one should bow? Is that not obvious? I submit that what we have here is a reworked version of Matthew

23:9, "Call no man on earth your father, for you have one Father who is in heaven." That Matthean coinage had its meaning in the situation of controversy between Matthew's Christian Judaism and the emerging authority of the Yavneh rabbis, among whom the very terms "Rabbi" ("my teacher") and "Abba" ("father") were just then coming into use. Matthew represents typical sectarian egalitarianism, eschewing the supposed advantages and superior dignity of the learned. For Matthew, the least scribe who is discipled unto the kingdom of heaven (Matthew 13:52) is greater than those who pompously (as he supposes) sit enthroned on the Seat of Moses in the synagogue. Thomas 15 is another version of this saying: no human deserves the respect Jews give to their religious leaders, only God. All religions, no matter how radically egalitarian at the beginning, eventually start to accord reverence to their leaders, kissing their rings and their posteriors if they think it will help them attain a heavenly reward.

(Let me confess that here I fear I may be yielding to the temptation to "naturalize" a strange-sounding saying, missing some esoteric significance in my impatience to understand it. Am I whittling it down to manageable size? On the other hand, I want to bring Occam's Razor to bear on the text: should we be quick to resort to an elaborate explanation when a simpler one lies ready to hand?)

16 Jesus says, "Perhaps people think I have come to spread peace on the earth, not suspecting I have come to create schisms upon the earth: fire, sword, war! For there shall be five in a dwelling, and three shall be pitted against two, father versus son and son versus father, and only the solitary will stand fast."

This is Thomas' version of the Q saying which he would have heard read from Matthew 10:34–36 and/or Luke 12:51–53. They borrowed it in turn from Micah 7:6, "for the son treats the father with contempt, the daughter rises up against her mother, the daughter-in-law against her mother-in-law; a man's enemies are the men of his own house." It is not that someone remembered Jesus quoting Micah; they picked it up from Micah and eventually ascribed it to Jesus by accident. It seemed to apply so well to the challenge facing Christians in times of martyrdom, as we see in the awful martyrology of the second-century Saint Perpetua. Her confession of faith won her an appointment with wild beasts in the Roman arena. She had just given birth, and her family brought the infant to her in her cell on the eve of her execution, begging her to abandon her pointless grandstanding and return to her family who loved her, to her baby who needed her! She wouldn't give them the time of day. She had chosen Jesus and made incredulous enemies of her own household. This still seems pretty fanatical to us, and we would quote to her, "If anyone does not provide for his own, and especially those of his own household, he has denied the faith and is worse than an unbeliever" (1 Timothy 5:8).

Note that Thomas adds his characteristic "standing as single ones," an encratite hallmark. While the encratites certainly encouraged the break-up of families, it is surprising that the least appropriate division, that between father and son, is retained from the Micah/Q saying, when "mother/daughter" and "mother-in-law/daughter-in-law" would have fit the encratite setting much better.

The conclusion, "They *shall stand* . . . ," implies a connection with the "divided house" parable in Mark 3:25, "a house divided against itself *shall not stand.*" Such a contrast would imply a household may survive if they all embrace a holy existence as "solitaries," a situation more easily described than managed, as we read in 1 Corinthians 7. Spouses who agree henceforth to live like angels, neither marrying nor giving in marriage, may find they have bitten off more than they can chew and are inviting scandal.

Saying 16 seems obviously to depend on both Matthew and Luke. It conflates details of both versions, as if careful to leave nothing out. Thomas picks up the "sword" from Matthew 10:34 and "division" from Luke 12:51—plus "fire" from the similar (and near-by) Luke 12:49.

17 Jesus says, "I will give you what eye has never seen, what ear has never heard, what hand has never touched, and what has never even occurred to the mind of man!"

There are a number of versions of this saying in early Christian literature, and by comparison to them, Thomas' is seen not to be the most primitive. 1 Corinthians 2:9 says, "But, as it is written, 'What no eye has seen, nor ear heard, nor the heart of man conceived, what God has prepared for those who love him,' God has revealed to us through the Spirit."

The Acts of Peter ascribes these words to that apostle: "O Jesus Christ, . . . thou art the All, and the All is in thee; and thou art, and there is naught else that is save thee only. Unto him, therefore, do ye also, brethren, flee, and if ye learn that in him alone ye exist, ye shall obtain those things whereof he saith unto you: 'Which neither eye hath seen nor ear heard, neither have they entered into the heart of man.'"

The Apocalypse of John the Lord's Brother, a minor Apocryphon incorporated into an "Encomium on John the Baptist" by Pseudo-Chrysostom, has virtually the same words as the 1 Corinthians version, only, as in Thomas and the Acts of Peter, they are attributed to Jesus, where 1 Corinthians ascribes them to scripture, presumably Isaiah 64:4, "From of old no one has heard or perceived by the ear, no eye has seen a god besides thee, who works for those who wait for him," though it is not that close a fit.

It is striking that none of the other versions has Thomas' extra phrase, "what hand has never touched." Why? Because it is a gnosticizing, docetizing addition. Notice the antithetical parallel to 1 John 1:1, "which we have heard, which we have seen with our eyes, which we have looked upon and *touched with our hands,*" an explicit rebuttal to the docetism condemned in 1 John 4:2, the notion that Jesus has not "come in the flesh." We might almost wonder if Thomas17 is not perhaps a rejoinder to 1 John 1:1.

Finally, there is at least one more version of the saying, this one in the Manichaean Turfan Fragment: "I will give you what you have not seen with your eyes, nor heard with your ears, nor grasped with your hand." But, remember, the Manichaeans used the Thomas Gospel, so it is no surprise if their literature reflects its gnosticized, docetized form.

The saying means to depict Jesus as the revealer of a *gnosis* that is suprasensory, not the product of empirical observation, a heavenly knowledge that could never have occurred to the human mind with its incurably worldly frame of reference—though in that case one might wonder how, even once revealed, it could make any sense to the human mind.

The saying must have been used as a Naassene initiation formula, the mystagogue speaking for Jesus. Note that the 1 Corinthians version occurs in a context of initiation of the "mature" into secret wisdom (verse 7).

18 The disciples say to Jesus, "Tell to us our destiny!" Jesus says, "Oh, does that mean you have discovered your origin, that you ask about your destiny? For where your origin is, there, too, shall be your destiny. Blessed is the one who shall arrive at the beginning, for he shall know the end, and he shall not taste death."

Jesus asks ironically if they have already fathomed the secret of their origin, seeing as how they ask only concerning their destiny. But then they cannot have asked the protological question, since, if they had, they should not need to ask the eschatological question. The solution to the one is the solution to the other. Their origin holds the key to their destiny. Jesus answers the question in simple terms elsewhere in Thomas: "Blessed are the solitary and elect, for you shall find the kingdom; because you come from it, and you shall go there again" (saying 49). "If they ask you, 'Where have you originated?' answer them, 'We have come from the Light . . . we are his children and the elect of the Living Father" (saying 50). In question is the postmortem return of the divine spark to the divine Pleroma (Fullness) from which it was primordially stolen and held captive in the material cosmos. Such salvation could be gained only by the Gnostic elite who understood the secret of their divine origin. I would guess that the disciples' question is derived from the opening of the Olivet Discourse, the Synoptic Apocalypse, probably Matthew's version: "the disciples came to him privately, saying, 'Tell us, when will this be, and what will be the sign of your coming, and of the end of the age?'" (Matthew 24:3).

19a Jesus says, "Blessed is he who existed before he came into being."

This saying rightly belongs with saying 18. It certainly reinforces the Gnostic reading of saying 18, referring it to the preexistence of the soul with God. A longer version appears in the Gospel according to Philip 112:9: "The Lord said . . . , 'Blessed is he who is before he came into being. For he who is, was and shall be.'" Philip's version looks to be the more original since it preserves the complete form of a beatitude, including the reason that so-and-so is considered blessed, e.g., "Blessed are the meek, for they shall inherit the earth" (Matthew 5:5). However, a beatitude does not absolutely require such an explanation, as in Luke 11:27, "Blessed is the womb that bore you and the breasts that nursed you."

19b "If you become my disciples and hear my words, these stones will turn to bread and feed you. For you have five trees in Paradise which are unchanged from summer to winter, and their leaves never fall. Whoever knows them will not taste death.

The image of stones turning to bread need not reflect the Temptation narratives in which Satan suggests Jesus do just this to assuage his hunger.

The connection is suggested by the visual similarity between smooth stones and common barley "loaves," which looked like our dinner rolls. Here the thought is of the miraculous plenty during the millennial kingdom to come, when want and hunger will be no more, as in Luke 6:21, "Blessed are you that hunger now, for you shall be satisfied." The trees in Paradise, yielding fruit all year round, are mentioned in Ezekiel 47:12 and Revelation 22:2. Pistis Sophia 1:3 mentions "the five trees in the treasury of light."[70] The related Books of Jeu (chapters 41, 42, 44, 55) mention them, too. But there being five trees in Paradise (the third heaven, as in 2 Corinthians 12:2–3) is not a uniquely Gnostic theme. It also appears in the Apocalypse of John the Lord's Brother, where luckily, we are told just which trees we are to eat in order to gain eternal life: the date palm, the fig, the cedar (possibly intending the juniper), the apple, and the thourakion tree. "Blessed is every one who shall be worthy to inherit these good things, which eye hath not seen, nor hath the ear heard thereof, nor hath thereof entered into the heart of man. These are the things which God has prepared for those who love him."[71]

> **20 The disciples say to Jesus, "Tell us what the kingdom of heaven is like." He says to them, "It is like a mustard seed, smaller than all the rest of the seeds. But when it falls on the tilled earth, it produces a large branch and becomes lodging for the birds of the sky."**

The parable of the Mustard Seed also occurs in Mark 4:30–32, whence, I judge, it is derived here. The principle difference is that Thomas has the disciples pose the question, whereas Mark makes Jesus himself raise it, rhetorically and reflectively: "What is the kingdom of God like? With what may one compare it?" My guess is that this saying was independent and originally meant that the kingdom cannot be expressed in human language at all, a Marcionite theme. The saying reads almost like a condensed version of this famous statement by Marcion himself:

O Wonder Beyond Wonders,
Rapture, Power, and Amazement is it,
That one can say nothing at all
[About the Gospel]
Nor even conceive of it,
Nor even compare it to anything.

We also observe a gnosticizing modification in that Thomas specifies that the phenomenal growth of the mustard seed is likely only when the seed falls into *tilled* ground, ground made ready by careful preparation, hinting at the catechesis required of the Gnostic initiate.

In Mark, most scholars think the parable means to measure the growth of the work of God in the kingdom of Jesus and its aftermath: it begins unobtrusively amid the excitement over one more itinerant faith healer, a tempest in a teapot, but before too many years have elapsed, the deposit of Jesus has grown to a sizeable organism/organization with room for everyone who seeks it out. As James Breech[72] says, this retrospective character of the parable means its creator is looking back from the far end of the process. It is not a saying of the historical Jesus. On the other hand, there is really no telling what Thomas may have understood it to mean. Could it refer to the fantastic and luxurious (though poisonous) growth of the Demiurge's mud pie cosmos once the photons stolen from the Pleroma have been scattered into it like potent seed into a fallow field?

21 Mariam says to Jesus, "Who are your disciples like?" He says, "They are like young children who have made a fort for themselves in someone else's field. When the owners of the field come, they will say, 'Get out of our field!' They strip off their clothes in order to vacate it to them and to return their field to them.

As Jonathan Z. Smith[73] shows, this is a baptismal text. That is, it used to be read or repeated at baptismal ceremonies. The "children" are the new initiates (cf. 1 Peter 2:2, "Like newborn babies, thirst for the pure spiritual milk, that by it you may grow up to salvation."). The "field not theirs" is this world, under the dominion of the *archons* of this age, the evil Powers from whom Christ has saved us. The "owners of the field" are, of course, the archons themselves. (And it was not only Gnostics who believed in malevolent angels barring the way of the soul's ascent; many Jews, Jewish Christians, Mithraists, etc., believed in them, too.)[74] In the parable's story, we are to picture the mischievous children "mooning" the irate owners (like Mr. Wilson in a Dennis the Menace cartoon) as they scatter and run away. This stands for the baptismal candidate's renunciation of Satan and his Powers (still part of baptism rites today) in the act of baptism, which entailed nudity, since the baptized had to trample his or her clothing, symbolizing the "old man," before entering the baptismal water of the "womb" and being reborn. Emerging from the water, he or she would be given a white linen robe to symbolize the new self in Christ. And naturally the change in vesture also symbolized the sloughing off of the sinful body of flesh at death and the donning of the "spiritual body" at the future resurrection. The Christian had died with Christ and risen with him already in an anticipatory form. Colossians 2:11–15 speaks in the same terms:

> In him also you were circumcised, not in a physical sense, but by being divested of the flesh; this is Christ's way of circumcision. For in baptism you were buried with him, in baptism also you were raised to life with him through your faith in the active power of God who raised him from the dead. And though you were dead because of your sins and because you were morally uncircumcised, he has made you alive with Christ. For he has forgiven us all our sins; he has cancelled the bond that pledged us to the decrees of the law. It stood against us, but he has set it aside, nailing it to the cross. On that cross he discarded the cosmic powers and authorities like a garment; he made a public spectacle of them and led them as captives in his triumphal procession.

Their fleshly bodies are part of the material cosmos of the Demiurge and his *archons*, and salvation requires the abandonment of both, beginning with asceticism and monastic isolation here and now. We will require this background again for sayings 22 and 37.

For this reason I say: If the master of the house is forewarned of the burglar's coming, he will stay awake before he arrives and will forestall his digging through into his house, or his kingdom, to make off with his vessels. You, then, must watch out for the world. Arm yourself with great strength in case the thieves discover a way to get to you, because if you know of an opportunity, you can be sure they will find it, too.

This is a saying parallel to the Q saying Matthew 24:42–44 // Luke 12:39–40. But whereas that saying urges vigilance in the face of the coming of the Son of Man in judgment, Thomas' version (obviously secondary from its cumbersome, overloaded character) eliminates the eschatological element in line with Thomas' redactional interest in realized eschatology. Now the reader is warned against incursions of "the world," the enemy of spirituality in any age.

We also detect elements of the "Strong Man" parable in Mark 3:27, itself based on Isaiah 49:24–25: "Can the prey be taken from the mighty, or the captives of a tyrant be rescued? Surely, thus says Yahve: 'Even the captives of the mighty shall be taken, and the prey of the tyrant be rescued, for I will contend with those who contend with you, and I will save your children.'" Note the references to "strength" and to "carrying away his goods." We also catch an echo of Luke 12:35, "Let your loins be girded and your lamps burning," an adjacent vigilance text in Luke, and a uniquely Lukan ("L") saying. This again implies Thomas is memory-quoting Luke as well as Mark, not drawing on independent but parallel tradition.

Let there be among you a man of discernment like the one who saw when the fruit was ripe, came quickly with his sickle in his hand, and reaped it. Whoever has ears to hear, let him hear!

Here is an abbreviated version of the otherwise uniquely Markan parable of the Seed Growing Secretly (Mark 4:26–29), giving only the conclusion (Mark 4:29). The "man of understanding" is the one who is able to "discern the signs," the significance, "of the present time" (Matthew 16:3). He is able to tell when the iron is at the right heat to strike. In Mark the framework was apocalyptic. The apocalyptic image of reaping is widespread: 4 Ezra (2 Esdras) 4; James 5:7–8; Revelation 14:14–16. But does Mark compare the situation to that in James, where the reader is told to be patient since the harvest must inevitably come, even if not soon?[75] Or is the point like that in Revelation, where we are to recognize that the appointed time has finally arrived? The harvest of the human race is at hand. Therefore repent! Can't you see the lateness of the hour? Which does he mean? Well, that is why discernment is required!

The call for understanding is also a stock feature of apocalyptic literature, as in Mark 13:14 and Revelation 13:18 and 17:9. That attests the origin of the apocalyptic genre, with all its strange-sounding ciphers and symbols, in scribal circles. They clothed their revelations (actually speculations) in puzzle form so only those worthy of their mysteries could penetrate them.[76]

22 Jesus saw children being nursed. He says to his disciples, "These nursing children are like those who enter the kingdom." They say to him, "Are we, then, to become children in order to enter the kingdom?" Jesus says to them, "When you make the

two sexes one, and when you make the inner reality as the outer appearance and the outer body as the inner spirit and the heaven above as the earth below, and when you make the male and the female into a single one, so that the male will no more be male nor the female be female; when you make eyes in the place of an eye, and a hand in the place of a hand and a foot in the place of a foot; an image in the place of an image, then you shall enter the kingdom."

This saying is parallel in many ways to the sayings complex on display in Mark 9:33–10:16. With the first part of the Thomas passage ("Jesus saw children being nursed. He says to his disciples, 'These nursing children are like those who enter the kingdom.' They say to him, 'Are we, then, to become children in order to enter the kingdom?'") compare Mark 10:14–15 ("But when Jesus saw it, he was indignant and said to them, 'Let the children come to me, do not hinder them; for to such belongs the kingdom of God! Amen, I tell you: whoever does not welcome the kingdom of God like a child shall not enter it.'") and, less clearly perhaps, Mark 9:37 ("Whoever welcomes one such little child in my name welcomes me; and whoever welcomes me welcomes him who sent me.") and 42 ("Whoever trips up one of these little ones who believe in me, he would be better off weighted with a huge millstone and thrown overboard.'").

Once we turn to the rest of saying 22, we may be surprised to see that, for all its off-putting strangeness, it is only equivalent to another portion of the same Markan complex. With Thomas' "When you make the two sexes one" and "make the male and the female into a single one, so that the male will no more be male nor the female be female" compare Mark 10:6–8, "But the pattern of creation is this: 'Male and female he created them.' And 'This is why a man will leave father and mother, and the two shall be one flesh.' This means they are no longer two but one flesh." The encratite interpretation I am pursuing in this commentary would imply a reversal of the sense of the Genesis passage (2:24) Mark quotes: instead of the unity of the sexes in marital intercourse, encratites would seek to undo that union and its results, by abolishing marriage and sexual union—and so, I think, would Thomas.

And the rest of the strange conditions, they for the most part come from Matthew and Mark: "when you make the inner reality as the outer appearance and the outer body as the inner spirit and the heaven above as the earth below" reflects Matthew 6:10 ("may your kingdom come; let your will come to pass as in heaven also on earth") and 23:27–28 ("Woe to you, scribes and Pharisees, hypocrites! Because you are just like freshly whitewashed graves, which, while indeed appearing externally to be beautiful, are filled inside with the bones of the dead and with all impurity! Thus you, too, indeed appear externally to others to be righteous, but internally you are stuffed with hypocrisy and disdain for the Torah!"). As for Thomas' "when you make eyes in the place of an eye," it amounts merely to Mark 9:47: cultivating new habits, no longer coveting or lusting. When Thomas speaks of "making a hand in place of a hand," it is no more mysterious than the advice of Mark 10:43 to undertake honest manual ("hand") labor, instead of stealing, just as in Ephesians 4:28. To put a foot in the place of a foot means the same as Mark 9:45: new habits of not trespassing, no more sneaking into stores after hours, no more liaisons with your neighbor's wife. Native Aramaic speaker George M. Lamsa[77] explained how "plucking out the eye," "cutting off the hand and foot" remain common idioms for repenting of lust or covetousness, of theft and trespassing. The idea is set forth plainly in Romans 6:19, "just as you once yielded your members to impurity and to greater and greater iniquity, so now yield your members to righteousness for sanctification."

We need not stumble at "making an image in the place of an image." This, too, speaks only of Christian initiation, the replacement of an old self with a new one, and in the same terms as saying 22, and it does so with the same group of ideas we find in Colossians 3:5–11 (which also recalls the "cutting off offending members" metaphor of Mark 9:43–47):

So *amputate your members* on the earth: prostitution, impurity, passions, illicit desire, and covetousness which amounts to idolatry. It is because of these things the wrath of God is on its way. Indeed, this is how you used to behave, when you lived this way. But now cleanse your mouths of all rage, anger, malice, blasphemy, and abuse. Do not lie to one another, since you have stripped off the old self with his duplicitous ways. Having *donned the new self*, being renewed by means of enlightenment, *in the image of the one who created it*, where "Jew" and "Greek" have no place, neither "circumcision" nor "uncircumcision," nor "Barbarian" nor "Scythian," "slave," "free," but Christ is all and is in all alike.

If we had grown up hearing this saying from the pulpit or in Sunday School classes, it would not sound strange to us at all. Maybe it's not too late.

23 Jesus says, "I shall choose you, one out of a thousand, and two out of ten thousand, and they shall stand fast as a single one."

A similar numerical comparison occurs in Psalm 91:7. There the notion is the invulnerability of the one who invokes the protective names of God. Here some sort of elite status is promised, but what? I cannot help linking this saying to saying 62: "I entrust my mysteries to those who are worthy of my mysteries." Understood in this way, the saying would be preparing the ground (fictively, in retrospect) for Gnostical claims to have received a chain of transmission restricted by Jesus to a tiny fragment of his disciples, a clever way to explain why most Christians had never heard of the strange-sounding teaching in question. This way, if you object to the newly announced teaching as heretical, you are made to sound like a dolt (or the successor of dolts from whom it had originally been withheld).

But it is also possible the saying refers to the future judgment and envisions only a tiny minority of humanity surviving it. "Many are called, but few are chosen" (Matthew 22:14).

24 His disciples say, "Show us the place where you are, for it is needful for us to seek it." He says to them, "Whoever has ears to hear, let him hear! Within a man of light there is light, and he illuminates the whole world. When he fails to shine, there is darkness."

The disciples' question seems to presuppose the Last Supper discourse of John, especially 14:3–5, and may have been influenced by it. But then again, questioning an already exalted Jesus is a basic genre convention of resurrection discourses. Bertil Gärtner has suggested that Thomas is intended as one, and James M. Robinson[78] has pointed out that John's Last Supper discourse must originally have been imagined as placed after the resurrection (minus a few redactional verses which anchor it in its present Johannine Passion context).

Jesus' reply was originally an aphorism, the set-up question being a subsequent addition in order to pre-interpret the saying. The saying combines Matthew 5:14 with Matthew 6:22–23. It thus combines the idea of a righteous person lighting up the world by his or her good example with the notion of the skewed and distorted perspective of the one with the "evil eye," i.e., a miserly squint or a jaundiced eye. "Man of light" denotes the same thing as a "son of light" in the Dead Sea Scrolls and Luke 16:8: a righteous person who stands out in contrast with the wicked darkness all around him.

What is the result of adding this saying as an answer to the originally unrelated question? The disciples imagine the Risen Christ to be manifesting himself from heaven, where they hope one day to arrive. But he tells them he is the divine light within, if they will but recognize it. Again, the kingdom of heaven is within you.

But we might also read the question and answer as parallel to the last words of the Buddha. As he lay dying from accidental food poisoning, his disciples crowded around, pressing on him questions, since it would be their last opportunity to ask them. His only response was:

> Therefore, Ananda, be ye lamps unto yourselves, be ye a refuge to yourselves. Betake yourselves to no external refuge. Hold fast to the Truth as a lamp; hold fast to the Truth as a refuge. Look not for a refuge in anyone beside yourselves.[79]

Had they imbibed nothing of his wisdom? Had he not ignited the radiance of enlightenment within them? Then they can answer their own questions. Maybe that is what Jesus means here: when he departs, if he has done his job, they won't need him anymore—or if they do, they can always find him *within*.

25 Jesus says, "Love your brother as your own life. Guard him like the pupil of your eye."

The apple of your eye is the pupil of your eye. No one is slow to safeguard it! You ought to be just as careful about the welfare of your fellow disciple, or your friend, or your relative. Compare Ephesians 5:28, "husbands should love their wives like their own bodies. He who loves his wife loves himself. For no one ever lived who hated his own body, but he nourishes it and cherishes it."

Kahlil Gibran's masterpiece *Jesus the Son of Man*[80] features an imaginary reminiscence by Peter of his Master that might have been inspired by this saying, had Gibran known it.

> Your neighbor is your other self dwelling behind a wall. In understanding, all walls shall fall down. Who knows but that your neighbor is your better self wearing another body? See that you love him as you would love yourself. He too is a manifestation of the Most High, whom you do not know.

26 Jesus says, "You see the speck in your brother's eye, but you do not see the beam in your own eye. When you remove the beam from your own eye, then you will see clearly enough to pick the mote out of your brother's eye."

The connection of this saying with number 25 is not far to seek. Both treat of your brother, your eye, and caring for your brother. But this piece of advice, familiar from Matthew 7:3–5, takes a different approach. We are quickest to notice in others the same faults we ourselves have, only somehow ours are hidden from us! Your advice on dealing with such a problem may be wise, though you have never thought to apply it to your own case. Or you may not have a clue what to suggest, as attested by your continuing to suffer from the same problem.

27 Jesus says, "If you do not abstain from the world, you will not find the kingdom; if you do not observe the seventh day as a sabbath, you will not see the Father."

The text has, literally, "fast from the world," but I think the qualifier "from the world" implies more than just fasting from food, especially since saying 14 forbids that sort of fasting in no uncertain terms. I should think the point is, like the Old Testament prophets, to condemn the special religious discipline as a grudging token behavior, as if observing it makes it all right to do as one wishes the rest of the time. "Now that I've got *that* out of the way . . ." So drop the hypocritical observance and embrace the larger attitude symbolized by it: abstaining from the world, cultivating an inner detachment from it, much the same stance of which we read in Galatians 6:14, "the world has been crucified to me, and I to the world." Again, keep in mind where the Gospel of Thomas was discovered: a monastery. These men were certainly "fasting from the world," and not merely from some favorite snack. Colossians 2:16–23, alludes to this attitude of dropping the outward token to embrace the inner reality, exchanging the ritual shadow for the ethical or mystical substance:

> So don't let anyone condemn you in dietary matters or for not observing feasts or new moon celebrations or sabbaths, all this being no more than a charade pointing to things to come, Christ being the reality. Let no one deprive you of your rights by an appeal to self-abasement and the worship of angels, blundering into matters he has hallucinated, his

head being filled with the phantoms of his own imagination, out of touch with the Head, from whom the whole body, being nourished and knitted together by means of its various joints and ligaments, will grow with God's green thumb. So if you have died with Christ as far as the elemental spirits are concerned, why are you, like those native to the cosmos, living by decrees? "Do not touch, nor taste, nor handle." These all pertain to things destined to perish as they are used, and they stem from man-made commandments and teachings. Such things, it is true, have a reputation for wisdom by way of self-imposed devotions, self-abnegation and severity toward the body, but they have no merit as they merely satisfy the cravings of the flesh in their own, more subtle, way.

"Finding the kingdom" and "seeing the Father" are obviously two ways of saying the same thing, so we should expect that "keeping the Sabbath as Sabbath" (as the text reads literally) should mean pretty much the same thing as "fasting from the world." Accordingly, the Messianic Brotherhood translation has "unless you keep the whole week as Sabbath" (the word "Sabbath" meaning, after all, "seven" or "seven-day week"). This possibility has significant implications, especially in light of Thomas' teaching about attaining the condition of heavenly "rest" and "repose" here and now, as in Hebrews 3:11–4:11. "For whoever enters God's rest also ceases from his labors as God did from his" (Hebrews 4:10). One could take this as a reference to Reformation "faith versus works" soteriology, or to the yogic principle of "mere witness," an inner detachment from external works, so that one "acts apart from the fruits of action" and accrues no karma, good or bad. Either would make a lot of sense here. (Perhaps ultimately they amount to the same thing anyway.)

28 Jesus says, "I stood there in the middle of the world, and in flesh I appeared to them. I found no one among them athirst. And my heart was broken for the human race, because they are blind in their minds and do not realize that they have entered the world empty and that they are happy enough to leave the world the same way. But now they are in a stupor. When they have snapped out of it, then surely they will repent."

This, as Davies points out, is a perfect bit of Wisdom Christology, of which traces may be found in 1 Corinthians 1:30; Colossians 1:15–17; and Hebrews 1:3. If one expands Jewish Wisdom speculation to include Philo of Alexandria, we would have to classify John, along with Thomas, as full of Wisdom Christology. Not surprisingly, in both these last cases, Wisdom has crossed over the hazy line to Gnosis. At any rate, Jesus is depicted here as Wisdom as personified in Proverbs chapters 8 and 9, coming into the world to announce the free availability of her instruction to all who may seek it. But, whereas Proverbs leaves the offer open, later works like 1 Enoch are more negative, adding to the Wisdom personification the denouement that, after getting nothing but a cold shoulder, Wisdom abandoned the world and returned to heaven where she would be appreciated! "Wisdom found no place where she might dwell; then a dwelling-place was assigned her in the heavens. Wisdom went forth to make her dwelling among the children of men, and found no dwelling-place: Wisdom returned to her place, And took her seat among the angels" (1 Enoch 42:1–2). Thomas 28 comes awfully close to this pessimism but holds out a ray of hope: surely mankind will eventually awaken from its self-imposed stupor—don't you think?

What about the appearance of Jesus in the midst of humanity "in flesh"? Does that not remove the text from any Gnostic frame of reference? No. For we can find the incarnation also in the overtly Gnostic Hymn of the Pearl ("I snatched up the Pearl, and turned to the House of my Father. Their filthy and unclean garments I stripped off and left in their country."). Some Gnostics thought the assumption of sinful flesh too degrading for Christ to endure, while others viewed it as demonstrating the lengths to which Christ would go to redeem the lost sparks of light. There was a wide range of thought on the question. What exactly was incarnationism, anyway? The view of Basilides, Cerinthus, and others, that the Christ-*aion* had temporarily come to rest in the human Jesus, whom he used as a channeler, could be viewed as a type of Nestorianism, not so much a denial of incarnationism as a variety of it.

29 Jesus says, "If the flesh has come into existence because of the spirit, what a marvel! But if the spirit exists because of the body, that is the greatest of marvels! But I marvel at how this great wealth has come to dwell in such squalor."

Jesus reflects on the marvel of the soul/body dualism, how incompatible the two seem. It is so strange, so outrageous, the last thing one would have expected, that he can only guess how it has come about! And no guess seems very plausible. Was the body created to house, or perhaps even to imprison, the soul? One may find this idea in Plato, Origen, and the Kabbalah. Or was the soul created (or imparted) in order to give life to the body, hitherto inert, as in the Nag Hammadi retellings of Genesis? This seems less likely ("the marvel of marvels!"), since then you would have the greater created for the sake of the lesser.[81]

The flesh as "poverty" (I render it "squalor") recalls saying 3, where we learn that the one without benefit of knowledge of his own divine nature (and thus lacking divine nature) is not only "*in* poverty" but *is* poverty, i.e., mere flesh.

The enigma considered in this saying is central to Hinduism of many stripes as well. It is a way of explaining the existence of suffering. Vedic cosmogony has it that there are two types of entity: *Purusha* (souls) and *prakriti* (matter). *Purusha* are practically individual deities, bubbles of pure, self-contemplating sentience, omniscient yet unaware of external events, for this would render them capable of being conditioned or affected by them. Matter, on the other hand, has three possible modes latent within it: matter may be *obtuse and inert, active and energetic,* and *refined and intelligent.* Such consciousness is not the unchanging *Purusha* (or *atman*), for it is (as modern neuro-science tells us) purely chemical in nature, i.e., material. This is the shifting, changing, suffering ego-self. Somehow the souls and matter have become unnaturally mixed together. The entry of the souls into matter has stirred up the latter, causing the three modes to emerge and combine, yielding all the diverse creatures we see. Suffering is a consequence of the mixing. The ego-consciousness would feel no pain if it were not augmented and energized by the soul (*Purusha, atman*) within it. It is as if the ego-self were the flashlight, the trapped soul being the battery. Without inserting the battery in the flashlight, you see nothing. Once you insert it, the battery itself sees nothing, but the flashlight illumines everything in its path. The individual perceives (experiences) pain because of the "consciousness-raising" caused by the soul, while the soul itself, being unconditioned, still experiences nothing. The goal is to learn the difference between the two and to identify with the unconditioned, divine *Purusha*. When you attain this stage, you will no more experience pain (or you can think yourself into a state of "mere witness" of the pain). Breaking the link between the soul and material consciousness guarantees no more reincarnation, precisely as in Gnosticism which parallels the whole system and may have an historical connection with it.

30 Jesus says, "Wherever there are three gathered in the name of God, they are not without God; where there are two, or even one, I am with him."

My version is a reconstruction. The Coptic text reads, "Where there are three gods, they are gods . . ." This just has to be a copyist error. I am switching over to the form of the saying in the Oxyrhynchus papyrus fragment of Thomas. That original version has also been split between Coptic saying 30 and the conclusion of Coptic saying 77. This first half reflects both Matthew 18:20 ("For where two or three are gathered in my name, there am I in the midst of them.") as well as Matthew's probable source, Pirke Aboth, 3:7:

> When ten people sit together and occupy themselves with the Torah, the Shekinah abides among them, as it is said, "God standeth in the congregation of the godly." And whence can it be shown that the same applies to five? Because it is said, "He hath founded his band upon the earth." And whence can it be shown that the same applies to three? Because it is said, "He judgeth among the judges." And whence can it be shown that the same applies to two? Because it is said, "Then they that feared the Lord spake one to the other; and the Lord hearkened, and heard." And whence can it be shown that the same applies even to one? Because it is said, "In every place where I cause my Name to be remembered I will come unto thee and I will bless thee."

31 Jesus says, "No prophet is welcome in his own village; no physician cures those who know him."

There are two ways of looking at this well known saying. With sympathy toward the prophet, one may judge his boyhood acquaintances as petty and envious of the fame that he has attained, while they are still undistinguished townies. With skepticism toward the supposed prophet, one may suspect that those who have known him all along know him too well to take his claims of prophetic dignity and inspiration seriously. One thinks of Joseph Smith, founder of the Church of Jesus Christ of Latter-day Saints. Among his own townspeople he had to overcome the reputation of being a huckster and a faker, using a seer stone to find buried treasure, which always seemed to elude him.[82] No wonder he was able to make greater headway among those who did not know him from Adam. To them, he appeared as if from heaven, with no previous baggage.

Thomas' version looks like the original of the saying in Mark 6:4. One reason to think so is the Semitic form of the saying: it uses synthetic parallelism, the repetition of the first item in different words as the second. But that is not all. There is something very odd about the story in which this proverb appears:

> And he went out from there and comes into his birthplace, and his disciples follow him. And when a sabbath came, he began to teach in the synagogue, and the audience was astonished, saying, "Whence do these things come to him?" "And what wisdom is given him by God!" "And what powerful deeds come about through his hands!" "Isn't this the carpenter, the son of Mary and brother of James and Jose and Judah and Simon?" "And aren't his sisters here with us?" Yet they were scandalized at him. And Jesus said to them, "It just goes to show that the only place a prophet gets no respect is his own birthplace, among his relatives, in his dwelling." And he found himself unable to perform any powerful deeds except that, laying his hands on a few sick, he cured them. And he was shocked at their lack of faith. And he made the circuit of the villages teaching.

Notice that the story is going fast in one direction, then slams on the brakes and goes into another. Jesus speaks, and the crowd is delighted: local boy makes good! They love what he says and does. And in all likelihood, the original reference of "What powerful deeds come about through his hands!" was to healings he performed on the spot, though Luke 4:23 tries to harmonize that implication with the failure of Jesus to heal anyone according to Mark 6:5 by making the reference to previous miracles reported from Capernaum (even though Luke has recorded no visit there! Jesus is fresh from the Temptation in the desert). But no sooner does Mark describe the adulation of the hometown crowd than he arbitrarily has them take great offense at the native son! We are as shocked as Jesus himself that he can heal no one there. Why the inconsistency between the beginning and the end of the Markan passage? As Bultmann[83] suggests, Mark inherited a story about the glad reception accorded Jesus at home (a story, I would guess, culminating in the list of the Pillars of the Jerusalem Church, the brothers of Jesus, and tending to reinforce their authority). But he also had to make some sense of the proverb about prophets and healers among their own acquaintances. How was he going to harmonize them? Simply by positing that somehow, for some reason, the crowd *just turned ugly*. Then Mark turned the second part of the old saying into more narrative, narrative in which Jesus in fact fails to heal anyone.

32 Jesus says, "A city erected atop a high mountain and fortified cannot fall to a siege, but then neither can it be hidden."

This is a secondary version of the saying found in Matthew 5:14b: "A city set on a hill cannot be hid," where it has been linked with other sayings about being a good example to others. Any of these sayings may easily have started out in a Jewish context, where it would describe the unique duty of Jews to witness by their lives and faith the true God whose people they are. The application to Christians would be secondary. This one certainly seems to have a Jewish coloring, as the imagery, especially as embellished by Thomas, recalls that of the pilgrimage song in Psalm 122:3–4, where mighty Jerusalem, built upon Mount Zion, is said to be the city "to which the tribes go up" at festival time. To it one day the heathen nations will stream to learn the Torah (Isaiah 2:2–4; Micah 4:1–2).

The application of the Jerusalem metaphor to the Christian community also occurs in Galatians 4:25–26 and Revelation 21:2. In both cases, Christians are compared to the new or heavenly Jerusalem, as if to admit they have no claim on the literal, geographical Jerusalem, something it might have come in handy to remember back in the time of the Crusades.

Finally, the addition of the fortification imagery seems to introduce something of a trade-off: a mountaintop city is a conspicuous target, yet a defensible one. Perhaps the point of application to the individual reader is to suggest that, once one takes a public stand for Christ, one invites ridicule or persecution, but that one will be well able to withstand it.

33 Jesus says, "What you hear whispered in your ear by two different people, preach that from your housetops. For no one kindles a lamp only to place it underneath a bushel, nor does he put it in a hiding place, but he sets it on the lamp-stand, so all coming in or out may see its light."

Here is another version of a saying found in Matthew 10:27 / Luke 12:3 as well as in Matthew 5:15 / Luke 11:33. In the Sermon on the Mount it occurs adjacent to the "city set on a hill" saying, and it is from memory of this that the juxtaposition of this saying with 32 stems. Again, we see that Thomas is derivative from someone's recollection of the canonical gospels, not an independent source. The saying also appears in Mark 4:21 and Luke 8:16 in context with the "nothing hidden not to be revealed" passage. On the whole, the Thomas saying appears to be a parable reinforcing the command to broadcast the once-secret teaching of Jesus when the time is ripe. In other words, it is an apologetic for new teachings one wishes to attribute to Jesus but which no one has heard before. "If Jesus taught *this*, then why have I never heard it up till now?"

Why does it stipulate that a proper saying for propagation must come from two sources? The Coptic text is not exactly clear. What it says literally is "What you hear whispered in your ear," followed by a scribal addition in the margin, "and in your other ear." This is said to be an idiom for esoteric teaching, as if you must hear the exoteric meaning with your outer or fleshly ear and the inner, esoteric meaning in the inner ear. But it might possibly mean to recall the old juristic rule (Deuteronomy 17:6; 19:15) that every testimony must be corroborated if it is to prove anything, in which case we would have here an ancient occurrence of the form-critical criterion of "multiple attestation." But of course, the marginal words might as easily be a comment by a scribe as a restoration of words a previous scribe had accidentally omitted.

34 Jesus says, "When a blind man leads a blind man, both of them end up in the pit."

This one is a familiar mini-parable (a "similitude") pointing out the sad absurdity, in a Three Stooges-sort of way, of unenlightened religious leadership. The last person you want to hire as your guide is someone who knows the way less well than you do! They may know scripture but are clueless how to apply it in practical terms. They may be masters of rhetoric but have nothing edifying to tell you. Or, and I suspect this is what the monkish Gnostics had in mind, they may be unwitting servants of the Demiurge and the *archon*s, teachers of the worldly laws these beings have promulgated to secure the worship of the benighted human race for themselves.

35 Jesus says, "It is impossible to enter a strong man's dwelling and take it by force without first tying his hands. Then one may pillage the house."

Though a glance at this saying reminds one of saying 21, the point is not the same. There the saying is addressed to the vulnerable one and recommends vigilance. Here the words are directed instead to the invader, the attacker, as advice on how to approach a difficult job. It is, I believe, a bit of training for exorcism, a la Mark 9:28–29.

In both Synoptic versions of the Beelzebul Controversy, the scribes charge Jesus with "casting out demons by the prince of the demons," and he refutes the charge. But he does it in quite different ways. Mark 3:23 has him begin with a rhetorical question, "How can Satan cast out Satan?" The Q source underlying Matthew and Luke lacks this and instead substitutes two subsequent hypotheticals: "If I cast out demons by Beelzebul, by whom do your sons cast them out?" (Matthew 12:27 / Luke 11:19) and "If I cast out demons by the finger of God, then the kingdom of God has come upon you" (Luke 11:20; Matthew 12:28 has "Spirit" instead of "finger"). This complex is plainly a secondary midrash applying to Jesus' case the Exodus story of Moses' triumph over Pharaoh's magicians who finally had to acknowledge Moses' superiority, saying, "This is the finger of God" (Exodus 8:18–19). If you omit both Mark's rhetorical question and Q's questions and midrash, you get close to the primitive tradition lying behind them both. And what's left is no refutation at all! Indeed, we must take Jesus' words as an admission and a *defense* of his practice of "binding the strong man." In other words, he *did* bind the power of Beelzebul to do his bidding. He was at first regarded not as the Son of God, but rather, as Celsus and the rabbis maintained, a magician who used the power of Satan against Satan, so that Satan's kingdom would come crashing down.

I have just performed exegetical surgery to uncover what I imagine to be the original meaning of the saying, but can we expect that ancient readers or the Thomas redactor did the same? The core saying by itself might have continued on in oral tradition alongside the written and augmented versions. But I think it would have been by no means difficult to see the force of the "binding" language, and since Christian magic continued for some centuries,[84] I am guessing that the saying, even in its Synoptic versions, was still clear enough in its implications.

36 Jesus says, "Do not spare a thought from morning till evening or from evening to morning for what you will wear."

This saying is a cut version of the one in Matthew 6:25, "Therefore I tell you, do not be anxious about your life, what you shall eat or what you shall drink, nor about your body, what you shall put on. Is not life more than food, and the body more than clothing?"

The Matthean mentions of food and drink as worrisome necessities have been omitted here in order to sharpen the saying's focus, not for its own sake, but to make it more appropriate to introduce saying 37, which has to do with clothing, though in a different sense.

Who was originally in view as the audience of this saying? It might be directed to the wandering charismatics[85] who prophesied in the name of Jesus, the itinerants dismissed sarcastically in 2 Corinthians 11:5; 12:11 as "super-apostles."[86] The Synoptic Mission Charge (Mark 6:711; Matthew 10:5–23; Luke 9:1–5; 10:1–16) was their charter, and they were to subsist on whatever their hearers donated, just like Buddhist monks and ancient Cynics. But the saying makes sense as directed to householders and parents, too, in short, regular laity. One may work for a living and still trust God for provision, knowing that, in his providence, it all comes from him anyway. Will there be enough? Can we get by in times of economic reversal? The saying warns us that if we focus all our attention on necessities, we will have our noses to the grindstone to the point where we begin to dehumanize ourselves, as if money were all that mattered. One may be rich or poor and make that mistake. One may be an itinerant apostle or a family man and not make that mistake.

The most interesting point of divergence from the Matthean original is the note about not being concerned *all day* with matters of mundane provision. What we look to have here is a typical amelioration, a whittling down of a radical saying, as in Matthew's command not to be angry with one's brother (Matthew 5:22) to which obliging scribes have added "without cause." Or the Markan prohibition of divorce on any grounds (Mark 10:11–12) to which Matthew has added the mitigating clause, "except for immorality" (Matthew 5:32; 19:9). Similarly, I think the Coin in the Fish's Mouth tale (Matthew 17:24–26) originally encouraged non-payment of the temple tax, but that subsequent Christians found a way to amend the story (adding verse 27) so as to avoid needless friction with other Jews who perceived their stance as arrogant sectarianism—which it was. In all such cases, the original rigorous version was found to be just too stringent, too difficult a demand (especially as the Christian community began to reassimilate familiar social mores, formerly rejected, as always happens in the second generation of a new sect.

So, just as never getting angry with another seemed too tall an order (what about "righteous indignation"?), so did it seem to be asking too much for people not to be at all concerned for life's necessities. So maybe all Jesus had meant was being carefree in faith, ah, *most* of the time. Not all.

> **37 His disciples say, "When will you be revealed to us, and when will we see you return in glory?" Jesus says, "When you are able to take off your clothes without shame and trample them under-foot like innocent children, then you shall be ready to behold the son of the Living One without fear.**

The question concerns the Parousia (what we call the Second Coming), and the effect of the saying is to sweep away all futuristic expectation, precisely as in John 14:22–23, "Judas, not the False One, says to him, 'Lord, what can have happened, that you are about to manifest yourself to us, and not to the world at large?' Jesus answered and said to him, 'If anyone loves me, he will keep my commandment, and my Father will love him, and we will come to him and we will make our dwelling with him.'" As I suggested in the introduction, Thomas is far from innocent of futuristic eschatology, as if no one had yet introduced it into the tradition, but rather dismissive of it. Here the disciples are made to speak with the voice of the *psuchikoi*, the pew potatoes, conventional believers. In this saying, the resurrection transpires *now* in baptism, through which gate one enters the angelic existence already here in earth. (This view comes in for condemnation in 1 Corinthians 15, as well as in 2 Timothy 2:18.) Again, Edenic, pre-sexual innocence is the prerequisite for salvation. And the saying is, once again, a baptismal formula,[87] as implied in the reference to disrobing, ritually trampling one's clothes as the symbol of the old, unregenerate self in order to put on the white linen signifying the renewed, reborn, risen identity, or the resurrection body, already beginning to gestate within, to be revealed in glory one day (Romans 8:19–23). Additionally, the old clothes represented the demons which dominated one's former life as a sinner, as well as the "coats of skin" with which God had clothed Adam and Eve, namely the fleshly body that imprisons the soul.

A similar saying occurs in the Gospel according to the Egyptians. It takes the form of a dialogue between Jesus and Salome, as in Thomas, saying 61. "Now when Salome asked when what she had inquired about would be known [i.e., become manifest], the Lord said, 'When you have trampled on the garment of shame, and when the two become one, and the male with the female is neither male nor female" (Clement of Alexandria, *Stromateis* 3, 13.921–93.1). See also the parallel in Thomas 22, also a baptism saying. In saying 21, which has the same themes, Mary, not Salome, is the interlocutor. It almost seems as if Thomas 21, 22. 37 are an expanded version of the saying from the Gospel according to the Egyptians. Taken together, these four sayings convey the idea of a teaching on the transcendence of sex difference through baptism, a teaching handed down from the women disciples ("Mary, Salome, the disciples").

> **38 Jesus says, "You have many times desired to hear these words which I speak to you, and you have no one else from whom to hear them. The days are coming when you will seek me and you will not find me, so take advantage while you have it."**

This one reflects four distinct canonical sayings: First, *Matthew* 13:17: "Amen, I tell you: many prophets and saints longed to see what you now see, yet never saw it." Second, *John* 6:68: "Simon Peter said to him, 'Lord, to whom should we go? You have the words of eternal life." Third, *Luke* 17:22: "The time will come when you will long to see one of the days of the son of man and will not see it." Fourth, *John* 13:33: "Little children, yet a little while I am with you. You will seek me, and as I said to the Jews, where I am going you cannot come." I should imagine that various phrases from these verses were all that our redactor remembered, and that over time they coalesced into this mélange. But to what end? Here I think we may catch a glimpse of the prophetic drama that ensued when the wandering charismatics got "in character" and spoke portentously of their role as channelers for the risen Christ. The saying reminds the hearers of the valuable opportunity they have for this brief moment. Ask away! And your Lord will answer, as he once promised (or so the same prophets claim he did!): "Whoever hears you hears me."

> **39 Jesus says, "The Pharisees and the scribes have received the keys of knowledge, but they have hidden them. They did not enter, nor did they allow entrance to those who wished to. But as for you, become shrewd as serpents and yet naive as doves."**

This is another version of the Q saying found in Matthew 23:13 ("But woe to you, scribes and Pharisees, hypocrites! because you shut the kingdom of heaven against men; for you neither enter yourselves, nor allow those who would enter to go in.") and Luke 11:52 ("Woe to you lawyers! for you have taken away the key of knowledge; you did not enter yourselves, and you hindered those who were entering.") What was the key to knowledge, or to the kingdom? If it is knowledge, are we to understand it as the key *to* knowledge, or the key that *is* knowledge? I think the latter: the knowledge needed if one is to enter in. Matthew does not actually mention keys here, but he does elsewhere, when he bestows the halakhic keys upon Peter (16:19) (or his successors in Antioch), who will henceforth be able to make binding decisions on kosher and other ritual matters, as well as cases of excommunication, whence we get the folklore image of Peter as the keeper of the Pearly Gates. That is the use of the keys to "shut the kingdom of heaven against men." In view for Thomas are Christian leaders who, lacking the spark of divine Gnosis, are unable to tell their flock the true way of salvation, much less following it themselves.

The saying about the wisdom of serpents and the purity of doves did not originally fit here. It occurs elsewhere in the Matthean Mission Charge (Matthew 10:16b) as advice not to underestimate the cleverness of their persecutors while also not stooping to use their tactics against them, or to save one's own skin. But here, juxtaposed with the keys of knowledge, the saying must intend a Gnostic application: the knowledge of the way to the kingdom requires the esoteric wisdom which the Ophites (notorious champions of this gospel) ascribed to the Edenic serpent, a revealer of Gnosis to the hapless creations of the Demiurge.

40 Jesus says, "A vine has been planted that the Father did not create. As it is alien to the soil, it will be pulled up by the roots and destroyed."

This is another version of Matthew 15:13, "Every plant which my heavenly Father has not planted will be rooted up." This in turn presupposes Isaiah 60:21, "Your people shall all be righteous; they shall possess the land for ever, the shoot of my planting, the work of my hands, that I might be glorified." But it seems to have picked up features from other gospel sayings as well. Thomas has a "vine" substituting for Matthew's more generic "plant."

The vine comes perhaps from the parable of the Wicked Tenants (Mark 12:1), itself a reference to Isaiah 5:1–7, which makes Israel the carefully tended vine of God's planting. So maybe Thomas here advocates Gentile suprasession of Israel in the good graces of God, the triumphalism combated in Romans 11:13–24.

The plant is uprooted because it is, literally, "not established," which harks back to the parable of the Sower" (Matthew 13:20–21) where, due to the shallowness and rockiness of the soil, the gospel seed has failed to take adequate root.

Matthew 15:13 says merely that the plant will be uprooted, but Thomas goes on to predict its destruction. That is taken for granted in the original, but the explicit term comes from Mathew 3:10 and 7:19; Matthew has both John the Baptist and Jesus warn of the fate of trees barren of righteous fruit. See also Matthew 13:35, 38–39; John 15:6.

So who or what exactly is the doomed vine? In Matthew, at least on the level of the narrative, the vine has to be the priestly and scribal leadership of the Jews, morphing subtly into the Yavneh Rabbinate, Matthew's competitor for Jewish allegiance in Galilee and/or Syria. Or, just as likely, as in the related, uniquely Matthean parable of the Wheat and the Tares/Weeds (Matthew 13:24–30,36–43), the weeds cleverly inserted by the Enemy may well be Pauline, anti-Torah would-be Christians (Matthew 5:17–19; 7:21–23; 23:15).

Note the Zoroastrian imagery: poison plants, like vermin, are the creation of Ahriman the evil anti-god, or the Demiurge, as implied in Luke 10:19. Evil is not in the world at the behest of the good God. It owes its existence to another Power, and God will in the end extract and destroy it. For the description of evil as a plant, see Hebrews 12:15 ("See to it that no one fail to obtain the grace of God; that no root of bitterness spring up and cause trouble, and by it the many become defiled.") and its source, Deuteronomy 29:18 ("Beware lest there be among you a man or woman or family or tribe, whose heart turns away this day from Yahve our God to go and serve the gods of those nations; lest there be among you a root bearing poisonous and bitter fruit.").

41 Jesus says, "Whoever has something in his hand, to him shall be given; and whoever is lacking, from him shall be taken even the little he has."

A Synoptic saying, in Mark it reads, "For to him who has will more be given; and from him who has not, even what he has will be taken away." In Mark the saying is made to reiterate the admonition, "Take heed what you hear," implying that one had better *get* an ear to hear, or nothing Jesus says will make any sense to you. The same point is made in 1 Corinthians 2:13–15, "And we impart this in words not taught by human wisdom but taught by the Spirit, interpreting spiritual truths to those who possess the Spirit. The unspiritual man does not receive the gifts of the Spirit of God, for they are folly to him, and he is not able to understand them because they are spiritually discerned. The spiritual man judges all things, but is himself to be judged by no one."

Both Matthew 13:12 and Luke 8:18 reproduce Mark's version, though Luke changes it at one point to "even what *he thinks* he has will be taken," an attempt to clear up the minor confusion over how one may have nothing and have it (what?) taken away? The Q version also appears in both Mathew and Luke (of course, that is what we *mean* by "Q"). Matthew 25:29 and Luke 19:26 associate the identical saying with the parable of the Talents or Minas, so the point becomes: What have you done with your life? In fact, one might fill in the implied blank in the saying thusly: "To him who has much *to show for himself* more shall be given; from him who has nothing *to show for himself*, what little he has shall be taken away." The servant who was too timid to make an investment did have something, the money originally given him, and now that is taken away.

But it is also possible that the saying is a specimen of pessimistic worldly wisdom equivalent to "The poor you have always with you." It need not be taken as an approval of this condition, just sober realism: no matter how much one does for the poor, the problem will never be completely banished, and yet that is only added incentive to do what one can toward solving it.

42 Jesus says, "Be as those who pass by."

Yoga teaches the attitude of detachment, or "mere witness," abstention from worldly distractions, acting, when it is necessary to act, without worldly motivation, e.g., for reward. Such "acting without the fruits of action" renders one immune from karma, good or bad, and thus does not oblige one to yet more incarnations in which to be rewarded or punished. That is the life-stance, if not the metaphysic, implied here. It is "disinterestedness" in that one no longer plays favorites or has any vested interests, but it is most certainly not "uninterestedness," i.e., apathy or unconcern, since now one is free to look upon all things and persons with unbiased, unselfish compassion. Such is the attitude of the bodhisattvas as well.

> **43 His disciples say to him, "Who are you that you say such things to us?" Jesus says to them, "From what I say to you, you cannot deduce who I am? No, you have become like the Jews, for they love the tree but hate its fruit; again, they love the fruit but hate the tree."**

For the theme of questioning Jesus' authority to teach, see Mark 6:2–3 ("Where did this man get all this? What is the wisdom given to him? What mighty works are wrought by his hands!") and 11:28 ("By what authority are you doing these things, or who gave you this authority to do them?"), plus John 3:2 ("Rabbi, we know that you are a teacher come from God; for no one can do these signs that you do, unless God is with him."). John 14:9–11 is the clearest parallel to Jesus' reply: "Have I been with you so long, and yet you do not know me, Philip? He who has seen me has seen the Father; how can you say, 'Show us the Father'?"

The specific sources for the rest are Matthew 7:16–18 ("You will know them by their fruits. Are grapes gathered from thorns, or figs from thistles? So, every sound tree bears good fruit, but the bad tree bears evil fruit. A sound tree cannot bear evil fruit, nor can a bad tree bear good fruit.") and its parallel Luke 6:43–45 ("For no good tree bears bad fruit, nor again does a bad tree bear good fruit; for each tree is known by its own fruit. For figs are not gathered from thorns, nor are grapes picked from a bramble bush."), plus Matthew 12:33 ("Either make the tree good, and his fruit good; or else make the tree bad, and its fruit bad: for the tree is known by its fruit.") In this last text, Jesus is speaking to the Pharisees, hence the reference to "the Jews" here in Thomas.

Thomas seems to suggest that it is perverse to seek to verify Jesus' teaching as coming from a legitimate source before you decide whether or not to heed it. Rather, the truth about Jesus is to be found nowhere else but in his words. If they are good, the source is good, good enough at any rate. No fancy title could make true sayings truer, no matter who the speaker is. Nor could it make dubious sayings into true ones. This is why, I think, Thomas has no Christological titles: it is not that no one had yet thought of any. Rather, it is that no title bestowed on Jesus is either necessary (as in this saying) or adequate (as in saying 13).

This saying seems to flow so well into saying 45 that we must suspect some scribe, late in the process, has interpolated saying 44 and interrupted the natural sequence.

44 Jesus says, "Whoever blasphemes against the Father, it shall be forgiven him, and whoever blasphemes against the Son, it shall be forgiven him, but whoever blasphemes against the Holy Spirit, it shall not be forgiven him, either on earth or in heaven."

Here is a much later version of a saying found in both Mark and Q: "Amen, I say to you, all sins will be forgiven the sons of men, and whatever blasphemies they utter; but whoever blasphemes against the Holy Spirit has not forgiveness unto the age but is guilty of an age-long sin" (Mark 3:28–29).

"And everyone who speaks a word against the son of man will be forgiven; but he who blasphemes against the Holy Spirit will not be forgiven" (Luke 12:10).

Matthew 12:31–32 combines the two: "Thus I tell you, all sins and blasphemies will be forgiven men, but the blasphemy against the Spirit will not be forgiven. And whoever says a word against the son of man will be forgiven, but whoever speaks against the Holy Spirit will not be forgiven, whether in this age or in the one to come." Here Matthew has clipped the two "age" references from Mark's version to add them in a new construction at the close of the appended Q version. Thomas' version looks to be based on Matthew's version. Which is the earlier version, Mark or Q? The Q version is puzzling, really senseless, if we take "son of man" as a title for Jesus, but it makes perfect sense if taken as meaning "mankind," "human beings" as in Psalm 8:4, "What is man that thou art mindful of him, or the son of man that thou dost care for him?" (It is the equivalent of Mark's "sons of men" as in Psalm 115:16: "The heavens are Yahve's heavens, but the earth he has given to the sons of men.") Matthew and Luke seem to have understood this. But Mark's version seems earlier. It contrasts not the severity of blaspheming God and blaspheming humans, as in Q, but rather the gravity of blaspheming God with all other sins mortals may commit. In Mark humanity is the envisioned class of sinners, while in Q humanity is the less serious object of blasphemy. Mark says that blasphemy against God is worse than all other sins. Q says that blasphemy against God far outweighs blasphemy against our fellow human beings. "Blasphemy" used to denote simply slander or maligning, no matter whose reputation one was blackening. It was not a sin specially directed toward God (or religious sensibilities), as we use it today. One might paraphrase Q: one may curse men and get away with it, but cursing God is fatal to the soul, as when Job's wife urges him, "Curse God and die already!" (Job 2:9).

Why specify "Holy Spirit" if the object of blasphemy is simply God instead of puny humans? The saying, so to speak, backs away as far as it can from the offense it discusses by using a reverential paraphrase: "Holy Spirit." Here it really means "Divine Spirit," i.e., God. Thomas' version, however, does not grasp this and takes the Holy Spirit to be one of the persons of the Trinitarian Godhead. "The son of man," accordingly, must refer to Jesus, and "son of man" is shortened to "Son," in accord with Trinitarian formulae. In that case, Thomas' redactor thinks he had better include the Father, too! There is just no telling why he thought blasphemy against one person of the Trinity should be much more serious than against the others. He must have thought so, though, just because, as he read it, "blasphemy against the Third Person of the Trinity alone has no forgiveness."

45 Jesus says, "They do not gather grapes from thorns, nor do they pick figs from thistles, for these give no fruit. A good man produces good out of his treasure, while a wicked man produces wicked things out of his wicked treasure, which is in his heart, and so speaks evil things. For out of what fills the heart he brings forth evils."

Add Matthew 12:34b-35 ("For out of the abundance of the heart the mouth speaks. The good man out of his good treasure brings forth good, and the evil man out of his evil treasure brings forth evil.") to those forming the basis for saying 43, and it becomes necessary to understand saying 45 as the original direct continuation of saying 43.

46 Jesus says, "From Adam up to John the Baptist, there is among mortal men none higher than John the Baptist, so that his eyes will not be blinded. But I have said to you that whoever among you becomes as a child shall experience the kingdom, and he shall become higher than John."

This is a slightly garbled version of the Q saying in Matthew 11:11: "Amen, I say to you, among those born of women, there has risen no one greater than John the Baptist; yet he who is least in the kingdom of heaven is greater than he." Thomas' introductory phrase, "From Adam to John the Baptist" reflects bits of the same Q complex (i.e., adjacent verses): "*From the days of John the Baptist until now* the kingdom of heaven has suffered violence, and violent men take it by force. For all the Prophets and the Law prophesied *until John*, and if you are willing to accept it, he is Elijah who is to come" (Matthew 11:12–14) and "The Law and the Prophets were until John; since then the news of the kingdom of God is preached, and everyone enters it violently" (Luke 16:16). The phrase "so that his eyes will not be . . ." ends in a lacuna (a hole rubbed in the manuscript), and scholars tend to fill it in "broken" or "lowered." I suggest "blinded." John was the only one since Adam to be worthy of looking at God and surviving it unimpaired.

Thus the saying heaps upon John the greatest praise imaginable: he is the greatest figure in all history! But then what to make of the following, where he is relegated to a lower place than the least important member of the new age which superceded John? It may be the original continuation, a way of co-opting John into the Christian system with full honors (so as not to offend the many still loyal to John's sect) and yet explaining why one would be best advised to abandon John's sect for Jesus'. That is the same point as in Acts 19:1–7, where Paul shows some Baptist ascetics that, as great as John was, he had no means of imparting the eschatological Spirit, which was the job of the one to come after, namely Jesus.

> **47 Jesus says, "It is impossible for a man to mount two horses at once and to stretch two bows, and it is impossible for a servant to serve two masters. If he tries, he will inevitably find himself honoring the one and, by the same act, offending the other. No one drinks old wine and immediately desires to drink new wine. And they avoid putting new wine into old wineskins, so as not to burst them; nor do they put old wine into new wineskins, to avoid spoiling it. They do not sew an old patch on a new garment, because it would result in a new tear."**

The first half of this saying centers upon a loose version of the Q saying found in Matthew 6:24 / Luke 16:13: "No one (or no slave) can serve two masters; for either he will hate the one and love the other, or he will be devoted to the one and despise the other. You cannot serve God and Mammon." Thomas lacks the last line, which might mean he had access to a more primitive version which did not yet apply and explain the saying for the reader. Indeed, the God and Mammon business does look secondary though it is quite apt in any case. But I think Thomas had only heard the canonical version(s) and then forgot the God and Mammon part. To venture a bit of Reader Response Criticism, I should think that after one has become familiar with the whole thing, one more or less hears the two masters as meaning God and Mammon from the start.

The familiar "two masters" saying is preceded by what looks like a "homologous formation" by which someone thought to add to the stock of Jesus sayings by extrapolating to a new set of metaphors to make a familiar point. In truth, one has but a single behind, though one might try to ride two horses rodeo-style, with a foot on each steed's back (which is presumably how Matthew pictured Jesus riding both "an ass and a colt, the foal of an ass.").

The second half of the saying is a jumble of two Markan similitudes in Mark 2:21–22, only Thomas has taken them from Luke's adaptation of Mark (Luke 5:36–38): "No one tears a piece from a new garment and puts it upon an old garment; if he does, he will tear the new, and the piece from the new will not match the old. And no one puts new wine into old wineskins; if he does, the new wine will burst the skins and it will be spilled, and the skins will be destroyed. But new wine must be put into fresh wineskins." Luke adds to the Markan text his own verse 39: "And no one after drinking old wine desires new; for he says, 'The old is good.'" Luke has an anti-Marcionite agenda, and he does not like Mark's talk of sweeping away the old (Judaism) in favor of the new (Christianity), so he simply negates the sense of what has gone before. If one is interested in new wine, he had best not use old wineskins, true enough, but in fact only a fool would prefer new wine to old! Thomas tales the Lukan text and stands it on its head: he begins the complex with Luke's parting shot about the superiority of vintage wine. Then he backtracks to the wineskins similitude, then to the patched garment.

And this is not all. As for the wineskins business, Mark and Luke warned the reader not to pour new wine into old skins, since the new wine had not yet finished expanding (fermenting), while the skins had expanded as much as they could with the last wine they held. Putting new wine in them now would make them burst. But Thomas says not to pour old wine, already done expanding, into new skins which can expand but will not need to! Similarly, Mark and Luke said not to patch an old, threadbare shirt with a piece of new cloth because the next time you washed it, the patch would shrink, while the old cloth surrounding it has finished shrinking, and so the patch would rip away. Time has come to throw away the old rag! But Thomas envisions taking a patch from some old shirt and using it to patch the hole in a new shirt. The shirt would still be ruined, but this time it would be the rest of the shirt shrinking away from the patch. So the punch line would be the same, but who is going to do it? Who is likely to ruin a new garment by cutting out a piece of it to patch an old, worn garment?

I suspect it would be over-subtle to read some meaning into the reshuffling of the components of this sayings complex. I think it more likely that Thomas was just passing on texts and metaphors he did not fully understand—just as we modern readers often do!

> **48 Jesus says, "If two make peace with each other in this one house, there is nothing they cannot do by joining their forces. They shall say to this mountain, 'Be moved!' and it shall be moved."**

This seems simply to be a combination of two sayings about the power of faith in prayer and on unity in prayer. One is Matthew 18:19: "Again I say to you, if two of you agree on earth about anything they ask, it will be done for them by my Father in heaven." The other is Mark 11:23: "Amen, I say to you, whoever says to this mountain, 'Be taken up and cast into the sea,' and does not doubt in his heart, but believes that what he says will come to pass, it will be done for him." Even omitting the Markan clause "and does not doubt in his heart," these sayings seem to ascribe the power of answered prayer to the prayer itself rather than to God. It is a question of how much of this miracle-working power one can summon up by sheer will-power, and whether one can double it by augmenting the power source, another praying unit.

> **49 Jesus says, "Blessed are the solitary and the elect, for you shall find the kingdom; because you come from it, and you shall find your way there again."**

This is, in form, a beatitude, or blessing, a familiar type of saying in the New Testament and in Jewish literature generally. This one blesses the "solitary ones," Thomas' favorites, those who are single-mindedly devoted to Christ inwardly because celibate outwardly, not distracted by domestic duties or by the pleasures of the flesh. However, since "the solitary" seems to overbalance the saying, since the elect are already present as the object of blessing, we might suspect that "the solitary" is an addition to specify who is among the elect. What qualifies one as "the chosen"? Now we know, at least according to the Thomas redactor: one who has chosen the ascetical lifestyle of the celibacy gospel. To be "chosen" implies one is "choice," i.e., worthy to be chosen because of recognized excellence. Just as Thomas elsewhere has a wise fisherman choose the biggest fish and dump the smelt, he says here that the Father, or Jesus, will choose the ones who have made themselves worthy.[88]

The saying appears to teach the pre-existence of the soul, a venerable belief shared by Gnostics, Origen, Orphics, Pythagoreans, and, today, by Mormons. Only those will attain unto the heavenly Pleroma who came from there. True, in the meantime, they have come to forget all about their true origin (and nature), and this accounts for the lostness and alienness they feel in this world. But, once illumined by the Revealer, they (Jesus) remember or at least can be taught the way back.

It is quite possible that, if an encratite emphasis is intended, the place of origin is thought of as Eden, and the departure from there as God's exiling of Adam and Eve. In that case, the baptismal renunciation of sex would be a rebirth into the once-lost Paradise.

Some do not want to see Thomas teaching preincarnation and so pretend that the reference to "coming from" the kingdom means merely "belonging to" the kingdom, but I must admit that seems awfully strained to me.

> **50 Jesus says, "If they say to you, 'Where did you originate?' tell them, 'We have come from the Light, where the Light originated through itself. It arose and it revealed itself in the image of its offspring.' If they say to you, 'Who are you?' say, 'We are his sons, and we are the elect of the Living Father.' If they ask you, 'What is the identifying mark of your Father in you?' tell them, 'It is both movement and repose.'"**

It is possible these questions constitute preparation of the Gnostic in case he should be discovered and questioned by the bishops, cf. saying 13. The questions are somewhat reminiscent of those in Mark 9:11 ("Why do the scribes say that Elijah must come first?") and 12:35ff ("Why do the scribes say the Christ is the son of David?" They may all be catechetical and/or apologetic, prepping the neophyte how to answer critics of the faith.

But it seems more likely to be preparation for the postmortem astral journey, imparting the passwords enabling the soul to pass the planetary *archon*s, who otherwise seek to devour souls seeking to ascend back to the Pleroma (realm of heavenly Light) after death. This was a major feature of Gnostic teaching. Full-fledged resurrection/revelation discourses such as Pistis Sophia and the Gospel of Mary contain detailed instructions as to what to say to the guardian of each celestial portal. Here one must be able to satisfy the archon of one's right to ascend to the Pleroma by furnishing the secret sign of kinship with the Light (God).

The Light has originated from itself, which is true only of the ultimate Godhead. The Light "stood," which refers to the epithet of God in Gnostic and Samaritan circles, "the Standing One." That "it" revealed itself in their image, i.e., that of believers, harks back to the Priestly creation account in which Elohim (originally "gods") created the human race in the divine image. Later we will find that this aspect of the creation story has been reinterpreted by Gnostics to take into account their belief that the true Deity did not create the material world. In that case, the God-reflecting images must be the celestial counterparts of the elect, of which we read in 2 Corinthians 5:1–2 and Thomas saying 84.

The sign of divine paternity is "a movement and a rest," which reminds us of Wisdom speculation: "Wisdom is more mobile than any motion; because of her purity she pervades all things." In turn, this characterization reflects Greek philosophy, e.g., Aristotle's view of God as the Unmoved Mover. And who will not recognize here a striking parallel to the Atman, the true divine self, in the Vagasaneyi-Samhita-Upanishad? "That one, though never stirring, is swifter than thought . . . Though standing still, it overtakes the others who are running . . . It stirs and it stirs not; it is far, and likewise near. It is inside of all this, and it is outside of all this" (verses 4–5; Max Müller trans.).

Indeed, the whole question and answer sequence is reminiscent of a passage in the Kaushitaki-Upanishad, when it maps out the heavenward course of the ascending soul and its requisite encounters with various gods along the way:

> On this couch sits Brahman, and he who knows this mounts it first with one foot only. Then Brahman says to him: "Who art thou?" and he shall answer: "I am a season, and the child of the seasons, sprung from the womb of endless space, from the light. The light, the origin of the year,

which is the past, which is the present, which is all living things, and all elements, is the Self. Thou art the Self. What thou art, that am I." Brahman says to him: "Who am I?" He shall answer: "That which is, the true" (verses 5–6). And so on.

51 His disciples say to him, "When will the repose of the dead begin? And when will the new world come?" He says to them, "What you look for has already come, but you fail to recognize it."

It looks like someone has confused two passages, fortuitously conflating them together. The disciples' question comes from Mark 13:4, while the answer comes from Jesus' reply to a similar question from the Pharisees in Luke 17:20–21. The latter verse means, in accord with Luke's redactional agenda, to choke off and to sweep away all apocalyptic horizon-gazing such as the Olivet Discourse (Little Apocalypse) embodies. The eschatological state of "rest" or "repose" (cf. Revelation 6:9–11; Matthew 25:34; Hebrews 4:1–11) is like that of Elohim upon completion of the creation (Genesis 2:2) or the ideal repose of the Epicurean deities.

52 His disciples say to him, "Twenty-four prophets spoke in Israel, and every one of them predicted you!" He said to them, "You have disregarded the Living, who is right in front of you, to prattle on about the dead!"

One day in the streets of Hippo, some pamphleteer handed none other than Saint Augustine a tract containing this saying. "But when the apostles had asked how they should regard the prophets of the Jews, who are thought to have prophesied in the past about his coming, he answered, surprised/ annoyed that they still harbored such an idea: 'You have forsaken the Living One who is before you and speak about the dead.'" The tract and the man turned out to be Marcionite. So is the saying. The disciples are made to mouth the sentiments of Catholic Christianity: Jesus is the messiah predicted by the biblical Prophets. You see, there are 24 books in the Rabbinic canon, the same ones in the Protestant Old Testament, but the 12 Minor Prophets are combined into one single book, while Samuel, Kings, and Chronicles are each a single book, not divided in two. The Marcionite Jesus sweeps all this away in tones of contempt. The old prophets are so many dead men moldering in their fancy tombs; Jesus is the Living One. Which are you going to quote? Marcionites, of course, rejected the whole Jewish canon.

The envisioned scene is quite funny: imagine, the disciples commenting on how Jesus is predicted in this and that scripture passage, as if this should impress him, as if he were a movie star and you, a star-struck fan, are marveling over mentions of him in the newspaper. Do you think he is impressed with such things, or even notices them any more? Your own seeming assumption that he is as impressed as you are is an insult, drawing him down to your own pitiful level!

Joachim Jeremias, seemingly desperate to "save" an attractive saying from such bastard heretical origins, wanted to take it as a Christian *defense* of messianic prophecy from the Old Testament, and a critique of a Rabbinical opinion that there would be no future messiah at all: he had already come, once and for all, in Isaiah's time. He was King Hezekiah. (There is a point to that in that there is reason to believe that the passages, now quoted as predictive messianic prophecies in Isaiah chapters 9 and 11 were really birth or enthronement oracles for Hezekiah, but then they are not really messianic in the usual sense at all. At any rate, Jeremias is grasping at straws and must take the sayings as meaning "the prophets of the Jews had spoken of his (the Messiah's) coming in the past," i.e., Hezekiah. Not likely.

But one might suggest an origin and meaning for the text that are not Marcionite and which would nonetheless have appealed to Marcionites (as the saying obviously did). The point might be to contrast the disciples' (=Christians') preoccupation with the merely preparatory at the expense of the present fulfillment. That is just the point of Jesus' rejection of fasting, penitence to prepare for the kingdom—which is here! The question bout prophetic prediction is in fact another way of asking about when the end or the repose of the dead will come, only to be told not only that it is already here, but that remaining in this anticipatory mode prevents them from seeing it! See John 5:39–40 for the same point.

> **53 His disciples say to him, "Is circumcision worthwhile or not?" He says to them, "If it were, men would be born that way automatically. But the true circumcision in spirit has become completely worthwhile."**

This saying cannot come from the lifetime of Jesus. If it we cannot really imagine Jesus debating Palestinian Jewish scribes using the hated Greek Septuagint Bible, as Mark 7:6–7 has him doing, neither can we picture any conceivable scenario in which Jews would ask him concerning the propriety of circumcision. That would be like asking, "Rabbi, what do you think of monotheism?" On the other hand, circumcision was the great debate in the early church, as in Romans 3:1; Galatians 5:2–12; Acts 15. The question was whether Gentile pagans or God-fearers (Gentiles who believed in Judaism and attended synagogue but stopped short of circumcision and dietary laws) who wanted to become Christians needed to be circumcised as Jews first. Some (like Matthew) said yes, some (like Paul) said no. This saying has been coined by one faction in order to posthumously enlist Jesus on their side. Had he said this in the first place, how could the subsequent debate ever have come about? He would already have settled the question. But in fact he didn't. Nice try.

Opponents of form criticism and the notion that many sayings were coined in the early church in order to make Jesus rule on some issue after the fact often gloat, saying, in that case, why no attempt to make Jesus address the later circumcision debate? They simply overlook this saying because of a bias toward the official canon of scripture. Thomas' inclusion or exclusion from that list does not change the fact that it forms part of the gospel tradition, and that it offers us just such a piece of evidence as the anti-critics dare us to supply. So there!

54 Jesus says, "Blessed are the poor, for yours is the kingdom of heaven."

This one resembles both Matthew's and Luke's version of the famous beatitude. Matthew 5:3 reads: "Blessed are *the* poor *in spirit*, for *theirs* is the kingdom of *heaven*." Luke 6:20, on the other hand, has: "Blessed are *you poor*, for *yours* is the kingdom of *God*." Thomas, then, does not spiritualize "the poor" as Matthew does. But he does piously substitute "heaven" for "God" as Matthew does. Matthew speaks of the blessed poor consistently in the third person, whereas Luke consistently uses the second. Thomas starts with Matthew's third person and switches to Luke's second-person address. All this clearly shows that Thomas' version is secondary, a conflation of the two other versions, probably by means of imprecise memory quotation.

Scholars usually (and plausibly) take the saying, in any of the three forms, to imply a future reversal of fortunes: when the kingdom of God ends history as we know it, ushering in the Final Judgment and the Millennial

Kingdom, those who are destitute now will find themselves sitting upon the thrones, judging the wicked rich who ruled this fallen age. But nothing in the beatitude requires that. It may simply refer to the "repose" or reward of the poor after death, as in the story of the beggar Lazarus and the damned Rich Man (Luke 16:19–31).

55 Jesus says, "Whoever does not hate his father and his mother will not be able to qualify as my disciple; and whoever does not hate his brothers and his sisters and does not pick up his cross in my wake, will not prove worthy of me."

The Q document had a version of this saying. Luke 14:26–27 has: "If any one comes to me and does not hate his own father and mother and wife and children and brothers and sisters, yes, and even his own life, he cannot be my disciple. Whoever does not bear his own cross and come after me, cannot be my disciple." Matthew 10:37–38 reads: "He who loves father or mother more than me is not worthy of me; and he who loves son or daughter more than me is not worthy of me; and he who does not take his cross and follow me is not worthy of me." Matthew has toned down the "hatred" business lest someone misunderstand it. Luke's (Q's) version does not mean to inculcate fanaticism, only to warn the reader not to renounce his faith in a time of persecution at the urging of his family. We see just the sort of scene envisaged here in *The Martyrdom of Perpetua and Felicitas*, in which Perpetua, young Roman matron with a newborn infant, is on death row, waiting to be fed to the beasts in the arena. Her family tearfully pleads with her to renounce her crazy determination and return home with them to nurse her new baby. She will not budge, and we wind up with a lion who is blessed for having eaten her (Thomas 7). A Christian martyr, bearing his cross, is to "hate" family in precisely the same sense as Jesus himself freely went to the cross "despising the shame" (Hebrews 12:2). In other words, he didn't let it weaken his resolve, nor should anyone who follows him let his or her family become a siren-like distraction.

Mark has his own version: "If any man would come after me, let him deny himself and take up his cross and follow me" (Mark 8:34). This Matthew reproduces exactly in Matthew 16:24, while Luke slightly alters it: "If any man would come after me, let him deny himself and take up his cross daily and follow me" (Luke 9:23). Luke adds "daily" in order to transform a martyrdom saying into a saying about daily self-sacrifice.

Thomas' version is closer to Q. It is most likely a memory-quote conflation of the Matthean and Lukan versions, as it seems to preserve some redactional features of each (retaining Matthew's "worthy of me" and Luke's "brothers and sisters"), while rounding off others. Thomas has lost Matthew's euphemizing of "hating" relatives as well as Luke's addition of "wife" as among the list of those to be sacrificed in the line of duty.

56 Jesus says, "Whoever has recognized the world for what it is, has found a rotting corpse. And whoever has found it to be a corpse, of him the world is not worthy."

Note the catchword connection with the previous saying: as the would-be disciple who cannot bring himself to abandon family "is not worthy" of Jesus, neither is this world worthy of the ascetic who sees it for the rotting heap that it is.

The saying advocates asceticism in terms reminiscent of Galatians 6:14 and Hebrews 11:15–16, 24–26, 38, and especially of Buddhism, where one kills any desire for the world by meditating on the mass of corruption it contains and soon becomes.

57 Jesus says, "The kingdom of the Father is like a man who had good seed. His enemy came by night and sowed weeds among the good seed. The man did not allow them to pull up the weeds, telling them, "in case you go to uproot the weeds and uproot the wheat along with it. For at harvest time the weeds will appear. That's the time to uproot and burn them."

One might naturally read saying 46 as the conclusion to this saying. There as here, it looks as if the point is to discourage premature judgment of fellow-believers, since this only ruins everything with sectarian feuding. The supposed righteous and the ostensible wicked are necessarily too intricately interwoven, given the interdependent nature of human society. Chaos will result if one tries to have the final judgment now, which is what sectarian, "holier than thou" churches often do. 1 Corinthians 5:10 puts it this way: the only way to completely steer clear of the wicked would be to leave the planet!

In a broader sense the parable may be trying to account for continuing evil in a world supposedly under the direction of Divine Providence (as in 4 Ezra 4:22–32). It would be counterproductive to try to eliminate all the wicked, since human beings are not either totally evil or totally good. As Tillich said, that is what makes the notion of heaven and hell impossible. Who really, unambiguously deserves to go to either? Can even God tell what is in the heart if the contents of the heart are unsettled, ambiguous, neither this nor that? If it is gray, not even God can be right if he calls it black or white.

The "enemy" is probably Paul, the weeds his Gentile converts who do not keep the Jewish Torah, though the parable loses no force if this original identification is forgotten.

It has been pointed out that the farmer is wrong: the only feasible time to uproot the weeds without destroying the wheat along with them would be *now*. The longer you wait, the more intertangled the root systems will become. The parables often portray farming or animal husbandry techniques that are unrealistic or erroneous. Some interpreters find in this an intended irony on Jesus' part, trying get his hearers to ask "What's wrong with this picture?" But I reject that. The simpler explanation is that the creator of the parable in such cases did not know what he was talking about, having no first-hand acquaintance with the rural setting in which Jesus is depicted as functioning.

Thomas' version of the parable of the Wheat and the Tares (Weeds) lacks the pedantic interpretation that we find in Matthew 13:37–43. Is this evidence that Thomas has an earlier version? I believe not. Rather, the interpretation of the parable had become so well known that it eventually seemed superfluous to repeat it along with the parable.

58 Jesus says, "Blessed is the one who has suffered; he has found the Life."

Is this not the equivalent of the exhortation of Paul and Barnabas in Acts 14:22, "It is through many tribulations that we must enter the kingdom of God"?

59 Jesus says, "Look upon the Living One as long as you live, in case you should die and seek in vain to see him."

The saying is parallel to John 12:35–36: "The light is with you a little longer. Walk while you have the light lest the darkness overtake you; he who walks in the darkness does not know where he goes. While you have the light, believe in the light, that you may become sons of light." See also Luke 16:19–31, the parable of Lazarus and the Rich Man: if you don't get down to business and seek God in this life, it will be too late once you die. In other words, "Seek the Lord while he may be found" (Isaiah 55:6).

> **60 They see a Samaritan carrying a lamb on his way to Jerusalem. He says to his disciples, "Why does this man carry the lamb with him?" They say to him, "So he may kill it and eat it." He says to them, "As long as it is alive, he will not eat it, but only if he has killed it and it has become a corpse?" They say, "Otherwise he will not be able to do it." He says to them, "As for yourselves, seek a place of repose for yourselves, so you do not become a corpse and get eaten."**

What's this? A Samaritan on his way to offer sacrifice at the Jerusalem temple? Did they not repudiate that holy place in favor of Mount Gerizim (or its ruins)? Yes, all but the Gorothene and the Dosithean sects, both groups of Samaritans who observed the Jewish calendar of holy days and therefore went to Jerusalem to celebrate. The parable bids us to choose to identify with either the man seeking the holy place of divine rest (literally the temple, figuratively salvation in heaven) or with the doomed lamb whose trip to the big city will issue in his being eaten, though he cannot suspect it, obliviously going long for the ride. In fact, you are already pretty much identified with the oblivious lamb, living, without realizing it, for someone else's ends and headed for your death. The point is to snap out of it and become like the Samaritan who is in charge and is taking responsibility for his life's direction, aiming at salvation.

It seems worth asking if perhaps saying 60 has grown from someone trying to make sense of what little he could remember of Luke 17:11–19, where Jesus himself is on his way to Jerusalem for the Passover (where he must sacrifice a lamb) and is met by a party of ten lepers, one of whom is a Samaritan. Thomas cannot remember much of it and gets it confused: he has Jesus spot the Samaritan going to Jerusalem for Passover.

> **61 Jesus says, "Two will rest on a bed: one will die, and one will live." Salome says, "Who are you, sir, and whose son? You reclined upon my couch and ate from my table." Jesus says to her, "I am he who is from the Same, and some matters were committed to me by my Father." Salome says, "I am your disciple!" Jesus says**

to her, "Therefore I say, if one is the same, he will be filled with light, but if he is divided, he will be filled with darkness."

Jesus' initial saying is a version of Q saying Matthew 24:38–41 / Luke 17:26–36, but only Luke has the reference to a pair of sleepers in the same bed, one turning over to find the other gone, taken in judgment. Thomas has retained only that scene, dropping (or forgetting) the other two: two working at a mill, two laboring in the field. Did Matthew omit the bedfellows from Q, or did Luke add them? If the latter, then Thomas is following Luke, as I think likely. Ancient readers were left asking the same question we do: *where* will the missing have been taken? Luke glosses the passages by having the puzzled disciples ask just this, to which Jesus replies that you will be able to find their dead bodies by looking for the circling vultures (Luke 17:37). Since Luke, not Matthew, says they have been "taken away" like the doomed by Noah's Flood, and Thomas says "one will die," it looks again like he is following Luke.

When Salome, a frequent interlocutor in Gnostic revelation dialogues, replies, "Who are you, sir (or lord), and whose (son)?" I must think of Mark 6:3, "Is this not the carpenter, the son of Mary?" It is a clumsily worded version of the same thing: Salome marvels at Jesus' wisdom, so extraordinary in someone she has known from his youth.

As for reclining on her couch, no romantic dalliance must be entertained: she refers merely to the posture of dining, propped upon one's elbow, reclining on the floor or a couch parallel to the dinner table (or at a tangent if the table is round). He is an itinerant who receives God's providential provision through the generosity of those to whom the itinerant preaches (Matthew 10:9–11). But the couch reference does connect back to the "two in one bed" reference, implying that, of these two, Jesus is the living one, Salome the dead, or doomed to die—until, that is, she embraces discipleship and receives life and illumination.

How does Jesus answer her question? Whose son is he? He is the son of ("from") the Undivided, the highest point in the Neo-Platonic hierarchy of Being. Undifferentiated being is his origin, the Ultimate Father, not divided into subject or object, not yet even Thought reflecting upon itself. As Jung described it, at the summit rests the One, where there is no division, no polarity. As we move downward to mortal perception, refracted by the clouds of finitude, we seem to see a god named Abraxas, who embodies the reconciled coexistence of opposites, not their absence. Jesus is like Abraxas, the one distinguished, but barely, from him who is the Same, the Self-identical One. His Father, the One, has committed (to use personalistic metaphors) certain matters to the differentiated "son," reflecting the Q passage Matthew 11:27 / Luke 10:22: Jesus is the unique revealer of the Godhead. But why not "all things" as in the Q passage? Perhaps because the Revealer, necessarily climbing down the ontological ladder in order to manifest himself, must become an entity among entities, one among others in the realm of opposites, of the subject-object distinction. Thus only *some of the things of my Father"* can appear in such an entity.

To this declaration Salome replies with an affirmation of discipleship. One may see here a rewriting of Luke 10:38–42, in which Jesus is similarly depicted as dining with female admirers, one of whom takes Salome's role as host, the other her new role as disciple.

Jesus' cryptic comment on her offer of allegiance is another version of Matthew 6:22–23, "The eye is the lamp of the body. So, if your eye is sound, your whole body will be full of light; but if your eye is not sound, your whole body will be full of darkness. If then the light in you is darkness, how great is the darkness!" Literally what it says is, "If your eye is *single*," which explains the meaning of the Thomas text "if one is the same," etc. A disciple must become "single," a "solitary" like Jesus himself who is "from the Same."

62 Jesus says, "I entrust my mysteries to those who are worthy of my mysteries. What your right hand may do, do not let your left hand know about it."

The first half of the saying reiterated Jesus' unwillingness to cast his pearls of esoteric wisdom before swine who cannot appreciate them. Remember, that is why he spoke in parables, to protect the mystery of the kingdom of God from the thick-headed crowds who did not have "ears to hear" (Mark 4:11; Matthew 13:111 and Luke 8:10 both have the plural "mysteries," as here in Thomas 62). The second half of the saying, which in Matthew 6:3 urges secret giving, here means not to betray the secrets of Jesus to the uninitiated, no matter how close you are to them otherwise. Remember, Thomas (saying 13) dares not even confide in his fellow disciples!

63 Jesus says, "Once there was a rich man who had great wealth. He said, 'I will invest my money in a farm so I may sow and reap and plant and fill my barns with produce, so I will lack nothing.'

So he resolved—and that night he died! Whoever has ears, let him hear!"

Ultimately the saying would seem to descend from Ecclesiastes 2:18–19, "I hated all my toil in which I had toiled under the sun, seeing that I must leave it to the man who will come after me; and who knows whether he will be a wise man or a fool? Yet he will be master of all for which I toiled and used my wisdom under the sun. This also is vanity." But the immediate source must be Luke 12:16–21, "And he told them a parable, saying, "The land of a rich man brought forth plentifully; and he thought to himself, 'What shall I do, for I have nowhere to store my crops?' And he said, 'I will do this: I will pull down my barns, and build larger ones; and there I will store all my grain and my goods. And I will say to my soul, Soul, you have ample goods laid up for many years; take your ease, eat, drink, be merry.' But God said to him, 'Fool! This night your soul is required of you; and the things you have prepared, whose will they be?' So is he who lays up treasure for himself, and is not rich toward God." Thomas' version is a condensed memory quotation of Luke's, not some earlier version from oral tradition. The original looks to me like a Lukan creation. Given Luke's emphasis on giving alms, one would expect him to use the saying to encourage it here, too: "You can't take it with you!" And that no doubt is the point of "being rich toward God." For Luke one gains heavenly riches by donating one's earthly riches to the poor (Luke 12:33, "Sell your possessions, and give alms; provide yourselves with purses that do not grow old, with a treasure in the heavens that does not fail, where no thief approaches and no moth destroys." In Thomas, though, the point seems just slightly different, more a case of "Man proposes, but God disposes," as in James 4:13–16.

64 Jesus says, "A man had professional acquaintances, and when he had finished preparing a banquet, he sent his servant to invite the associates. He went to the first and said to him, 'My master invites you.' He said, 'I have some claims against some merchants. They will come to me this evening. I will go to give them my orders. I must request to be excused from the banquet.' He went to another and said to him, 'My master has invited you.' He said to him, 'I have bought a house, and they will need me for the day. I will have no time.' He came to another and said to him, 'My master invites you.' He said to him, 'Wouldn't you know it? My friend is to

be married the same day, and I am to cater the reception! I shall not be able to attend. Please have me excused from the banquet.' He went to another and said to him, 'My master invites you.' He said to him, 'I have bought a farm, and I am just on my way to collect the rent. I shall not be able to attend. Please have me excused.' The servant returned and said to his master, 'Those you have invited to the banquet have excused themselves.' The master said to his servant, 'Go out to the roads and bring in whomever you find, so they may dine!' Tradesmen and merchants shall never enter the places of my Father."

This is the parable of the Great Supper, also found in Q and freely adapted by both Luke (14:15–24) and Matthew (22:1–10). Here it is tempting to think Thomas has preserved an independent and more primitive version, or that he had independent access to Q. But I judge it more likely that he remembers, a bit vaguely, hearing both versions read, and he has, in trying to recall the essentials, accidentally filtered out both Matthew's and Luke's most extravagant additions.

The original version is to be found back behind Q, albeit preserved in a source written down much later, the Jerusalem Talmud, where we read of the nouveau riche publican Bar Majan and a poor scholar, an improbable pair who happened to drop dead on the very same day. A forlorn friend of the scholar couldn't help but see the publican's funeral, as the whole town left off work to attend the procession. The scholar complained to God: "Why allow the wicked to be celebrated in death while the righteous pass unnoticed?" He is told that Bar Majan's funeral was the reward for his single good deed, in the midst of doing which, he died. As he could not go on to cancel the merit of the deed by subsequent sins, he had to be rewarded for it here on earth! (What was the good deed? See below.) In a dream the scholar beheld the afterlife of the two departed souls: "A few days later that scholar saw his colleague in gardens of paradisal beauty, watered by flowing streams. He also saw Bar Majan the publican standing on the bank of a stream and trying, like Tantalus, to reach the water, but unable to do so." Obviously, this much is the original of the parable of the Rich Man and Lazarus (Luke 16:19–31).[89]

But what was the publican's good deed? Bar Majan had hoped to cultivate favor among the leading men of the city by inviting them to a great banquet. All refused, apparently unwilling to let themselves be used in such a cheap ploy for undeserved respectability. Furious, yet unwilling for the food to be wasted, Bar Majan ordered his servants to round up the town's street people for the meal instead; that ought to show those high-and-mighty who had snubbed him! This part is the basis of the gospel parable of the Great Supper.[90] It explains why and how *all* the guests turned down the host's last-minute reminder (they must initially have accepted the invitation: we see them bowing out at the last minute); also why all were prosperous land-owners, farmers, merchants, etc.

For his part, Luke has placed the parable into a "symposium" context which he has used in order to link several general "supper" sayings. He has made it a "great" banquet to justify the addition of a second invitation later on. He lets the cat out of the bag early on (14:8), telling us in advance that no one will come! He has a groom rather than a wedding caterer. He has also changed passersby and street people into "the poor, the maimed, the blind, the lame," as in 14:13, just above. Finally, he has added a second substitute summoning, representing the Gentile Mission, after the first one, representing the outcasts within Israel. None of this is all that memorable.

Matthew, on the other hand, adds major new features to the parable: He has added a separate parable,[91] that of the Guest without a Wedding Garment (22:2, 11–12), to which he has also added one of his hellfire appendices, vv. 13–14. This brief parable is the same in intent as that of Rabbi Yohonon ben Zakkai (if not actually another version of it), preserved in the Babylonian Talmud. Here is Joachim Jeremias's summary: "A king . . . issued invitations to a banquet without specifying the hour. The wise attired themselves, while the foolish went on with their work. Suddenly the summons came, and those who were not dressed in clean clothes were not admitted to the banquet . . . The festal garment is repentance . . . Put it on today!"[92] Matthew, in order to make room for what he is going to add, summarizes the excuses, simply saying what two of them did rather than what they said they had to do: "they went off, one to his farm, another to his business," which seem to echo the first and second excuses in Luke's version. The here-pointless violence accorded the servants has been borrowed from the parable of the Wicked Tenants (Mark 12:1–11; Matthew 21:33–41). The multiplication of servants from one set to two seems to intend an allegory for Old Testament prophets and New Testament apostles/missionaries. The destruction of the murderers' city is surely supposed to stand for the fall of Jerusalem in 70 CE. So alien is this whole subplot to the original parable and so ineptly has Matthew jammed it in that he fails to see the comical disparity between verses 7 and 8:

after the razing of the city in a military campaign, the original feast to which the vanquished had been invited is still hot on the table!

For Matthew, the invitation of substitute guests refers only to the "Plan B" Gentile Mission. The Guest without a Wedding Garment now thus refers to the admission of the unwashed pagans; only let them be sure they have repented! They dare not take their improbable election for granted (as in Romans 11:17–24).

There is very little in the way of substantial Lukan redaction, nothing that seriously alters the parable. Thomas, having heard it read from Luke, would not likely remember Luke's changes. By contrast, if he remembered the basic plot-logic, it is not surprising he would forget Matthew's gross zigzags. As for Thomas' own changes, they, too, are fairly minor. Luke preserved the original threefold structure (three excuses, then lower the boom). Thomas shows his derivative character by complicating the pattern; only whereas Matthew chopped an excuse and summarized the rest, Thomas adds a fourth. Thomas adds a new conclusion: "Tradesmen and merchants shall not enter the places of my Father." Especially since "place" is often used for "temple" (as in John 11:48), the conclusion looks to be based on Zechariah 14:21b: "And there shall no longer be a trader in the house of Yahve Sabaoth on that day."

Any way you look at it, the parable warns of the danger of worldly preoccupations crowding out the urgent business of repentance and salvation (or, as Heidegger would say, sacrificing meditative thinking to calculative thinking). This is the danger depicted in Mark 4:19 and Shepherd of Hermas, Vision 3, chapter 5; Mandate 10:4–6; Parable 1.

65 He says, "A good man had a vineyard. He entrusted it to share-croppers to work it, and he would receive his share of its fruit from them. When the time came he sent his servant for them to give him his share of the produce of the vineyard. They grabbed his servant and beat him. They stopped just short of killing him. The servant returned and told his master. His master said, 'They must not have recognized him!' So he sent another servant, but the sharecrop-pers beat him, too. Finally the owner sent his son, thinking, 'Surely they will respect my son!' But since those sharecroppers were well aware this one was the heir of the vineyard, they grabbed him and killed him. Whoever has ears to hear, let him hear!"

See just below.

66 Jesus says, "Show me the stone which the contractors spurned as unsuitable; in fact, it is the very cornerstone!"

This pair of sayings is found in all three Synoptics. The link between the two is not readily apparent unless one looks at Mark's narrative context. The cornerstone saying is a quotation of Psalm 118:22. In that Psalm it is juxtaposed with the temple entrance liturgy: "Blessed is he who comes in the name of Yahve." That acclamation, originally the greeting of any and every pilgrim, had come to be interpreted as prefiguring Jesus' Triumphal Entry to the city (Mark 11:9), so the cornerstone text, adjacent to it in the Psalm, was thought to prefigure something in Jerusalem during the Passion, too. Matthew and Luke simply reproduce this sequence (with minor changes) from Mark. Thomas preserves the pairing of the sayings, which means he derived them from the Synoptics. Out of context, the connection would never suggest itself. If he had any particular gospel version uppermost in his mind, it must have been Luke, since he omits the same material: the initial back-story about the elaborate preparation of the vineyard (derived from Isaiah 5:2), as well as half of the Psalm citation. But Thomas no longer even knows that the cornerstone text *is* part of a Psalm. The "show me" is taken rather from the "show me a denarius" saying (Luke 20:24). Finally, why does Thomas describe the landlord as "a good man"? Perhaps in order to account for his persistent optimism, believing the best of his share-croppers despite mounting evidence to the contrary.

The parable looks back on the rejection and execution of Jesus (the "son") as the climax of Israel's age-long rebuff of the prophets, and the subsequent substitution of Christians for Jews as the heirs of God's favor. There is no use in trying to reinterpret the parable to fit into an imaginary *Sitz-im-Leben Jesu*, as many today attempt, as if Jesus told the parable to signal the end of the Sanhedrin's custody over the temple—in favor of whom? And despite Jeremias's sophistry, anyone can see the parable is nothing but a Christian allegory of redemptive history focusing on the death of the Son of God.

67 Jesus says, "Whoever knows all things yet fails to know himself, lacks everything."

This is a Gnosticizing version of the well-known saying, "What will it profit a man to gain the whole world at the cost of his soul (or life, or self)?"

The true wealth is self-knowledge. The lack of it, as saying 3 tells us, is the real poverty.

68 Jesus says, "Blessed are you when you are hated and persecuted, for the place where they persecuted you will be wiped off the map!"

This saying looks like a corrupted conflation of Matthew 5:11 (*"Blessed are you when you when men revile you and persecute you* and utter all kinds of evil against you falsely on my account. Rejoice and be glad, for your reward is great in heaven, for so men persecuted the prophets who were before you.") and Matthew10:23 ("When they persecute you in one town, flee to the next; for truly I say to you: *you will not have gone through all the towns* of Israel before the Son of Man comes.") plus Matthew 10:14–15 ("And if anyone will not welcome you or listen to your words, shake off the dust from your feet as you leave that house or town. Truly, I say to you: it shall be more tolerable on the day of judgment for the land of Sodom and Gomorrah than for that town.").

But does not the blessing/beatitude form have to supply some enviable outcome for the one addressed? But it does: the persecuted will get the last laugh.

69a Jesus says, "Blessed are those who have suffered in their hearts from persecution; it is these who have truly known the Father."

That is, as opposed to external, physical suffering, more easily shrugged off than the deep wounds of betrayal and the loss of loved ones. Since God obviously cannot suffer physical pain but is often said to feel anguish at the futile antics of mortals, the only way God may be said to be "persecuted" is "in heart." Hence whoever feels such anguish empathizes with God.

But it seems quite likely that this saying is no more than a corruption and conflation of two of Matthew's beatitudes: "Blessed are you when men revile you and persecute you," etc. (Matthew 5:11), and ""Blessed are the pure in heart" (Matthew 5:8). If it makes little apparent sense, this may be why.

69b "Blessed are the hungry, for the belly of him who desires will be filled."

This is clearly a memory quotation of Luke 6:21, "Blessed are you that hunger now, for you shall be satisfied," though it mixes in Matthew's third-person address. It is superfluous to translate as some do: "Blessed are they that go hungry in order that the belly of the poor may be satisfied." This is just the piety of Politically Correct affluent liberals being read into the text, to make it a proof text for vicarious, conscience-salving pantomimes.

70 Jesus says, "If you bring out what is inside you, what you have will save you. If you do not have it inside you, what you lack will be the death of you."

This saying recalls, and indeed, is based on the Q saying in Matthew 25:29: "For to every one who has will more be given, and he will have abundance; but from him who has not, even what he has will be taken away." (Luke 19:26 hardly differs). Thomas' version moves in a Gnosticizing direction and seems to be posed as a riddle: what is it that will save you if you have it and retrieve it, but the lack of which will destroy you? The divine photon of the Pleroma? I can see no textual basis for the widely quoted paraphrase by Elaine Pagels: "If you bring forth what is in you, what is in you will save you. But if you do not bring forth what is within you, what is within you will destroy you." I once asked how she arrived at such a translation result, and she replied it was the best sense she could make of it.

71 Jesus says, "I shall destroy this house, and no one will be able to rebuild it again."

The saying about the temple ricochets around the New Testament in various forms:

Mark 14:58: "We heard him say, 'I will destroy this temple that is made with hands, and in three days I will build another, not made with hands.'"

Matthew 26:21: "This fellow said, 'I am able to destroy the temple of God, and to build it in three days.'"

John 2:19: "Jesus answered them, 'Destroy this temple, and in three days I will raise it up.'"

Acts 6:14: "for we have heard him say that this Jesus of Nazareth will destroy this place, and will change the customs which Moses delivered to us."

Mark and Matthew deny Jesus said it. Acts transfers the saying to Stephen, even while denying that he said it either. John and Thomas admit Jesus said it, though John says he was not referring to the temple but to his own body. What does Thomas intend? I cannot help recalling Dhammapada 153–154: "Looking for the maker of this tabernacle I ran to no avail through a round of many births; and wearisome is birth again and again. But now, maker of the tabernacle, thou hast been seen; thou shalt not rear this tabernacle again. All thy rafters are broken, thy ridge-pole is shattered; the mind approaching the Eternal has attained to the extinction of all desires." (Irving Babbit trans.).

72 A man says to him, "Tell my brothers to divide my father's possessions with me!" He says to him, "O man, who appointed me executor?" He turned to his disciples and said to them, "Surely I am no executor?"

Here is a memory quotation of Luke 12:13–14: "One of the multitude said to him, 'Teacher, bid my brother divide the inheritance with me.' But he said to him, "Man, who made me a judge or divider over you?" The scene certainly rings true: in antiquity (and even today) people would approach itinerant holy men, asking them to act as arbiters for disputes. After all, the saint has neither worldly interests nor favorites to play. He cannot be bribed and is so holy that he will more readily discern the will of God even as the ancient prophets did, like Moses (Exodus 18:13–16) and Deborah (Judges 4:4–5). So the man's request seems both reasonable and biblical. Why does Jesus repudiate the role? Simply because the saying, uniquely Lukan among the Synoptics, is Marcionite in origin and tendency: it means to contrast Jesus with Moses, not to parallel him, in just the same way it contrasts Jesus with Elijah (contrast Luke 9: 61–62 with 1Kings 19:19–21 and Luke 9:51–56 with 2 Kings 1:9–12) a development of the Markan-Marcionite motif of the Transfiguration: heed Jesus, not Moses and Elijah (Mark 9:4–7; Luke 9:30–36). Similarly, for Marcionites God was no judge (Luke 13:1–3a, 4–5a), and neither was Jesus, which is why he repudiates the role here. Not surprisingly, the saying is based on a line from a Moses story, Exodus 2:14, "Who made you a prince and a judge over us?"

73 Jesus says, "There is so much waiting to be harvested, but how few laborers there are! So plead with the Lord to send laborers into the field!"

Thomas quotes Luke 10:2: "And he said to them, 'The harvest is plentiful, but the laborers are few; pray therefore the Lord of the harvest to send out laborers into his harvest.'" The saying sounds like an early Christian recruitment exhortation: more and more people were expressing interest in the Christian message, too many to keep up with! So this prophecy of the risen Christ, similar to that in Acts 13:1–3: "Now in the church at Antioch there were prophets and teachers, Barnabas, Simeon who was called Niger, Lucius of Cyrene, Manaen, a member of the court of Herod the tetrarch, and Saul. While they were worshiping the Lord and fasting, the Holy Spirit said, 'Set apart for me Barnabas and Saul for the work to which I have called them.' Then after fasting and praying they laid their hands on them and sent them off."

74 He says, "Lord, there are many gathered round the cistern, but no one is using it!"

Origen (*Contra Celsum* 8:16) tells us he found this saying in the Naassene text *Heavenly Dialogue*. The author of that work may have been quoting Thomas, since we know his sect used Thomas. Their version goes: "How is it that many are around the well, and no one goes into it?" The point of it would seem to be the irony that, despite protestations of pious faith, few are willing to "take the plunge" into the well of living waters. The strange thing about the saying is that Thomas seems to understand the saying as spoken *to* Jesus rather than *by* him, as a set-up question which Jesus will go on to answer (e.g., Mark). Perhaps we are to understand the scene as occasioned by the disciples noticing that, among those crowded round the well, no one seems to be drawing water from it (could this reflect John 5:1–7?). Jesus then replies with saying 75.

75 Jesus says, "Many are standing at the door, but only the solitary will gain entrance to the bridal chamber."

The Bridal Chamber was a Gnostic and Jewish-Christian sacrament in which the initiate encountered his astral self or heavenly twin = his guardian angel = the Risen Christ.[93] Here Thomas stands for the twin of Jesus who has reached the necessary enlightenment. Paradoxically, of all those assembled, the only one worthy to enter the bridal chamber is the "solitary," the celibate! This is because one marries Christ (Revelation 19:7, 9; 21:9; 2 Corinthians 11:2), one's higher self, and thus cannot be the mate of any mortal. This idea survives today among nuns who are betrothed to Christ alone. The well imagery recalls the living spring from which Thomas (Jesus' allegorical twin) drinks and so becomes Jesus' equal (saying 13). Anyone to whom this happens becomes the same as Jesus (saying 108), thus one with him.

> **76 Jesus says, "The kingdom of the Father is like a man who was a merchant, who owned much merchandise and found a pearl. That merchant was shrewd: he sold off all his stock so he could buy the single pearl for himself. You, too, seek the treasure that never gives out, which lasts, in a place where no moth approaches to devour and no worm ruins."**

This saying conflates Matthew 13:45–46 ("Again, the kingdom of heaven is like a merchant in search of fine pearls, who, on finding one pearl of great value, went and sold all that he had and bought it.") with Matthew 6:20 ("lay up for yourselves treasures in heaven, where neither moth nor rust consumes and where thieves do not break in and steal."). It is a natural and effective combination, interpreting the parable with the exhortation, no doubt correctly.

> **77 Jesus says, "I am the light that shines down upon all. I am the All! All things emerged from me, and all reached their goal in me! Split a log and I am revealed. Pick up a stone and you will find me underneath."**

Here Jesus speaks as the Logos, the Word, personified. Remember, the notion of the Logos (John 1:1–5) comes from Philo, and he received it from Stoicism. The Logos was both the agent of creation and revelation and the divine reason that permeated all things. Here, permeation is equated with pantheistic identity, but that, too, is classic Stoicism. What does it mean that he is the goal of all things, an idea also found in Ephesians 1:9–10? That, too, is pantheism: all things were emanated from the Godhead, the Pleroma, and must eventually return there. In a Gnostic context this does not include the material world, but refers to the Pleromatic photons that have been introduced to the previously inert cosmos to lend it motion and life. But one day all these sparks will be regathered, and the mud-pie world of the Demiurge's creation will collapse back upon itself.

It is difficult to imagine a flesh-and-blood human speaking this way about himself without measuring him for a straightjacket. It is far more natural, as D.F. Strauss said, to understand such a statement as the adoration of a worshipper for his deity, only transferred figuratively onto the deity's own lips, an incarnation of the praise rendered him.

> **78 Jesus says, "What are you doing in the desert? Did you come all the way out here just to see the wind shake the reeds? To gaze on a man clad in silks? Behold, your mortal kings and celebrities are the ones clad in silks, and they will never be able to know the truth."** [94]

They came out to hear a prophet who does know the truth, either Jesus himself or John the Baptist. In Q (Matthew 11:7–9 / Luke 7:24–26), this saying introduces a eulogy of John the Baptist. Part of that is found in Thomas 46. Here the emphasis is on the decadent rich and their having cut themselves off from the truth.

> **79 A woman in the crowd calls out to him, "Blessed is the womb that carried you, and the breasts that nursed you!" He says to her, "Blessed are those who have heard the commandment of the Father and have truly kept it. That alone abides, for there will be days when you will say, 'Blessed is the womb that never conceived and the breasts that never nursed'!"**

This logion combines two Lukan sayings: Luke 11:27–28 ("As he said this, a woman in the crowd raised her voice and said to him, 'Blessed is the womb that bore you, and the breasts that you sucked!' But he said, 'Blessed rather are those who hear the word of God and keep it!'") and Luke 23:28–29 ("But Jesus turning to them said, 'Daughters of Jerusalem, do not weep for me, but weep for yourselves and for your children. For behold, the days are coming when they will say, "Blessed are the barren, and the wombs that never bore, and the breasts that never gave suck!"'"). Elaine Pagels[95] plausibly suggests that the second saying was originally encratite in character, and that Luke has introduced it into a secondary context, that of the future fall of Jerusalem, matching Mark 13:17: "Woe to those with child or nursing in those days!" Thomas separated the saying from the Lukan context probably by accident (being unable to recall where it had belonged originally). In thus allowing the saying to resume its original isolation, he allowed its pro-celibacy emphasis to come to the fore once again.

80 Jesus says, "Whoever has understood my references to 'the world' has discovered it means 'the body,' and whoever has mastered the body is too good for this world."

This logion is but a slight variation on saying 56. I am taking this one as an interpretation of that one.

81 Jesus says, "Let him who has become rich become king, but let him who has attained true power renounce the throne."

This is a contrast between two forms of power. False, worldly power is mere riches. Kingship is available to one with such power (as he thinks), but the real power is that exercised by Prince Siddhartha, Amitabha, and St. Francis of Assisi: to renounce worldly power to seek a higher kingdom, as in saying 2, the spiritual "reign over all things."

82 Jesus says, "Whoever is near me is near the fire, but whoever is far from me is far from the kingdom."

Origen knows this as a saying attributed to Jesus, occurring in the Gospel according to the Hebrews. The point of it seems to be that, while allegiance to Christ is dangerous, presumably because of possible persecution, it is the only game in town: "Where else would we go? You're the only one with the words of eternal life!" (John 6:68).

83 Jesus says, "The images are manifest to human perception, while the Light which is within them is hidden in the image of the Light of the Father. But he will manifest himself, and then it is his image that will be overshadowed by his Light."

For now, all we see are human forms, made in the image and likeness of God. The divine light itself is concealed within the material human body, itself but an image of the light, but a marred one because of sin, obscuring the light more than revealing it. But one day the divine light will shine forth unobstructed from the resurrection body.

84 Jesus says, "When you see your likeness in a mirror you rejoice. But when you see your prototype images which came into being before you in the mind of the Creator, those which neither die nor are visible to the eye, you will be overwhelmed!"

I am taking the words, "When you behold your likeness" in the sense of James 1:23–24, but it is possible, as Winterhalter[96] suggests, to see here a reference to Adam first beholding his likeness in the newly-formed Eve and rejoicing (Genesis 2:23). There is certainly a protological context here, as seen in the preceding and subsequent verses. But I see it as leading up to the contrast with the eschatological revelation of the heavenly body-prototype (= the resurrection body) in the Last Day. In that day we will see no longer in a cloudy metal mirror, but rather face to face—with our higher, divine *doppelgänger*. The sacrament of the Bridal Chamber is an anticipation of this consummation.

85 Jesus says, "Adam came into being from a great Power and a great wealth, and still he was not your equal. For if he had been, he would never have tasted death."

Note the encratite contrast between the mortal sin of Adam and the greater worthiness of the encratite who does not make (or who reverses) Adam's mistake by renouncing sex. The language of "great Power" and "great wealth" sounds Gnostic (and may be, for the writer), but it need not be. These terms began as reverential paraphrases for the holy name of God, even for the generic word "God." We see this in Simon Magus' epithet "the Great Power" (Acts 8:10) and the title of the Mandaean scripture, the *Ginza*, or Treasure of Life. See also Mark 14:62; 1 Corinthians 1:24; 2 Corinthians 8:9; 1 Peter 1:4; Ephesians 1:17–19 (wisdom, treasure, power).

86 Jesus says, "Foxes have their burrows, and the birds have their nests, but man has no natural place to rest his head."

This Q saying occurs, in a context of discipleship, in Matthew 8:20 and Luke 9:58. Thomas has forgotten the context and perhaps the secondary

Christological reference as well. By itself, as it must have originated, the saying speaks, in Cynic (or nomad) fashion of the natural homelessness of the human species (literally, "the son of man," as in saying 44), either destined to wander (Cynics, nomads) or requiring no one type of habitat. The contrast with lower animal species is reminiscent of Matthew 6:26–30, though it serves as a counterpoint to the animal-human similarity there.

87 Jesus says, "Wretched is that body which subsists on another body, and wretched is the soul that depends on these two!"

Thomas here advocates vegetarianism, the avoidance of eating "dead things."

88 Jesus says, "The angels and the prophets will come to you, and they will mete out what is due you. And for your part, render to them what you have in your hands. In the meantime, say to yourselves, 'Which day will they come and demand what is due them?'"

Compressed here is a judgment scene like that in the Koran, where the prophets, warners against sin, will testify that you knew better (Luke 16:31), and the guardian angels will testify to what they saw you doing (Matthew 18:10). "If thou couldst see, when the wrong-doers reach the pangs of death and the angels stretch their hands out, saying: Deliver up your souls" (Koran VI:94, Muhammad Marmaduke Pickthall trans.) You will, as in the parable of the talents (Matthew 25:14–30), be called to account for your life and what you have made of it. So you should live mindfully of that day.

89 Jesus says, "Why do you wash only the outside of the cup? Don't you realize that the same artisan made both the inside and the outside?"

This is another version of Luke 11:40: "And the Lord said to him, 'Now you Pharisees cleanse the outside of the cup and of the dish, but inside you are full of extortion and wickedness. You fools! Did not he who made the outside make the inside also?'" (And see Matthew 23:25–26.) A mini-parable on hypocrisy, urging its hearers/readers to make the inner as the outer, this saying is a moralizing adaptation of a real scribal debate over the question whether the ritual pollution attaching to the outside of a vessel is automatically communicated to the liquid inside if it does not actually touch it. In the original scribal context this reasoning would mean that the inside is automatically polluted as soon as the inside is. Has such a scribal original been simply misunderstood, or re-applied to moral concerns?

90 Jesus says, "Come to me, for my yoke is easy to bear and my lordship is lenient, and you shall find repose for yourselves."

Here is an abbreviated version of Matthew 11:28–30: "Come to me, all who labor and are heavy laden, and I will give you rest. Take my yoke upon you, and learn from me; for I am gentle and lowly in heart, and you will find rest for your souls. For my yoke is easy, and my burden is light." (Haven't you ever had trouble trying to quote the whole thing from memory?) Matthew has in turn abbreviated Sirach 51:23–27:

> Draw near to me, you who are untaught; and lodge in my school. Why do you say you are lacking in these things, and why are your souls very thirsty? . . . Put your neck under the yoke, and let your souls receive instruction; it is to be found close by. See with your own eyes that I have labored little and found for myself much rest.

Wisdom may seem a troublesome path, but in fact it is sin that complicates things. The wise man steers clear of many entanglements. Naturally, Thomas sees "rest" and thinks of the wider promise of the elect entering into the eternal Sabbath rest of the Creator, as often elsewhere in his gospel.

91 They say to him, "Tell us who you are, so we may make you into a creed!" He says to them, "You can assess the appearance of the sky and the earth, but as for him who stands right in front of you, you have failed to recognize him, for you do not grasp the meaning of the present moment!"

Most of Jesus' reply here comes from the Synoptic refusal of Jesus to produce an authenticating sign from God ("heaven"). One might well ask, "A sign authenticating *what*?" That Jesus' mission or message was really ordained of God, presumably. Thomas adds that specificity to Jesus' reply: "as for him who stands right in front of you, you have failed to recognize him." "They" may stand for Jesus' enemies or his disciples here; each is equally ignorant in that they seek a definition for Jesus, just as the emissaries of the priests do when they interrogate John the Baptist in John 1:19 ff. Their error is the same as that of Peter and Matthew in saying 13: must they have a title, a Christology, before they can respond to Jesus' challenge? Must you learn something *else*, something *about* Jesus, besides what you see of him? The danger is to substitute for the living Jesus some theological construct. What pretends to convey only obstructs and replaces. Carl Michaelson[97] explains how demythologizing enables us to free faith in Jesus from the categories of first-century thought which inevitably tend to subsume Jesus under general categories and thus rob his uniqueness. He has become a "son of God," a "messianic king," a Hellenistic "Kyrios." But no. He is Jesus of Nazareth. You must encounter *him*. (Naturally, however, this is much easier said than done, as no such Jesus is available anymore. All that one can do is consider what Tillich called "the picture of Jesus as the Christ" mediated to the church by the gospel accounts. But then these are already heavy with Christological interpretation, so that one is already encountering someone else's reinterpretation of a lost historical Jesus. And how many even of his contemporaries can have had even a moment of significant encounter with him? Very few were so lucky.)

92 Jesus says, "Once I told you, 'Seek and you will find.' But those things you asked me in those days, I refused to tell you then. Now the time has come to tell you, and you are no longer interested!"

They have prematurely given up the search, contra saying 2. Jesus is made to quote himself from Matthew 7:7, "Ask, and it will be given you; seek, and you will find; knock, and it will be opened to you." I would conjecture that this saying began as a rebuke by an early Christian prophet (channeler) rebuking lazy compatriots. It presupposes the Johannine (John 16:12–15) and generally Gnostic belief that the deeper teaching of Jesus would be revealed only after his departure from historical existence, by agency of the Paraclete, and this is the pose of the speaker, who has a message that no one is very anxious to hear. What preacher, albeit with fewer delusions of grandeur, has not felt precisely the same way?

93 "Do not give what is holy to the dogs, for then it will only end up in the dungpile. Do not throw pearls to swine, for they will only make it defiled."

Here is an abbreviated version of Matthew 7:6 "Do not give dogs what is holy; and do not throw your pearls before swine, lest they trample them under foot and turn to attack you." The advanced teaching of the Gnostic is not to be leaked to a public not ready for it. It will only be exposed to blasphemy and ridicule that way. What else can you expect from those not ready? What else can they do with it? It will be your fault, not theirs. This is why disparate religious groups over the centuries, including the eleventh-century Druzes and the modern Moonies, have indulged in "heavenly deception." Sufis, too, kept mum, learning well the lesson of the great mystic Al-Hallaj, who, rapt in divine ecstasy, went about proclaiming, "I am the Truth!" only to be crucified by those conventional Muslims who of course had no way of understanding his nondualism. Thomas knows this danger and seems to warn of it in saying 13, though here he lacks Matthew's element of danger, the dogs or boars tearing you to pieces. His concern in this saying is to protect the truth from unseemly ridicule.

94 Jesus says, "Whoever seeks will find, and whoever knocks, the door will swing open for him."

A memory quote from Matthew 7:7, on optimism in prayer: "Ask, and it will be given you; seek, and you will find; knock, and it will be opened to you."

95 Jesus says, "If you have money, do not lend it out at interest. Rather, give it to him from whom you can expect no return."

This abbreviates Luke 6:34–35, "And if you lend to those from whom you hope to receive, what credit is that to you? Even sinners lend to sinners, to receive as much again. But love your enemies, and do good, and lend, expecting nothing in return; and your reward will be great, and you will be sons of the Most High; for he is kind to the ungrateful and the selfish." Giving is understood here as a categorical imperative, always right for its own sake, not merely a hypothetical or prudential imperative, one that might or might not make sense as an advantageous strategy. Notice that Thomas lacks any assurance that God will repay you what you lose lending to a deadbeat.

96 Jesus says, "The kingdom of the Father is like a woman who has taken a pinch of leaven and hidden it in the dough, and has made large loaves from it. Whoever has ears, let him hear!"

It is only another version of Matthew 13:33: "He told them another parable. 'The kingdom of heaven is like leaven which a woman took and hid in three measures of flour, till it was all leavened.'" Like the parallel parable of the mustard seed (saying 20), this one looks back on the remarkable growth of Christianity from a later historical standpoint. Some read great significance into the use of leaven as a metaphor for the kingdom of God, since leaven is otherwise universally used in Judaism as a metaphor for corruption. On such a slender basis some understand Jesus to have been undermining or sweeping away traditional categories of sacred and profane.[98] But that is nonsense. If it means anything, the use of leaven here rather marks the teller of the parable as a Gentile utterly unacquainted with such niceties.

97 Jesus says, "The kingdom of the Father is like a woman carrying a jar full of meal. While she was walking a distant road, the handle of the jar cracked. The meal trickled out behind her on the road. She was wholly unaware of it, having noticed no accident. Once she arrived at her dwelling, she put the jar down and found it empty!"

If we are not vigilant, our spiritual life steals away on little cat feet! It is also possible that the saying comments on the forfeiture by Judaism of its privileges by a gradual spiritual neglect, perhaps an excessive reliance upon the accumulated "merits of the Fathers"[99] ("Don't go reassuring yourselves, 'We don't need to repent! We have Abraham for our father!'"). We need not envision here a Christian jeering at Judaism as an outmoded religion. The gradual character of the envisioned loss more implies an intra-Jewish prophetic rebuke.

98 Jesus says, "The kingdom of the Father is like a man who plans to kill a powerful opponent. He drew his sword in his house and thrust it into the wall, to see whether he was strong enough to strike the death blow. Then he killed the powerful man."

Parallel to the twin parables of Luke 14:28–33, this one urges its audience not to make a religious commitment impulsively, without considering whether one is prepared for the long haul and the needful sacrifices. The scene envisioned is that of a Zealot preparing to assassinate some Herodian aristocrat, as often happened.

99 The disciples say to him, "Your brothers and your mother are waiting outside." He says to them, "Those here who obey the will of my Father, they are my brothers and my mother, for they are those who shall enter the kingdom of my Father."

Mark 3:31–35 is another version of this saying. Mark's story serves his polemic against Jewish Christian authority factions, in this case that of the Heirs or *Desposunoi*, namely James the Just, Simeon bar-Cleophas, etc. Unlike Moses who, in a similar scene (Exodus 18) welcomed his visiting relatives and heeded their advice to ease his workload lest he have a breakdown, Mark has the relatives of Jesus decide he is insane and then come to take custody of him. Jesus, then, rebuffs them, serving notice that henceforth no one is closer to him than those who hear God's commands and perform them—unlike his apostate blood relatives. Luke 8:19–21 tries to iron out the factional disputes. For this reason he carefully cuts words from Mark's original, implicitly making the scene parallel to the Moses scene in Exodus 18: now, alerted to his family's presence, Jesus seems to eulogize them precisely as stolid examples of those who heed God's will! Thomas seems to remember the Lukan version. He is far from hostile to the James faction, as per saying 12.

100 They show Jesus a gold coin and say to him, "Caesar's agents demand taxes from us." He says to them, "Give Caesar's things to Caesar. Give God's things to God. And give me what is mine."

The repentance and commitment the disciple owes to Jesus far outweigh petty concerns such as taxation and temple offerings, once considered so important, as in the original version of this text, namely Mark 12:13–17: "And they sent to him some of the Pharisees and some of the Herodians, to entrap him in his talk. And they came and said to him, 'Teacher, we know that you are true, and care for no man; for you do not regard the position of men, but truly teach the way of God. Is it lawful to pay taxes to Caesar, or not? Should we pay them, or should we not?' But knowing their hypocrisy, he said to them, 'Why put me to the test? Bring me a coin, and let me look at it.' And they brought one. And he said to them, 'Whose likeness and inscription is this?' They said to him, 'Caesar's.' Jesus said to them, 'Render to Caesar the things that are Caesar's, and to God the things that are God's.' And they were amazed at him." Originally the point of Jesus' reply must have been to legitimate Jewish payment of Roman taxes, paid with Roman *denarii*, by appealing to the fact that these same coins were no good for buying sacrificial animals in the temple. No one faulted Jews for using any type of coinage for common business, but it was considered idolatry to offer God Roman coins with human profiles on them. Hence the notorious money changing tables in the temple court. A sacrificing pilgrim bought pre-inspected beasts on site and then had them butchered at the altar. Coins used to buy them had to be aniconic Jewish or Phoenician. Well, then, reasons Jesus, it can involve no religious compromise to give Caesar his own coins which God will not take at the temple anyway! It is no clever trick, but a genuine case of halakhic reasoning. But it is irrelevant to Thomas, written in Syria where golden *denarii* were current, and all thoughts of temple sacrifices were long gone.

Why does Thomas add to Jesus' reply, "And render to me what is mine"? It may simply be a transformation of his indignant initial response to the hypocrisy of his interrogators; it may just mean: "Be honest with me" or "Give me the respect I deserve." On the other end of the spectrum, it is conceivable we have here a reflection of Gnostic soteriology whereby, as one ascends heavenward after death, one has to "pay" the guardian of each celestial sphere, either casting aside the various layers of "clothing" (the concentric physical, appetitive, astral, and etheric bodies) appropriate to each sphere, as Jesus did when he ascended, or by giving the guardians the proper password. Can it be that Caesar stands for the lord of this world, the Demiurge? Is "God" the true deity? Does one somehow render appropriate tokens, perhaps of a righteous life, to each, and to the Christ-*aion* (now back in heaven), as one ascends?

101 "Whoever does not hate his father and his mother following in my way will not be able to be a disciple of mine. My natural mother gave me death, but my true Mother gave me the Life."

The first half of the saying is the same, basically, as saying 55. The second half contrasts physical descent with spiritual. The true Mother is the Holy Spirit. "Spirit," *ruach*, is feminine gendered in Hebrew and Aramaic, so that she was personified as "sexually" feminine. The saying bespeaks Marcionite encratism: Marcion condemned marital procreation as only producing more slaves for the Demiurge, the Creator God. Spiritual rebirth, however, is a different matter entirely.

102 Jesus says, "Woe to them, the Pharisees! For they are like a dog sound asleep in the ox trough, who neither eats nor allows the oxen to eat."

Socrates uses the same metaphor, which is precisely equivalent to that of the hidden keys in saying 39. If you have no plans of going in, or of eating, then get out of the way so others can do what you won't! But how does one occupy the manger, making the oxen starve? How does one hide the keys? Of course, hiding saving knowledge which you could be communicating would be one way to do it. Another would be to allow one's apparent spiritual unconcern to form a bad example for others. Others will look at you and say, "Well, I guess there's no real rush; *he's* in no hurry to settle things with God!"

103 Jesus says, "Blessed is the man who knows which watch of the night in which the burglars will arrive, so he may get up and collect his weapons and be ready for them before they come in."

This is but another version of saying 21b. Why are there so many repetitions, and all clustered here toward the end? I would have to guess that the compiler heard slightly different versions and wanted to make sure not to lose any of the sacred words. He was motivated by the same scribal anxiety that led Mark to include two versions of the loaves and fishes miracle: they had slight differences in detail, even though they are plainly variants of the same story; he dared not leave either one out in case they weren't!

104 They say to him, "Come, let us observe this day of prayer and fasting." Jesus says, "Oh? Which sin have I committed? Where has sin defeated me? Wait till the bridegroom emerges from the bridal chamber, signaling the feast is over; then let them fast and let them pray."

Another version of the first half appears in the Gospel according to the Nazoreans, "Behold the mother of the Lord and his brethren said to him: 'John the Baptist baptizes unto the remission of sins; let us go and be baptized by him.' But he said to them: 'Wherein have I sinned that I should go and be baptized by him? Unless what I have just said is a sin of ignorance." Ismo Dunderberg[100] is right: this apologia represents an advanced stage of development along the same trajectory we find in the canonical gospels and into the later apocryphal ones. It puts Thomas later than the canonical texts.

The second half, taken from Mark 2:18–22, has often been over-theologized. It may have nothing at all to do with subsequent Christian fasting to commemorate Jesus (the bridegroom of the Church) being taken away and crucified *on Friday*. The point may simply be to say that "For everything there is a season and a time for every matter under heaven . . . a time to weep and a time to laugh; a time to mourn and a time to dance" (Ecclesiastes 3:1, 4). One need not fast all the time! But then that would appear to be obvious to all; how could it be in controversy?

105 Jesus says, "Whoever can identify father or mother shall be called the son of a harlot."

Anything short of spiritual rebirth is tantamount to the most degrading bastardy. The true ascetic disciple of Jesus renounces all natural family connections.

106 Jesus says, "When you make the two one, you will become true humans, and when you say, 'Mountain, be moved!' it will indeed be moved."

This logion is another version of saying 48. Literally, "you will become sons of man," implying a recovery, by means of celibacy, of the image of the androgynous Adam before the split into male (*ish*) and female (*ishshah*).

107 Jesus says, "The kingdom is like a shepherd with a flock of a hundred sheep. One of them, the largest, wandered off. He left the ninety-nine to themselves while he went in search of the one, till he found it. He was exhausted, but he said to the sheep, 'I love you more than ninety-nine!'"

The original version of this Q parable, whether one prefers Matthew 18:12–14 or Luke 15:3–7, raises the question why on earth a shepherd would leave ninety-nine helpless sheep to fend for themselves, at the mercy of wolves and bears, to go look for one single sheep that had wandered away. The rhetorical question with which it is introduced in Q implies any shepherd would do the same, when in fact none would. This I judge to be one of many such errors implying the parables originated far from the romanticized Galilean landscape in which they are placed. Thomas must have asked himself the same question, but his answer was that the lost sheep was the favorite of the shepherd! To hell with the others! The parable then becomes parallel to that of the Dragnet in Matthew 13:47–48 and the Pearl of Great Price in Matthew 13:45–46 (see Thomas saying 8). The shepherd no longer stands for the compassion of God or Jesus who will not let the *least* of his brethren go astray,[101] but rather for the wise person who knows that something supremely valuable is worth the sacrifice of all else.

> **108 Jesus says, "Whoever drinks from my mouth shall become as I am, and I myself will become he. And the hidden things shall at last be revealed to him."**

This is just what happens to Thomas in saying 13, the spiritual twin of Jesus, who attaining his insight, is no more to be counted a mere disciple, but the very equal of Christ, who was not intended to be unique, but rather the firstborn of many brothers and sisters. Thomas stands for the ideal reader.

> **109 Jesus says, "The kingdom is like a man who had a treasure buried in his field without knowing it. When he died, he left it to his son. The son did not know about it either, and once he inherited the field, he sold it. And he who bought it went to it and, while plowing, discovered the treasure. He began lending money to whomever he wished."**

This saying appears to combine elements from two parables. One is Matthew 13:44: "The kingdom of heaven is like treasure hidden in a field, which a man found and covered up; then in his joy he goes and sells all that he has and buys that field." The other comes from the Midrash on Canticles V:13:

> It is like a man who inherited a place full of rubbish. The inheritor was lazy and he sold it for a ridiculously small sum. The purchaser dug therein industriously and found in it a treasure. He built therewith a great palace and passed through the bazaar with a train of slaves whom he had bought with the treasure. When the seller saw it he could have choked himself.[102]

The rabbinic parable seems to teach the lesson that one cheats only himself by his laziness. Unwilling to expend much labor on his opportunity, he is unable to discern its worth. By contrast, the one who is willing to pour much effort into realizing his opportunity will find a great reward. The buyer spent a small sum on it in terms of money and gained a huge amount, true, but what he really paid was the labor he expended on the plot of land, so the reward did not come cheap. The seller sold a fortune for peanuts, and it was his own fault. The gospel parable similarly requires a great sacrifice to gain a great reward. Thus the two are compatible.

But we must not too quickly laugh off (as Davies does)[103] the Gnosticizing interpretations offered by Bertil Gärtner[104] and Robert McLachlan Wilson.[105] According to the former, the succession of generations in the parable stands for successive incarnations of the divine spark/soul until it finally comes to self-realization. According to the latter, the field stands for the Christian message/scripture passed down obliviously by the unenlightened Catholic authorities into the hands of those who discover the esoteric, Gnostic meaning and enter into spiritual riches unsuspected by their catechists.

110 Jesus says, "Whoever has found the world and become rich, let him renounce the world."

Another version of saying 81.

111a Jesus says, "The sky and the earth will be rolled up like a tent flap before your very eyes, and he who subsists on the living shall taste neither death nor fear."

Whoever coined this saying had certainly not despaired of a soon-coming apocalyptic denouement! See Isaiah 34:4: "All the host of heaven shall rot away, and the skies roll up like a scroll. All their host shall fall, as leaves fall from the vine, like leaves falling from the fig tree." Also Revelation 6:14: "the sky vanished like a scroll that is rolled up, and every mountain and island was removed from its place." The saying means to guarantee the salvation (only) of vegetarians, those who subsist on spiritual food and do not eat "dead things," animal carcasses.

111b Jesus says, "Whoever finds himself is too good for this world."

Another version of saying 80.

112 Jesus says, "Woe to the flesh which depends upon the soul! Woe to the soul which depends upon the flesh!"

The physical body is doomed; let it not be the focus of one's life, as with the worldlings. The second half looks like a repetition of saying 87: blessed are the vegetarians who do not prolong their lives by eating animal flesh.

113 His disciples say to him, "When will the kingdom come?" Jesus says, "It will not come in a way you expect; they will not be able to say, 'Look, here!' or 'See, there!' Rather, the kingdom of the Father is spread out over the earth without people recognizing it."

Another version of saying 51, based in turn upon Luke 17:20–21. The very attitude of anticipation of a thing prevents one from seeing it if it has already arrived. One looks in the wrong direction, and so it seems Godot never comes.

114 Simon Peter says, "Tell Mariam to leave us, because women are unworthy of the Life." Jesus says, "Behold, I shall lead her to make her male, so that she, too, may become a living spirit, like you males. For every woman who makes herself male will enter the kingdom of heaven."

In the terminology of Philo, used here, the "male" element of the personality is the rational, while the "female" is the emotional. Passion must be mortified and controlled by reason, or salvation is impossible. Despite the insulting imagery, the point of the saying is to affirm that women are equally capable of discipleship, against the carping of church misogynists, symbolized here by Peter. This is another way of saying that, in Christian discipleship, the two become one, so that the male is no longer male, the female no longer female. There is no denying, however, a certain element of back-handedness, of grudging chauvinism, hardly surprising given the times. We find the same combination of forward and backwards looking in a pair of Buddhist parallels.

Yasodhara had three times requested of the Buddha that she might be admitted to the Sangha, but her wish had not been granted. Now Pajapati, the foster-mother of the Blessed One, in the company of Yasodhara, and many other women, went to the Tathagata entreating him earnestly to let them take the vows and be ordained as disciples.

And the Blessed One, foreseeing the danger that lurked in admitting women to the Sangha, protested that while the good religion ought surely to last a thousand years it would, when women joined it, likely decay after five hundred years; but observing the zeal of Pajapati and Yasodhara for leading a religious life, he could no longer resist and assented to have them admitted as his disciples.

Then the venerable Ananda addressed the Blessed One thus:

"Are women competent, Venerable Lord, if they retire from household life to the homeless state, under the doctrine and discipline announced by the Tathagata, to attain to the fruit of conversion, to attain to a release from a wearisome repetition of rebirths, to attain to saintship?"

And the Blessed One declared: "Women are competent, Ananda, if they retire from household life to the homeless state, under the doctrine and discipline announced by the Tathagata, to attain to the fruit of conversion, to attain to a release from a wearisome repetition of rebirths, to attain to saintship.[106]

And in the Mahayana scripture *Saddharma-Pundarika* XI:51, we read how:

Then the venerable Sariputra said to that daughter of Sagara, the Naga-king: Thou hast conceived the idea of enlightenment, young lady of good family, without sliding back, and art gifted with immense wisdom, but supreme, perfect enlightenment is not easily won. It may happen, sister, that a woman displays an unflagging energy, performs good works for many thousands of Aions, and fulfils the six perfect virtues (Paramitas), but as yet there is no example of her having reached Buddhaship. [Then she presents the Buddha a gem as an object lesson, which proves her worth.] At the same instant, before the sight of the whole world and of the senior priest Sariputra, the female sex of the daughter of Sagara, the Naga-king, disappeared; the male sex appeared and she manifested herself as a Bodhisattva.[107]

Conclusion

Well, have we done it? Have we cracked the code? Where do we turn in our papers? When will we get the grades? And how high a score does it take to win eternal life? And who is to say that, even if we have imbibed from the bubbling spring that Thomas has measured out, we are really wise? We may understand him, his gospel, but are we any closer to understanding life and death, or God, or our moral duty? These, the really important questions, cannot be resolved in a book like this.

4 THE NECRONOMICON

Introduction

At the outset of his masterful survey *Arabic Literature: An Introduction*, H. A. R. Gibb warns his readers that "Arabic literature has ... shared the fate of the classical literature in that many valuable works are, it is to be feared, irretrievably lost."[1] So as wide-ranging and detailed as Dr. Gibb's study is, it can provide at best a representative cross section of an originally much larger corpus. The same is true of that obscure corner of Arabic literature with which we are concerned—the *Necronomicon*, or the *Kitab al-Azif*, of Abdul Alhazred. For despite both its inherent interest and the wide curiosity it has provoked, the book has survived only in scattered fragments. And not only has most of the text itself been lost to scholarly scrutiny. Myriad popular misconceptions have also clouded the correct interpretation of what portions of the text remain. Hence the need for the present work, a critical commentary on Alhazred's work.

Surprisingly, little work has been done in this field. As Saul Lieberman[2] wisely pointed out, even though mysticism may be nonsense, the history of nonsense is a proper task for scholarship! Alas, too few scholars have caught this crucial distinction. Thus most have been put off by the arcane character of the *Necronomicon*. The regrettable result is that the field has been left to cranks and occultists. Two works that readily come to mind in this connection are Laban Shrewsbury's *Cthulhu in the Necronomicon* and Joachim Feery's *Original Notes on the Necronomicon*. The scarcity of both works would of itself make a new study advisable. But beyond this, both texts are quite unsatisfactory. For one thing, both draw freely from secondary as

293

well as authentic material, oblivious of the distinction (more about which momentarily). For another, neither author maintains the slightest scholarly detachment, a trait indispensable in this kind of study. One may fault Sir James Frazer for the unreliability of his sources in *The Golden Bough*, or one may criticize the extravagance of Margaret Murray's theories in *The Witch-Cult in Western Europe*,[3] but one cannot fault the academic impartiality with which they approached their subjects.

By contrast, *Cthulhu in the Necronomicon* is manifestly the product of a fanatic who has come not only to catalogue the nonsense, but finally to believe it. Departing completely from the calm balance of Shrewsbury's earlier work *An Investigation into the Myth-Patterns of Latterday Primitives with Especial Reference to the R'lyeh Text*, the book in question here represents little more than a doom-saying jeremiad worthy of Chicken Little.

Like some field anthropologists of whom one occasionally reads, Shrewsbury had "gone native." And unable to find a legitimate publisher for his rantings, he resorted to the vanity press to produce *Cthulhu in the Necronomicon*. Had he lived a generation or so later, Shrewsbury would not have wanted for a publisher. No doubt his theories would have been ideal fare for those sensationalist paperback houses which have so profitably spread the pseudoscientific gospels of Von Däniken,[4] Sitchin,[5] and Velikovsy.[6]

Feery's *Original Notes on the Necronomicon* presents the scholar with even greater problems of credibility. Even those occultists who use the book note its dubious reliability. It often "quotes" passages that seem not to have appeared in any known version of the *Necronomicon*. In fact, Feery's book seems to be the result of a mediumistic rewriting of the text (Lumley calls it an "often fanciful reconstruction"[7]), rather than a commentary on it. In this, Feery resembles Levi Dowling,[8] the author of *The Aquarian Gospel of Jesus the Christ*, who "transcribed" this "New Age" life of Jesus from the ethereal "Akashic Records" floating around somewhere in the universe or, more likely, in the occultists' imagination.

A word should be said of Mark Owings's *The Necronomicon: A Study*. Though this work does not suffer like Shrewsbury's and Feery's from being the product of uncritical fanaticism, neither is it much of a work of scholarship. Mainly, it offers a compilation of previous writings (by Lin Carter, Laban Shrewsbury, H.P. Lovecraft, and others). The only original material consists of a revisionist chronology of the various editions of the *Necronomicon*, together with a summary of copies rumored still to exist. On both subjects,

Owings' study is to be approached with caution. And in neither case does the pamphlet take us much beyond Lovecraft's authoritative but regrettably brief article "History of the *Necronomicon*" to which we shall make reference in what follows.

If previous efforts have been so meager and so disappointing, how will this one do better? Briefly, in four respects. First, we will analyze all known fragments of the *Necronomicon*, clarifying the meaning of hitherto-puzzling passages by referring to parallels in other ancient texts. Second, we will employ various critical criteria to distinguish authentic material (i.e., that actually written by Alhazred) from later interpolations. Third, we will employ the results gained by the preceding methods to elucidate the history and development of the "Cthulhu Mythos."[9] Fourth and finally, we will propose a verse-numbering system to facilitate future reference to the *Necronomicon*.

The basic ground-plan is as follows. Preliminary chapters will deal with what biblical scholars have come to call "problems of introduction," i.e., the propriety of the critical approach to the text, the identity of the author, Abdul Alhazred, the genre of the *Necronomicon*, the sources used in writing it, etc. Then we will proceed to the discussion of the various surviving fragments, both exegeting them and evaluating their genuineness.

A final note on the sources for this study. Most readers are familiar with the *Necronomicon* through the quotations of it appearing in the works of fiction writers including H.P. Lovecraft, August Derleth, and Clark Ashton Smith. Many writers of pulp fantasy fiction, though not occultists themselves, pored over occult works ancient and modern with the zeal of true acolytes simply because they recognized them as rich resources for fiction.[10] As most readers will already know, the complete text of the *Necronomicon* is no longer extant, having apparently perished sometime in the early Renaissance as a result of the repeated ecclesiastical attempts to suppress and destroy the infamous work. As far as we can tell, these inquisitors were finally successful. Even John Dee's notorious version is lost. One must not be misled by the fiction of Lovecraft and others here. For purely fictional purposes they have represented stray copies as having survived into the present day. Would that it were so! The task of the scholar would thereby be made infinitely easier. No, we have only the fragments preserved for posterity, ironically enough, in the obscure works of medieval Church demonologists and heresy-hunters. Since these works are virtually inaccessible to most laypersons, we will instead give the references to the modern works of fiction in which the *Necronomicon* fragments appear. Please keep in mind that our fiction writers did not restrict themselves to the few surviving fragments, but when these ran out, they felt free to fabricate their own. Needless to say, we will deal only with the actual quotes; thus not every supposed *Necronomicon* passage in every work of fiction comes in for discussion.

The situation that we face has a close analogy. We find a famous precedent in the intriguing Gospel According to the Hebrews. M.R. James describes this work as "a divergent yet not heretical form of our Gospel according to St. Matthew."[11] This is a second century A.D. work, written in Hebrew or Aramaic, and used by a Jewish-Christian sect, though extant quotations come from Greek translations. The book was commented upon and quoted by several ecclesiastical writers including Irenaeus, Jerome, Clement of Alexandria, Origen, Epiphanius, Nicephorus, and Haimo of Auxerre. These writers range from the second to the ninth centuries A.D. The complete text was accessible to them, yet today it survives only in the form of several fragments; but this does not make it impossible to exegete these passages and to characterize the work as a whole. No more does the fragmentary state of the *Necronomicon* disallow its exposition.

Section One: Preliminary Questions

The Critical Approach

One of the intellectual pivots on which Western history turned from the Dark Ages to the Renaissance was the discovery of critical historiography. Previously, historians saw their task as that of mere chroniclers, setting out the order of all events recorded in the available sources. Few thought to question whether the old records deserved the credence, even the credulity, they received. In the realms of historical as well as natural science, the rule was *magister dixit*; the mere citation of "authorities" settled any question. If the ancients said the hyena gave birth through its ear, why then it must! If Livy said Rome had been founded by Romulus, dare anyone question it? But eventually, the winds changed, and the rule became *ipse dixit*. "The thing itself" must decide the issue. If Galileo wanted to know about the relative speed of falling bodies, he didn't take Aristotle's word for it. Instead, he dropped two iron balls, larger and smaller, from the Tower of Pisa to find out for himself. Church authorities jailed him for trying it. Historians, too, raised ecclesiastical ire when they examined the so-called "Donation of Constantine," which purported to be a charter signed by that emperor, granting eternal possession of the Papal States to the Church. This land-grant charter was discovered to bear the marks of a later day than Constantine's, and so to be a "pious fraud."

As the foregoing examples make clear, the use of critical investigation was perceived from the start as subversive. If historians dared to reject the claims of the past, they might soon come to question those of contemporary authorities as well. And if they presumed to label secular history or Church documentation as spurious, what was to stop them from laying the critical blade to Holy Scripture as well? It seemed only a matter of time.

And it was; from the seventeenth century up to the present, cries of outrage have echoed as critical historians have honed their techniques and applied them to the traditions of the Bible. Astruc, Spinoza, Graf, Wellhausen, Von Rad, and Noth have led research on the Old Testament, Reimarus, Strauss, Baur, Schweitzer, and Bultmann on the New.[12] As the value of such study for elucidating the origin and meaning of biblical texts became apparent, the use of the methodology became more and more widespread. Nowadays there are few quarters of the religious and academic world where one does not feel the influence of the "higher criticism." This term refers to the critical investigation of the authorship, historical accuracy, and literary unity of texts, together with the influences on them of other texts and traditions. For instance, such historical and literary criticism of the Gospel of John has led most scholars to doubt that it is an eyewitness account preserving genuine discourses of Jesus. Instead, the work seems largely to embody the theological meditations of a late first-, early second-century writer or school. It is heavily influenced by Gnostic philosophy and addresses issues current later than Jesus' day.[13]

"Lower criticism" or textual criticism is, by contrast, the comparative study of different manuscripts of a work, with a view to weeding out copyist errors and establishing the original reading. Whereas textual criticism is usually welcomed by all,[14] historical criticism is another story. Since it tends to discredit miracle stories as legendary (did Jonah really get swallowed by a whale?) and to challenge traditional ascriptions of authorship (did Moses really write Deuteronomy, which recounts his death?), many religious conservatives are threatened by it. They claim that the historical-critical method makes it impossible truly to enter into the spirit of the work in question, since the historical critic's presuppositions are so alien to those of the ancient writers. For instance, it is on this basis that Muslim scholar Seyyed Hossein Nasr attacks the modern study of scripture.

> The inner meaning of the Quran can be understood . . . only through the inspired commentaries each of which seeks to elucidate and elaborate certain aspects of the Book. These commentaries, however, have nothing to do with the so-called higher criticism which during this century has become an almost diabolical distortion of Sacred Scripture, making it a kind of second rate handbook of archaeology which one tries to understand through sheer historical methods rather than trying to penetrate inwardly into the meaning of the symbolism involved.[15]

Some may feel inclined to voice a similar objection to the present study, since, as is by now clear, we are treating the Cthulhu Mythos as indeed nothing but myth. As such, it may indeed embody psychological depth and may deserve respect as a cultural monument of some kind. But to those who might prefer an "inspired commentary," say one like Feery's, we would ask a little patience. It may be that the disinterested stance of the scholar may allow him to discover insights initially unnoticed by the eye of faith.

But the critical study of a work like the *Necronomicon* might encounter objections from another source, and of another kind altogether. For it has been argued by serious historical scholars that the critical approach is wrong-headed in this particular area because of the confused and corrupt condition of the material involved. In *The Secret Lore of Magic*, Idries Shah contends,

> There is no known magical book which fulfills the requirements of original authorship. The fact is that every extant book of spells, charms, divination or magical conjuration . . . is a work which has gone through innumerable hands, been edited and re-edited, and translated in many cases two to three times between different languages. . . . No, the Grimoires should be studied from any point of view but that of bibliographical criticism: for here we have absolutely no criteria to apply.[16]

How are we to respond to this challenge? Surely the sad textual state of affairs described by Shah reads as if he had in mind the *Necronomicon* itself. According to Lovecraft, the original Arabic text was probably lost by the eleventh century, after having been translated by Theodorus Philetas a century earlier. In the seventeenth century the Greek text was translated into Latin by Olaus Wormius[17] and into Spanish by persons unknown. Finally it was rendered into English by the Elizabethan magus John Dee. Besides this family tree of translations (sometimes more than one in the same language), Lovecraft also lists several editions. According to various notices, some editions were published with the more shocking sections expunged. Other privately owned copies seem to have been bastardized collections of passages hand-copied severally from this and that printed edition. With this haphazard and incestuous inbreeding of different text-families, and the fact that we have only snippets from various of these text types, should we not throw up our hands and surrender to Shah's conclusion? Isn't our task hopeless?

We think not. In view of the preceding factors, one can at least answer the question of original authorship strongly in the negative. It is almost certain that the extant corpus of *Necronomicon* fragments is seriously corrupt, and as a whole, definitely does not represent the *al-Azif* of Abdul Alhazred. But whether or not any of these fragments is genuine is quite another question, and admittedly one more difficult to answer. Granted, the opportunities for interpolation and falsification of the text were so plentiful that a good deal of both must have occurred; still, it is hard to imagine that the original voice of Alhazred could have been completely smothered under such accretions. Chances are that at least some of those distinctive words (which, after all, provided the impetus for the centuries-long fascination with the book) must survive as gems among the rubbish.

The problem, as Shah says, is one of criteria. Admittedly, criteria for inauthenticity are much easier to come by. We can sometimes detect later glosses and interpolations by the tell-tale presence of references to historical events or to religious conditions later than Alhazred's day. An analogy would be the mention in John 9:22 that the Pharisees had announced they would excommunicate any Jew who professed faith in Jesus as the Messiah. This account seems to reflect conditions in Christian-Jewish relations near the end of the first century rather than during Jesus' own ministry. Thus the speech attributed to Jesus on this occasion was probably not spoken by him. Likewise, the so-called Second Epistle of Peter contains a reference to a collection of Paul's epistles (3:15–16). However Paul's letters were collected long after the date of Peter's death (ca. A.D. 65). Any similar anachronisms in our *Necronomicon* passages would immediately denote inauthenticity.

Other, stylistic, criteria may be considered in the course of the commentary. A different sort of criterion is one of comparative mythology. If we can establish the authenticity of one passage, and the conception of the Cthulhu Mythos in a second passage shows disagreement or substantial development, the latter will be judged inauthentic since it can scarcely be the work of the same author. We will be able to gain some idea of how the myth-cycle developed over the centuries as we peel back various layers representing attempts to "update" the text according to the evolving beliefs of Cthulhu cultists.

So we must dissent from Shah's conclusion; there is some possibility of getting back to the actual words of Abdul Alhazred amid the luxuriant growth of redactional expansion and textual corruption. Yet we may agree with Shah that, in another sense, questions of authenticity and interpolation are irrelevant: if the spells and myths incorporated into the "received" form of the text, with all its secondary accretions, are true, then it does not much matter who discovered and wrote them down.[18] The situation would be like that of "Grandma's Cookbook," passed down from mother to daughter. Through the generations, new recipes may be added because they are deemed as tasty as the originals. And as long as they are, who will hesitate to cook them up merely because they were not literally the work of Grandma?

This analogy applies to the *Necronomicon* regardless of whether one accepts the implied belief in magic. In a larger sense, it is hard to dispute that the "post-history" of a book is just as important as its "prehistory." That is, no matter how erratic and checkered the process of a book's compilation, this need not reflect on the subsequent influence of the work on human imagination.[19] Consequently, no matter how many passages end up, so to speak, on the cutting room floor during this study, no one need hesitate to refer to the whole body of material as the *Necronomicon*, and to enjoy it as such in the fiction in which it is used.

Abdul Alhazred

The author of the *Necronomicon* is, of course, Abdul Alhazred. As L. Sprague de Camp[20] points out, this form of the name is a corruption, having been passed down through several languages. De Camp's own hypothesis is that the original form was something like "Abdallah Zahr-ad Din" ("Servant of God, Flower of the Faith").[21] This is about as close to the truth as anyone is likely to come. To avoid confusion, however, we will continue to use the common form. According to Lovecraft's article "History of the *Necronomicon*," Alhazred was born somewhere around A.D. 700. We may surmise that he was born sometime during the last half of the seventh century, rather than during the beginning of the eighth. It is certain that he died in A.D. 738, and there is nothing to suggest that he was particularly young when he died. If this guess is correct, then Alhazred only narrowly missed being a contemporary of the Prophet Muhammad, who died in A.D. 632. Alhazred was for most of his life a resident of Sanaa in Yemen, moving to Damascus in the years preceding his death. Tradition makes him something of a traveler, having him visit the ruins of Babylon, the catacombs of Memphis, and the Arabian wilderness called the Roba el Khaliyeh ("Empty Space"). He had also visited Irem, the "City of Pillars" mentioned in the Koran as having been destroyed for its wickedness. Some of the stories of his wanderings may be erroneous, based on a literalistic misreading of certain passages of the *Necronomicon* (see the commentary on Fragments 5 and 6).

Abdul Alhazred is sometimes referred to simply by his epithet "the mad Arab" or "the mad poet." Actually, the latter form is virtually redundant. In their *Introduction to the Qur'an*, Richard Bell and W. Montgomery Watt report that in Arabic "poet," "soothsayer," and "madman" were pretty much the same.[22] The idea was that all three were inspired by the jinn or spirits of the desert (the "genies" of the *Arabian Nights*). Thus they might all receive the appellation *majnun* "affected by jinn." By Alhazred's century, however, the word had simply come to mean "mad."[23] This is why it prefixes the title "poet" in Alhazred's epithet; the two terms are no longer strictly speaking synonymous.

The connection in meaning between the two terms, however, remains undisturbed. During the same period, the term *kahin* was used to refer to a class of "Arabian oracle-mongers" (H.A.R. Gibb). Corresponding roughly to the shaman ("medicine man" or "witch doctor") of other preliterate societies, the *kahin* might be consulted to predict the future, to solve mysteries of the past, or to arbitrate legal questions. His utterances were in "a sinewy oracular style cast into short rhymed phrases, often obscure" (Gibb).[24] He was a seer or poet (possibly both) who was possessed or inspired by jinn. The jinni served the seer as a familiar spirit, whispering (actually "cackling") into his ear secrets overheard in heaven. The spirit inspired the poet in the manner of a muse, enabling one formerly ungifted and illiterate suddenly to compose and recite. Claiming to be a revealer of supernatural truths given him by spirits, Alhazred was naturally put into this category.

These data about the religious and cultural setting of Abdul Alhazred immediately clarify two things. First, the title of his work in Arabic, the *Kitab al-Azif* (literally "the book of the buzzing") refers to the nocturnal insect-like chirping of the jinn. In view of what we have just seen about the divination practices of Alhazred's fellow *kahins*, the title takes on new meaning. This "buzzing" denotes the whispering of supernatural secrets into Alhazred's ear. Thus *al-Azif* means something like "Revelations of the Jinn," or with just a bit of license, "Secrets of the Demons."

Second, the legends surrounding the death of Alhazred are seen in an entirely new light. His twelfth-century biographer Ibn Khallikan records a gruesome tale of the "mad poet" being "seized by an invisible monster in broad daylight and devoured horribly before a large number of fright-frozen witnesses."[25] Of course, no one in his right mind is going to give credence to a story like this, at least in the modern West. But it would be shortsighted not to realize that the cultural assumptions of medieval Arabia were much different from our own. There, this story commanded belief for a long time. The legend was probably interpreted in either of two ways. First, story-tellers may have pictured the episode as what evangelist Robert G. Lee used to call "payday someday." That is, Alhazred must have, like Faust, made an infernal pact to gain his supramundane knowledge. We find an example of such a contract in the so-called *True Grimoire*.

The demon Lucifuge: "I will agree [to do thy bidding] only if thou wilt agree to give thy body and soul to me after twenty years, to use as I please."

Sorcerer: "I promise the Great Lucifuge to reward him after twenty years for treasures given me."[26]

Thus, according to one possible reading of the legend, Alhazred must have made such a pact, and now it was time to pay up.

The second possibility is that we are to understand Alhazred's grisly death as punishment by occult forces for the impropriety of recording the demonic secrets in book form for all to see. In this form, the legend would have served to frighten the curious away from delving into forbidden lore. No doubt this is also the origin of the several analogous scare-stories of owners or readers of the *Necronomicon* in the intervening centuries. It might be interesting to note that the same tactic is employed today against other magic books more readily available than the *Necronomicon*. Lutheran specialist on the occult

Kurt Koch[27] provides several eerie anecdotes concerning individuals who have used *The Sixth and Seventh Books of Moses*. He tells of one man who "all his life indulged in black magic using *The Sixth and Seventh Books of Moses*. His home was a place of unrest and discord. At his death he suffered many agonies and later the house was pervaded by a terrible stench."

At any rate, we are forced to make some sense of Ibn Khallikan's account of Alhazred's death. Is there any core of fact to the bizarre tale? Yes, indeed there is, and the solution to the puzzle turns out to be fairly simple. Ibn Khallikan lived at a time when the *kahins* were presumably no longer familiar to a devout Muslim population hostile to pagan diviners. In his ignorance, he has misunderstood what was originally simply the account of Abdul Alhazred's "prophetic calling." The initiation of a *kahin* was a rather violent hysterical fit. Tor Andrae describes the typical experience:

> The Arabian poet was thrown to the ground by a jinni who kneeled upon his chest. . . . To the bystander the attack appears as a falling to the ground, where the victim writhes in cramps, as if he were struck down by an invisible hand. But the victim himself experiences the spell [of hysteria] as a literal attack, in which something frequently chokes and crushes him like a demon. At times he imagines that his body is being cut to pieces or pierced.[28] (emphasis mine)

Such a story is told of the poet Hassan Ibn Thabit, who at the time of his "calling" was walking down a street in Mecca. Thus his fit of possession was the object of shocked public observation just as we read of Alhazred. Similarly, Muhammad himself was said to have been called to his prophetic vocation by a vision wherein the angel Gabriel choked him, commanding him to "Recite!" From then on, the Prophet was constantly compelled to deny charges that he was a mere *kahin*. "No, your compatriot is not mad . . . nor is this the utterance of an accursed devil!" (Koran 81:22, 25). "It is no poet's speech; scant is your faith! It is no sooth-sayer's divination; how little you reflect!" (69:41–42).

Can there be any doubt, in light of all this, that what Ibn Khallikan described as Alhazred "being seized by an invisible monster in broad daylight and devoured horribly," was actually the story of the "mad poet's" first fit of mantic inspiration? We may take as settled, then, that we have hit upon the real meaning of Ibn Khallikan's narrative, a meaning missed by Ibn Khallikan himself. Ironically, this means that while we understand more about Alhazred's "death narrative," we know less about his actual end, since the only surviving account of it turns out not to refer to it at all! However, the story, rightly understood, does confirm the portrait of Abdul Alhazred as a *kahin*, or a pagan diviner merely pretending to adhere to the new Islamic creed, but actually worshipping older "entities whom he called Yog-Sothoth and Cthulhu."

What Kind of Book?

Though a hurricane of controversy may rage over other questions on the *Necronomicon*, there would at least seem to be a stillness at the eye of the storm. Surely on one issue all are agreed—the *Necronomicon* is a book of magic. This, it is true, may be taken for granted. But the apparent ease with which such a conclusion may be drawn should make us suspicious. Can scholars not find anything to fight about here? Rest assured, they can. For when we have used the term "magic book," we have left much unsaid. A book dealing with occult subjects may deal with them in several possible ways. There are several kinds of books treating the occult. For example, there are the scripture, the grimoire, the demonology, and the book of marvels. Our task is to decide into which category the *Necronomicon* falls.

We must bear in mind that these four categories represent "ideal types." Reality seldom obediently pigeonholes itself according to the taxonomy of scholars, so it will not be surprising to discover a certain amount of overlap between these categories. A book may straddle the line between two or more types. Indeed the *Necronomicon* itself may be such a hybrid.

First is the category of occult scripture. Recent books belonging to this genre are Anton Szandor LaVay's *The Satanic Bible*[29] and *The Witches' Bible* by Gavin and Yvonne Frost. Charles G. Leland compiled such a book called *Aradia: The Gospel of the Witches* at the end of the nineteenth century, though it is supposed to consist of very ancient oral tradition.[30] Finally, Gerald Brosseau Gardner, one of the modern revivalists of witchcraft, published the *Book of Shadows* around 1960. It purports to be another collection of ancient witch lore, but on the whole is not. All these works function as scriptures to regulate the beliefs and practices of occult religions, whether of Satanism or of pagan nature-worship. They contain the mythology of the faith (descriptions, visions, speeches of the gods, etc.), as well as liturgical material (directions for ceremonies, chants, and spells).

What differentiates these books from scriptures like the Hebrew Bible, the New Testament, the Koran, or the Pali Canon? We might mention two criteria. One is that occult scriptures are the writings of "underground" religions, alternatives to the major traditional faiths. Like Satanism, such a religion may constitute an intentional repudiation or negation of traditional faith. Like paganism, it may simply seek an alternative to mainstream faith. Like Gnosticism or Kabbalism, it may see itself as a more enlightened elite form of orthodox belief. But in all cases, the self-definition is in some significant measure "over-against" a traditional religion.

The other distinctive of occult scriptures is that they seem to ignore Frazer's line between religion (worshipful adoration and ethical obedience to the Divine) and magic (manipulation of supernatural forces for selfish ends). Occult scriptures and religions do not linger only on the side of magic, or we would not use the term "religion" to describe them at all. But one is far more likely to find magical spells in an occult scripture where he might find psalms of praise in a mainstream scripture. (On the other hand, maybe the difference is not so great after all, since hymns of praise surely originated as attempts to "butter up" the deity.)

Might the *Necronomicon* fall into this classification? There is a good case to be made for this possibility. Abdul Alhazred, after all, is said by Ibn Khallikan to have "*worshipped* entities whom he called Yog-Sothoth and Cthulhu" (emphasis mine).

At this point, the Greek title of the book, supplied by Philetas in his translation, assumes some importance. There have been several hypotheses, mostly ill-informed, about the meaning of the word "Necronomicon." Colin Wilson[31] took it to mean "the Book of Dead Names." George Wetzel interpreted it as "The Book of the Names of the Dead." Both, obviously, took the syllable "nom" as representing the Greek word for "name," *onoma*. "Necro-" of course, by everyone's reckoning, means "dead." Manly Bannister understood the title to mean "The Book of the Laws of the Dead," a suggestion very close to that of H.P. Lovecraft who proposed "The Image of the Law of the Dead."[32] Bannister and Lovecraft took the syllable "nom" to refer to the Greek word for "law," *nomos*, though the former makes it plural, the latter singular. The only other difference is that, while all the interpreters take "-icon" to denote the Greek word for "image" or "picture" (*ikon*), Lovecraft rendered it literally, whereas Wilson, Wetzel, and Bannister gave the idiomatic equivalent "book."

Surprisingly, all of these guesses are seriously off target. The key to the meaning of "Necronomicon" lies in its analogy with the title of Manilius' first-century A.D. poem on astrology, the *Astronomicon*. Though written in Latin, the title was Greek, in accord with contemporary literary convention. S.T. Joshi has pointed out that, in both titles, the third syllable "nom" must come from neither *nomos* ("law") nor *onoma* ("name"), but rather from the verb *nemo* ("to consider"). Likewise the end of the word, "-icon," has nothing to do with *ikon* ("image"). Instead, it is a neuter adjectival suffix, such as we still find in Greek-derived words like "nautical" or "evangelical."[33] Thus the title means simply "Concerning the Dead" or (since "treatise" or "book" is implied) "The Book of the Dead."

Now if the title of the *Necronomicon* is to be interpreted this way, we are immediately tempted to associate it with two other famous works sharing that title, the Egyptian and Tibetan "Books of the Dead." Both of these texts are most definitely scriptures. Each has to do with questions of "eschatology"[34] (the "last things"), albeit far different questions. *The Egyptian Book of the Dead* deals with the final judgment of the soul after death. *The Tibetan Book of the Dead* guides the individual in seeing through the illusory mind-spawned terrors that will accost him on the point of death. If he disregards these fearful shadows, he will not be frightened "downward" toward another birth. He will be liberated from the wheel of birth-and-death.

Might Alhazred's book fall into this category? We need not be daunted by the fact that he himself did not give the book its Greek title. In both of the other cases the appellation "Book of the Dead" was also supplied later because it seemed so appropriate to the contents. As will be seen when we delve into the fragments themselves, Philetas, too, picked the appropriate title, for many passages do in fact deal with "the dead." The trouble is that, though there are various types of material in the *Necronomicon* treating "the dead," none of them deals with eschatological questions like the fate of the common soul after death. So even though we cannot yet rule out the possibility of the book being intended as an occult scripture, it is not supported by the similarity in title to the Egyptian and Tibetan "Books of the Dead." This analogy turns out to be a false one.

Our second genre is that of the grimoire. Grimoires might be called "magical cook books." They generally inform one as to how to go about summoning supernatural aid for various specific purposes, say revenge on an enemy, knowledge of the future, or winning someone's love. There is a large number of such texts, including *The Key of Solomon*, *The Sword of Moses*, *The Book of Sacred Magic of Abramelin the Mage*, *The Sixth and Seventh Books of Moses*, *The True Grimoire*, *The Great Grimoire*, *The Book of Power*, and *The Fiery Dragon*.[35] Sometimes spells are little more than recipes of chemicals and incantations that should bring desired results. But some inform the seeker how to exploit the power of demons or the devil. This can be done in two basic ways. The magician may be a faithful Christian or Jew. In this case he will force the demon to act under the compulsion of sacred names or symbols, before which, like Count Dracula, the spirit must yield. This belief goes far back into history, for instance, in the legend of King Solomon enslaving the demon Asmodeus to carry the stones for building the Temple at Jerusalem.[36]

The other approach is to make a contract with the demon. He will serve you now if you will deed yourself to him for the future. Do not various allusions to the book suggest that the *Necronomicon* contained spells with which both to call forth and to banish supernatural beings? This is true, but remember, occult scriptures also contain ritual invocations. So the presence of such material would fit the *Necronomicon* being either a scripture or a grimoire. The fact that Alhazred is said to have "worshipped" the supernatural powers involved would tend to support the book's being a scripture rather than a grimoire. One might command or bargain with the beings listed in a grimoire, but one would not worship them.

Some have construed Abdul Alhazred as a repentant sorcerer and his book as a demonology (the third category). Lin Carter saw it this way, as is implied by his term "the Alhazredic Demonology." A demonology is a descriptive system of the beliefs of occultists, drawn up by someone opposing those beliefs. Several famous books belong to this category, including the *Demonolatry* of Nicolas Remy, the *Malleus Malificarum* of Heinrich Kramer and James Sprenger,[37] and the *Compendium Malificarum* of Francesco Marice Guazzo. These volumes contain material extorted from witches and warlocks during the course of the European persecutions. The work of the demonologist Wierus[38] would also be placed here. In any case, Ibn Khallikan's notation that Alhazred worshipped the supernatural beings described in the *Necronomicon* disqualifies the book as a demonology.

Fourth and finally, we have to consider the genre of the "book of marvels."[39] These books were collections of alchemical formulae, the lore of roots and gems, local legends, and rumored oddities, a la Charles Fort. The books were written by compilers or "encyclopedists" across many centuries. Aelius Aristides (A.D. 170–235), for instance, wrote on many disparate subjects. One of the most interesting sections of the work *Sacred Tales* describes his own numerous dreams of Asclepius the healing god. Isidore of Seville (A.D. 602–36) uncritically assembled legends of strange creatures living in the unknown southern hemisphere (the "Antipodes"), together with quotations of Papias' traditions of the apostles. The *Lata'if Al-Ma'arif* ("Book of Curious and Entertaining Information") of Thalalibi was written in eastern Persia in the eleventh century. It contains history, information on the Prophet Muhammad and Islam, the lives and works of poets, geographical data, and accounts of odd coincidences. The most famous of all such works is the *Book of Secrets*, falsely attributed to Albertus Magnus. It was written in the sixteenth century. This text catalogues lore on the imagined properties of herbs, stones, and animals, a section on astrology, and a summary of the "marvels of the world." There were many, many such collections.

In the "book of marvels" we have at last arrived at the genre of the *Necronomicon*. Like many of the books just described, Alhazred's volume is a compendium of bizarre information of various kinds. Such an observation anticipates some of the results of our inquiry into the authenticity of the fragments. But for the moment, suffice it to say that the apparently genuine *Necronomicon* material does fall into different categories, both dealing with different topics and employing different literary forms. As this sort of "catch-all," the book could, like an occult scripture, contain testimonies of the author's faith (just as in the books of Thalalibi and Aelius Aristides). But whereas some of the other types of curious information appearing in the *Necronomicon* would be out of place in a scripture, they could be juxtaposed with religious confession quite nicely in a grab-bag "book of marvels."

The principal respect in which the *Necronomicon* differs from most of the other books of marvels (besides its greater concentration on occult beliefs and curiosities) is in its function as a Bible for the Cthulhu cult. Should not this consideration make us hesitate to remove it from the "occult scripture" category? No, because in its composition the book is a "book of marvels" no matter how it may have subsequently come to be used. There is no indication that Alhazred intended his book to be used as a scripture. By contrast, only a century earlier, Muhammad had produced the Koran with the explicit intention of providing a revelation to guide the fledgling Muslim community. No doubt the *Necronomicon* eventually came to play the role of a scripture because it was unique in the breadth of its information on the cult's lore. But what we are interested in is gaining a correct understanding of Alhazred's text as he intended it to be understood.

The answer to the question of genre is at the same time the answer to the question of intended audience. For books of marvels were decidedly not for the specialist. Scholars usually ignored, even despised, them. They felt, correctly, that the texts merely propagated superstition and misinformation. These books were popular literature. Their whole premise was to share the secrets of the wise man with the workers and peasants who had neither the ability nor the occasion to search out the lore for themselves. The tone of practically every extant passage of the *Necronomicon* implies this intended audience.

How then did the volume come to be known as a rare and suppressed tome? A moment's thought yields a satisfactory answer. It was not Abdul Alhazred, but rather the conventional religious authorities, who thought that this knowledge should remain secret. We have already suggested that the legend of Alhazred's grisly death may have served exactly this end. If the mad poet himself was destroyed for daring to publicize the demonic lore, the curious ought to take the hint! But the suppression of the book did not stop at mere legend-mongering. In A.D. 1050, the Eastern Orthodox Patriarch Michael had the Greek translation of Philetas burnt. In A.D. 1232, the book was again banned, this time in the West by Pope Gregory IX. This practice was hardly unprecedented. Early Church Fathers had tried to destroy all copies of heretical gospels and Gnostic treatises. They were so successful that only in the last century have hidden copies of some of these texts been discovered.[40] Nor has the practice ceased. In recent decades several attempts have been made to prohibit by law the sale of *The Sixth and Seventh Books of Moses*.[41] Incidentally, there is nothing particularly shocking or revelatory in either this book or the Gnostic texts. The lesson is that it only takes a bit of heterodoxy to prompt ecclesiastical suppression if the authorities are in the proper mood. Though the *Necronomicon* is often held to be mind-blasting in its implications, it could easily have been banned for less.

Alhazred's Sources

As a "book of marvels," the *Necronomicon* contains, in part, the original researches of Abdul Alhazred. The language of individual passages confirms this, where Alhazred speaks of "cases" of this and "instances" of that, which he has personally collected or witnessed. But like most other compilers of books of this type, he does not hesitate to make extensive use of other written sources. We will briefly describe two of the major written sources which appear in the extant fragments of the *Necronomicon*.

First, there is the lost book of Ibn Schacabao. The occurrence of this name in two passages of the *Necronomicon* (4:3; 8:3) has intrigued and perplexed many students. Very little is known about him. The name itself presents difficulties as it stands. It seems to have been garbled in transmission (just as, for instance, "St. Nicholas" became "Santa Claus"). Some take the original to have been "Ibn Shayk Abol," or "Son of the Sheik Abol."[42] This is quite possible, but another hypothesis is even more attractive. On this view, the name is derived from the Arabic root *shacab*, "to sit down, inhabit, or dwell." The prefix mu- would be added to personalize it as a name, resulting in "Ibn Mushacab," or "Son of the Dweller." To anyone familiar with the Cthulhu Mythos, the ring of this name is unmistakable.

It may well be that we have here the meaning of "Ibn Schacabao," and that the person in question was a devotee, like Abdul Alhazred, of the Old Ones. A third possibility is to derive the name from the Hebrew word *shakhabh*, meaning "bestiality," in which case the nefarious sage would have been reputed to be the offspring of a mortal woman and some nonhuman Entity. Such a dual nature might have been accounted the reason for the superhuman knowledge Alhazred attributes to him.

If Alhazred quotes or alludes to some lost work of Ibn Schacabao twice in the handful of *Necronomicon* fragments that survive, it is safe to surmise that he must have used the work extensively throughout. He attributes to Ibn Schacabao the information on the Gulf of S'glhuo (4:3–7), and quotes a verse from him relating to the powers of wizards after death:

Happy is the tomb where no wizard hath lain,

And happy the town at night whose wizards are all ashes. (8:3)

One more allusion to Ibn Schacabao occurs in some eighteenth-century correspondence. An eccentric, apparently subject to frightening hallucinations, thinks he has conjured up "Yogge-Sothothe." He relates how he "saw for the first time that face spoken of by Ibn Schacabao in the_____."[43] It is hard to account for the tantalizing omission of the name of Ibn Schacabao's volume, but we are at least told that the source was a written book, rather than, say, a floating oral tradition. At any rate, the reference, scant though it is, shows that Ibn Schacabao wrote of Yog-Sothoth as did Alhazred.

Given the range of subjects touched upon in these three references, we may form some rudimentary idea of the scope and nature of the lost volume. Dealing as it did with other dimensions, necromancy, and Yog-Sothoth, Ibn Schacabao's lost book would seem to have served as the prototype for Abdul Alhazred's own *Necronomicon*.

The second major written source employed by Alhazred is *The Book of Thoth*. There is a large range of ancient Egyptian literature that passes under this name. But what is probably in view here is the Hermetic Literature, a series of Hellenistic, Egyptian, and Arabic tracts dealing with mysticism and alchemy.[44] They date from the second or third century A.D. on into the early Islamic period. These disparate books concern "Hermes Trismegistus," or "Thrice-Great [i.e., Most Great] Hermes," the Greek name for the Egyptian Thoth, a divine revealer of supernatural secrets. Characteristically, the writer somehow gains an audience with the great Thoth/Hermes or his representative, either in the heavens, in an unspecified mystical state, or in an underground chamber. Sometimes the enthroned revealer is associated with the "Ancient of Days" who is pictured in the Old Testament vision of Daniel, or the "Head of Days" in the apocalyptic book I Enoch. The divine secrets are then presented in book form, dictated from a book, or presented in a series of visions, as in the following passage from Poimandres:[45]

My Thoughts being once seriously busied about the things that are, and my Understanding lifted up, all my bodily Senses being exceedingly holden back, as it is with them that are very heavy of sleep . . . Methought I saw one of an exceeding great stature, and an infinite greatness call me by name, and say unto me, "What wouldest Thou Hear and See? or what wouldest Thou Understand, to Learn, and Know?" Then said I, "Who art Thou?" "I am," quoth he, "Poemander, the mind of the Great Lord, the most Mighty and absolute Emperor. . . ." When he had thus said, he was changed in his Idea or Form and straightway in the twinkling of an eye, all things were opened unto me: and I saw with an infinite Sight. . . . But after a little while, there was a darkness . . . , coming down obliquely, fearful and hideous, which seemed unto me to be changed into a Certain Moist Nature, unspeakably troubled, which yielded a smoke as from fire, and from whence proceeded a voice unutterable, and very mournful, but inarticulate.[46]

In our fragments, Alhazred seems twice to make reference to one or another of these "Books of Thoth." In one, the revealer is named "The Most Ancient One" (parallel to the "Ancient of Days"); in the other he is called "Soul of the Creator Spirit" (parallel to "Mind of the Great Lord" in *Poimandres*). Alhazred is aware of the Hermetic form of revelation, but does not seem favorably disposed towards it. Perhaps it seems to him too dangerous.

To conclude this section, brief mention might be made of form criticism,[47] since it provides yet another fruitful approach to the question of source-material. The technique is that of identifying distinctive types of written or oral material incorporated into a work. Sometimes it is simply a matter of pointing out figures of speech customary for an ancient author but unfamiliar to us. For instance, the identification of *Necronomicon* 3:13–14 as a special "punishment story" of the kind we find in the Bible and the Koran, helps us understand that when Alhazred describes the doom of Kadath and R'lyeh, he means to warn his readers that they are in the same danger.

Sometimes form criticism enables us to detect that an earlier unit of material has been woven into a later context. For instance, a list of place names occurring in a passage (16:7) about exorcising the minions of the Old Ones, is recognized by its symmetrical pattern as the poetic incantation to be used in the rite. A copyist had obscured this fact by writing it all in prose. The very same thing has occurred several times in the New Testament. For instance, Philippians 2:6–11, though it appears at first sight to be a simple prose paragraph, is revealed by its meter, accent, and parallel structure, to be a fragment of a hymn, quoted by the writer.[48]

Form criticism reveals the presence in the *Necronomicon* of several literary forms common in the ancient world. They include the punishment story (3:13–14); the apocalypse (Fragments 14 and 15); the exorcism rite (Fragment 16); the "myth of the fall" (Fragments 11, 12, and 13); the poem (2:6–7); the beatitude (8:3); the attestation oath (9:1; 10:1); and the testament (Fragment 19).

The History of the Cthulhu Religion

One of the greatest strides in biblical criticism occurred in the nineteenth century, when Tübingen scholar Ferdinand Christian Baur unveiled his reconstruction of the history of early Christianity. He showed how the various New Testament documents could be better understood when placed in a hypothetical order of development. Baur and others had been puzzled over what to make of the many contradictions and different viewpoints present among the several gospels and epistles. Taking his hints from these differences, Baur was able to sketch out a tentative outline in which New Testament-era Christianity was divided between Jewish Christians, led by Peter, and Gentile or Hellenistic Christians, led by Paul. After serious factional feuding, the two were gradually melded into a synthesis corresponding more or less to orthodox Catholicism. Some New Testament documents represented Jewish Christianity (James, Matthew, Hebrews), while others represented Hellenistic Christianity (The Epistles of Paul, The Gospel of John). Still others represented the mediating synthesis (1 Peter, The Acts of the Apostles). The differences between the various books, then, seemed to stem from their different positions along this time-line of ideological development.

Though several details of Baur's schema have since been challenged, no one has disputed the value of his methodology. Essential to the critical exegesis of an ancient text is the effort to arrive at some kind of *Sitz-im-Leben*, a setting in the life of the movement from which the document was written.

This approach is inescapably necessary in the study of the *Necronomicon*. For any wide-awake perusal of the extant fragments makes it immediately clear that there are in its pages competing and mutually contradictory viewpoints. For instance, some texts speak reverently of Cthulhu and Yog-Sothoth, while others gleefully predict their imminent destruction. Some speak of a pantheon of "Elder Gods," while these deities are altogether absent from other texts. The same person (Abdul Alhazred) cannot have written all these passages. As we have anticipated, there are some criteria for deciding which he did, and which he probably did not, write.

But it is just as important to account for the inauthentic passages. How would anyone sincerely attribute to Alhazred writings in which he condemns what earlier texts show to have been his own views? Where did new characters like the Elder Gods come from? Finally, when were such interpolations made? In hopes of enabling the reader to make a little more sense of the texts to follow, herewith is presented a preliminary reconstruction of how the Cthulhu Mythos and its religion developed. The outline, like Baur's, is based on hints in the documents themselves.

The religion of the *Necronomicon* seems to have begun as a form of ancient Gnosticism. This was a movement closely related to early Christianity, though not all Gnostics were Christians like Basilides or Valentinus. It was called the "hydra-headed heresy" because of the bewildering variety of sects and schools that proliferated under its canopy (like any religion today!). Common to all forms of Gnosticism, however, was a dualistic worldview, whereby the world of matter was denigrated as the ill-advised creation of an imbecilic "Demiurge," the last (and least) in a series of Aions, or divine emanations from a distant and unfathomable Godhead. Incidentally, this use of the term Aion may have been derived from the Jewish apocalypticism of Jesus' era. In this scheme of things, there were to be two successive world ages (aions), the present one ruled by Satan, with the future Golden Age to be ruled by God. Eventually, the word aion may have come to be used derivatively to indicate not only the world-age, but also the power who ruled it. The Gnostics may have picked up the term in this way. Alternately, the term may have come from the lion-headed Iranian god of Time, called Aion.

The Gnostics worshipped the Aions but found themselves stranded, imprisoned here in the world of matter by malevolent archons, or planetary rulers. The goal of Gnostic salvation was to learn the secret knowledge (gnosis) necessary for the soul, upon death, to slip past the vigilant archons and soar free into the Aions' realm of light. Here some striking similarities between Gnosticism and the Cthulhu cult come into view. Both groups regarded themselves as strangers in a strange land. They were devotees of entities obscured from sight in the present age. True, the Gnostics hoped to flee the world and join their gods, whereas our cultists sought to restore the direct rule of the Old Ones on this earth. But both labored for future salvation by overcoming the alienation between the world in which they lived and the gods whom they served.

In both religions, the world was seen as the creation of a mindless Demiurge (called "Azathoth" by Cthulhu cultists). Gnostics generally vilified the creator as either a malevolent prankster or a dimwitted bungler. For though he is one of the Aions, not the archons, he represents the emanation farthest removed from the perfection of divinity and is sort of a deformed monster. It can hardly be mere coincidence that we find the same odd deprecation of a creator-god in the Cthulhu Mythos. Azathoth "the blind idiot god," unlike the rest of the Old Ones, seems to be held in derision even by his own minions:

"I am His messenger," the daemon said
As in contempt he struck his Master's head.[49]

And as for the act of creation itself, Cthulhu cultists, like Gnostics, dismissed it as the act of a lunatic. The earth was "moulded in play" by an "idiot chaos" (though later traditions confuse the entities Azathoth and Nyarlathotep at this point).[50]

Finally, both groups envisioned a future "transvaluation of values," negating the moral standards of the present order. While some Gnostics practiced radical asceticism as their manner of world-negation, others more notoriously trod the path of wild libertinism. The fourth-century heresiologist Epiphanius of Salamis, in his *Panarion* (an early precursor to Von Junzt's *Die Unaussprechlichen Kulten*) detailed the stomach-turning practices of various Gnostic sects. For example, the Marcosians ritually imbibed urine and menstrual blood. We are reminded of the "mad cacophonous orgies" of the Cthulhu cultists.[51] The disgusting rites of Gnostics and Old Ones-cultists were alike symbolic of their repudiation of the present world order, and of the utterly alien order to prevail when they basked in the direct rule of their gods.

In light of these parallels, it is hard to resist the conclusion that the religion of Alhazred was one of the lesser known branches of the Gnostic religion. The Old Ones were known in that context as Aions.

At some point in the history of the religion, the worship of the Old Ones themselves was supplemented by that of a group of subordinate entities connected in some way with the same Mythos. They were lesser beings, but had the advantage of being less aloof and far-off than the Old Ones. This, in fact, is a common, almost predictable, development once a religion's deities have become more transcendent. In exactly the same way, a new generation of demigods (Heracles, Asclepius, etc.) began to replace the Olympians in Greek piety, once Zeus and his kin were made more abstract by philosophers. In Zoroastrianism and Judaism, the cult of angels flourished in direct proportion to God's increasing transcendence. And as Jesus Christ evolved from the Galilean savior to the divine Pantocrator represented on the dome of Santa Sophia, the Virgin Mary and the saints assumed greater importance to fill in the gap.

By Alhazred's day, Cthulhu, Yog-Sothoth, Nyarlathotep, and Shub-Niggurath had filled the vacuum, mediating between the Old Ones and their worshippers, but were distinct from the Old Ones (*Necronomicon* 3:6–7, 15). The situation was analogous to that prevailing in most West African mythologies, where a primordial god has retreated far into the sky. The day-to-day business of religion is handled by a number of lesser godlings and spirits who receive sacrifice and answer prayers. So here: the Old Ones are far away, beyond dimensioned space. One day they will return, but for now one may venerate the sea-monster Cthulhu, the messenger Nyarlathotep, and the universal gatekeeper Yog-Sothoth.

The final step in this direction was taken when Cthulhu and the rest actually came to be identified with the Old Ones. Alhazred had taken the dangerous risk of predicting that the return of the Old Ones was near (3:21). As the *Necronomicon* soon came to function as the "Bible" of the cult, this prophecy was widely heeded. Thus, when many years passed and the apocalyptic return failed to materialize, far-reaching adjustments had to be made.[52] The Old Ones were brought home in word if not in fact when believers began to worship Cthulhu, Yog-Sothoth and the others *as* the Old Ones. Probably none of this was the product of anyone's deliberate decision. It must have been a gradual and unconscious process.

The next major shift must have occurred many years later, when careful students of the *Necronomicon* noticed that these developments did not square with the text. Seizing upon an ambiguous passage that suggested to them a punishment of Cthulhu by the Old Ones (3:14–15), these reformist zealots repudiated the conventional pantheon as "fallen angels." Instead, they called for a return to the worship of the original, transcendent Old Ones. Perhaps for clarity's sake, they did not try to reclaim the original term "Old Ones," still used by the Cthulhu-worshippers, whom the reformers regarded as apostates from the pure faith. They regarded the title as irrevocably polluted by heresy, and decided to adopt henceforth the synonymous nomenclature "the Elder Ones," or "Elder Gods." The slight shade of difference in meaning ("Elder" versus "Old") connoted that the reformists' Old Ones were older than the usurping Old Ones of the Cthulhu-worshippers.

The single passage 3:14–15 was made the basis for an elaborate "Fall of Cthulhu" myth, wherein he was imprisoned by the Elder Gods in a sunken crypt bearing their seal. In this manner, the reformists had indeed returned to Alhazred's conception of Cthulhu, et al., as servants of the Old Ones. But whereas Alhazred had venerated them, the reformists vilified them as rebellious servants. This reversal, though radical, is by no means without precedent. The Asuras of Vedic Hinduism were second-tier, sometimes demonic, divine entities, while the Devas were the ruling gods. But Zoroastrianism, which arose out of Vedism, worshipped the Asuras (e.g.,

Ahura Mazda) and vilified the Devas as devils. Hence the later Latin word *deus* (god) reflects the Vedic theology, while the word "devil" reflects that of Zoroastrianism.

At first Cthulhu and his allies were conceived in the new theology as having been banished forever following their revolt. But at some point, they were expected to rise to power again briefly—immediately before the final coming of the Elder Gods, just as Antichrist precedes and heralds the return of Christ.

Eventually, the reformists composed new texts setting forth these beliefs in detail. Some were pseudonymously attributed to Alhazred himself, a practice quite acceptable by ancient and medieval literary standards. Other texts may simply have been bound with the *Necronomicon* for reference purposes, the distinction between the two later being forgotten. They came finally to be taken for part of the text. Needless to say, the pro-Cthulhu sect may already have made interpolations of their own (one occurs in Fragment 13:1–2, 4–5, where it has been mixed into other material by the reformists). But the older faction probably maintained a purer textual tradition. In any case, from the time of the schism onward, there must have been two different canonical texts, one with the reformist interpolations, the other without.

From the time of the split, the history of the religion seems to have been primarily taken up with sectarian in-fighting. Both groups, the Cthulhu-cultists and the reformist worshippers of the Elder Gods, considered themselves faithful disciples of Abdul Alhazred. Neither side noticed how its doctrines diverged significantly from those of Alhazred, who had neither reviled Cthulhu and Yog-Sothoth, nor identified them as being the Great Old Ones. Our knowledge of the reformist faction is greater because most of the spurious *Necronomicon* fragments stem from this group.

Is there any way to tell when the addition of new material began? Our only real clue is Ibn Khallikan's characterization of Alhazred as a worshipper of Cthulhu and Yog-Sothoth. He betrays no awareness either of the reformist picture of Alhazred as a warner against Cthulhu, or of the whole controversy. Ibn Khallikan is cognizant of many legends about Alhazred's death, the most fantastic of which he does not hesitate to report. So if he were aware of various opinions about whether Alhazred served or opposed Cthulhu, Ibn Khallikan would probably not have recorded unambiguously that the mad Arab was a Cthulhu-devotee. Since the biographer lived in the twelfth century, the origin of the reformist interpolations cannot be quite this early.

We might be able to narrow down the date further if we had the thirteenth-century Syriac commentary on the *Necronomicon* by the Nestorian monk Zecharias. Written perhaps a full century later than Ibn Khallikan's day, Zecharias' commentary would no doubt indicate whether any of the interpolations had already crept into the text by that time. Obviously, if he commented on them, they must have appeared in the text of the *Necronomicon* he had in front of him. The discovery of this remarkable document was announced in 1968 by Dr. Franklin E. Tillinghast.[53] Nine years earlier, the commentary had been acquired in a purchase of several Arabic and Syriac manuscripts once belonging to the collection of H.R. Englehart. Tillinghast's announcement stirred a good deal of excitement at the time, and just as much disappointment a few months later when it reportedly vanished in a fire of dubious origin, which also claimed the life of the great scholar. Of such importance was this manuscript that it is no exaggeration to say that its loss was felt quite as keenly as was that of Dr. Tillinghast himself. In any case, the intriguing document can no longer offer any help in our investigation.

At least some of the interpolations may date from late medieval times, since they suggest that the reformists may have been influenced by a decadent form of Jewish Kabbalism. Exorcistic techniques mentioned in two fragments include the "Tikkoun elixir" (perhaps drawn in a garbled form from fifteenth-century Kabbalism) and an amulet in the shape of a five-pointed star (based on the magic "pentacle of Solomon"). Furthermore, during this period the Elder Gods were depicted as "Towers of Fire," an image clearly borrowed from the Jewish representation of God as a "pillar of fire" (Exod. 13:21). This incidentally, helps account for the similarity many have pointed out between the biblical mythos and late forms of the Cthulhu legend-cycle.

The Verse-Numbering System

The discussion of any text is facilitated if there is some kind of system for dividing it into sections and shorter passages. The utility of the chapter and verse divisions in the Bible, or the Surah and verse numbering in the Koran, or even the Act, Scene, and Line divisions in Shakespeare's plays, is obvious if one has ever had to look up a quote in any of these works. As serious research and discussion of the *Necronomicon* commences, scholars will no doubt feel the need for a reference-system of this kind. The system proposed here, though simple enough to follow, may at first seem slightly puzzling in its rationale. A bit of explanation is in order.

The reader may note that some fragments that are numbered later would seem, from their subject matter, to have occurred earlier in the original text than passages that precede them according to our numbering. For instance, the so-called "Preface" occurs last! How can this be? Two considerations have dictated this. First, though some numbering system seems to have existed in various editions of the complete *Necronomicon*[54] no such texts are available today. Thus ours is a system for numbering fragments in their order of study, not sections in their order of occurrence. That latter order we cannot hope to discern. In the present state of things, there is often no way to be sure which passage followed which. Second, at least some of the extant passages seem to be inauthentic. Therefore, though once interpolated they may (like the "Preface") precede older passages in the text, they actually follow those passages chronologically. We have endeavored, then, to follow the chrono- logical sequence insofar as this can be determined. Within the categories thus established, we have grouped passages more or less according to subject. In this chronological ordering, we are not unprecedented. Pretty much the same approach has been adopted by Bell, Rodwell, and Dawood in their translations of the Koran, and by Barclay, Schonfield, and others in their versions of the New Testament. In these cases, naturally, the verse-numbering had already been established, but the translators did rearrange the order of presentation chronologically, supplying charts enabling the reader to locate traditionally numbered passages in their new placement. We avoid this difficulty by making the numbering and the order of presentation coincide.

As for the numbering system itself, the first number will denote the fragment or passage as a whole, while the second will refer to an individual verse (a sentence or lengthy clause). Thus a notation like "3:12" should be read as "Fragment 3, verse 12."

Section Two: The Authentic Material

That Which Came Before Men

Fragment 1

Text: [1]The book of the black name, containing the history of that which came before men. [2]The Great Old Ones were both one and many. [3]They were not separate souls like men, yet they were separate wills. [4]Some say they came from the stars; [5]some say that they were the soul of the earth when it was formed from a cloud. [6]For all life comes from the beyond, where there is no consciousness. [7]Life needed a mirror, therefore it invaded the world of matter. [8]There it became its own enemy, because they possess form. [9]The Great Old Ones wanted to avoid form; [10]therefore they rejected the heavy material of the body. [11]But then they lost the power to act. [12]Therefore they needed servants.[55]

Version: Uncertain; the fragment survives only in the thirteenth-century commentary of the monk Martin the Gardener, written in oddly mixed Greek and Latin.

Commentary: We have here the beginning of the entire book, which (at least in its first section) deals with pre- and inhuman life. "The book of the black name" seems to be Martin's attempt at translating Philetas' title "*Necronomicon*." Martin's knowledge of classical languages seems to have been spotty. He has mistaken the suffix -icon for "image" or "book," and -nom- for "name." He has somehow confused *necro-* ("dead") with *nigro-* ("black"), resulting in a completely erroneous translation. The verse should read simply "The *Necronomicon*, containing the history of that which came before men." (Of course the original Arabic would have had "*Al-Azif*, containing the history," etc.)

There are different senses in which the Old Ones may be described alternatively as singular and as plural. We have here something on the order of the Christian doctrine of the Trinity. It is explained in v. 3.

v. 3 This verse shows the influence of Christian theological debates in the Near East in the late seventh century. The denial that the Old Ones had "separate souls" recalls the Christology (= doctrine of the nature of Christ) of the churches in Alhazred's region. It was Monophysite Christology, meaning that Christ had one (*monos*) nature (*physis*), instead of two (divine and human) as Western Christians thought. "Dithelitism" (or "two-will-ism") was another doctrine, one which defined Christ as having two distinct though harmonious wills, each stemming from one of the two natures of Christ. Obviously one would not espouse the Monophysite and the Dithelite doctrines simultaneously, since the first removes the rationale for the second. But something like a combination of the two ideas had already surfaced in order to define the doctrine of the Trinity. Accordingly, the Godhead shared one divine nature, yet existed as three distinct persons (Father, Son, Spirit).

In the same way, Alhazred has borrowed the Christological jargon of his day to explain his conception of the Great Old Ones. They, too, are ultimately one, though they possess individual wills. This was no doubt his updating of the original Gnostic doctrine that the Aions (the Old Ones here) were a series of emanations from the ultimate Godhead, thus sharing the divine nature even when differentiated as individual beings.

v. 4. Alhazred is aware that some would make the Old Ones mere angels. This is probably what is meant by the reference to "stars." This was a common image for angels, occurring for instance in the Book of Revelation, "The mystery of the seven stars that you saw in my right hand . . . is this: The seven stars are the angels of the seven churches" (Revelation 1:20).

Another current theory was that the Old Ones were the spiritual nature of the physical world, the rational principle by which the primeval chaos was formed into an ordered cosmos. (A similar doctrine had been taught by Philo concerning the divine Logos.) According to this version, the Old Ones would have functioned like Plato's archetypal forms.

Alhazred understands why these theories were formulated, because it is true that life comes from beyond the earth as we know it. Life is not indigenous here. But the truth of its origin lies with neither of the theories he has mentioned. Instead, life comes from the mindless Demiurge Azathoth, who is referred to here by the phrase "the beyond where there is no consciousness." The phrase is similar to others elsewhere, to the effect that Azathoth is the "blind idiot chaos beyond angled space."

This verse refers to the original coming of the Old Ones to earth (cf. Fragment 3). The word "invaded" denotes that their presence there is utterly alien. The next verse explains why.

V.8 Apparently the reference here is to the dawn of the conflict between the Old Ones and the living creatures of earth. The source of this conflict was that the Old Ones are "undimensioned and to us unseen" (3:3), while earthlings "possess form." The enmity described here accounts for the threats posed in 3:18–19.

vv. 9–10. The utter revulsion felt by the super-dimensional Old Ones in the face of embodied life-forms is here given as the reason for their departure. This is why, according to 3:21, they do not presently rule the earth. Verse 10, incidentally, is one of the clearest traces of the Gnostic origin of the religion of Alhazred. He refers explicitly to the spirit vs. matter dualism of

Gnosticism. "Therefore they rejected the heavy material of the body." This is closely parallel to the Gnostic Hymn of the Pearl, in which one of the Aions visits earth and is benumbed and confused by the materiality of the world: "And with guile they mingled for me a deceit, and I tasted of their food . . . . and by means of the heaviness of their food I fell into a deep sleep." Soon he comes to his senses and recoils in horror at his careless entrapment in material flesh: "And I stripped off the filthy garment and left it in their land, and directed my way forthwith to the light of my fatherland" (Hymn of the Pearl, vv. 32, 35, 62, 63). So did the Old Ones flee the mire of the material world.

Yet this self-imposed exile left them at a disadvantage. How might their will be done on earth? "They needed servants," and this of course is the origin of the religion of the Old Ones. Someone had a visionary experience in which he received the "gospel" of the Old Ones, summoning men to their service. However many ages it might take, the human followers must tirelessly prepare for a "second coming" of their Masters, who will say to them "Well done, good and faithful servants." They will transfigure them into a purely spiritual state and proceed to wipe the earth clean of other human life.

Fragment 2

Text: [1]Whosoever speaketh of Cthulhu shall remember that he but seemeth dead; [2]he sleeps, and yet he does not sleep; [3]he has died and yet he is not dead; [4]asleep and dead though he is, he shall rise again. [5]Again it should be shown that

[6] That is not dead which can eternal lie,

[7]And with strange aeons even death may die.[56]

Version: Either Latin or Greek; the citation is ambiguous.

Commentary: vv. 1–4. The meaning of this passage seems fairly straightforward. It refers to the primeval monster Cthulhu imprisoned in uneasy slumber in the sunken city of R'lyeh in the Pacific. An old piece of cult-liturgy reads

"In his house at R'lyeh
Dead Cthulhu waits dreaming."[57]

The idea is that Cthulhu is lying in wait, biding his time in a state of suspended animation that only resembles death. The sense of v. 1 is "Don't write him off—he only seems dead."

It is interesting to note the ambivalent manner in which Cthulhu's hibernation is described. Vv. 4 and 6 remind us that this apparent death sleep has not the finality of death, but is instead a lying in wait, even if the waiting seems to take forever. Verse 7 flatly calls the torpor "death" but again hints that it is not. For unlike genuine death, this slumber will end. The idea is very similar to that expressed in chapter 11 of the Gospel of John. There Jesus' friend Lazarus has become gravely ill. When told of this, Jesus replies "This sickness will not end in death" (v. 4). Two days later he tells his disciples, "Our friend Lazarus has fallen asleep, but I am going there to wake him" (v. 14). But hadn't Jesus already assured them that the illness would not issue in death? The whole point of the "sleep" metaphor is that, though technically and actually dead, Lazarus will not remain that way. Jesus will resuscitate him, so the "end" is not death. A true death from which one may yet awake is aptly compared to sleep. The idea surfaces in several other places in the New Testament, e.g., a hymn-fragment preserved in Ephesians 5:14:

Awake O sleeper
Rise from the dead
And Christ will shine on you.

The *Necronomicon* couplet simply reverses the metaphor, so that a sleep from which one wakes seems like death if it lasts for ages.

The puzzling term "strange aeons" denotes periods of time "strange" by the reckoning of human time-frames, epochs that are unimaginably vast. Once more we have biblical parallels, e.g., 2 Peter 3:8: "With the Lord a day is like a thousand years, and a thousand years are like a day." Psalm 90:4 makes the same point:

A thousand years in your sight
are like a day that has just gone by
or like a watch in the night.

And the point is that for beings who have no mortality there is virtually no time either. When the "eternal lying" in wait (v. 6) has ended, then "death itself [will] die." Cthulhu will awake from dreaming exile to rise from his watery grave.

vv. 5–7. So far our exegesis has been fairly unexceptionable, but at this juncture we must introduce a note of controversy. For we wish to suggest both that the rhymed couplet of vv. 6–7 has a deeper meaning that is far from apparent on first reading, and that while it is authentic *Necronomicon* text, it is not the work of Abdul Alhazred. Rather it is a much older piece of Cthulhu-cult lore quoted by him. That he might quote earlier material should occasion no surprise. After all, the Gnostic cult of the Old Ones goes back considerably before Alhazred's time.

First of all, the couplet is presented as a quote in the text of the *Necronomicon* itself. The verses appear set off from the surrounding prose with what is clearly a formulaic introduction to a quotation. "Again it should be shown that . . ." (v. 5).

The second important factor militating against Alhazred's authorship here is that the poem seems to reflect in its linguistic structure an older milieu than his. The poem manifests the repetitive parallelism of Hebrew poetry such as we find in the Old Testament Psalms. As is well known, Hebrew poetry did not have to rhyme, depending instead on the device of paraphrasing one thought in slightly different ways. For example:

> The heavens declare the glory of God
> The firmament showeth his handiwork. (Psalm 19:1)

There are several possible variations, including antithetic parallelism, wherein an idea is emphasized by juxtaposing it with its corollary:

> The heavens are the Lord's
> But the earth he has given to the children of men.
> (Psalm 115:16)

There is also staircase parallelism, wherein each phrase repeats the last but adds a new element:

> Blessed is the man who
> walketh not in the counsel of the ungodly,
> nor standeth in the way of sinners,
> nor sitteth in the seat of the scornful.(Psalm 1:1)

Obviously the verses from the *Necronomicon* are of this last type, exhibiting the same kind of parallel structure. Each of the two lines echoes the other, though the second adds a new emphasis: not only have men mistaken for death that which is only age-long sleep, but it is promised that this dormancy will eventually reach its end.

Thus far, the Hebraic cast of the couplet would seem to push it further back in time than Abdul Alhazred's day, but how much further? Another clue is provided by the appearance (in English translation) of the words "eternal" (v. 6) and "aeons" (v. 7). The parallel, noted above, between the verses is made more distinct once we realize that they were originally composed, not in Alhazred's Arabic, but in Greek, where the words "eternal" and "aeon" are simply different forms of the word *aion*, or "age." English "eternal" would then translate the Greek phrase *eis tous aionous*, literally "unto the ages," "always," or "forever."

Our poem seems to have been written in the Greek language, yet according to the pattern of Old Testament Hebrew poetry. These factors make it probable that it was composed under the influence of the Septuagint, the Greek translation of the Hebrew Old Testament. This would place the poem back near the very beginning of the religion, in the context of Hellenistic-Hebrew Gnosticism. It is thus a very old and valuable piece of cult lore.

We find the same kind of "Hebraism with a Hellenistic flavor" in documents like the Gospel of John. The prologue to that gospel is a long poem or hymn on the Logos, written in Greek but employing Hebrew staircase parallelism. The same technique appears again in chapter three, in Jesus' dialogue with Nicodemus: "Unless a man is born again, he cannot see the Kingdom of God . . . unless a man is born of water and the Spirit, he cannot enter the Kingdom of God" (3:3, 5). Though the technique of parallelism is Hebraic, the parallel itself is clinched by the pun implied in the equivocal use of the Greek word *anothen*, which can mean either "again" or "from above." Here it is supposed to mean both, implying a heavenly birth and a rebirth. In exactly the same way, the word *aion* is used with a double meaning in *Necronomicon* 2:6 and 7. It all depends on the pun implied in the two uses of the word *aion* as "age" and as a hidden divine entity.

On the surface, as we have seen, the subject of the poem is Cthulhu. On this reading, it is he who "lies eternal" waiting for the passing of "strange aeons," i.e., unimaginably vast ages. Then his apparent "death [will] die," and his exile of slumber will end. But those readers with the "gnosis" will perceive themselves as the subject of the rhyme. Now the faithful cultists are "that [which] is not dead [and] can eternal lie." According to this interpretation, to "lie eternal" (*meinai eis tous aionous*) means not "to abide forever" (as does Cthulhu in R'lyeh) but rather "to await the Aions," i.e., the Old Ones. Those who do await them faithfully are "not dead," because death itself will pass away "with strange aeons"—not "with the passing of unimaginable ages," but rather "with the advent of unearthly Aions." The poem promises eternal reward to the human servitors of the Old Ones. According to the oral tradition of the cult, "then mankind would have become as the Great Old Ones; free and wild and beyond good and evil, with laws and morals thrown aside and all men shouting and killing and revelling in joy."[3] And, though the conception of salvation is much different to say the least, there are parallel promises in the New Testament. "He who endures to the end will be saved" (Matt. 24:13). "He who believes in me will live, even though he dies; and whoever lives and believes in me will never die" (John 11:25–26). For those who keep faith, death itself will die.

Fragment 3

Text:[1] Nor is it to be thought that man is either the oldest or the last of earth's masters, or that the common bulk of life and substance walks alone. [2]The Old Ones were, the Old Ones are, and the Old Ones shall be. [3]Not in the spaces we know, but between them, They walk serene and primal, undimensioned and to us unseen. [4]Yog-Sothoth knows the gate. Yog-Sothoth is the gate. Yog-Sothoth is the key and guardian of the gate. [5]Past, present, future, all are one in Yog-Sothoth. [6]He knows where the Old Ones broke through of old, and where They shall break through again. [7]He knows where They have trod earth's fields, and where They still tread them, and why no one can behold Them as They tread. [8]By Their smell can men sometimes know Them near, but of Their semblance can no man know, saving only in the features of those They have begotten on mankind; [9]and of those are there many sorts, differing in likeness from man's truest eidolon to that shape without sight or substance which is Them. [10]They walk unseen and foul in lonely places where the Words have been spoken and the Rites howled through at their Seasons. [11]The wind gibbers with Their voices, and the earth mutters with Their consciousness. [12]They bend the forest and crush the city, yet may not forest or city behold the hand that smites. [13]Kadath in the cold waste hath known Them, and what man knows Kadath? [14]The ice desert of the South and the sunken isles of [the] Ocean hold stones whereon Their seal is engraven, but who hath seen the deep frozen city or the sealed tower long garlanded with seaweed and barnacles? [15]Great Cthulhu is Their cousin, yet can he spy Them only dimly. [16]Iä! Shub-Niggurath! . . . As a foulness shall ye know Them. [18]Their hand is at your throats, yet ye see Them not; [19]and Their habitation is even one with your guarded threshold. [20]Yog-Sothoth is the key to the gate, whereby the spheres meet. [21]Man rules now where They ruled once; They shall soon rule where man rules now. [22]After summer is winter, and after winter summer. [23]They wait patient and potent, for here shall They reign again.[58] [[24]And at Their coming again none shall dispute Them and all shall be subject to Them. [25]Those who know of the gates shall be impelled to open the way for Them and shall serve Them as They desire, [26]but those who open the way unwittingly shall know but a brief while thereafter.][59]

Version: The above is a translation of Wormius' Latin version. There is also a hand-copied English translation from a text of unknown version and edition. Its readings (including the verses bracketed here), when they differ, are inferior. Nonetheless, the more interesting ones will be briefly noted.

Commentary: Our passage represents the continuation of a longer discourse, now lost. This is evident from the opening of this verse, "Nor is it to be thought . . . " "Nor" implies a previous "neither." The opening of v. 1 might be paraphrased, "Not only that, but here is something else about so-and-so." What was the "that," the subject matter of the missing text? The present passage discusses how man has not always ruled the earth and will not do so forever. Thus the preceding discourse must have qualified the rule of man in other ways. The whole section must have said in effect, "Man is not the unchallenged lord of his world that he imagines himself to be. For one thing, his control is limited (or threatened or whatever) by _____. For another, his rule is of short duration, since he once did not rule, and one day will be deposed."

The variant version attempts to round off the fragment artificially, by changing "Nor" to "Never." Thus the copyist had no more of the text than we do.

This verse, perhaps originally a liturgical chant, is parallel to Revelation 4:8b,

Holy, holy, holy
is the Lord God Almighty
who was, and is, and is to come.

The idea is that, unlike man whose rule is insecure and ephemeral, the Old Ones are eternal. They are "the same yesterday, today, and forever" (Hebrews 13:8). The verse follows the statement of v. 1 precisely in order to underline this contrast.

Note that the Old Ones do not at the present time, or by nature, inhabit dimensioned space as we know it.

"Yog-Sothoth" is an important entity in the Cthulhu Mythos. He is named by Ibn Khallikan as one of the beings worshipped by Alhazred. The name seems at least partially derived from, or influenced by, the Egyptian "Thoth," the god of enchanters. Given the important role of Egypt as the breeding ground for many early Gnostic sects, this is not surprising.

A series of more or less synonymous metaphors are used to describe Yog-Sothoth's role. He is the "gate," but also the "key" to and the "guardian" of the gate. We have a close parallel in the "Good Shepherd" discourse of John chapter 10: "Jesus said again, "I tell you the truth, I am the gate for the sheep . . . I am the good shepherd" [i.e., the guardian of the gate to the sheep pen] (vv. 7, 11).

Yog-Sothoth is able to serve as a gate of passage for the Old Ones because, like them, he is oblivious of the strictures of time. The parallel to v. 2 shows this.

As is already implied in v. 5, Yog-Sothoth is not to be included as one of the Old Ones. He is clearly distinguished from them here. The importance of this point cannot be overstressed. We will have more to say in this vein in connection with v. 15.

This verse informs us as to why man is "neither the oldest nor the last" of earth's rulers: The answer is that the Old Ones "broke through" long ago, and will do so again in the future. That is, they somehow pass into our space-time continuum. A kind of apocalyptic "second coming" of the Old Ones is hinted at here, though the very next verse seems to confuse this point somewhat.

"They still tread them"—these words imply that the Old Ones are not altogether absent from the terrestrial scene even now. The fact that "no one can behold Them as They tread" might be taken, in concert with v. 3, to suggest that the Old Ones are not directly present in our dimension, but are peering in from the outside. Yet this cannot be the correct interpretation, since their present "treading" is explicitly made equivalent in kind to their past presence on earth ("where They have trod") in their "first coming." They would seem to be present in the same way now.

Why can "no one behold Them as They tread"? We may guess that their translation into earth's dimensionality is incomplete, rendering them only partially susceptible to human senses (as in Lovecraft's story "From Beyond"). But in any case, our understanding of the passage is sufficient without an answer to this question; Alhazred's point is that Yog-Sothoth alone knows the answer.

The "beholding" of the previous verse referred strictly to sight, for v. 8 admits that the Old Ones can, at least sometimes, be detected by the other senses. Human beings can smell them. In the following verses we are told that their smell is a terrible stench—cf. v. 10, "They walk unseen and foul"; v. 17, "as a foulness shall ye know Them." The variant reading incorporates a marginal gloss into the text at this point: ". . . by Their smell, which is strange to the nostrils, and like unto a creature of great age."

Their "semblance," i.e., visual image, can be deduced only as it has been adapted into human terms, by the siring of children by human hosts. This is a common theme in virtually all mythology, e.g., in the cases of Gilgamesh and Heracles, whose divine paternity gave them telltale traits including superhuman strength. Only here, it is actual physiognomy that is affected.

The variant reading adds after "mankind" the words, "which are awful to behold, and thrice-awful are Those who sired them."

One cannot always gain an impression of how the Old Ones look, since some of their earthly offspring are indistinguishable from true men, while others seem to bear no human characteristics at all. A parallel range in Greek mythology would be that between Perseus, Heracles, and Apollo. All three are sons of Zeus by mortal women, yet Perseus is an entirely human hero, while Heracles is a superpowerful mortal, and Apollo is a god pure and simple.

We may detect a sinister implication here. In case of either extreme, the spawn of the Old Ones would be undetectable, either as impervious to our senses as the Old Ones themselves, or exactly like ourselves with no sign of their unearthly parentage. Who knows but that Alhazred himself did not harbor the delusion of being a literal son of his gods?

v. 10 We discover that the transition of the Old Ones into our world requires the agency, not only of the entity Yog-Sothoth, but also of initiated mortals. Incantations and rituals must be performed in "lonely places." The use of the word "howled" implies that the words to be spoken were originally designed for other-than-human throats, or that they represent a human adaptation shouted in imitation of animal howling to recall the nonhuman character of the original.

The verse also implies that the Old Ones are free to walk only in places prepared for them by such incantations. Perhaps we have the key to the apparent contradiction between vv. 6 and 7, where it is first said that they "shall break through," but then that they "still tread." The "breaking through" would seem to refer to a large-scale invasion, in sufficient numbers as to rule the earth again. This point has not yet been reached because sufficient preparation has not yet been made. Where the ground has been prepared, some Old Ones do "tread" even now, but not in sufficient strength to rule. Of course, the goal of the cult of the Old Ones was to restore the earthly dominion of their gods. This verse indicates that the preparatory rites could be enacted only at selected times ("in their Seasons"). For this reason, the faithful had to be patient. Through their tireless work, a sufficient number of the Old Ones would be invoked to reestablish their reign.

v.11 The "gibbering" of the wind with the voices of the Old Ones might reflect the universal tendency to understand weather phenomena as divine acts, such as the attribution of thunder and lightning to Zeus or Thor. But the reference here might be to the "buzzing" of desert insects heard in the wind, believed to be the whispering of demons, the source of Alhazred's revelations. In this verse, then, we would have the origin of the title of the work, *Al-Azif*.

However, on this understanding it remains to be seen just what the "murmuring of the earth" would refer to. Another possibility presents itself if this verse is read in closer connection with the following sections, as was quite likely intended. In this case, the murmuring of the earth would denote earthquakes. (See commentary immediately below.)

v.12 The winds of v. 11 are what "bend the forest"; the earthquakes of that verse "crush the city" of this verse. In both cases, no one "beholds" the Old Ones themselves, since they have employed "natural" disasters as their weapons. This verse introduces the unit comprised of vv. 13–14, which is technically known as a *mathna*, a formulary "punishment story" of the kind employed several times in the Koran and the Bible as a warning to sinners. The well-known doom of cities or peoples of the past is rehearsed in order to warn hearers (or readers) of their present danger.

Hast thou not seen how thy Lord dealt with Ad,
At Irem adorned with pillars,
Whose like have not been reared in these lands?
And with Themoud who hewed out the rocks in the valley; And with Pharaoh the impaler;
Who all committed excesses in the lands,
And multiplied wickedness therein.
Wherefore thy Lord let loose on them the scourge of chastisement.(Koran 89:5–12)

"Sodom and Gomorrah and the surrounding towns gave themselves up to sexual immorality and perversion. They serve as an example of those who suffer the punishment of eternal fire." (Jude 7)

Woe to you, Chorazin! Woe to you, Bethsaida! If the miracles that were performed in you had been performed in Tyre and Sidon, they would have repented long ago in sack cloth and ashes. But I tell you, it will be more bearable for Tyre and Sidon on the day of judgment than for you. And you, Capernaum, will you be lifted up to the skies? No, you will go down to Hades. If the miracles that were performed in you had been performed in Sodom, it would have remained to this day. But I tell you that it will be more bearable for Sodom on the day of judgment than for you. (Matt. 11:21–24)

In exactly the same way, the following verses attribute the doom of various cities to the vengeance of the Old Ones. The reader is to understand that he is potentially helpless before the same fate.

It is possible that the desolation of Kadath in the cold waste is derived from Psalm 29, one of the hymns sung yearly at the Feast of Tabernacles to commemorate the mythical victory of Yahweh over the lesser deities ("sons of God," Psalm 29:1), whereupon he became king of the gods. In the course of praising Yahweh's might, the psalmist writes:

The voice of Yahweh breaks the cedars,
Yahweh breaks the cedars of Lebanon . . .
The voice of Yahweh shakes the wilderness,
Yahweh shakes the wilderness of Kadesh.
The voice of Yahweh makes the oaks to whirl,
And strips the forest bare . . . (vv. 5, 8–9)

It is not hard to see the similarity between these verses and the present *Necronomicon* text: "The wind gibbers with Their voices, and the earth mutters with Their consciousness. They bend the forest and crush the city, yet may not forest or city behold the hand that smites. Kadath in the cold waste hath known Them, and what man knows Kadath?" Note how both texts symbolize the divine voice as wind which destroys the forest and devastates Kadath/Kadesh in the waste/wilderness. This might be coincidence, but such a close parallel implies rather that Alhazred was at least vaguely familiar with the psalm (not inherently unlikely anyway given the ancient Jewish community in his native Yemen) and that its imagery, whether consciously or unconsciously, shaped his poetic praise of the power of the Old Ones.

Kadesh was the wilderness in which the children of Israel wandered under the leadership of Moses. "Kadath" looks to be a variant form of Kadesh, especially in view of the parallel texts just discussed. As far as we know, no city existed in the wilderness of Kadesh, though it may be that in Alhazred's day some local legend claimed that there had been a city, and that for some great sin the gods had destroyed it. The point of such a legend would have been to explain the desolation of the area: it seemed cursed by the gods, so there must at one time have been people (i.e., a city) there to have sinned grossly and deserved the divine wrath.

Recalling the legend of Atlantis, this verse adds mention of once-inhabited islands sunk by the earthquakes of the Old Ones' making. There is a hint of special punishment, as the buildings of the sunken cities bore the seal of the Old Ones. Presumably they have been destroyed for some kind of unfaithfulness.

v. 15 The mention of sunken cities evokes mention of Great Cthulhu, who according to the belief of the cult, lies in repose in R'lyeh. It is just possible that Cthulhu is somehow to be understood as an object of the Old Ones' punishment, and that the drowned city of v. 14 is none other than R'lyeh.

As with Yog-Sothoth in v. 6, Cthulhu is here differentiated from the Old Ones. He shares in the infirmity of human beings: the Old Ones are very nearly as invisible to him as they are to us. He is related to them in some fashion, but the same statement that he is "Their cousin" simultaneously serves to distance him from them. He is merely related to them, not one of them. Remember that Cthulhu and Yog-Sothoth both came to be confused with the Old Ones. But this is a later development in the mythology. Alhazred himself was careful to distinguish them.

v.16 The ejaculation "Iä! Shub-Niggurath!" occurs here as a spontaneous exultation of praise. The exclamation expresses the author's pious joy at the truths he has just penned. Such literary outbursts are not unusual. The Apostle Paul makes occasional use of them in his epistles. For example he concludes a summary of the religious privileges of the Jewish people with a paean of praise:"God who is over all be forever praised!" (Rom. 9:5). And at the close of an appeal to his readers to contribute to a charitable relief effort, Paul cries, "Thanks be to God for his indescribable gift!" (2 Cor. 9:15).

As to the identity of "Shub-Niggurath," there is quite an element of mystery. Elsewhere in the lore of the cult, Shub-Niggurath is referred to as "cloud-like" or, alternatively, as the "Black Goat of the Woods" or the "Goat with a Thousand Young." The "black goat" imagery recalls the medieval depiction of Satan as a black satyr with a goat's head. The name "Shub-Niggurath" would seem to have some connection with this image, as it may derive in some way from the Latin *niger* ("black"). The "thousand young" would suggest a fertility god or goddess. Unless all this is purely metaphorical, Shub-Niggurath would seem to be, like Cthulhu and Yog-Sothoth, some sort of lesser entity connected with the Old Ones, but not strictly speaking one of them. The attributes as described are too earthy in their reference for their subject to be one of the transdimensional Old Ones.

Once again Alhazred states that the Old Ones may be detected by their foul odor. See v. 8.

This striking image, drawn readily from the world of Alhazred's day with its treacherous alley-ways haunted by cut-throats waiting to pounce, vividly illustrates the danger posed by the Old Ones to those oblivious of their presence.

Whatever fortification men might think to build against them, they have already breached it. Or perhaps the idea is that no protection intended against earthly foes can hope to avail against the invisible threat of the Old Ones.

Again, Yog-Sothoth is asserted to be the gate whereby the Old Ones may pass over. The use of spheres external to each other but touching tangentially, is interesting. Usually "sphere" cosmology entailed a system of concentric spheres, one inside the other, as in the Ptolemaic system.

vv. 21–23. These verses form a unit, comprising a classic apocalyptic warning, almost precisely parallel to James 5:7–8:

> Be patient, then, brothers, until the Lord's coming. See how the farmer waits for the land to yield its valuable crop and how patient he is for the fall and spring rains. You, too, be patient and stand firm, because the Lord's coming is near.

Both texts employ the image of the change of seasons. The idea is not that of an endlessly repeated cycle. Rather, it is that as surely as one season follows another, the dreary present must soon give way to the eagerly anticipated future. "Winter" in v. 22 refers to man's rule in v. 21, while "summer" is, of course, the rule of the Old Ones. James uses the analogy to exhort his readers to have patience, while Alhazred uses it to explain why the Old Ones can afford to be patient, but the point is the same

It is important not to pass quickly over the word "soon" in v. 21. With this single word, we discover that Abdul Alhazred, like many another prophet, has embarrassed his followers by virtually setting a date for the end. Like early Christians who had to cope with the delay of the Parousia, believing readers of the *Necronomicon* eventually had to come up with some expedient "when prophecy failed." However, on the positive side, it should be noted that the presence of this unfulfilled prediction in the text weighs heavily in favor of its authenticity; it is hard to imagine a later writer adding such an embarrassment when it didn't already exist!

vv. 24–26 occur only in the variant version of the passage, and are almost certainly inauthentic.

Fragment 4

Text: [1]Verily do we know little of the other universes beyond the gate which YOG-SOTHOTH guards. [2]Of those which come through the gate and make their habitation in this world none can tell; [3]although Ibn Schacabao tells of the beings which crawl from the Gulf of S'glhuo that they may be known by Their sound. [4]In that Gulf the very worlds are of sound, and matter is known but as an odor; [5]and the notes of our pipes in this world may create beauty or bring forth abominations in S'glhuo. [6]For the barrier between haply grows thin, and when sourceless sounds occur we may justly look to the denizens of S'glhuo. [7]They can do little harm to those of Earth, and fear only that shape which a certain sound may form in Their universe.[60]

Version: The version and edition from which this quote is taken are unknown.
Commentary: The reference to Yog-Sothoth and his guarding a gate between universes implies that this passage followed closely the one just discussed. It is assumed that the reader will already know who Yog-Sothoth is and why he serves this function.

Note that Alhazred admits his ignorance about other-worldly matters which do not directly concern the lore of his gods, the Old Ones. However, he does assume that there are still other universes, apparently to be identified with the cosmological "spheres" of 3:20. Thus Yog-Sothoth is the gate of passage between all the universes. This means he is part of Alhazred's larger worldview, and not especially of the Cthulhu Mythos proper. This would explain how it is that Yog-Sothoth knows where the Old Ones broke through into our world, while not being one of them. He is aware of all interdimensional crossings, whether of the Old Ones or of others, as in the present text.

v. 2 Just as the other universes are largely a mystery to us, even so, those who pass over from there are virtually undetectable. Here Alhazred admits that the invisibility of the Old Ones, stemming from their extramundane origin, is a quality common to all interdimensional travelers. And while he as an adept of the Old Ones knows how to detect them, he now confesses that he is as much in the dark as anyone else when it comes to other aliens.

His only clue about the only other alien race he names, the dwellers in "the Gulf of S'glhuo," is that they are detectable by distinctive sounds. (The distinctive element is named in v. 6.) Note the analogy with the Old Ones who may sometimes be detected by their smell (3:8).

There seems to be an element of confusion here. Whereas the previous verse indicated that a distinctive sound was a sign of their presence, v. 4 makes their very presence nothing but sound. The effect would be the same for the observer, but they are two different conceptions. Alhazred seems to return to the "sign" conception when he remarks that, in parallel fashion, earthly matter is perceived by these aliens as odor.

Musical sounds made by us (whether randomly or intentionally designed as an incantation, is not made clear) are creative of new reality in their universe. Once again, the conception of these aliens as being nothing but sound (rather than represented by sound) seems to be uppermost, since what would be mere sounds to us, upon penetrating their world, are by definition forceful realities. All in all, the logic here is familiar from Alhazred's belief that

"Rites howled through in their Seasons" (3:10) may penetrate the dimensions and enable the Old Ones to cross over.

vv. 6–7. It is not explained precisely why "the barrier grows thin" between their universe and ours. Presumably this is a periodic occurrence determined by purely cosmological considerations, just as the rites summoning the Old Ones may be performed effectively only at certain times, "in their Seasons" (3:10).

The denizens of the Gulf of S'glhuo pose no threat to humanity, so why does Alhazred bother recording this information? He merely wishes to relate this explanation for why we sometimes seem to hear sounds with no evident source. That is the whole point of the passage. This is one of the clearest examples of the superstitions and curiosities that form the stock-in-trade of the "book of marvels" genre to which the *Necronomicon* belongs.

From the Book of Thoth

Fragment 5

Text: [1]And while there are those who have dared to seek glimpses beyond the Veil, and to accept HIM as guide, [2]they would have been more prudent had they avoided commerce with HIM; for it is written in the Book of Thoth how terrific is the price of a single glimpse. [3]Nor may those who pass ever return, for in the vastnesses transcending our world are shapes of darkness that seize and bind. [4]The Affair that shambleth about in the night, the evil that defieth the Elder Sign, the Herd that stand watch at the secret portal each tomb is known to have and that thrive on that which groweth out of the tenants thereof: [5]—all these Blacknesses are lesser than HE WHO guardeth the Gateway: HE WHO will guide the rash one beyond all the worlds into the Abyss of unnamable devourers. [6]For He is 'UMR AT TAWIL, the Most Ancient One, which the scribe rendereth as THE PROLONGED OF LIFE.[61]

Version: Unfortunately, the edition and translation from which this quote is taken are unknown. However, we do possess a parallel version of the same text, taken from a Kufic recension of unknown edition.[62] Variant readings, where noteworthy, will be supplied in the commentary, since the Kufic seems better to represent the original, retaining words and phrases omitted by other copyists and/or translators.

Commentary: v. 1. The beginning "And" implies that we have once again a fragment of a longer passage in the original. The subject seems to be the gaining of extramundane knowledge. "Beyond the Veil" is extremely common terminology for revelation in esoteric mysticism.

The Kufic recension has "And while there are those who have had the temerity to seek glimpses of beyond the Veil . . ."

v.2. The few who have sought esoteric knowledge in this fashion were foolish to have done so. (The technique in question was presumably discussed in the preceding text, lost to us.) The price is one of extravagant danger. What sort of danger? The text itself supplies no real clues, but the legend of the Patriarch Atal and his companion Barzai the Wise, which may have been known to Alhazred, may provide the solution.

It seems that the two sages once set out to gain a glimpse of their gods as they danced in the starlight atop a certain forbidden peak. Though both made the climb, only Barzai dared peer over the peak. For this Promethean act, he was "drawn screaming into the sky." Apparently this means that the vision drove him mad, and that he died soon after. The more reticent Atal survived to descend the mountain and live in peace.

This seems to be a somewhat late and confused version of the Talmudic story of "the four who entered Paradise," Rabbis Akiba, Ben Azai, Ben Zoma, and Aher. The four made a visionary ascent to the divine throne-room and each met with a different fate. Ben Azai was overcome at the sight of divine glory and died. Ben Zoma went insane. Aher became a heretic, and only Akiba returned completely unharmed. The later version seems to have substituted Atal for Akiba, and to have combined the fates of Ben Zoma and Ben Azai. The name "Barzai" would seem to represent a corruption of "Ben Azai," perhaps involving the substitution of the Aramaic *bar* for its Hebrew equivalent *ben* (both, like the Arabic *ibn*, meaning "son of"). At any rate, the lesson of both tales is clear: the vision of supramundane reality is all too likely to prove too much for mortal senses. Insanity, heresy, or even death may result from a journey "beyond the Veil." Thus, Alhazred warns against it. The Old Ones may penetrate the Veil from the other side, but humans should not try it.[63]

The reference to *The Book of Thoth* reveals the Hermetic background of this passage. The reference to the legend described above accords with this. Gershom Scholem considers that the "Merkabah" ("Throne") mysticism from which that legend stems, was the Jewish counterpart of Hermetic mysticism.

We will find more evidence for our hypothesis in vv. 5–6 below.

Apparently, those who actually "pass" beyond the Veil have done more than merely to "seek a glimpse" of that realm. According to this verse, their doom is sealed by the presence of monsters there.

The Kufic version reads: "and none who pass may return, for they will be firmly bound by those who lurk in the vastnesses that transcend our world."

The three horrors listed here are probably cumulative, synonymous descriptions of the same thing—ghouls of some kind. They "shamble" in darkness, violating tombs which have been vainly sealed for protection with the "Elder Sign," apparently the charmed sigil of some conventional religion. The cryptic reference to "that which groweth out of the tenants" of the tomb is the subject of Fragment 8. Further comment will be reserved for that passage.

For a later interpretation of v. 4 by the reformist sect, see the commentary on 16:8–11.

The Kufic reading is rather different, and apparently confused: "The terrors of the night, and the evils of creation, and those who stand watch at the secret exit that it is known each grave has, and thrive on that which grows out of the tenants thereof . . ."

The ghouls are less terrible than the guardian of the Gateway. Why is this? The ghouls and "the Most Ancient One" (named in v. 6) are paralleled in their role as guardians. The ghouls "stand watch [i.e., guard) at the portal" of the grave and devour the corpse, but the Most Ancient One presides over the Gateway leading "beyond all worlds into the Abyss of devourers" who are much worse than ghouls. The ghouls devour the dead, but these devourers consume the living soul of the mystic. This is a complicated way of saying that the Most Ancient One brings the visionary a fate worse than death.

The Kufic text has "They are lesser powers than he who guards the Gateway, and offers to guide the unwary into the realm beyond this world and all its unnamed and unnamable Devourers." Here the "devourers" represent not those more fearsome than the ghouls, but the earthly ghouls themselves. This seems to be a simple copyist error. On such a reading, the parallel between the ghouls and the Most Ancient One is destroyed and no reason is left for fearing him.

V. 6 Finally the guardian is named. He is "the Most Ancient One." From the two previous fragments, the reader might have expected to find the name "Yog-Sothoth." He is, after all, described in both Fragments 3 and 4 as the guardian of a gate between the worlds. Technically 5:5 speaks of a gate "beyond all worlds," not between worlds. But beyond this perhaps merely semantic difference, there is a good reason that Yog-Sothoth does not appear here. We have suggested that the whole of Fragment 5 is derived, not from Alhazred's own Cthulhu Mythos, but rather from the Hermetic *Book of Thoth*. Later readers of this passage have missed this, and so have sought to identify the Most Ancient One and Yog-Sothoth.("Yog-Sothoth . . . whose aspects on earth are 'Umr At-Tawil and the Ancient Ones"—15:4). That they are quite different entities with no connection will become apparent.

According to the text as it now stands (in both recensions), the name of the guardian is "'Umr At-Tawil," which is rendered "Most Ancient One." Yet 'Umr At-Tawil does not mean this at all; rather it quite clearly means "speaker of allegorical interpretations."[64] Here it is to be taken as a title of "the scribe" mentioned in our passage. The extant reading of the text can be explained quite simply as a copyist's error. We may confidently surmise that the text of v. 6 originally had "For He is 'the Most Ancient One' [written in Greek], which the scribe 'Umr At-Tawil rendereth as 'THE PROLONGED OF LIFE [the same title, only in Arabic]." 'Umr At-Tawil was the title of the scribe, not the name of the Guardian of the Gate.

"The Prolonged of Life," then, is the translation of "the Most Ancient One." The reason that both forms survive side by side in this manner is this: The Hermetic tract used by Alhazred was originally written in Greek, though he himself worked from the Arabic translation by 'Umr At-Tawil. Tawil had reproduced the original Greek for "the Most Ancient One" and followed it with the Arabic equivalent. Alhazred decided to record both the original and the translation. When Philetas translated Alhazred into Greek, he translated the Arabic translation back into Greek, leaving two synonymous versions of the title ("Most Ancient One" and "Prolonged of Life"). The effect would be the same as if an Aramaic speaker had translated John 1:41 from Greek back into the Aramaic originally spoken by the characters in the scene. It reads, "We have found the Messiah [Aramaic] (that is the Christ [Greek])." Translated back into Aramaic, it might read "We have found the Messiah (that is the Messiah)."

Fragment 6

Text: [1]" . . . the Place of the Blind Apes where Nephren-Ka bindeth up the threads of truth."[65]

Version: This fragment is cited as being from a rare Arabic version.

Commentary: v. 1. This brief sentence-fragment is usually thought to allude to the legend of the "Black Pharaoh" Nephren-Ka, a corrupter of the religion of Egypt. Nephren-Ka was supposedly a hierophant of Nyarlathotep, messenger of the Great Old Ones. Like the Pharaoh Imhotep (Ikhnaton) who sought to convert Egypt to the new faith of Aten the Sun, Nephren-Ka's "reforms" were of short duration. They were especially atrocious, involving necrophilism and human sacrifice. He apparently symbolized Nyarlathotep as an ape, i.e., probably in human form with the head of an ape in accord with the style of traditional iconography. In this form, Nyarlathotep was venerated as "The Blind Ape of Truth." For his excesses, Nephren-Ka was eventually overthrown. He is said to have sought refuge with his acolytes in a vast underground tomb.

The *Necronomicon* is supposed to outline this much of the story, which is continued in greater detail by the Flemish wizard Ludvig Prinn in *De Vermis Mysteriis*. There it is said that the Black Pharaoh somehow sacrificed his remaining attendants in a Faustian bargain with Nyarlathotep. In return he received knowledge of all the future ages of Egypt, which he managed to inscribe on the vast walls of his tomb before he expired. The cult of Nyarlathotep survived him, eventually discovering the tomb and covering the oracular inscriptions with a tapestry to be rolled back each day to uncover that day's events.

It is not inherently improbable that Alhazred did record at least part of this legend. However the wording of the single surviving sentence about Nephren-Ka does raise intriguing questions. We are going to argue that the story related by Prinn is a later version of the legend, which appeared in the *Necronomicon* in quite a different form. Like the preceding fragment dealing with "the Most Ancient One," the present passage is dependent on a Hermetic text. Even in the brief sentence we have, there are strong hints both that Alhazred's version did not coincide with Prinn's, and that it is Hermetic in origin.

First, who was "Nephren-Ka"? Later legend seems to have seized upon the similarity of his name to that of the Egyptian queen Nephertiti, a combination of the divine names "Neph" and "Thoth." Thoth has already been discussed briefly above with reference to the Hermetic tracts. Neph was the creator, the "spirit of god" which hovered over the primeval waters. It was common for rulers to be named for gods, but we suspect that Nephren-Ka was actually supposed to be a divinity. Ka was the word for one's soul, or spirit-double, which survived death. "Nephren-Ka" would then denote either "Soul of the Spirit of God," or "Double of the Spirit of God," i.e., his visible manifestation on earth.

Or perhaps, under the earth. Concerning the Hermetic literature, Geo Widengren writes,

> The entering of a dark, subterranean chamber in order to find a book of revelation is a theme often recurring in Egyptian and Hellenistic tales . . . only in Egypt do we meet with the idea of a descent into an underground edifice in order to acquire the unsurpassed wisdom of preceding ages.[66]

The present *Necronomicon* fragment agrees with Prinn's legend in placing Nephren-Ka in an underground chamber of some sort. This in fact is the significance of the mention of "the place of the blind apes." This phrase has nothing to do with Nyarlathotep or any other god. Instead, it is merely a figure of speech denoting a lightless underground place of mysteries. Alhazred uses an analogous expression in 8:1. But the cavern is not a burial vault. It is simply the underground chamber of revelation mentioned by Widengren. It can hardly be a crypt according to our fragment, since Nephren-Ka is described as still alive there ("bindeth" is present tense).

The implied image of Nephren-Ka is like that of the Fates in Greek mythology. He is "binding up the threads of truth," or weaving a tapestry that records the wisdom of the ages. Those who find their way to his subterranean abode may seek revelations from this tapestry. Presumably the Egyptian Hermetic text Alhazred used purported to contain such revelations. Whether all this represented someone's actual visionary experience or was merely a literary convention we do not know. At any rate, the whole scene was later garbled so that the "blind apes" metaphor was taken literally and combined with the word "truth" in the expression "threads of truth." The tapestry was retained in the legend, but as the covering for the revelation rather than the medium of it. Finally the revelation itself was transformed into a forecast of future history.

The mischief of later misunderstanding is evident elsewhere as well. Ibn Khallikan records that Alhazred had visited the crypts of ancient Memphis. He probably derived this information from this passage of the *Necronomicon*, failing to realize that the "underground journey in Egypt" was simply part of an older document adapted by Alhazred and incorporated into his book of curiosities.

Fragment 7

Concerning the Dead

Text: ¹Many and multiform are the dim horrors of Earth, infesting her ways from the prime. ²They sleep beneath the unturned stone; they rise with the tree from its root; they move beneath the sea and in subterranean places; they dwell in the inmost adyta; ³they emerge betimes from the shutten sepulchre of haughty bronze and the low grave that is sealed with clay. ⁴There be some that are long known to man, and others as yet unknown that abide the terrible latter days of their revealing. ⁵Those which are the most dreadful and the loathliest of all are haply still to be declared. ⁶But among those that have revealed themselves aforetime and have made manifest their veritable presence, there is one which may not openly be named for its exceeding foulness. ⁷It is that spawn which the hidden dweller in the vaults has begotten upon mortality.[67]

Version: Unknown, though possibly Wormius' Latin in light of the next fragment.

Commentary: With vv. 1–5, we seem to have the beginning of a new section, that grouping of material which led Philetas to give the work its Greek title *Necronomicon*, or "Book of the Dead." The next passages all refer to matters of necrophagy and necromancy. Interestingly, it is apparent that Alhazred himself was revolted at the curiosities and practices he set before the reader.

The "horrors" seem, from the context, to be monsters or creatures which are "dim" to us, i.e., we neither perceive nor understand them at all clearly. There are many of them, and they come in many varieties. They have always dwelt unwholesomely ("infested" earth's "ways"). The "ways" are the various channels and recesses of the planet. They are enumerated in the next verse. (Also, see commentary on 8:6.)

Like disgusting bugs and vermin, they hide beneath stones. Like root-rot disease, they seep into the trees alongside more wholesome nourishment from the soil. Some are sea-monsters prowling the knighted depths; others hibernate in unsuspected lairs far beneath earth's surface. All in all, they are hidden away in the "adyta" or secret places.

"Betimes" is probably a mistranslation. It means "in good time" or "soon," but the context seems to demand "sometimes." At any rate, these particular "horrors" emerge from the tombs of rich as well as poor. Both grand and humble tombs are described as having been secured ("shutten" and "sealed") but to no avail, since the monsters have appeared there. How? Perhaps via "the secret portal each tomb is known to have" (5:4). These "horrors" might be ghouls, though another possibility will concern us below, in verse 7.

Some of the many monsters are already familiar, such as those of the previous verse. Others are still unsuspected, at least to humanity by and large. Obviously, Alhazred is not ignorant of them or he would not be writing about them. The reference to "terrible latter days of their revealing" has a distinctly apocalyptic ring. We may wonder if the author is not making a sidelong reference to what most of mankind deems (or would deem if they knew) the ultimate horror—the coming of the Great Old Ones. The conspiratorial tone is reminiscent of the smug and taunting Fragment 3, which deals with the return of Alhazred's gods.

The point is the same as in v. 4. The worst horrors may perhaps ("haply") yet lie in the future.

Here Alhazred begins his consideration of several specific monstrosities, to which the first five verses have formed a preface. Of those terrors which have already revealed their presence before the final onslaught, there is one in particular about which he is reticent to speak in detail.

Incidentally, the thought-pattern here is familiar. Though the reference is not to the Old Ones, we are reminded of 3:17, "as a foulness shall ye know them." Compare 3:17 with 7:6: "one which may not openly be named for its exceeding foulness." Though the point is not quite the same in context, both verses share the notion that an alien entity may not be known except by the simple fact of its "foulness."

Some have interpreted the "spawn . . . of the hidden dweller in the vaults" as the fruit of a blasphemous union between ghouls and the dead. This is possible on a reading of this text taken by itself. But if ghouls are in view, then we must read into the passage some explanation for their presence in a sealed tomb. We have hazarded such a guess above, but the problem can be avoided if we restore the passage to its full context. We suggest that the present fragment was originally followed immediately by the next one, which places the verses discussed here in a whole new light. The following fragment will relate how the disembodied souls of wizards linger in the grave, forming a new host body from the very worms which devour the old one. Such a disembodied soul is the "hidden dweller in the vault" of the present fragment. It entered secretly along with the corpse. Its "spawn" is the new walking humanoid worm that issues from the terrible process, and leaves the tomb to plague mankind ("mortality").

Fragment 8

Text: [1]The nethermost caverns are not for the fathoming of eyes that see; for their marvels are strange and terrific. [2]Cursed the ground where dead thoughts live new and oddly bodied, and evil the mind that is held by no head. [3]Wisely did Ibn Schacabao say, that happy is the tomb where no wizard hath lain, and happy the town at night whose wizards are all ashes. [4]For it is of old rumor that the soul of the devil-bought hastes not from his charnel clay, but fats and instructs the very worm that gnaws; till out of corruption horrid life springs, [5]and the dull scavengers of earth wax crafty to vex it, and swell monstrous to plague it. [6]Great holes secretly are digged where earth's pores ought to suffice, and things have learnt to walk that ought to crawl.[68]

Version: This passage comes from Wormius' Latin version.

Commentary: "Eyes that see" at first appears to be a redundancy. Actually, it is a reference to the blind creatures, e.g., fish who inhabit the deepest caves and grottos. Of course the eyes of such a species have simply become atrophied through evolution. There is no need for them to have functional eyes since there is no light. But Alhazred uses the creatures as a striking metaphor:in such depths there are things to be seen that are so terrible, nature has mercifully blessed innocent creatures who live there with blindness. Alhazred is about to describe, or at least hint at, these awful beings which disgust even him.

v. 2 In this and the next verse, Alhazred has juxtaposed a set of woes with a set of blessings, combining his own imprecation formulae with benedictions by Ibn Schacabao. The evangelist Luke has used the same technique in his Sermon on the Plain, taking the list of beatitudes from the earlier source he shares with the Gospel of Matthew, and adding a matching set of "woes" of his own (Luke 6:20–26, cf. Matt. 5:3–12).

The two imprecations are parallel and may originally have formed an independent poetic epigram. "Dead thoughts" (i.e., the thoughts of the dead) proceed from a disembodied mind (one that is "held by no head"). Just how these thoughts became "[em]bodied" in a "new and odd" manner is elaborated in vv. 4 and 5.

v. 3. Ibn Schacabao is once again quoted (cf. 4:3). "Happy" (or "blessed") is any tomb housing the remains of anyone but a wizard. The same goes for any townspeople wise enough to have cremated their wizards' remains (or perhaps to have burnt them at the stake!). In each case, the point is that one must not bury the body of a sorcerer. The reason is given below.

Note, incidentally, that the wizard's anticipated mischief would occur "at night" as in the vampire legends.

v. 4. This verse provides more evidence that the *Necronomicon* is not a grimoire, for Alhazred seems to despise pacts with the devil. He describes wizards as "devil-bought" and does not seem to approve.

At any rate, the soul of a dead wizard is believed to haunt the grave. It "fats and instructs" the worms that come to consume the corpse. That is, it imparts both new substance and intelligence to the carrion creatures. This is how "dead thoughts" come to be "new and oddly bodied"—the mind of the wizard possesses and transforms the flesh of the worm, giving itself a new host. The result is a hideous resurrection: "out of corruption horrid life springs."

The worms, normally "dull," thus grow clever enough to "vex" the earth they used to scavenge. Their bodily shape "swells monstrously" into a parody of humanity, in which form it will plague the earth.

The "vexing" and "plaguing" of the earth primarily takes the form of burrowing large tunnels in the earth's fabric, instead of merely slipping through the soil's natural pores as they used, as small worms, to do. In their new humanoid form, the wizard-possessed creatures need cavernous passages through which to move. This is probably in view in 7:1, with the phrase "infesting [earth's] ways from the prime."

It is probably also the phenomenon described here that Alhazred alludes to in 5:4 as "that which groweth out of the tenants" of the tomb. Together Fragments 5 and 8 would imply that the nightmarishly resurrected wizards still have one danger to cope with—the threat of ghouls waiting to devour them in their new incarnation.

Fragment 9

Text: [1]It is verily known by few, but is nevertheless an attestable fact, that the will of a dead sorcerer hath power upon his own body and can raise it up from the tomb and perform therewith whatever action was unfulfilled in life. [2]And such resurrections are invariably for the doing of malevolent deeds and for the detriment of others. [3]Most readily can the corpse be animated if all its members have remained intact; [4]and yet there are cases in which the excelling will of the wizard hath reared up from death the sundered pieces of a body hewn in many fragments, [5]and hath caused them to serve his end, either separately or in a temporary reunion. [6]But in every instance, after the action hath been completed, the body lapseth into its former state.[69]

Version: This passage comes from the original Arabic, and is omitted from Wormius' Latin. Presumably Philetas included it and Wormius likely omitted it simply by accident. See below.

Commentary: Note again the tone of an insider deigning to reveal his secrets to a wider audience. This is typical of the "book of marvels." Also, the introduction is a standard "attestation formula," repeated in 10:1.

This verse begins the discussion of another version of the "wizard's resurrection" theme familiar from the preceding passages (Fragments 7 and 8). According to the present version, the deceased wizard's mind also survives the death of the body, but whereas before he abandoned his corpse for a new body, now he merely reanimates the corpse for temporary use. The goal here is not to continue one's life indefinitely, but rather simply to "tie up the loose ends" remaining from one's affairs, cut short by death. After the mission is accomplished, the wizard (apparently) resigns himself to death. The whole notion is parallel to that of a ghost seeing to the affairs of the departed, e.g., gaining proper burial.

Such resuscitations are never for any wholesome purpose. We are not, for instance, to imagine the wizard sending his remains back to rectify some error in the distribution of his goods. No, the purpose is always malicious. But this passage probably refers only to the gaining of vengeance on those responsible for the wizard's death.

The resurrection may be effected with least difficulty if the body is still more or less intact.

Yet even if the wizard's murderer has tried to prevent such revenge from the grave by chopping the corpse to pieces, he may not be safe. If a wizard's will is extraordinarily strong, even the dismembered pieces may be marshalled for vengeance.

Note the terminology of a compiler of curiosities "there are cases where . . ."

The wizard may reanimate the body parts singly or in reassembled form.

In any case, the resurrection is finally temporary. The goal, again, was not the resumption of life as before.

Does the conception of "wizard's resurrection" in this passage not contradict that found in Fragments 7 and 8? Obviously so, but compilers like Alhazred were seldom greatly concerned with absolute consistency. He is concerned only to catalogue and relate the curious superstitions he has assembled from whatever source.

Incidentally, the text is said to have supplied an elaborate formula for exorcising such a spectral visitor. It involved rare Arabian spices and lists of a hundred or more names of ghouls and demons, as if to "cast out demons by Beelzebub" (Matt. 12:27). One wonders how many of these names the frightened reader could get through before the reanimated skeleton attacked?

Fragment 10

Text: [1]'Tis a veritable & attestable Fact, that between certain related Persons there exists a Bond more powerful than the strongest Ties of Flesh and Family, [2] whereby one such Person may be aware of all the Trials & Pleasures of the other, yea, even to experiencing the Pains or Passions of one far distant; [3]& further, there are those whose skills in such Matters are aided by forbidden Knowledge or Intercourse through dark Magic with Spirits & Beings of outside Spheres. [4]Of the latter: I have sought them out, both Men & Women, & upon Examination have in all Cases discovered them to be Users of Divination, Observers of Times, Enchanters, Witches, Charmers, or Necromancers. [[5]All claimed to work their Wonders through Intercourse with dead & departed Spirits, [6]but I fear that often such Spirits were evil Angels, the Messengers of the Dark One & yet more ancient Evils.] [7]Indeed, among them were some whose Powers were prodigious, who might at will inhabit the Body of another even at a great Distance & against the Will & often unbeknown to the Sufferer of such Outrage. [8]Yea, & I discovered how one might, be he an Adept & his familiar Spirits powerful enough, control the Wanderings or Migration of his Essence into all manner of Beings & Persons [9]—even from beyond the Grave of Sod or the Door of the Stone Sepulcher.[70]

Version: Unknown, but translated into English by Joachim Feery.

Commentary: vv. 1–2. Alhazred repeats the formula of attestation with which he began the preceding passage. As we will see, the present section follows 7, 8, and 9 with basically the same theme, the powers of a wizard after death. He begins by describing what we would call a telepathic link between certain individuals. Such alleged phenomena are notoriously difficult to verify, but such as seem to occur usually involve identical twins. Surprisingly, Alhazred seems to rule out such "ties of flesh and family," unless he simply means that natural family loyalties, even strong ones (very strong in his day, when blood-feuds were not uncommon), pale in comparison to such telepathy.

Some thus gifted have augmented their psychic abilities through occult study and spiritualistic contact with alien beings. They are described as the inhabitants of "outside spheres," terminology characteristic of Alhazred's cosmology (cf. 3:20).

Alhazred has made special efforts to learn the secrets of this latter group. "In all cases" (again, the telltale language of the collector of curiosities), these individuals turned out to be full-fledged practitioners of the black arts. Did he not already know they had sought occult aid? Perhaps the point is that his suspicions were confirmed that no one who dabbles in magic can avoid becoming completely enmeshed in it.

vv. 5–6. These verses seem to be an interpolation by Joachim Feery, in whose *Original Notes on the Necronomicon* the whole passage is preserved. The mention of "evil angels" and the devil are more likely to represent Feery's religious beliefs than Alhazred's. Feery is notorious for rewriting quoted materials, and we seem to have an example of his doing it here. However, it may be that Feery meant only to make a parenthetic observation: Alhazred accepted the occultists' claims, but Feery himself does not. If this is the case, Feery's omission of appropriate punctuation gives the impression that Alhazred himself disputed the claims of his informants.

v. 7. Some of the occultist-psychics were able not only to share perceptions with others, but also to possess them, replacing the hosts' senses with their own. This they could do over long distances and against the host's will. It could even be done without the victim's knowledge. Presumably the person, upon regaining his senses, would merely seem to have suffered memory loss, unaware of what had happened. Obviously, the purpose of such an operation would be nefarious; for instance, to employ someone else's body to commit some crime. Today we call it "identity theft."

We have now passed beyond telepathy to astral projection, or soul travel. Alhazred confides that, with sufficient expertise and supernatural assistance, one may even occupy minds and bodies other-than-human.

Such astral projection is yet another means by which a wizard may continue to work his will after death. Neither a grave dug in the ground nor a carved mausoleum can imprison the wizard who had, in life, mastered soul-travel and psychic possession.

With this passage, we have reached the end of Alhazred's material on the powers of the wizard beyond the grave. He has outlined how a dead sorcerer may return in a hybrid body of worm-flesh, how he may send his skeletal remains on a brief mission of revenge, and finally how he may send only his disembodied soul to do his bidding in the body of another.

As a sidelight, this passage is of particular interest for the light it sheds upon Joachim Feery himself. We have remarked upon Feery's notorious practice of freely augmenting and rewriting ancient texts. He is said to have received his inspiration to do this from dreams. Fragment 10 of the *Necronomicon* describes just what Feery thought he was doing—acting as host for the mind of Alhazred and others! In his own estimate, he was the medium whereby the ancient writers revised and updated their work. The same sort of delusion has been shared by other eccentrics in our day, including various UFO-contactees and bus-station prophets through whom, e.g., Jesus Christ has rewritten the gospel for the space age.

Section Three

The Apocryphal Material

The Fall of Cthulhu

Fragment 11

Text: [1]'Twas done then as it had been promised aforetime, that he was taken by Those Whom he defied, and thrust into the nethermost deeps under the sea, [2]and placed within the barnacled tower that is said to rise amidst the great ruin that is the sunken city (R'lyeh), and sealed within by the Elder Sign, [3]and, raging at Those who had imprisoned him, he further incurred Their anger, [4]and They, descending upon him for the second time, did impose upon him the semblance of death, but left him dreaming in that place under the great waters, [5]and returned to that place from whence they had come, namely, Glyu-Vho, which is among the stars, [6]and looketh upon earth from the time when the leaves fall to that time when the ploughman becomes habited once again to his fields. [7]And there shall he lie dreaming forever, in his house at R'lyeh, [8]toward which at once all his minions swam and strove against all manner of obstacles, and arranged themselves to wait for his awakening, powerless to touch the Elder Sign and fearful of its great power [9]knowing that the cycle returneth, and he shall be freed to embrace the earth again and make of it his kingdom and defy the Elder Gods anew. [10]And to his brothers it happened likewise, that they were taken by Those Whom they defied and hurled into banishment, [11]Him Who is Not to Be Named being sent into outermost space, beyond the stars, [12]and with the others likewise, until the earth was free of them, [13]and Those Who came in the shape of Towers of Fire, returned whence they had come, and were seen no more, and on all earth their peace came [14]and was unbroken while their minions gathered and sought means and ways with which to free the Old Ones, [15]and waited while man came to pry into secret, forbidden places and open the gate.[71]

Version: This fragment comes from a collection of translations of random chapters, each out of different editions and versions, no longer specifiable.

Commentary: v. 1. "He," as is evident from the context, is Cthulhu. Vv. 1–8 of this fragment seem to have originally constituted an independent unit of tradition, a narrative of the "Fall of Cthulhu," elaborated from the ambiguous passage 3:14–15. The beginning of the narrative is lost, as v. 1 begins in the middle of the action ("'Twas done then . . ."). For some unspecified action, perhaps described in the preceding lost text, he is imprisoned in a tower beneath the sea.

This is all said to have been previously prophesied. A summary of the epic of the Elder Gods and the Old Ones preserved elsewhere[72] mentions the Prophet Kish of Sarnath, who may be intended here. We are reminded of how frequently the Koran names pre-Muslim prophets, co-opting them as precursors of Islam. In the same way, the writer of the present text has appropriated the legendary figure Kish as a proponent of the Elder Gods against the Old Ones, a scenario that arose long after Alhazred.

Parenthetically, "the Prophet Kish" is perhaps to be identified historically with King Saul of Israel! The latter was also known as a prophet and as the son of Kish: "What has come over the son of Kish? Is Saul also among the prophets?" (1 Sam. 10:11). The "Prophet, son of Kish" has become the "Prophet Kish of Sarnath."

"R'lyeh" is apparently a marginal gloss, incorporated into the text. And the seal of the Old Ones (3:14) has been identified with the "Elder Sign" of 5:4.

It is not clear just how Cthulhu, trapped in an undersea tower, could have "further incurred their anger." It looks as if this verse is a kind of patch intended to harmonize two originally independent (and divergent) versions of the punishment of Cthulhu: that he was imprisoned (v. 2), and that he was put to sleep (v. 4).

v. 4. The phrase "for the second time" has been added for the sake of harmonization (see above, v. 3).

v. 5. The Elder Gods are the subject here.

The late origin of our text is evident from the confusion of the cosmology of Alhazred. According to 3:3, the Old Ones (= the "Elder Gods" here; see Chapter V) exist beyond dimensioned space. Here they are located simply far away in space. Similarly, "Glyu-Vho" seems to be a corruption of "S'glhuo" (4:3), which originally had nothing to do with the Old Ones.

The star is visible from the writer's perspective during fall and winter. This may be an explanatory gloss, since it interrupts the flow of thought.

This verse, the conclusion of the original "Fall of Cthulhu" unit, supposes that Cthulhu has been laid to rest "forever." Thus, this unit of tradition dates from a time after the reformist faction had rejected Cthulhu as a rebellious demon, but before his temporary return was expected. It has been inserted here in a later context.

vv. 8–9. The theology of v. 7 has been updated, so that Cthulhu is now attended by a host of demons who await his liberation. The idea is parallel to that of Revelation 20:2–3, "He seized the dragon, that ancient serpent, who is the devil or Satan, and bound him for a thousand years. He threw him into the Abyss, and locked and sealed it over him, to keep him from deceiving the nations any more until the thousand years were ended. After that, he must be set free for a short time."

Also note a Zoroastrian parallel from the fourth book of the Bundahishn:

It is said in the Religion that when the Destructive Spirit [Ahriman] saw that he himself and the demons were powerless . . . he was thrown into a stupor. For three thousand years he lay in a stupor. And when he was thus languishing, the demons with monstrous heads cried out one by one (saying), 'Arise, O our father, for we would join battle in the material world that Ohrmazd and the Amahraspands may suffer straitness and misery thereby.[73]

How strikingly this image has resurfaced in the reformist sect's mythology: Cthulhu, vanquished, "waits dreaming" while his minions seek vainly to awaken him before the appointed time to do battle against the Elder Gods.

vv. 10–12. This story of Cthulhu's punishment has been summarily applied to the rest of "his brothers."

v. 13. The Elder Gods are described as "Towers of Fire," an image borrowed, ultimately, from Exodus 13:21.

vv. 14–15. The reference is to the worshippers of Cthulhu, whose worship is construed by the reformist faction as the mere attempt to call up demons.

Fragment 12

Text: [1]Eternal is the Power of Evil, and Infinite in its contagion! [2]The Great Cthulhu yet hath sway over the minds and spirits of Men, [3]yea, even though He lieth chained and ensorcelled, bound in the fetters of The Elder Sign, [4]His malignant and loathly Mind spreadeth the dark seeds of Madness and Corruption into the dreams and Nightmares of sleeping men . . .[74]

Version: From the English translation of John Dee.

Commentary: Evil's power does not fade, and there is no limit to its corrupting influence ("contagion").

The specific "evil" in view is Cthulhu, who still controls human minds. Thus this passage is the work of the later, reformist faction. Alhazred did not consider Cthulhu evil.

The writer refers to 3:14–15. The "seal," said there to be engraved on the sunken buildings, is interpreted as the "Elder Sign" from 5:4. Originally, however, its meaning in 5:4 was that of a largely powerless talisman of some conventional religion.

Interestingly, our author has attributed to Cthulhu the power of telepathic projection discussed by Alhazred in connection with dead wizards in 10:8–9.

Fragment 13

Text: [1]Concerning the Old Ones, 'tis writ, they wait ever at the Gate, [2]and the Gate is all places at all times, for They know nothing of time or place but are in all time & in all places together without appearing to be, [[3]& there are those amongst Them which can assume divers shapes & features & any given shape & any given face][4] & the Gates are for Them everywhere, but the first was that which I caused to be opened, namely in Irem, the City of Pillars, the city under the desert,[5] but wherever men set up the stones and say thrice the forbidden words, they shall cause there a Gate to be established & shall wait upon them Who Come through the Gate, [6]even as the Dhols, & the Abominable Mi-Go,[75] & the Tcho-Tcho[76] people, & the Deep Ones, & the Gugs, & the Gaunts of the Night & the Shoggoths, & the Voormis, & the Shantaks which guard Kadath in the Cold Waste & the Plateau [of] Leng. [7]All are alike the children of the Elder Gods. [8]But the Great Race of Yith & the Great Old Ones failing to agree [one with another, & both] with the Elder Gods, separated, [9]leaving the Great Old Ones in possession of the Earth, [10]while the Great Race, returning from Yith, took up Their abode forward in time in earth, land not yet known to those who walk the Earth today, [11]where they wait till there shall come again the winds & the voices which drove them forth before [12]& that which walketh on the winds over the earth & in the spaces that are among the stars forever.[77]

Version: This fragment comes from a collection of translations of random chapters, each out of different editions and versions, no longer specifiable.

Commentary: This fragment is particularly difficult to decipher. Not only does it seem to represent a condensed summary of some original, but the original is itself a puzzling conflation of three unrelated units.

vv. 1–2, 4–6. This section was originally a tribute to Alhazred (put pseudonymously into his own mouth) as the first mortal to open the way for the return of the Old Ones. It is comparatively late, as can be seen from the legendary embellishment of Alhazred's journey to Irem. His twelfth-century biographer Ibn Khallikan listed as one of the marks of his madness that Alhazred claimed to have visited the ruined "City of Pillars," whose ancient destruction was chronicled in the Koran:

> Hast thou not seen how thy Lord dealt with Ad,
> At Irem adorned with pillars,
> Whose like have not been reared in these lands? (89:5–7)

Nothing is said or implied about Alhazred performing any rites on this occasion, and certainly nothing is said about it being an occasion of such importance as it is made here. Since it shows such development from the simpler version known to Ibn Khallikan, the passage must have been composed after the twelfth century.

Alhazred is made to promise that any readers performing the appropriate rites will be aiding the Old Ones in their return. A technical apocalyptic phrase is used in this connection: "Them Who Come." This recalls John the Baptist's title for the expected Messiah, "He That Cometh," as well as the Shi'ite title for the Mahdi, "He Who Shall Arise."

This section, celebrating Alhazred as the harbinger of the Old Ones, is the only surviving interpolation stemming from the pro-Cthulhu faction.

vv. 3, 5–7. These verses, woven clumsily into the context, are the product of the reformist sect, the adherents of the Elder Gods. The unit is a sort of "bestiary," enumerating a vast catalogue of legendary creatures, probably from local folklore. "Kadath" appears in 3:13, and "Leng" is mentioned in 17:3. Kadath is perhaps the biblical Kadesh in the Sinai desert, while Leng is an alternate name for Tibet. The Plateau of Leng was mentioned by Alhazred in connection with a sphinx-like talisman used by a necrophagous cult of some kind. But the passage has been lost.

In the original unit, all these creatures were said to be creations of the Elder Gods, as if to incorporate random folklore into the official pantheon. But by their inclusion here, they are being shunted into the ranks of the Old Ones.

vv. 8–12. These verses form another originally distinct unit. The translation is very poor, confusing tenses and resulting in overall incoherence. In general, the fragment merely rehearses the myth of the "Fall of the Old Ones."

The bracketed words seem to be a still later addition. The copyist did not understand the term "Yith," and read the "Great Race of Yith" as a third group distinct from the "Great Old Ones." In fact "Yith" seems to be an abbreviation of "Y[og-Sotho]th." This is a case of what Old Testament critic D. R. Ap-Thomas calls an "unresolved abbreviation." Ancient scribes seem on occasion to have abbreviated plurals and proper names, assuming later scribes, making new copies from their own, would understand the abbreviation. If later scribes did not understand the abbreviations, various confusions crept into the text. Sometimes such abbreviations were conjecturally and wrongly resolved.[78] We might also find a parallel in the scribal use of "Nomina Sacra" in some Greek New Testament manuscripts. These were recurring abbreviations of holy names, perhaps to prevent the destruction of the names when eventually the manuscripts, worn out, would be burned and replaced.[79] Thus the "Great Race of Yog-Sothoth" and the "Great Old Ones" are the same. The terms are mentioned together in poetic parallelism twice in the passage.

The Old Ones rebelled against ("failed to agree with") the Elder Gods and "possessed the earth." The text suddenly jumps to the temporary return of the Old Ones before their final defeat.

Verse 10 has particularly suffered in translation. The sense seems to be that the Great Race will return through (not "from") "Y[og-Sotho]th" who is understood as the Gate of the spheres (cf. 3:4). This return to make their abode again on earth is to occur in the future, though exactly when, no one knows ("forward in time ... not yet known to those who walk the Earth today"). Their ultimate defeat is predicted in v. 11, but much of the terminology is obscure.

Apocalyptic Tracts

Fragment 14

Text: [1]Then shall they return & on this great returning shall the Great Cthulhu be freed from R'lyeh beneath the sea [2]& Him Who Is Not To Be Named shall come from his city which is Carcosa near the Lake of Hali, [3]& Shub-Niggurath shall come forth & multiply in his hideousness, [4]& Nyarlathotep shall carry the word to all the Great Old Ones & their minions, [5]& Cthugha shall lay his hand upon all that oppose him & destroy, [6]& the blind idiot, the noxious Azathoth shall arise from the middle of the World where all is chaos & destruction where he hath bubbled & blasphemed at the centre which is of all things, which is to say infinity, [7]& Yog-Sothoth, who is the All-in-One & One-in-All, shall bring his globes, [8]& lthaqua shall walk again, [9]& from the black-litten caverns within the earth shall come Tsathoggua, [10]& together shall take possession of earth and all things that live upon it, [11]& shall prepare to do battle with the Elder Gods when the Lord of the Great Abyss is apprised of their returning & shall come with His brothers to disperse the evil.[80]

Version: From a seventeenth century Latin edition, presumably that of Olaus Wormius.

Commentary: v. 1. Though the text as we have it is missing its introduction ("Then . . ." implies something previous), it is a substantially complete apocalypse, or predictive outline of the end of the age, such as we find in Mark 13, Matthew 24, Luke 21, and the Book of Revelation. The Old Ones will return to power. Cthulhu is listed first, as usual.

vv. 2–9. Various of the Old Ones, presumably the chief villains, are enumerated as returning from their places of exile/refuge.

There is an almost humorous description of Yog-Sothoth "bringing his globes." The writer lives so far after the time of Abdul Alhazred that he no longer understands the "spheres" of 3:20 and 10:3 to refer to the several universes linked by Yog-Sothoth.

v, 10. The Old Ones resume their ancient rule, but only briefly.

v. 11. They prepare for Armageddon, deceiving themselves into hoping they may overcome at last. But the Elder Gods will surely destroy them.

Interestingly, the leader of the Elder Gods is designated "the Lord of the Great Abyss," an epithet pretty much equivalent to the terms in which Azathoth is described in v. 6. There is no reason to believe that Alhazred had referred to Azathoth in the *Necronomicon*'s authentic sections as actually being one of the Old Ones, nor one of their subordinates like Cthulhu. Recalling that the reformist sect's "Elder Gods" are the same as Alhazred's "Old Ones," it is surprising that Azathoth was repudiated along with Cthulhu. Perhaps only a semantic change is involved, as in the change from the title "Old Ones" (conceded to the "apostates") to that of "Elder Gods." Perhaps the reformists regarded the name "Azathoth" as polluted from its use by the "apostate" branch, and simply left it to them to avoid confusion. The original entity, ruler of the center of cosmic chaos, was henceforth designated simply as "Lord of the Great Abyss."

Fragment 15

Text: [1]Ubbo-Sathla is that [unbegotten] source whence came those daring to oppose the Elder Gods who ruled from Betelgueze, the Great Old Ones who fought against the Elder Gods; [2]and these Old Ones were instructed by Azathoth, who is the blind, idiot god, [3]and by Yog-Sothoth, who is the All-in-One and One-in-All, and upon whom are no strictures of time or space, [4]and whose aspects on earth are 'Umr At-Tawil and the Ancient Ones. [5]The Great Old Ones dream forever of that coming time when they shall once more rule earth and all that universe of which it is a part. [words missing] [6]Great Cthulhu shall rise from R'lyeh; [7]Hastur, who is Him Who Is Not To Be Named, shall come again from the dark star which is near Aldebaran in the Hyades; [8]Nyarlathotep shall howl forever in the darkness where he abideth; [9]Shub-Niggurath, who is the Black Goat with a Thousand Young, shall spawn and spawn again, and shall have dominion over all wood nymphs, satyrs, leprechauns, and the Little People; [10]Lloigor, Zhar, and Ithaqua shall ride the spaces among the stars and shall ennoble those who are their followers, who are the Tcho-Tcho; [11]Cthugha shall encompass his dominion from Fomalhaut; [12]Tsathoggua shall come from N'kai [words missing]. [13]They wait forever at the Gates, for the time draws near, the hour is soon at hand, [14]while the Elder Gods sleep, dreaming, unknowing there are those who know the spells put upon the Great Old Ones by the Elder Gods, and shall learn how to break them, [15]as already they can command the followers waiting beyond the doors from Outside.[81]

Version: This fragment comes from a collection of translations of random chapters, each out of a different edition and version, no longer specifiable.

Commentary: vv. 1–4. The translator must have inadvertently written "unforgotten" for "unbegotten" in v. 1. We have emended the text accordingly.

This section seems to be a fragment of a demonology, a systematizing of the various Great Old Ones, their powers and duties. It is reminiscent of the hierarchical rankings of demons catalogued by Wierus and other medieval demonologists. Note, incidentally, the ever-growing number of Old Ones as listed in the following verses.

The demonologist had before him portions of the original *Necronomicon* corresponding to our Fragments 3 and 5. Failing to understand the Hermetic context of 5, he felt compelled to harmonize 'Umr At-Tawil with Yog-Sothoth. Thus the scribe has been doubly deified!

vv. 5–15. These verses form an apocalypse, seemingly another version of Fragment 14. But there are a few interesting variations which deserve note.

v. 5. This may be identical to the lost introduction to Fragment 14.

v. 7. "Him Who Is Not To Be Named . . . is named! His secret identity is "Hastur." Apparently someone could not resist the temptation. The same sort of thing has occurred in Matthew's use of his source, Mark 8:27. In the earlier form, Jesus asks the disciples, "Who do people say I am?" But in Matthew's version, Jesus himself is made to answer his own question in midsentence: "Who do people say the Son of Man is?" (Matt. 16:13).

In this version, Nyarlathotep is shown howling in the darkness. This sounds at first as if he is still imprisoned. But the context has all the Old Ones pouring forth from their lairs like a swarm of hornets from their nest. Probably we are to understand his howling as equivalent to 14:4, i.e., as his manner of "bearing the word" to the rest of the Old Ones.

To Shub-Niggurath is attributed control over various creatures drawn from European folklore. This implies that our writer is himself a European.

v. 13 uses classical apocalyptic imagery. The Old Ones "wait at the Gate." Cf. Matthew 214:33, "When you see all these things, you know that he is near, right at the door"; also "The Judge is standing at the door!" (James 5:9b). Our passage warns that "the time draws near; the hour is soon at hand." Cf. Mark 1:15, "The time is fulfilled; the Kingdom of God is at hand."

vv. 14–15. The point here is not that the Elder Gods are literally oblivious of all this mischief. Rather, they have "closed their eyes to it." They are patiently "giving the Old Ones enough rope to hang themselves." The minions of Cthulhu may imagine they are making real progress. Yet they are playing right into the hands of the Elder Gods, who are only waiting for the Old Ones to rise up like clay pigeons to be shattered.

Rites of Exorcism

Fragment 16

Text: [[1]There is no curse that has no cure and no ill against which no remedy exists. [2]The Elder Gods dwell remote and aloof from the affairs of men, [3]yet They have not abandoned us to the wrath of them from Outside and Their abominable minions:[3]]

[4]Armor against witches and daemons, against the Deep Ones, the Dholes, the Voormis, the Tcho-Tcho, the Abominable Mi-Go, the Shoggoths, the Ghasts, the Valusians and all such peoples and beings who serve the Great Old Ones and their Spawn [5]lies within the five-pointed star carven of grey stone from ancient Mnar, which is less strong against the Great Old Ones themselves. [6]The possessor of the stone shall find himself able to command all beings which creep, swim, crawl, walk, or fly even to the source from which there is no returning.

[7]In Yhe as in great R'lyeh,

In Y'ha-nthlei as in Yoth,

In Yuggoth as in Zothique,

In N'kai as in K'n-yan,

In Kadath in the Cold Waste as at the Lake of Hali,

In Carcosa as in lb,

It shall have power

[8]yet, even as stars wane and grow cold, even as suns die and the spaces between the stars grow more wide, so wanes the power of all things-[9]of the five-pointed star-stone as of the spells put upon the Great Old Ones by the benign Elder Gods, [10]and there cometh a time as once was a time, when it shall be that

[11]That is not dead which can eternal lie

And with strange eons even death may die.[82]

Version: From a seventeenth century Latin edition, presumably that of Olaus Wormius.

Commentary: This poetic phrase introduces what is essentially the text of a rite of exorcism.

The aloofness of the Elder Gods is stated in terms reminiscent of the theology of Epicurus.

As in Deism, the Gods are pictured as having bequeathed to man what he needs for survival, though now it is up to him to fend for himself.

Note: The first three verses are absent from some manuscripts. Also those sources which contain it reverse the order of vv. 4 and 5.

v. 4 The terminology "armor against witches and daemons" indicates the medieval origin of this fragment. It is the product of the reformist sect, followers of the Elder Gods.

Various creatures of fable and folklore are here considered servants of the devilish Old Ones, in agreement with the redactor of Fragment 13.

v. 5 The pentacle (derived from that of Solomon) is the chief weapon in this arsenal. It has some power, though not much, against the Great Old Ones themselves.

v. 6 Armed with the five-pointed amulet, one may consign the unclean creatures to the bottomless pit ("from which there is no returning")—cf. Luke 8:30–31, where the demons "begged Jesus repeatedly not to order them to go into the Abyss."

v.7 This is the incantation. The names are evidently those of the refuges of the demons. The formula extends the power of the amulet to all of them, cutting off any escape. Thus the demon cannot disobey the exorcist's command to enter the bottomless pit.

Note: In Feery's version the formula is slightly different after the third line, reading:

In N'kai as in Naa-Hk & K'n-yan

In Carcosa as in G'harne

In the twin Cities of Ib and Lh-yib

In Kadath in the Cold Waste as at the Lake of Hali.[83]

Obviously, this version is the later one; the original symmetry has been clumsily interrupted.

vv. 8–11. But the incantation is only a stopgap measure against the Old Ones' minions in the time before the final outbreaking of the Old Ones themselves, preparatory to their final destruction by the Elder Gods. So if the charm should seem less than effective, all is still not lost. It simply means that the final triumph of the Elder Gods is close at hand. The purpose of these verses is to provide fail-safe protection for the would-be exorcist's faith—he wins either way.

This notion of the eventual waning of the five-pointed "Elder Sign" may have been derived from the reformists' exegesis of 5:4. There they read of some "Evil that defieth the Elder Sign." Alhazred seems only to have intended a reference to ghouls against whom no tomb is effectively sealed. But these later interpreters have linked the text (out of context) to 3:1, 4–15 which, as they interpreted it, depicted Cthulhu as imprisoned with the "seal" of the Elder Gods. Together the reinterpreted passages seemed to suggest that one day Cthulhu would be able to "defy the Elder Sign," i.e., the seal of the Elder Gods, which had long entombed him in R'lyeh.

Verse 11 quotes 2:6–7, referring that passage to the reawakening of Cthulhu. The double meaning has been forgotten.

Fragment 17

Text: [1]Men know him as the Dweller in Darkness, that brother of the Old Ones called Nyogtha, the Thing that should not be. [2]He can be summoned to Earth's surface through certain secret caverns and fissures, [3]and sorcerers have seen him in Syria and below the black tower of Leng; [4]from the Thang Grotto in Tartary he has come to bring terror and destruction among the pavilions of the great Khan. [5]Only by the looped cross, by the Vach-Viraj incantation and by the Tikkoun elixir may he be driven back to the nighted caverns of hidden foulness where he dwelleth.[84]

Version: From the fifteenth century Black Letter edition of some Latin translation prior to Wormius but often mistaken for Wormius' edition on the basis of Lovecraft's mistaken dating of Wormius.

Commentary: "Nyogtha" is called "that brother of the Old Ones," recalling a similar phrase in 3:15 ("Great Cthulhu is their cousin"). The point of the passage as a whole is how to exorcise him.

The image is a striking one. Nyogtha passes the ages in a vault deep beneath the earth, connected to the surface only by a haphazard chain of ruptures in the earth's crust. He interrupts his hibernation to heed the psychic call of sorcerers, his dark bulk struggling against gravity ever upward through the dry beds of magma-rivers, like Lucifer climbing slowly up from hell.

vv. 3–4. The local origin of the legend is indicated as being Tibet or Central Asia, for various reasons, as will become clear. "Leng" (see commentary on 13:6) is another name for Tibet.

The fact that Nyogtha is described as being "seen below a tower" implies that he was seen in a vision.

The passage is revealed as inauthentic by its reference to "the pavilions of the great Khan." He lived in the thirteenth century! The present text could obviously be no earlier than that time. Actually it seems to speak of the ravaging of the Khan's camp as an event of some distance in the past, so the text must be later still. The mention of the great Khan again betrays Central

Asia as the origin of the traditions included in this text.

v. 5. The looped cross is the "ankh," the Egyptian symbol of life or wind.

The Vach-Viraj incantation must be an otherwise-unknown formula used by Tantric mystics. Tantra is the type of Hindu-Buddhist yoga carried from India into Tibet by Padma Sambhava, a magician, exorcist and living Buddha, in A.D. 632. In Hinduism, Tantra is usually found in Saiva (i.e., Siva-worshipping) contexts, while Buddhist Tantra (especially the Tibetan Vajrayana and Japanese Shingon sects) forms part of the great Mahayana school. The goal of Tantra is to overpass the perceived dualities of Samsara and attain unto the ultimately real, primal oneness of Nirvana or Dharmakaya. The mythological schema employed is one whereby the multiform universe as we know it was produced by a sexual union of the self-divided halves of the original divine One. In Saiva Tantrism, the original One is Siva. His creative power (= *shakti*) is at least logically differentiated from himself as his bride Kali (or Durga, the famous mother goddess). The sexual union of the two begets the phenomenal world. In Buddhist terms, it is the Adi-Buddha who divides himself into the passive and mental *garbha* ("womb") element and the active and material *vajra* (alternately "lightning bolt," "adamantium," i.e., irresistible force), or "penis" element. The vajra impregnates the garbha and begets the phenomenal world.

By various means (whether the "left-handed path" using the "five forbidden substances," or the "right-handed path" of pure meditation) the yogi seeks to pass beyond the phenomenal world to the noumenal world of the primordial Oneness. As in all yoga, concentration formulas, or mantras, play a crucial role at this point, and the "Vach-Viraj incantation" must be such a mantra. "Vach" is simply another name for the garbha, while "Viraj" is just an alternate transliteration into English of "vajra."[85] The incantation, then, was a meditation formula to enable the yogi to pass beyond the duality represented by vach and viraj to the original One underlying both. Its use as a magical charm is obviously debased superstition.

The terminology occurs in both Buddhist and Hindu Tantra, but in either case the mention of the Vach-Viraj incantation, together with the tacit assumption that any reader will be familiar with it, is further evidence that this piece of tradition originated in the Tibet-Central Asia area. The reference to "the Tikkoun elixir," however, is jarring, as *tikkun* is the Hebrew word for "purification." It does not fit at all in the same cultural context as Tantric incantations. We must suppose that this reference has been added by our anonymous interpolator, himself a Near Easterner, not a Central Asian, because he was convinced of the potency of this purification tonic, or holy water, and felt no qualms about adding it to the exorcistic recipe of the original Nyogtha tradition. The reference to this Hebrew magical elixir is an intriguing hint toward further narrowing down the date of the interpolation. Tikkun only gained currency as a technical term in Kabbalist mysticism around the fifteenth century A.D. It referred alternately to the Heavenly Adam ("Adam Kadmon") or, as Blavatsky calls him, the "Manifested Logos," or to the ritual acts of piety prescribed by Kabbalistic guru Isaac Luria in the 1500s.[86] However, since a "Tikkun elixir" has no evident relationship to either of these items of Kabbalistic lore, we must assume a more general meaning of "purification elixir" or "holy water," which gives us no real historical marker.

Finally, the origin of this passage is not hard to explain. Some collector of legends and marvels, like Alhazred himself, merely incorporated the Tibetan-Central Asian legend of Nyogtha the Dweller in Darkness, together with a recommendation of the Tikkoun elixir, into his copy of the *Necronomicon*. It seemed like the same kind of material he found there, and so he added it for the benefit of future readers. Such expansions of texts were not unusual, especially when the text was already a collection of oddities and wonder-tales. No more deceit was intended than is involved when new entries are added to "Webster's" dictionary as the years go by. Noah Webster himself did not write them, and no one is intended to think he did.

Christian Interpolations

(Note: Up to now, this section has dealt with interpolations made by the reformist faction of Alhazred's followers. The final fragments, however, are the work of Christian readers of the *Necronomicon*. We know of two Christian commentators on the book. Both were monks of the thirteenth century. Zecharias was a Nestorian, while Martin the Gardener was a Roman Catholic. The work of the former has perished, and publication of the latter's text has been held up interminably. Thus it is not yet available for general study. But we do know of Martin that he actually sought to fit the teachings of the *Necronomicon* into the categories of Christian demonology.[87] Therefore it is quite possible that he is the source of these interpolations. Another possibility is that John Dee is our interpolator. Though something of an occultist himself, he did write in a Christian setting. Besides it is thought that his copy of the *Necronomicon* was heavily interpolated. Some passages, in fact, appeared in no other edition, and the obvious implication is that he himself composed them. Fragment 18 may be one of these. It comes from Dee's edition, and the copyist actually cites it as being from "John Dee's *Necronomicon*," implying that Dee not only translated it, but actually authored it.

Fragment 18

Text: [1]The cross is not a passive agent. [2]It protects the pure of heart, [3]and it has often appeared in the air above our sabbats, confusing and dispersing the powers of Darkness.[88]

Version: John Dee's English translation.

Commentary: Though a gross oxymoron, "passive agent" might refer to something that does not act on its own initiative, but is rather used by another. It is far from clear how this would apply one way or the other to the symbol of the cross. Probably this is simply a poor translation. The general sense of this verse would seem to be that the cross is not powerless.

When worn as a talisman (?), it will protect the righteous.

The scene evoked is a witches' sabbat suddenly thrown into chaos and terror by the miraculous appearance in midair of a luminous cross.

This passage can be neither authentic nor an interpolation by either of the factions. Alhazred is presenting himself as a villain, and as informing readers how they may thwart his evil designs! He would be likely neither to do this, nor to describe his Christian opponents with a noble-sounding epithet like "pure of heart." What we have here is a clumsy interpolation by ecclesiastical authorities. The rationale of the fiction would be to have the master-warlock himself attest to the effectiveness of the Church's power.

Fragment 19

Text: [1]I, Abdul Al-Hazred, say this to you: [2]The Elder Gods have put the damned to sleep. [3]And they that tamper with the seals and wake the sleepers, too, are damned. [4]And I say further, herein lie those spells to break the seals that hold in thrall Cthulhu and his ebon horde. [5]For I have spent my life to learn them all. [6]So, fool, the darkness is pent up in space: the gates to Hell are closed. [7]You meddle at your own expense: When you call they will wake and answer you. [8]This is my gift to mankind—here are the keys. [9]Find your own locks; be glad. [10]I, Abdul Al-Hazred say this to you: I, who tampered, and am mad.[89]

Version: Unknown.

Commentary: The introductory formula reveals this text as a "testament." This is one of the most common pseudonymous devices in ancient and medieval literature. The function of "testament" texts is to invoke the sagely wisdom of a famous authority at the culmination of his career. The speech put into the mouth of the dying patriarch Jacob in Genesis chapter 49 is a famous example; others would be the Farewell Discourse attributed to Jesus in John chapters 14–16, or the pseudonymous 2 Timothy where the Apostle Paul is presented as giving final instructions and delegating authority to Timothy. An extrabiblical example is The Testaments of the Twelve Patriarchs. The pseudonymous testament seeks to appropriate the authority of "famous last words" for the work of a later writer, the real composer of the testament. What commences in this verse is such a document.

This verse shows that the passage presupposes the later mythology, wherein the Great Old Ones play devils to the Elder Gods.

Anyone who ranges himself with the Old Ones incurs for himself the wrath of higher powers.

vv. 4–7. This text has departed completely from either faction's conception of the return of the Old Ones. Both expected an apocalyptic return of the Old Ones (whether successful or abortive) to rule the earth. But here they are imagined as petty demons, genies captured in lamps which one only need rub to free them. They come and go, and when they come, the world is not changed. The summoner merely risks his own sanity (v. 10). The stakes have been lowered considerably.

This state of affairs assumes that the author himself does not belong to either branch of Alhazred's followers. He is an outsider who simply fears for the sanity or the (Judaeo-Christian) orthodoxy of any who read the dubious book. So he writes this preface, as if to say "Keep Out."

vv. 8–9. The phrase "be glad" does not fit in here. Perhaps it has been displaced by a copyist's error from its original position at the end of v. 6, where it would seem to fit better.

v. 10. The repetition of the name "Abdul Al-Hazred" is intended to underline the fact that even he could not "find new locks" to replace the ones with which he had tampered. He is mad as a result. Who is the reader to think he can do better?

Spurious testaments like this one are not rare even today. Church authorities have circulated similar apocryphal tales about the deathbed recanting of Thomas Paine, Voltaire, Lenin, and Charles Darwin. They are all of a piece with the present text.

5   JESUS CHRIST SUPERSTAR

A Modern Gospel

What is a gospel? And why do I consider the rock opera *Jesus Christ Superstar* to be one? Isn't a gospel by definition one of the books of the Bible? If so, then nothing written in recent centuries could be counted as a gospel. This is because the "canon" of scripture (the official table of contents) was settled back in the fourth century C.E. Who settled the matter? Who decided what writings should be included, excluded? Various synods of bishops meeting here and there in North Africa and Rome. Who gave them the authority to make such a decision? Keep in mind that the Bible is a book many people have lived by and died for, believing the book to be the written Word of God. But no one ever claimed that the voice of God suddenly rang out and told the bishops which books to include. Being an editor of fiction anthologies myself, I know this would make the selection process a lot simpler. But, no, like me, the bishops made their own judgment calls. Did they make the right choices? Some religious leaders tell us that we must simply accept their ancient editorial decisions as if the bishops were just as divinely inspired as the original Bible writers themselves were supposed to have been. This is quite ironic, since on all other matters the same clergymen will warn us to listen only to the Bible, not to the words of mere mortals—and yet it was the opinions of mere mortals like ourselves who determined what was Bible and what wasn't.[1]

Today many people, including religious people, are beginning to realize we must think for ourselves in this as in all other matters. Religious questions are potentially too important to leave in anyone else's hands. This means that it is we who must choose what we will consider to be our "Bible." We might choose some other sacred text, like the Koran or the Bhagavad Gita, to replace the Bible, or to be added to it. Or we might take a second look at some of the books excluded from the official Bible long ago. Luckily, copies of several of them managed to survive the attempts of churchly inquisitors to burn all of them. To decide what is going to be sacred scripture is to control people's beliefs in advance by eliminating other sources of ideas.

If you're thinking about choosing a new set of "biblical" writings for yourself, you might even decide to write your own. That is what the writers of the Bible did, after all. And that is what Tim Rice did, too.

But, someone may object, the ancient apostles and scribes had an advantage over us: they were infallibly directed by the Holy Spirit to write what they wrote. That's why it's so trustworthy. In fact, critical, scientific study of the Bible, begun back in the eighteenth century, has revealed that the Bible writers quite often contradicted themselves and each other. They regularly treated myth and legend as fact, just as credulous rumor-mongers do today. They took for granted superstitions and pre-scientific beliefs common in their day. They disagree with one another even on major theological issues. Whether the Bible is "divinely inspired" or not seems to be a moot point. Even if it is inspired, that hasn't protected it from the same sort of errors and corruptions that all human writings are liable to. So what the Bible writers did was apparently no different from what modern writers are doing, whether they are poets, philosophers, essayists, fiction writers, whatever. All these literary genres are present in the Bible. It is, as is often said, a library of books, not a single, unified composition.

Which one of these genres does a "gospel" belong to? Actually, several at the same time. A gospel is a writing in which a writer expresses his faith about Jesus and perhaps seeks to awaken the same faith in the reader. The word "gospel" is an English word, a contraction of the Old English "good spell," i.e., good report, good news. It is a translation of the Greek word *euangelion*. This means something like "the big news." Literally it breaks down to "good news," but by the time of early Christianity, the prefix "eu-" had been overused, beaten to death (just like our words "marvelous," "awesome," etc.). It was used to refer to things like the announcement that the Emperor would be staying the night in your village on his way back to Rome. Now this might be good news, or it might not be. He might commandeer your food, your horses, or use your home as a stable for his horses, leaving you to sleep on the street.

Either way, it was certainly the "big news." And the early Christians' big news was Jesus. It might be good news or bad depending on your reaction to it: "This sounds great! What must I do to be saved?" (Acts 16:30). Or "What can this babbler be trying to say?" (Acts 17:18).

At first the message preached by evangelists ("Believe in Jesus and you will be saved!" Acts 16:31) was called the gospel. It didn't mean a book, as when we refer to the four gospels, according to Matthew, Mark, Luke, and John. This was a later stage, when some Christians decided they needed written documents to use as long-distance evangelistic tools. Luke may have written his gospel and its sequel, the Acts of the Apostles, in order to persuade his reader, a man named Theophilus, to accept the Christian faith, which Luke tried to make look as attractive as he could (Luke 1:1–4). John wrote with pretty much the same purpose in mind (John 20:30–31). Matthew rewrote and expanded the earlier Gospel of Mark to use as a catechetical manual for missionaries teaching their converts (Matthew 28:19–20). Mark was probably an evangelistic tract (Mark 2:10; 13:10; 14:9).

If a gospel is a story of Jesus, does that mean a gospel is a history? It's not that simple. The New Testament gospels are mainly narrative, but the writers used earlier source material, including previous gospels: Matthew and Luke both used most of Mark's text. They tend to treat their material with creative license, changing the order of events, rewording what Jesus said, apparently attributing to him sayings of their own. In short, they are quite close to writing "historical fiction" like many novels and docudramas today. For instance, the Disney movie *Pocahontas* is certainly based on historical characters, but no adult thinks Pocahontas and John Smith spoke these words or did these things. Or think about Oliver Stone's movies about JFK and Nixon. Many scholars think that the gospels are ancient novels, largely fictionalizing the original events of the life of Jesus. A few even think that there was no historical Jesus in the first place, that he is a fictional character based on myths and legends of many Middle Eastern and Hellenistic gods and heroes.

The importance of these facts for our discussion is this: many viewers, readers, listeners of modern Jesus fictions like Nikos Kazantzakis's *The Last Temptation of Christ*, Kahlil Gibran's *Jesus the Son of Man*, Webber and Rice's *Jesus Christ Superstar* are offended, even shocked at what they view as the blasphemy of a mere mortal rewriting the holy story of Jesus to suit their own tastes. And yet a close study of the New Testament Gospels of Matthew, Mark, Luke, and John makes it absolutely plain that this is precisely what they did! This is the major reason for there being four different gospels in the first place. None of them is a perfectly accurate account of what Jesus did and said. Nor were they trying to be. In this book I am going to be trying to demonstrate how the same techniques scholars apply to the New Testament gospels can help us to understand the riches of Tim Rice's lyrics. But for the moment, we should realize this: we will understand the four gospels better once we recognize they were doing essentially the same thing as Tim Rice.

But isn't *Superstar* a different sort of writing from the canonical gospels? It tells a story, but it is a musical libretto. Really this is not much of a difference. It has been known for a long time that the sayings of Jesus in the New Testament gospels, like those of the Old Testament prophets Isaiah, Jeremiah, Amos, etc., are composed in verse. Modern translations try to indicate this by indenting the sayings like blank verse poetry. It doesn't rhyme very often (not even in the original Greek text of the gospels), but Hebrew and Aramaic (the languages Jesus would have spoken as a first century Palestinian Jew) usually didn't either. Instead, biblical poetry relied mainly on meter and parallelism (immediately paraphrasing an idea just stated, both versions put in poetic diction). The teachings of Jesus in the four gospels manifest just these characteristics. They read, in fact, very much like the lyrics of *Jesus Christ Superstar*.

What Language Shall I Borrow?

Another similarity is that of poetic diction. Matthew, Mark, Luke, and John have Jesus speak in common idiom, the language of the peasants, simple but very powerful and beautiful in its effect. Any reading of, say, the Sermon on the Mount will verify this. Kahlil Gibran, in his gospel *Jesus the Son of Man*, follows this path faithfully, with the result that one often catches himself thinking that these words might actually be slipped into the New Testament without anybody knowing the difference. Nikos Kazantzakis (*The Last Temptation of Christ*) went in the opposite direction. There Jesus, like everyone else, speaks powerfully, strikingly, with colorful metaphors, but in "secular" speech, not overtly poetic, though Kazantzakis's writing as a whole certainly comes across as powerfully poetic. But Tim Rice settles down right in the middle. His characters, Jesus included, speak a strange prosy poetry, rhyming but mundane, somewhat the same effect of Rap lyrics, more clever than movingly poetic.

Many reviewers of the rock opera couldn't get past this and commented on the seeming dullness, even the silliness, of Rice's lyrics. They felt the effect was not so much profane as trivializing. Clive Barnes concluded that Rice "does not have a very happy ear for the English language. There is a certain air of dogged doggerel about his phrases . . . His language is unforgivably pedestrian."[2] Catharine Hughs agreed: "There is a banality to Mr. Rice's lyrics, a persistent lack of originality in his relentlessly pursued rhymes, that even their eager courting of the vernacular does not excuse."[3] "The lyrics are pedestrian and often absurd" (Harold Clurman).[4] Jack Kroll of *Newsweek* opined that "The lyrics, like those of most opera librettos . . . , often seem numb and dull," though he is ready to admit that "sometimes [they] are dulcetly melted or dramatically tempered in the flow of the music."[5] Cheryl Forbes of *Christianity Today* (where, as in some of the Roman Catholic magazines just quoted, one sometimes feels that reviewers are striking the pose of the aesthete and finding piddling reasons to discourage readers from viewing films the reviewer really wants them to shun on dogmatic grounds, but dare not overtly say so since he knows no cultured despiser of Christian dogma would take that kind of warning seriously) disdains Rice's lyrics as "emptied of meaning,"[6] while Martin Gottfried, reviewing for *Women's Wear Daily*, speaks of "miserable lyrics."[7]

Others, pious Christians, as we have seen already, condemned *Superstar* for its departures from Holy Writ. But both criticisms amounted to the same thing. Those who blamed *Superstar* for not being the Bible were much like "superfans" of Stephen King or Tolkien who are guaranteed to despise any film adaptation of their favorite author's work. One feels that nothing would satisfy these people short of a movie in which someone simply sits there and reads the written text. If a fundamentalist Christian picketed the theater in outrage at *Superstar*, his indignation was essentially that of the fan, a kindred breed of "true believers."

But the drama and music critics, ostensibly not theologically motivated, were not too far removed from the same sort of pedantry. They had their own Procrustean bed into which all literary works must fit by hook or by crook. Allowing no variation on a theme, they operated on the basis of certain customary genre conventions, insisting that an epic theme must be expressed in an elevated and dignified manner. They displayed the bean-counting narrowness of the dried up schoolmarm, for whom the greatest sin is to, God forbid, end a sentence with a preposition. God save us from splitting an infinitive. The irony here is that *Jesus Christ Superstar* is not such an innovation even on these grounds. We already had modern, hip versions of great classics. And critics applauded *West Side Story* (which set Shakespeare's *Romeo and Juliet* in the midst of urban street gangdom) and Archibald McLeish's *JB* (a ghetto version of the biblical book of Job) for essentially the same thing others panned *Superstar* for. (Uh-oh: I ended a sentence with a preposition.)

But there were a few reviewers who saw a glimmer of Rice's technique and its effect. An anonymous *Time* reviewer praised Rice's Muse with faint damnation, commenting that, "Tim Rice's lyrics occasionally turn mundane in their otherwise commendable effort to speak in contemporary terms, but his psychologically aware variations on the Gospels are often adroitly arresting." [8] Walter Kerr of *The New York Times Theater Reviews* recognized that it was not an either/or choice when it comes to mundane words and psychological acuity: "Lyricist Tim Rice has found for the rock musical a personal, and I think persuasive tone of voice. This tone of voice is not merely mod or pop or jauntily idiomatic in an opportunistic way. It sheathes an attitude. It speaks, over and over again, of the inadequate, though forgivable, responses ordinary men always do make when confronted by mystery. These are blunt, rude, pointed unlyrical lyrics . . . meant to . . . catch hold of thought processes-venal, obtuse, human. Delivered in the jargon we more or less live by, they become woefully and ironically recognizable." [9] Kerr was right on target, I believe, in seeing the importance of the lyrics' use of jargon as a kind of anti-poetic poetry and of irony to reinforce the element of ambiguity that accompanies the human response to mystery. I will develop these themes presently.

Gordon Clanton, writing for *The Christian Century*, described the lyrics as "generally [being] theologically provocative and laden with double meaning." Rice's version of the Words of Institution at the Last Supper Clanton calls "stunning." [10] George Melloan of *The Wall Street Journal* was on Rice's wavelength, or in New Testament terms, he had ears to hear: "the words have an engaging simplicity and special poetic quality." [11] How can reviewers differ so radically over the quality of the lyrics? Each reader or critic will draw different conclusions or make different evaluations of a text depending on the particular set of criteria or categories he brings to the text. If you think poems all ought to be sonnets then maybe you're not the right reviewer for a book of blank verse.

Poetic diction is ever a mystery. Even if one can explain what makes it transcend mere prose, even if the critic manages to explain how poetic diction bewitches, the risk is that the critic will have to ruin the effect in order to explain it. J.B. Phillips, himself an extraordinary translator of the gospels into colloquial, yet poetic, prose, once observed that the danger is to kill the text and do an autopsy on it. You will then have discovered what made it tick, but you have stopped it from ticking. You can appreciate the beauty of a butterfly more closely if you kill it and pin it to a display board, but you have lost the most beautiful thing about the butterfly: its life. But let's take the risk.

Tim Rice has, as I see it, taken familiar if extravagant expressions ("you've backed the right horse," "he's top of the poll," "when John did his baptism thing"), and troped them. That is, Rice has used them slightly out of their ordinary context, turning them a bit, removing them an extra step from their usual references, making them metaphors *for* metaphors. He arrests our attention by maintaining the poetic structure one might expect in a gospel, and yet filling it with rough-hewn speech. Poetic diction is in many ways a creative use of words beyond their ordinary reference. A word may not usually be employed as a metaphorical comparison for some emotion or abstraction, and yet there is a basis for metaphorical use, perhaps some overlooked point of analogy or similarity. Traditional Christian poetry might speak of the wounds of Christ eloquently speaking of the savior's love. Come to think of it, though we usually wouldn't, wounds could be compared to open mouths. So if a wound is evidence of something that caused them, the wounds may metaphorically be said to speak of that cause.

The understandable yet unusual figure of speech serves to "defamiliarize" the subject described (as Viktor Shklovsky and Boris Tomaschevsky, two of the greatest Russian Formalist critics, say), so we see it as new.

> After we see an object several times, we begin to recognize it. The object is in front of us and we know about it, but we do not see it—hence we cannot say anything significant about it. Art removes objects from the automatism of perception . . . And art exists that we may recover the sensation of life; it exists to make one feel things, to make the stone *stony*. The purpose of art is to impart the sensation of things as they are perceived and not as they are known. The technique of art is to make objects "unfamiliar," to make forms difficult, to increase the difficulty and length of perception because the process of perception is an aesthetic end in itself and must be prolonged.[12]

Tim Rice does the same thing. Only he uses the familiar and the prosaic as metaphoric tropes (figurative turns of phrase) for things we have sealed away behind stained glass. If poetry usually brings out the unnoticed sacred beauty in the ordinary, Rice has set himself the task of defamiliarizing the extraordinary. For we take even the extraordinary for granted. Because the gospel events are extraordinary, superhuman, we have elevated them to the status of religious myth and dogma. And, ironically, these we take for granted! Once one has heard them embedded in dull sermons for years, clubbed to death by an army of Sunday School teachers, the shocking mandates of the Sermon on the Mount come to seem as familiar as the words of a TV commercial. Thus it comes to be that tales of a crucified god rising from the dead seem as dull as reruns of *Green Acres*. And so, if the tale is to strike us again, it must be defamiliarized. And the only way to defamiliarize it is to make it sound mundane, profane. Once the cross, the ancient Roman device of execution by slow torture, has become a piece of gold jewelry, we may have to depict Jesus dying in the electric chair. It was a trope to make the splintery cross a golden throne. Now, to communicate afresh the original point, we may have to trope that throne into one of today's engines of brutality.

It is one thing to remind oneself that the Shakespearian eloquence of the Bible's Jesus must have been put forth in common speech for the original audience. But it is quite another thing to have it rendered directly in today's slang. While the new wording of *Superstar* is faithful in spirit to the original, the fact that Jesus and his disciples are made to speak our own vernacular, even our own slang, gives it all an arresting quality. Linguists call what *Superstar* does "dynamic equivalence" translation. That is what Bible versions like the *Living Bible* and the *Good News Bible* do. The same basic idea, but in familiar modern speech. But there are additional elements in Rice's version of the gospel drama.

If You'd Have Come Today

One of these is an intentional use of *anachronism*. Anachronism is placing something in a story of the past that didn't exist at the time. For instance, the rumor is that if you slow down the DVD when you are watching *Ben-Hur*, you can spot one of the ancient Roman chariot drivers wearing a wrist watch. Or in *The Shadow*, one museum guard suggests to another that they order a pizza. But they couldn't have ordered one. The Shadow's adventures occur in the 1930's, and Americans only encountered pizza in Naples after World War Two. In *Jesus Christ Superstar* the crowd of gawkers dogging Jesus' footsteps while he is led, bound, to Caiaphas' palace suddenly become a crowd of pestering reporters. And one of them fires off the mock assurance, "You'll escape in the final reel!" Obviously this presupposes the audience knows about B-movies with last-minute rescues. But movie theaters were scarce in first century Palestine, to say the least. A colossal anachronism in the movie version of *Superstar* occurs when Judas, writhing in self-reproach at conspiring with Jesus' enemies, is buzzed by warplanes. He has unleashed against Jesus the dogs of war, and the modern weaponry drives this home with a force that a Roman chariot with sword-bearing legionaries could never do.

What is the point of Rice's constant use of anachronism? We see it most clearly in the scene near the end where the glorified Judas descends from heaven confessing his continued bafflement. Though assumed into heaven in acknowledgement of his innocent complicity in God's dirty scheme, Judas is no more enlightened as to the point of it all than he was before his suicide. "Every time I think of you, I can't understand . . . If you'd have come today, you've reached a whole nation. Israel in 4 B.C. had no mass communication." Judas speaks from the still-baffled perspective of the twentieth century. That is the "today" of which he speaks. Judas, both here and elsewhere, serves as the reader's representative, the sympathetic but skeptical outsider. In our day, many would hasten to admit Jesus was among the most admirable figures in history. But they feel they can no longer share the religious worship of Jesus. They feel confused both at why Jesus should be given religious veneration ("He's not a king; he's just the same as anyone I know"), and at their own sense that there is something important about him that they are missing ("I don't know how to love him." "Neither you, Simon, nor the fifty thousand . . . nor Judas . . . understand").

The most obvious, as well as the most important, piece of poetic anachronism in *Superstar* is the very title of the work. The term "superstar" comes from the modern entertainment industry, especially movies and rock music. Tim Rice has explained that his intent was, as he has Judas say, to "strip away the myth from the man." He wanted to portray Jesus as a real human being, not a god in human guise. Theoretically, this should offend no one, no matter how theologically orthodox, since the official Christian claim has always been that, no matter how fully divine Jesus was, he was also fully a human being. Now, on the human level, what would it have meant for Jesus to be such an object of popular adulation? And how would he and others have perceived the sudden abandonment of Jesus by the fickle crowds? Surely the best equivalent is the figure of a superstar, a celebrity who exercises potent charisma on the crowds and yet is dependent on their adulation as the source of the charisma he wields over them. When the cheering stops, when the ratings drop, the helium leaks swiftly from the balloon, and it soars no more.

One must at the same time pity and admire the celebrity actors and singers whose heyday was the 40's through the 60's, the icons of the old musicals and night clubs. Many of them realize they are lampooned as grotesque caricatures by the baby boomers who had to sit through their appearances on *The Hollywood Palace* show because their parents controlled the TV set. So they make the best of it and appear on *David Letterman* and MTV as living parodies of themselves. When Robert Goulet shows up on *Letterman* singing the theme song for the "Supermarket Finds" segment, and glad to get the work—well, it's kind of pathetic. Like Bela Lugosi being directed by Ed Wood, or anybody sitting on Joe Franklin's splitting Naugahide couch.

Suddenly the fate of the martyr, or of young, dead showbiz icons venerated as if they were martyrs (James Dean, Elvis, Marilyn Monroe), starts to look pretty good. For a former superstar, fading quietly away must be an even more agonizing way to go. Is it possible Dr. King would have sunk to the annoying has-been status of his surviving colleague Ralph Abernathy, had King not perished at the height of his fame? This is what the Superstar Jesus begins to realize in Gethsemane when he demands to know from God, whose advice he will grudgingly follow as if God were his agent, "Why, why, why must I die? Would I be more noticed than I ever was before? Would the things I've said and done matter any more?" You bet they would, and it is perhaps because Jesus himself begins to realize this that he is willing to see the whole thing through. Better a short life with an immortality of fame than a long life followed by historical oblivion for its sequel. At the Last Supper, after all, his principle fear is long-term historical insignificance: "I must be mad thinking I'll be remembered; I must be out of my head! Look at your blank faces! My name will mean nothing ten minutes after I'm dead!" But the cross remains his best hope of remaining at the "top of the poll." His strategy is "to conquer death, you only have to die."

So anachronism is a means of forcing the story into the present, and forcing the audience into the narrative world in which the opera takes place.

We are practically on stage. Strangely, the idea is not unlike the Roman Catholic idea of transubstantiation, the miracle of the mass, whereby the past event of Jesus is drawn forward into the present, so that the communicant is brought to stand at the foot of Calvary.

I am not trying to attribute some kind of religious motive to Tim Rice, much less to suggest that *Jesus Christ Superstar* is a sacramental ritual. No, the point is just the reverse: the similarity between the rock opera and a sacramental ritual points up the fact, long known to anthropologists and liturgical theologians alike, that the effectiveness of rituals is in their character of *theater, drama*. This is not the place for it, but I am prepared to argue that the only "faith" necessary for religion to work for you is what Coleridge called the "poetic faith," the "temporary willing suspension of disbelief" we experience whenever we find ourselves drawn into a movie or a play. If it gets especially suspenseful, romantically tragic, or frightening, we have to remind ourselves that "it's only a play." As long as you become drawn into the drama of religion during the weekly service, it does the trick; you hardly have to bother trying to believe in the supernatural for the rest of the week.

Don't Crowd Me—Heal Yourselves!

Anachronism is not only a device for defamiliarizing the gospel story so it can speak to us anew. It also helps create the element of *ironic distance* which permeates *Superstar*. Irony usually suggests satire and parody, if not even outright mockery. I do not mean to suggest that *Superstar* subjects Jesus to mockery. To the contrary, the scene in which Jesus is made sport of by Herod Antipas strikes many listeners either as sadly poignant or, on the other hand, as doubly ironic since the joke seems ultimately to be on Herod himself who is too dull-witted to see what counts as real Messianic glory. It has little to do with walking across swimming pools, much to do with the cross.

Ironic distance is something else. Irony is used by the author in this case as a technique for pulling the reader back from a complete and comfortable absorption in the story. You begin to see a gap opening between what the characters think is going on and what the narrator thinks is going on. He is inviting you to share his privileged, extra-textual standpoint. Usually authors try to get you to agree to that "temporary willing suspension of disbelief" Coleridge talked about. Usually this works well in a movie or a book. It has worked very well indeed when we find ourselves crying at the sad events in a fictional drama. Or when we are as scared as the victims in a horror movie. In fact, our anxiety may grow so great that we try to get hold of ourselves and say, "Hey, calm down! It's only a *movie* for Pete's sake!" Ironic distance is the same sort of reminder. The author is telling the reader: "Wait just a minute! What's wrong with this picture?" To take an extreme example, I see the cartoon *The Simpsons* and the sitcom *Married with Children* as being based entirely on the device of ironic distancing. Unlike the old sitcoms like *Father Knows Best*, where you were to identify with the characters so as to share vicariously in their trials and triumphs, the presupposition behind every minute of *Married with Children* is "What a bunch of jerks!" One does not sympathize with Al Bundy's disasters for a split second, since they are the predictable results of his own shifty schemes. The Bundys are one and all bad role models, so the show does not urge us to identify with them; on the contrary, it forbids us to empathize with them.

It is worth noting that narrative irony, ironic distancing, is not alien even to the four canonical gospels. Robert C. Tannehill has demonstrated how Mark's Gospel first depicts the twelve disciples of Jesus in an enviable and admirable role, confidants and colleagues of Jesus. They are privy to Jesus' plans and privileged to hear more of his teaching than anyone else. The reader is led to think, "If only I could be like them!" But gradually, as Mark's story unfolds, a rift opens up between the reader and the disciples. Mark writes with irony, winking to the reader who soon comes to realize that he understands Jesus better than the disciples did! It becomes apparent that the disciples never seem to get the point of any of the parables; they ignore Jesus' predictions of his death and resurrection; it never sinks in that he can do miracles to get them out of a jam, even though they have seen him do enough of them. The author is in the know; so is the reader. It is the thick-headed disciples who are lost in confusion.

> Mark shapes a story which encourages the reader to associate himself with the disciples . . . However, the relation between the disciples and the Christian reader does not remain simple as the portrait of the disciples becomes clearly negative; the tendency to identify is countered by the necessity of negative evaluation. A tension develops between these two attitudes, with the reader caught in the middle . . . [And] as the inadequacies of the disciples' response to Jesus become increasingly clear, the reader must distance himself from the disciples and begin to seek another way.[13]

What is Mark's point? It is hard to be sure, but we may venture a guess or two. It may be that Mark sides with the Apostle Paul and wanted to make Paul's rivals, the Twelve, look inept, unworthy of the faith many Christians had placed in them and their teaching. Or it might be that he is warning the reader: see where the Twelve strayed off the path? Is it can happen to them, it can happen to you. Watch your step! Tannehill opts for the latter.

So much for Mark. Why does Tim Rice employ ironic distance throughout *his* gospel, *Jesus Christ Superstar*? A moment ago I tried to explain how modernizing gospel language helps make the story of Jesus available to us freshly in the present. But at the same time, as paradoxical as it may seem, the anachronisms, as well as the slang language, keep us aware that we are in our own time looking back to the time of Jesus. Unlike the old TV show, Rice is not telling us, "All is as it was then, only YOU ARE THERE!" No, we are here. If *Superstar* sometimes sounds almost parodic ("You'll escape in the final reel"), it is trying to remind us that we are outsiders, no matter how much we might wish to be insiders. Otherwise the temptation will be too great to do what people do when they read the four gospels: to identify so closely with the text, imagining that we are part of it, that we begin subtly to rewrite the text even as we read it, filtering it through the grid of our beliefs and expectations. It is from such a too-comfortable acquaintance with the gospels that we need to be disengaged if they are to have any power to speak anew to us, to surprise and amaze us, as Jesus is shown amazing and affronting his disciples.

Thus it is Judas Iscariot, not Jesus, nor even Peter, whose viewpoint we share. "Basically, the idea of our whole opera was to have Christ seen through the eyes of Judas."[14] Like Judas, we are interested in Jesus, admiring of him, yet eternally puzzled. No serious reader of the gospels can easily satisfy his curiosity. There is no obvious solution to the mystery hymned by the chorus, "Jesus Christ, Jesus Christ, Who are you? What have you sacrificed?" Legions of theologians as well as simple believers have pondered these same questions throughout the Christian centuries. There was a whole series of debates among theologians and bishops in the fourth and fifth centuries over these questions. Was Jesus simply a great man? Was he an incarnation of God? Was his human aspect merely a sham? Was he a man who "channeled" the voice of God? Was he something like an angel come to earth? The early Christian thinkers handled these great questions gingerly, as if they were handling explosives. Salvation seemed to depend on arriving at the proper orthodox conclusions. Little room remained for error. At stake was not whose theory would win acceptance, as when philosophers or scientists debate today. At the end of the series of Ecumenical Councils, the bishops had adopted the dogmas enshrined in the Nicene-Constantinopolitan and Chalcedonian Creeds.

Essentially the punch line was that Jesus Christ was one person possessing (or partaking of) two natures, divine and human. He was fully human as well as fully divine. But his identity, his personhood, came from the divine side: there would never have been a man known as Jesus of Nazareth had God not planned to incarnate himself as a man. So Jesus is a divine person with a divine nature and a human nature. And that divine person is one of three divine persons, Father, Son, and Holy Spirit, who share divine nature and are one single God.

Did any of this make any sense? Even the framers of this theology had to say both yes and no. On the one hand, they made quite clear that if you didn't hold these beliefs about Jesus, you were cursed of God and damned to hell. But on the other hand, they implicitly admitted that there was nothing positive to believe here. In other words, they admitted they hadn't really explained anything. What they had done was to eliminate various false ideas about Jesus. The dogmas were really boundary markers beyond which lay mystery, before which one might only bow in humble faith. The result of this double bind was a situation in which one need only have "implicit faith;" i.e., one could not understand *what* precisely it *was* that one was required to believe, so all one had to do was to believe that whatever theologians understood these beliefs to mean—must be true. Rather like holding a sealed envelope and saying "Whatever it says in here is true! I know it, even though I have no idea what is written in here!" Incomprehensible creeds do not tell the believer anything in the long run except that he'd best not question the party line, or there'll be hell to pay. As Pontius Pilate says, "But what is truth? Is truth unchanging law?" Theologian Don Cupitt makes this point well: "From early times there has been a tendency to treat doctrines defined by official gatherings of the hierarchy as something like laws, and deviations from them or failure to uphold them as something like a crime."[15] In other words, "thought crime," as George Orwell called it in *1984*.

When you are a "law-abiding" believer in this sense, you have "lost something kind of crucial" (as the Jesus of *Godspell* would say), namely the felt need to search for truth. Somebody has told you that you already have all the truth you could need, and that to question that truth is blasphemy. What a result: religion telling you not to bother seeking the truth. Spiritual and intellectual complacency is the result. The soul and the mind become "comfortably numb." And religion starts badmouthing the intellect. Job is blamed for daring to question God. Paul condemns the wisdom of philosophers and intellectuals as the merest foolishness in the eyes of God. No, God prefers the ignorant and has made them his chosen people (1 Corinthians 1:26–29). We are congratulated insofar as we can manage to believe without sufficient evidence (John 20:29). We are told it is a woeful lack of faith to see any plan as unrealistic. We are told to become childlike; otherwise we will be excluded from the kingdom (Matthew 18:3).

And it is such religiously reinforced childishness that made many pious people protest *Superstar* as blasphemy when it first appeared. Some reproached the libretto for not keeping literally to the words of the gospels, for adding new ones, for sketching in the details of vague gospel characters. Bob Larson (famous nowadays for his radio talk show, then for his rock record burning rallies) even went so far as to claim that Tim Rice was literally inspired by a demon who dictated the lyrics to him![16] Larson "knew" this because he later had occasion, he reported, to exorcise the same spook from a teenage rock listener, and the demon confessed the whole thing. There you have it, right from the Pale Horse's mouth, I guess.

I suggest that this outrage on the part of the faithful was much the same as the indignation of the little child who wants the bedtime story told in the very same words each and every night. If the parent wants to skip a part for time's sake, or begins to summarize, embroider, paraphrase, the child will sternly bring him or her back to the letter of the text. You see, it is the familiarly formulaic drone of sameness which helps the child go to sleep, and likewise, it is the slavish adherence to biblical literalism that is required for the true believer to keep his intellect snoozing peacefully. Changes, especially like those we see in *Jesus Christ Superstar* and *The Last Temptation of Christ*, sound like an alarm clock, jolting one suddenly awake from one's "dogmatic slumber" (Kant).

Strange Thing Mystifying

A creed full of affirmations can be put under one's pillow to make one sleep tight. But a creed that is more like a set of questions will keep you awake, prodding and needling you, a constant irritant. And this is what the religious person needs, lest the frostbite of spiritual complacency steal over him. In his book *Lost Christianity*, Jacob Needleman argues that we must be shoved into a state of disorientation, knocked off balance, before the Spirit can breach our defenses.[17] This explains why Zen masters try to jolt their novices into *Satori* (enlightenment) by unexpected jokes, slaps, non sequiturs, even blasphemies! There is a spirituality of blasphemy. Accordingly, in Kazantzakis's *The Last Temptation of Christ* Jesus retorts to the High Priest Annas: "Didn't they tell you? I'm Saint Blasphemer!"

Once you think you've got the truth wrapped up in a creed, the danger is smugness, bigotry, the assumption that one need not listen to anyone else's viewpoint. Absolute Truth corrupts absolutely. Just look at the people who are pretty sure they've got it. Gotthold Lessing, one of the great religious Rationalists of the eighteenth century, saw this and wrote, "If God held all truth in his right hand and in his left the everlasting striving after truth, so that I should always and everlastingly be mistaken, and said to me, 'Choose,' with humility I would pick on the left hand and say, 'Father, grant me that. Absolute truth is for thee alone.'"[18] When mere human beings think they have the truth all wrapped up, you get religious wars, book burnings, etc.

What does all this philosophizing have to do with the way *Jesus Christ Superstar* is written? As Paul would say, "Much in every way" (Romans 3:2). Tim Rice has used anachronism and irony to keep us close enough to be involved in the saga of Jesus yet at enough of a distance that we remain haunted with our Twentieth-Century doubts and questions about Jesus. Accordingly, he never brings the saga to a genuine resolution. He leaves the listener suspended between faith and doubt, between heaven and earth, just like Judas, who, again, is our representative, who voices our own sincere confusions, who shares Jesus' plaint: "I look for truth and find that I get damned!" And the medium is the message. Some literary techniques accomplish this, where others would impede it. Rice wants to leave us with a sense of wonder (the crucial ingredient of worship, in my humble opinion).

If *Superstar* had come to a pious and "safe" conclusion, like, for instance Franco Zefferelli's *Jesus of Nazareth* TV miniseries did (thanks to Bill Bright of Campus Crusade for Christ, who advised Zefferelli not to end with the mysterious empty tomb as he had planned, but rather to have a flesh-and-blood risen Christ on hand), one satisfying to Bob Larson and his affronted brethren, it would have dead-ended in pious, stale certainties, lulling the listener back into a peaceful dogmatic slumber ("Sleep and I shall soothe you ..."). But *Superstar* aims to disturb, just as Jesus himself did ("He scares me so!"). This is why I think reviewer Henry Hewes, who made several insightful observations at other points, veered off the track at this one. He judges *Jesus Christ Superstar* to be "the life of Jesus as seen by modern agnostics, who don't seem to want to take a discernible position on the crucial question of Christ's divinity. Such equivocality is undramatic."[19]

This was in the days before the currency of Reader Response criticism. Since then it has become clear through the writings of Wolfgang Iser (*The Act of Reading; The Implied Reader*), Stanley Fish (*Is There a Text in This Class?*), Umberto Eco (*The Open Work*),[20] and others that the open-ended, open-textured character of literary texts compels the reader/viewer/hearer to fill in certain "zones of indeterminacy" left open by the author. Thus the reader becomes an active collaborator in producing the text as the reader experiences it. We could almost go so far as to say that if the text, the drama, were completely univocal, if there were a single, definitive meaning visible to every reader/viewer, then the literary work would be merely a dead stone. There would be no real role for the reader save for passive reception, and this is not really reception at all. Good luck trying to get the catharsis of pity and terror (as Aristotle said) from a drama that is just dumped in front of you as a *fait accompli*.

Or think of a detective mystery. The whole point of this genre is to involve the reader as a silent rival of the investigator: the reader eagerly assembles a hypothesis using every fresh piece of evidence tossed him by the author, trying to figure out the ending in advance. If the mystery writer cannot place the reader in this kind of suspense, the story has already crashed before it could take off. So the case of a mystery story well illustrates the crucial importance of indeterminacy precisely in order to make the story dramatic. And this much Hewes would probably not deny. He would rightly point out that any and every detective mystery story resolves itself. Sooner or later we discover the identity of the guilty party; the mystery is solved, and we can breathe freely again.

But the drama of *Superstar* is not of this kind, and a "dramatic" resolution of its suspense will destroy its (aesthetic or religious) effect. For the mystery of religion, the mystery of the gospel, is not like the mystery of a detective story. The latter is just a problem, an empty blank that Sherlock Holmes or Philip Marlowe will eventually fill in with the correct answer. Paul Tillich explains that the religious mystery, what Rudolf Otto[21] called the "*Mysterium Tremendum*," is something altogether different:

> Whatever is essentially mysterious cannot lose its mysteriousness even when it is revealed. Otherwise something which only seemed to be mysterious would be revealed, and not that which is essentially mysterious . . . Nothing which can be discovered by a methodological cognitive approach should be called a 'mystery.' What is not known today, but which might possibly be known tomorrow, is not a mystery.[22]

In Very Many Ways He's Just One More

Tillich speaks of the religious reality per se, but one can apply the same principle to Jesus and religious evaluations of him, as Carl Michaelson does: "When the early church wanted to talk about Jesus of Nazareth, what did it do? It borrowed myths from everywhere. That was a big mistake."[23] Why? Because to say Jesus is the "son of God" is to put him in the same general classification as Perseus, Theseus, Hercules, Pythagoras. To make him the "messiah" is to make him merely one more candidate for the job of nationalistic deliverer of Judea; to say he is a dying and rising savior is just to build him a shrine alongside those of Attis, Adonis, Tammuz, and Osiris. There was no dearth of supposed sons of God, messiahs ("You Jews produce messiahs by the sackful!"), and dying saviors in the Greco-Roman world. Whatever uniqueness Jesus may have had was not highlighted but rather obscured by defining him in terms of these ancient religious categories. You hear him described with one of these categories and you say, "Oh, another one of *those*. Right, gotcha." What happened to any idea that Jesus had anything distinctive to say?

The early Christians tried to safeguard the uniqueness of Jesus by saying all the other sons of God, messiahs, and dying gods were fakes, Satanic counterfeits, and that Jesus was the only real one. Just like a commercial I heard on TV tonight while searching for one of the books I have quoted: "Don't believe any of those phony bunko psychic hotlines you see advertised on TV. There's only one genuine one—ours!" Hey, I've got news for you: if you shut down all the other psychic 900 numbers, you've still got nothing left but fakes. What the early Christians did not see was that even if they eliminated all the competing name-brand sons of God, messiahs and saviors, if Christians cornered the religious market, as they eventually did, they had still reduced Jesus to the conventional stereotypes represented by all these categories they had applied to Jesus. The categories defined Jesus; Jesus had no chance of redefining them or religion in general. And Jesus of Nazareth was lost, absorbed in familiar mythic-religious categories one could easily take for granted. And pious Christians are still taking him for granted, like a comfortable teddy bear, like a convenient ventriloquist dummy to mouth their own opinions in a King James accent. Jesus has become habitualized. We can no longer see him, because we think we have him all figured out. I don't need to stop and try to figure out how to tie my shoes. I can do it automatically by now. John the Baptizer said he was unworthy to tie Jesus' shoelaces. We have made Jesus as predictable and ignorable as tying our own laces.

These considerations, Michaelson said (and as Dietrich Bonhoeffer[24] had already pointed out some two decades earlier in a letter written in a Nazi death row cell), explain why Rudolf Bultmann thought it necessary for us to "demythologize" the gospels to get at the distinctive element of Jesus ("If you strip away the myth from the man, you will see . . ."). And this is precisely why the common believer takes such umbrage at theologians and Bible scholars like Bultmann and like today's Jesus Seminar who do try to strip away the myths (at least to interpret them in modern terms).

Why is it important to strip away the myths? Theologically, it is to take away a grand excuse Christians have given themselves to ignore the perilous, radical ethical demands of Jesus. Turn the other cheek? Give your riches to the poor? Not me, pal! It is quite convenient, as Max Scheler pointed out,[25] to say that such things are impossible for mere human beings, that Jesus was able to live like this only because he was really God. And because he did it, and then died to save us from the penalty of our miserable, mediocre existences, we can sit back and breathe a sigh of relief. Not only did he take away our sin, but he took away our responsibility, too. As Bonhoeffer called it,[26] that's "cheap grace."

For these or other reasons, orthodox Christianity has always given lip service to the notion of Jesus' genuine and full humanity while silently putting the thumb on the divine side of the scales. They wanted Jesus to be basically, primarily God. Thus the official creed which makes Jesus a divine person with a human nature. The humanity turns out to be a sham. It is to stop playing these evasive and logic-twisting games that many theologians and historians, both within and without the churches, have tried to "strip away the myth from the man." They wanted to take an unflinching look at Jesus and his demands. They suggested trying to redo "Christology from below," to reformulate our views of Jesus from the standpoint (insofar as we may be able to imagine it) occupied by Jesus' contemporaries, both followers and opponents.[27]

In this attempt to get a fresh look at Jesus, Jesus' humanity must be given priority, not his supposed divinity. Why? Because Jesus must have been perceived as man, albeit a remarkable one, not as a haloed demigod striding the earth. If Peter, Andrew, James, John and the others came to faith in Jesus, they must have initially had faith in one they deemed a man. Only gradually, after much hindsight reflection, could they have come to deem him God. John's gospel makes this quite clear (John 2:22; 16:12–13; 20:9). Otherwise it is senseless to speak of a gradual coming to faith, such as the gospels describe. If Jesus had been something like Superman or Hercules, what room could there have been for a single instant's doubt? And, by the same token, how could anyone *not* have believed in him? There remained sufficient of ambiguity, plenty of it, for faith in Jesus to be a real risk, a leap of faith. There is no faith where you have pat and evident certainty about something.

Just the Same as Anyone I Know

We can draw two inferences from all this. First, you have to do what Tim Rice admitted he did: to look at Jesus as a man, not as God. You're going to have to choose between the superhuman and therefore inhuman Jesus (well played, i.e., robotically, by Max von Sydow in *The Greatest Story Ever Told*) or the human Jesus. In the former case, you explain Jesus and what he did simply by appealing to the sovereign will of God. Jesus did not have to think over his priorities, his beliefs, his strategies. He just went to the cross in the same way an equation reaches its sum, impassively, thoughtlessly, inevitably. But as a man, Jesus would have been motivated by fears and ideals, would have struggled over important decisions, been the sort of person we can all identify with. His sacrifice, like that of Gandhi or Dr. King, would be all the more noble and poignant because it would have been genuine and costly and avoidable though not avoided.

Martin Kähler, in a book called *The So-called Historical Jesus and the Historic Biblical Christ*,[28] rejected any attempt to make Jesus understandable in human psychological or historical terms. He said that such an explicable and accountable Jesus was simply not the Jesus Christ of Christian faith who was the Son of God and did nothing but the will of God. In short, he opted for the myth, not the man. Rice, like today's revisionist historians and theologians, has chosen the man. And yet it is possible to start from the New Testament gospel texts and reach either conclusion, since the gospels are mixtures of history and myth. Most of the time, I think, we see the mythic Jesus, the son of God, messiah, rising god (the Jesus Kähler wanted) in the pages of the gospels, but occasionally we see an echo of something else, of someone else: a human Jesus. And these passages are the ones Tim Rice has chosen as his starting point. These are the places where Jesus is shown speaking or acting with uncertainty, ignorance, irritability, or petulance. There are five important passages.

The first is the scene of the anointing of Jesus in Bethany, where Mary the sister of the resurrected Lazarus pours expensive balm on Jesus to show him special honor. Judas raises a ruckus over this extravagance, while Jesus defends her action in seemingly self-serving terms (John 12:1–8). The second is the unsuccessful visit of Jesus to his home town Nazareth; he gets a distinctly chilly reception and is astonished at their lack of faith, which inhibits his ability to heal any of them. It occurs first in Mark 6:1–6. The later gospel writers found this portrayal disturbing enough to rewrite the story in various ways, omitting both the element of Jesus being taken by surprise and that of his being rendered incapable of healing (see Matthew 26:6–13; Luke 7:36–50; John 12:1–8). This, by the way, is a good example of redaction criticism, a method I will be using to interpret the *Superstar* libretto throughout this book. More on that soon.

The third key text for the characterization of Jesus in *Jesus Christ Superstar* is Mark's conclusion to the "Little Apocalypse" on the Mount of Olives: "But of that day and that hour no man knows, not even the angels of heaven, nor the Son, but only the Father" (Mark 13:32). The fourth major passage is the Garden of Gethsemane scene (Mark 14:32–42), in which Jesus' resolve to follow the redemptive plan seems to falter momentarily and he pleads with God to let him skip the whole thing. Why not? After all. God is all-wise: surely he must be able to think of some other way to accomplish his purpose. The fifth is Mark 15:34, the Cry of Dereliction, part of the crucifixion story, when Jesus laments, in the words of Psalm 22, "My God, my God, why have you forsaken me?" Here is another text that Luke and John (though this time not Matthew) have rewritten because they found it unworthy of the more-than-human Jesus they had come to believe in. Jesus? Reproaching his heavenly Father for abandoning him? None of these five passages portrays Jesus in a manner that emerging orthodoxy was coming to brand as heresy, i.e., thought crime.

When critics like Bob Larson and other fundamentalists upbraid Tim Rice for depicting Jesus in an unworthy manner they seem not to notice that they are upholding a Jesus who is more biblical than the Bible. I suppose that generations of gospel readers have managed to ignore the same passages that later gospel writers tried to editorially de-fuse.

Leighton Ford, an evangelistic colleague of Billy Graham, wrote in a leaflet called *Jesus Christ Superstar-Or Son of God?*, "The rock opera, 'Jesus Christ Superstar,' leaves us with a haunting question: 'Who are you? Who are you?' The New Testament leaves us with a triumphant affirmation. He is not 'Superstar.' He is the Son of God. He is not dead. He is alive, forever more." On the whole, of course, Ford is quite correct: the gospels and epistles are full of theological affirmations about Jesus, but, as we have just seen, there are a few lingering traces of an earlier stage where such certainties had not yet solidified. And he is equally correct in saying that Rice's *Superstar* leaves us with a haunting question. I have been trying to suggest that, even religiously speaking, haunting uncertainty is not a bad thing. Paul Tillich even said that "faith" should not be understood as unwavering acceptance of a prescribed set of beliefs, but rather as an ultimate concern with a set of issues or questions. Faith is not the antithesis of doubt; rather, faith *includes* doubt. In some ways doubt is even constitutive of faith, since without an element of uncertainty we would not speak of "faith" at all, but of knowledge. Uncertainty, doubt, "haunting questions" keep the nerve endings sensitized; certainties make them comfortably numb.

From the standpoint of secular literary theory, Tzvetan Todorov makes exactly the same point in his discussion of what he calls "the fantastic," what Lovecraft tended to call "the weird tale." Such is a tale of the unexpected, the eerie, a tale that raises uneasy suspicions, fears and dreads. They are not fears of a concrete known danger, but rather of what awesome thing *may* be awaiting. It is the element of *uncertainty* that keeps the adrenalin pumping, the chills running down the spine. Todorov distinguishes the *fantastic* tale from the tale of the *uncanny* on the one hand and that of the *marvelous* on the other. The uncanny tale is one which begins with unsettling and alarming possibilities of ghosts or the supernatural but ends with a rational, naturalistic explanation, as in Poe's "Murders in the Rue Morgue" or Doyle's *The Hound of the Baskervilles*. The tale of the marvelous, by contrast, also resolves itself, only in the opposite direction. The reader learns that the ghost or vampire is real. Todorov regards both the marvelous and the uncanny (defined in these specific senses) as less effective than the tale of the fantastic in which the suspense, the dramatic tension, is never resolved. One is left with the frightening feeling, "Suppose it *was* a vampire?" Shiver. But if the detective proves it was all an elaborate ruse, the suspense leaks away. We feel a sense of relief even though the ending is anticlimactic, disappointing. We like this because we want not to be disturbed. We don't like haunting ambiguity. We want to *know* one way or the other.

If the vampire turns out to be real, the dramatic tension drains away, too. Instantly the terms of the story change. As van Helsing pursues Dracula, we still have an exciting movie, but the supernaturalism is no longer so fearful, having come out into the light of day. Now the vampire is just a dangerous opponent in a world in which the supernatural has been reclassified as mundane. We take it for granted, and all we have left for thrills is to hope the hero has the speed to avoid the deadly fangs and the strength to plunge in the stake. Really just an action-adventure film (or story). The wonder and the breath-holding awe are dissipated. But the author of the "fantastic" tale refuses to let you off the hook. The tension, the mystery, is sustained.

> The fantastic occupies the duration of this uncertainty. Once we choose one answer or the other, we leave the fantastic for a neighboring genre, the uncanny or the marvelous. The fantastic is that hesitation experienced by a person who knows only the laws of nature, confronting an apparently [but possibly not genuinely] supernatural event.[29]

One leaves the theater or puts down the book, but it's still not over. You look over your shoulder as you head for your bed.

Tim Rice is on record (no pun intended!) as saying, "We've just tried to tell a story. It's a fantastic story."[30] It is even "fantastic" in Todorov's specific sense. Rice knew that a resolution of the film either way (Jesus was just a self-important media idol, now fallen—or Jesus was the redeemer Son of God) would dissipate the crucial mystery: "our intention was to take no religious stand on the subject, but rather to ask questions."[31] We could dismiss Jesus in the same terms Pilate does ("Yes, he's misguided, thinks he's important

. . .") or we could become one of Eric Hoffer's "true believers"[32] ("Jesus, I am with you! Did you see? I waved! I believe in you and God, so tell me that I'm saved!"). Those options, that question, were open in the days of Jesus. They remain open now, as Judas still knows at the end of the opera, from the perspective of 2,000 years later. Leighton Ford is glad that the canonical gospels resolve the story of Jesus into a tale of the marvelous, but then it is simply one more drifting dream in our dogmatic slumber. Judas wants to be done with the whole thing, and he will be if he can only reduce the story of a once-mysterious Jesus to a tale of the uncanny, of a "jaded mandarin" who has to be turned in "like a common criminal." But he knows better: he knows that he does not know, can never know for sure. His hell is to be ever tormented with the question "Jesus Christ, Jesus Christ, who are you? What have you sacrificed? Don't you get me wrong—I only want to know!" That, Tillich would say, is faith, the wrestling with one's ultimate concern. "He scares me so . . . Does he love me, too? Does he care for me?"

Then When We Retire We Can Write the Gospels

One reviewer dismissed *Jesus Christ Superstar* as "A sorry redaction, in short, of one of the greatest books we possess" (Brendan Gill). [33] What is a redaction? It is, quite simply, an edited and/or revised version of a prior document. It may have been redacted by the original writer, trimming it of what now seem superfluous verbiage or erroneous notions. Or it may have been redacted by a later author. In the latter case, the original writer may himself have submitted his manuscript to an editor, believing the latter has a more objective judgment. Or it may be that a much later editor/redactor has taken it upon himself to update, revise, improve an older work.

The gospels of the New Testament all represent works of redaction. None of them seem to have been written up from whole cloth, like a novel or an original biography. None seems to have been eye-witness reportage, either. Mark, apparently the oldest of the official four, seems to have been working with various traditional individual sayings attributed to Jesus as well as stories about him. These had filtered down over some decades by word-of-mouth transmission—yes, like a game of "Telephone." There is no telling how much of it really goes back to Jesus at all, much less in its extant form. But at any rate, Mark must have edited these various bits and pieces. How much flexibility, how much creative freedom did he allow himself? Opinions differ. It is beginning to look as if the wording is pretty much all his, i.e., he preserved very little of the wording as he had heard it but felt free to put everything into his own distinctive idiom.[34] A modern parallel would be one of those celebrity "autobiographies" that credit authorship this way: "By Charles W. Kingsfield [and in fine print:] with Michael de Leeuw."

Other scholars think Mark preserved a good bit of the wording of the sayings and anecdotes as he received them, but that he combined the bits and pieces in new ways with little regard for their original context (which he was in no position to know anyway, though often we can surmise it). This seems to be what the writer of John's Gospel did with the various pieces of Jesus tradition available to him. He may have taken individual striking sentences and combined them into wholly different meaning-units than we find in the other three gospels. It almost looks like someone had thrown into the air a collection of words scissored out of a newspaper, and then did his best to make what sense he could of the snippets, trying to recombine them.

A couple of intriguing ancient manuscript fragments, *The Secret Gospel of Mark* and the Egerton Papyrus are even better examples. One reads them with a sense of *deja vue*: the individual sentences are all familiar from the gospels, but they never appear in the gospels in precisely these combinations. The puzzle has been put together a different way. Mark may have followed this "jigsaw puzzle" method in assembling his gospel.

On the other hand, his narrative moves so fast, spending virtually no time on scenery, characterization, description, that it reads almost like an abridgement of some earlier, more fulsome document now lost. There's probably no way to tell for sure. We have the same problem with *An Ephesian Tale*, a second century C.E. novel written by Xenophon of Ephesus. Scholars still debate whether Xenophon was just a hasty, sketchy writer, or whether he had for some reason condensed a longer original into a sort of *Reader's Digest* version.

Matthew and Luke both independently made their own redacted versions of Mark, preserving by far most of his original verbatim, cutting superfluous, confusing, or embarrassing bits here and there. Matthew and Luke each had on hand another document that must have been as popular and well-known as Mark's gospel, and that one, now lost, scholars call simply "Q," for *Quelle*, German for "source." (It was German scholars who first figured all this out.) It was a lengthy compilation of sayings of Jesus, with only a few short pieces of narrative. There was no crucifixion or resurrection in Q. The

Gospel of Thomas, one of the many gospels excluded from the official list of the churches, is very much like Q in these respects: mainly sayings with no narrative context, no cross, no resurrection. A lot like the Book of Proverbs, actually.

How do we know there was such a thing as the Q Gospel? It seems a safe bet, since there is quite a bit of material, a number of sayings, that both Matthew and Luke have in their gospels which they couldn't have gotten from Mark, since Mark doesn't have it. When we look carefully at the differences between Matthew, Luke, and Mark in those places where all three overlap, we soon get an idea of the ways, stylistically and theologically, that both later gospel writers made changes in their common source-document Mark. Then, when we take a look at how Matthew and Luke differ in their wording of non-Markan sayings they share in common, we can hardly escape the impression that here, too, Matthew and Luke were working on a prior document, one independent of Mark. And this is what we dub "Q" for want of any information of whatever title it may actually once have had.

Matthew and Luke each have a good deal of "extra" material of their own, stories or sayings not to be found in Mark or in Q. Where did Matthew and Mark come by this material? There are several possibilities. Each may have had access to traditional, orally transmitted sayings or stories (such material continues, in fact, to surface, quoted by various Christian writers through the next couple of centuries) that the other had never heard of. Or some of it may have been included in Q but used by only one evangelist (= gospel writer). Or Matthew and Luke may have separately made up various new stories and sayings and attributed them to Jesus. This sort of thing was quite common in early Christian gospels including the *Pistis Sophia*, *The Dialogue of the Savior*, *The Apocryphon of James*, *The Gospel of Mary Magdalene*, etc. I think that very much of the uniquely Matthean and Lukan material is their own invention. Usually their style and their theology have left fingerprints all over the text at these points.

A comprehensive comparison of the gospels suggests to most New Testament scholars that it is possible to draw up a profile of each evangelist based on the tendency or pattern of changes he made in producing his own redacted version. By seeing what Matthew added to Mark or omitted from Mark, or what he tried to "clarify" (really, to correct) in Mark's text so that Matthew's own readers might not be left with the "wrong" idea. You can catch the drift of Luke's changes to Mark (or Q) in the same way, and it turns out that Matthew's and Luke's beliefs and agendas differed from one another as much as either differed from Mark. Of course there must have been more agreement than disagreement, or Matthew would never have used Mark in the first place. Not enough of it would have suited him. So with Luke. And Matthew and Luke cannot have been drastically different in belief, or they never would have used the same sources.

John, on the other hand, must have found himself a lot less satisfied with Mark (or the other two, all of which he may had in front of him as he wrote) since he did pretty much a wholesale rewrite. The Fourth Gospel is so radically different from the other three in events, order of events, the type of teaching attributed to Jesus, etc., that one does not at first notice that they have much specific in common at all. A closer scrutiny does, however, imply that John knew Matthew, Mark, and Luke. He never simply reproduces their wording, as Matthew and Luke often reproduce Mark's. Sometimes John seems to have been acquainted with another version of a story or a saying and preferred it to Mark's or Luke's. Sometimes he seems to have been freely creating out of his own head (or, as he put it in John 16:14, from the inspiration of the *Parakletos* of Jesus). Other times he actually seems to be referring to an earlier gospel's version but only by way of refutation.

An illustrative example might be appropriate at this point. Both will be instances of later evangelists smoothing out Christological "rough spots" in their sources. In other words, places where the earlier gospel did not presuppose such an exalted and superhuman understanding of Jesus as the later writers themselves held.

Let's take the baptism of Jesus at the Jordan River by John the Baptizer. As we read the story in Mark 1:2–11, the scene presents several elements that made later orthodoxy cringe. For one thing, what's Jesus doing there in the first place? It's a baptism of *repentance*, for Pete's sake! *Jesus?* Repenting? That's pretty much like going forward at a Billy Graham rally. Mark apparently had no problem with the idea. He had as yet no dogma of Jesus' absolute sinless perfection to worry him. Similarly, in Mark 10:17–22, an inquirer approaches Jesus with polite flattery, "Good rabbi, what must I do to inherit eternal life?" With the nit-picking correctness of the holy man ever on guard against pride, Jesus prefaces his answer with this humble disclaimer: "Why do you call me good? No one is good but God alone."

Matthew distinctly did not like what he read here. For Matthew, Jesus shares the perfect goodness of God, so he rewrites the same scene (Matthew

19:16–22) so as to circumvent Jesus' denial of having Godlike goodness. Now the inquirer asks him, "Rabbi, what *good thing* must I do to inherit eternal life?" Jesus' reply? "Why do you *ask me about what is good?*" There's nobody here either affirming or denying the goodness of Jesus. Problem solved! And this is a consistent pattern with Matthew. When he comes to certain points in Mark he flinches and reaches for the white-out.

So how would we expect Matthew to handle the baptism of Jesus? We would expect some kind of abrupt, even clumsy alteration to allay his readers' fear of heresy. And that's exactly what we do in fact find. As Jesus is about to be baptized, "John tried to prevent him, saying, 'It is I who need to be baptized by you! And you come to me?' Jesus reassured him, 'Let it be so, for we must fulfill all the obligations of righteousness.'" The reasoning attributed to Jesus here seems a bit vague, but one thing is clear: whatever the reason Jesus was there to be baptized, it *wasn't* because he was a sinner pledging to change his ways! And that's the only point Matthew wished to make.

Another sticking point with the Markan baptism story was the mere fact that Jesus had come to receive spiritual ministry from John, implying he viewed John as a guru superior to himself. As we just saw, Matthew took care of that one, too. Not only does Matthew's John the Baptizer tell Jesus that Jesus doesn't need his baptism; he says that he himself stands in need of Jesus' spiritual empowerment. Luke had the same problem, and his way of dealing with it is scarcely more felicitous than Matthew's crowbar approach. He relates the facts about John's baptizing ministry (Luke 3:1–18), then concludes it with John's arrest by the minions of Herod Antipas (3:19–20), which brings the Baptizer's public activities to an end. Only then does Luke get around to telling the reader about Jesus' baptism, and that in a brief flashback squeezed into a subordinate clause: "Now when all the people were baptized, Jesus, also having been baptized, was praying, the heaven was opened . . ." (verse 21). John's name does not even appear in the sentence. Luke seems to be trying to draw as little attention as possible to John's role in the matter.

John's Gospel is the boldest of all. He cuts the Gordian knot in one decisive blow by omitting the baptism of Jesus completely. We read about John the Baptizer immersing people, and about Jesus being in the vicinity, and about the Spirit having descended upon Jesus at some recent time, but what we never read in this gospel is that John the Baptizer baptized Jesus.

I imagine these examples are sufficient to show how one can trace patterns and tendencies of redaction, or editorial alteration, in a single gospel writer or from one to another. One can surmise with some degree of confidence what was in a redactor's mind when he made this or that change by placing it in the context of the general pattern and direction of his changes. This whole way of studying the gospels is called "redaction criticism." It presupposes the hypothetical division of each gospel into the primary units of oral tradition, the individual anecdotes and sayings, and the many sub-types of each. This preliminary process is called "form criticism," or the history and classification of the smallest self-contained units of the Jesus tradition. The sniffing out of the relationships between the various gospels, which used which, etc., is called "source criticism."

Allow me a brief parenthetical comment here. The whole edifice I have tried to describe here implies something scholars often do not seem to notice. Doesn't it imply a surprisingly limited range of available information about Jesus even in the early days of Christianity? If Jesus had indeed been so widely known and spectacular a figure as the gospels portray, mightn't we expect to see evidence about him coming to the gospel writers from all manner of sources? Would we expect the canonical four to be so incestuously interlocked and overlapping as they patently are? In fact it is their redundancy and interdependence more than anything else that rules out the old tradition that they were separate memoirs of eye-witness disciples. If that were the case, there is just no way they would have to rely on earlier texts for their information. And they would have more different, distinctive stories to tell. Instead, the impression we receive is that there were only two basic sources of information for Luke and Matthew to use when they wanted to produce new and definitive versions of the story of Jesus. These two were, as we have seen, Mark and Q, and only the former is a story. The second is a collection of wise sayings with no definite narrative context implied.

To make matters worse, you only have to examine Mark's passion narrative to suspect that he really had no prior historical information to work from, even on the crucial point of the crucifixion itself. This is because his whole crucifixion account in chapter 15 seems rather too close to the text of Psalm 22, though Mark does not necessarily want his reader to notice this, since he nowhere says that Psalm 22 was a messianic prophecy or that Jesus' crucifixion was a fulfillment of it. So Mark may be suspected of having created the very first version of the passion story, and that not from historical sources but rather from literary ones. And this, in turn, was all Matthew and

Luke had to work with. Where they give more "information," they, too, seem to have created it.

You Hold Every Card

In this commdentary, I am going to be using redaction criticism more than any other method. Little need be said about form-critical matters (though a little bit will come up at appropriate points), but in *Superstar* as in the New Testament gospels, redaction criticism presupposes source criticism. We have to know, or we must try to find out, what was the source of what. When two versions of the story differ, who changed which?

What were Tim Rice's sources for his gospel, *Jesus Christ Superstar*? Ostensibly, the rock opera is an adaptation (a redaction) of the passion narrative of John's gospel. A passion narrative is the sequence of episodes leading up to and including the crucifixion of Jesus. But it immediately becomes apparent that Rice has made creative and eclectic use of all four gospels. That is, he has treated them as mines of sayings and incidents that he felt free to recombine like tiny colored stones into a new mosaic. The result is very much his own, but he has not simply rewritten the story. Rather he has chosen carefully and done fine-tuned micro-surgery on the bits he has chosen. Rice has never been given adequate credit for his creative and exegetical achievement.

Fundamentalist critics had only to notice a departure from the letter of the original texts to start howling heresy. For their purposes, they needed to read no further. A thorough scrutiny was the last thing they wanted to waste their time on. By contrast, mainstream reviewers tended not to look closely enough at either the New Testament or Rice's libretto to notice the importance of either the differences or the similarities between *Superstar* and the gospels. Richard Watts, reviewing the opera for *The New York Post*, reported that "The narrative . . . is dutifully faithful to the New Testament accounts."[35] Hubert Saal of *Newsweek* saw the play "staying well within limits prescribed by the Gospels."[36] One hates to say it, but such bland assessments only confirm the fears of the *Time* reviewer who commented, "It is depressing to imagine what certainly is the case, that too many Americans, whether religious or not, will know no more of the Gospels and the Passion than *Superstar* represents."[37] No reviewer seems to have taken a close enough look at either the gospels or the libretto to catch the subtle and dialectical relationship between them. It is no mere question of *Superstar* being "accurate" or "inaccurate."

In what follows, I aim to compare each line of Tim Rice's lyrics with its source in the four gospels, showing why Rice made what changes, major or minor, he did, as well how the Jesus story is reinterpreted in the process. I hope that the application of the methods of biblical criticism will help us more fully to appreciate *Jesus Christ Superstar*. And I suspect that once we have a deeper insight into Rice's creative methods, we will find ourselves also having a deeper understanding of the gospels and the differences between them.

Finally, we must draw one more instructive parallel between the composition of *Superstar* and that of the canonical gospels. Just as Matthew, Mark, and Luke represent three different redactions of the same original work, even the libretto of *Superstar* has now come to circulate in at least three different redactions, all from the hand of Tim Rice. The shortest and earliest, thus corresponding to Mark, is the studio version of the rock opera. The stage adaptation of the album added more text to existing songs and even added a whole new song. This one might be compared to Matthew, who essentially padded out Mark. Finally, the film version added still more transitional material, including another song. Certain words, appearing in the first two, have been changed in the cinematic retelling. This might be Rice's "Luke." We may even find hints of *Superstar*'s influence on the film version of *The Last Temptation of Christ*. And this implies, correctly, that one might profitably undertake similar redactional studies of all the various Jesus movies and gospel novelizations. It would be quite revealing as to the theological tastes of the various writers and redactors, as well as of the publics for whom they wrote. But all that is beyond our scope this time out.

Heaven on Their Minds

The first song/scene opens with Judas fretting over the future of the movement headed by Jesus, a movement Judas himself once believed in very strongly, though something seems recently to have changed his mind. As we will see, Judas has not turned away from the Jesus movement; he is no betrayer. Rather, he has come to realize that the Jesus movement is no longer what it was when he joined it. As he will say later, "Our ideals die around us." The movement has parted company with him, not he with the movement.

(I use the term "Jesus movement" for Jesus and his followers in *Superstar* because of a felicitous coincidence. Today's New Testament scholars realize that it would be anachronistic to use the term "Christianity" for Jesus' own following since, as Acts 11:26 tells us, the name "Christian" was first applied to Jesus-sectarians in Antioch many years later. Surprisingly, that term appears only three times in the entire New Testament, and it is always at least implicitly an outsider's term for them. So scholars like Richard Horsley, Gerd Theissen, Burton Mack,[56] and others have taken to calling Jesus' sympathizers and disciples the Jesus movement. And, as it happens, journalists had dubbed the Jesus fad among American youth in the early 1970's the Jesus movement, too. Some social commentators associated *Jesus Christ Superstar* with this Jesus movement: "One striking gauge of this movement's phenomenal growth potential is the success of the hit album *Jesus Christ Superstar*."[57] "Its recorded score has been a big hit throughout this country and in several others, chiefly among the young, who appear to have found in it an outlet for their new religious stirrings."[58])

Whom exactly is Judas addressing here? Himself, certainly. He begins with what is in effect an aside to the audience, a "you" who is presumed to be outside the action. It is possible he could be envisioning another listener on the spot, a fellow disciple, but there seems to be no clue of this. Judas is really talking to himself. It is an interior monologue given voice, a common device on the stage, as witness Hamlet's famous soliloquy ("To be or not to be . . ."). In terms of the action of the play, Hamlet's plotting and deliberation is meant for no ears but his own, but of course the audience must be privy to his thoughts. In a movie Hamlet's (or Judas') inner thoughts might be given in a voice-over. In a comic book this song would be contained in a thought balloon.

Even when Judas begins to address Jesus after the fourth line, he is still inwardly reflecting. We are not to imagine he is present with Jesus, only speaking as he would like to speak to Jesus but apparently fears he cannot. As we will shortly see, Jesus in fact proves unwilling to listen to any criticism from Judas.

My mind is clearer now-at last all too well
I can see where we all soon will be

Something has only now snapped Judas out of the fool's paradise he had been happy to live in up till now. What did it? I will suggest an answer after the comments on the next couple of songs. But meanwhile, what is Judas now clear about? He has seen a truth, hitherto invisible to his faith-glazed eyes, about the consummation, nay, the denouement of their movement ("we all"). It will, or it threatens to, end in a disastrously different manner than he had believed. Judas had, like the others, had "heaven on his mind," but unlike the others he has returned to terra firma.

> **If you strip away the myth from the man**
> **You will see where we all soon will be**

The near identity of the fourth line with second implies "you, too, will see what I now see if you only do what I did: strip away the myth from the man." That is what Judas has done, what some recent event seems to have forced him to do. So Judas now perceives a disparity between a growing mystique about his old comrade and the facts behind this smoke screen. We will hear similar remarks from Herod Antipas, Caiaphas, and Pontius Pilate. Does Jesus, can he possibly, measure up to the hype they have all heard—and which they assume is of his own making? In those scenes Jesus will refuse to acknowledge that any of the fantastic rumors actually emanated from him. Could Judas, too, be wrong? Perhaps Jesus is simply being carried along with the flood, not riding the wave. We'll see.

Why does Judas alone see the problem? "Why are we the prophets? Why are we the ones? Who see the sad solution?" Tim Rice explains. Whether Judas actually sees the truth of the matter, he does indeed discern more than the other disciples: "In the Gospels . . . Judas is a cardboard figure. Every time he is mentioned, there is a snide remark. I believe that Judas was the most intelligent of the Apostles, and that's why he got into such a dilemma."[59]

> **Jesus! You've started to believe**
> **The things they say of you**
> **You really do believe**
> **This talk of God is true**

Up to now Judas has been aware of an increasingly volatile fan worship centered on Jesus. The Sanhedrin will later refer to the same burgeoning phenomenon as "this Jesusmania," "his half-witted fans" going "out of control." We can already see at this early point how Judas' own grasp of the situation has begun to coincide with the Sanhedrin's. Apparently the exaggerated character of the Jesus mania had already made him uneasy. He feared things might somehow get out of hand. And some straw has now broken the camel's burdened back. Something has made clear to Judas that Jesus himself has at last come to share the delusions of the crowd. Like a modern political or musical superstar, Jesus seems to have succumbed to their adulation. For Judas, this is the turning point. Jesus has gone round the bend to looming disaster. There was perhaps some hope while Jesus maintained a realistic hold on the situation, but if he has at last allowed himself to accept the inflated role in which his fans have cast him—they're all alike in big trouble.

Judas was particularly surprised at the excesses of the people. Fans of a celebrity will wind up saying anything. He has in effect become the object of their worship (just think of all the Elvis worshippers on pilgrimage to the Holy Shrine of Graceland). But what has taken Judas aback is the astonishing development that Jesus, too, has begun to believe the same fantasies about himself. That amazes Judas: "You really do believe . . ." He couldn't credit such a thing before, but it really seems to be true after all.

And what are the crowds saying of Jesus? There must be many "things," as implied in the gospel passage known as Peter's confession, the earliest version of which appears in Mark 8:27–30. Jesus asks the disciples, "Who do men say that I am?" The idea is that the disciples are in a better position to overhear the talk of the crowd than Jesus himself, since they function as something of a buffer shielding him from the enthusiastic throng (c.f., Mark 9:17; 10:13–14; *Monty Python's Life of Brian*: "Don't jostle the Chosen One. Please! Don't push that baby in the Saviour's face.").[60]

They supply a list of options they have heard whispered among the people. "John the Baptist; and others say, Elijah; and others [say] one of the prophets." Then he asks what conclusion the disciples themselves have reached. Peter speaks up: "You are the Messiah." Mark attributes no quote to Jesus in response to this but only says, "And he charged them to tell no one about him." It is by no means clear from this, or from Luke's very similar version (Luke 9:18–21), that Jesus acknowledges the truth of any of these estimates, even Peter's. In fact, in Mark Jesus almost immediately turns on Peter and blasts him with "Out of my sight, Satan! Your mind is full of the worldly, not the divine!" Some scholars have taken this to mean that Jesus vociferously repudiates Peter's flattery.

But things are rather different when we compare Matthew's version of Peter's confession (16:13–20). For one thing, Matthew's Peter does not simply make Jesus the Messiah (as in Mark) nor even "the Messiah of God" (as Luke has it), but rather "You are the Messiah, the son of the Living God." For another, now, though Jesus still tells them to keep the secret under their turbans, he gives a big Yes to Peter: "Blessed are you, Simon bar-Jona! For flesh and blood did not reveal this to you [i.e., no human agency; it's no mere opinion. Cf. Galatians 1: 11–12; 2 Peter 1:20–21], but rather my Father who is in heaven. And I tell you, you are Peter [= Rock], and upon this rock I shall build my church," etc.

Is it possible that Tim Rice, scrutinizing the gospels, has noted the progression of Peter's statements from more modest to more spectacular, as well as the movement from Jesus' reticence or hostility to his enthusiastic acceptance of even the most extravagant praise? If for a moment one were to suppose that the three versions of Peter's confession represented three different occasions, that Jesus periodically polled the delegation on their views, and that the three scenes happened in pretty much the order in which the gospels were written, Mark to Luke to Matthew, then you would arrive at a scenario in which Judas could indeed trace the change of Jesus' attitude towards the crowd's beliefs about him till finally Jesus could no longer resist the temptation and accepted them.

"You've started to believe this talk of God is true." Out of context, this statement could mean that Jesus, formerly an atheist, has now begun to be convinced otherwise by someone's plausible talk about God, but I think we can rule this possibility out since the line is parallel in structure (and therefore, in meaning) to the previous one. "Believe the things they say of you" is tantamount to "believe this talk of God is true."

None of the gospel scenes we reviewed has anyone say they think Jesus is God himself, though after the resurrection of Jesus in John 20:28, Thomas calls Jesus "My Lord and God!" But this is pointedly not something anyone says even in John's gospel before the death of Jesus. It was not, as far as we know, among the popular opinions during the lifetime of Jesus. So where does it come from? I believe the reference here to Jesus' fans calling him God is an intentional anachronism. Rice is raising the issue of whether Jesus believed himself to be what traditional Christianity has proclaimed him to be in all the official creeds of Nicea, Constantinople, and Chalcedon. Did Jesus believe himself to be God? To be a "hypostatic union of two natures in one person"? Did he think he was the second member of something called the "Trinity"? Did such ideas ever enter his head?

Of course not even the gospels have Jesus or anyone else saying such things about him. It is fairly obvious that such sophisticated philosophical theology must have grown up long after the time of Jesus, but the gospels themselves do raise the same general issue. Their writers do certainly believe that Jesus was the Messiah, the Son of God, etc. And they have presented the story of Jesus as if he, too, held these beliefs. Most scholars believe such portrayals represent later retellings of the Jesus story in light of the faith of the Christians who told them, and that Jesus himself held no such conceptions of himself. Thus the gospels are already anachronistic. And yet none of them goes so far as to have Jesus actually say, "I am the Messiah," "I am the Christ," "I am the Son of God." At most, Jesus seems once or twice to accept such praise as uttered by others, but as I will argue, even here the meaning of those gospel texts is by no means certain.

And all the good you've done
Will soon get swept away
You've begun to matter more
Than the things you say

"And . . ." introduces the consequences. What follows is going to be the tragic result of Jesus' caving in to his followers' adulation. He will be undoing the great good he has done which brought him to this point. He will have become the worst enemy of his own cause, because the transfer of emphasis from what he stood for to him as a popularity cult figure will eclipse his principles, and not even his followers will care about them any more. (And to some degree exactly this has happened in the history of Christianity!)

We must pause to ask what "good" done by Jesus it is that Judas thinks is now in danger of being undone. Since the first and fourth lines seem to be parallel here, presumably the good done by Jesus has something to do with the things he says, his teaching. And it cannot be any teaching about himself, since it is Jesus' recent acquiescence to the crowd's Jesus-focus that threatens to negate the earlier good. So what was it? What does *Jesus Christ Superstar* assume that Jesus taught and that brought him such a following in the first place? There is precious little evidence anywhere in the libretto. This is so for two reasons. First, *Superstar* restricts itself to only one particular type of gospel episode-sequence, a passion narrative. In all the gospels, most of the teaching is out of the way by this point anyway. This is where it all comes down. Second, *Superstar* takes its chief inspiration from the Gospel of

John, where, more than in any other gospel, the central focus is Jesus himself. Most of his teaching in John's story, as Rudolf Bultmann has shown,[61] is about his own centrality. In John Jesus is above all the Revealer; and what does he reveal? That he is the Revealer!

In the New Testament, when we read summary statements that Jesus has "done good," the reference is usually to his miracles of healing and exorcism (e.g., Acts 10:38; Mark 7:37; John 10:31), but such miracles are put in question in *Superstar*. We never see him perform one. When Jesus is thronged by people seeking miracles, Jesus refuses to have anything to do with them. And, from "Herod's Song," we would have to infer that the miracle tales are part of the hype. When Judas compares Jesus with the Prophet Muhammad later on, his ironical question "Could Mahomet move a mountain, or was that just PR?" seems to imply the same skepticism about Jesus' reported feats.

So teaching it must be. *Superstar* seems to presuppose Jesus taught something about the Kingdom of God, the coming Golden Age or Utopia to be inaugurated by a miracle of God. On that day, soon to come, the poor would be made rich, and the rich poor. The lepers would be cleansed, the blind given sight, the dead raised, Satan bound in hell, the Romans vanquished from the Holy Land. The temple would be given over to a legitimate, godly priesthood unlike the politicians and collaborators like Annas and Caiaphas who were lapdogs of Caesar and Pilate. In the gospels, especially Mark, but scarcely less in Luke and Matthew, Jesus' teaching about repentance and piety is all related to the Kingdom of God—how to live righteously to prepare for its coming and to survive the Final Judgment. "The time is fulfilled; the Kingdom of God is at hand! Repent and believe the News!" (Mark 1:15). Nonetheless, much is taken for granted, left implicit or confused.

In *Superstar* it is the same. Pilate and Herod are said to know Jesus is somehow supposed to be a king of the Jews. The disciples hear this teaching, as they do in the gospels, as a prediction of imminent military action to be led by Jesus, with themselves the beneficiaries of a worldly *coupe d'etat*, and Simon Zealotes urges him to get on with it. And yet Jesus seems not to share this view of the matter. He apparently meant something else by his preaching of the kingdom. From what we will hear in Judas' next number, the teaching must have involved repentance from sin and redistribution of the property of the rich to the poor. A moral and social reordering, then, and this Judas feels is about to be undone.

Listen Jesus I don't like what I see
All I ask is that you listen to me
And remember-I've been your right hand man all along

Judas was once Jesus' closest confidant, his campaign manager, as it were. But no more. Now Jesus listens to no one but his flatterers, or to the voice of God, which may turn out to be the same thing, as it was for Jim Bakker and other assorted TV evangelist con men. Judas knows that it has now come to the point where just to get Jesus to consider his opinion would be a major compromise, unlike the old days when the movement was going strong and in the right direction. Will he be open to the perspective of his old friend and advisor just one more time?

What does Judas "see"? He sees the movement straying off its original track, heading for disaster. His remarks in this song strikingly match the deliberations of the Sanhedrin, who see the same eventual bloody outcome if the Jesus movement goes political and gains the unfavorable notice of the Roman occupiers. Judas sees this future; he like Annas and Caiaphas is cursed with the muse of prophecy. And like Cassandra, Judas' prophecies are doomed to be met with stubborn unbelief by those to whom they are addressed.

You have set them all on fire
They think they've found the new Messiah
And they'll hurt you when they find they're wrong

Here's one of the lines that so upset orthodox Christians. What? You mean Jesus wasn't the messiah? Ordinarily, no Christian reader or listener would be inclined to get very upset over what the villain Judas Iscariot said. Not exactly an unimpeachable source! And the press kit for *Jesus Christ Superstar* made it plain that Rice intended *Superstar* to be presented from Judas' standpoint: "Basically, the idea of our whole opera was to have Christ seen through the eyes of Judas."[67] One reviewer said that made it "the Gospel according to Judas."[63]

But Judas may be what Wayne Booth[64] calls an "unreliable narrator." Just as there may be a gap of ironic distance opened by the author between the reader and the characters, so that the reader understands what's going on better than the characters who are right in the middle of it, the author may place an implicit question mark beside the voice of the narrator, who may himself be a participant in the narrated events, telling his version of the story. It may eventually become clear to the reader that the narrator does not fully grasp the significance of the events in which he participates and now recounts. Judas in *Superstar* may be just this kind of narrator. Though the story is told from his standpoint, it by no means follows that his version of the events is to be credited. His own tale may "unwittingly" preserve evidence for a different understanding of the events. He may have said more than he realized he was saying. The author behind the fictive narrator may have been winking at us all along. As will become clear, I believe that is just what is happening in *Jesus Christ Superstar*. Judas seems to see more about Jesus than he can readily make sense of, and he leaves it for the viewer to make his or her own sense of the lingering questions "Who are you? What have you sacrificed? Did you mean to die like that?"

It is a natural enough metaphor when Judas says Jesus has "set them all on fire," but it is worth noting that Rice may have derived it from Luke 12:49, "I have come to cast fire upon the earth; and would that it were already kindled!"

Another detail: why does Judas say the crowd (mistakenly) deems Jesus "the *new* messiah"? Had there been one already? Judas is speaking of "messiahs" not in a theological sense, but in a historical and sociological one. Every now and again, under conditions of foreign oppression, there will arise a prophet, a bandit chief, a peasant king who rallies the people to strike for freedom. He claims a divine mandate. The generic category for such leaders, whatever they may dub themselves, is "messiah," a term obviously derived from Jewish expectation of a new Davidic monarch to ascend the throne of an independent Israel and protect her from her national enemies. And in the couple of centuries surrounding the time of Jesus there were many messiahs who tried to gain Jewish independence from Rome. Luke even admits Jesus was seen by outsiders as just another of these (Acts 5: 36–37). And it is that long view of the matter that Judas is depicted as taking here, echoed later by Pilate ("You Jews produce messiahs by the sackful!").

Judas speaks, of course, with the perspective of later history. Probably he wouldn't have seen it that way at the time. It's like in *Gone with the Wind*, when Rhett and Scarlett look out over the blazing ruins of Atlanta, and Rhett says, "Take a look; that's the end of the Old South!" He speaks from the audience's perspective. When Judas says "And they'll hurt you when they find they're wrong," he speaks as if with knowledge of how the story's going to come out. And the viewer of *Superstar* knows precisely what he means because we know the gospel story pretty well already. We know that the same crowd (apparently) that welcomed him into Jerusalem as the King of Israel on Palm Sunday would have reassembled on Good Friday to howl for his blood.

Tim Rice has anticipated this scene and supplied dramatic motivation: this otherwise inexplicable rage is that of betrayed love. The mob passes over the razor's edge between love and hate because Jesus seemingly disappoints their hopes for a Messianic Utopia to begin that very weekend. Death to the false prophet! Think of the fan-worship directed to maverick candidate Ross Perot in the 1992 presidential campaign—until he dropped out of the race, and then his former fans began denouncing and suing him! Thus is the fate of the media superstar: toast of the town one day, down the garbage disposal the next.

> **I remember when this whole thing began**
> **No talk of God then-we called you a man**

Judas reiterates that the deification of Jesus is a new and dangerous development without precedent in their movement ("this whole thing"). There was none of this talk "of God," that is, of Jesus being God, back then. Does this imply Jesus is calling himself God now? No, for Judas contrasts today's "talk of God" with what *they used* to call him, a man. So it is the talk of others about Jesus that has changed. We do not know what Jesus may have said about himself, but the clear implication is that his supposed Godhood was extravagant praise offered by others. It is not unlikely that what is in view here is the scene in Mark 10:17–22, in which, as we have seen, Jesus sharply repels the honorific bestowed on him by an admirer, "good rabbi," since God alone can truly be called "good," not a mere mortal like Jesus. In fact, I have to wonder if this particular episode did not originate among the early Jesus followers as a polemical tale aimed at debunking the growing Christian belief in Jesus' divinity.

Here I think we can be pretty sure Judas is voicing the belief of Tim Rice: "We [Bob Larson would take this to mean "Satan and I"] were basically trying to tell the story of Christ as a man. I think he increases in stature by looking at him as a man."[65] If Jesus were at root God, no matter how long and hard you protest he was fully human, in the end you're going to be saying that

Jesus lived and acted as he did because he was God (in other words, because he was a "strange visitor from another planet with powers and abilities far beyond those of ordinary mortals"). Thus we need not trouble ourselves to try to imitate him. ("How con*ven*ient!")[66] These are pretty much the terms in which they carried on the debate that issued in the Nicene Creed which made official the full divinity of Christ.

> **And believe me-my admiration for you hasn't died**
> **But every word you say today**
> **Gets twisted round some other way**
> **And they'll hurt you if they think you've lied**

So it is not Jesus himself who is to blame. Judas allows that he has not begun to make these fantastic and overblown claims which have put them in such danger. Jesus remains the same inspiring example in Judas' eyes as he was when Judas, attracted by Jesus' character and ideals, first signed on as a charter member of his movement.

And yet, this very appeal to Jesus (even if it is merely what Judas would like to say if he dared) implies the current excesses are somehow Jesus' fault. Judas must feel Jesus could put a stop to it if he wanted. And the reason he doesn't is that he has begun to find all the absurd hype gratifying. And one cannot enjoy such worship with a guilty conscience. Notice how when Peter is worshipped by an admirer (Acts 10:25-26) Peter will have none of it and at once sets Cornelius straight: "I too am a man." John of Patmos abases himself before an angel who, no doubt remembering the trouble Lucifer got into, at once tells him, "You must not do that! I am a fellow servant . . . Worship God!" (Revelation 19:10). To enjoy receiving such adulation one must convince oneself that it is entirely proper, that one indeed deserves it. Herod Agrippa I deigned to receive the worship of flatterers and yes men and was struck dead at once (Acts 12:20-23). Judas sees Jesus flirting with the same temptation. And if he doesn't stop playing the dangerous game, he will perish at the hands of those whose hopes he will have fanned to a height so great that no man could fulfill them.

The twisting of Jesus' every word into some distortion for which he will eventually be blamed is a repeated theme throughout *Superstar*. We will see it again when Herod Antipas tells Jesus everyone at his court hangs on every report of his miracles, his Godhood, his kingly destiny, and when Caiaphas says he has seen publicity leaflets supposedly circulated by Jesus, but certainly on his behalf, that style him the Son of God. The implication is that Jesus has said exactly none of these things. They are the very distortions Judas mentions here.

But we might wonder also if we find here a reference to the disparity between the sayings of Jesus in the Bible and the more rough and slangy version in *Superstar* that met with such disapproval with some reviewers. Is Rice saying that what Jesus said would have been harsh, would have been all too clear, forcing you to make a decision for or against him? But that Christian scribes have done their best to polish these sayings into aesthetically pleasing poetic nuggets easy to admire for their style and to ignore for their content? It seems possible. Incidentally, in flattening out the poetry attributed to Jesus,[67] Rice, like Kazantzakis, is only doing what Luke did, who regularly breaks up Mark's poetic parallels and paraphrases his metaphors.

Nazareth your famous son should have stayed a great unknown
Like his father carving wood-he'd have made good
Tables, chairs and oaken chests would have suited Jesus best
He'd have caused nobody harm—no-one alarm

Here I think we find reflected the cynical words of Nathanael, a rookie disciple mentioned only in John, the main inspiration of *Superstar*, though not in the passion section of John. "Philip [himself a new recruit and full of enthusiasm] found Nathanael, and said to him, 'We have found him of whom Moses in the Torah and also the prophets wrote, one Jesus ben-Joseph, from Nazareth.' Nathanael said to him, 'Can anything good come out of Nazareth?'" (John 1:45–46). He must have felt pretty embarrassed soon after, when he meets Jesus who convinces him he heard every insulting word at long distance. This is enough to convince Nate, and he joins up.

This passage may itself have been suggested by a passage in Mark, elements of which John has split up and redistributed at various points throughout his own gospel. I am thinking of Mark 6:1–6, where Jesus returns to Nazareth and preaches to a cold crowd. They can be heard muttering: "Isn't this that carpenter, the son of Mary, the brother of James, Joses, Judas, and Simon? Sisters, too." The point is essentially the same as Nathanael's, even though these people actually live in Nazareth! "He can't be much if he's from *this* crummy burg!" I should also note that in Matthew's version, as well as in some ancient manuscript copies of Mark, one of which Matthew may have been reading, it says "Isn't this the son of the carpenter?" meaning Joseph, though he is never otherwise even referred to, much less named, in Mark.

I suspect that Judas' words combine allusions to both these passages, referring to Jesus' humble origins, his father's trade of carpentry, and Jesus' abandoned career in that vocation. Jesus came from obscurity and should have remained there. Granted, he would have been hiding his light under a bushel basket (Matthew 5:15), remaining a great unknown as far as the wider world was concerned, but that way at least the impending disaster would have been averted. Great as Jesus turned out to be, he has now threatened to become more trouble than he is worth. Here Judas has already arrived at the canny logic of Caiaphas, who reasons that it is better for one man, Jesus, to die, regrettable as it might be, than for the whole people to face disaster at the hands of the Romans.

By the way, in ancient Judaism, to call someone a "carpenter" in a situation like Mark depicts in chapter 6 in the Nazareth synagogue, is to commend him for doing a fine job explaining a difficult scripture passage, which is what Jesus would have been doing. So it may be that the gospel writer has misconstrued what was intended as praise from the congregation. If so, it is amusing to see what has grown from this seed. Justin Martyr, a Samaritan philosopher who converted to Christianity in the mid-second century, claimed that some Christians still had and still used farm implements made by Jesus in his old carpenter shop! I think I know where these would have come from. Remember disk jockey Don Imus's Billy Saul Hargis character? The radio evangelist whose scams got wilder and wilder with each broadcast? Once he was offering whole bed room and dining room sets made personally by the Son of God.

> **Listen Jesus don't you care for your race?**
> **Don't you see we must keep in our place?**
> **We are occupied-have you forgotten how put down we are?**
> **I am frightened by the crowd**
> **For we are getting much too loud**
> **And they'll crush us if we go too far**

If we have seen Judas already speak with the wisdom of historical perspective about the doomed course of the typical messiah which Jesus appears to be following, now we see that he has also learned history's lesson about the outcome of such God-inspired revolutions. They always come to nothing. Once they begin to make enough noise to persuade the populace they have a chance to succeed, others hear that noise, too, and act swiftly to nip the growing movement in the bud.

It is worth noting that, whereas in the other gospels we must read between the lines to pick out any signs of revolutionary plans or dangers, they appear full-blown in the Gospel of John. There, after the miraculous feeding of the multitude, Jesus himself begins to be "frightened by the crowd." In John 6:14–15 we read that "When the people saw the sign which he had done, they said, 'This is indeed the prophet who is to come into the world!' Perceiving then that they were about to come and take him by force to make him king, Jesus withdrew again into the hills by himself."

> **It was beautiful but now it's sour**
> **Yes it's all gone sour**
> **Listen Jesus to the warning I give**
> **Please remember that I want us to live**
> **But it's sad to see our chances weakening with every hour**
> **All your followers are blind**
> **Too much heaven on their minds**
> **all gone sour**

A parting plea to listen, as if Jesus could hear. But, just as surely as after the betrayal, he can't: "Christ, I know you can't hear me, but . . ."

Judas wants to stress that he has not lost faith in the cause. No, his reason for wanting Jesus to put on the brakes, to turn things around, get them back under control, is that it has now become a question of survival. What good will it do anybody if they all get themselves killed? Then his voice of moral guidance will be silenced forever. Will that serve any purpose? Jesus himself will be asking the same question of God later on in the Garden of Gethsemane.

Chances of survival are shrinking very rapidly. It's all coming to a head. At least that's Judas' reading of the situation. And that's why he will not wait to see what happens. He will very shortly take decisive action, taking in hand the decision Jesus himself should make but apparently will not. Jesus could make it without any bloodshed ensuing. Judas cannot end things so neatly, but he will do what he has to do. It seems the only choice left.

Why is Judas the only one who feels this way? Because the others are too heavenly-minded, as the cliché alluded to here has it, to be of any earthly good anymore. In short, the crowd of disciples are out of touch with reality.

Judas alone has come back down to earth with a thump. He used to share their starry-eyed enthusiasm. In the old days "it was beautiful"—the cause, the life together, the good they did as people's lives were changed by the hope Jesus brought of the kingdom and the healing it would bring to the sick, the blind, the mad, even the dead. But that's finished. He might mean to say, as Jesus will say at his arrest, "Can't you see that it's all over? It was nice but now it's gone." Only Judas can see that it was over long before Jesus himself could see it. Or maybe Judas means it had been nice to live for awhile among the clouds in a fool's paradise, but that beautiful narcotic dream has suddenly popped like a bubble, and he is now sober and surly. But someone has to be.

I want to propose that, relative to the time-line of events covered by the play, what we have just heard must be understood as having occurred *after* the scene we will see next, i.e., as fitting into the temporal sequence after the events in Bethany on Friday night, the interchanges between Jesus and the other disciples ("What's the Buzz"), Jesus, Mary Magdalene, and Judas ("Strange Thing Mystifying" and "Everything's Alright"). It is related *before* these other events/songs just so as to tip the reader off to the significance Judas will see in the events of Friday night, so that he will be able to see them as Judas does while they are depicted. As if in hindsight. It is as if the Bethany events are a long flashback to what it was that led Judas to conclude things had now gone too far for him to count on Jesus turning them back. These events, these words from Jesus, are what made it all seem clearer to Judas, so that he could see where they would all soon end up.

Notice that at the head of the lyrics to "Heaven on Their Minds," there is no marginal note of when Judas' soliloquy is supposed to take place, as with all the subsequent songs, so the libretto expressly avoids making it appear that "Heaven on Their Minds" precedes "What's the Buzz," "Strange Thing Mystifying," and "Everything's Alright." Where does it fit into the sequence of events? Either on Saturday, when there is no song (the libretto chronology seems to skip Saturday altogether), or on Sunday, simultaneously with "This Jesus Must Die." Things are coming together quickly: just at the time the hierarchy is gathering to deliberate the fate of the interloper Jesus, Judas is coming to feel he must do something about Jesus for all their sakes.

Matthew and Mark both make Judas' visit to the priests follow directly after the anointing in Bethany, implying some sort of connection between the two events, as if Judas were disillusioned by what he had seen and heard in Bethany and soon headed off to confer with Caiaphas as to what to do about it. If "Heaven on Their Minds" does presuppose some immediately preceding event as the thing that opened Judas' eyes, it has to have been the Bethany scene in the next three songs, all the more since the indignation of Judas in "Strange Thing Mystifying" seems to be fresh and stinging, a nasty surprise. Thus it preceded "Heaven on Their Minds."

What's the Buzz

In Mark, followed by Matthew, the identity of the woman who anoints Jesus remains unspoken, despite the irony that Jesus said her deed of kindness would be repeated when and where ever his story might be told! Maybe it *was* in Mark but was censored at some point, because this lady eventually fell from apostolic favor for some reason. In any case, it is only the Gospel of John that identifies her as Mary the sister of Lazarus, an old friend of Jesus, along with her sister Martha. In John chapter 11 Jesus has raised Lazarus from the dead (in a story probably based on the parable of Luke 16:19–31, where a man named Lazarus dies and someone requests that he be sent back to earth to his brothers). At a celebration feast (possibly worked up by John from Luke 15:32, "It is needful to make merry and be glad, for this your brother was dead, and is alive; he was lost, and is found") Mary, Lazarus' sister, anoints Jesus' feet with perfume. It was customary to wash the feet of a guest, since everyone wore sandals and had been walking a dusty road. Mary is pouring it on, using expensive perfume for the purpose, in a gesture reminiscent of the saying ascribed to John the Baptizer: "I am not worthy to untie his sandal thongs."

Judas protests, and will soon make his way to Caiaphas, but in John the connection between the anointing and the conspiracy to kill Jesus is a bit different. It is because of the spreading of the shocking news of Lazarus' resurrection that the Jerusalem crowds are on hand to greet Jesus on Sunday at the Triumphal Entry, and it this new height of fame that convinces the Sanhedrin that Jesus must be gotten out of the way. Thus in John both the decisions of Judas and of the hierarchy stem ultimately from the resurrection of Lazarus and its aftermath.

Here is one of those instances where John has either inherited an alternative version of a story or has rewritten a story from the earlier gospels. In Mark and Matthew, the scene is quite different. We have already observed that the anointing woman is not said to be Mary the sister of Lazarus, but she really cannot be Mary, because the occasion of the dinner is not the resurrection of Lazarus (which does not happen in any gospel but John's). And the place is not the home of Mary, Martha, and Lazarus, but rather that of one Simon the Leper, a man who no doubt did little social entertaining! And, while in John Mary anoints the feet of Jesus, in Matthew and Mark the unnamed woman anoints Jesus' head with the perfume. And in either case there is no reason to think the woman was Mary Magdalene as we have it in *Superstar*. Why is she taking this role in Rice's gospel?

In the original draft of the libretto, the anointing woman was, as in John, simply Mary of Bethany, the sister of Lazarus, even though the setting for the feast was, paradoxically, the house of Simon the Leper![68] And originally Mary Magdalene had nothing to do with it. The song "Everything's Alright" was to be sung as a duet by the two sisters, Mary and Martha. By introducing Mary Magdalene, Rice seems to be taking for granted the traditional (though legendary) identification of Mary of Bethany with Mary Magdalene. No suggestion of such a thing appears in any gospel. And if we understand the epithet "Magdalene" to refer to her home town, thus "Mary of Magdala" or "Mary of Magadan," we can completely rule out the two Marys being the same, because Lazarus' sister is plainly and explicitly associated with Bethany. But Rice had no occasion to do all this unraveling. People in general tend to think Mary of Bethany was Mary Magdalene, and if that'll give Rice a more colorful character, why not?

Luke's version has the anointing occur in the house neither of Lazarus nor of Simon the Leper, but of Simon the Pharisee. The woman doing the anointing (and she anoints Jesus' feet, as in John, not his head as in Matthew/Mark) is not named but is said to be a notorious sinner, perhaps a prostitute. Church tradition/legend identified this sinful woman as Mary Magdalene, with the result that Mary Magdalene is pictured as a reformed prostitute, though the New Testament never says any such thing. But it is this identification of Luke's sinful woman as Mary Magdalene, as well as the similar identification of Mary of Bethany (John's anointing woman) which has made possible Mary Magdalene's taking over the role in *Jesus Christ Superstar*.

What's the Buzz? Tell Me What's Happening

This refrain, repeated throughout the song, is attributed to the whole company of disciples (apparently excluding Judas who already knows, or thinks he knows, what is happening). Thus they function somewhat like a Greek chorus, punctuating the action with interpretations and urgings. But there is a biblical parallel as well. The Bible often makes the crowd speak with one voice, since they share a single actantial role. They are there to serve a common narrative purpose: to represent the obtuseness of the disciples. We don't need to hear too many variations on the theme to get the point.

The first draft of *Superstar* had an introductory sequence in which Simon the host welcomed the whole group into his home, greeting each of the disciples by name, kidding Thomas that "there was no need to doubt the quality of the table wine."[69]

The disciples are called "the Apostles" in the libretto, another of the anachronisms that abound in the rock opera. The irony here is that this bunch of dim-witted bumblers are the ones who will bear the haloes of venerable apostles for all of Christian posterity. What a joke! We will see more of this, rest assured. By the way, Mark's gospel treats the disciples the same way. He depicts them as failing to understand everything Jesus says, constantly saying something stupid as Jesus rolls his eyes and groans.

They ask, "What's the buzz?" In other words, they have heard some sort of scuttlebutt, enough to alert them that things are about to get moving. What is it? What's going on?

Why should you want to know?

This retort comes right from John 21:22, though the context is a bit different. In the Bible, the scene is just after the resurrection reunion of Jesus and his men on the shore of the Sea of Galilee (Tiberias). Jesus predicts Peter's eventual death by crucifixion, whereupon Peter asks him what will become of another disciple. "Jesus said to him, 'If it is my will that he remain until I come, what is that to you?'"

Don't you mind about the future, don't you try to think ahead
Save tomorrow for tomorrow, think about today instead

These lines are a close paraphrase of a fatalistic proverb from the Sermon on the Mount: "Do not be anxious about tomorrow, for tomorrow will be anxious for itself. Let the day's own trouble be sufficient for the day" (Matthew

6:34). And the fatalism is appropriate in the new context in which Rice has placed it. Now it refers to the foreordained events in which Jesus' destiny, unsuspected by the disciples, is about to be played out. Jesus himself seems sullen and introverted under the weight of it.

I could give you facts and figures—
I could give you plans and forecasts
Even tell you where I'm going

A major difference between *Superstar* and the gospels is that the latter have Jesus make several clear predictions of his death, even though the disciples remain confused and obtuse, seeming not even to hear him. Thus when Jesus is arrested, they are completely flummoxed and totally ill-prepared. Scholars have long recognized these "passion predictions," as they are called, as being creations of Mark (taken over by Matthew and Luke). They are previews of "next week's episode." Their artificiality is obvious from the fact that all the predictions go right over the heads of the characters in the scene, not registering at all, having no impact on the events to follow. Instead, they are aimed at the readers to assure them that Jesus' arrest and death did not take him by surprise. As bad as it might look, Jesus had everything under control. In fact, it must have been the predestined will of God. It is exactly parallel, one can hardly help thinking, to what an embarrassed child says when he has come crashing down off his bike in a humiliating manner: "I *meant* to do that!"

Tim Rice has omitted these predictions. He is in no haste to dispel the mystery of the fate of Jesus. Jesus speaks only in veiled, ominous hints. And the result has much more verisimilitude than the gospels. When the disciples scatter in panic, it seems entirely natural. And in these lines, Jesus seems pointedly to reject the option of giving the disciples the sort of forecasts Mark had Jesus give, as if purposely to disappoint the audience's expectation. The "facts and figures" he could give them are the specifics of what is to happen, just as we read in Mark's passion predictions: "Behold, we are going up to Jerusalem; and the son of man will be delivered to the chief priests and the scribes, and they will condemn him to death, and deliver him to the Gentiles; and they will mock him, and spit upon him, and scourge him, and kill him; and after three days he will rise" (Mark 10:33). There are the "facts," so cut and dried that it is hard to imagine the disciples not being fully prepared for the events to come. There are the "figures," the three days of death. And the whole is both plan and forecast, since not only does it lie ahead for him inevitably (thus predictably), but he will go forth to embrace it willingly (thus a plan). And he does tell them where he's going: Jerusalem. But he says none of these things to the disciples in *Superstar*.

And Jerusalem is not his final destination, only a significant stop along the way. Here we cannot help but think of the words of Jesus at the Last Supper in John, as he responds to the questions of the floundering disciples: "Simon Peter said to him, 'Lord, where are you going?' Jesus answered, 'Where I am going you cannot follow me now . . . And you know where I am going, and you know the way.' Thomas said to him, 'Lord, we do not know where you are going; how can we know the way?'" (John 13:36; 14:4–5). Rice has produced the same effect of caginess on Jesus' part. He will not give the disciples straight answers.

When do we ride into Jerusalem?

So they do know something: the coming of the heavenly kingdom predicted by Jesus is to happen in Jerusalem soon. They expect it will be a military assault on the capital. Their heads are filled with grand scenes of entering the city astride white chargers (cf., Revelation 19:11–16). My guess would be that Rice has derived this from the childish jockeying among the disciples for positions of power in the messianic regime they feel sure will soon dawn: "'Rabbi, we want you to promise us a favor—whatever we ask.' And [no doubt saying to himself, 'This ought to be good!'], he said to them, 'And what is it you have in mind?' And they said to him, 'Grant us to sit, one at your right hand and one at your left, in your glory.' But Jesus said to them, 'You do not know what you are asking . . . Whoever would be great among you shall be your servant, and whoever would be first among you, let him be the slave of all" (Mark 10:35–38).

> **Why should you want to know?**
> **Why are you obsessed with fighting times**
>   **and fates you can't defy?**
> **If you knew the path we're riding you'd understand it less than I**

The second line here seems to combine two bits from the Acts of the Apostles, the sequel to Luke's gospel. This is fitting since here Jesus is talking with the future Apostles. The first part is taken from one of the three accounts of Saul's encounter with the Risen Jesus on the road to Damascus. Confused by a sudden outburst of blinding light, Saul hears a commanding voice address him by name: "Saul, Saul, why are you persecuting me?" Saul, you see, was on his way to Damascus to hunt down any Christians who had managed to escape him in Jerusalem. "You're only hurting yourself when you kick at the ox goad" (Acts 26:14). This last was a well-known Greek proverb or cliché, recalling the dumb ox, chafing at the sharp ox-goad behind him, but learning soon enough that if he tries to kick it away, it will only hurt him worse. The same rhetorical question is aimed at the Twelve by Jesus here in Bethany in *Superstar*.

The other source text seems surely to be Acts 1:6–7, which takes place forty days after the resurrection, immediately before the ascension. He has been giving the disciples final instructions, and yet after all that has transpired, they seem as doltish as ever: "So when they had come together, they asked him, 'Lord, will you at this time restore the kingdom [i.e., national sovereignty] to Israel?' He said to them, 'It is not for you to know times or seasons which the Father has fixed by his own authority.'" God has his own timetable for the dawning of the kingdom; you can't hasten it. Or, as he later says to Pilate, "Everything is fixed and you can't change it."

"If you knew the path we're riding," i.e., not just into Jerusalem as you think, you'd be even more baffled, like me!, not less. So you're better off knowing no more than you do. The plain implication is that Jesus himself wishes he might defy the times and fates set by the Father, though he knows it would be futile. These themes will be sounded again and elaborated in the Gethsemane prayer. Jesus knows well enough what awaits him, by the decree of God, but as to its purpose, there he must follow in faith—or grudging resignation.

In general, the foregoing exchange between Jesus and the apostles seems to correspond to the Last Supper discourse in John chapters 13 through 17. Both the back and forth style of questioning and the business about "telling them where he is going" suggest this, as these are two distinctive features of that Johannine discourse. But if this is correct, why doesn't *Superstar* place the discourse where it belongs, at the Last Supper, on Maundy Thursday? *Superstar*'s chronology (based on Fulton J. Sheen's *Life of Christ*)[70] reflects the Gospel of John's peculiar juggling of the gospel events. Since John understands Jesus as the sacrificial lamb of God, a sacrifice to eradicate human sins (John

1:29), he wants him to be crucified at the same hour the Passover lamb is being slaughtered (John 19:14, 31, 36, cf. Exodus 12:46). Since Jesus' last meal with his disciples must have taken place on the previous evening, just before his arrest, this means John cannot portray the Last Supper as a Passover supper. Matthew, Mark, and Luke, on the other hand, do understand the Last Supper to have been a Passover supper, and accordingly they all have Jesus speak the famous "words of institution" about his body and blood during that meal as a kind of reinterpretation of the Passover symbolism in Christian terms. John seems to know that the sayings about eating the flesh of the son of man and drinking his blood have to be placed in a Passover setting. But since the Last Supper is for him no longer a Passover meal, he has Jesus talk about other things at the Last Supper and moves the flesh-and-blood sayings up to an earlier point in his story, to chapter 6, where Jesus is speaking to a Capernaum synagogue about the manna in the wilderness—at Passover time.

As I read him, Tim Rice has reversed John's order, but using John's technique. Rice decided he wanted to include the words of institution at the Last Supper, but this meant the Last Supper discourse of John must be given some time before, at another supper of the disciples with Jesus ("As you prattle through your supper . . ."). So why not tack it onto the scene of the anointing at Bethany? That, too, was a supper. So in a sense *Superstar* has two Last Supper scenes.

Let me try to cool down your face a bit

Here is the anointing, and it does not yet match either the Matthew/ Mark head anointing or the Luke/John feet anointing. Here she applies the soothing ointment/oil to his face, a possible reference to the post-biblical legend of Veronica's veil: As Jesus staggered and fell on his way to the cross, Veronica took pity and hastened to wipe his bloody, sweat-grimed face. And, lo, the cloth miraculously picked up the image of the savior! It was a tall tale to make a particular relic sound impressive.

> **That feels nice, so nice . . .**
> **Mary that is good-**
> **While you prattle through your supper-where**
> **   and when and who and how**
> **She alone has tried to give me what I need right here and now**

In the gospels Jesus speaks in the anointing woman's defense, but only after someone objects to her action. Here, however, it is Jesus who makes it an issue.

When Jesus contrasts the ruckus of the disciples during supper with the considerate attention given him by Mary Magdalene, we can detect a surviving trace of the original draft version in which the anointing was performed by Mary of Bethany. In the one other New Testament story in which Mary and Martha appear (Luke 10:38–42), Martha invites Jesus to dinner and is running around seeing to the fancy spread while her sister Mary leaves domestic chores aside to sit at the feet of Jesus, listening to him discoursing. Martha storms out of the kitchen and irritably upbraids her guest, "Lord, do you not care that my sister has left all the serving to me? ["Of course I care!"] Well then, tell her to help me!" Jesus tries to calm her down: "Martha, Martha! You are anxious and troubled about many things; only one thing is really necessary. Mary here has made the proper choice, and I for one am not going to take it away from her."

"While you prattle through your supper" = "You are anxious and troubled about many things [in preparing supper]." "She alone has tried to give me what I need" = "One thing is needful, and she has chosen the better part." The self-important disciples cannot see the individual trees for the forest! Are they devoted followers of Jesus? Then why are they ignoring him? Their minds are full of their own ambitions, for which they see Jesus basically as a means of fulfilling. Mary Magdalene leaves such windy talk to the men and resolves to show some kindness to Jesus, not as a messiah but as a human being. And in this she (like her counterpart in Luke 10:38–42) has penetrated to the true essence of discipleship.

Strange Thing Mystifying

Here is the moment of Judas' disenchantment with Jesus and his movement. We are about to see what "clarified" things for him.

> **It seems to me a strange thing, mystifying**
> **That a man like you can waste his time on women of her kind**
> **Yes I can understand that she amuses**
> **But to let her stroke you, kiss your hair, is hardly in your line**

It's not that I object to her profession
But she doesn't fit in well with what you teach and say
It doesn't help us if you're inconsistent

Tim Rice follows John in making it "poor old Judas" who objects to the extravagant use of the anointing oil. But Rice has deferred the lines John gave his Judas until a bit later, when "Strange Thing Mystifying" invades "Everything's Alright" (below). Judas starts off instead with the objection Simon the Pharisee levels in Luke's version of the anointing. Simon had said to himself, "If this man were really a prophet, surely he would realize what sort of a woman this is who is touching him, since she is a sinner" (Luke 7:39). When Judas says "a man like you," clearly he means one in Jesus' public position as a prophet. In the same way, accepting such a display "is hardly in your line," i.e., definitely unbecoming behavior for one seen as a holy man. It is the same "inconsistency" Simon the Pharisee remarked, and which forecloses any possibility of Jesus really being a prophet. Is it beginning to have the same effect on Judas?

Mary Magdalene is obviously supposed to be a whore, and it is by no means apparent that she has deserted the oldest profession, despite her interest in this Galilean preacher of repentance. Judas speaks as if she is still active on the circuit. And yet he tries to make clear that he means no moral criticism of her. He has nothing against prostitutes (apparently, neither did the Old Testament laws, which, as far as I can see, condemned only married women who made a little extra spending money while hubby was away by plying the trade. See Proverbs chapter 7). He just realizes that higher standards are expected of a prophet. He doesn't want Jesus to be taken down, like Elmer Gantry and Jim Bakker, by some kiss-and-tell floozy.

We have already noted the traditional identification of Mary Magdalene as a repentant prostitute. Is there any basis at all for this characterization of her in the gospel texts? It may just have a narrow toe-hold. Jewish counter-blasts to Christianity often used clever word play to ridicule Christians. For instance, they referred to a gospel book (Greek: *euangelion*) as if the title came from Hebrew, where one could match it with a similar-sounding Hebrew phrase *awon-gillayon*, "sin of the margin" or "copying error," as when one scholar dismissed a book by a rival scholar in the same field as "one huge typographical error." In the same way, some rabbis confused Mary the mother of Jesus with Mary Magdalene and punningly derived "Magdalene" from a similar sounding Hebrew word meaning "hair dresser," a euphemism for prostitute. This made Jesus the bastard son of a whore—and of a Roman legionary named Pandera (a pun on the Greek *parthenos*, virgin).

But it is possible that with the supposed meaning of Magdalene they had struck pay dirt. Maybe this is what the epithet originally meant, whether it was the truth or a slur. Perhaps she had been known from very early times, already before the gospels were written, as Mary the Prostitute, and it was later cleaned up by reinterpreting it as meaning "from Magdala."

Mary Magdalene is not simply wiping Jesus' furrowed brow with a hot towel like an airline stewardess. She is stroking him, kissing his hair. We might have expected, as more natural, "to let her kiss you, stroke your hair," and it is interesting to see that in the movie version, this is what Judas says. Did Rice change the line, or did Judas slip and sing it the way it made more sense to him? Who's the redactor here?

At any rate, this somewhat risqué performance is based on Luke's anointing, where the sinful woman is described as bathing Jesus' feet with her copious tears (apparently she was grieving for her past sins), wiping them off (wiping off the road dust) with her long, unbound hair, then kissing his feet (and for some length of time: "from the time I came in she has not ceased to kiss my feet"!) and finally smearing the ointment on his feet. This rather elaborate process, Luke says, had been continuing for some time while Jesus' hostile host sat there fuming but saying nothing, giving the false prophet rope enough to hang himself. Even to the modern Western reader it seems the woman is perhaps pouring it on a little thick! It has even been suggested[71] that the word "feet" here might possibly mean what it does sometimes in the Old Testament, a pious euphemism for "penis." (See Exodus 4:25, "Then Zipporah took a flint and cut off her son's foreskin and touched Moses' feet with it, and said, 'Surely you are a bridegroom of blood to me!'" Isaiah 7:20, "In that day Adonai will shave [Israel] with a razor . . . the head and the hair of the feet [were they Hobbits?], and it will sweep away the beard also." Ruth 3:7, "Then she came softly and uncovered his feet and lay down"). Nuff said!

Rice has simplified the process somewhat. Now the woman kisses *his* hair rather than kissing his *feet* and wiping them with *her* hair.

They only need a small excuse to put us all away

This might be a little extreme. At the most, such gossip might discredit Jesus in the eyes of some, but it would hardly lead to arrest and imprisonment for any or all of them. Besides, such rumors did make the rounds. Jesus himself is made to quote what was said against him by his critics: "Behold, a glutton and boozer, bosom buddy of traitors and apostates!" (Matthew 11:19).

Who are you to criticise her? Who are you to despise her?
Leave her, leave her, let her be now
Leave her, leave her, she's with me now
If your slate is clean-then you can throw stones
If your slate is not then leave her alone

Didn't Judas just say he had no problem with Mary Magdalene herself? If she wants to sell herself, let her! That wasn't the issue. And yet here Jesus comes out swinging, defending Mary Magdalene as if she were the one attacked. As often in the Bible, when you trip over an inconsistency like this, you begin to suspect that the story you are reading has been cobbled together from a couple of different ones that don't quite fit together. And that is manifestly the case here. Redactor Rice has just jumped out of any New Testament version of the anointing story and into the very different story of the woman taken in adultery (John 8:1–11), a brief tale some early scribe decided to preserve by tacking it on to his copy of John's Gospel, though the earliest manuscripts of John do not have it. In it an outraged mob drags a frightened and half-dressed woman across the marketplace and dumps her unceremoniously in front of Jesus, who is writing in the dust, like Socrates in the *Meno* dialogue. Sure enough, we are about to hear Jesus tie his opponents in knots by means of a couple of shrewd questions hurled like bolos.

A spokesman (the woman's husband?) announces that she has been caught in the act of adultery. (It takes two to tango, doesn't it? Where is her partner in crime? Already murdered by the cuckolded husband?) Well, should they go ahead and stone her to death? That's what the Torah would say. The story is not historical, because it seems to picture Jesus, like the Prophet Muhammad, as a theocratic ruler who can decide capital cases by his Solomon-like wisdom. But in Roman-occupied Jerusalem, he would have no such power. It's really a later Christian invention designed to provide a Christian divorce law. Should the Old Testament law apply or not? Someone is imagining what Jesus would say, could we bring the dilemma to his heavenly throne of adjudication.

Notice that Jesus does not deny she is guilty. He grants for the sake of argument that she is. But who is qualified to execute the scriptural penalty? Unless one wants to pretend to superior righteousness, an absurdity, and thus reveal himself as the blackest hypocrite, one might think again. "Let him who is without sin cast the first stone. Okay, who's first?" Well, now that you put it that way . . . Better drop it, guys. Listen, there's still time to make the cock fight if we hurry.

Are we to understand that none of them were innocent of adulterous affairs of their own? At any rate, this story is certainly the source for Jesus' ill-aimed reply to Judas.

I'm amazed that men like you can be so shallow thick and slow
There is not a man among you who knows or cares if I come or go

Jesus takes Judas' rebuke as evidence that the whole bunch of the disciples are superficial, stupid, slow to catch on. There is a deeper thing going on here, and all of them without exception have utterly failed to grasp it. We had already seen Jesus' disgust for them just a bit earlier when he dismissed their questions as not worth answering because they would only be more confused. Many viewers of *Superstar* took offense at such a portrayal of Jesus, whom all imagined as unfailingly compassionate and sweet, like a first-century Leo Buscaglia. But contrast such a picture with that sketched by Mark 9:14–20. Jesus comes upon his disciples engaged in a shouting match with a complaining customer. The irate man had brought his demon-possessed son, hoping to have Jesus heal him. The disciples assured him that in Jesus' absence, they'd be happy to care of it. But no go. The kid still gave off a heavy aroma of burning sulfur. "I want to see the manager! And right now!" "Yes sir? Now what seems to be the problem here? I'm sure we can fix it." And he does. Of course, I'm paraphrasing. But here's the crucial point. On being filled in, Jesus bursts out in impatience: "O faithless generation! How long am I to be with you? How much longer must I endure you? Bring him to me." See also Mark 4:13. But I suspect Rice drew his inspiration from the scathing words of yet another passage, Mark 8:17–18, "Do you not yet perceive or understand? Are your hearts hardened? Having eyes, do you not see? Having ears, do you not hear?" Sounds like they're pretty shallow, thick, and slow.

It sounds a little strange for Jesus to accuse them of not even noticing whether he comes or goes. But we might think of two gospel passages. The first is Mark 1:35–39. After a full day of healing the crowds, Jesus nonetheless wakes up early, "a great while before day . . . and went out to a lonely place, and there he prayed. And Simon and those who were with him followed him, and they found him and said to him. 'Everyone is looking for you.'" Jesus announces that they will just have to keep looking, because he must be off to the other surrounding villages, to spread his message there, too. Imagine the disciples, basking in the glow of being the hangers-on of this new celebrity. He is their ticket to greatness, and they seem to feel possessive of him, perhaps seeing themselves as his managers ("Don't crowd the savior, ma'am!" as the Peter analogue in *Monty Python's Life of Brian* says), and—lo and behold, where *is* he? We've *lost* him!" That about describes the portrayal of the disciples drawn by Jesus in this scene of *Superstar*.

The second text possibly reflected here is Matthew 24:44, "Therefore you also must be ready, for the son of man comes at an hour you do not expect!" The same kind of admonition to vigilance is found in Luke 21:34, "But take heed to yourselves lest your hearts be weighted down with dissipation and drunkenness and cares of this life [sounds like the disciples as we will see them at the Last Supper!], and that day come upon you like a snare."

So the gospels do show the disciples being so sleepy and inattentive that they do not notice whether Jesus has left them behind or whether he is about to surprise them in his arrival.

No you're wrong! You're very wrong!
How can you say that?

These are the stung words of all the disciples with the significant exception of Judas, the libretto informs us. He is silent because, even though Jesus plainly meant to include him in the general accusation (it was Judas' remarks that prompted Jesus' outburst, after all), Judas does not think it fits. He needn't try to bat it back, because it didn't come anywhere near him. Besides, he agrees with Jesus! At least as far as the others are concerned. He says as much in "Heaven on Their Minds." He is ahead of them, though, as we will be led to suspect, a crucial step behind Jesus. Or put it this way: Judas *does* know the path they're riding, right into the fanged maw of Pilate, but he understands it less than Jesus. Unwittingly he will further Jesus' own mystifying plans.

The protests of the disciples here seem to be an anticipation of their denials at the Last Supper that they will deny and abandon Jesus despite his prediction: "But [Peter] said, 'Even if they all fall away, I will not . . . If I must die with you, I will not deny you!' And they all said the same" (Mark 14:29, 31). Why has Rice doubled the disciples' protestations of loyalty? It is simply the logic of the Last Supper scene and, remember, he has doubled the Last Supper, in order to include both the versions of John's gospel and of the other three.

Not one-not one of you!

This is a clue to the audience that Judas is mistaken to hold himself aloof and exempt from Jesus' accusation. He is not as smart as he thinks he is. As Jesus will later say, "Neither . . . Judas nor the Twelve . . . understand at all." Jesus knows not to simply lump Judas together with the others, yet he is at one with them in his ultimate failure to grasp the point of it all.

Everything's Alright

We continue with the anointing scene, in accord with the primary version of *Superstar*, the libretto issued with the studio album. The movie severs the continuity of the scene by inserting an entirely new song at this point, following "Strange Thing Mystifying" and "Everything's Alright." We will defer comments on this song, "Then We Are Decided," till after "Everything's Alright."

> **Try not to get worried, try not to turn on to**
> **Problems that upset you oh don't you know**
> **Everything's alright yes everything's fine**
> **And we want you to sleep well tonight**
> **Let the world turn without you tonight**
> **If we try we'll get by so forget all about us tonight**

Mary Magdalene intervenes to stop the shouting, knowing that it is the last thing the exhausted Jesus needs. There's nothing really wrong (she naively supposes).

And yet she speaks with powerful, albeit unwitting, irony. Soon enough the world will truly be turning without him, for he will taken from them.

He will, depending upon one's opinion, be dead or ascended to the heavenly throne, but the cruel Palestinian sun will cast his shadow no more. They will have to try their best to get by without him then. This is a theme which Jesus will shortly make explicit. These lines of inadvertent prophecy (a theme drawn perhaps from John 11:51) correspond to what Jesus says of the anointing in Mark 14:8, "She has done what she could; she has anointed my body beforehand for burial." Needless to say, that was the ironic significance Jesus saw in it. It is hardly likely that the woman herself had anything like that remotely in mind—nor does Mary Magdalene in *Superstar*.

Everything's alright yes everything's alright yes

This refrain is sung by "the Apostles' women" (which puts me in mind of a student's answer to the quiz question "What were the Epistles?" He ventured "The wives of the Apostles"!). Who, pray tell, are the apostles' women? Rice seems to be making them apostolic groupies. This is in keeping with the celebrity rock star metaphor that permeates the work. But it is no less in keeping with the gospels of Mark and Luke which also relate that a group of women traveled about Galilee and on to Jerusalem with Jesus and the Twelve. Mary Magdalene is listed among them. "There were also women looking on [the crucifixion scene] from afar, among whom were Mary Magdalene, and Mary the mother of James the younger and of Joses, and Salome, who, when he was in Galilee, followed him, and ministered to him; and also many other women who came up with him to Jerusalem" (Mark 15:40–41; cf., Luke 8:1–3). We may be sure, based on the reactions to similar practices by second- and third-century itinerant prophets who followed this pattern, that suspicions abounded as to precisely what kind of "serving" the women did. If Rice raises suspicions that they were a harem, even as Judas implies in his accusation, they are not new suspicions.

> Sleep and I shall soothe you, calm you and anoint you
> Myrrh for your hot forehead oh then you'll feel
> Everything's alright yes everything's fine
> And it's cool and the ointment's sweet
> For the fire in your head and feet
> Close your eyes close your eyes
> And relax think of nothing tonight

Mary Magdalene just wants him to relax and concentrate on enjoying the relief of the ointment, as he was doing before that nasty old Judas upset him.

What's cool? The "it" would at first seem to refer to the ointment, but it probably refers instead to "everything." It's cool, it's all right. The ointment is mentioned next, implying it has only now become the subject.

Now we hear that Mary Magdalene has anointed not just Jesus' face but his head and feet as well, which is a harmonization of the feet-anointing of John and Luke with the head-anointing of Mark and Matthew.

But Jesus' rest is delayed again, for Judas is not to be so easily silenced.

Woman your fine ointment-brand new and expensive
Could have been saved for the poor
Why has it been wasted? We could have raised maybe
Three hundred silver pieces or more
People who are hungry, people who are starving
Matter more than your feet and hair

Here is the complaint of Judas in the Gospel of John. The original reads: "Why was this ointment not sold for three hundred denarii [= silver coins each worth a day's wage] and given to the poor?" Judas' point will be lost if we do not bear in mind that this is not some innovative idea of Judas', but rather reflects the general policy preached by Jesus. *Superstar* does not tell us that Jesus was in the habit of telling the rich to cash in their property and distribute the proceeds to the poor. But then again, neither does the Gospel of John! It seems to presuppose the reader has read texts like Luke 12:33, "Sell your possessions and give alms," or Mark 10:21, "Go, sell what you have, and give to the poor, and you will have treasure in heaven."

Thus Judas means to charge Jesus with hypocritically casting aside his own most important principles when it suits his fancy. As long as luxury is showered on *him*, then it is suddenly all right! "You've begun to matter more [to *yourself*!] than the things you say." The clay feet of the idol have been revealed. "Our ideals die around us, and it's all because of you!" Jesus doesn't seem to believe them himself, so why should we? Just like the scrawny guru of the Breatharian sect who publicly maintained that the body would thrive without any food intake whatsoever. Fresh air and sunlight had all the nutrients a body needed. He seemed, with that chic "Auschwitz look," to be a convincing if repugnant argument for the truth of his position. But then somebody spotted him sneaking out nightly to the Seven Eleven for clandestine hamburgers! "They think they've found the new messiah, and they'll hurt you when they find they're wrong."

> **Try not to get worried, try not to turn on to**
> **Problems that upset you oh don't you know**
> **Everything's alright yes everything's fine**
> **And we want you to sleep well tonight**
> **Let the world turn without you tonight**
> **If we try we'll get by so forget all about us tonight**

Mary repeats herself here, but not redundantly. She repeats her soothing words right after Judas' scathing attack as if to say, "Now don't you listen to a word he says! This is just the kind of thing I want you to forget about till tomorrow." Jesus' comfort is uppermost to his fans. They want to shield him even from the truth if that should turn out to be unpleasant. This is the strategy of the sycophant, the yes-man. It flatters a prima donna leader but insulates him from reality until it is too late, and danger looms from a direction from which he has been hitherto shielded. Being indulged by admirers is just as numbing and dangerous as self-indulgence. Mary Magdalene is providing just the sort of blind adulation Judas was lamenting in "Heaven on Their Minds."

The movie version omits the last three lines of this verse and has Mary Magdalene sing it to *Judas*, trying to calm him down, not Jesus! Jesus himself does not need music's charm to soothe the savage breast, since he is already serene, in total contradiction to the logic of the scene as written. If Jesus is not on edge and upset, he scarcely needs such comforting, so on the big screen she offers it instead to Judas. This is but one of many signs of misguided direction and misinterpretation in the film.

> **Surely you're not saying we have the resources**
> **To save the poor from their lot?**
> **There will be poor always, pathetically struggling-**
> **Look at the good things you've got!**
> **Think! while you still have me**
> **Move! while you still see me**
> **You'll be lost and you'll be so sorry when I'm gone**

Jesus can't believe Judas is serious! Is he really implying it would make an ounce of difference to the problem of poverty if Mary Magdalene cashed in the myrrh for poor relief? If it will become meaningless, without effect, as a mere drop in the vast bucket of poverty, then why not let her use it in a situation where it can have a meaning?

Don't kid yourself! No matter what you and I do, poverty will go on till the end of the world just as it is as old as the world. As Jesus says in Luke 12:46, "Why are you incapable of interpreting the present time?" He draws the contrast between something that, precisely because it is a perennial problem, can be dealt with any old time. There is no great urgency, since nothing permanent can be done about it anyway. But the clock is swiftly ticking away on another, more acute matter. The passion drama must be played out to the end, as arbitrary as it may seem, even to Jesus himself. They must come to their senses before it is too late and their chance for understanding is gone. All Judas can see here is Jesus being narcissistic. But he isn't necessarily being petulant, as a *New Yorker* reviewer said ("I personally thought Christ seemed a little petulant."[72]) though that's one way to read it. Judas does. But in fact Jesus is frustrated with their obtuseness. It will become clear what you squandered once I'm gone. And then it will be too late.

All this is quite scriptural. Jesus' lines here are based squarely on three gospel passages. The first is, again, John's version of the anointing, where Jesus' response to Judas' carping goes this way, "Let her alone, let her keep it for the day of my burial. The poor you always have with you, but you do not always have me" (12:7). The second is Mark 2:18–22, where Jesus is reproached for not directing his followers to share in the austerities of Jewish piety. Hasidic sects like the Pharisees and the followers of John the Baptist fasted frequently to mourn for their sins and to hasten the coming of the Kingdom of Heaven. But Jesus ignores the fasts. What possible reason can he have? The Markan text as we read it has suffered some clumsy editing which results in two different answers canceling each other out. The one relevant to our purpose may be found in verses 19 and 20, "Can the wedding guest fast when the bridegroom is with them? As long as they have the bridegroom with them they cannot fast. But the days will come when the bridegroom is taken away from them, and then they will fast in that day." The point seems to be that, a la Ecclesiastes 3:1–8, there is a time to fast, and a time to feast. The time Jesus shares with his friends is a time to celebrate, analogous to a wedding reception. But once he is gone, they will have plenty of reason to fast.

Notice the parallel between the anointing story and this one. In both, we have a celebration of abundance (a wedding feast, the extravagant anointing), followed by a pious objection (why don't you fast?/why was this ointment wasted?). In both cases, the objector feels it is required to practice some kind of ascetical self-denial (abstain from food/sell your treasures for almsgiving). And in both Jesus' reply is to the effect that such rules, though quite proper as a norm, do not govern special situations where asceticism would be gauche (when the friend's wedding feast is over, or maybe when it comes time for the same friend's funeral!, it'll be back to fasting//when you don't have me anymore, you can give your ointment for poor relief).

In both cases the problem is that the objectors cannot see that it is a special occasion! The fasters cannot see that the time for feasting has arrived! Judas fails to see that things are not business as usual, and that there is something more urgent than one's common duty. Pretty much the same point is made again in Mark 2:23–28, the controversy over Jesus allowing the disciples to glean grain from the fields on the Sabbath. The Torah stipulated that farmers leave some of the grain unharvested so the destitute could pick it. Jesus and his group qualify, being wandering mendicants. The trouble is that it's the Sabbath, and work is prohibited. But does this count? His opponents say yes; Jesus says no, because human need constitutes a legitimate exception to an otherwise valid rule.

Third, in the Last Supper discourse of John, Jesus supplies what can be taken as the most childish remark of all, if one fails to see what motivates it: "A little while, and you will not see me . . . Truly, truly I say to you, you will weep and lament, but the world will rejoice" (John 16:19–20; cf., John 7:33, "I will be with you a little longer, and then I shall go to him who sent me."). Obviously this is the source of *Superstar*'s "You'll be lost and you'll be so sorry when I'm gone." It is not a petulant "You'll be sorry! Just wait!" Here is a fine example of the double entendres Gordon Clanton notes. "The lyrics are . . . laden with double meaning."[73]

    Sleep and I shall soothe you, calm you and anoint you
    Myrrh for your hot forehead oh then you'll feel
    Everything's alright yes everything's fine
    And it's cool and the ointment's sweet
    For the fire in your head and feet
    Close your eyes close your eyes
    And relax think of nothing tonight

Close your eyes close your eyes and relax

The repetition of Mary Magdalene's soothing words brings closure to the scene. Her purpose of calming Jesus down is back on track after a bothersome interruption. A nuisance is all it seems to her, when in fact the scene just ended will prove pivotal, since, as I have argued, what Judas has just seen has decided him, made everything clear to him at last. "What more evidence do we need?"

On the studio album, Jesus finishes Mary's refrain by singing, "And I think I shall sleep well tonight," just before he dozes off in her protective arms. Has she lulled him into a false sense of security, both of them ignorant of the fatal significance of what has now transpired? Or is it just the opposite? Does Jesus relax because he knows the last piece has just been put into place toward the fulfillment of his enigmatic destiny?

Then We Are Decided

This is the additional song that appears in the film but not in the studio album or any of the stage versions. Its purpose is not clear, except perhaps to confirm Judas' fears that the popularity of the Jesus movement is attracting unwelcome attention from the authorities. But even in this respect, as in all others, the song seems to be superfluous, merely a redundant paraphrase of "This Jesus Must Die." Only, coming as it does before "This Jesus Must Die," it threatens to make that song appear redundant instead. And it interrupts the scenic continuity of "Strange Thing Mystifying" and "Everything's Alright." (That is why I have discussed these songs out of order, to make clearer the thematic links in the original order.) One suspects that it owes its presence between these two songs to the simple fact that otherwise it would come immediately before "This Jesus Must Die," and the redundancy would be just too blatant. Such a reshuffling might have made sense had there been any particular reason for inserting "Then We Are Decided" anywhere in the first place. But as it stands, it's a strange thing, mystifying.

The settings, costumes, and scenery in the film *Jesus Christ Superstar* are strictly minimalist. There are no crowds, even when the scene calls for them. Roman soldiers look absurdly like construction workers with T-shirts and chrome helmets (only what they can have been constructing is a mystery, since the movie seems to take place on the lunar surface!). One feels none of this is due in the least to aesthetic preference; all of it looks like the result of a production budget of $1.75. But in fact, director Norman Jewison did it this way on purpose. "The one thing I knew for sure I didn't want was a 'King of Kings' job ... I've seen Passolini's 'The Passion According to Saint Matthew' at least eight times [—and he still couldn't get the title (*The Gospel According to Saint Matthew*) straight! He must have been thinking of Bach's "Saint Matthew's Passion."]; it's so spare and simple and close to the Bible—and that's what I had in the back of my mind. The first scenario that Andrew Lloyd Webber and Tim Rice came up with—can you believe it—was pure 'King of Kings' with all the trappings; a cast of thousands, you know. They had this very modern concept for the music but when it came to the visuals they lapsed right back to sheer Hollywood '30s."[84] In fact, as many music critics noted, Webber's music was highly eclectic, by no means all faddish rock, and the result is a style and feel that wears well even after thirty years. Jewison's movie, on the other hand, fairly reeks of the '70s, hopelessly dated already. It has none of the dignity of Passolini's film, though it does share with it the crude feeling of being a home movie of a bunch of amateurs parading around in bed sheet costumes. Too bad Jewison utterly misunderstood the tendency of *Superstar* to play off of traditional depictions of Jesus, so as to turn them against themselves. The whole notion of Jesus as a pop superstar demands the kind of "cast of thousands" crowd that Jewison so despised. And the result is an unintentionally hilarious juxtaposition of Caiaphas' fears of Jesus' growing strength with the sight of Jesus accompanied by a following about the size of a Cub Scout troop!

And yet in one point the cut-rate minimalism does work to good advantage. The sequence in "Then We Are Decided" takes place in the palace of the high priest Caiaphas. Annas makes his way through the gate, up the broad steps, and into his fellow-cleric's presence, all by firelight, a meeting in clandestine darkness. And the long walk, as well as the worried pacing that follows, gives us a good look at Caiaphas' residence. It is bare and roofless stone, its mighty columns reaching up helplessly into an empty void, like so many stalagmites. What worries the canny priests is a growing threat to their position: if the Jesus movement continues unchecked, it may bring the wrath of Rome down upon them, so that nation and temple will alike be swept away. And as they deliberate the best way to forestall it, they are already standing in the midst of a field of ruins! The temple's doom is already sealed. "Everything is fixed, and you can't change it." True, it will not be Jesus who pushes the plunger, but a subsequent generation of angry messiahs in 70 C.E.

We've been sitting on a fence for far too long

Caiaphas feels it is time that some decision be made: to take preemptive action against Jesus or not? This does not quite match John's gospel, though for a good reason. John actually has the Jewish authorities gunning for Jesus from the beginning (5:16; 7:25–26, 32; 10:31, 39) but unsuccessfully. As J. Ramsey Michaels has noted,[85] John seems not only to have a much longer passion narrative than Matthew, Mark, or Luke; John has in effect made the entire gospel into a passion narrative, which is why Jesus' public career starts with the cleansing of the temple, whereas in all three of the others, the cleansing brings it to a close. John knew good and well that the cleansing rang down the curtain, and in his own gospel it still does. It's just that the curtain takes a long time to descend in John. This is because John wants to use the story of Jesus as a frame for presenting long, revelatory monologues, considerably expanding the story.

And, again, as Michaels observes,[86] the striking recurrence of judicial terminology ("bearing witness to me," "testimony," "will be your judge," etc.) implies that John has cast the whole public ministry of Jesus in the form of one long trial before the Jewish authorities. And several times the trial almost issues in Jesus' execution, as of course it does in the older passion narratives. His enemies make moves to stone or capture him. Since John needs more time to insert more discourses of Jesus, he has to contrive to have Jesus, so to speak, gain reprieve after reprieve. He does this somewhat unimaginatively, simply having Jesus hide or slip away unseen, or with no explanation at all, or with the explanation that it was not yet God's appointed time for him to die (7:30; 45–46; 8:59; cf., Luke 4:28–30). What Tim Rice has done is to substitute a more believable reason for the Sanhedrin not having done away with Jesus long before. Thus Caiaphas explains that they had not yet made up their minds. John's gospel does depict a tiny amount of dissent within the ranks, making Nicodemus and Joseph of Arimathea speak up for Jesus, to the scorn of their colleagues. But an occasional note of dissent is not the same thing as indecision.

Why let him upset us? Caiaphas let him be
All those imbeciles will see
He really doesn't matter

Annas, depicted here as pretty much a yes-man and a toady, plays a role quite parallel to that of Mary Magdalene in the "Strange Thing Mystifying"/"Everything's Alright" scene taking place simultaneously with this one. He thinks poor Caiaphas is worried over nothing and tries to set his mind at ease.

Annas' advice is quite likely derived from that of Gamaliel to the Sanhedrin in Acts 5:33–39 (in turn probably modeled on Cadmus' sage advice to Pentheus in Euripides' *Bacchae*, not to persecute the new religion of the savior Dionysus). The Sanhedrin is trying to silence the preaching of Peter, but he refuses to cooperate, so they consider erecting twelve more crosses! And Gamaliel warns, "Keep away from these men and let them alone; for if this plan or this undertaking is of men, it will fail, but if it is of God, you will not be able to overthrow them. You might even be found [on the wrong side,] opposing God!"

The contempt for Jesus' disciples (and his larger following, as we will see in a moment) as "imbeciles" no doubt comes from John 7:49, "This crowd, who do not know the Torah, is accursed." Annas says the whole thing will blow over simply because there is less to Jesus than meets the eye, and even the stupidest must sooner or later see it. There may be a sucker born again every minute, but even they have to wake up eventually!

Jesus is important
We've let him go his way before
And while he starts a major war
We theorize and chatter

The source of these sentiments of Caiaphas is John 11:46–48, the worried musings of the Sanhedrin in the aftermath of Jesus' raising of Lazarus. "What are we to do? For this man performs many signs. If *we let him go on* thus, everyone will believe in him, and the Romans will come and destroy our place (= our privileged position? our temple?) and our nation." This last is the "major war" whose prospect haunts Caiaphas. He fears Roman reprisals to put down such a revolt.

Here is an anachronism, in my judgment: it is as if Caiaphas has in mind the destruction of the temple and priesthood in 70 A.D (C.E.) as well as the deportation of all Jews from the Holy Land after the defeat of Simon bar-Kochba in 136 C.E. We have seen that Tim Rice uses anachronism as a device for keeping the viewer aware that, no matter how the play catches him up, the viewer is in the twentieth century and shares the long perspective of the twentieth century. Here the informed viewer is to know, as poor Caiaphas does not, that the very events he fears from Jesus will overtake Judea and the priests anyway.

But it is no less anachronistic in John's original, since he, too, makes Caiaphas sound as if he knows of the future events under warrior messiahs Simon bar-Giora and Simon bar-Kochba, and wants to fend them off as long as possible. This is John's own irony, making the same point and for the same reason. It remains to ask why Caiaphas and the Sanhedrin should ever have viewed the Jesus movement in such a light to begin with. Were they either so militant or so numerous? We will return to that question.

As for the impatient comment about empty theory and chatter, we think of a similar passage in John a chapter later: "Then the Pharisees said among themselves, 'You see how you are getting nowhere. Look, the whole world has gone after him'" (John 12:19).

Annas is partly right: in himself, Jesus is insignificant. But he represents danger nonetheless. At the start, Hitler seemed a buffoon no one could take seriously—until the mob of imbeciles swept him to power!

He's just another scripture-thumping hack from Galilee

Annas still cannot take Jesus seriously as a threat. For him, Jesus is merely the equivalent of a dime-a-dozen TV evangelist (or as E.K. Hornbeck, the H.L. Mencken analogue in *Inherit the Wind* calls Matthew Harrison Brady [William Jennings Bryan], a "Bible-beating bunko artist"). Revival preachers often pounded their fist on the Bible in front of them to emphasize a point, rather like a judge slamming down the gavel. "Scripture-thumping" is a clever comparison, though no one would have had closed Bibles to thump in Jesus' day, since the various biblical writings were written on individual scrolls. The bound book had not yet been invented. Another dimension of the metaphor is that revival preachers are notoriously ignorant of the very Bible they pound. They repeat a few sloganeering phrases from it but have little idea of the larger context. Annas assumes Jesus' knowledge of the scriptures, from which he pretends to teach, is likewise superficial and vacuous. I believe the jibe comes from John 7:15, "How does this man know the scriptures without an education?"

I suspect that the dismissive placing of Jesus on a par with other Galilean would-be prophets comes from the same Gamaliel passage, Acts 5:33–39. Gamaliel gives his colleagues the big picture: "Before these days Theudas arose, giving himself out to be somebody, and a number of men, about four hundred, joined him; but he was slain, and all who followed him were dispersed and came to nothing. After him Judas the Galilean arose in the days of the census and drew away some of the people after him; he also perished, and all who followed him were scattered. So in the present case . . . let them alone . . . If this plan . . . is of men, it will fail." Or as Mary will say, "He's not a king, he's just a man . . . he's just one more."

We can also sniff out a reference to John 7:51–52, where Nicodemus tries to forestall the rush to judgment by objecting, "Does our Law judge a man without first giving him a hearing and finding out the truth about his deeds?" The response is sarcastic: "Are you from Galilee too? Search [the scriptures— cf., John 5:39] and you will see that no prophet is [predicted] to rise from Galilee." Here is the cluster of terms "scripture, Galilee, false prophet" which Annas' remark presupposes.

> **The difference is, they call him king**
> **The difference frightens me**
> **What about the Romans?**
> **When they see King Jesus crowned**
> **Do you think they'll stand around**
> **Cheering and applauding?**

Again, provided Jesus is taken seriously enough and by enough fools, we could be in big trouble! The Romans will not stop to deliberate Jesus' political and theological merits. They won't be among the crowd of well-wishers at Jesus' inauguration. Far from it: they'll shoot first and ask questions later.

Do we detect here an ironic anticipation of the mockery and abuse of Jesus by the Roman soldiers who *will* crown him with a diadem of thorns and cheer and applaud him as "King of the Jews" with cruel sarcasm (John 19:2–3)?

> **What about our people?**
> **If they see we've lost our nerve?**
> **Don't you think that they deserve**
> **Something more rewarding?**

Caiaphas feels that, in view of the Sanhedrin's responsibility to the Jewish people, they simply cannot take the risk Annas advises. They cannot wait and see what happens with Jesus. The danger from Rome is too great. They deserve better than that, a leadership that considers their security first and does not gamble with it.

Historically, it seems much more likely that Caiaphas would still have his Roman masters in view. What if Pilate and Tiberius Caesar get the impression that Caiaphas and his cronies are too weak-willed to do what is necessary to protect Rome's interests? It is they who will hardly look dispassionately on a wait-and-see attitude toward a possible threat. Why give a baby serpent the chance to mature and become more deadly? Crush it now! The Romans will feel entitled to something better if Caiaphas and company do not act decisively and quickly.

So why is Caiaphas suddenly concerned for the welfare of his people? Simply because this allows for another double entendre: as a startled glance from Annas in the film implies, Caiaphas almost seems to have admitted that the people need a better leadership than the Sanhedrin provides and that they are seeking it in Jesus! This is no doubt why Caiaphas was made to say that they deserve, not something "better," but rather something "more rewarding." That implies they'd get more for their money if they switched to a different brand now on the market: Jesus.

They've got what they want
They think so anyway

Annas has indeed caught Caiaphas' unintended implication. The people do prefer Jesus. Since Caiaphas had just been talking about the Jewish population as a whole, and now Annas refers back to "they," we get the impression that support for Jesus is nearly universal! The gospels never quite suggest this, but they come close when they note that the Sanhedrin fears rioting among the populace if Jesus should be arrested in public during the Passover feast, when the city will be jammed with pilgrims from all over the country (Mark 14:2).

Of course Annas thinks Jesus is the opiate of the people. They think he's what they need, but they'll sooner or later realize they've played the fool, and then, like certain disgruntled fans of Jimmy Swaggart or Deepak Chopra, they'll sue to get back the money they contributed to their guru.

If he's what they want
Why take their toy away?
He's a craze

A craze nothing, craze nothing, craze, nothing more. A flash in the pan. Why fan the flames by lighting the martyr's stake? He'd be more powerful dead than alive! Jesus knows this, too: "Would I be more noticed than I ever was before? Would the things I've said and done matter any more [than they already do]?"

Put yourself in my place
I can hardly step aside
I cannot let my hands be tied
I am law and order

Annas, Caiaphas here points out, can only take the view that he does because he does not bear on his shoulders the burden of responsibility. Caiaphas does not have the luxury to speculate as Annas does: "Maybe Jesus won't be so dangerous; why not wait and see?" No, Caiaphas does not have that option. He is no more a private citizen, nor a mere advisor: he is the embodiment of the public order. The buck stops at his desk, and he alone will be blamed for a failure. His words "I am law and order" remind one superficially of (and may have been inspired by) the conceit of Louis XIV of France, the "Sun King," who proclaimed "I am the state!" The difference is that Louis was claiming absolute power, while Caiaphas is almost lamenting the final responsibility that rests in his hands. And here is an irony: in a real sense, his hands *are* bound. His options are far more limited than Annas seems to think.

What about our priesthood?
Don't you see that we could fall?
If we are to survive at all
We cannot be divided

At least not on this crucial issue. Caiaphas needs to secure Annas' agreement now, so that the two of them can persuade their fellow justices to present a united front before Pontius Pilate, the Roman prefect, in this ticklish matter. So voices like Nicodemus' must be silenced, must be convinced. And

JESUS CHRIST SUPERSTAR 439

certainly an appeal to common self interest is the best ground for solidarity. As Benjamin Franklin said to the other plotters for American independence, "Gentlemen, if we do not all hang together, we shall most assuredly hang separately!"

Mark's gospel tells us that the Sanhedrin's verdict indeed was a unanimous vote (Mark 14:64), Joseph of Arimathea's subsequent pious concern to see to the burial of the dead (Mark 15:43) notwithstanding. To get an idea of the sort of parliamentary disaster Caiaphas dreaded, take a look at Acts 23:1–10, where the Sanhedrin has Paul on the spot, in a scene highly reminiscent of (and no doubt based on) the Sanhedrin trial of Jesus. Paul, a former stooge of this august body, suddenly realizes that he can exploit the sectarian loyalties of the bipartisan council before him, some of whom are Pharisees, others Sadducees. The first were well known to have embraced Zoroastrian doctrines at odds with traditional Judaism, pointedly the belief in a resurrection of the dead at the end of the age. The conservative Sadducees scoffed at such wild notions. So Paul sees where to drive the wedge and claims that his preaching about the Risen Christ is simply a special case of the larger doctrine of resurrection per se, and that he stands in continuity with Pharisaism at this point. As he was counting on, this remark plunges the duped Sanhedrin into internecine theological bickering, and in the comical melee Paul manages to make a fast exit. The story is obviously a piece of fiction and parody, but it does constitute a sort of rewritten version of the trial of Jesus before a high priest, and its outcome is precisely that envisioned by Caiaphas unless he and Annas get on the phones right now and start calling in favors.

> **Then say so to the council**
> **But don't rely on subtlety**
> **Frighten them or they won't see**

Annas, now convinced there is no budging his senior partner, quickly reverses himself and starts talking tactics. The best way to ensure total unanimity of the kind Caiaphas wants is to frighten the herd into a stampede. And as we will see in "This Jesus Must Die," Caiaphas follows this advice to the letter.

> **Then we are decided?**
> **Then we are decided**

The first link in the conspiracy has been firmly forged. Caiaphas' question is repeated verbatim as Annas' answer. And soon enough the whole council chamber will be ringing with it.

In short, "Then We are Decided," though a vintage bit of Tim Rice, seems merely to echo (beforehand!) "This Jesus Must Die," and that, as we will see, virtually line for line. In fact, if one wanted to compare yet a third version of the same song, give a listen to Rice's "Be Prepared" in *The Lion King*.

This Jesus Must Die

Instant replay! This time Caiaphas and Annas are meeting with the assembled Sanhedrin. "Then We Are Decided" ended waiting for the other sandal to drop, namely this meeting in which Caiaphas hoped to persuade the members of the high council to unite behind a plan of swift and dramatic action. But once we get to *This Jesus Must Die*, we see that there is little persuading to be done. The whole body sings the refrain with one voice: "He is dangerous!" Though Caiaphas will indeed have occasion to push them along further to the conclusion he wants, there is no real debate, no indecision. His colleagues are merely at a loss for practical ideas (as committees always are; indeed that is the point of them, a pooling of mediocrity and ineptitude, eight or ten committee members trying to screw in the same bulb but too dim to do it). Caiaphas, a strong individualist, will not be confined by the Lazarus bands of collegiality. His will shall prevail, if only by default. He sees they need but a prod, and momentum will carry them the rest of the way.

The scene, as the libretto's notes inform us, is Sunday in Jerusalem. Of course this means it is what we call Palm Sunday, and in fact, the Triumphal Entry is in process even as Caiaphas and the council deliberate.

Good Caiaphas the council waits for you
The Pharisees and priests are here for you

What was the Sanhedrin? It is a Greek word for council. The use of a Greek word is one of several indicators of how deeply Hellenistic (Greco-Roman) culture had penetrated even the supposed strongholds of orthodoxy. Even the Rabbinate, emerging about the end of the first century C.E., was based on the Greek model of a Socratic figure surrounded by volunteer disciples. The precursors of the later rabbis ("rabbi" is Hebrew for "my teacher") were the scribes with whom Jesus is often shown debating. The Sanhedrin is said to be composed of seventy prominent Jews from several categories: scribes, priests, elders, Sadducees, and Pharisees. (The high priest, president of the Sanhedrin, counted as number seventy-one.) We must pause for a moment to define these elements.

As already noted, "Sadducees" were aristocrats, the "major shareholders," so to speak, in the Jewish Commonwealth. Their name, defined (or redefined) as meaning "Zadokites," would refer to their descent from the priestly lineage of Zadok, whose prerogatives King David had sponsored. And no doubt this was true: they represented the descendants of those who had returned from the Babylonian-Persian Exile and had, against popular feeling, been installed with the aid of foreign (Persian) backing. It seems likely, however, that, as T.W. Manson[87] theorized, "Sadducee" simply meant "councilmen, syndics." They were not exactly a religious sect. They were simply traditionalist Jews, though no doubt with a good soaking in Hellenistic culture. They only seem to stand out religiously over against the Pharisees whose innovations the Sadducees did not approve.

"Pharisees" was (re-)defined as meaning "pure ones," thus equivalent to the English "Puritans." But, again, Manson[88] had an intriguing, well-nigh irresistible suggestion. He thought "Pharisee" meant the same thing as "Parsee," Persian, still the name for Zoroastrians living in India today. The religion of Zoroaster began perhaps as early as the 1800s B.C.E. in Persia/Afghanistan. It was a revolt against the polytheistic religion of the Vedas shared with the Indus Valley. Zoroastrianism paired off God (Ahura Mazda or Ormuzd) with an evil counterpart (Ahriman or Angra Mainyu), each having a great abundance of angelic/demonic servants at his disposal. All history was a protracted war of Good and Evil. At the consummation of this age-long jihad, a descendent of the Prophet Zoroaster would appear, born of a virgin, to raise the dead for the final judgment. Jews must have encountered Zoroastrianism (the religion of Cyrus) during the Exile, and apparently many liked what they heard. Old Testament writings dating from before the Exile are bare of ideas that sound Zoroastrian, while afterward such doctrines abound. They include the transformation of God's security chief Satan into his arch-enemy, the doctrine of end-time resurrection, angelology and demonology, the apocalyptic division of history into predetermined epochs, etc. Those Jews who embraced these views (by no means all of them did) were suspected (rightly) of religious syncretism and called "Pharisees/

Parsees," the latter being the name given Persian expatriates wherever they lived.

The Pharisees, contrary to the popular imagination, were not a group of clergymen. They were a pietistic movement of the laity, something on the order of today's Orthodox and Hasidic Jewish communities. Like their modern counterparts they were marked by distinctive, strict religious scruples about fasting, tithing, almsgiving, and prayers. In general they tried to maintain the strictest standards of ritual purity, comparable to those required of temple priests on duty. Their regulations were extrapolations from the literal commands of the Torah, admittedly stricter than the letter of the commandments. The goal was to keep oneself from getting within breaking distance of the actual commands by "building a fence" of secondary rules "around the Torah."

When in *Monty Python's Life of Brian* poor Matthias son of Deuteronomy of Gath is about to be stoned to death, what is his heinous crime? "Look, I'd had a lovely supper and all I said to my wife was, 'That piece of halibut was good enough for Jehovah.'"[89] Did the Torah of Moses really condemn anyone to death for uttering the divine name? Not exactly, but it did sternly prohibit "taking the name of Yahve/Jehovah your God in vain." After several centuries, no one was really sure any more what that meant. So why not play it safe and never say the divine name at all? Only the high priest (Caiaphas!) was allowed to speak the sacred syllables, and that once a year on the Day of Atonement. Jesus, too, was reportedly concerned with the issue: "Our Father in heaven, may your name be hallowed." See the logic? That was the approach of the Pharisees. They had such elaborations of many of the commandments, more and more as time went on. The Talmud is the result some four centuries later.

Other Jews either weren't willing to take the trouble, while others thought the whole business unnecessary. The former group would be the mass of the common people, who admired the Pharisee sect but wouldn't actually join, while the latter would include the Sadducees, who thought the written Torah text by itself was good enough. The Sadducees were the aristocrats, but the Pharisees had long been a force to be reckoned with, since they enjoyed widespread popular support (and occasional royal patronage during Hasmonean times). Thus the Sanhedrin had to provide seats for Pharisees. Only rarely was the high priest chosen from the Pharisees. Annas and Caiaphas, like most, were Sadducees. A more recent parallel might be the uneasy coexistence in the Church of England of dour Calvinist Puritans or pious Methodists alongside worldly, red-nosed Anglo-Catholic princes of the Church.

Who elaborated the extra rules the Pharisees followed? This is where the scribes came in. These were the experts on the Bible. Who would be more familiar with the text than those whose job it was to hand-transcribe new copies? Many of the scribes belonged to the Pharisee sect, though not all. They had frequent debates, recorded in the Mishnah, and these are in general reminiscent of the gospel scenes where Jesus debates the scribes, only the gospel writers, no longer acquainted with the issues, tend to garble them, making the scribes into vicious fanatics with absurd opinions and inflexible rules. The positions on the sabbath, vows, healing, etc., taken by Jesus in the gospels practically in every case match up with the tenets of liberal Pharisaism of the House of Hillel, as Harvey Falk has shown.[90]

The priests were of three sorts. There were the well-heeled priests of Jerusalem, the Establishment. Then there were underlings, sacred flunkies: vergers, sextons, choral singers, night watchmen, and armed temple guards. These were collectively called Levites because of their pedigree as members of the pre-Zadokite priesthood of Levi. Since Levi means "serpent," I would guess they originated as priests of the divine serpent of wisdom, Nehushtan, worshipped in the temple for centuries (2 Kings 18:4). It was also called Leviathan, and the Levites would have been "those who are skilled to rouse up [i.e., invoke in worship] Leviathan" (Job 3:8). These priests were in big trouble when King Josiah interdicted the worship of these gods. They were kept on in subordinate positions and never advanced in status. The scare-story of Korah's challenge to Moses and Aaron in Numbers chapter 16 was written by the elite priests in the fourth century B.C.E. to keep the Levitical guild of choristers, the sons of Korah (see, e.g., Psalm 87), in their place.

The third group was composed of rural and village priests whose ancestors had once officiated at local hilltop shrines ("high places") all over the countryside. King Josiah put them out of business, too. Since they had practiced polytheistic worship, and might return to it once the "Feds" or "Revenuers" left, the only way to stamp out polytheism in the outlying districts was to shut them down altogether. As a minor consolation, these men were allowed to take shifts of minor temple service when it was their order's turn twice a year, and even then one might sit on the bench cooling one's heels. Remember John the Baptist's father Zachariah who, as a member of the Abijah order, happened to be in Jerusalem when the reserves were called up, so to speak, and once there he was lucky enough to win the drawing of lots and take a turn doing his priestly thing. And this was no more than making the incense offering. Animal sacrifices, of which the celebrant took a portion and sold what he could not use to the meat markets, were the prerogative of the elite priests only. Well, the Levites' ancestors had asked for it, picking the wrong gods to serve!

So the priesthood was a mixed bag, and the priests depicted in the gospels (and in *Superstar*) were of the elite class, not the Levites (though one of them takes it on the chin in the Good Samaritan parable, too!) or the rural part-timers.

One last thing: In "Then We Are Decided," which in the movie version directly anticipates the present scene, we find the line "We've been sitting on the fence for far too long." And also in the movie, the Sanhedrin is shown meeting on ramshackle scaffolding erected against the wall of the city. They are literally sitting on the fence. Yuk yuk. Again, it is hard to fathom the elusive esthetics of "scenery on the cheap," but perhaps the ludicrous arrangement is meant to symbolize the role of the Sanhedrin as the "power structure." It seems perhaps to owe something to *Godspell*'s depiction of the Pharisees in "Alas for You," where the Pharisees are standing on one another's shoulders, each carrying or wearing part of an elaborate monster costume. Here the imagery, perhaps more profound, is that the structures of established religion with vested interests is transhuman, an insidious reified collectivity greater than the sum of its parts. This is the New Testament doctrine of the Principalities and Powers ruling the present age of darkness.

Ah gentlemen-you know why we are here
We've not much time and quite a problem here

"Gentlemen"—a polite address to a group of self-satisfied gentry, stolid pillars of the community whose charge it is to protect the status quo. This is not an attempt to stir up a lynch mob; it is a call to action to those whose job is to maintain order and decorum.

The Jesus menace seems to have blown up to frightening proportions since the last meeting of the Sanhedrin. If they are to quash it, it's now or never. And this is an emergency meeting called for that express purpose. If anyone is in doubt as to what course to take, His Holiness will make that clear soon enough.

Hosanna! Superstar!

As if to lend emphasis to his words, Jesus' minions are audible right outside! Their proximity in space is a metaphor for the close approach of the danger they represent. The whole scene is based on John 12:19, where we see the Pharisees commiserating during the Triumphal Entry, "You see that you can do nothing; the whole world has gone after him!" (This in turn is probably based on Luke 19:39–40/Matthew 21:15–16, to be considered below.)

In the movie version, with its cast of tens, the juxtaposition of the twenty or so Jesus partisans laughing and singing like refugees from *Godspell* on the one hand, with the fretting Sanhedrin on the other, comes across as pathetically ludicrous. *This* is a mass movement liable to start a war against Rome? The Sanhedrin is losing sleep over *these* guys? We would have to see Caiaphas as suffering from the worst kind of Nixonian paranoia.

"Hosanna" is an old Hebrew acclamation shouted in worship. It is a call to God and seems to mean "Save now!" In the gospels, it is what the crowd cries out at the entry of Jesus to the city of Jerusalem. That is what the Sanhedrin is overhearing. It is a living "Exhibit A" for Caiaphas to use in making his case.

The crowd hails Jesus not as "King of Israel" (John 12:13; cf., Luke 19:38) or "Son of David" (Matthew 21:9), but rather simply as "Superstar." Again, characters in the play are speaking from the perspective of the twentieth century. They are not speaking their own minds, but are made to mouth an outside observer's view of them, as if a pious person were to say, "I'm a fanatic for Jesus," or "I'm all wrapped up in Orthodox Jewish legalism!" (—Though it is not uncommon in socio-religious history for a group to adopt what had been a mocking taunt as a proud badge: Moonies, Methodists, Queer Nation.) More about this in a moment.

Listen to that howling mob of blockheads in the street!

Annas' contemptuous words come directly from John 7:49, "This mob that knoweth not the Law is accursed!" (Rice has xeroxed this line for "Then We Are Decided," where Annas calls Jesus' adoring fans "these imbeciles.") The pejorative word "mob" weights the scales already, implying a ticking bomb of a crowd, just waiting for the signal to go off.

A trick or two with lepers and the whole town's on its feet

Just as in John, the principal scriptural source of *Superstar*, the ovation given Jesus on his entry into Jerusalem is the result of his miraculous healings. In John, the miracle in question is the resurrection of Lazarus. Rice has substituted for this another miracle possibly implied in the Mark/Matthew version of the anointing story. Just as John had the anointing occur during a dinner with Jesus as the guest of honor in the home of Lazarus, the beneficiary of his miracle, may we infer from Mark/Matthew that the dinner honoring Jesus at the house of Simon the Leper was a token of gratitude for Jesus having healed his leprosy? Any way you look at it, Simon cannot have still been a leper, or no one would have attended this little soiree! Victims of "leprosy" (anyone with psoriasis would have qualified) were considered ritually unclean and to be avoided till certified as cured. Maybe it was Jesus who cured him. And so Simon the Leper (as Radar said to Hawkeye who had just called him "Stinky," "A name like that kind of sticks to a fellow, sir!") may have been another, more modest, version of Lazarus before the legend grew to that of a full-fledged resurrection.

John Dominic Crossan[91] believes that when it says Jesus raised the dead, it actually meant that he accepted lepers and other "untouchables" and social outcasts. He saved them from the living death of being pariahs. Similarly, Barbara Thiering[92] ventures the theory that Jesus had rescinded the excommunication of his compatriot Lazarus and welcomed him back into the fellowship of the Qumran Essenes, a move highly displeasing to the supreme council of that body, who then engineered his death.

He is dangerous

No one's doubting that!

Jesus Christ Superstar-tell us that you're who they say you are

The mob calls on Jesus to stop teasing them. Much in the spirit of the devotees of the late Lubavitcher Rebbe Menachem Mendel Schneerson, Jesus' followers feel sure that Jesus is the messiah (and more), but he says nothing explicitly either to confirm or to deny it. We think of a similar passage in John: "How long will you keep us in suspense? If you are the Christ, tell us plainly!" (John 10:24). And that is precisely what he refuses to do. Notice that Jesus' enemies will badger him with the same question: Caiaphas, Herod, and Pilate will all ask him to acknowledge or repudiate the claims made on his behalf. And he will give none of them satisfaction. Nor can it be taken as cowardice. True, a clear affirmation would send him to the gallows, but he is obviously headed there anyway. A clear denial might well have spared him, though at the cost of his followers abandoning him in disillusionment (which is exactly what happened to most of the followers of the seventeenth-century messiah Sabbatai Sevi who had boasted that he would get the Turkish sultan to convert to Judaism but wound up renouncing Judaism to embrace Islam when threatened with martyrdom!).

On another level, we must remark the element of sustained mystery that is so effective both dramatically and theologically. Here we have the never-dispelled numinous chill of the fantastic. If the question were resolved either way, Jesus is the Christ, Jesus is not the Christ, we would lose the aura of awesome possibility, and both the story and the fearful charm of Jesus would collapse. If Jesus is merely one more scripture-thumping hack from Galilee, the story switches over to the uncanny, a tale which has mystery—until we see the man behind the curtain. If Jesus is the messiah, then it's off into the marvelous, where miracles must be accepted as the ground rules of a redefined universe—but by the same token they are rendered mundane, to be taken for granted.

But, no, Jesus keeps us guessing, because that is the only way he can maintain his religious mystique. Like a candidate for president. He only seems to be a bearer of new hope as long as he has not entered the Oval Office yet. As soon as he sits behind the desk it's over. Now he must disappoint, since reality can never measure up to fond hopes. In the same way, the mythic figure of a Messianic Deliverer is by definition a metaphor for *future* hope, a hope that by definition can never arrive! As it says in Romans 8:24, "Who 'hopes' for what he sees?" In the harsh world of reality, it will be crushed by gravity. Jesus can only remain the messiah by *not* claiming to be messiah! He can only be messiah for as long as he does not announce himself as such. He can only be the bearer of hope, the incarnation of hope, as long he remains the object of hope, future hope. The excitement around Jesus was generated by the thought that he *might* well be the Christ himself (John 4:29, "Can this be the Christ?" John 7:25–27, 31: "When the messiah comes, will he do more signs than this man?").

Jürgen Moltmann was right: the essence of messianic religion is not faith but rather hope.[93] Faith only becomes needful when a supposed messiah has stepped out of the holy zone of hope, the future, and touched down in the present. Even though Jesus is present to his contemporaries, his messiahship remains in the future so long as he has not announced it or acknowledged it. He is still at least a few moments into the future, the zone in which messiahship can exist, as long as his possible announcement has not been made. Till then he remains surrounded by the mysterious aura of what H.P. Lovecraft called "adventurous expectancy."

The man is in town right now to whip up some support

This anonymous priest has a brilliant gift for stating the obvious. He seems to picture Jesus on the lines of a presidential hopeful glad-handing the yokels in advance of Super Tuesday. On one level, that is surely a misunderstanding. The mission of Jesus in *Superstar* has not one thing to do with worldly politics. But on another level, it is a shrewd perception. It reinforces Rice's delicate picture of Jesus' movement: its true character is not "revealed by (or to) flesh and blood" (Matthew 16:17), but the form it takes here on earth as a social and historical reality is that of a mass movement with a charismatic leader, whether a political one or of a segment of Rock fandom.

A rabble-rousing mission that I think we must abort

Another nameless priest seconds that statement but adds that understanding it right is not enough. The support Jesus is apparently trying whip up is among the shiftless surly rabble, the dregs, "worthless fellows," as the Bible calls such people. And these, the proletarians and untouchables, are the natural enemies of any aristocracy. Peasant revolt will in fact erupt into a revolutionary reign of terror in a few decades, so their instincts are sound. And in contrast to the pessimistic Pharisees of John 12:19 who see the Triumphal Entry and decide to throw in the towel, the Sanhedrin here feels that it is not yet too late. They may yet "abort" it; i.e., it is still aborning, not ready to do its destined harm.

Look Caiaphas they're right outside our yard

The first of the priests who has just commented speaks again: they're too close for comfort! Maybe it's later than we think! Like Cyrus' invading armies, they've breached our stronghold before we even knew they were here!

Quick Caiaphas-go call the Roman guard

This would not have been hard to do, since Roman peace keepers were garrisoned just down the street in the Antonia fortress. In fact, there were more than usual stationed there during Passover season for fear of revolutionary outbreaks exploding during this traditional celebration of the liberation of Jews from Egypt. The panicked reaction of this, the other anonymous priest (in other words, any priest, speaking as the voice of the whole group), perfectly typifies the underlying factor that invited revolutions in the first place: the collusion between the foreign occupying power and the Jewish leaders. These not-so-strange bed fellows are strikingly parallel to the relationship between American oil interests and the dictators of the Arab states who oppress their own populations and get rich off the profits of selling oil to the United States. The Arab popular resistance takes the form of terrorism for the same reasons bandits and messiah-kings fomented revolt against Rome—there was no use looking to their own governments to take action against foreign oppressors, since Caiaphas and the modern oil sheikhs are in bed with them.

No wait-we need a more permanent solution to our problem . . .

Caiaphas will not settle for something so mild as calling in the riot police to disperse a crowd of trouble-makers. That's like chasing a serpent back into its hole. It will only reemerge more deadly next time. The thing to do is to kill it now, though he leaves them to put two and two together and discover the Final Solution for themselves.

What then to do about this Jesus of Nazareth
Miracle wonderman-hero of fools?

In the original libretto, Annas really does not know what to suggest. He plays a role similar to that of Peter in the gospels, saying the wrong thing or asking a naive question like a straight man in a comedy dialogue, feeding lines to the star. If, however, we try to reinterpret these lines in light of "Then We Are Decided," we have to take Annas to be feigning befuddlement so as to prime the pump and get somebody to say what needs to be said, so it will not appear to come from himself or Caiaphas. The Sanhedrin members will more likely approve the plan if it seems to have emerged from their own ranks, not imposed from the top by the high priest.

Annas implies that Jesus is the hero of fools only because he was able to wow them with miracles, presumably fake ones, as in Caiaphas' earlier reference to "a trick or two with lepers." This line of attack to discredit Jesus' exorcisms is broached in Mark 3:22; Matthew 12:24; Luke 11:15, where skeptics assure the gaping crowds that it is all cheap magical conjuring: "It is only by invoking Beelzebul, prince of demons, that he is able to cast out demons."

An interesting issue arises here, namely that, though Christians have always been eager to try to prove Jesus' messiahship by appealing to his miracles, he himself is shown disparaging the idea of basing faith on miracles (John 4:48; Luke 16:27–31; Mark 8:11–12) if for no other reason than that false prophets can manage such feats, too (Mark 13:22).

No riots, no army, no fighting, no slogans

A priest marvels upon reflection how Jesus has been able to secure such an impressive following already and without the use of any of the traditional methods, whether political or military. Here is a glimmer of anticipation of Jesus' reply to Pontius Pilate, especially in the Johannine original: "My kingdom is not of this world; if it were, then my servants would fight to forestall my being handed over to the Jews" (18:36). In *Superstar* it becomes "I have got no kingdom in this world," with somewhat different implications, as we will see later.

Another of the strange reinterpretations in the movie is that the priest addresses this line to Caiaphas, as if to warn *him* not to use such measures as these *against Jesus*! Not likely. A riot is the last thing they want. Indeed, that's the whole point.

One thing I'll say for him-Jesus is cool

How so? Not "way cool," but rather "cool as a cucumber." That is, he uses subtler methods of winning support than any of the crude conventional ones the priest has just listed. And yet, later on, in the trial, Caiaphas will accuse Jesus of pamphleteering.

Caiaphas admires Jesus as a clever, perhaps even a worthy, adversary. But that is precisely what makes him so exceedingly dangerous. His influence is insidious, not overt. And this is why they must act now even if it may not seem like things have reached a state of crisis. The son of man comes like a thief in the night.

We dare not leave him to his own devices
His half-witted fans will get out of control

Again Annas derides the followers of Jesus who must ipso facto be nit-wits or they wouldn't be following him in the first place! We might be tempted to think the same of PTL Club members, Pat Robertson supporters, Christian Coalition and Moral Majority brownshirts.

If Jesus is allowed to continue his activities unchecked (cf., "We've let him go his way before" in "Then We Are Decided"), things will boil over. His true believers will "get out of control"—whose? Out of the control of the government? In a revolt? Yes, certainly. But maybe it is implied here that the fans of Jesus will spin out of Jesus' own control, as in the scene in *The Last Temptation of Christ* (film version) where Jesus is preaching salvation for the poor and doom for the rich, and some over-eager listeners jump up and run after a fleeing rich man, and Jesus cries, "Wait a minute! I didn't say anything about killing! I said love!" It seems, after all, that to some extent this has already happened, since someone seems to be making extravagant claims on Jesus' behalf that are rapidly getting him into deep trouble. This seems to be what Judas was alarmed by, as he said in "Heaven on their Minds": "All your followers are blind! Too much heaven on their minds! And they'll [the authorities] crush us if we go too far." Annas is thinking the same thing exactly. Funny how their pragmatic assessments neatly coincide. "Annas, you're a friend; I know you sympathize!")

But how can we stop him? His glamour increases
By leaps every minute-he's top of the poll

From this quizzical remark by another priest, one might imagine oneself in a tactics meeting of a trailing candidate's campaign committee. How can they undermine a rival candidate? Or, worse yet, it sounds like a meeting of mainline denominational officials bemoaning their decline in the face of fundamentalist sects. On such occasions one feels compelled to jump to one's feet and shout, "It's *you*! *Look* at you! *You're* the reason we're slipping!" Fools will follow the fool who rushes in where angels fear to tread. By definition, moderation does not attract zealots. Zealots attracts zealots. Even so, Mark explained that Jesus' popularity arose from the fact that "he taught with authority, not like their scribes," whose every ruling was carefully put through the dialectical strainer.

This may all be true, but as Caiaphas will thunder forth presently, the real problem is much more grave than who's ahead in the Nielsen Ratings. But the priest's remark is fundamental for understanding the premise of the whole rock opera. Henry Hewes, who reviewed the Broadway version of *Superstar* for *Nation* came nearer to this critical insight than anyone else:

> The new rock opera *Jesus Christ Superstar* begins promisingly as if it were going to look back in anger at all the negative results of merchandizing Jesus as a supernatural hero whose crucifixion justifies our acceptance of pain and poverty as the necessary path to an eternal paradise . . . Unfortunately, neither the lyrics of Tim Rice nor the music of Andrew Lloyd Webber sustain the original concept very consistently . . . The crucifixion itself shifts back to the show's original unfulfilled concept, the grotesque tragedy of myth-making. There we see Jesus impaled on a gold triangle [unlike the movie, where it is a traditional cross] that is spectacularly pushed forward to rebuke the audience for the vulgar myth they enjoy and evidently prefer to a real man of wisdom and compassion who should have been allowed to continue his good work until a ripe old age.[94]

I am not sure where Hewes judged Rice and Weber to have strayed from the path, but I do think he correctly pegged the tendency of *Superstar*, though Rice might not put it precisely the same way. But it is true that the rock opera implies radical criticism of traditional and popular Christianity on two levels. First, there is the scathing treatment of Jesus fandom as superficial, bubble-headed, wrongly directed—pretty much everything Judas and Annas say about it. The same kind of enthusiasm outlasted the Jesus groupies and hangers-on and has survived through the ages as a Jesus personality cult. (Indeed, Hewes himself seems to echo Annas' sentiments about the "vulgar" half-wits in the Broadway audience.) When we are told that no one can be "saved" without having a "personal relationship with Jesus Christ," we are in the theological equivalent of the Elvis cult. Even the Epistle to the Romans sees it this way. "Through him we have obtained access to this grace in which we stand" (Romans 5:2). Compare this to the picture drawn in John 19:16,

"So the other disciple [John? Judas?], who was known to the high priest, went out and spoke to the maid who kept the door, and brought Peter in." It's okay; he's with me. It's not what you know, it's who you know.

Second, *Superstar* carefully refrains from providing or even implying any understanding of Jesus as an atoning sacrifice, a saving event. Bultmann[95] once wrote that Christian faith ought to renounce all theological speculation on how the death of Jesus saves, because the danger is that we will come to require acceptance of a particular theory of the atonement before one can qualify for salvation. That would be salvation by "cognitive works," not by the existential faith in God as the open future. If you could boil it down and explain it, account for it, then the formula of salvation would lie well within the grasp of human resources. But this is a case where our reach must needs exceed our grasp, since we are reaching for the arms of a rescuer who must meet us more than half-way.

Superstar is saying something like this, though strictly speaking, salvation is nowhere up for consideration. But it does hold up the destiny of Jesus, the enigma that even he could not solve, as a factor serving to elevate his actions and motives above worldly aims and calculations. As the resurrected Judas, not damned for all time after all, will say, the mystery of Jesus remains a mystery. He was not merely a product of the superstar industry like a thousand other flash-in-the-pan celebrities, though many could see nothing higher or deeper in him because they themselves were "shallow, thick, and slow." Nor was he something so understandable, however *outré*, as a god masquerading in human flesh. That is a comfortable category that domesticates mystery by reducing it to cartoonish myth. The question, the case, remains open.

> **I see bad things arising-the crowd crown him king**
> **which the Romans would ban**
> **I see blood and destruction, our elimination because of one man**
> **Blood and destruction because of one man**

Thus far, none of the council members has voiced more than general concern. They seem to see something ominous, but not acute danger (no more than Pilate will). Thus at last Caiaphas cuts to the chase and tells what he sees on the horizon. The phrase "I see . . ." is purposely reminiscent of the language of the oracle, the fortune teller, the prophet, as if Caiaphas is reporting on the shapes taking form in a crystal ball. This need mean no more than that Caiaphas is a particularly shrewd interpreter of events. Able to see more subtle factors, he can discern better than most how things are to unfold. This is what we (or somebody!) pay futurists for.

Tim Rice has taken the idea from John 11:51, "He did not say this of his own accord, but being high priest that year he prophesied that Jesus should die for the nation," etc. It is admittedly strange for John to be crediting the scheming Caiaphas with a genuine prophecy, but then this is just a reflection of the double attitude most Jews held toward the high priest. The office must be respected, while the occupant might be despised (cf. Acts 23:1–5). Matthew 23:2–3 shows the same attitude: "The scribes and Pharisees sit on Moses' seat, so pay heed to and practice what they say. But do not imitate them, for they do not practice what they preach." In the same way, today's Roman Catholics may have stark disagreements with certain policies or statements of the Pope and yet feel bound to hearken to his decrees on the rare occasion he speaks *ex Cathedra*, from the throne of Peter, with apostolic authority.

And though that is doubtless the implied theology, the literary function of John's comment is simply to say, "He spoke more truly than he knew." More irony, since the Christian reader of John's gospel knows that Jesus' death was for the sake of the nation in an altogether different way than the short-sighted Caiaphas intended. As Joseph had said to his betrayers, "You meant it for evil, but God meant it for good" (Genesis 50:20).

What Caiaphas says in this stanza has served for the basis of the earlier song (earlier in sequence in the movie version, but actually added subsequently) "Then We Are Decided." Again we read about the danger that the Romans will get fed up. The rebels crowning Jesus King of the Jews will push them too far, and the Roman legions will sweep over the land like a flood, carrying both temple and priesthood with it, as indeed happened some forty years later.

> **Because, because, because of one man**
> **Our elimination because of one man**
> **Because, because, because of one,**
> > **'cause of one, 'cause of one man**

The three lines, the first and third sung by the whole Sanhedrin, the second by Caiaphas, simply demonstrate that all are now in agreement as to the danger they face. All that remains on the table is the hard part . . .

What then to do about this Jesusmania?

So what next?, asks a priest, as if there can be more than one answer.

How do we deal with a carpenter king?

According to the original libretto, we must take Annas' worried question here to be sincere, denoting that he has not arrived at the ruthless clarity of Caiaphas. If we follow the movie version, we have to see Annas as feigning ignorance, posing as a confused and worried Sanhedrinist desperate for a solution, helping to build this sentiment among the group, who will then be ready to accept whatever plan is offered them. He is priming the pump, trying to "whip up some support" for the preordained solution already decided by Caiaphas in the earlier, private, session.

The oxymoron "carpenter king" sums up what is so difficult in dealing with Jesus. He is no traditional rebel. Unlike Judas the Galilean, Athrongas, Menachem, and others, he does not employ as his weapons riots, armies, fighting, or slogans. Rather, as a peasant tradesman, he slowly builds a base of support brick by brick and board by board, a common man appealing to common men, and thus winning a following attached to himself by personal loyalty and love. This is a kind of Gandhian bloodless guerilla warfare, an effective "winning of hearts and minds."

Some listeners, with esoteric or Masonic leanings[96] might be tempted to read a deeper significance into the epithet "carpenter king," namely a reference to Hiram, king of Tyre, who served King Solomon as chief architect in building the Jerusalem temple in the tenth century B.C.E. and, some speculate, encoding its design with occult wisdom. It has been argued that when Jesus was hailed as Son of David after exorcizing demons, he was being hailed as another Solomon, the great sorcerer-king.[97] But a Hiram-Solomon-Jesus connection would seem far-fetched. And certainly there is no reason to read in such a meaning here.

Where do we start with a man who is bigger
Than John was when John did his baptism thing?

Another priest confesses himself equally baffled. He doesn't see how they can do other than start from scratch. He has not the slightest idea how to respond to such a cleverly covert program on the part of Jesus. If it were an overt military threat, that would be different, but this! Anybody have any ideas?

At the beginning of John's gospel we have a scene implicitly alluded to here. When John is building his own following, baptizing people in the Jordan, the chief priests send a delegation of inquisitors to determine precisely what he is claiming. John answers, "I am not the Christ," if that's what you're afraid of. "What then? Are you Elijah?" This prophet's second advent was believed by some to signal the end of the age. "I am not." "Are you the Prophet?" Many, especially Samaritans, expected not a royal Davidic messiah, but rather a latter-day successor of Moses, based on Deuteronomy 18:15–16. Centuries later, the Prophet Muhammad stepped forth to take this role. "And he answered, 'No.'" They are running out of alternatives. They want to be able to pigeon-hole him, not necessarily so they can accept his claim, but just so they can know what kind of dangerous imposter they're dealing with (just like King Herod in Matthew 2:3–8). So they ask, "Who are you? Let us have an answer for those who sent us. What do you say about yourself?" He answers, "I am the voice of one crying in the wilderness, 'Make straight the way of the Lord,' as the prophet Isaiah said." So for John, the issue is not his identity, for he has no title, but rather his function, to fulfil prophecy. Barbara Thiering suggests that "The Voice" was indeed a prophetic title, implying something like the one inspired to rightly interpret the prophetic texts of the Bible to the Essene community. She makes John the Baptizer the same as the Teacher of Righteousness, the guru of the Dead Sea Scrolls brotherhood.[98] John did eventually attract too much attention for his own good, at length arousing the suspicion and hostility of Herod Antipas (the "King Herod" of *Superstar*), who imprisoned him and subsequently beheaded him, forever silencing "the Voice." As far as we know, the Sanhedrin had nothing to do with it.

Whence the note that Jesus had become more popular than John had been at the height of the latter's fame? This comes from John 3:22–30; 4:1–3. One of the Gospel of John's major departures from the earlier gospels is in the relative chronology of John and Jesus. Following Mark 1:14, Matthew and Luke have Jesus begin his public ministry just after John's imprisonment, as if to take up the banner from his fallen comrade. But John's gospel has Jesus start his activity while John the Baptist is still at large. In fact John's gospel imagines Jesus baptizing converts just as John did. "Jesus was making and baptizing more disciples than John (although Jesus himself did not baptize, but only his disciples)" (John 4:1–2).

There is evidence to indicate that following John the Baptizer's death, some baptized by him decided he was the messiah. There was competition between John's posthumous sect and Jesus' over who had been the true messiah. John's sect may well survive today, in a much evolved form, as the Gnostic sect of the Mandaeans or Nazoreans who live in Iraq. They venerate John as a prophet and denounce Jesus as a deceiver and a false messiah.

It is very likely that some of Luke's and John's statements about the Baptizer have been shaped so as not to give any aid and comfort to the John sect, to keep the John character safely within Christian bounds (c.f., Matthew 11:11–15/Luke 7:28–30; a Hebrew version of Matthew preserves the original wording, lacking the interpolation which served to cut John down to size: "Nevertheless, I tell you, he who is of least repute in the kingdom of heaven is greater than John.").[99] Similarly, John 4:1–2, the note about Jesus conducting a more successful baptizing mission than John, is an anachronism squeezed in clumsily to remind the readers of the gospel that in their day Christianity was numerically much greater than the antiquated and shrinking John the Baptizer sect.

It is all too reminiscent of the boast of another John, John Lennon, that "We're more popular than Jesus Christ," a remark that goaded the pious to fury (like that attributed to the stone-hefting Pharisees!) simply because it hit a nerve. It was too close to the truth. Some of these ecclesiastics must have smiled gratefully when Mark David Chapman dispatched this jaded mandarin for them. "What do you think you are? A superstar? Well, right you are!" One delightful bit of irony that might have been: at one point, Rice was hoping to get John Lennon to play the role of Jesus in the Broadway version. "We felt Lennon would be ideal . . . He is sincere in his efforts for peace—at least he is trying to do something."[100]

The anachronistic nature of the gospel scenario of John and Jesus engaged in friendly competition is clearly admitted in the back-peddling proviso that of course it was not Jesus himself who immersed people, but rather his disciples. In other words: it didn't really happen in Jesus' own time. It was his successors who borrowed the practice of baptism and did it in their master's name. Equally anachronistic is the notion of Jesus and John already enlisting members for some kind of church, organizations that would have come into existence only after their deaths. In their lifetimes, both men were more like wandering preachers exhorting fellow synagogue-going Jews, not evangelistic recruiters.

Nonetheless, Rice has taken the text about both baptizing at face value, and it comes in handy here. John had already been enough to throw a good scare into the authorities (Mark 11:30–32). And in the end they hadn't had to make any decision about him; Herod Antipas had saved them the trouble. Now they were caught up short! What are we going to do *this* time?

> **Fools! You have no perception!**
> **The stakes we are gambling are frighteningly high!**
> **We must crush him completely-**
> **So like John before him, this Jesus must die**
> **For the sake of the nation this Jesus must die.**

All his followers are blind. Only Caiaphas can see where they all soon will be—unless swift and deadly action be taken now.

The metaphor, "The stakes we are gambling," originally (in the libretto) referred simply to the decisive situation in which they now find themselves. Any action they take will be a throw of the dice. Hence the care taken to choose the best available option, since there will likely be no second chance. But the movie's addition of "Then We Are Decided" reinterprets the gambling metaphor. Now "we are gambling" refers to continuous, habitual action, their usual practice of ignoring the problem and hoping it will go away. This in itself has caused the present danger, since it has allowed the threat to grow to more dangerous proportions in the meantime. It has brought us to this point.

Annas' advice in "Then We Are Decided," when he says, "But don't rely on subtlety. Frighten them or they won't see," was intended as the loop by which to hang that song onto the peg provided by this one: "The stakes we are gambling are frighteningly high." It brings us back to the original juncture.

"For the sake of the nation this Jesus must die." Caiaphas is thinking of political expediency, something made even more clear in the Johannine original: "You know nothing at all [= "you have no perception"]; you do not understand that it is expedient that one man should die for the people, and that whole nation should not perish" (John 11:49–50). John, as we have seen, sees this as a great irony: the joke is on Caiaphas. But in fact, there is not so great a gap between what Caiaphas says and the martyr theology of Hellenistic Jews. In 2 and 4 Maccabees we read of the terrible persecution of Jews who defied Antiochus IV's prohibition of Judaism. As they die, two of these heroes pray that God may accept their spilt blood (obviously not shed for any sin of their own, since they are dying in witness to their faith) as an expiation washing away the sins of Israel, which they suppose have led to this persecution. In this way the debt may be paid and perhaps God will call off the Seleucid tyrants.

> **Must die, must die, this Jesus must die**
> **So like John before him, this Jesus must die**
> **Must die, must die, this Jesus must, Jesus must, Jesus must die!**

These three lines, divided between all the priests (first and third) and Caiaphas (second) simply tell in shorthand that the whole body has fallen in line with his thinking with nary a note of dissent.

> **Hosanna Heysanna Sanna Sanna Ho**
> **Sanna Hey Sanna Ho Sanna**

This jaunty rendering of the Palm Sunday acclamation "Hosanna!" strings the shout out into a long refrain by means of the children's ditty called "The Name Game," which goes: "Banana Fana Fo Fana, Fee Fie Fo *Fana-Banana!*" Something like this becomes necessary simply in order to depict the scene, instead of scantily summarizing it as the gospels do. The duration of narrative time is by definition greater in a scene than in a summary, so the narrator must pad out the scene with more detail, more dialogue, more description.

> **Hey JC, JC won't you smile at me?**
> **Sanna Ho Sanna Hey Superstar**

Like the parallel refrain below, the point here is to demonstrate the adulation which makes Jesus into a pop superstar. It is just what disturbed Judas so much; the focus has shifted dangerously. Jesus himself has come to matter more than the things he says. The crowds render him fan worship, like Madonna wanna-bes or Trekkies. The Jesus movement has become a mere personality cult.

> **Tell the rabble to be quiet we anticipate a riot**
> **This common crowd is much too loud**
> **Tell the mob who sing your song that they are fools**
> **and they are wrong**
> **They are a curse, they should disperse**

As anticipated above, Rice has here combined the Johannine and Matthean/Lukan versions of the Sanhedrin's disdain for the followers of Jesus. The specific urging for him to silence the crowd matches Luke 19:39, "The whole multitude of the disciples began to rejoice and to praise God, saying, 'Blessed is the king who comes in the name of the Lord! Peace in heaven and glory in the highest!' And some of the Pharisees in the multitude said to him, 'Teacher, rebuke your disciples!'" Matthew 21:15–16 is quite similar: "When the chief priests and the scribes saw the wonderful things that he did, and the children crying out in the temple, 'Hosanna to the Son of David,' they were indignant; and they said to him, 'Do you not hear what these are saying?'" (Then why are you letting them continue?)

John's version of the Sanhedrin's disdain for the crowd occurs earlier in his chronology, but remember, this only reflects his expansion of the passion narrative backward through the whole extent of the gospel. All the little scenes in which the reader eavesdrops on the Sanhedrin (John 7:45–52; 11:45–53; 12:19 which does occur coincident with the Triumphal Entry) seem to be components of one original council scene such as Tim Rice has recombined. John 7:49 says, "This crowd who do not know the Law [else they should never fall for Jesus!] is accursed." This comment Rice has spliced together with the demands in Matthew and Luke for Jesus to shut them up.

Why should they think Jesus would want to silence them? In Matthew and Luke it is plain that they do not hold Jesus accountable (not yet, anyway) for the improprieties of his followers. Their rhetorical questions imply that surely Jesus must see what is wrong in their cries. It is the content of what they are shouting, not the volume of it, that disturbs the curators of the temple. What they seem to be disturbed by is the identification of Jesus as the Son of David, the destined messianic king who will overthrow the Romans. It is not that they don't wish to see the advent of the messiah. It is just that they cannot imagine that this unimpressive Galilean might be he. Nor can they imagine that Jesus himself could countenance such wild talk either. Talk like that can be dangerous within Roman earshot. Surely Jesus doesn't want reprisals any more than they do.

In *Superstar* this is pretty much the attitude of Judas, at least for a while. He thought Jesus' half-witted fans might go out of control unless Jesus put a stop to the inflated claims they were spreading on his behalf. But then he began to see that Jesus himself was beginning to be taken in by their flattery, and there was no more help to be expected from that quarter.

But Caiaphas professes only to be concerned over the fact of the ruckus itself. He is afraid that the match of fan excitement may ignite the tinder of the dull-witted crowd who only need to behold their own numbers to get the itch to go on a destructive rampage. We might think of the way the peaceful rallies of Dr. King often became the occasions for rioting, as certain roustabouts on the fringes of the crowd, too obtuse to grasp King's gospel of nonviolence, boiled over into rioting. Many Southerners, (I remember all too well, being a child in Mississippi at the time), already unsympathetic with King's message of equality, were only too happy to hold him responsible for the carnage, though in a real sense, he was the main victim of it! Again, remember Jesus in *The Last Temptation of Christ*: "Wait a minute! I didn't say kill! I said love!"

For the Sanhedrin to make such an appeal to Jesus is to politely give him the benefit of the doubt, to make it easier for him to back down without losing face. "Of course, we don't hold *you* responsible! In fact, we're asking for your cooperation!"

Hosanna Heysanna Sanna Sanna Ho
Sanna Hey Sanna Ho Sanna
Hey JC. JC you're alright by me
Sanna Hey Sanna Ho Superstar

More of the herd's bellowing, as Caiaphas would call it. "You're alright by me" implies partisanship. Jesus is a figure of some controversy, but he's certainly okay with these people! This is a challenge to the Sanhedrin, and they know it.

Why waste your breath moaning at the crowd?
Nothing can be done to stop the shouting

Rice has transferred this much of Jesus' reply from John 12:19, the Pharisees' confession of impotence to reverse the course of events they see happening around them on Palm Sunday, "You see that you can do nothing; look, the world has gone after him."

If every tongue was still the noise would still continue
The rocks and stones themselves would start to sing:

This comes directly from Luke 19:40, "I tell you, if these were silent, the very stones would cry out." Matthew has something rather different at this point. As we have seen, it is the acclamation of the children that so upsets the authorities. And there Jesus' reply takes a different form: "Have you never read, 'Out of the mouths of babes and sucklings thou hast brought perfect praise'?" (Matthew 21:16). Jesus is pictured as quoting from Psalm 8:2. The trouble is that he is made to cite the mistranslated form in the Septuagint, the Greek version of the Jewish Bible used around the Mediterranean world. The Hebrew original translates like this, backing up half a verse, "Thou whose glory above the heavens is chanted *by the mouths of babes and infants* [= "sucklings"], *thou hast founded a bulwark* because of thy foes, to still the enemy and the avenger." The Hebrew wouldn't be relevant as a proof-text, only the Greek mistranslation, and there's just no way Jesus would be quoting the Greek version to the Jerusalem Sanhedrin scribes! This is Matthew's work. He has rewritten a scene (as he frequently does) from an obscure note in his sources. It was a source he shared with Luke, presumably the Q source, where the Triumphal Entry story had a reply of Jesus involving *ebeni*, Aramaic for "stones." Each gospel writer made what sense he could of the text. Luke produces the saying with the phrase "the very stones would cry out," while Matthew evidently suspected a typo and came up with "out of the mouths of babes," *beni*, "sons" in Hebrew. Whole stories in the Bible seem to have come from etymological guesswork of this kind. Though Tim Rice passed Matthew's version by, the movie version does include it by placing young children among the Palm Sunday crowd. Now you know why.

Hosanna Heysanna Sanna Sanna Ho
Sanna Hey Sanna Ho Sanna
Hey JC, JC won't you fight for me?
Sanna Hey Sanna Ho Superstar

Jesus' last line ended with a colon in the libretto, "sing:" In other words, they will sing what follows in the present stanza. And the libretto's notes make clear what the listener cannot readily pick out, that Jesus himself joins in the chorus.

This is rather surprising, since the third line raises a volatile new note, "Won't you fight for me?" This is what the Sanhedrin feared was in the offing. It was implied in Matthew, Luke and John, where the crowd hails Jesus as King Messiah. In John there is also the earlier scene in which the miracle-bedazzled crowd decides Jesus would make a good figurehead for a peasant revolt. But there he recoiled at the idea and, so to speak, took it on the lam of God (John 6:15). Now he himself takes up the song at just the most dangerous part! Why? Thus far, Rice has given us no solid evidence for any revolutionary aims of Jesus. And in just a moment, in "Simon Zealotes," he will explicitly repudiate the whole notion. So what's going on here?

I think the key is in the note of inevitability: "nothing can be done to stop the shouting." This may sound as if he is saying the popular adulation is just too great; they will not listen even to Jesus himself. As in *The Life of Brian* when reluctant messiah Brian of Nazareth tries to reason with the crowd: "Look . . . you've got it all wrong. You don't need to follow me. You don't need to follow anybody. You've got to think for yourselves. You're all individuals." The reply comes back from hundreds of mouths but in a single voice: "Yes, we're all individuals . . ."[106]

But this is another of those double entendres, so characteristic of John's gospel as well as of Rice's redaction of it. Jesus means that the train of his secret destiny is chugging resistlessly on to its undisclosed destination, and this is part of the route. No matter what trouble it will get him into, no matter how misconceived the crowd's shouting, it has to be. He can vary from the path neither to the left nor to the right. And, as for the singing, if you can't beat 'em, join 'em.

"Hosanna" continues through a few more lines in the movie version. Instead of joining in, Jesus sings something else to the crowd. It is, in fact, almost as if he is acceding to the request of Caiaphas! He tries to change the focus, to take the spotlight off himself and shine it on the audience, as when an Oscar winner dutifully refuses any credit and thanks "all of you" instead. Here are the added lines:

Sing me your songs but not for me alone
Sing out for yourselves for you are blessed
There is not one of you who cannot win the kingdom
The slow, the suffering, the quick, the dead

It is tempting to speculate whether these lyrics, vaguely reminiscent of the Matthean Sermon on the Mount (chapters 5–7) were not added to fend off the impression given of Jesus being an ego-maniac, an impression many received from the earlier version. Here he shows he is still concerned with others at least as much as himself. It is not himself as king that should matter to them, but rather the kingdom of God to which all of these humble people are the heirs. The third and fourth lines reflect nothing in John's gospel but rather a Q saying used in Matthew 11:5–5 and Luke 7:22, "The blind receive their sight and the lame [=″the slow″] walk, lepers are cleansed, and the deaf hear, and the dead are raised up, and the poor have good tidings announced to them." Presumably the tidings are the news of the nearness of the approaching Kingdom of God. That great blessing is especially for these, "the least of his brethren," with no one any longer left out, like the street derelict Lazarus who spent his monotonous days in the gutter outside the rich man's mansion (Luke 16:18–21 ff.).

This new verse also anticipates the scene in which Jesus is ambushed by a crowd of lepers and demoniacs who, we must suppose, had taken these words as an open invitation to come up and join the healing line.

Hey Sanna Ho Sanna Sanna Sanna Hey
Sanna Hey Sanna Hosanna
Hey JC, JC would you die for me?
Sanna Hey Sanna Ho Superstar

This stanza also appears only in the movie version. Jesus hears it and freezes, or at least the camera does (in a gimmick right out of a college sophomore film assignment).

The crowd does not anticipate the crucifixion as such, not even as the possible outcome of a failed revolution. It was, after all (according to the attractive suggestion of Geza Vermes)[107] the death of the failed messiah Simon bar-Kochba in 135 C.E. that gave rise to the widespread Jewish doctrine of a Messiah ben-Joseph who would die in battle against the heathen, after which time a second messiah, Messiah ben-David, would finish the task of national liberation. A failed messiah might still be a messiah, even if he must yield to a greater messiah to come. In the same way, Jesus' own death was construed as the first, saving stage of the messiah's career, to be followed by a second phase in which he would come as the roaring Lion of the Tribe of Judah. But the crowd has no thought of this.

No, their point seems to be to ask for Jesus' reassurance of loyalty to them. They have made sufficient protestations of their own undying love, and they will make more. But does their idol reciprocate their love? It is rather like the scene in John chapter 21 when the Risen Jesus questions Peter, "Do you love me?" Or the Last Supper pledges of Peter and the others, "Even if I must die with you, I will not deny you!" (Mark 14:31). "I will lay down my life for you!" (John 13:37). Only this time, the disciples require such commitment from Jesus. "Would you die for me?" He alone knows it is soon to come to exactly that.

Simon Zealotes

Christ you know I love you
Did you see I waved?
I believe in you and God
So tell me that I'm saved
Christ you know I love you
Did you see I waved?
I believe in you and God
So tell me that I'm saved
Jesus I am with you
Touch me touch me Jesus
Jesus I am on your side
Kiss me kiss me Jesus

The repetition in the words of the crowd drives home the fact that they are chanting in religious ecstasy. Here is the behavior which justifies Annas' term "Jesusmania." Mania is of course a dissociative state in which the individual is lifted up beyond himself, with the implication that it is not a higher, enlightened level that he has reached, but rather a cutting loose from rational self-control, and especially by way of absorption in a collective crowd mentality. Either way, normal judgment and normal inhibitions are vanquished. Euripides' play *The Bacchae* depicts the women of Thebes as having been overcome with a divine madness, understood by them as inspiration or possession by their Lord Dionysus. In a scene probably derived from *The Bacchae*, Luke shows the apostles swept away in glossolalic frenzy, speaking in tongues like the Oracle of Delphi. Peter regains his senses long enough to defend the crowds from the mockery of outside observers: "These are not drunk as you suppose: it is only nine in the morning!" (Acts 2:15; c.f., 1 Corinthians 14:23, "If . . . all speak in tongues, and outsiders or unbelievers enter, will they not say that you are mad?").

This is the way Jesus' disciples are being depicted in this song, as chanting Maenads for Jesus. They believe in Jesus and expect salvation; in other words, they speak in the very language of fundamentalist/Pentecostal pietism. Any political element we might have sensed in the song "Hosanna" has vanished. This is because the present song "Simon Zealotes" is taking a rather different approach. The idea will be that, even though Jesus' followers have no prior interest in political matters, their devotion might easily be turned in that direction, if only Jesus will see the political potential of the great power he commands. In the late 1970s Republican campaigners approached fundamentalist TV preacher Jerry Falwell and convinced him to marshal his credulous minions on behalf of partisan politics. Thus was the Moral Majority born. And Simon the Zealot has similar intentions.

> **Christ, what more do you need to convince you**
> **That you've made it and you're easily as strong**
> **As the filth from Rome who rape our country**
> **And who've terrorized our people for so long?**

Were the Romans as bad as all that? Not all of the time, though the tenure of Pontius Pilate was a singularly bad time for Jews. But many of the religious nationalists did not need a specific list of grievances. Rather it was the principle of the thing: the only rightful allegiance of Jews was to God, and certainly not to the Roman Empire. The famous episode of the coin rendered unto Caesar (Mark 12:13–17) presupposes this attitude. Jesus is asked if paying the denarius to Caesar in taxes represents idolatry or a lack of patriotism. That was certainly the position of the Zealots and those like them.

Simon speaks as if supposing that Jesus' reluctance to politicize his mission up to now has stemmed simply from an underestimation of his influence among the people. And the present show of support must be enough to allay any such doubts. It does not even occur to Simon that such thoughts may never have entered Jesus' mind. Not everyone thinks as Simon does, but like all "zealots" he cannot realize that. Everyone either thinks as he does—or ought to.

> **Did you see I waved?**
> **I believe in you and God**
> **So tell me that I'm saved**
> **Christ you know I love you**
> **Did you see I waved?**

I believe in you and God
So tell me that I'm saved
Jesus I am with you
Touch me touch me Jesus
Jesus I am on your side
Kiss me kiss me Jesus

Simon pauses for Jesus (and the listener) to hear again the cheering and chanting of the crowd, this time in a new light. See? There is power there.

There must be over fifty thousand
Screaming love and more for you
Every one of fifty thousand
Would do whatever you ask him to
Keep them yelling their devotion
But add a touch of hate at Rome
You will arise to a greater power
And we will win ourselves a home
You'll get the power and the glory
For ever and ever and ever
Amen! Amen!

Simon must be overestimating, but then statistics are always in the eye of the beholder. The magnitude of the cause makes the number seem greater, as when Elisha can see invisible angels encamped on the side of Israel (2 Kings 6:15–17). Their devotion is such that they would do anything Jesus asked. If the 900 of Jonestown would drink a deadly eucharist at their mad master's request, so would the devotees of Jesus shed the blood of others if he asked. But will he ask?

Note the cynical manipulation urged by Simon. He is a true politician who sees John Q. Public as the slave of Pharaoh but tries to keep him from seeing it himself. The vanguard of the proletariat knows best. In other words, Simon views the crowd exactly as Caiaphas does: an ignorant and potentially volatile mob, a source of great power to be manipulated to the advantage of some and the disadvantage of others. The Sanhedrin is afraid that Jesus thinks like Simon Zealotes.

Notice, too, that Simon Zealotes also shares the opinion of Judas on Jesus. He evidently feels he can manipulate Jesus to his political purposes as easily as Jesus can manipulate the crowd, by appealing to his own presumed lust for self-aggrandizement. "You will arise to a greater power . . . you'll get the power and the glory." It is as if he doubts that political liberation of his people means that much to Jesus, but he might be attracted to it if it were presented to him as a means to advance what he *is* (supposedly) primarily interested in, namely his own glorification. Judas was afraid Jesus would stumble blindly into a deadly confrontation with Rome by taking all the praise too seriously, letting it go to his head. Simon, on the other hand, is trying to engineer precisely this! Simon thinks there is a good chance to succeed. There, too, he is overestimating, as events will make all too clear some four decades hence.

John's gospel lacks any scene in which Satan attempts to tempt Jesus off his ordained path. But Simon the Zealot is His Satanic Majesty's stand-in here. He is only paraphrasing the devil's wily offer in Luke 4:5–7, "And the devil took him up and showed him all the kingdoms of the world in a moment of time, and said to him, 'To you I will give all this authority and their glory; for it has been delivered to me, and I give it to whom I will. If you, then, will swear fealty to me, it shall all be yours.'" In John's gospel, the temptation of a worldly power-grab is presented in a non-mythic form. It is the Galilean crowd who seek to take him by force and make him king (John 6:15).

Tim Rice wants to make the issue explicit by having an individual character appear before Jesus to make the offer in no uncertain terms, but it would destroy any semblance of reality to have the devil come on stage, so why not follow the lead of the gospels in a different place, and have a disciple take the unwitting role of the devil's mouthpiece? Mark makes Peter Satan when he tries to save Jesus from his fate (Mark 8:31–33; c.f., Matthew 16:21–23). John makes Judas "a devil" (6:70), so why not Simon Zealotes? He's certainly the man for the job if we're talking about politics.

How insidious of Simon to couch his offer in the words of the Lord's Prayer. "You'll get the power and the glory for ever and ever and ever." This line shifts smoothly from the words of the devil, "To you I will give all this authority (political power) and their glory," with the doxology of the Lord's Prayer as it appears in the King James Version, "Thine is the kingdom and the power and the glory for ever and ever. Amen." Only now the implicit prayer is addressed to Jesus, not to the heavenly Father. In the balance here is whether Jesus will become the Christ or the Antichrist.

The double Amen is appropriate for lyrics based on John, since, where the other gospels have Jesus preface many sayings with the single Amen

("Amen ["truly" or "verily"], I say unto you . . ."), John systematically changes the formula to "Amen, Amen, I say to you." The Jerusalem Bible is the only version to translate it literally like this.

It only remains to note that the movie version flubs this scene, adding silly choreography that would have been more at home in the purposely non-verisimilar *Godspell*. It looks as if Simon is conducting some kind of aerobics class in front of Jesus for his entertainment while he gives him political coaching. Jesus appears to be forcing a polite smile at the inane square dancing, waiting, like the viewer, for it to be over. And how could director Jewison imagine he was correctly depicting a scene in which a character points out to Jesus that at least fifty thousand people are right there cheering him on!

Poor Jerusalem

Neither you Simon, nor the fifty thousand
Nor the Romans, nor the Jews, nor Judas nor the Twelve,
Nor the Priests, nor the Scribes,
Nor doomed Jerusalem itself,
Understand what power is
Understand what glory is
Understand at all . . . understand at all

Jesus responds to Simon's exhortation, but, like Pilate later on, Simon would probably have to say, "That is not an answer!" Jesus essentially shoos away the Zealot's suggestion as being simply out of the question. Nor does he even attempt to explain why. The answer is a mystery that only he knows. Compare a parallel scene in Gibran's *Jesus the Son of Man*, when Judas has made a suggestion similar to that of *Superstar*'s Simon Zealotes: "Get you behind me, Satan. Think you that I came down the years to rule an ant-hill for a day? My throne is a throne beyond your vision. Shall he whose wings encircle the earth seek shelter in a nest abandoned and forgotten? Dare you tempt me with a crown of dross, when my forehead seeks the Pleiades, or else your thorns?"[108]

All this is certainly a faithful rendering of the gospels' picture of the ambitious disciples and their being utterly out of touch with Jesus' goals and priorities, unsuspecting of the hidden purpose that drives him on, sometimes almost against his will. Even Jesus himself does not quite understand the why of it, according to *Superstar*. And, though there are isolated gospel texts pointing in the direction Tim Rice has charted ("But of that day and that hour knoweth no man, nor the angels in heaven, nor even the Son, but the Father only," Mark 13:32), at this point we do have a key disjuncture between the rock opera and the gospels. In the latter, Jesus certainly does know the secret. In historical retrospect, as already suggested, Jesus' tragic fate has been transformed into a predestined plan of God, just because, if Jesus was truly the Christ, he *cannot* have been taken by surprise, overcome by unforeseen events. No, he must have been in control. The Gospel of John makes this clumsily clear in its arrest scene, where Jesus' merest word is enough to send the arresting guards toppling like tenpins, and yet he carries through the charade of being arrested, coming along quietly.

We find the same naive myth-making tendency running riot in later, apocryphal Infancy Gospels, where we read that Jesus, though trapped in an infant body, was already wise with the wisdom of the omniscient God and patiently condescended to the dull-witted mortals around him, including Mary and Joseph who come off sounding (already in the Gospel of Luke!) like a couple of typical sit-com nit-wit parents. The same tendency was early at work in Buddhist piety. Gotama the Enlightened became such an object of idolatrous veneration that Buddhists could no longer bring themselves to believe that he had ever been an ignorant mortal like themselves. So, they imagined, he had descended from the heavens in a human likeness, merely posing, first as a carefree dandy, then as an introspective seeker, a humble *chela* to other gurus, and finally as the discoverer of the Dharma. Don't be fooled: he knew it all the time.

In the same way, early Christians started by deciding, as the grieving often do, that God *must* have had *some* purpose in letting Jesus die. They proceeded to decide what that purpose must have been, i.e., to die as a sacrifice to purify the uncleanness of the Gentiles. They figured Jesus must have known that divine plan and been obedient to it. But then they essentially identified Jesus *with* that divine will. He becomes the wisdom of God incarnate. And his human life becomes a passion play, a sacred sham.

Superstar, itself a kind of passion play, must diverge right here, because Tim Rice knew there is no way to make what Todorov calls "the plot of predestination"[109] into a genuine drama. How can there be any real suspense? How can there be any narrative tension, if the protagonist already knows (and, worse yet, *tells the audience!*) what's going to happen? "Don't worry, folks! I've seen the script and I'll escape in the final reel!" Stanley Kauffmann, in *The New Republic*, saw the difficulty in his review of the Broadway version of *Superstar*. "The real agony manifested here was not that of Jesus but of Tom O'Horgan, the director, as he struggled to give drama to a story that, in its very being, is undramatic. The whole point of the Passion is that, though Jesus questioned, he did not struggle."[110]

Some early Christians believed Jesus did not die on the cross. Maybe someone took his place, Simon of Cyrene perhaps. Others believed it was an illusion created by God to hide the fact of an empty cross (as in *The Last Temptation of Christ*). Others believed it had indeed been Jesus up there on the cross, but that he had survived the ordeal, as some did. Other Christians (like the writer of the Gospel of John) thought such views endangered the doctrine of divine redemption through the cross. And yet to have Jesus die and stay dead only a couple of days is just a variation on the very same theme. Real deaths are, sadly, forever. And how can you take such a death as tragic?

Thus Rice has given Jesus a kind of resigned awareness that he is heading toward death, but, as the Gethsemane scene will show, hardly a detailed understanding of what it is all to accomplish. All he knows is that the mills of God grind slowly, and in ways mere mortals, such as Jesus himself, can never understand. Rice has, in effect, split the Jesus character right down the middle, almost in imitation of the traditional doctrine of the divine and human natures of Christ. In other words, there is a side of Jesus that is moving on an altogether different plane than his disciples. It is from that perspective that he speaks to Simon the Zealot, dismissing the latter's childish dreams and schemes. And yet there is another side to Jesus which is no more clued in, really, than the disciples about the necessity for his death. We will catch a hint of that in his lament over "doomed Jerusalem" in the next lines.

I believe that Tim Rice has in this fashion managed to provide the requisite element of drama. On the one hand Jesus is the one who leads the action along by creating the mystery that Judas (and the chorus: "Jesus Christ, Jesus Christ, Who are you? What have you sacrificed?"), speaking for all the others, seeks to penetrate: "Did you mean to die like that?" And on the other, Rice's Jesus is one of the mystified, following the call of the mystery within him to see how it will all turn out, and what it may turn out to mean. In a sense, Jesus is both the protagonist and his own antagonist.

Jesus knows quite well the fears, lusts and machinations of all those he catalogues here. He knows they are all playing a blind game in the dark. Simon the Zealot offers him the sure reward of power and glory? He doesn't know the first thing about them. What are power and glory? Nothing that any of them would seek if they knew what they were seeking, and nothing they, any more than he, can avoid.

The whole scene is in fact based on a similar one, already referred to, in Mark, where two of the disciples, James and John approach Jesus with a tall order: "Master, we want you to grant us whatever we may ask of you." Jesus replies, "And what is it you want?" They look at one another, and one speaks: "We want the seats of honor at your right and your left when you enter into your glory." Shaking his head, Jesus says to them, "You do not know what you are really asking! Are you able to drink the bitter cup I am going to drink? Are you ready to suffer the baptism of fire I am about to suffer?" These are rhetorical questions, assuming what the gospels elsewhere do not, that the two disciples understand what fate awaits Jesus in Jerusalem. Jesus seems to be saying that they can't hope simply to ride to power on his coat tails. One must gain such privilege the hard way, as he himself will do. But, cocksure, James and John are not about to back down. Looking at each other with a small note of worry, they nonetheless buck up, throw their chests out, and answer, "Indeed we can!" And with irony undetected by the poor fools, Jesus answers them, "As a matter of fact, you *will* undergo my cup of pain, my immersion in suffering. But I'm still afraid you're too late. The seats you want have already been spoken for" (my paraphrase of Mark 10:35–40).

There follows some basic reeducation. Jesus tells them just what sort of glory he will have. Then see if you still want a piece of it: "The son of man came not to be served, but rather to serve, even to give his life a ransom for many" (Mark 10:45). This is clearly the model for the Simon-Jesus exchange in "Simon Zealotes" and "Poor Jerusalem." Simon bids Jesus to seize power, so that his followers may share his glory. And Jesus pops his bubble: "You know not what you ask." (Later he will be saying the same thing in answer to a similar question from Pontius Pilate.)

> **If you knew all that I knew, my poor Jerusalem**
> **You'd see the truth, but you close your eyes**
> **While you live your troubles are many, poor Jerusalem**
> **To conquer death you only have to die**
> **You only have to die**

This portion of the song is based on Jesus' lament for Jerusalem as he is about to enter it, from Luke 19:41–44: "And when he drew near and saw the city he wept for it, saying, 'Would that even today you knew the things that make for peace! But now they are hid from your eyes. For the days will come upon you, when your enemies will cast up a bank about you and surround you, and hem you in on every side, and dash you to the ground, you and your children within you, and they will not leave one stone upon another in you; because you did not know the time of your visitation.'"

This theme of Jesus' true glory being death, the consummation of God's mysterious plan for him, is a major Johannine theme. Jesus speaks in John's gospel in a distinctive idiom of John's creation. It is an idiom filled with double meanings for the tuned-in reader. Jesus speaks of being "lifted up," of being "glorified," and, given the context, it often seems he is referring to his coming crucifixion (John 7:39; 8:28; 12:16, 23, 32, 34; 13:31–32; 17:5, 24). Apparently the ambivalence adds up to the idea that Jesus is soon to return to his long-vacant place of heavenly glory with the Father, and the manner of his exit will be his death on the cross, whether this anticipates postmortem appearances to his disciples or not. But some, especially in the Lutheran tradition, take John's point to be a *theologia crucis*, theology of the cross, which reverses all worldly distinctions and finds glory in self-sacrificing love. Joachim Kahl is one of the few to raise the question whether such a religious *summum bonum* is not really something more on the order of spiritual masochism.[111]

But Jung would certainly agree with the basic insight, at least as it is expressed in a more down to earth manner in the Mark 10 text: for the spiritually mature (a redundancy for Jung), glory is precisely in the serving of others, because one has transcended one's selfish ego to become a Self, an expanding circle with a center but no circumference any more. In serving others one is not setting aside his own interests in favor of the interests of others. Quite the contrary, one's "own" interests have expanded exponentially to *include* those of "others." Only they are no longer really perceived as others, but as parts of one's larger Self. It is only the ever-defensive ego, the childish bully, who finds glory in lording it over others.

What is it that Jesus knows that Jerusalem does not allow itself to recognize? In the Lukan original, the point of Jesus' apostrophic address to the Holy City seems to be that peace is within her grasp, if only she will see it. In Luke's terms, "peace" for Jerusalem means the coming of the Kingdom of God, the earthly golden age, as in Luke 2:25 ("the consolation of Jerusalem"),

38 ("the redemption of Jerusalem"). And yet, face to face with this hope, she has closed the door upon it, and now there will be hell to pay. The Roman conquest of 70 C.E. will descend like an axe. Compare Luke 10:10–12, "Whenever you enter a town and they do not receive you, go into its streets and say, '. . . nevertheless, know this, that the kingdom of God has come near.' I tell you, it will go easier for Sodom and Gomorrah on that Day than for that town." In other words, towns hostile or indifferent to the message of Jesus will face terrible doom. Thus, Luke (writing decades after the destruction of Jerusalem) looks back in hindsight at the disaster as divine judgment on Jerusalem for rejecting the messianic bringer of peace.

But in *Superstar* we almost get the impression that Jesus speaks with a dark fatalism, with resigned cynicism, as if what Jerusalem does not suspect is that the things that make for peace *are* destruction and death! It's a black-humor truism that the dead have their troubles behind them. Think of the old black slave spiritual: "Soon ah will be done wit de troubles of de world"— by dying! That is what Jesus knows, and thus he is past all anxieties (or is he?) about death. Caiaphas and Annas are so anxious to fend off any risk of Roman reprisals, and yet all their schemes will come to nothing in another generation. Trying to secure your life against death is as futile as the Maginot Line was to stop the German advance. "He who seeks to save his life will lose it. But whoever loses his life . . . , the same shall find it" (Mark 8:35). In some form or other, this seems to be what Jesus is telling Jerusalem. It is what he has learned, or is learning.

Rudolf Bultmann makes this insight the core of the New Testament message: only if we will abandon the delusive attempt to secure our own future (it didn't do the Rich Fool any good, after all—Luke 12:16–21) and commit our lives into the hands of a faithful (though admittedly unpredictable) God can we henceforth live as Jesus lived, with the freedom of inner detachment from all worldly anxieties. Perhaps without the religious coloring, the same insight might be just as well expressed in terms of the contemporary Epicurean philosophy, which taught there was neither reward nor punishment after death, only oblivion. Epicurus taught that death is nothing to be afraid of. It is not some sort of unpleasant experience—it is no experience at all! You won't be hanging around somewhere bemoaning the fact that you aren't alive anymore! And if death no longer holds any fear for you, what else can possibly scare you? Paul (Romans 8:31) quotes Psalm 118:6: if God be for me, what can any man do to me? Epicurus might say, If

Death be my friend, who can be my enemy? And this seems to be what Jesus advises Jerusalem: "To conquer death, you only have to die," or as Heidegger said, to face and accept the stark fact of your own mortality now, to get that out of the way is to stop living a cowardly, inauthentic existence spending your life denying and avoiding what cannot finally be avoided.

Granted, one might considerably simplify the explanation of Jesus' words here by supposing he intends no reference to anyone's fate but his own. In this case all the occurrences of "you" in the lines, "While you live your troubles are many, poor Jerusalem. To conquer death, you only have to die," though addressed figuratively to Jerusalem, really would have to mean "one." "While one lives, one's troubles are many, poor Jerusalem. To conquer death [or the fear of death] one only need die." And this would be seen to mean, "While I live, my troubles are many, poor Jerusalem. To conquer death, all I have to do is die." But this seems unlikely, however clever, since in this case there would be no reason to call Jerusalem "poor." It is the troubles of Jerusalem which are plainly in view. Likewise, remember that earlier in the same song Jesus calls her "doomed Jerusalem." It is Jerusalem who will find her peace, her consolation (to use the Lukan vocabulary) in the soothing chill of Lethe's waters.

A marginal note: in the original draft of the libretto another scene was to have been inserted at this point. As Ellis Nassour summarizes it, it took place "outside of Jerusalem where the disciples and Jesus ran out of food. Judas is quick to blame the shortage on Jesus and said that he would sell his soul for a piece of camel pie. Christ countered that he did not need his advice and that he and the other apostles have noticed that Judas was not much on self-sacrifice. The sequence ended with a rather mystifying bit about a fig tree bearing fruit."[112] We may speculate whether Judas' complaint was intended to reflect back on the waste of the ointment by Mary in the earlier scene. Had it not been gratuitously squandered on a gesture of devotion, it might have been cashed in for enough money to feed the lot of them now. This scene would have made Judas appear self-seeking, and its omission fits better with the sympathetic view of Judas given by the rest of the opera.

Another inconsistency eliminated by the loss of the scene would have been the on-stage working of a miracle by Jesus. What Nassour seems not to have grasped was the implicit connection to the strange passage Mark 11:12–14, just before the entry into Jerusalem (as here), where Jesus looks for figs on a wayside tree and, finding none, irritably curses the tree to remain forever barren. The miracle is that it soon (immediately, according to Matthew's version) withers up. Rice's proposed version would have involved a creative reversal of the story, in which the hunger of the disciples, not just Jesus' own itch for a snack, prompts him to cause a barren fig tree to produce fruit to feed them all, a variation on the theme of Jesus miraculously multiplying fish and bread for a crowd of thousands (Mark 6:35–44; 8:1–9). The point would have been much the same as in the story of the stilling of the storm (Mark 4:35–41), where Jesus silences the worried carping of the disciples by causing the wind and waves to cease. As in that tale, Jesus might have concluded Rice's miracle story with the rebuke, "Have you no faith?" Good gospelling, I'd say. But it is important for the whole course of events that we never know for sure whether Jesus' reputation for miracles was more than "just PR." To have him perform a juicy miracle right onstage would have resolved the issue and robbed the opera of its crucial dimension of "the fantastic."

Pilate's Dream

This scene is derived from Matthew 27:19, "Besides, while he was sitting on the judgment seat, his wife sent word to him, 'Have nothing to do with that righteous man, for I have suffered much on account of him today in a dream.'" This is one of several embellishments Matthew has added to the Markan passion narrative, trying to make the story more natural, more plausible. It is not that Matthew shuns prodigies and enormities—far from it: his gospel is the most extravagantly legendary of them all. But he knows that if one is describing the supposed actions of ordinary human beings, then one cannot leave them without motivation. What he is trying to make more believable is the surprising attempt of Pontius Pilate to free Jesus and controvert the plan of the Sanhedrin. What would Pilate care? Knowing what we know of him, it is hardly likely that Pilate would exercise any more concern for Jesus than for a mosquito. Matthew is stuck with this portrayal of Pilate. It is already this way in Mark, a well-known writing. So all he can do is to try to make it seem less arbitrary.

He has added the note that Pilate smelled a rat. "He knew that it was out of envy that they delivered him up" (Matthew 27:18), and Pilate does not care to be manipulated. His attitude is a disdainful indifference such as Luke attributes to Gallio, Proconsul of Achaia: "If it were a matter of wrongdoing or vicious crime, I should have reason to bear with you, O Jews; but since it is a matter of questions about words and names and your own law, see to it yourselves; I refuse to be a judge of these things" (Acts 18:14–15). We might suppose that Pilate was not trying to set Jesus free, but only playing devil's advocate to see how far he could press the Sanhedrin, all in order to get to the bottom of things. He surmises that they are hiding something, and in this way he hopes to find out what.

But Matthew apparently did not think this motivation sufficient. Perhaps he realized such a strategy would never account for the lengths to which Pilate goes on Jesus' behalf. At any rate, he adds the dream of Pilate's wife. Since here Matthew was no doubt creating freely, he could have had Pilate himself having the dream, but he doesn't. Why not? My guess would be that he doesn't think it would be in character for a hard-headed Roman official like Pilate to be spiritually sensitive enough to be receiving divine portents in dreams. Matthew does attribute such psychic sensitivity to Joseph (Matthew 1:20. 13, 19, 22) and to the Magi (Matthew 1:12) in his nativity story, but with Pilate—well, that would be casting pearls before swine. So Matthew falls back on the stereotype that women are more open to such things than men, a trait that also left them open to hysteria, religious mania (like the Bacchus religion), and deception by fraudulent gurus from the East (see Juvenal's Sixth Satire for a send-up along these lines). What Mrs. Pilate is supposed to know about Jesus in order for her to be dreaming of him is left unstated. Matthew has forgotten to explain what interest she has in the Nazarene. Remember, even Pilate doesn't even seem to know who Jesus is. But his wife's last-minute communiqué throws a superstitious scare into him, and he redoubles his efforts to free Jesus.

Early Christian legend had a lot of fun with Mrs. Pilate and her dream. Using a clever literary instinct, Christian story-tellers following in Matthew's footsteps eventually filled in the gaps Matthew opened while he was trying to close those he saw open in Mark. They decided that Mrs. Pilate must secretly be a disciple of Jesus (just as Nero's wife Pompeia had surprised everyone by converting to Judaism). Or, perhaps, the very dream mentioned here led to her conversion. What kind of suffering had she undergone in the dream? Probably Matthew simply meant that she had tossed and turned all night because of nightmares starring Jesus. But suppose she meant she had suffered physical harm in the dream, and this on account of Jesus. Maybe that meant she had experienced a clairvoyant dream of her own future martyrdom as a Christian! The Pilate legend continued to grow. You may find it represented in such apocrypha as *The Acts of Pilate* and *The Avenging of the Saviour*, in addition to modern pseudepigrapha like "The Report of Pilate" and *The Archko Volume.*

It is, then, Pilate's wife, not Pilate himself, who had the troubling dream. Tim Rice had at first intended to introduce Pilate's wife at this point, under the name that early Christian legend had given her, Procula. She would have appeared on stage to sing this number, obviously, with a few of the lyrics changed. She was eliminated in favor of her husband once "Barry Dennan came along and we were so pleased with him that we decided to bring him on early in the recording."[113] Rice's freedom in redrawing the scene is of a piece with the artistry that has expanded the story for centuries anyway. (Interestingly, Mrs. Pilate was similarly dropped from *Monty Python's Life of Brian (of Nazareth)*, where she had figured in a scene that did not make it into the final cut.)[114]

Rice wants us to keep Pilate's soliloquy recounting his dream in mind once we arrive at the later scene which the dream anticipates. It may explain, as Matthew intended, some measure of Pilate's interest in Jesus and the question of his guilt. This cannot be just one more criminal. "You Jews produce messiahs by the sackful! Who is this Jesus? Why is he different?"

This works especially well in *Superstar*'s version of the interrogation scene, since Rice has also drawn on the much longer version of John, where Pilate's curiosity about Jesus has reached the proportions of superstitious dread. He is almost afraid to crucify him. This is the effect Matthew seems to have desired, but he has added too little. The scare of the dream does not really seem to affect the remainder of the Matthean passion story. John, on the other hand, did manage to create that effect, and he didn't need the device of the dream to make it work. Rice has brought both together, making better use of the elements of both gospels. The only drawback is that, by having the dream happen to Pilate so early, Rice leaves us wondering why Pilate seems to be taken by surprise by the events once Jesus is brought before him. In Matthew, Pilate only hears of his wife's earlier dream once he is already considering Jesus' case. But if he himself had experienced the dream beforehand, why doesn't he experience a curious sense of *deja vue* once the dreamed-of events begin to transpire? And why does he allow them to come to the conclusion he does?

I dreamed I met a Galilean
A most amazing man
He had that look you very rarely find
The haunting hunted kind

I asked him to say what had happened
How it all began
I asked again-he never said a word
As if he hadn't heard

Let's note, first off, that what Pilate says here is almost a verbatim parallel to what he will say to Jesus once he meets him in waking reality: "How can someone in your state be so cool about his fate? An amazing thing, this silent king!" So even Pilate's musing on the dream is prophetic, foreshadowing events soon to transpire.

"He had that look you very rarely find." Pilate speaks like a connoisseur of condemned criminals, as if he is speaking of a particular vintage that "you very rarely find." He is in the position to evaluate these men, and this is one of the rare ones. Why? What sort of look did the dream-criminal have?

The figure in his dream seemed to be both running scared and able to throw a scare of his own into the observer. Fearsome in some strange way, and yet a victim of a stranger fear himself. I think of a similar scene in H.P. Lovecraft's story "The Music of Erich Zann": "Those haunting notes I had remembered . . . so when the player at length laid down his bow I asked him if he would render some of them. As I began my request the wrinkled satyr-like face lost the bored placidity it had possessed during the playing, and seemed to show the same mixture of anger and fright which I noticed when I first accosted the old man . . . As he did this he further demonstrated his eccentricity by casting a startled glance toward the curtained window, as if fearful of some intruder."

"I asked him to say what had happened, how it all began. I asked again. He never said a word, as if he hadn't heard." Again, Pilate will soon find himself having the same conversation with a waking-world Jesus, one, however, who is no less eerie than the dream. On that day Pilate will ask of the beginnings: "Where are you from?" He will badger Jesus until Jesus breaks his preoccupied silence. And Jesus will seem to him a bored adult whose mind is elsewhere as he waits for the children's game around him to be over.

Or think of the *Twilight Zone* episode in which a condemned criminal relives his trial over and over again, in dream after dream. It is always the same, except that the other people in his dream rotate the roles, being the prosecuting attorney this time, the judge next time, the chaplain the time after. The judge asks him, "Have you anything to say for yourself?" But the man is not even listening anymore. Why should he? It is only a wearisome charade, and he is sick of going through the motions. Jesus appears the same way to Pilate in the dream: just getting through it, knowing too well how it must end, according to the irrevocable will of God.

Like Erich Zann, Jesus is preoccupied with what haunts him, what hunts him. And that is the will of God. As he does in *The Last Temptation of Christ*, Jesus has tried to escape that plan, to change it, to outrun it, but it remains a monolith in his path. He is hunted by the Hound of Heaven:

I fled Him, down the nights and down the days;
I fled Him, down the arches of the years;
I fled him down the labyrinthine ways
Of my own mind; and in the midst of tears
I hid from Him, and under running laughter.
Up vistaed slopes, I sped;
And shot, precipitated,
Adown Titanic glooms of chasmed fears,
From those strong Feet that followed, followed after.
But with unhurrying chase,
And unperturbed pace,
Deliberate speed, majestic instancy,
They beat-and a Voice beat
More insistent than the Feet—
'All things betray thee, who betrayest Me.'"
(Francis Thompson, *The Hound of Heaven*).

And next the room was full of wild and angry men
They seemed to hate this man-they fell on him and then
They disappeared again

Pilate recalls how, as is typical of dreams, one event followed another with no discernible connection. Why would this mob be so crazed in its hatred against the pensive, otherworldly man?

The mob described is apparently not the Sanhedrin, who never lose their composure this badly in the verbal dueling with Pilate, but rather the crowd who will turn against Jesus, smarting from the fact of jilted hope. "They fell on him"—the same image occurs later, when it is actually happening, when Pilate, taken aback at the hostility called forth by this unassuming figure, announces, "But to keep you vultures happy, I shall flog him." The crowd is likened to circling birds of prey (we see them circling in the scene when Jesus is pestered by reporters, surely jackals even in our day), and as soon as they see their victim fall, they drop from the sky to tear and feast.

"They disappeared again," because in the panorama of the prophetic dream the scene is about to change, substituting a glimpse further ahead in time, when some strange aftermath has manifested itself.

Then I saw thousands of millions
Crying for this man

If Jesus is surrounded by legions of fans in his own day, they are nothing compared to the uncounted millions who will eventually come to worship him as Lord and God. The seeds of this had been sown already, in the rumors of the admiring crowds with their "talk of God." But what will ensure Jesus' future worldwide renown is, paradoxically, the very machinations of his enemies who seek to be rid of him once and for all. This is the implied connection, which of course Pilate himself cannot see, between the two scenes of his dream: first, Jesus is pounced on by the mob; second, he is worshipped by vastly larger crowds, whole populations! Ironically, the first led directly to the second. How? Jesus will later suspect as much: "Why should I die? Will I be more noticed than I ever was before? Will the things I've said and done matter any more?"

The billions envisioned by Pilate are crying for Jesus. It is not that they believe his death was the end, for Christianity will contain the doctrine of Jesus' resurrection. The crying referred to is ritual mourning in the yearly celebration of the passion, just as for ages the worshippers of other dying-and-rising deities (whose number Jesus will join) annually wept for Baal (Zechariah 12:11), Tammuz (Ezekiel 8:14), Osiris, Attis, Adonis, etc.

And then I heard them mentioning my name
And leaving me the blame

Here is the greatest surprise of all! Pilate had stood on the sidelines through the whole business, pretty much a detached observer—and now all men blame him for their savior's death! Now we see what the dream had to do with Pilate; why should the gods send him such a dream? It seemed almost like reading someone else's mail. But, scan far enough down the column of newsprint and, sure enough, there's your name! But what's it doing there?

This is narrative irony. The listener shares with Tim Rice the historical perspective that Pilate lacks. His very lack of it illumines the events in a new way for us, defamiliarizing them, restoring a bit of the way it must have looked at the time, without the filter of "historical knowledge," which is after all simply an accepted reading of the events to lend them some explicable meaning they lacked at the time. Seeing it through Pilate's eyes (not even having what little understanding he will have gained from the Sanhedrin once the events actually start taking place), we cannot take the event for granted, as our religious upbringing leads us to do. We see something of the arbitrariness, the mystery of the events, a mystery that traditional dogma rushed to domesticate and obscure with its theologies of atonement and redemption. Pilate (like Judas in his last song) has not the dubious benefit of these sophistical rationalizations. He bears the full brunt of the "strange thing mystifying." And, for a moment, so do we.

When Pilate hears billions of Christians mentioning his name, leaving him the blame, of course the reference is to the Nicene Creed and the Apostles Creed, in which Jesus is said to have "suffered under Pontius Pilate." It has been often and well remarked that, if not for his involvement in what must have seemed at the time a minor execution, Pontius Pilate would be as unknown to history as his colleagues and successors Cuspius Fadus, Felix, Festus, et. al. When Jesus gained immortality by becoming an object of worship, Pilate rode on his coat tails to a lower niche of notoriety. One imagines him entering the marble halls of history, referring the bouncer to Jesus: "I'm with him."

Money Changing Tables of the Law

Who are the "moneylenders and merchants" who harass the visitor to the Holy Place with deafening pitches? Though Rice has taken some liberties with the facts, the temple pilgrim did indeed have to navigate his way through whole acres of livestock stalls and tables of money changers. What on earth were they doing there? Actually, there had long been livestock stalls and money changing tables set up just outside, and all for the convenience of the pilgrims coming to the feast. According to the ancient stipulation of the Torah, all Jews were to visit Jerusalem three times a year for the major festivals of Tabernacles, Passover, and Pentecost. Once there, they were to offer animal sacrifices. Traditionally they had brought animals taken from their own herds, which, after all, was the original point of the thing: you were offering these animals in token of your gratitude to God for prolific animals, in the hope that God would smile on your remembrance and increase herd productivity even more. But there was a problem.

Once you arrived at the temple, the animals had to be "government inspected" by the priests and certified as perfectly healthy and not deformed, so as to insure no one was trying to palm off their "damaged goods" to God (Malachi 1:13–14). Suppose your sheep had broken its leg on the trip from the hillsides of Galilee all the way down to Jerusalem. No good! You were stuck. Knowing human nature, we may be sure there were "scalpers" present to replace your sheep at several times the fair price. To protect pilgrims from this, the temple authorities thoughtfully provided animals, already inspected, on site.

Now about the money changers. In ordinary commerce Jews used any of the various coins minted by local fiefdoms like Herod Antipas' Galilee and Peroea, or from neighboring provinces, or the official Roman silver coins, denarii (from which we get the Spanish word for money, "dinero"). As long as the coins had the proper weight of metal in them, nobody cared. But it was different in the temple. In its holy and emphatically Jewish precincts certain coins were no good, especially the Roman denarius and any others which bore the imprinted image of Caesar or any other living thing. Remember, the Ten Commandments forbade any "graven image." And the denarius had an image. Picture yourself in line to buy a sacrifice at the temple, and suddenly you reach nervously into your pouch and come up with only a handful of denarii! The innkeeper was happy enough to take them, but you realize the priests will be more choosy. What will you do? What *will* you do? Forget the American Express card.

To solve this problem and speed things up, the authorities provided money-changing service. Hand over the filthy lucre and get good Hebrew or Phoenician coins, which you would then take over to the sheep pens to buy a sacrifice. The temple tax was also collected there, and the IRS looked down on Roman coins, too.

Here I think we find the original meaning of the famous "Render unto

Caesar" passage that occurs only a bit later in Mark (12:13–17). Jesus is asked if it is apostasy from the Torah to, in effect, worship Caesar by paying him tribute in the form of state taxes. Judas the Galilean, remember, had once led an unsuccessful revolt over this very issue. Jesus redefines the problem by asking to see a denarius. Since it had an image of Caesar on it, it couldn't be offered to God (used to buy a sacrificial animal). So giving the denarius to Caesar instead, you weren't depriving God of what was rightly offered to him instead. He wouldn't take it if you did! So paying the Roman tax involved no religious compromise. "Render unto Caesar that [coin] which is Caesar's, and render to God that [coin] which is God's."

Something had changed under Caiaphas' tenure. He had the whole business brought indoors and set up in the Court of the Gentiles. This was an outer area of the temple where Gentiles could come to observe the rites of the temple. But since these were only for Israel, non-Jews could go no further, could get no closer. And yet there had been a place for them. Not any more, though! Good luck hearing or seeing any of the temple service with all the animal and human clamor surrounding you. Think what it would be like if you went to visit St. Patrick's Cathedral—only to discover they'd moved the New York Stock Exchange (or the Fulton Street Fish Market!) into the vestibule.

Mark seems to have understood Jesus as objecting to this shabby treatment of Gentile visitors, since he has Jesus quote from Isaiah 56:7: "My house shall be called a house of prayer *for all the nations . . .*" (Mark 11:17). There are, however, many different theories as to what motivated Jesus' outrage, all of them more or less plausible, in my judgment. One of the most important modern theories is that Jesus led an armed occupation of the temple, perhaps hoping to seize the temple treasury, aiming to use it to arm an even larger force. Note that Mark says "he would not allow anyone to carry any of the vessels through the temple" (Mark 11:16). How would this be practicable unless he had posted armed guards at the doors? Mark later describes Barabbas as having killed a man during "the insurrection" (Mark 15:7). *What* insurrection? The one Jesus himself had led in the temple? Jesus was, after all, crucified by the Romans, not stoned to death for blasphemy by the Jews. Crucifixion was a punishment reserved by the Romans for thieves, pirates, runaway slaves—and rebels.

If this is what was going on, then we have to conclude that Mark has erased the more explosive aspects of the story (albeit incompletely, leaving us these hints). Christians were falling under Roman suspicion in the next decades, and the last impression Mark would have wanted to convey was that Jesus had been an anti-Roman seditionist.

Jesus would have needed a sizable force to occupy the temple, which was about thirty-five acres in extent, with hundreds of tables to overturn. And there were armed temple police posted everywhere, precisely to prevent outrages like this one. Did they just stand by and watch? There was a garrison of Roman soldiers headquartered just down the street in the Antonia Fortress, also for occasions like this. So if anything happened at all, it must have been quite different from the scene as we now read it in the gospels, where it pretty much looks like Jesus is causing a ruckus at a church rummage sale, knocking over a few folding tables.

And if there really was such an assault on the temple, it would seem most probable for Jesus to have been arrested, if not killed, on the spot. In that case, the rest of the gospel story would be pure fabrication. The Last Supper would have been added as a liturgical text for the Christian eucharist, the Garden of Gethsemane scene as a lesson in prayer, the trials before the Sanhedrin and Pilate (both riddled with narrative and historical implausibilities) as models of courage for martyrs, and the crucifixion scene (cobbled together from unacknowledged borrowings from Psalm 22) simply to flesh out what little was known about Jesus' death.

On the other hand, the story as we read it is so anachronistic and misleading as to the implied description of the temple set-up that, we would be easily justified in dismissing the whole thing as a piece of fiction created by Hellenistic Christians writing after the destruction of the temple in 70 C.E., who had never seen the temple. (The Epistle to the Hebrews describes the temple incorrectly for the same reason.) Perhaps the scene was composed to provide a "fulfillment" of Malachi's prophecy: "Behold, the Lord whom you seek will suddenly come to his temple . . . But who can endure the day of his coming, and who can stand when he appears? For he is like a refiner's fire and like launderer's soap; he will sit as a refiner and purifier of silver, till they present right offerings to Yahve" (Malachi 3:1–3).

The traditional reading of the temple cleansing episode is that Jesus was disgusted by the commercialization of the temple and its worship. God had become big business. John's gospel seems to have understood the scene this way; it has Jesus say, "Take these things away; you shall not make my Father's house a house of trade!" (John 2:16). There was something similar at stake in the struggle of the Prophet Muhammad against the authorities of the holy city of Mecca. Mecca was the pilgrimage center of the pre-Islamic Arabs because the major shrines of the various gods were collected there, and the city lived off the tourist trade. Thus it was not well-received by the city fathers when Muhammad began to preach against the worship of all gods other than Allah.

John has substituted "You shall not make my Father's house a house of trade" for Mark's version, which has Jesus say, "It is written, 'My house shall be called a house of prayer for all the nations,' but you have made it 'a den of robbers.'" The first quote, as we have seen, is from Isaiah 56:17. The second is from Jeremiah 7:11, "Has this house, which is called by my name, become a den of robbers in your sight?" Jeremiah's point was to rebuke hypocrites who piously entered the temple to offer sacrifice without the slightest notion that God would be sickened by their shady business practices. Does Mark's use of the passage imply he wanted to show Jesus, like Jeremiah, condemning, not the temple authorities, but the unrepentant worshippers? No more sacrifices until you stop making them a mockery! That would make sense.

But Mark may have just quoted the single phrase he wanted, caring nothing for the original context. In this case he may have been aiming the jibe against the temple authorities after all. And this might imply he ascribed shady dealings to them. Might they have become the kind of scalpers that the whole system was originally established to avoid? Did they overcharge you for on-site sacrificial animals (like $7.00 boxes of popcorn in a movie theater?), since you really had no other option? Were their exchange rates unfavorable? Like the despised "publicans" (tax farmers), did they skim off an unfair commission for themselves? None of this is implausible, but we really have no evidence to support such charges. But if this is what Mark meant, then John has toned it down, making Jesus object not just to priestly gouging, but to the presence of trading in the temple per se.

That no one has learned anything from this passage in the many hundreds of years since John wrote it is evident from every tacky trinket counter one sees in any holy place. In any case, Tim Rice has zeroed in on this reading of the texts and, so as not to have to enter into the kind of explanations I have tried your patience with here, he has transposed the scene into more contemporary equivalents. The money-changers have instead become money lenders, something expressly prohibited by the Torah ("usury"). And the livestock offered for the pilgrim's convenience have become simply a meat market. Some deem it improper for the Roman Catholic Church to gain income from the supermarkets it owns. But the way Rice describes the scene, it is as if they actually set up the supermarkets inside their churches. (Bingo comes to mind, too.)

The concession stand/convenience mart array of merchandise has expanded to include an astonishing variety of sacrilegious items, like one of those shopping marts in the American South where you can buy a born-again romance novel or Bible-study book off the rack, then stop at the R- or X-rated video counter, then the potato chips, then the rifle and ammo rack.

The Temple

Roll on up-for my price is down
Come on in for the best in town
Take your pick of the finest wine
Lay your bets on this bird of mine
Roll on up for my price is down
Take your pick of the finest wine
Lay your bet on this bird of mine
Name your price I got everything
Come and buy it's all going fast
Borrow cash on the finest terms
Hurry now while the stocks still last

This melee of shouted sales pitches says it all. One comes to the temple to worship the Lord of Hosts in the splendor of holiness, perhaps meditating on the Psalm of Habakkuk, "Yahve is in his holy temple; let all the earth keep silence before him" (Habakkuk 2:20)—and then one's ears are met with this!

"Roll on up!" is the English equivalent of the American huckster's cry, "Step right up!" Remember, "Roll up, roll up, for the Mystery Tour!"

In the movie *Jesus Christ Superstar*, we behold a larger variety of merchandise on sale than the barkers actually mention in the song, including automatic rifles, racks of post cards, etc. The usurers are out in full force, too. And as the Old Testament makes clear, there was even prostitution taking place in the temple. Surely the most loathsome aspect of the temple trade as Rice imagines it is the betting on cockfights. It adds new meaning to Jesus' baleful prediction to Peter, "Before the cock crows twice, you will deny me three times."

My house should be a house of prayer
But you have made it a den of thieves
Get out! Get out!

Rice has taken this straight from Matthew 21:13/Luke 19:46, the same as Mark, minus the continuation "for all the nations." (Since Matthew and Luke must both have gotten their source material from Mark here, it seems not unlikely that the phrase "for all the nations" did not appear in the early copies of Mark they would have been reading. Perhaps the phrase has been added to the text of Mark by a later copyist who looked up the source of Mark's Isaiah quote and wanted to provide a note explaining what he took to be Jesus' motive, as suggested above.)

Incidentally, it is worth noting that what Mark did in his original version of the scene was pretty much what Tim Rice does throughout: he has created new dialogue by stitching together various snippets of scripture (in Mark's case, Old Testament scripture). This implies that what Mark has added to his Bible quotes is just as fictitious as what Rice has added to his. Apparently he didn't know what Jesus said on this momentous occasion, but he felt the occasion called for something appropriate, so what better than a bit of Isaiah and a bit of Jeremiah, prophetic figures like Jesus? Some suspect that the tradition/information available to Mark had Jesus saying, "I will destroy this temple made with human hands, and in three days I will build another, one not made with mortal hands" (Mark 14:58), but he didn't like the sound of this, made it a false accusation against Jesus, and substituted a couple of "safe" scripture quotes.

My time is almost through
Little left to do
After all I've tried for three years, seems like thirty,
Seems like thirty

Jesus is seen in soliloquy here. This is what he's thinking once the uproar at the temple is over. Rice follows the gospels in his surprising conclusion to the cleansing scene. Was there no reaction from the authorities?

Jesus speaks as if to say, "Well, now *that's* out of the way." One more hoop jumped through, one more item checked off the agenda, and soon it will all be over. We think of the Ghost of Christmas Past in Dickens: "My time is almost up. One shadow more." He is tired, but at least little work remains.

Once again, the whole idea of a predetermined divine plan cannot have belonged to the earliest Jesus tradition, nor to the life of Jesus itself. If there is any historical basis to the Jesus story at all, we must suppose many of these events to have occurred more or less spontaneously or even to have taken Jesus by surprise. It was only later, in hindsight, that Christians came to feel that everything that happened to Jesus must have been divinely ordained. And then they began to tell the tale as if Jesus himself had consulted with the script writer and knew what was going to happen scene by scene.

Rice's lyrics have no punctuation to speak of. And the melody inhibits ordinary intonation and stress. So we are left guessing whether Jesus' last two lines are unfinished, interrupted by the pleading crowd, or whether they are meant as a completion of the previous pair of lines. "My time is almost through" would then link up with "for three years, seems like thirty." And "little left to do" would contrast with "all I've tried." Does Jesus mean that all this time he has tried unsuccessfully? And if so, tried to do what? Get his message across? Even in the gospels we receive the impression that the disciples never in fact get what Jesus is telling them.

Or does he mean, as Albert Schweitzer thought, that Jesus saw few responding to his call to repentance, few taking seriously his proclaiming the soon-coming end of the world? If either of these guesses is anywhere near the mark, Jesus is sighing with frustration: like Sisyphus, he is getting nowhere for all his effort, but at least it will all be over soon. Or does he mean to despair over the unlikelihood of his getting his mission accomplished in the short time left to him, if he hasn't been able to do it already? We may get this clearer later, once Jesus resumes these musings in the Garden of Gethsemane, and finishes his thought.

The idea of Jesus having been in public ministry for three years comes from John's gospel, and even there a three-year duration is not actually stated as such. Rather, it is the inference of scholars from the fact that John has Jesus present and teaching on three Passover occasions. But then John is certainly the most fictional of the gospels. He feels free to reshuffle the traditional order of the story for topical purposes. So if he has Jesus teaching three times at Passover, it is just as likely that it means John had three Passover-related things he wanted to have his character Jesus say.

"Seems like thirty"—here Jesus probably means it seems he has been slaving at his task all his life. Luke tells us Jesus was "about thirty" when he began his public activities (Luke 3:23), though who knows if he had some information or just took a likely guess. There is some reason, as Alfred Loisy[115] showed long ago, to think John meant to give the impression that Jesus was fifty years old when he died (John 2:20–21; 8:57). This is certainly what Irenaeus (writing about 175–180 AD/CE) took John to mean.

> **See my eyes I can hardly see**
> **See me stand I can hardly walk**
> **I believe you can make me whole**
> **See my tongue I can hardly talk**
> **See my skin I'm a mass of blood**
> **See my legs I can hardly stand**
> **I believe you can make me well**
> **See my purse I'm a poor poor man**
> **Will you touch will you mend me Christ**
> **Won't you touch you can heal me Christ**
> **Will you kiss you can cure me Christ**
> **Won't you kiss won't you pay me Christ**

Suddenly Jesus is besieged by a crowd of the crippled, afflicted, and poor. They all expect, even demand, Jesus, now recognized as the Christ, the Messiah, to heal them, as if it's part of his job description. They'd been waiting for the messiah to appear and wanted to be first in line to receive his blessings. After all, that's why he came, isn't it? He owes it to them, they figure.

All these afflictions match those Jesus is said to have healed in the gospels: blindness, lameness, muteness, skin disease ("leprosy"). Jesus touched them, or they touched him, and they were healed. When Rice makes them offer professions of faith in his powers, we hear an echo of Matthew 9:28–29, "Do you believe I am able to do this? Then be it done unto you according to your faith."

> **There's too many of you-don't push me**
> **There's too little of me-don't crowd me**
> **Heal yourselves!**

In Matthew 21:14, immediately following the cleansing of the temple, it says, "And the blind and the lame came to him in the temple, and he healed them." This is what prompts the hosannas of the children that the Pharisees complained about. But Rice's Jesus is not in a healing mood.

Malcolm Boyd, the prototype for Paul Simon's "radical priest [who] come and get me released and we's all on the cover of *Newsweek*," was not amused. Boyd was known in his heyday as "the espresso priest," hence perhaps the "radical chic priest." And, despite the retrospective patina of silliness, he remained a voice for social justice. And like all such zealots, he sometimes grew a bit humorless. Boyd's review of *Jesus Christ Superstar* on Broadway showed that, despite his famous prayer, "Are you running with me, Jesus?" it was Boyd who could not quite keep in step with the mod messiah. As he saw it, the rock opera contained "enough theological travesty to boggle the mind. In a myriad of details gone wrong, the show bears little resemblance to the New Testament." Boyd? A biblicist? "Is this the Jesus of a significant counter-culture? Not at all. For we see him reject the sick and distressed victims of society who come to him for help."[116] The review is as unintentionally funny as Philip Berrigan's paranoid finger-wagging in a *Sojourners* magazine review of *Star Wars*, which the good father could see only as a propaganda tract for the military-industrial complex.

And yet it is hard to believe that Rice was not trying to throw a stumbling block in the viewer's path. This is the last way we would expect Jesus to react to "the least of these my brethren." In one of Boyd's own published prayers, his sentiments seem remarkably parallel to those of Rice's Jesus: "I want to anchor myself in the past and shed tears of self-pity. When I look ahead tonight I can see only futility, pain and death." But Boyd expects better of his personal savior, whose grace he asks: "But you call me tonight to love and responsibility. You have a job for me to do. You make me look at other persons whose needs make my self-pity a mockery and a disgrace."[117] Why does Rice's Jesus come up not as Christ-like as Malcolm Boyd?

Because Rice has recognized another opportunity to show the real humanity of Jesus. Sometimes you reach the end of your rope. You get "burned out," used up ("There's too little of me!"). Even if Jesus is God incarnate, he isn't Superman. The degree of umbrage one takes at Rice's portrayal of Jesus in this scene is a measure of just how human one thinks of Jesus as having been. If clay feet bother you, it just goes to show you've been worshipping an idol.

And as it happens, the same reluctance we seem to feel at this scene also blinds us to a few New Testament texts that seem to have escaped Boyd's notice. In Mark 3:20–21, we read that Jesus was under such pressure that his family feared for his sanity. "And the crowd came together again, so that they could not even eat. And when his family heard it, they went out to seize him, for they [presumably his family (cf. verses 31–32), or else the rumor-mongers] were saying, 'He is beside himself!'" Jesus is angered at their meddling and repudiates the lot of them (verses 33–35). But later on, he comes to see it their way. "The ones he sent returned to Jesus and reported to him all that they had done and taught. And he said to them, 'Come away by yourselves to a lonely place and rest awhile,' for many were coming and going, and they had not the leisure even to eat" (Mark 6:30–31). It doesn't work. Jesus is recognized, even on vacation, and the throng forms again. "And he had great compassion on them, for they were like sheep without a shepherd."

And again: "And he entered a house and would not have anyone know it; yet he could not be hid. But immediately a woman, whose little girl was possessed by an unclean spirit, heard of him and came and fell down at his feet . . . And she begged him to cast the demon out of her daughter" (Mark 7:24–26). Jesus rebuffs her in shocking terms: "Let the children first be fed, for it is not right to take the children's bread and throw it to the dogs." But she will not be daunted and retorts, "True enough, my lord, yet even the dogs under the table eat the children's crumbs, do they not?" Taken aback with delighted surprise that the woman has so cleverly outwitted him, Jesus congratulates her, his irritability gone, and assures her she will find the girl perfectly well when she returns home.

We are also told that Jesus took to avoiding the towns because "people came to him from every quarter" (Mark 1:45). He would teach on the sea shore and "he told his disciples to have a boat ready for him because of the crowd, lest they should crush him; for he had healed many, so that all who had diseases pressed upon him to touch him" (Mark 3:9–10).

Rice's scene of Jesus blowing up at the crowd, no matter how distasteful some may find it, seems in direct continuity with this theme in the gospels. Specifically, Rice would seem to have drawn it from the last passage quoted here, Mark 3:9–10. Mark shows Jesus using the same caution summed up well in Neil Peart's song "Limelight." "One must put up barriers to keep oneself intact." And, again, remember the crowd control measures in *Monty Python's Life of Brian*: "Incurables, I'm afraid you'll just have to wait for a few minutes. And keep the noise down a bit, please!! Those possessed by devils, try to keep them under control a bit, can't you . . . Come on, give him space, don't push, mind your backs . . . Don't jostle the Chosen One."[118]

Ex-Pentecostal preacher Sam Kinnison had the same idea. It seemed to be easier for him to envision Jesus as a real human being once he repudiated his religious faith. In one routine Sam asked the audience to imagine the kind of pressure Jesus must have been under, the kind of hours he must have kept. Imagine, he said, after a long day of healing the sick and casting out demons, Jesus retires to a local tavern for a relaxing drink. Suddenly the door flies open and in staggers a blind man, calling out, "Has anybody seen Jesus of Nazareth? I need him to heal me!" At once Jesus begins to put his finger in front of his lips in the *Shhh!* sign and to wave urgently, pantomiming that no one should let on that's he's there. The catch of the joke is that this too-human behavior would seem parodic or even blasphemous only if one assumed that Jesus was not really human, which, deep down, one suspects, Christians do believe. Imagine! Jesus acting like a human! What a riot! But, uh, wait a second—he *was* a real human, wasn't he? Doesn't even the Creed say so?

One cannot help suspecting that the *Superstar* scene we are discussing was a direct source for a scene, occurring in the same place, just after the temple cleansing, in Paul Schraeder's screenplay adaptation of Kazantzakis's *The Last Temptation of Christ*. There, too, Jesus is beset by the threadbare masses, throngs of lepers in mummy wrappings, crusty cripples, and thrusting club-limbs. He is momentarily overwhelmed, disoriented, and as Judas helps him away, he yells "You don't make demands on God!" There is no such scene in the original novel, but the similarity to *Superstar* is unmistakable. Here, I think, we can speak of Schraeder's redaction of Rice. He has shifted the focus from Jesus protecting himself from the demands of the crowds to Jesus rebuking the crowds for their presumption. They think God owes it to them. The messiah is Santa Claus, and he'd damn well better have the items on their lists.

Again, *Monty Python's Life of Brian* contains an instructive parallel. As Brian of Nazareth is making his way through the crowded marketplace (pretty much the same setting as in the *Superstar* scene), he is accosted by an agile and fit-looking beggar trying to pester a donation out of him.

Beggar: "Spare a talent for an old ex-leper, sir?"

Brian: "Did you say—'ex-leper'?"

Beggar: "That's right, sir . . . sixteen years behind the bell [lepers had to ring a bell before them where ever they went, to warn people to avoid them so as not to contact ritual impurity from them], and proud of it, thank you sir."

Brian: "What happened?"

Beggar: "I was cured, sir."

Brian: "Cured?"

Beggar: "Yes sir, a bloody miracle, sir. Bless you."

Brian: "Who cured you?"

Beggar: "Jesus did. I was hopping along, when suddenly he comes and cures me. One minute I'm a leper with a trade, next moment me livelihood's gone. Not so much as a 'by your leave.' (gestures in the manner of a conjurer) 'You're cured, mate, sod you' . . . Look, I'm not saying being a leper was a bowl of cherries. But it was a living. I mean, you try waving muscular, sun-tanned limbs in people's faces demanding compassion. It's a bloody disaster."

Brian: "You could go and get yourself a decent job, couldn't you?"

Beggar: "Look, sir, my family has been in begging six generations. I'm not about to become a goat-herd, just because some long-haired conjurer starts mucking about. (makes gesture again) Just like that. 'You're cured.' Bloody do-gooder!"

Brian: "Well, why don't you go and tell him you want to be a leper again?"

Beggar: "Ah yeah, I could do that, sir, I suppose I could. What I was going to do was ask him if he could . . . you know, just make me a bit lame in one leg during the week, you know, something beggable, but not leprosy, which is a pain in the arse to be quite blunt, sir, excuse my French but . . ."

Brian, giving him a coin: "There you are."

Beggar: "Thank you sir . . . half a denari for my bloody life story!"

Brian: "There's no pleasing some people."

Beggar: "That's just what Jesus said."[119]

Finally, what about what Jesus says to the crowd: "Heal yourselves!" Isn't this unnecessarily cruel? Isn't he mocking the poor and infirm? We can be sure that today's Political Correctness mavens would have him up on a cross for no more than saying this! It may be that the line is based on what Jesus says to those with faith enough to be healed in Mark 5:34, "Your faith has made you well." This saying has always raised the intriguing possibility that Jesus believed it was the power of faith in the seeker that wrought the healing, and not any power of his own. Faith healers and New Thought practitioners have been quick to seize on the passage. And in *Superstar* it may imply that Jesus was impatient with people who wanted everything done for them when in fact, if they really wanted it, they could have done it themselves.

But a more likely source for this line is Luke 4:23, where Jesus gratuitously infuriates a friendly audience of his own townspeople anticipating that Jesus ought to let charity begin at home, use his famous healing powers to cure some of his neighbors and kinfolk right here in Nazareth. "No doubt you will quote me this proverb, 'Physician heal yourself.'" But, sorry, you're out of luck! This turns the once-friendly crowd ugly in a hurry. They try to pitch him off a nearby ledge. In the same way, Tim Rice has Jesus use equivalent words to turn his one-time fans into disappointed and bitter enemies. *This is in fact a key turning point:* from here on in the crowd becomes a lynch mob, cooperating with Pilate and the Sanhedrin, eager to see the resented Jesus die.

Everything's Alright

> Try not to get worried try not to turn on to
> Problems that upset you oh don't you know
> Everything's alright yes everything's fine
>
> And I think I shall sleep well tonight
> Let the world turn without me tonight
>
> Close your eyes close your eyes
> And forget all about us tonight

In this brief reprise, we see Mary Magdalene trying once again to get Jesus to disengage himself from his hectic schedule with all its draining labor. This time it works; Jesus joins in the song, takes over some of the lines, internalizing them. He didn't seem able to do it before.

Even so innocent-seeming a scene as this is liable to strike some of the pious as blasphemous. Some feel a distinct unease at the intimacy shown here between Jesus and Mary Magdalene. Though nothing sexual is implied (her actions are more motherly than anything else), some critics of *Superstar* apparently share the squeamishness of Simon the Pharisee in Luke 7:39.

Besides this, there is the tendency to see Jesus as already an omniscient

God while on earth. In the same way that some readers of the gospels have trouble with Jesus being taken by surprise or having to be told information (Mark 5:30; 6:6), they stumble over the idea of Jesus sleeping and leaving his followers on their own. I suppose such pious readers, who have left behind any real notion of a genuinely human incarnation in Jesus, are imagining him as the providential, ever-vigilant God, like the Greek Argus. "He that guardeth Israel shall neither slumber nor sleep" (Psalm 121:4)

I Don't Know How to Love Him

This song, a soliloquy of Mary Magdalene, sung to her own heart, directly follows the reprise of "Everything's Alright," both in the sequence of songs (obviously) and in story time. It is not just the next thing told. It is the next thing that happens. It would be natural to picture Jesus sleeping on her lap as she sings.

> **I don't know how to love him**
> **What to do how to move him**

Romantic Christian legend has for many centuries flirted with the notion that Jesus and Mary Magdalene were lovers, had been lovers, or would have wound up lovers if given more time. Many listeners of *Jesus Christ Superstar* have inferred some sort of romantic or sexual relationship between the two based on "Everything's Alright" and "I Don't Know How to Love Him." But the initial lines of this song seem pretty clearly to rule out the whole idea. Here we witness the inner confusion of a woman who knows she loves Jesus, but she knows not how. This implies that she has had adoring feelings for the man Jesus, and yet she has not yet been able to decide the nature of those feelings, nor what to do about them.

> **I've been changed yes really changed**
> **In these past few days when I see myself**
> **I seem like someone else**

We saw back in "What's the Buzz" that Mary was commonly known to be a prostitute, notorious enough that Judas feared Jesus' association with her in the public eye would have the same effect it did when Elmer Gantry was photographed visiting a prostitute in order to counsel her toward repentance. This implies either that Mary had not yet repented of her sins, or that Judas could not take such repentance seriously. But here in "I Don't Know How to Love Him," we suddenly hear that Mary Magdalene's great life-change has come about only during the Passion Week ("in these past few days"). She doesn't even recognize this new Mary. And of course it is the influence of Jesus that is somehow responsible. She is beginning to realize that the great devotion she feels for him is of a strange new kind, not lust.

> **I don't know how to take this**
> **I don't see why he moves me**
> **He's a man he's just a man**
> **And I've had so many men before**
> **In very many ways**
> **He's just one more**

What is the cause for this special feeling for Jesus? It is not readily apparent to her, and she is a woman who knows men. What is it about Jesus? Because he's not apparently something other than a mortal man. When Mary sings "He's just a man," is she rejecting higher estimates of Jesus that she has heard? She must have heard "this talk of God" if Judas had heard it. But I think that to take her words as a rebuttal to these early Christologies would be over-interpretation. The implied contrast is not with other possibilities of who or what Jesus might be, but rather with all the other men she has known: something is different, but what? If he were some sort of demigod like Theseus or Hercules, that might explain it. Her love might be both romantic yearning and hero-worship, just like Lois Lane's love for Superman. But that can't be it.

Here is another place where pious critics lambasted *Superstar* for supposed heresy. Here, they said, was a clear declaration that the rock opera rejected Christian Christology of the divine incarnation in Jesus. Admittedly, we have already quoted Tim Rice as saying that he did want to portray Jesus as a man, not as God. But even this is not a denial of the incarnation doctrine. In fact, doesn't the very idea of God being made into a human being mean precisely that God, like Rice, was trying to "portray him as a man"?

However, let us remind ourselves that the careful reader never has the right to assume that any single statement by a character represents the author's view. Remember narrative irony. We have to derive our view of the author's intent from the whole work.

And yet Mary Magdalene herself seems to recognize that Jesus is not simply reducible to any man, to "Everyman." It is only "in very many [i.e., not all] ways" that "he's just one more."

Does the phrase "in very many ways" connect to the line preceding it ("And I've had so many men before") or with what follows ("he's just one more")? As Stanley Fish[120] says, the "meaning of the text" has got to be the whole history of meanings which have arisen in the reader's mind during the reading process, the red herrings as well as the others. It is not simply irrelevant that the reader has been allowed or invited to think one thing, only to be corrected in the next line. In this case, the author wants you to have both impressions, one after the other. You will miss the point if you manage to catch on the very first time.

Thus here I think we are first supposed to hear "in very many ways" as a continuation of "I've had so many men before." This stresses the variety of relationships, some definitely sexual, that she has had over the years. Then we read "he's just one more" and are for a moment left thinking that Jesus may be one of her customers. But the appearance of "he's just one more" sparks the realization that "in very many ways" means rather to modify "he's just one more." He is outwardly ordinary in most ways, so what is different about him is mysterious, hard to pinpoint. And this manipulation of the reader ("Fooled you!") means that we have suddenly understood that Jesus, despite his close company with Magdalene, has not been one of her customers as we had thought. We see, as she herself did, how oddly different he is. We are again confronted by the mystery of the unresolved "fantastic" (Todorov). What is the mystery of Jesus? He did not move ahead lock-step like the perfect martyr. He strained against his fate because in very many ways he's an ordinary mortal, not a demigod like Apollonius of Tyana or Pythagoras, merely pretending human frailty for the sake of dull-witted humanity.

> **Should I bring him down should I scream and shout**
> **Should I speak of love let my feelings out**
> **I never thought I'd come to this-what's it all about?**

Mary is dumbfounded. Neither alternative, to explode in the wrath of the woman scorned, or to whisper the secret pledge of love, seems at all appropriate in the situation. And how can that be? She couldn't have imagined herself flustered like a schoolgirl, and yet here she is!

Don't you think it's rather funny
I should be in this position
I'm the one who's always been
So calm so cool, no lover's fool
Running every show
He scares me so

This is why she never thought to find herself at such a pass: she has been the heart-breaker, not the broken heart. She has carefully guarded her heart. Like a nurse who must build a barrier around tender emotions since otherwise the troubles of her legion of patients will wear her out (again, think of Jesus rebuffing the lepers and the lame in "The Temple"), the prostitute must cultivate a feeling of impersonal detachment to her clients. The old story has the young man falling in love with the first whore he visits, because he is naive. He cannot yet disassociate love from sex. He becomes a "lover's fool." But the prostitute has gotten over such illusions long ago. So why is Mary so much like a teenager in puppy love? Simply because she is a new creature (2 Corinthians 5:17), in Johannine terminology (John 3:16) she has been "born again" or "born from above," "born of the Spirit." This is what she means when she says the looking glass yields a different reflection these days. So she has returned to a second naiveté. And her hard exterior is gone. She is all too vulnerable, and the feeling of love is as if she has never felt it before. And perhaps she hasn't! In the words of the title of the worst movie ever made (and, to give credit where credit is due, Paul Newman and Joanne Woodward starred in it) Mary is feeling "a new kind of love."

"Running every show" must refer to Mary's previous sense of command in all situations. It is because she was this kind of professional that she is astounded to be so moonstruck now. But as soon as we read the next line, "he scares me so," we begin wondering if "running every show" means now to attach itself to "He scares me so." This would be why Jesus is frightening to her. He assumes complete mastery of every situation. Whereas, up to now, it was Mary who had been absolute mistress of her fate, now it is the charismatic Jesus who wields an eerie dominance over her and the others. He is silently in charge of everything they think and do. How did she acquiesce to this so easily? And again, tracing the responses of the reader, first naturally linking "running every show" with the preceding lines, then just as naturally with the following, we can see how the predicate "running every show" has reinforced the point by switching abruptly from Mary to Jesus! Our own reading and sudden reinterpreting has repeated the turn-about Mary has faced when, as a devotee of Jesus, she yielded control of her life.

I never thought I'd come to this-what's it all about

Her confusion repeats itself, recapitulating the whole song up to this point. Such repetition mimics the way of worry: we turn things around again and again in our troubled minds.

Yet if he said he loved me
I'd be lost I'd be frightened
I couldn't cope just couldn't cope
I'd turn my head I'd back away

I wouldn't want to know
He scares me so
I want him so
I love him so

Mary shifts the focus from any possible approach she might make to Jesus: what if Jesus were thinking the same things and were finally to voice his love, letting his feelings out? And this makes it all a moot point, since she could never accept it anyway! Here is the biggest clue that she knows something would be terribly wrong in such a liaison, as if Zeus should ravish Coronis. Or perhaps more like a confession of love from a man who does not know she is his own long-lost daughter! Mary feels the urgency with which Marty (the Michael J. Fox character) in *Back to the Future* rebuffs the amorous advances of the teenage version of his mom (who of course does not suspect his true identity). No, the love she feels for Jesus is not the kind she is used to. There is something higher or deeper here. What it is, she does not yet know. And yet we will see another hint of it when Judas later, just before his suicide, sings Mary's song! He feels the same mysterious adoration, and from it comes the unbearable grief he feels for turning him over to the authorities, an act that would have made sense if Jesus had been nothing more than Judas had thought at the time.

As Tom Gearhart puts it, "the confusion of emotion which Mary Magdalene feels toward Christ—pain, bewilderment, and melancholy love— is exquisitely transmitted and touches deeply."[121] In fact in her plaintive words, we can see the trajectory to the erotic-sounding passion mysticism of St. Theresa of Avila already charted. Tim Rice, exasperated by the insistence of some listeners that Jesus and Mary were sexually involved, remarked: "Read the lyrics to 'I Don't Know How to Love Him.' Mary is in love with Jesus, but mentally, not physically. He had a frightening effect on her—she was awed, he scares her so. The only thing Mary could relate to was Jesus. The last stanza of the song makes that clear."[122]

Poor Old Judas

Gordon Clanton, in his *Christian Century* review, observed that "the portrayal of the betrayer is at least as complex as that in Nikos Kazantzakis' *The Last Temptation*."[123] As Tim Rice said, the Judas character is not complex at all in the New Testament gospels. He is one of what Todorov calls "narrative men," simplistic characters who do no more than embody their actantial role, the narrative function, they are created as devices to perform. In other words, as Frank Kermode [124] outlines it, there probably was no Judas in the first version of the Jesus story. There was the simple theological statement that "God delivered up his son" (cf., Romans 8:32; 1 Corinthians 11:23), implying nothing more than that God provided Jesus as a sacrifice, or even more simply, God let him die. The Greek word used in such statements is *paradidomai*, meaning "to give over," "to deliver up," "to hand over," or, sometimes, "to betray." Once someone decided to spin out a narrative version of the gospel preaching, this last nuance of *paradidomai* suggested a very dramatic plot element: suppose Jesus, like Julius Caesar, had been double-crossed, backstabbed by someone close to him? What to name such a character? How about "Mr. Betrayer"? For that is probably just what "Iscariot" means, representing a Greek transliteration of the Aramaic *Ish-qarya*, or "man of falsehood," "the false one," hence "the betrayer."[125] "Judas" was a pretty obvious choice for a personal name, given the anti-Semitic direction Christianity was by this time headed in. The belief was that Jesus had set himself forth as the messiah and was stubbornly rejected by the Jewish nation whom he had come to save. Thus Judas the Iscariot, Judas the Betrayer, stood, like a figure in a political cartoon, for the whole Jewish people, cast in the role of betrayers ("He came unto his own, and his own received him not," John 1:11).

Another reason for doubting that any such character as Judas originally belonged in the story is the superfluous nature of the role he plays in the passion narrative. Exactly what does the Sanhedrin need him for? It cannot have been difficult to trace the movements of Jesus and his considerable retinue. One hardly needed Judas in order to find Jesus at Gethsemane. And how little can they have needed him, or anyone, to do what he does in the story: pick Jesus out of the crowd so the troops will know whom to arrest! They are there to apprehend him at night precisely because Jesus is so well-known a figure that a public arrest might lead to rioting. And they need someone to point out which one he is? It seems rather that someone has looked and looked and finally found something for this new "betrayer" character to do.

Of course, even if there was a historical Judas, the derivation of "Iscariot" from "the false one" is no less likely. We would simply have to remind ourselves that Judas would not have been known as "Judas Iscariot" during his lifetime any more than Jesus would have been hailed as "Jesus Christ" by his contemporaries. In both cases we would have a retrospective reference from the gospel writer's standpoint, but from the standpoint of the narrative, an anticipation of the character's destiny. Alternately, it is possible that tradition had long ago dubbed Judas "the Iscariot," the Betrayer, but that Mark did not know what it meant and supposed it was a genuine surname borne by Judas.

Two other proposed meanings of "Iscariot" would seem to require a historical Judas, not a fictive one, since each seems to presuppose background information never mentioned as part of the story. One is that "Iscariot" means "of Kirioth," a patronymic, naming a man after the town he hailed from. Many Palestinian towns were pre-fixed with "Kirioth" or "Kerioth" or "Kiriath," which meant "cities" or "city of." As most of these were in Judea, this origin would make Judas the odd man out, since he would be the only non-Galilean among the Twelve. Some have inferred from this that he never quite felt a part of the group, and that this alienation somehow festered to the point of his becoming a traitor to them. There was an Edomite Kiriath as well, and from this possibility Nikos Kazantzakis inferred the Edomite (Idumaean) ethnicity of Judas, making him a redhead.

But "Iscariot" might also mean "the Sicarius," the dagger-man, the assassin. The Sicarii were a group of notorious assassins who made it their goal to pick off people they viewed as Quislings, collaborators with Rome. They used a dagger or short-sword (*sicca*) which was readily concealed within one's sleeve. Once they struck the fatal blow, they would join in the general melee, shouting in distress like everyone else, then slipping away as the crowd dispersed. If Judas was a member of this group, we must imagine Jesus' movement to have been at least somewhat sympathetic to the whole approach. One might guess that Judas had quit the Sicarii to join Jesus, but then it would be a little strange for him to continue to be known by an epithet standing for an allegiance he had repudiated. It would be like calling someone "Biff the Communist," even though he had quit to join the Republican Party years ago. On the other hand, again, it is quite possible that Judas was a Sicarii assassin and that Mark no longer understood the reference and just put "Iscariot" down as a proper name. Or, a la S.G.F. Brandon,[126] Mark may have known good and well what the name meant but suppressed it by making it into a proper name, so as to hide another clue to the originally seditious character of the Christian movement.

The Sicarius option has attracted many scholars and fiction writers because of the romantic possibilities it offers, depicting Judas as a heroic, though perhaps confused, man of the people who had followed Jesus as a charismatic leader with the potential to rally the people to rebel against Rome.

Mark gives no real motivation for Judas' act, unless Mark means to imply that the anointing of Jesus at Bethany somehow disillusioned Judas about Jesus (more about this presently). The notice about Judas going to collaborate with the priests follows immediately the anointing episode (where "some" complain) in Mark 14:3–11. Matthew rewrites it to make it "the disciples" who grumble about the anointing (26:8), but John makes the spoilsport none other than Judas (12:4–6). John adds that Judas was a sneak-thief, while Matthew also implies it was mercenary greed that motivated Judas to conspire against Jesus (Matthew 26:15—note Matthew's subtle rewriting of Mark 14:11 at this point). Luke and John both have Judas become possessed by Satan himself in order to betray Jesus (Luke 22:3–6; John 13:2). His characterization grows even blacker in subsequent legends.[127]

Given all this, the clearly artificial vilification of Judas, modern writers trying to adapt the gospels for dramatic performance have felt obliged to transform Judas into a believable character. Hence he has to be provided some sort of plausible motive. Kazantzakis's Judas is, I think, the best variation on the theory that Judas was a political revolutionist. In Zefferelli's version, *Jesus of Nazareth*, Judas is a confused but earnest lad who cannot understand why Jesus waits so long to strike. So he decides merely to arrange a meeting between Jesus and the high priest's servants who will come to the Garden of Gethsemane to escort him to Caiaphas' palace. He realizes he has been had once he sees them bearing weapons. In other versions, Judas arranges the arrest in order to force the hand of Jesus: it's now or never! In *The Last Temptation of Christ* Judas' revolutionary hopes are indeed disappointed, but he sticks with Jesus anyway, and it is Jesus who asks Judas to "betray" him so that he may die, since he has meantime discerned that this is God's will.

The process of reimagining Judas, alternating between rank vilification and rehabilitation, is a very old one, almost as old as the character itself. Judas is one of the great examples of an archetypal mythic figure that Hyam Maccoby called "the Sacred Executioner."[128] Combining insights from Maccoby and Rene Girard, with whom Maccoby's theories are partly compatible, we can briefly summarize the mythopoeic process. (I don't want to give the impression that Maccoby simply agreed with Girard, as Maccoby told me he intended to write a book refuting aspects of Girard's thesis. He never got around to it.)

Girard[129] studied various myths in which gods are executed or murdered. His belief was that all such myths reflected historical crises in which classes, castes, or other sub-groups of a society waged total war that threatened the continued existence of the society. Eventually all realize that the conflict must cease, but since neither side will admit its fault (no doubt sincerely believing themselves innocent), resolution is possible only via the expedient of scapegoating some innocent (or at least not especially guilty) third party, some sort of bystander or other marginalized figure (deformed, a holy man, a resident alien) and pinning the blame on him, as if he had brought on the conflict by sneaky or even magical manipulation of both sides. Such imagined power means he must be a sorcerer or a devil, and so he must be destroyed to bring about the peace. He (or she) is burnt at the stake, crucified, etc., and (not surprisingly for a self-fulfilling prophecy) it works. Peace settles in. But, in retrospect, the scapegoat starts looking very different. Now that his death has "miraculously" restored blessed peace, it is evident that he must have been no villain but rather a savior god incognito! Who else, by his death, could have wrought salvation? This in turn implies that we (both groups) jointly bear great guilt for persecuting and executing the divine savior.

But who can bear such guilt? So we nominate a secondary scapegoat whom, we say, *must* have incited the masses against the savior. This mitigates the guilt of the society as a whole. But the process hardly ends there. The delivery of the savior unto his sacrificial death becomes viewed as, in *effect*, a priestly act. Had the betrayer not betrayed the savior, there would have been no salvation. Hence the scapegoat himself begins to take on the halo of a secondary savior, who performed his priestly role by *intent*. He becomes a priestly offerer of sacrifice. He becomes the Sacred Executioner. And then he must be split into two, for someone must bear the villainy. There is still that aspect. So the story-teller's imagination splits the character into two: the priestly facilitator of the sacrifice and the villainous betrayer. So the Sacred Executioner gives birth to a shadow-counterpart, a tertiary scapegoat to bear the blame.

An important example would be the death of the Norse sun god Balder. According to the myth, Balder's mother Frigga had exacted an oath from all living things that none would ever harm her new son. The only exception was the sprig of mistletoe, which she deemed no threat in any case. Thus Balder grew up invulnerable to all weapons, since any arrow or javelin cast at him would remember the oath of its wood and veer aside. Loki, the god of malicious tricks, one day beheld a contest in which the gods took turns throwing weapons at Balder, who merely laughed as they turned aside. Loki then discovered the origin of Balder's invulnerability, as well as the loophole of the mistletoe. He found some mistletoe and fashioned it into a potent dart. Taking it to blind Hother, the winter storm god, Loki offered to help him join in the game, promising to guide Hother's hand. The dart found its mark, and Balder perished.

On Girard's principles, we must imagine the original story of Balder to have been one in which the gods' missiles did not turn aside, a story, in other words, in which they intentionally and collectively executed Balder as a scapegoat. (Again, this would have reflected real, though largely forgotten, events of an ancient social crisis.) But in retrospect Balder was venerated as a god and savior, henceforth universally beloved. Hother is blamed for his death, as is natural, Hother standing for the wintry blast, the opposite of Balder's sunny benevolence (just as Egyptian myth pitted Osiris, the grain god, against his brother Set, the god of the desert). Hother then becomes the scapegoat to exonerate the rest of the gods. But it is not long before Hother becomes the Sacred Executioner, so his guilt is shifted onto the shoulders of another scapegoat, Loki, the god of evil.

If we superimpose this template onto the gospels, how does it look? We might come up with a scenario in which it is the disciples as a group who betray Jesus (whether this meant merely their mass desertion in the Garden of Gethsemane or something more definite). Perhaps they have all lost faith in Jesus. After all, where Mark had "some" present complain at the woman's anointing of Jesus at Bethany, and John narrows it down to Judas, Matthew, right in the middle, has "the disciples" gripe about it. Were they all fed up? Maybe so. With their assistance, or even at their initiation, Jesus goes to his death. Does his death fit the pattern of the scapegoat? Indeed it does. As Caiaphas says (John 11:47–53), Jesus' death is meant to fend off a coming war between Jews and their Roman occupiers. If the blame for Jewish unrest can be laid on Jesus, Judea will be in the clear. As in Girard's pattern, the disciples come to view Jesus after the fact as an innocent savior, implying their own sore guilt. But then someone nominates one Judas as the secondary scapegoat, to embody and ameliorate the guilt of the disciples as a whole. We still glimpse this in the now-odd scene at the Last Supper when Jesus designates as his betrayer whomever happens at the moment to be dipping his bread into the sauce at the same moment Jesus does. It sounds like, not a revelation of an already-set state of affairs, as if Judas is already planning to turn him in, but rather as if the choice is being made then and there as to who will do it!

But if Jesus was a sacrifice for sin, that makes Judas the priest offering him (as the Cainite Gnostics actually taught, so this isn't pure conjecture). So Judas becomes the Sacred Executioner. And then he must be split into two (or more!) characters. The good Judas becomes Judas Thomas, twin brother of Jesus, master of gnosis, apostle to India. John calls him, about as bluntly as you can get, "Judas not Iscariot" (John 14:32). The bad Judas remains "Judas Iscariot," Judas the False One.

The "quest for the historical Judas," then, exactly parallels that for the historical Jesus: the data are few and enigmatic and susceptible of many interpretations, none without some plausibility, none capable of decisive demonstration. In both cases it is not even unlikely that the character is completely legendary or fictive.

Tim Rice, at any rate, has made Judas into a loyal friend (a la Kazantzakis) but also a hard-nosed pragmatist. He has reversed the typical portrait of Judas as a disappointed revolutionist. No, for Rice, it is Jesus who is tilting toward a violent denouement, or at least Judas believes so, and it is Judas who is more cautious. Rice shows him as reluctantly willing to see Jesus gotten out of the way in peace time rather than see a pointless and bloody war erupt with the same eventual result. Why let him take everyone else with him when he goes down?

Damned for All Time

Now if I help you it matters that you see
These sordid kinds of things are coming hard to me
It's taken me some time to work out what to do
I weighed the whole thing up before I came to you
I have no thought at all about my own reward
I really didn't come here of my own accord
Just don't say I'm
Damned for all time

It is well known that traitors are despised both by those whom they have betrayed and by those to whom they betray them. The latter are glad for the help rendered, but they hate traitors because they are inherently despicable, dishonorable, just as a prostitute's customer may despise her even as he enjoys her. In both cases, the ones offering the service have lost any real integrity, lost their soul, reducing themselves simply to the service they represent. Judas knows this well, and he hopes to exempt himself from such contempt. He wants to make sure his new allies understand his motives, because he knows what it must look like, what it has looked like to Christians for centuries now.

He knows what he is doing is a sordid affair, and he himself loathes it. It has been hard to make the decision, whereas if he were selling out Jesus just because he needed a few extra bucks, he would be so far beyond moral scruples that he wouldn't have hesitated. As it was, Judas only decided to come to them after long deliberations. There were cons as well as pros, and he had to balance them all carefully, give due weight to each. Yes, the situation was urgent enough, all right, but did it justify so extreme a measure as betraying a friend? In the end he was afraid that it did. Maybe he would have gladly sacrificed his own life if it would have somehow averted the impending catastrophe. But that wouldn't have worked. It must be Jesus. He is irreplaceable, and if he were taken out of the way, the danger of messianic revolution and Roman reprisals would be quelled.

That's why he's here, honest. It's not a question of Judas as a bounty hunter. No, to tell you the truth, it had not even entered his head to think about any monetary recompense. Nor does he want any. Hell, it wasn't even his choice, really. It just had to be done, dirty job, sordid sort of thing, that it is. This seems to be the intent behind Judas' saying, "I really didn't come here of my own accord," but there is a double entendre waiting in the wings.

With the shared narrative irony between Tim Rice and the listener, we can recognize in Judas' words something of a premonition of what he will later "see all too well." Then, when his mind is clearer, he will see that God has used him as a helpless pawn in a mysterious game, used Judas to do the terrible dirty work so as not to dirty his own divine hands. Judas did not approach the Sanhedrin of his own accord, his own free will. It was predestined. On some level, "poor old Judas" was fully as surprised as Caiaphas to see himself appear and make his offer.

"Just don't say I'm damned for all time." In other words, all I'm asking is, don't let history make a harsh judgment on me. Judas speaks with a sense of futility, as if knowing it's already too late to avoid universal opprobrium. History is not kind to those whose only remaining option is a tough choice no one would make if they had any alternative.

Here is a particularly clear example of Rice's ironic use of anachronism. Judas is really speaking to history, to the modern listener who has "known" all his life that Judas was worse than Benedict Arnold, that he is being slowly chewed like a beef jerky stick by Satan deep in Dante's Hell, along with Brutus and Cassius. Judas yells down the corridors of the centuries to us, hoping that at last we will put ourselves in his place and understand why he did what he did. He felt he had to. If you can understand him, then soften your judgment, can't you? That's all I'm asking! "Just don't say I'm damned for all time!" "Don't you get me wrong!"

> **I came because I had to I'm the one who saw**
> **Jesus can't control it like he did before**
> **And furthermore I know that Jesus thinks so too**
> **Jesus wouldn't mind that I was here with you**

"I'm the one [the only one] who saw [that] Jesus can't control it like he did before." In other words, "his half-witted fans" are about "to go out of control." And since Judas seems to be the only one who can see what is coming, it becomes his terrible responsibility to take action to prevent it. Would Jesus really not mind that Judas was here selling him out? Does Jesus really "think so too"? Does he share Judas' assessment of the situation? Of course Judas knows better. The crucial factor motivating his agony in "Heaven on Their Minds" was that Jesus had become so blinded by the adulation of his fans that he had lost touch with the real situation. He should have seen the danger his movement was drifting into, but he couldn't. Indeed, this is precisely why

Judas felt he was forced to take matters into his own hands.

So why does he insist that Jesus would whole-heartedly bless Judas' scheme? If he saw it Judas' way, Jesus would be turning himself in! Judas knows this. No, he is simply trying to rationalize his present behavior. His gut tells him too keenly that what he is doing is a despicable thing, and he is trying to silence this incriminating inner voice. If a few lines back he was really addressing the audience, not the Sanhedrin, here he is talking to himself, trying to convince himself that what he is doing is not what it seems. Sure, sure, Jesus wouldn't even mind if he knew what I was doing! Yeah, that's it! That's the ticket! If Judas can beguile himself into believing this nonsense, he can stop feeling guilty. The truth is, whatever Jesus might say, Judas himself minds that he is here with them.

But then Jesus will make no effort to derail the train of his destiny even when it is visibly bearing down upon him. So maybe he would not mind that Judas is here selling him out after all. But Judas cannot know this. He is even less privy to God's plans than his friend Jesus.

I have no thought at all about my own reward
I really didn't come here of my own accord
Just don't say I'm
Damned for all time

Why the repetition of these lines? It is the frantic agitation of the guilty soul seeking absolution by trying to persuade itself that it is not really guilty. And maybe if it repeats the defense often enough, it will manage to convince itself. You can always tell when someone's too-fulsome apologies are really aimed inward to the person's own unmerciful conscience.

Annas you're a friend a worldly man and wise
Caiaphas my friend I know you sympathise
Why are we the prophets? Why are we the ones?
Who see the sad solution-know what must be done?

Like Peter outside the high priest's palace later, during the trial of Jesus, Judas here seeks warmth from his new companions, so to speak, gathering around the fire with them. Judas can tell the others despise him as a miserable stool pigeon, though they are grateful for the information he brings. His nervous and transparent flattery is a vain attempt to close the gap between them by calling them "friend." Furthermore, he tries to draw them closer to sharing responsibility for his actions. "I know you sympathise." (In other words, "Caiaphas wouldn't mind that I was here with you.")

He says to Annas that the latter's well known Machievellian pragmatism ("a worldly man and wise") could lead him to no other conclusion than that which Judas has now reached. And indeed Judas is right. His motive for turning in Jesus was exactly the same as the motive of the Sanhedrin for concluding that "this Jesus must die."

"Why are we the prophets?" Here is a clever reference back to the Johannine irony of calling Caiaphas a prophet in John 11:49–52. He spoke more truly than he knew. In the scene/song "This Jesus Must Die" remember that Caiaphas berated the others for their short-sightedness: "Fools! You have no perception . . . I see bad things arising." Caiaphas is made to speak with a prophetic perspective that the others lack. Here Judas reintroduces the same theme. By seeing what none of his compatriots (the other disciples) see, Judas, too, is to be numbered among the prophets. So if Caiaphas despises Judas, let him know that he is despising someone just like himself.

He and Caiaphas, like a couple of bearded Cassandras, have a heavy cross to bear. Like Moses or Jeremiah balking at the burden of such a task, Judas asks for himself and Caiaphas: why me? "O Lord, I pray thee, send someone else!" (Exodus 4:13). It is a sad but inevitable solution that the acuity of both men reveals to them. And thus it lies with them to do it, on behalf of those who do not yet understand the need.

I have no thought at all about my own reward
I really didn't come here of my own accord
Just don't say I'm
Damned for all time

From here on in we start to see Jesus and Judas as parallel figures, growing more and more alike as we go. Many of their individual lines will sound almost indistinguishable. And here we see Judas speaking more to himself than to those around him, introspecting and musing ironically on his dimly-perceived and inescapable role in the divine plan—and we see Jesus doing the same in his trials before the Sanhedrin and Pilate. And this parallel, in turn, should cause us to realize that what we are seeing here in "Damned for All Time" is really the trial of Judas. In it, he is in effect accepting the verdict, issued by his own conscience, that he is eternally damned for what he does. He "protests too much," trying to mollify his own conscience. But it is a stern and severe judge. It will carry out its sentence soon when, again, like Jesus, Judas will die hanging from a tree.

Cut the protesting forget the excuses
We want information get up off the floor

Annas' completely unsympahetic words here show that Judas' apologia for his actions has not had the least effect. Annas quickly dismisses his words as excuses. But they are not interested either in Judas' pangs of conscience nor in how Judas may try to salve them. Annas is already anticipating the impassivity of the priests in Matthew 27:3–4 when Judas returns to them bemoaning what he has done. "What is that to us? See to it yourself."

There is a note of humor here, too, in that Judas' gymnastic dancing, as he writhes in an agony of conscience, should not really be visible to any other characters. It is strictly intended for the audience. It is just like the recitative in any opera. Since all the characters are singing their lines, it is not noticeable to any of them that they are doing it, much less how bizarre it would sound to hear people singing this way in real life. It's all for audience consumption. For the characters on stage, the world is working just the way it's supposed to. For Annas to notice Judas' choreography is as if Mary Magdalene suddenly turned to Peter and said, "Hey, why is it that you sing everything you have to say, anyway?" Or if one character should say to another, "Don't you remember what you said on the previous page?" The medium of the action and speech is unknown to the characters; they are like fish in the sea; the water surrounds them invisible and unseen. Thus it is pretty funny when Annas directly addresses the oddity of Judas' actions: "Get up off the floor."

Annas is seeing something only the audience should be in a position to notice. It is another of those constant ironic reminders that this is not a recreation of reality, as if you were there, but rather a glance back with long hindsight at an ancient event. We are perhaps trying to share Annas' perspective, when suddenly Rice shatters this willing temporary suspension of disbelief by forcing Annas to take our perspective, as if he, too, could see what we as viewers see.

We have the papers we need to arrest him
You know his movements-we know the law

Judas had said, "If I help you," apparently expecting that his offer would come as a godsend to the worried but baffled priests. Little did he know they would already have Jesus in their sights, just waiting for an opportunity. This becomes clear once Caiaphas explains the exact nature of the assistance they will need from Judas. Just help them locate Jesus.

Caiaphas speaks of the requisite papers for Jesus' arrest. It sounds like he has a warrant of some kind. It must contain some citation from the Torah, for it is surely the Jewish Law of which he speaks. The two we-phrases should be read as parallel in meaning: "we have the papers"="we know the Law." They will be arresting him on the basis of some supposed transgression of the Torah, blasphemy perhaps.

Your help in this matter won't go unrewarded

Annas assures Judas that he will be remunerated, as if he were a bounty hunter, even though Judas has already clearly stated that he has no desire or expectation of a reward. No more than does someone who jumps into a rushing river to save another. Judas sees himself as doing his civic duty as to avert a disastrous uprising, even though he has begun to feel he was somehow wrong and is now doing the wrong thing, hence his excuses.

Note the euphemism Annas uses: "this matter." As if the whole "business" is distasteful to him. It must not be too distasteful, since he still intends to prosecute "the matter." It is as if speaking of the thing delicately will hide its stench under a cloud of verbal perfume. If we don't look at what we're doing straight on, perhaps we can forget what it is that we are doing, or that it is indeed we ourselves who are doing it.

We'll pay you in silver-cash on the nail

Caiaphas says Judas will be paid in cold, hard cash as soon as he delivers the goods, as soon as the job is done. "Cash on the nail" means just that, like the phrase "cash on the barrel head." As soon as the merchandise is delivered. In this case, the merchandise is Jesus himself. And "cash on the nail" is a wonderful double entendre pointing forward to the nailing of Jesus to the cross. (By the way, that Jesus was *nailed* to the cross (instead of being tied, for instance) is said in only a single verse in all of the gospels, namely in the Doubting Thomas story in John 20:25, and this is not even a crucifixion scene.)

We just need to know where the soldiers can find him
With no crowd around him
Then we can't fail

These three lines are divided between Caiaphas (first and third) and Annas (second). Here is a particularly overt reminder of what has been implicit from the start: Annas and Caiaphas are two characters dividing a single narrative role between them. They are a single "actant"[130] or character-function fleshed out in however many individual characters it takes. In *Superstar*, the utility of having both of them, redundant as they seem, is that the doubling of the character allows us to hear the thoughts of the "High Priest" character(s) in the form of dialogue instead of yet another soliloquy. The effect, very obviously in "Then We Are Decided," is that of overhearing the thoughts of a man inside his head.

Blood Money

I don't need your blood money!

Judas cuts through the euphemisms. It is clear to him they are treating him as a bounty hunter (just as he himself will later call Jesus "a hunted criminal," or as Pilate has already described him as the "hunted kind"), and he will have none of it, especially because of what it implies about his motives. Matthew does actually use the phrase "blood money" in 27:6. "I don't need it" denotes "that's not what I'm after here."

Oh that doesn't matter our expenses are good

Caiaphas responds as if Judas is generously foregoing payment because he knows the temple treasury funds are needed for more important things. Caiaphas says, in effect, "Don't worry about us, old man. We're good for it. Our expense account can easily afford it."

Interestingly, we seem to have some sort of eerie parallel with the scene in which Judas has protested the squandering of the expensive ointment for the sake of Jesus. This time, he is protesting the spending of temple funds on himself! And, sure enough, the money does go back into the pool to be used to help the poor, because Matthew has the priests decide to use the money, once Judas returns it to them, to buy a cemetery for the indigent (Matthew 27:6–7).

I don't want your blood money!

No, you don't get me, cries Judas. It's just that that's not what
    I'm interested in!

But you might as well take it-we think that you should

Annas is quick with a rejoinder. Okay, we understand: you don't want it and you don't need it. But, still, why not take it? Would it hurt you to take it? What's the point of *not* taking it?

Let us turn the question back upon Annas and Caiaphas: why should Judas accept the money? Why does it even matter to the priests? I think we can get a hint when we see Judas reluctantly reach out and take the bag of coins: the look on his face in the movie version (where Judas is rendered with the best acting in the movie, by Carl Anderson) shows he is acting against his own better judgment and against his own conscience. As Stephen King puts it in *The Gunslinger*, Judas can feel a moral value uncoupling, like train cars, inside him. Annas really is a worldly man and wise. He is shrewd enough to know that if he can manipulate Judas into accepting the money he will have corrupted his motives, gotten him to compromise himself. And he will have in fact become a paid flunky of the Sanhedrin. He will have switched sides. They own him now. Thus it is really himself that Judas is selling to the priests, not Jesus.

Think of the things you can do with that money
Choose any charity-give to the poor
We've noted your motives-we've noted your feelings

Caiaphas knows where to attack, the vulnerable points. If Judas is all that high-minded as he has told them, or at least if he thinks he is, then one appeals not to selfishness (as the cliché phrase, "think of the things you can do with that money," spoken to countless lottery winners by reporters, usually does). Rather he appeals to the very same instinct that made Judas take such umbrage to the "waste" of the ointment earlier in the story. If Judas eschews selfish waste, fine. It doesn't have to be that way. Unlike Annas earlier in the song, Caiaphas now professes to have understood Judas' qualms and self-justifications. One gets the impression that Caiaphas can see clearly enough that, just as Annas said, Judas was protesting too much, trying to rationalize his terrible actions, to convince not Annas and Caiaphas, but himself, of his innocence. But now he's trying to manipulate Judas by going along with Judas' self-deception, accepting his excuses at face-value. Anything, as long as he will take the silver and thus seal his implicit oath of fealty to them.

This isn't blood money-it's a fee nothing
Fee nothing, fee nothing, fee nothing more.

You don't want to be in the position of accepting bounty money? Fine, it isn't bounty money. If you don't like that, we'll just call it something else, that's all. It's really quite simple, don't you see? Just as Jesus said to his disciples when he sent them off to do missionary work: they shouldn't hesitate to accept donations of food and shelter from the people they preach to, since "the laborer is worthy of his hire" (Luke 10:7). In short, Caiaphas argues, it's only fair that, since Judas is rendering them a service, he be compensated for his valuable time. In all this evasion, Caiaphas is giving Judas the chance to do what Annas had done a moment before: to cover the nasty truth of the matter with an inoffensive euphemism: "This isn't 'blood money.' It's a fee, nothing more." A fee, yeah, that's it! That's the ticket! And then with a wink: "Know what I mean?" They have welcomed Judas into their fellowship (if only better to manipulate him), and he senses he has indeed changed sides. He is a card-carrying enemy of Jesus now, however much he may wish to deny it.

On Thursday night you'll find him where you want him
Far from the crowds in the garden of Gethsemane

Judas speaks as if he is the mouthpiece for someone else's voice. He cannot associate himself with the words he is saying. It is too late to turn from his disastrous course. The best he can do is to pretend it is someone else selling secrets, someone named Judas, but surely not himself. Judas' slow, soft, trailing voice as he makes the arrangements, his blank look of disbelief, is reminiscent of the stunned disbelief of Peter and the others at the Last Supper. They just cannot believe Jesus' prediction that one will deny Jesus, another betray him. Only where Peter and the others cannot credit what Jesus says they will do, Judas is already refusing to believe what he sees himself doing right now! No, I can't be doing this.

He assures the Sanhedrin that they'll find him "where [they] want him." Do they especially want to apprehend Jesus in the Garden of Gethsemane? No, "where" they want him is anywhere away from the crowds, who would more than likely intervene to protect Jesus and spirit him away. "Now we've got him right where we want him!"

Well done Judas
Good old Judas

The chorus, like the traditional Greek chorus in ancient dramas, assumes a collective function as an oracle, speaking out the dangers that the heedless character somehow fails to see impending because of what he has done. The chorus is a single actantial role played by a group of women who speak, like the witches in *MacBeth*, all in one voice. Here they speak ironically, patting Judas on the back. He can take pride in a job well done. And it's just what we would have expected from him. Got a job to be done? Judas won't let you down, reliable old Judas! You can count on him. The chorus will return with a mocking farewell after his suicide.

What about the motives of Judas? As I said earlier, there is a variety of motives attributed to him in the gospels, all of them villainous and scurrilous. He began his literary life as a mere incarnation of the actantial role of "the Betrayer." Mark does not explain what moved him. Neither does Mark have Judas going to the priests with the design of making some money ("You gave away the things you loved, and one of them was me") as if he were cashing in Jesus at the pawn shop. Judas goes to them and offers to hand Jesus over. Only then do we hear, "They agreed to give him money." We don't hear whose idea the money was. Tim Rice draws the altogether legitimate inference that it was the priests who brought up the issue. Matthew drew the opposite inference, rewording the scene so that Judas approaches them with money, and only money, in mind. "How much will you give me to turn Jesus over?" Let's bargain.

The Last Supper

Look at all my trials and tribulations
Sinking in a gentle pool of wine

Don't disturb me now I can see the answers
Till this evening is this morning life is fine

We begin the Last Supper with a major departure in detail from the gospel texts. In them there is no hint of the disciples being drunk. And yet inebriation would go far toward explaining some otherwise rather contrived details in the gospels. For one, there is the thick-headedness of the disciples who seem dumbfounded at everything Jesus says to them, despite the fact that they have heard most of it, even most of the esoterica revealed in John's lengthy version, several times over in the previous story. This remarkable stupidity is probably an unintended effect of the gospels being written on two levels. Everything Jesus is made to say in the gospels he is really saying (in other words, each gospel writer is saying) to the reader. But for the purposes of the narrative frame, Jesus must be shown saying it to characters on stage with him. And much of what he says does not easily fit in with the logic of the story level. The disciples have to be surprised at Jesus' fate as it unfolds. They panic at his arrest and flee. They cannot believe it when he rises from the tomb. And all this despite the fact that the evangelists have had Jesus give them a blow-by-blow preview of what will happen. Weren't they listening? Mark, Luke and the others have to resort to the most arbitrary *deus-ex-machina* devices to keep the disciples ignorant. For no stated reason, we are told that they simply didn't comprehend the early warnings. They can't have, or we don't have any story! Tim Rice has decided that at least this scene will have some narrative plausibility, so he makes the disciples tipsy. No wonder they don't remember.

Similarly, the irresistible assault of the Sandman who arrives in the Garden of Gethsemane just ahead of Judas, leaving the disciples lost in Slumberland, seems completely arbitrary. Mark (followed by Matthew and Luke) seems to have written it that way just to give Peter the opportunity for sleeping at the switch, a theme he may have derived from Jesus' apocalyptic parable of the servant who was supposed to keep watch for the return of his master but was rudely surprised when the master woke him up!

Mark didn't care a fig for narrative motivation. As Todorov says, in the plot of predestination, one event does not really lead to another. All alike are simply given by the mysterious will of God, none of them following contingently from other events in an indeterminate series of causal links. So who cares why they were asleep? Tim Rice does. He is not trying to present a systematic series of passion cameos, like the Stations of the Cross depicted in a Roman Catholic sanctuary. No, he wants to restore the sort of natural causal linkage we see in real life, or at least that we portray as realistic in fiction. In short, Rice recognizes the need for motivation. And, again, being drunk would easily explain the disciples repeatedly falling asleep in the garden even though Jesus has already rebuked them in no uncertain terms more than once.

The disciples are glad to bid their troubles good-bye, though even in their growing stupor they realize full well that they will be back waiting for them tomorrow (even sooner, as it turns out). They are drowning their sorrows, in the words of the old cliché, which they are paraphrasing here: "my trials and tribulations sinking"="drowning my sorrows."

"Don't disturb me now; I can see the answers." Apparently it is Jesus who is disturbing their boozy reverie. But they are not in the mood to hear more enigmas from him when the answers come so easily from the bottle. The implied image of the disciples, like the patriarch Joseph, scrying in a divination cup, is ironic (Genesis 44:2, 4–5, 15).

> **Always hoped that I'd be an apostle**
> **Knew that I would make it if I tried**
> **Then when we retire we can write the gospels**
> **So they'll still talk about us when we've died**

Here we get a glimpse of the kind of thing James and John had in mind when they asked Jesus to promise them the seats of honor alongside him, in the Messianic Kingdom: lolling about, banqueting, and drinking. Indeed Paul might easily have been speaking of the disciples in this very scene: "Already you are filled! Already you have become rich! Without us you have become kings! And would that you did reign, so that we might share the reign with you!" (1 Corinthians 4:8). That is the prestige that comes with being among the elite group of apostles! But they are hardly acting the role of an apostle. "Apostle" means, literally, "sent one" and implies an ambassador or delegate bearing a message, a spell of news, a gospel. But this is hardly what the disciples had always hoped to become. They are thinking of "the Holy Apostles" just as we do in long retrospect. Such an office did not even exist at the time of this scene, so they cannot have any such thing in mind. This is another piece of Rice's ironic distancing. It makes the listener think, "You mean *these* guys became the successors of Jesus? No wonder the religion is so screwed up!" (It is not unlikely that Mark had already written with the same strategy in mind, showing readers that the lords of the church were really incompetent and understood no more of the message of Jesus than the donkey he rode into Jerusalem.)

"Then when we retire we can write the gospels, so they'll all talk about us when we've died." According to the traditions passed down by the second-century bishops Papias and Irenaeus, the four gospels were indeed the work of the apostles during their autumn years, or of their assistants who recorded the apostle's reminiscences to preserve them after the apostles died. Justin Martyr calls them "the memoirs of the apostles." Papias said that after Peter's death his assistant Mark wrote down what Peter used to say about his days with Jesus. However, he doesn't say he means our Gospel of Mark. He may as easily be referring to one of the spurious "Petrine" writings like *The Preaching of Peter*, written about the same time. He says Matthew wrote down the sayings of Jesus in Aramaic, and that these were later translated by various people into their own Greek versions. Is this a reference to our Gospel of Matthew? Or to the Q source incorporated in it? Papias also said Matthew wrote first, then Mark. But this is the opposite of the relation our Matthew and Mark bear to one another. It seems instead that Matthew's gospel uses Mark's, copying most of the text verbatim, something quite odd if the author of Matthew had been an eye-witness of Jesus. Why would he not have relied upon his own, no doubt copious, memories?

Papias had apparently never heard of gospels going under the names of Luke or John. But Irenaeus relates that Luke the evangelist was the same as Luke the physician (Colossians 4:14) who accompanied Paul on his journeys. And he wrote down what Paul used to preach about Jesus. But it is plain from Paul's epistles that he had little interest in and nothing to say about the earthly Jesus. And Luke's portrayal of Paul as a character in the Book of Acts is so different from the Paul we meet in his own epistles that most scholars doubt seriously that Luke even understood Paul or had read his letters. In short, it is highly unlikely Paul's personal physician compiled our Gospel of Luke. Luke and Mark were the most common male names in the Roman civilization, so that doesn't do much to narrow down the search for the true identities of the gospel writers. They could have been anybody with those two names.

Irenaeus makes John the son of Zebedee the author of the Fourth Gospel, but this one is the least likely of all to have come from an eye-witness disciple. It is both the most consciously literary and the most factually loose of all the gospels. It is steeped in Hellenistic, Gnostic, and Essene-Zoroastrian currents of thought. Not likely for John the Galilean fisherman. Rice knew something odd was going on in John: "Matthew, Mark, and Luke seem more dependable, even though John is supposed to have been present most often. He tends, however, to lean more on the supernatural and visions."[131] Rice has the disciples as authors of the gospels simply because that is the tradition. And verisimilitude is a matter of conforming not to what actually is true, but to people's expectations of what is true.

Listen to the disciples' apparently realistic but pathetic estimation of their own worth. What sort of careers do they expect to lie ahead of them if they already know they will only be remembered to history for riding Jesus' coat tails? Just as Pilate will only be remembered by future generations for the single act of condemning Jesus to the cross, so will the otherwise utterly insignificant disciples only escape their richly deserved obscurity by means of writing the gospel accounts of Jesus, his sycophantic hangers-on in death as in life.

The end . . .
Is just a little harder when brought about by friends

Jesus somehow knows before the fact that death will come looking for him this very night. He seems ready, resigned to his fate, though despondent. Just as Mark has him say after the Supper as he enters the garden, "My soul is sorrowful even unto death."

Though he will shortly tell them what their roles in the ensuing denouement will be, he already pins the blame on them. As he refers to "friends" in the plural, he cannot have only Judas in mind. By their cowardly unfaithfulness, the others will contribute to his death as well. But he is not telling them this now. Rather, he seems to be musing, muttering to himself while the others are preoccupied. Here he is, sitting at table with his comrades, all of whom have pledged to him their lives and fortunes. And as they recline at ease in the peaceful zone of accustomed friendship, Jesus knows matter-of-factly that the hidden truth of the situation is the exact opposite of what it seems. As if a hidden briefcase containing a bomb were sitting under the table, ticking away the minutes until Armageddon, he knows the Grim Reaper sits silently among them, perhaps in the empty chair reserved for Elijah, if this is supposed to be a Passover meal. One thinks of Poe's "The Masque of the Red

Death," where the intruder has already breached the barricades and chats convivially among the guests he will soon mercilessly dispatch.

For all you care this wine could be my blood
For all you care this bread could be my body
The end!
This is my blood you drink
This is my body you eat
If you would remember me when you eat and drink

Having just vilified his own disciples as treacherous foes, Jesus suddenly comments disgustedly about their indifference to his impending death, which he seems to think they know about. Perhaps he, too, is a bit tipsy. Here he is like a man on death row listlessly chewing his last meal, and the others have so little sensitivity that they are making merry at the same table. ("If Jesus wants to be a wall-flower, let him!")

Following up the theme that death is invisibly present (in the person of Judas), Jesus speaks as if he is dead already. He says the disciples really are eating his flesh, drinking his blood—or might as well be. "You could be eating my flesh, drinking my very blood, and you wouldn't know it!" "Hey, Pete, did Jesus say something?" "Dunno, Phil. Here—this one's on me." He means nothing more to them than a meal ticket, anyway. That's all he is to them.

But how to put together the menace Jesus ascribes to his companions with the plain indifference toward him that he also condemns them for? Are not the two antithetical? Yes, but Jesus does not really blame them. He can forgive them since they know not what they do. They are simply tragic stooges of the will of God, the puppet master. Judas (remember, according to Rice, he is the most intelligent of the disciples) is the only one who will eventually understand this. In "Judas' Death," sung just before he hangs himself, he realizes how he has been maneuvered into his wretched act by God. And he yet he seeks no excuse, attempts no evasion. He still cannot live with what he has done. Malcolm Boyd is right: it is "Calvinism with bitters." Judas is predestined to do what he does, but this takes away none of the guilt, not even in his own eyes.

"This my blood you drink; this is my body you eat. If you would remember me when you eat and drink . . ." This is *Superstar*'s version of the Words of Institution, a formula repeated in nearly all Christian observances of the eucharist (Holy Communion, the Lord's Supper, etc.). Mark has "Take it. This is my body . . . This is my blood of the covenant which is poured out for many" (Mark 14:22–24). Matthew has, "Take, eat, this is my body . . . All of you drink of it [the cup]; for this is my blood of the new covenant poured out for many for the forgiveness of sins" (Matthew 26:26–28). Luke has "Take this and divide it among yourselves . . . This is my body" (Luke 22:17–19a). Some manuscripts of Luke continue with " . . . given up for your sakes . . . This cup [a second one!] is the new covenant in my blood, poured out on your behalf" (Luke 22:19b-20). John has "the bread which I will give for the life of the world is my flesh . . . Unless you eat the flesh of the son of man and drink his blood, you have no life in you. He who eats my flesh and drinks my blood has eternal life," etc. (John 6:51b, 53–54a). 1 Corinthians 11:24–25 has, "This is my body, which is on your behalf; do this in remembrance of me. This cup is the new covenant in my blood. Do this as often as you drink it in remembrance of me." Some of these have variant versions in other manuscripts of the same gospel.

It is all a piece of early church liturgy. It seems extremely doubtful that any such words were spoken by the historical Jesus on this or any other occasion. The episode is a fiction attempting to link the sacramental meal of Hellenistic Christians to the supposed Judaism of Jesus. In fact, it must have been derived from the similar feasts of the Mystery Religions. The initiates of Osiris drank beer as his blood, ate bread as his body. So the gospels are using anachronism, too, but not for the same reason Tim Rice often does. The evangelists are trying to give the rite an unimpeachable pedigree by constructing a scene in which Jesus himself explains the symbolism like a stewardess demonstrating the use of the seat belt and the oxygen mask.

The gospel texts vary so much because each gospel writer or copyist perhaps inadvertently copied out by memory what he was used to hearing at the eucharistic service in his church, not noticing that the text he was copying had it a bit different. Rice has obviously stuck closest to his main source, John, but he has taken the phrases about remembering him from 1 Corinthians. And in doing so he is doing the very same sort of thing the evangelists did: recombining and reshaping the earlier versions. The important difference is that he purposely avoids anachronism here. The last thing Jesus has in mind is instituting a ritual in his own memory that will endure through the ages. He only hopes, by providing a sort of mnemonic trick, to spur their thoughts to return to him at mealtime. "Hey, Andrew, pass me another slice of pizza.

Hmm, remember the old days when we used to sit around the table with Jesus?" "Yeah, yeah, I guess I do, now that you mention it. As I remember, he got kind of sullen toward the last, didn't he?" And maybe even this is too much to ask, with this bunch.

Rice is assuming, as he does throughout, that there really was a core of facts behind the stories and sayings in the gospels, but that "every word you say today gets twisted round some other way." How? In this case it isn't hard to see why. They are hearing whatever he's saying through the daze of uncomprehending drunkenness! And future years will distort their recollections even more. So when they retire and write the gospels everything gets rewritten. And what Rice has endeavored here is to provide natural motivation for Jesus comparing his blood and body to wine and bread. Forget about him trying to establish a Christian rite. What would bring a man awaiting death to say something like that?

> **I must be mad thinking I'll be remembered-yes**
> **I must be out of my head!**
> **Look at your blank faces! My name will mean nothing**
> **Ten minutes after I'm dead!**
> **One of you denies me**
> **One of you betrays me—**

Jesus is on edge, to say the least, near the end of his life and mission, unsure why it must all end in death. He knows that it must so end only because Rice has combined his natural human anxieties, based on ignorance of the future, with an anachronistic knowledge of how the story turns out. It is as if the butler had read the end of the very novel he is in, discovers that "the butler did it," and infers that his act is predestined. Of course it is, but not on the narrative level, the butler's own level. The gospel writers confuse the two levels by using Jesus as the mouthpiece for their own authorial perspective, making direct asides to the reader. And yet they also show Jesus as anxious, as in the Garden of Gethsemane. But Rice more deftly weaves the two together. Jesus somehow knows, but he doesn't know why. Thus he is worried, though still determined to go through with it.

The first two lines above are an expression of his fears that it will all have been for nothing. He will be making the supreme sacrifice for no reason. These are his understudies, his disciples, his trainees? And his ongoing influence rests in their hands? Then he is finished. Their bovine stares show what they have learned "after all I've tried for three years"—nothing at all. This is all quite close to Mark's dismal portrayal of the disciples, and to Marcion's some decades later.

Are they likely to remember his words and to convey them? Hardly, in light of what they are about to do: betray, deny, and abandon him. How could you expect such a crew to become his mediators to posterity? Jesus groans at the absurdity! How could he have been so stupid to choose idiots like these?

Somewhere in the background of these lyrics must lie the promise of John's Jesus to send them the Paraclete, the Spirit of Truth, who will bring to mind all that he had said to them, as well as much they were not advanced enough to hear while he was still with them (John 14:25–26; 16:12–14). It is evident that these Johannine sayings are like the Words of Institution. They are an anachronism created in order to give the (false) impression that Jesus had written John a blank check in advance: "Whatever you guys want to say I said, fine with me. Even if it sounds strange to people, just tell them it is they who have poor memories. And that's why the Spirit restored the true knowledge of what I really said. And if you have to admit I didn't actually say this or that—no problem! Just tell them I conveyed new information by means of the Paraclete. Who can prove you wrong, after all?" Are Jesus' words in John more accurately remembered and recorded than in the other gospels? Not by a long shot. And Rice explains this by saying that the disciples were in no state to remember anything the next morning! The ecclesiastical euphemism is that they were filled with the Holy Spirit, even though the shrewd eye, trained to see that the Emperor had no clothes on, recognized that they were instead filled with a different spirit, that of "new wine" (Acts 2:13).

Jesus' disgusted rebuke, "Look at your blank faces!", is an unusual kind of apostrophe (addressing someone absent as if present, pretending to say things one would never dare to their faces). Here the speaker's intended addressee is actually in front of him, but the speaker knows the addressee is so uncomprehending that the speaker's rebukes fall on deaf ears that might as well not be in earshot. Their blank faces will be just as blank when he is done lambasting them.

The whole scene thus far is strikingly reminiscent of saying 29 of the Gospel of Thomas: "I took my stand in the midst of the world, and in flesh I appeared to them. I found them all drunk. I found none among them athirst. And my soul was afflicted for the sons of men, because they are blind in their hearts and do not see that empty they have come into the world, and that empty they seek to go out of the world again. But now they are drunk. When they have shaken off their wine, then they will repent." Whether Rice had Thomas in mind, I do not know. It may simply be a spontaneous parallel, suggested by the communication gap between Jesus and the Twelve in the gospels.

Not I! Who Would? Impossible!

In the gospel versions of the Last Supper scene, the disciples display the same storm of sheer incredulity. They sincerely cannot imagine what he says. But this is because their subsequent actions of betrayal, denial, and abandonment will not arise naturally from their own motives. They will have been maneuvered into a situation where they have only bad choices, none they would have chosen. And even at the time they will look at their own actions with a sense of horrified detachment as if some demon (or God!) had taken over their bodies and now used them to do terrible things.

There are two kinds of suspense in fiction. The first is when we do not know the solution to the crime, the identity of the villain, the outcome of the story. We find ourselves perched on the edge of our seat, eager to see, heart beating fast. The second arises when we know what is supposed to happen, and yet we cannot see how things could turn plausibly in that direction. It must happen, yet it seems things are headed another way. How will they coincide? Think of the folktale "Appointment in Samara," where a slave gets wind of the fact that the Grim Reaper is closing in on him. He reasons that the Death Angel will come for him at his accustomed address and so he swiftly flees to far Samara. His master wishes him well. Who would think of looking for him there? The master soon beholds the Grim Reaper in a roadside tavern. The Reaper approaches him and sits down. "If you've come for my servant, I fear you've come too late. He's away on a journey." "Oh, that's all right," replies the Reaper, pouring himself a glass, "I'm not due to see him today. Tomorrow I've an appointment with him in Samara."

The suspense comes not from what will happen, but rather from the curiosity of *how* it may happen. The predestined character knows full well what awaits him and thus would seem to be forearmed against it. And yet, inevitably, whatever path he takes will bring him face to face with his fate. How? That is what we cannot yet see, though we do in the end, feeling like we do when a stage magician explains an illusion that looked so real while he was performing it.

This is the sort of suspense raised here, to be answered as the events continue to unfold.

Peter will deny me in just a few hours
Three times will deny me—and that's not all I see
One of you here dining, one of my twelve chosen
Will leave to betray me—

The suspense is heightened, the dramatic tension raised yet another notch: Jesus gives them specifics. He had anticipated this at the previous meal with the disciples, in Bethany, days ago: "Why are you obsessed with fighting times and dates you can't defy . . . I could give you facts and figures . . ." Now he has, and, even so, they want to fight the times and dates they can't defy, in Peter's case, mere hours hence. ("In just a few hours" replaces the original wording of John 13:38: "Jesus answered, 'Will you lay down your life for me? Truly, truly I say to you, the rooster will not crow, till you have denied me three times." In other words: "So you will remain loyal till death, eh Peter? How ironic! The fact is, you'll have repudiated me not once, but three times before dawn tomorrow!"

This news shocks the disciples, as it implies a mysterious reversal of their most steadfast belief and hope about themselves. What can possibly happen between now and then that could make them become their own opposites? The answer: the resistless will of God, which no human determination can gainsay. One can imagine them beginning to doubt Jesus' sanity. Judas in particular can see his worst suspicions coming to bloom; Jesus has passed from delusions of grandeur to delusions of paranoid persecution.

And yet, on second thought, the cold knife of the realization cuts him to the heart: "He *will* be betrayed, and I'm the one who'll *do* it!" And while the others are dumbfounded at the prediction that they will shortly do that which they hate most, Judas is awakening to the fact that he has already done it! "I do not understand my own actions! The good that I wish, I do not do, while the evil which I hate is the very thing I do instead!" (Romans 7:15). Soon, once he sees the issue of the matter, he will recoil in self-loathing. And as he will say in "Judas's Death," his horror will not be because he didn't expect it all to end this way. What else did he expect? Rather, his reproach, directed in equal measures to himself and to God, will be that in retrospect he cannot imagine how he had decided on such a course, how God must have used him as a pawn, forced him to make Sophie's Choice.

"And that's not all I see . . ." Here we are reminded of Caiaphas' prescience, "I see bad things arising." Jesus, too, is looking with prophetic second sight through the roiling mists of the future. This note of clairvoyance probably comes from John 13:19, "I tell you this now, before it takes place." And yet in John the idea seems to be not so much what *will* happen as what *must* happen. He doesn't exactly know the future; he doesn't have to. He knows the script. Somehow he is privy to what God has mapped out for all of them, though he still does not grasp why it must go that way. And, remember that in all likelihood the whole notion that Jesus did know the plan beforehand is a result of the gospel story tellers gradually attributing to the Jesus character their own knowledge (standing outside the story) of how the story will end. We see the same thing in comedies when a character will turn to the audience and say he knows what to do because he has read the script already.

The next lines predict that, of all people, members of his own chosen inner circle will be the ones to sell him out. They seem to be a paraphrase of the rest of John 13:18, the verse immediately preceding the one just discussed. It tells what it is he is telling them before the fact: "I know whom I have chosen [plug in here a phrase taken from a twin verse, John 6:70, "'Have I not chosen you, the twelve? And yet one of you is a devil.' He spoke of Judas . . ., for he, one of the twelve, was later to betray him"]; it is that the scripture may be fulfilled, 'He who ate my bread has lifted his heel against me.'" Many scholars think that the whole scene we are discussing has been imaginatively constructed on the basis of that verse, quoted from Psalm 41:9 (which is, of course, not actually a predictive prophecy in its original context).

Cut out the dramatics! You know very well who—

Judas does not have so much heaven on his mind that he is easily tricked into the mysterious stupor possessing the others. Jesus has bewitched them with ominous hints, keeping the straight facts behind the curtain so he can lead the disciples along by the nose as he always does. But Judas is not fooled by such charismatic trickery. He stopped being fooled some days ago. His mind is clearer than theirs now.

In particular, Judas resents Jesus making it look like he is gazing into some crystal ball in which the future is still hazy, still taking form. Bunk!

Judas knows at once that Jesus must somehow have heard some whispered rumor of the Sanhedrin's plan. It is not mystery but only machinations. And so Jesus must know which one of them is the culprit. And yet he insists on milking even this fact for all the fraudulent theatrics he can.

Why don't you go do it?

Well, then why are you standing there? Get to it! You, Judas, are the one who is doing the play acting! But there's no need for pretense. We both know where it stands. There is a hint of Jesus calling Judas' bluff, as if he can see Judas is undecided, temporizing, hesitating, as if maybe he will not rendezvous with the Sanhedrin's goon squad after all. Think of the stereotyped scene in which the police officer faces a young crook cornered on his first caper. The kid is more nervous than afraid, his hand shaking as he holds a gun on the cop. The latter tries to soothe him as he slowly inches toward the lad with a fatherly demeanor: "C'mon, son, put the gun down. We both know you don't want to shoot me . . ." Jesus almost sounds like that, as if to say, "Judas, I don't think you're as resolute as you thought you were about this thing. What keeps you here now that the truth is out? Go ahead, if you want to. I'm not stopping you. I think it's your conscience making you hesitate. Isn't that right?"

But it might as easily be that Jesus is appealing to his schoolyard sense of honor, daring him to go through with it, calling him a coward, goading Judas to go through with it because Jesus actually *does* want him to go through with it, as Judas says next.

You want me to do it!

Judas may be replying to what he thinks is Jesus' accusing sarcasm. Why are you reproaching me? It sounds like you *want* me to! Then don't blame me! Of course, as the Gethsemane scene will make clear, it is the last thing Jesus wants. He speaks to Judas with bitter resignation. He is God's puppet; he will do the deed because the script says he will, and that's that. So get on with it! Why prolong the inevitable? Jesus speaks to Judas here as he will to Pilate in a later scene. He is impatient with someone who imagines himself to wield life-and-death power, but who in fact has as little real initiative in Jesus' death as the cross beams and the nails. God is the real culprit.

Then again, Judas may be replying with bafflement: You want me to do it? You mean you know, and you've taken no steps to prevent it? You're just willing to go along quietly, like a lamb to the slaughter? What *is* this? What's going on here? Not what I thought.

Or we might take Judas to be answering Jesus' question as if it were not merely rhetorical, a piece of sarcasm. "Why don't I go do it? Because you want me to, that's why!" So he's just being contrary. If Jesus wants Judas to betray him, then he's not really injuring Jesus, so he'll do the opposite, since his only real aim is to frustrate Jesus one way or another. Pure spite. And yet we have not been given to believe that personal animosity motivates Judas at all—though these very developments will soon make Judas despise him.

Finally, when Judas says, "You want me to do it," we might not be mistaken if we detect a hint of self-justification, parallel to his excuse-making before Caiaphas and Annas: "Jesus wouldn't mind that I was here with you."

Hurry they are waiting

Jesus speaks as Annas did: "Cut the confessions, . . . get up off the floor." Where does Rice get the notion that Jesus would tell his betrayer to get a move on? As usual, from the Gospel of John. John 13:27 reads, "Jesus said to him, 'What you are going to do, do quickly.'"

If you knew why I do it . . .

. . . then you wouldn't be angry with me! He senses, whether correctly or not, that Jesus has nothing but contempt for him as a miserable turncoat. But actually Jesus seems more irritated at God! It is as if Jesus is telling God, "Cut out the dramatics!" Why all this melodrama? Cut to the chase! Don't play cat and mouse like this! And Judas tries to justify his despicable actions as he did before the Sanhedrin. But, strangely, even though what he says is all true, it is not convincing even to Judas himself. He is uneasily aware of things being terribly amiss.

I don't care why you do it!

Huh? How can that be? Simply because Judas is not really the one responsible, God is. And as the Gethsemane prayer reveals, Jesus cares very much why God does it. Judas is exploding with explanations, but God, the mastermind of the scheme, remains silent.

Judas, however, can only imagine that Jesus has some insanely grandiose "reason for . . . wanting . . . to die," perhaps because it would assure that he "would be more noticed than [he] ever was before." Dying as a martyr is going out with a bang: people remember you, dedicate churches to you. But those who merely fade away? They get a gold watch, maybe a painting hanging dustily in some hall someplace. I tell you, they have received their reward in full. So Judas begins, but *only* begins, to understand. He had thought Jesus carried away with ambition, but he thought it was the ambition of "the man who would be king." Judas, of course, the cold-eyed realist, thought he could see that Jesus was obliviously hurtling toward disaster. Little did Judas realize before this moment that Jesus' ambition was to rush to a martyr death with eyes wide open.

Real life examples of such ultimate grandstanding are not unknown. One such is an early Christian-Cynic preacher names Proteus Peregrinus, of whom Lucian tells (*The Passing of Peregrinus*): he had gained a following among the poor and credulous, who dutifully visited him in prison. After his release, he announced that he would walk straight into his own funeral bonfire and there be assumed into heaven. In the event, Proteus did not shun the fiery embrace. Lucian himself was there for a few chuckles. As he turned to leave, a late-comer asked what he had missed. Unable to resist the temptation to mischief, Lucian told the poor yokel that he had missed nothing less than the sight of Proteus rising from the pyre in the form of an eagle, bound for heaven. As he walked back to the city limits what should Lucian hear but a credulous believer telling the same story as he himself had witnessed the marvel!

Or think of Bishop Ignatius of Antioch in the second century. A set of spurious letters attributed to him pictures him writing various individuals and churches from several points along the way to Rome where his captors were taking him to be fed to wild beasts in the arena. Time and again, Ignatius writes that his friends and followers should in no case try to rescue him or gain his freedom in any way. No, he looks forward with eager expectation to the moment when the lions will grind his pious bones between their fangs and his spirit will soar aloft to the heavenly Valhalla reserved for martyrs. Isn't the idea of martyrdom that you succumb resignedly to die as a witness for your faith when no chance of escaping remains? You figure your time has come. But Ignatius was practically volunteering to serve as lion lunch! This is a bit hard to respect. It is just taking the short (though painful) path to pie in the sky, the express elevator to heaven.

So this is now what Jesus intends, or so Judas thinks. And of course he is half-right: Jesus is going to death as part of a vaster plan, but much more is going on than Judas (or even Jesus himself) imagines.

To think I admired you
For now I despise you

Remember "Heaven on Their Minds"? Judas said then, "My admiration for you hasn't died," even though he was beginning to worry. Now his admiration for Jesus has been destroyed. Jesus appears no longer as the noble teacher of enlightened morality and piety, but rather as a fanatic bent on self-glorification even to the point of death.

You liar—you Judas

Jesus accuses Judas of lying, but about what in particular? I would guess that Judas' expressed contempt for the supposed charlatan Jesus is a smokescreen. What is really going on is Judas' rationalization of his betrayal. If Judas can convince himself that Jesus is unworthy of the love and devotion Judas had given to him all these long months, then he may be able to live with the terrible act he has committed. It will seem not such a bad thing to hand this faker over to the authorities. Good riddance! "You're a joke! You're not the Lord! You're nothing but a fraud! Take him away, he's got nothing to say . . . Get out of my life!" Herod Antipas will say it and mean it. Judas says pretty much the same thing, but he will soon be echoing Mary Magdalene's song, "I don't know how to love him." And Jesus can see it. He knows Judas better than Judas knows himself.

But what does Jesus mean by calling him "You Judas!" It sounds as if the name Judas had already become synonymous with "betrayer, traitor." It hadn't yet, but this is another one of Rice's creative anachronisms. By this modern usage, Jesus is as much as telling Judas his fate will be eternal execration. Judas will certainly "be more noticed than [he] ever was before," but as with Pilate, millions will spit his name as a curse, "leaving [him] the blame." Ironically, "Iscariot" seems to have started out as an epithet and ended up as a name;

"Judas" began as a name and wound up an epithet!

> **You want me to do it!**
> **What if I just stayed here**
> **And ruined your ambition?**
> **Christ you deserve it!**

Again, Judas thinks at last he sees what is going on. And what he sees is that Jesus has been manipulating him, using him to engineer his own death. Thus he says that it looks like Jesus is getting nervous that Judas may have a change of heart! And that's the last thing the glory-seeking Jesus wants! Or so Judas imagines. Knowing that Jesus plans to go to his death, he is still largely in the dark. "If you knew the path we're riding, you'd understand it less than I." Even so, it has happened. Judas knows the path. He *is* the path, the Via Dolorosa, Jesus will walk to his death. What Judas will soon be blaming God for ("I've been used—and you knew! I'll never know why you picked me for your crime, your foul, bloody crime!"), this he is now accusing Jesus of. Only later will he know (as Jesus will say in Gethsemane) that Jesus, too, was a pawn in God's enigmatic chess game.

"Christ, you deserve it!" Yeah, he's rationalizing it, all right. Judas is actually secretly relieved that he doesn't have to feel so bad about what he's about to do.

Notice that in *Jesus Christ Superstar* his disciples and friends almost always call their master "Jesus," his own name. It is outsiders who call him "Christ." Herod Antipas: "Hey! Aren't you scared of me, Christ? Mister wonderful Christ?" Centurion: "Someone Christ, King of the Jews." Pontius Pilate: "Talk to me Jesus Christ." The crowd: "Tell me, Christ, how you feel tonight." The fans on Palm Sunday, particularly Simon Zealotes, call him Christ, not Jesus: "Christ, you know I love you." "Christ, what more do you need to convince you?" The point, as Jesus' subsequent lament, "Poor Jerusalem," demonstrates, is to relegate the Zealot and the fervent crowd to the rank of outsiders, since they completely misunderstand his mission. They are as near insiders as anyone can be, but still they are outsiders—just the point Mark makes over and over again. Privileged to hear the secret explanations of the parable, they still do not get it. In the enviable position of seeing all the miracles up close, they are in the end no more enlightened than anyone else. Now Judas has distanced himself from Jesus. He calls him "Christ," not "Jesus."

Hurry you fool, hurry and go,
Save me your speeches, I don't want to know—Go!

Why does Jesus think Judas a fool? Judas thinks Jesus has made him a pawn in his insane scheme, and yet Judas is still willing to go ahead with it, since he now (says he) thinks Jesus deserves death. But, from Jesus' perspective, Judas is still acting the fool, the dupe, just like the self-important Pilate, only they are pawns of God's plan, not Jesus'. In fact, Jesus fears he himself may be playing the fool. It is Jesus' own morbid and resentful attitude toward his imminent death that makes him heedless of Judas' feelings and impatient at Judas' implicit apologies and excuses. No words will change anything or mitigate anyone's guilt. Because ultimately Judas bears no responsibility. As he will soon be saying, the bloody crime (if crime it is) is God's. So Jesus is willing to save his own speeches, speeches of reproach, for the Garden where he will call God to account. Judas is a mere stooge. His role is unimportant, and therefore so is his guilt, his soul-bearing. "Cut the confessions, forget the excuses." Jesus just wants to get the damn thing over!

Look at all my trials and tribulations
Sinking in a gentle pool of wine
What's that in the bread it's gone to my head
Till this morning is this evening life is fine
Always hoped that I'd be an apostle
Knew that I would make it if I tried
Then when we retire we can write the gospels
So they'll still talk about us when we've died

The boozy chorus of the twelve is repeated here to remind us that the disciples are drunk, since we will need to know this shortly when they find themselves unable to keep awake with Jesus to support him in prayer. Also, we need to be informed as to why there is no intervention by anyone else on the scene during this altercation between Jesus and Judas. Are we to imagine them hearing all this plain speech about how Judas is going right now to call the authorities to arrest Jesus? No, of course not, or they would not be taken by surprise when it comes to pass. So Rice reminds us they are beyond all worries. In John 13, this question does not arise so sharply, since the interchange between Jesus and Judas is much briefer and less explicit ("What you are planning to do, do it quickly"). John says that at this point

Judas rose and left, and that the others speculated that Jesus might have sent him out to buy provisions for the Passover seder the next night, or to make a holiday contribution to the poor. Under these mistaken impressions, they would naturally be surprised later to see Judas show up with an armed mob. But since Rice has had Judas spill his guts during his heated words with Jesus, he has to account for how this news escaped the other disciples. Thus their drunken stupor.

Incidentally, the egotistical motivation Rice attributes to the disciples here, that they will write memoirs of Jesus just so they can continue riding his coattails in death as they have in life—this is pretty much what Rice actually thought of the gospel writers' motives. In an interview he speaks of "the ego-trip" of Matthew, Mark, Luke and John, as if to explain why each made the changes in the gospel story he did. Like a hack staff writer who has to make it look like he's earning his pay by making gratuitous changes in a perfectly good script, ruining it just to look busy.

Finally, note that there is a new line as opposed to the last time we heard this refrain. "What's that in the bread? It's gone to my head." This is certainly a sly reference to the later church doctrine of Transubstantiation. What is special in the communion bread? The Real Presence of Christ, whereby the wafer becomes sacramental and salvific. In the Aristotelian terms of Thomas Aquinas, the inner essence of the bread has changed into the essence of the body of Christ, though the external properties are still those of bread. There is a mysterious something "in the bread" that's "gone to my head," i.e., caused a change in spiritual consciousness. We can well imagine that something in the wine, namely alcohol, has gone to the disciples' heads, but what can it be in the bread?

> **You sad pathetic man-see where you've brought us to**
> **Our ideals die around us all because of you**
> **And now the saddest cut of all-**
> **Someone had to turn you in**
> **Like a common criminal, like a wounded animal**
> **A jaded mandarin**
> **A jaded mandarin**
> **A jaded faded [jaded faded jaded] mandarin**

Judas again parallels Pilate, in that both speak dismissively to Jesus from a self-assured, but completely mistaken, perspective. Pilate will describe

Jesus in very nearly the same terms used by Judas here: "He's a sad little man, not a king or god . . . He's just misguided, thinks he's important."

Neither Judas nor Pilate, however, means to characterize Jesus as feeling "sad," subjectively unhappy. No, they mean he is a sad spectacle, pitiable especially in his obliviousness to reality. He is pathetic in that you can't take him seriously enough to be very mad at him. Judas seems to have resolved his inner struggles for the moment. Jesus' seemingly petulant and arbitrary behavior in the last few moments has confirmed Judas' half-imagined suspicions. Jesus is just a grandstander who has now gone so far as to become a danger to himself and others. For everyone's good he must be taken in hand. It's just pitiful.

When Judas speaks of "ideals" which have tragically succumbed to Jesus' fatal narcissism, we have a valuable clue as to what the Jesus movement had meant to him. He cannot have been hoping for a political-military revolution that would make him one of Jesus' powerful lieutenants. Such were the silly daydreams of James and John, but when Judas saw such vain imaginings growing among the disciples and the larger circle around them, that's when he started to worry. He never thought such a thing had any chance of succeeding. In "Heaven on Their Minds," he lamented the eclipse of "the things you say." He had pinned no hopes on Jesus the king but rather on Jesus the teacher. It was, then, a movement of ethical renewal and religious reform that had attracted Judas. These are the "ideals" that are already going to the cross, thanks to Jesus. Jesus does not teach them or embody them any more. Judas finds himself in precisely the role he had predicted (in "Heaven on Their Minds") the disappointed crowds would eventually take: "You have set them all on fire; they think they've found their new messiah, and they'll hurt you when they find they're wrong . . . and they'll hurt you when they think you've lied." Judas is now so mortally stung with disappointment at Jesus that his love has soured into hate, and he is ready to hurt Jesus whom he sees as having lived a lie.

"The saddest cut of all" recalls Shakespeare's phrase "the unkindest cut of all." The subtle difference between the two expressions would seem to be that "the unkindest cut" denotes the needless cruelty of the one who delivers the sword stroke to his defeated opponent," while "the saddest cut of all" envisions not Jesus, but Judas and the other disciples, as the victims, even though it is Jesus who is being handed over to death. It is Jesus who has dealt *them* this mortal blow. How has he done it? By going so badly off track, sending his once-hopeful movement of renewal into a tailspin, and for sheer self-aggrandizement's sake. How pathetic! How tragic!

"Someone had to turn you in." Not only is Judas commenting on Jesus' terrible fall from grace: "you've finally come to this, have you?" He is in the same moment trying to excuse himself from the responsibility of what, deep down, he knows is a betrayal of his friend. "If it wasn't me, it would have been somebody else." All his invective here is an obvious distancing device (subconsciously) aimed at burying Judas' still-living love and devotion to Jesus. If he can convince himself (and that's really who he's talking to in this tirade) that Jesus no longer deserves his affection, then maybe his conscience will stop throbbing.

"Like a common criminal"—in other words, Judas does not think Jesus has been caught out, like Moliere's *Tartuffe*, as a rogue pretending to be a saint, now exposed as a crook. No, Jesus was destined for better things. He had the potential to do great things for the human spirit. But in fact, he has disgraced himself, making himself appear as one more trouble-making hooligan. No doubt Judas is thinking of a specific act of Jesus, and it is not difficult to figure out which one he has in mind. It was the "cleansing" of the temple. Not surprisingly, the authorities saw only a fanatic making a scene to no apparent purpose other than gaining a few moments' notoriety, like a Presidential assassin who will go to any length to capture the limelight. What a fatal blunder Jesus had made, so that there could really be no other outcome than this.

"Like a wounded animal"—that is, Judas means, Jesus has so mismanaged things that he winds up getting hunted down and cornered in his lair by his pursuers. The image does not seem to recall the scene of a hunted animal becoming more dangerous because of a wound, but rather that of the prey retreating to its den to await the inevitable. And thus the "common criminal" and "wounded animal" are the same: "We know you're in there! Come out slowly with your hands up!"

Mandarins were Chinese nobles and emperors with fantastic wealth, power, and pomp. Regaled with brilliantly hued silks and sporting six-inch lacquered fingernails (signaling their sublime disdain of manual labor), they often sank into the sadistic decadence that their power and position made possible, even inevitable, since there was no exotic thrill left for these jaded sufferers of ennui to try. Or at least this is the stereotype. One can find vivid treatments of the theme in Sax Rohmer's novels of Fu Manchu and in Robert Bloch's tale, "The Mandarin's Canaries." Is Judas making Jesus a "jaded mandarin" in this sense? Not directly, no. But there is perhaps the implication not only that his time is past, he is yesterday's news, but also that, having tired of his original mission, he has decided to let hell break loose just so he can go out with a bang. "Would I be more noticed than I ever was before?" That's how Judas sees Jesus' motivation in first bringing on his arrest and then his refusal to do anything to avert it. A martyr death will ensure that his name will after all be remembered more than "ten minutes after I'm dead."

Get out! They're waiting! They're waiting for you!

Judas, then, has not "saved [Jesus his] speeches" as he asked. And Jesus can put up with no more, since everything Judas says is predicated on such a complete misunderstanding that there is no reason at all for Jesus to take it seriously. Jesus just wants to cut to the chase, to get the whole thing over with since nothing can be done to stop it anyway. In this line we almost get the impression Jesus feels Judas has been stalling with all this verbal abuse, as if he secretly hopes Jesus will listen to him and escape, or that the arresting party will grow tired of waiting and return to their beds. And this Jesus does not want! No, he means to hurry Judas up: "Get on with it! Before it's too late! Don't make them wait!"

Everytime I look at you I don't understand
Why you let the things you did get so out of hand
You'd have managed better if you'd had it planned—

"Every time I look at you," i.e., in the present state of pathetic dissolution, "I don't understand." That is, I wonder "why you let the things you did get so out of hand." Judas knows good and well that Jesus has not simply been overtaken by unforeseen events. No, for some reason he must have allowed it to happen. And that is the mystery: what possible reason could there be? Jesus will, in Gethsemane, soon be asking God the very same question.

The terminating dash, equivalent to an ellipse, indicates that Judas meant to go on but lets his sentence trail off. We will hear the continuation soon enough, in his postmortem retrospective. But then we will hear his voice from the far future, from our own day, when Judas has seen much more but is no closer to understanding it.

Contrast his bafflement here with his earlier clarity: "My mind is clearer now. At last I can see . . ." And yet now he cannot see what is going on. It is more of a mystery than ever. What he could see clearly then, that Jesus had passed into perilous danger, and that Judas might have to do something to prevent it, he sees now only in a glass darkly. Ironically, it is now, in the very moment that he is to follow through on his much-considered plan ("I thought this whole thing out before I came to you") that he grows unsure of the situation. "I don't understand." And it is his own role in the affair that he understands least of all. And while he imagines the whole mess is the result of Jesus "letting things get out hand," he does not suspect that all is in fact proceeding according to schedule.

> **Look at all my trials and tribulations**
> **Sinking in a gentle pool of wine**
> **Don't disturb me now I can see the answers**
> **Till this evening is this morning life is fine**

This reprise of the drunken ditty of the other eleven disciples brings closure to the Last Supper scene, making it end where it began. It also serves to remind us that the disciples are so drunk, there is no way they will be able to stay awake with Jesus in his garden vigil. Peter, harmonizing boozily with his companions, has entirely forgotten Jesus' shocking prediction that he will betray him "in just a few hours." And yet the very words he obliviously sings betray his looming destiny. "Till this evening is this morning life is fine." Jesus said Peter would deny him before the cock crows to announce that the evening has given way to the morning. That's when Peter will fail so miserably. That's when life will cease being fine.

> **Always hoped that I'd be an apostle**
> **Knew that I would make it if I tried**
> **Then when we retire we can write the gospels**
> **So they'll still talk about us when we've died**

The selfish, worm's eye view ambition of the disciples, so evident in Mark's gospel, is highlighted here. Achieving apostleship is viewed as making it into the big time, an honor and an advantage. Technically they will be apostles (authoritative emissaries of an absent Christ) only once Jesus dies. Till then they are mere apprentices, "disciples," learners. So the impending death of

Jesus means to them the sooner fulfillment of their cherished dreams. With him out of the way, they will have the spotlight all to themselves. But what about when they die? Won't their public forget about them?

They've already got that one figured out: during their comfy retirements in Patmos or Rome or Ephesus they will relax and write their memoirs, the gospels, as something to be remembered by. In other words, the gospels will not be written for the sake of perpetuating the memory of Jesus, but rather as public relations for themselves ("Or was that just PR?"). "So they'll still talk about"—whom? Jesus? No, us. This is precisely the motive Judas is attributing to Jesus for allowing himself to be done in! Just like Proteus Peregrinus. But Jesus forms a stark contrast with his self-absorbed sycophants.

Notice again the intentional anachronism here. The disciples speak of "the gospels" just as we would: as well known literary works already penned. Such terminology would be appropriate only in retrospect, not in prospect. The disciples are being pictured as on the scene with Jesus at the Last Supper, but Rice makes them speak as if from the future, the time of the *Superstar* audience. He does this in order to force us to make the same connection he is making: "See? This is how the 'holy' gospels came about!"

> **Will no-one stay awake with me?**
> **Peter? John? James?**
> **Will none of you wait with me?**
> **Peter? John? James?**

In the gospels, Jesus issues this rebuke only after they have left the upper room and walked to the moonlit Garden of Gethsemane, and once he has returned to the sleeping trio after having prayed by himself. "And they went to a place which was called Gethsemane; and he said to his disciples, 'Sit here, while I pray.' And he took with him Peter and James and John, and began to be greatly troubled. And he said to them, 'My soul is very sorrowful, even to death; remain here, on vigil'" (Mark 14:32–34). But he returns to find them snoring, not praying. "On vigil" might mean, in accord with religious idiom, either "keep watch" or "continue in prayer" (Psalm 63:6). Jesus awakens them with these stinging words, "Simon! Are you asleep? Could you not watch one hour? Stay awake and pray not to have to be put to the test" (Mark 14:37–38a).

Scholars suggest that what Mark has done here is to create the whole episode on the basis of a parable in the Markan apocalypse, Mark 13:33–36: "Take heed, watch and pray; for you do not know when the time will come. It is like a man going on a journey, when he leaves home and puts his servants in charge, each with his assigned duties, and commands the doorkeeper to be on the watch. Watch, therefore, for you do not know when the master of the house will come, in the evening, or at the stroke of midnight, or when the cock crows [!], or at mid-morning, lest he come suddenly and find you asleep." That Mark has indeed created the scene out of whole cloth is plain from the fact that he is somehow privy to the "information" of what precisely Jesus said in prayer—while the only possible witnesses were sound asleep! He "knows" it because he made it up.

Why is Jesus shown to leave the greater part of his men waiting on the periphery and to take along with him an inner circle of three? And this is hardly the only such occasion. Peter, James, and John are also the only three privy to the Transfiguration (Mark 9:2) and the resurrection of Jairus' daughter (Mark 5:37). This fact, which one might think noteworthy, goes unexplained in the gospel texts. But the likelihood is that the writers, or the traditional stories they were using, had tried to read back into the time of Jesus a later church authority structure. Paul in Galatians 2:9 refers to "the Pillars" in Jerusalem: James, John, and Cephas (apparently the same as Peter).

This term suggests the mythic image, frequent in the Old Testament, of the cosmic pillars supporting the solid dome of the firmament above the flat earth. Solomon's temple had sported two great pillars with names: Boaz and Jachin, which were supposed to represent the central pillars supporting the heavens. Perhaps in Israelite mythology they had been two brother Titans turned to stone as a punishment for their rebellion, just as Zeus consigns the Titan Atlas to shoulder the burden of the heavens. Castor and Pollux, too, had something to do with such a myth, since "Pollux" means "Upholder of the vault of heaven." My guess is that originally, Boaz (who still survives as a character in the Book of Ruth) and Jachin were the Hebrew versions of Castor and Pollux.

And so were James and John, who carried the enigmatic epithet "Boanerges" (Mark 3:17), which Mark dopes out as possibly meaning "Sons of Thunder." This would be significant since another of the Titans was named "Brontes," which means "Thunderer." But "Boanerges" does not in fact seem to be a recognizable Hebrew, Aramaic, or Greek word, or combination of words. The most sense anyone has made of it is John Allegro's suggestion[132] that it is equivalent to the hypothetical Sumerian term, *Geshpuanur*, which simply makes the suffix "-ges" in Boanerges into a prefix. (In Semitic names the prefix and suffix were often interchangeable anyway, as in the twin names Hananiah and Yohannon, "gift of Yahve" and "Yahve's gift.") If the syllable order were the same, we would have *Puanurgesh*, "upholder of the vault of heaven." And Peter comes from *petros*, "rock," in this case denoting the great foundation stone of the universe, symbolically identified with the foundation of the Jerusalem temple.

The three of them, "Boanerges" and "Petros" or "Kepha" (the Aramaic equivalent), were collectively known as "the Pillars." Just as the Pillars of Islam were originally the immediate relatives of the Prophet, and later the fundamental practices upon which the Islamic community squarely rests, these three men were the foundations of the Christian Church—at least in their own eyes. The "James" who belonged to the Pillars was supposedly the same as "James the Just," the brother of Jesus, while the James who accompanies Jesus up Mount Olivet and into Gethsemane is James, son of Zebedee, brother of John. Roman Catholic tradition understands James the Just to have been a cousin, not a brother, to Jesus, and thus possibly identical to James, son of Zebedee. And Samuel Sandmel[133] and other scholars have questioned whether "Cephas" and "Peter" were not originally two different figures. Perhaps Peter was the disciple, Cephas the Jerusalem Pillar Saint, only later identified with each other so as to give the Pillar Saint a pedigree stemming from Jesus' own ministry. Just as the two Jameses may have been combined, so may an originally distinct Simon Peter and Cephas. And the early church fairly teems with seers and apostles named John. John of Patmos, seer of the Revelation, was probably not the same as John son of Zebedee, and yet tradition identified the two. So the long and short of it is that the scenes of Jesus taking only Peter, James, and John with him into the inner circle, may simply be a fictitious retrojection of the later Pillar Saints into the ministry of Jesus, so as to buttress their authority once the Twelve disciples had risen to prominence, threatening to eclipse the authority of the Pillars. The spin doctors went to work to co-opt apostolic authority for the Pillars, pretending they had been the same as three of the original disciples, and the top three at that.

An alternative explanation would be that there actually were three specially intimate disciples, and it was to them that Jesus entrusted certain advanced teachings he knew he dared not vouchsafe to the others. This is just what the Gnostic Christians of the second century claimed. Basilides claimed to have received his teaching from Peter via Peter's assistant Glaukias. The

Gnostic *Secret Book of James*, discovered in the Egyptian desert only some seventy-five years ago, makes James the receiver and purveyor of secret, elite truths. The Gnostics claimed that these chosen disciples transmitted the "inside stuff" only to certain chosen disciples of theirs, knowing that the run-of-the-mill Christians would never understand or accept their revelations. In this case, the gospels might record the existence of this inner circle of three without any explanation, since the gospel writers did not know the point of it, not being acquainted with either the fact or the content of the secret teaching.

But why did Jesus want them to stay awake with him? Did he really suppose that their prayers, added to his, would avail something that his own alone would not? It seems more likely that, even though Mark has taken the story off in a different direction, the point of Jesus' instructions was for his disciples to stand guard to alert him in case an arresting party should be spotted headed their way. If they told him in time, there might still be time to escape. And then they would all be spared the trials to come. Their failure has led directly to his capture. They were asleep on guard duty, awakened only as the enemy arrived on the scene. This reading of the situation fits better than any other the curious fact that Jesus is shown praying for nothing else than to escape arrest and execution! It is surprising, given the artificial ubiquity of the "divine preordination" motif, that such clear reminders of an earlier version, in which Jesus sought to escape his death, survived at all. Everywhere else, the story has been rewritten wholesale to have Jesus walk forward into Death's embrace with eyes wide open because it is the will of God.

Why does Rice move these lines back into the scene of the Last Supper? It makes more sense to picture the disciples as passing out drunk around the table, but then how do they manage to be with Jesus in the Garden? The movie version neatly solves this problem by setting the Last Supper out in the open air in Gethsemane itself. Thus Jesus has only to get up from the picnic and walk a few yards to a more isolated spot to pray. For what it may be worth, even this ambiguity reflects the Gospel of John, where, probably because of clumsy editing, there is some confusion over when Jesus and the disciples had risen from the table and walked to Gethsemane. Jesus seems to leave the upper room at the close of chapter 16, and yet where does he offer the "high priestly" prayer of chapter 17? John probably didn't care much. As long as he had the right words mouthed by the right characters, matters of geographical and chronological continuity were strictly trivial to him.

Gethsemane (I Only Want to Say)

Peter and the others are on hand here in the garden, but Jesus must have awakened them only long enough to make the short walk. As soon as they found nice soft spots on the ground they collapsed into their stupor once again. As they sleep it off, Jesus bares his soul to God. As always, such a prayer is really more of a self-realization than a revelation to God who must presumably know our hearts already. But our latent feelings are crystallized as we are moved to speak them out. And it may be at this point that we ourselves first discover how we feel about something.

> I only want to say
> If there is a way
> Take this cup away from me for I don't want to taste its poison
> Feel it burn me . . .

This opening, "I only want to say . . ." implies that Jesus might be expected, given his demeanor, to say something more than he in fact plans to say. One might expect him to rebel and refuse the plan of God, to flee like Jonah did. Indeed he does not relish the prospect of what is ahead for him, but he isn't refusing to go through with it. All he's asking is that God change his plans, work out some Plan B that does not entail Jesus' "messy death." This scene may be the most outrageous of all to pious listeners, and yet it is directly based on the gospel text, though not John's. In Mark 14:36, Jesus prays, "Father, all things are possible to thee; remove this cup from me." Introducing the scene, Mark summarizes Jesus' words first in indirect discourse: "he fell on the ground and prayed that, if it were possible, the hour might pass from him."

There is an interesting difference between the words Mark attributes to Jesus and the words of Mark's own summary. Jesus assumes that his deliverance from crucifixion is definitely possible for God, should he be persuaded to do it. The question is, will God do it or not? It will be a matter of his will, not of his available options. Mark, on the other hand, seems to suppose that even God almighty has no room to maneuver in the present situation. We might take this difference to denote Mark's redaction of the traditional story in order to eliminate any remaining element of contingency. Otherwise we seem to end up with God depicted as demanding the death of Jesus even when other alternatives remained to him. Thus Mark might be seen as trying to control the reader's interpretation of Jesus' prayer before he reads it.

This would make sense in terms of redactional motivations, since we have already seen how the gospels tend to freeze the indeterminacy of history-as-experienced into the inflexible givenness of fate. But since the prayer of Jesus is manifestly Mark's own composition, we must look for some other explanation. And one lies ready at hand. Scholars have long realized that one of Mark's chief compositional techniques is "doubling," describing the scene in the third person, as a narrator, and then following it with a comment by Jesus that repeats much the same wording, but with slight variation, achieving the same effect as Old Testament Hebrew poetry, which used the technique of paraphrasing what has just been said: "The heavens are telling the glory of God, the firmament showeth his handiwork." This is probably all Mark is doing in the present case, putting a slightly different spin on the element of possibility: "if it were possible"/"All things are possible." Similarly, notice the substitution of "this cup" for "this hour." Just poetic license.

In the Bible, "the cup" is a frequent metaphor for a time of trial and suffering. It is the cup of sufferings, and one must endure, must drink it to the bitter dregs. But Rice has activated another potential dimension of the metaphor: a cup of poison, suggesting a parallel with the death of Socrates, sentenced by the authorities to commit suicide by drinking a cup of hemlock. In the gospels, Jesus is often depicted in terms of a Cynic philosopher (emulators of Socrates), or even as a kind of Jewish Socrates, as when in John 8:6 he casually writes in the dust with his finger, giving his opponents time to consider the implications of what he has said. The scene recalls the dialogue of Socrates with Meno. Lucian calls Jesus "the crucified sophist," and the Gospel of Thomas has Matthew characterize him as "a wise philosopher." So the allusion to Socrates is by no means unlikely.

But it seems equally likely that what Rice has done is to move forward the business about the hyssop-sponge dipped in vinegar or poison from the crucifixion scene (John 19:28–30). John says there was a bowl of vinegar (i.e., cheap wine that had gone sour, kept on hand, too long, to dull the pain of the sufferers), but his having Jesus "fulfill" Psalm 69: ("They gave me poison for my food and vinegar to drink") may imply Jesus died quickly from being mercifully poisoned.

If this element of the story comes from John's gospel, the prayer of Jesus, as we have just seen, comes instead from Mark (echoed by Matthew and

Luke with slight variations). John repudiates the whole idea. In one of the clearest cases of John attempting to correct the previous gospel tradition, he has Jesus hypothetically raise the question of shirking the cross only to dismiss it contemptuously: "Now my soul is troubled. And what shall I say? 'Father, save me from this hour?' No, it was for this purpose that I came to this hour!" (John 12:27). Contrast this with Mark 14:33–34, Jesus "began to be greatly distressed and troubled. And he said to them, 'My soul is very sorrowful, even unto death.'"

This change is part of a larger redactional tendency in John. He seems to want to cut the ground from beneath an interpretation current in his day that Jesus did not die on the cross but rather survived and showed himself three days later. To this end he made Jesus repudiate the original prayer in which he had asked God to let him escape the cross, since the narrative function of such a request is to anticipate an actual deliverance from the cross, albeit in an unexpected way: by a premature seeming death because of the numbing "vinegar." John has also inserted the note about Jesus being stabbed in the side to verify his death, even though the soldiers had supposedly already decided he was dead. The spear thrust releases a torrent of blood and water, indicating that he was definitely dead. John is trying to verify Jesus' death for the reader's benefit. But he protests too much with his frantic oath-taking: "And he who saw it bears witness, that you also may believe" (John 19:35).

And after the resurrection, John transformed an earlier story, still extant in Luke 24:36–43, where Jesus showed the disciples his hands and feet to demonstrate he is flesh and bone, not a ghost, i.e., still alive, not risen, as a ghost, from the dead. John's version is in John 20:19–20, and he has Jesus indicate his hands and *side*, all wounded, to demonstrate that he really did die. John adds to this the redundant Doubting Thomas episode to make things even more explicit. John has even replaced the ambiguous raising of Jairus' daughter (Mark 5:21–23, 35–43) with the definitive resurrection of Lazarus (John chapter 11). Whereas Jairus' girl had only just "died," and Jesus says "She is not dead, but only sleeps," John has Jesus say the same of Lazarus, then has one of the disciples pointedly ask if he means Lazarus is sleeping off his fever. Jesus then says, No, he's dead all right, but not for long. When they get to the tomb, Lazarus is already decomposing: "By this time, he stinketh." So this one's no coma. And so with John's Jesus.

One last note: in Mark, the Gethsemane prayer is our deepest glimpse into the intimacy between Jesus and his heavenly Father (well rendered by

Mark's artistry, in fact, his own creation). But Rice has dropped the whole relationship. While Mark and the Q source common to both Matthew and Luke have Jesus call God his Father fairly infrequently, Luke's special material, added to Mark and Q, his main sources, and Matthew's distinctive material, as well as John en toto all raise the percentage significantly: Jesus is calling God his Father all the time in these later rewrites. But Rice has eliminated the tendency. The one and only time Jesus will call God his father is the last line of the play, when he is about to die on the cross. This vaguely reminds us of Mark, where the first time someone outside the circle of Jesus' disciples calls Jesus the Son of God is when he dies.

> **. . . I have changed I'm not as sure**
> **As when we started**
> **Then I was inspired**
> **Now I'm sad and tired**

Apparently Jesus started out on his mission, somewhat ill-defined in *Jesus Christ Superstar*, in the full knowledge that it would eventually come to this. Then he was willing to shoulder the cross manfully. In fact we might say he had been shouldering the cross from the beginning, laboring under the dreadful knowledge that he was only heading for crucifixion. But bearing this invisible burden for these three years has at length taken its toll. Jesus is worn out with it. He has not yet gotten his second wind. The Via Dolorosa looks right now like a marathon course that he just cannot finish. As the finish line, the deadline, approaches him now, he flinches. It all seems more terribly real than before.

Jesus had in the beginning been inspired, filled with the prospect of accomplishing great things for his God. Why is he sad and tired now? Probably because he has seen so little accomplished. His efforts seem to have been largely wasted, as witness the impenetrable stupidity of even his closest disciples. If even they cannot in the least comprehend him, how can he expect to have made any mark on the rest? Jesus does not yet suspect, though momentarily the thought will flit across his mind, that the fulfillment of his work will come with his death.

> **Listen surely I've exceeded expectations**
> **Tried for three years seems like thirty**
> **Could you ask as much from any other man?**

"Listen," that is to say, "Look at it this way," and you'll see my point—and relent. Jesus is bargaining with his Master. "You've gotten your money's worth—and more. Isn't that enough?" He is saying to God, as God said to mortals in Isaiah 1:18, "Come, let us reason together." Or, even more to the point, it almost sounds as if Jesus has made some sort of deal with the devil, as in *Faust* or "The Devil and Daniel Webster." Zero hour is about to strike, and he is desperate.

Jesus feels that God couldn't have expected as much from him as he has gotten. One wonders in what respect Jesus sees himself as having done more than he might have. Perhaps nothing specific is in view. All we need to know is that he thinks that God must agree he has more than discharged his duties. It would be fair to let him off the hook even though technically the original contract stipulated Jesus' death as well. Jesus is trying to negotiate some slack. And it could hardly be said that Jesus has proven unequal to the job, the wrong choice for the task. Any other man would not have done half as much. And Jesus implies he has, paradoxically, both done more than God expected of him and yet less than God has demanded of him!

What precisely has Jesus been trying for three years, that made them seem like three decades? Usually when we say that days felt like years slowly dragging we mean that the days were full of difficulty or frustration or pain. "I thought the day would never end!" I would guess that Jesus means there has been too much to do, and little to show for it. Think of his outburst at the lepers a bit earlier. Why did he explode at them? They must have wondered themselves! Probably because there had been just too much of it and too often. He has had enough!

(On the other hand, is it possible that the lepers accosted Jesus based on groundless rumor? It is never clear in *Superstar* that Jesus has actually healed anyone. Everyone keeps mentioning his miracles, but we never see him doing any or even acknowledging that he has done any. And often miracle stories are not the ground of faith but the result of it. When a charismatic individual has inspired someone, given them new hope, this healing of despair is soon mythologized into a rumor of literal healing.)

But if I die
See the saga through and do the things you ask of me
Let them hate me hit me hurt me nail me to their tree
I'd wanna know I'd wanna know my God
I'd wanna see I'd wanna see my God

Why I should die

Jesus would still be willing to die on one condition: if God would at last explain the purpose of his dying. Here Jesus is made to ask the question Judas will soon ask, posthumously, voicing the questions of modern people who no longer take for granted the need or the meaning of the death of Jesus: "Did you mean to die like that?" "Jesus Christ, Jesus Christ, who are you? What have you sacrificed?" Even he does not know. And this raises a major question. What has Jesus been thinking he was about? What is it that he was trying to accomplish for those long years? He must have had something in mind. Presumably he thought his purpose was to teach and to persuade people to embrace a higher righteousness, a more enlightened piety. We have seen little of this in the story so far (unless you count the token excerpt from the Sermon on the Mount in the movie version). But this is entirely natural: *Superstar* takes place, remember, only at the very end of Jesus' career, when all the teaching is past. This is not an entire gospel, but only a passion narrative.

So we have a double ambiguity as to Jesus' purpose and mission. On the one hand, the public activity of Jesus (the particular things he has been trying for three years) is all left unclear and implicit. On the other hand, the only piece of his predestined program of which we hear, and we hear it over and over again, is the inevitability of his death, and yet we do not, nor does Jesus, know why this must be. As Burton Mack[134] has underscored, there is no obvious link between the activity of Jesus in any of the gospels and his final fate in Jerusalem. The temple cleansing does not seem to follow at all from the teaching and healing ministry. There is no strategy or doctrine manifest in the main portion of the gospel story that would seem to come to fruition at Jerusalem. Mack denies that the temple incident ever happened at all, partly based on the arbitrary character of it.

Henry J. Cadbury,[135] on the other hand, believed the temple cleansing was an historical fact, but that it was a spontaneous act of outrage provoked by the visit of the Galilean holy man to the temple (his first?). He hadn't planned to cause a disturbance but could not contain his indignation at the commercialization of the holy place. Cadbury knows it does not read like this in the gospels as we now read them. He sees as well as anyone how Mark has, from his position of hindsight, made the cataclysmic events of those days into a preordained plan of God. To eliminate the suggestion that Jesus was overwhelmed by events out of control, Mark and early Christians generally retrojected their belief in the divine plan into the story with the result that Jesus already knows the plan and is actually controlling events, steering them toward their puzzling but divinely decreed goal. So we receive the clear impression that there is an important divine providence in play, a method to the seeming madness. But we are left with no clear impression of what it was supposed to accomplish. There are a couple of vague references in Mark to Jesus giving his life to seal a covenant with God on behalf of an unspecified "many" (Mark 14:24), and to the son of man not coming to receive the services of others but to offer "his life as a ransom for many" (Mark 10:45). These appear to be odd bits of early Christian eucharistic liturgy inserted into the story by Mark or by some early interpolator. Luke cuts both of them in his rewrite. But even if Mark himself had included them, they do little to offset the impression that the events of the passion simply had to occur because they had to occur! The story had to go this way. "The scripture must be fulfilled." That assumes that the Prophets and Psalmists had predicted the sufferings of Jesus, another piece of hindsight theology. In reality, it is the *script* which "must be fulfilled." This is why Rice's Jesus puts it as he does: "If I . . . see the saga through . . ."

And all to avoid the implication that Jesus was a failed messiah since God neglected to rescue him from a shameful death. So Christians redefined the Jewish doctrine of the messiah (the anointed king of David's dynasty, who would restore national independence) in terms of what had in fact happened to Jesus. If Jesus was the messiah, then what he did must have been exactly what the messiah was supposed to do! So what was his mission? Simply to do what he did! And so he must have been actively trying to bring about his death for the simple reason that the prewritten story will end as it ought to. This spoils any narrative tension in the gospels. How can there be any suspense when Jesus not only knows everything before it happens, but does not hesitate to inform the reader in advance, and this several times? It recalls the joke about the Calvinist Scot who stumbles and falls down the stairs, breaking his leg. He exclaims, "Ach! I'm glad *that's* over!" As if it had been a scheduled appointment. The wisdom of the joke is great: if things were really predestined as Calvinists stoutly maintain, it would screw everything up. If you knew the future was set in advance but did not know how, one would still not be forewarned and forearmed. One would only be more anxious than ever, as if some kook had called in a bomb threat but didn't say where he had planted the thing.

Superstar gets this right, deconstructing the traditional passion narrative so as to let the original impetus of the story break out of the artificial restraints imposed by the subsequent dogma of Jesus' saving death. The arbitrariness and theological superfluity of that doctrine is clearly demonstrated by E.P. Sanders[136] who shows what trouble Christians had explaining why any new way of salvation was necessary, since Judaism already had adequate, biblical provisions for repentance and forgiveness for sinners. What was the damning sin from which belief in Christ saved? Why, the sin of not believing in Christ!

So Jesus in *Superstar* has been cast in the position of knowing in every detail what events must overtake him, just as in the gospels, but as not knowing why God has written this script when he could as easily have written a different one. All this is a beautiful example of Tim Rice's juxtaposition of hindsight anachronism ("You liar, you Judas!" "We can write the gospels") with realistic, on-the-scene, character motivation. The effect is much the same as in *The Last Temptation of Christ*, the novel as well as the film, when Jesus is shown knowing what later Christian dogma said he must have known (that he is God incarnate) and yet reacting to this shattering fact as a genuine human being would: with tormenting fits and nightmares, his mortal brain struggling to absorb the great overload of divine knowledge. The Jesus of the gospels and of orthodox Christianity never has this problem since he is really imagined as a mythic demigod with a superficial human likeness.

Would I be more noticed than I ever was before?
Would the things I've said and done matter any more?

At first hearing or reading these words seem to put Jesus in a bad light, marking him as a narcissistic glory-seeker who is willing even to die if it will cement his fame (it worked for Elvis), but who can see no other reason for a martyr death. Dying for personal glory, not for a selfless cause. But I think this would be premature. The second line interprets the first. Jesus speculates whether God means to use his death to give a long-lasting echo to his words, to speed them on their way as nothing he might do in life ever could. He seems to toss this off as an option, a possibility for God's determination that Jesus die, albeit not a very likely one. But I suspect that here we see Jesus ironically and unwittingly playing the prophet as Caiaphas, Pilate and Judas have already done. They have all spoken, as does Jesus here, much more truly than they know. The wisdom of God appears as rankest folly to the mortal mind (1 Corinthians 1:25). And so the truth of God appears in the guise of irony and jest. The jester is a prophet, and his silly antics are dead serious truth, but we are so deaf and insensitive to the truth that it strikes us as a joke.

I would submit that here we have hit upon the answer that Jesus seeks. He has himself hit upon it though he does not linger long enough over it to recognize it. The reason Jesus has not accomplished anything notable in his three years of toil is that he has, so to speak, only loaded the gun. His death will pull the trigger. Or, to vary the metaphor, "unless a grain of wheat falls into the ground and dies, it remains alone; but if it dies, it bears much fruit. He who loves his life loses it, and he who disdains his life in this world will keep it for eternal life" (John 12:24–25).

The cases of Martin Luther King, Jr., and Mohandas Gandhi illustrate the point perfectly. Though these men did great good in their public careers, it was the fact of their tragic deaths that ensured the powerful continuance of their mighty messages for the future. Had they remained active voices in the debate in subsequent years or decades, chances are they would have been superseded by events and new viewpoints, and soon forgotten. Albert Schweitzer, a giant easily on the level with King and Gandhi, is nonetheless being quickly forgotten for the simple reason that he lived to a good old age and died more or less peacefully. His thoughts survive in book form, but few among the general run of people will read that kind of book. King and Gandhi wrote several books, too, all of them filled with great ideas, but no one reads them either. Their immortal influence lies in the fact that their shocking deaths made their lives and causes to be forever engraved on the hearts of the world and passed down as common knowledge to posterity. As Jeremiah said, a covenant etched upon the heart far outlasts one merely written on paper or stone. Jesus and Socrates were assured the same immortality for themselves and their truths because they, too, underscored their teaching with their blood. They are far more eloquent dead than alive. But this is hard for Jesus to envision before the fact. "My name will mean nothing ten minutes after I'm dead." It's a fair trade: longevity in the flesh for immortality of influence. This is how one gains the boon of eternal life by being willing to let go this earthly life.

I'd have to know I'd have to know my Lord
I'd have to see I'd have to see my Lord
If I die what will be my reward?

Again, petulant selfishness—or is it? "What's in it for me?" A fair question. Jesus after all is not dying for a cause he believes in. He doesn't know what the point is. Why die arbitrarily? Here we can see the same point that is always missed by advocates of Peter Abelard's "moral influence theory" of the atonement. Abelard found all the traditional explanations of how Jesus' death provided salvation to be grotesque and silly. He could not take seriously such notions as that Jesus' death had tricked the devil out of his hostages (damned human souls) or that on the cross Jesus had invisibly battled Satan and despoiled him of his prisoners. Or that Jesus' death was like that of a sacrificial animal whose shed blood washed away sins. Instead, he proposed, Jesus' death was a winning lesson of the Father's love for his wayward children. We respond to love and are reconciled to God.

This sounds pretty good, except that it is also completely arbitrary, because no reason is given why a death without cause on other grounds would be a lesson in love. If I leap in front of an oncoming bus and die because that is the only way I can hurl you out of its path, then my death demonstrates my love for you. But if there is no danger to you, yet I see a bus coming and say, "Watch this! It ought to prove my love for you!" and I jump needlessly into the path of the bus, I have only demonstrated my own insanity. So if Jesus' death were not intrinsically accomplishing something *else*, then his merely dying can be no demonstration of sacrificial love. Even so, Rice's Jesus understands that he must go to the cross, but what makes the act any different from throwing himself under the wheels of the bus?

I'd have to know I'd have to know my Lord
Why should I die?
Can you show me now that I will not be killed in vain?
Show me just a little of your omnipresent brain
Show me there's a reason for your wanting me to die
You're far too keen on where and how and not so hot on why

Through all this venting, Jesus is rapidly running through Elisabeth Kübler-Ross's stages of the acceptance of death. The person told by his doctor that death will be soon in coming first feels denial, then rage, and then admits the truth but tries to bargain with God ("If you'll spare me, I promise I'll turn over a new leaf. Anything!"). Finally there is resigned acceptance. We will see that last step in a moment.

In these lines we cannot escape the undertone that Jesus knows he is arguing a lost cause. His accusing questions are not really demands so much as rhetorical questions. "You're not going to give me the satisfaction of knowing what I'm dying for, are you?" He does not seriously think to shirk the cross, only to shout his frustration. There is never a real question of turning aside from the path.

The phrase "omnipresent brain," while clear enough, at first seems to be mixed up, confusing "omnipresent" with "omniscient." The first means that God is everywhere present, the second that God knows all things at once. Shouldn't he have said "Show me just a little of your omniscient brain?" Maybe, but the word "omniscient" would have broken the rhythm! Beyond this, however, the word "omnipresent" is really truer to the underlying point. Structuralist critics have shown how the sense of temporality, the forward motion of action in a narrative, is an illusion crafted by the writer. In reality, everything is determined in advance. The logic of the plot is static, already present simultaneously throughout the literary work as a skeleton. The individual scenes are all meat packed onto these bones. They are waiting for you when you get there. The whole film is already on the reel; you seem to see forward-moving action progress through time because you are seeing the frames of the film in succession. The only real progression into the temporal future is that of your perception, not that of the thing you are perceiving. And this is exactly the picture we see in Superstar. Though Jesus moves from event to event, he knows it is a charade. He knows that the narrative structure is already in place below the surface. This is why he is so contemptuous toward and impatient with the disciples who are genuinely optimistic or sometimes frightened at the prospect of what (they think) may happen in the future. He cannot take their anticipations seriously, since for him things cannot happen any other way than in God's script. The deck is stacked before the game, with all chance contingency eliminated. And yet Jesus does not see the crucial piece of the puzzle. Or rather he sees the outline of the missing piece from the outlines of the pieces surrounding its place: it has the shape of his death. But the content of the missing piece, that remains a mystery. What is written or painted on that piece? That is the answer he needs.

Alright I'll die!
Just watch me die!
See how I die!

It is no real surprise that Jesus finally drops the futile appeal. He hears no voice denying his petition. He simply accepts the inevitable because he knows it is inevitable. We are reminded of Camus's "The Myth of Sisyphus," where he gives an existentialist spin to the old myth of a man banished to the netherworld and assigned the eternal and pointless task of rolling a boulder up a steep hill, only to see it roll back down every time. And then he has to walk back down and start the whole process all over. Camus speculates that Sisyphus has learned to accept the futility of his fate, to rise above it by disdaining it. Is this the resolution at which Jesus arrives in these lines? He will struggle no more, as if to see him rage against his fate was somehow entertaining for God.

The logic is reminiscent not only of Camus's parable, but of Jesus' own, in the Sermon on the Mount, when he advises fellow Jews living in Roman-occupied territory how to respond when a Roman soldier presses you into service to carry his field pack for a mile (which the law allowed): "If any man should force you to accompany him one mile, make it two!" (Matthew 5:41). Take away the satisfaction he has in thinking himself your master by refusing to be coerced. But instead of fighting him, a foolish gesture in any case, you ought to comply freely. It becomes evident that you are doing it from your own decision, and therefore from a position of condescending strength, once you reach the end of your legal obligation and continue voluntarily. God has ordered Jesus to carry his cross "the last mile," and Jesus replies, in effect, "Yeah? Watch me carry it two!" He has become at last the master of his fate by submitting to it. "Why kick against the goads?" (Acts 26:14).

Then I was inspired
Now I'm sad and tired
After all I've tried for three years seems like ninety
Why then am I scared to finish what I started
What you started-I didn't start it

Jesus himself is surprised at his sudden lack of resolve. Had he not embraced his dharma back at the beginning, knowing full well what must happen in the end? And again he recalls the three long years, in retrospect more like ninety. Even more trying and grueling than he had remembered only moments before. Only now he sees them as so many years full of working to get to precisely this point. He has at last neared his goal, and only now does he begin to reconsider. Why? Jesus' rhetorical question is aimed at himself, not at God.

As if in answer to his own question, as if in sudden realization, he turns upon God and levels the accusing finger at him. Maybe Jesus isn't cooling on his own plan. It was never his idea, as he seemed to think. No, God started the whole thing, and only now is Jesus beginning to realize how much of a pawn he has been! Here he sounds exactly like Judas will sound just before he hangs himself. He, too, awakens too late to the terrible truth. He has been tricked and maliciously used by God.

But Jesus also sounds more than a little like Judas back in the Last Supper scene, when he accused and insulted Jesus in order to convince himself that he did not still love him and was not betraying his friend. Jesus turns the blame back on God so as to justify his own rage at God. But he remains faithful, and yet what choice has he got in the matter?

God thy will is hard
But you hold every card

By means of a wonderful metaphor, God having all bets covered, Rice has transformed Jesus' meek submission to God ("Yet not what I will, but as thou willest" (Mark 14:36b) into a grudging resignation. Mark's Jesus says, "May your will be done," an affirmation in the third person imperative. Rice's Jesus curses a victorious foe who has outwitted him, using a simple indicative: You drive a hard bargain, but then you don't really leave me any choice, damn you. That God will win this hand of poker is a forgone conclusion: you can't hope to beat a man who's clutching four aces and three kings.

I will drink your cup of poison, nail me to the cross and break me
Bleed me beat me kill me take me now—
Before I change my mind

The point seems to be that Jesus has been unable to convince himself to flee and save his life. The God he was beseeching was really his own sense of dedication to the mysterious cause. Jesus has taken the place of Peter in Matthew 16:22–23 or of Simon Zealotes earlier in *Superstar*: he has become his own Satan, tempting himself with cool logic to abandon his path. The voice of Jesus' prayer in Gethsemane was the voice of his own fears. He has for the moment fought them down. But who knows how long this new determination will last? Hence, "Take me now—before I change my mind."

It is just as he said to Judas before the betrayer slipped out into the night: "Hurry, they're waiting!" He knew Judas was beginning to waver, and if Judas chickened out at that point, he would have, as he said to Jesus, "just stayed here and ruined your ambition." Jesus tried purposely to antagonize him, to goad him into continuing with his plan before he can change his mind. Now he goads himself: up and meet the soldiers, quickly, before you waver again and decide not to go through with it after all.

Jesus has just accused God of wanting to abuse and execute him, albeit through the agency of hapless stooges like Judas, Pilate, and Jesus himself. As these lines are sung on the original studio album, there is a slight but significant departure from the libretto (whether a last-minute change by Rice, or an ad lib): Instead of "Nail me to the cross," Jesus says, "Nail me to your cross." This just serves to underline the point. God is the one shouting to Pilate "Crucify him!"

The Arrest

There he is! They're all asleep-the fools!

Judas has arrived like the blood hound leading the hunters to their prey. It looks like it will be even easier than he thought. The disciples are asleep and thus can neither warn Jesus of his captors' approach nor defend him. Their mission should meet with no resistance.

Judas—must you betray me with a kiss?

Though Mark, the earliest version, gives Jesus no line to speak at this climactic juncture, Matthew and Luke supply the lack, filling the dramatic vacuum. Tim Rice has pretty much borrowed Luke's version, "Judas, would you betray the son of man with a kiss?" (Luke 22:48). The point is the same in Rice's redaction: this is "the saddest cut of all," that Judas should not only betray him, but do so with the sign of friendship. This is cruel and spiteful villainy. Judas need not be so malicious.

What's the buzz? Tell me what's happening

Towards the beginning of the play, the eager disciples asked the same question, hoping soon to ride into Jerusalem for a war of liberation. Jesus dampened their enthusiasm then, saying they would be more in the dark than ever if he should share his real plans with them. And now, in the Garden, those plans are unfolding before their bloodshot eyes. Now when Peter asks what's the buzz, he means that the noise, some noise, has disturbed his drunken slumber. Blinking and squinting under the weight of his hangover, he tries to get a focus on whatever is happening around them.

What's the buzz? Tell me what's happening
Hang on Lord we're gonna fight for you

Peter's question wakes the others, similarly disoriented and asking Peter's question themselves. It doesn't take long to put the pieces together. There's only one way to take what is transpiring before them. Here is the fighting they had expected ("When do we ride into Jerusalem?"), but they are hardly prepared for it now that it has come. Nonetheless, to their credit, they are prepared to give it a go, rather, one supposes, in the manner of a belligerent drunk only too eager to land a punch on the police who have raided the bar. "Hang on, Lord!" We're coming! Like the cavalry over the hilltop "in the final reel."

Put away your sword
Don't you know that it's all over?
It was nice but now its gone
Why are you obsessed with fighting?
Stick to fishing from now on

Once again, the disciples are as much in the dark as the arresting party. They haven't a clue as to what's going on. Jesus' aims (to die, as he has just acquiesced in doing, in prayer) would be ruined if they fought and somehow managed to protect him, just as surely as Judas would have "ruin[ed] your ambition" had he "just stayed here" instead of keeping his appointment with the authorities. But in fact, it's moot. They haven't a chance against this armed mob which already has the drop on them.

"Don't you know that it's all over? It was nice, but now it's gone." Easy come, easy go. It almost sounds like a bank robber or an embezzler being apprehended by the police. The crook knew it had to end sometime. But while his crooked career was going well, he was on Easy Street. Now it's all over?

No surprise; he knew it would be. He's ready to pay the piper, no complaints.

And yet there is a gospel basis even to this cynical nonchalance. In Luke's Last Supper scene, he has added an interesting Socratic mini-dialogue between Jesus and the disciples which functions as a kind of plot-hinge, signaling the closing of the previous chapters, the public ministry, and the opening of a new one, the passion and the birth of the Jerusalem Church in Luke's second volume, the Acts of the Apostles. "'When I sent you out with no purse or bag or sandals, did you run short of anything?' They said 'Nothing.' He said to them, 'But now, let him who has a purse take it, and likewise let him who has no sword sell his cloak and buy one'" (Luke 22:35–36). The period of halcyon peace and easy success has come to an end. Beginning with Jesus' arrest, it is not going to be so easy any more. The storm clouds have gathered. When they go on preaching journeys in the future, they will not be able to count on God's special protection as they have in the past, when those to whom they preached the coming of the Kingdom of God gladly fed and sheltered them, when they traveled the roads unmolested by such brigands as mugged the poor wayfarer on his way to Jericho in the Good Samaritan story.

I do not mean to say that Tim Rice means to make Jesus say something tantamount to this, but only that this passage in Luke may have formed the inspiration for these quite different lines of Jesus. As elsewhere, the idea may be that these humble and worldly words, or something like them, have been re-edited in the haze of later piety according to which Jesus could never have said anything that didn't sound like it was written to go in Holy Scripture.

"Why are you obsessed with fighting?" This is an obvious reference back to the earlier, longer version of "What's the Buzz" at the beginning, as well as to the militant sentiments of Simon Zealotes and the crowd at the Triumphal Entry. Jesus' remark underscores that a military challenge has never been part of his agenda, only of theirs, and that it stems from some strange fixation with violence.

Though all the disciples seem to be in view here, Jesus must be speaking to one in particular, since he commands "Put away your sword," singular. This is no doubt a reference to the statement of all four gospels that one of the disciples lashed out with his sword, trying to cleave the skull of one of the arresting party, but missed and succeeded only in neatly slicing the man's ear off. John's gospel alone identifies the inept swordsman as Peter. That tendency, to identify "some disciple" by name as Peter (or Judas) is found elsewhere in the gospels. It is a novelizing touch, to lend greater concreteness to the narrative.

"Stick to fishing from now on." Here is a nod to John 21, in which after the death of Jesus we find Peter, Andrew, James, John, and Nathanael having returned to plying their trade in the Sea of Galilee. They are startled to recognize a familiar figure silhouetted against the dawn light. Jesus' remark in *Superstar* is a crack at their expense ("As fighters, you make great fishermen. Stick to something you're good at."), but it also anticipates the resurrection scene which we will not actually see, since *Superstar*, being a Passion, does not go on to the resurrection.

> Tell me Christ how you feel tonight
> Do you plan to put up a fight?
> Do you feel that you've had the breaks?
> What would you say were your big mistakes?
> Do you think that you may retire?
> Did you think you would get much higher?
> How do you view your coming trial?
> Have your men proved at all worthwhile?

In a brilliant instance of creative anachronism, Rice has made the taunting of the vindictive crowd equivalent to the harassment of the jackal-pack of paparazzi. They are like reporters who get in the face of tragedy survivors and pester them with cruel and annoying personal questions in their darkest hour when such questions are most invasive and least welcome. Specifically, we are to imagine Jesus surrounded by the ankle-weight chorus of reporters dogging the steps of a fallen superstar, a defeated basketball coach, a losing prizefighter, a politician who has failed to be reelected.

> Come with us to see Caiaphas
> You'll just love the High Priest's house
> You'll just love seeing Caiaphas
> You'll just die in the High Priest's house
> Come on God this is not like you
> Let us know what you're gonna do
> You know what your supporters feel
> You'll escape in the final reel

Now we pass into out and out sarcasm, childish derision. Who are these people? What have they got against Jesus? One thing is obvious: they are familiar with him ("This is not like you!"). Though the gospels never explicitly say so, readers have traditionally supposed that the crowd mocking and hounding Jesus, demanding his crucifixion, is the same crowd that welcomed him with such adulation on Palm Sunday. And this is a natural assumption, since "the crowd," like the chorus in an ancient Greek tragedy, may be presumed to be the same people throughout, unless we are told differently. But perhaps we *have* been told differently, since Mark specifies that it was "the crowd of his disciples" who hailed his entry into the city, whereas no such identification is made of the bunch of rowdies gathered before Pilate's Praetorium. Similarly, in John's account the welcoming crowds are merely outsiders curious about the reports of Jesus' raising Lazarus, not committed disciples.

It is important for *Jesus Christ Superstar* that the crowds should be one and the same, because the "superstar" paradigm on which the rock opera is based entails both a meteoric rise to celebrity and a subsequent abandonment by the fickle crowd. Such support is a mile wide and an inch thick. It vanishes as soon as there is "a new kid in town." Jesus has been spoken of this way before: "He's top of the poll." Similarly, the taunting question "Did you think you would get much higher?" implies Jesus was climbing the charts and that he must have known it was just a matter of time before he starting slipping, dropping in popularity as quickly as he had gained it. The same thing happened to Elvis. Once the King, he was abruptly dethroned by the Beatles. His career went on to settle in for the long haul as one of the living museum of Big Names, performing for vacationing business men in bad suits in the night spots of Las Vegas, like a defeated Samson clowning for the Philistines. Indeed, this is the ignominious mode in which Jesus continues to exist today, as the grotesque figurehead of the Religious Right and the spiritual party doll of pious fundamentalists.

Incidentally, it is noteworthy that in an off-Broadway revival of *Jesus Christ Superstar* in the late 70s, Herod Antipas, freed of the ludicrous crustacean costume in which a hallucinating Tom O'Horgan had imprisoned him, was depicted as a cross between Elvis and a member of KISS. He postured like Elvis and added the line "I'm the King, Jesus!" That's more to the point.

"You know what your supporters feel: you'll escape in the final reel." Do you think they're right? This bit of anachronism well expresses a major issue in early Christianity. The death of Jesus, especially his execution as a criminal, must have fallen like a major blow to the early Christians, just like the totally unexpected apostasy of Sabbatai Sevi, a messiah of the seventeenth century, who boasted he would miraculously convert the Ottoman sultan to faith in Judaism. When instead the sultan offered Sabbatai two choices, to convert to Islam or to die, the ostensible messiah lost no time in crowing like a rooster (i.e., a chicken): *Allah ho Akbar*! This seemed to spell it out pretty clearly. Such a man could be no messiah. The same with Jesus: if the role of the messiah was to liberate Israel and bring about a golden age of peace and piety, then Jesus simply did not qualify. Of course the Christian response to this was to redefine the mission of the messiah in hindsight, making it conform to what Jesus had done, and not vice versa. The messiah was *supposed* to die. This apparently did not persuade many Jews. But Gentiles, who did not care and perhaps did not even know anything about Jewish messianism, were attracted to the quite different idea of Jesus as a dying-and-rising savior god like Tammuz or Osiris. For them, "Christ" (messiah in Greek) was simply a proper name, Jesus' last name (which is how it is used in *Superstar*, anachronistically, in Jesus' own lifetime).

But other Christians tried to do an end run around the problem, claiming that Jesus had not in fact died. Someone else took his place, voluntarily or not, and Jesus ascended to heaven without either crucifixion or resurrection. This belief held on in some places for several centuries, since early Christian converts to Islam in the eighth century brought this belief with them, from whence the Prophet Muhammad seems to have adopted it. It found a place in the Koran and remains the belief of Muslims the world over to this day. Other early Christians, as we have already seen, believed Jesus had been crucified, perhaps tied to the cross, narcotized into a seeming death, taken down alive and later revived. Obviously, according to all these versions of the story, Jesus did escape in the final reel.

Tell me Christ how you feel tonight
Do you plan to put up a fight?
Do you feel that you've had the breaks?
What would you say were your big mistakes?

Come with us to see Caiaphas
You'll just love the High Priest's house
You'll just love seeing Caiaphas

You'll just die in the High Priest's house

More of the same. And of course, while Jesus will not actually be executed in the palace of Caiaphas, he will be judged as deserving death by the Sanhedrin there. This is the figure of speech called metonymy, the use, in this case, of the outcome to stand for the process leading to it. And, as if anyone missed it, "you'll just die in the High Priest's house" is raw sarcasm, as if Jesus has been offered an audience with the Big Man, as if he will be overcome with the marvelous decor, like a foreign dignitary taking Jackie Kennedy's tour of the White House. "Simba, it's to die for."

Now we have him! Now we have got him!

This is predatory gloating, but it makes more sense coming from Annas and Caiaphas, who have been looking to "get him" for some time, unlike the crowd, who have turned coats only recently. But it makes sense nonetheless. Again, as A.J. Greimas explains,[141] there are certain narrative roles, narrative functions, that characters in a story must assume. Such a role is an "actant" or "actantial role," and we may find two or three different actors playing the same actantial role through the course of the story. In this case, we have a single actantial role played alternatively by Annas, Caiaphas, Judas, Herod Antipas, Pontius Pilate, and the crowd. In precisely the same way, in Mark's gospel, we first see Jesus in conflict with the Galilean scribes who become so incensed that they lay plans to kill him, then with the Jerusalem Pharisees and the possessed demoniacs, and finally with the Sadducees and the Sanhedrin in Jerusalem who put him to death in collusion with the Romans. All play the same role of the actant "rejecter of Jesus," providing a kind of monolithic continuity that tends to blur all the "enemy" characters into one in the reader's mind. Since in *Superstar* the crowd is now playing the actantial role of "enemy of Jesus," and the Sanhedrin will assume the role next, it is no transgression of narrative logic to have the crowd say what would technically be more appropriate for the Sanhedrin. It only reinforces the actantial identity of the two groups.

Jesus you must realize the serious charges facing you
You say you're the Son of God in all your handouts—well is it true?

Caiaphas is, so to speak, reading Jesus his Miranda Rights. Be on your guard. Consider carefully what you say. Your words here may be your last. Surely you know that, don't you?

What actually are the charges against Jesus? In the gospels, the Sanhedrin seems to be trying to punish Jesus for the cleansing of the temple; at least they bring forward witnesses claiming to have heard Jesus threaten to destroy the temple, but these charges are thrown out for lack of agreement on some unspecified point. Scholars think it not unlikely that Jesus did indeed make such a threat in some form. But that would make Jesus a fanatical seditionist of some kind, an impression the gospel writers are not likely to have wanted to leave with the reader. Thus those charges are dismissed— not by the Sanhedrin, mind you, but by the gospel writers. John dispenses with them early on, reinterpreting the words figuratively (John 2:19–21) during the cleansing scene itself. And at the trial he does not have anyone mention it. For him, the charge against Jesus was blasphemy. Luke retains the charge of fomenting revolution, but all alike make the final charge that of blasphemy, too. The Sanhedrin is depicted as taking any claim to messiahship as blasphemy. This is probably an anachronism, later Christians reading the point of controversy between Christians and Jews in their day back into the trial of Jesus. Jews regarded the Christian claims of Jesus being messiah as blasphemous in these later years only because Christians had redefined the messiah as a divine being, not part of the job description according to Jewish belief. If a Jew claimed to be messiah, it would be a terrible mistake to believe him (as the followers of Simon bar-Kochba discovered about a century after Jesus). But in no case was it to be considered blasphemy.

Superstar indulges in the same anachronism. From the very first song, "Heaven on Their Minds," we have been hearing "this talk of God." The crowd, once fans of Jesus, just called him "God," albeit mockingly, and yet their very sarcasm assumes they had previously held this view sincerely ("Come on, God, this is not like you"). They are rejecting the disappointed view they once held. Herod, too, will quip, "But now I understand you're God. At least that's what you've said." This was not at issue in the lifetime of Jesus. It is a later piece of Christian theology. But Rice reads it back into the gospel story, because he is not concerned to depict the way things were in Jesus' own time, but rather to hold the distorting lens of modern controversy up to Jesus for whatever light it may shed either on those controversies or on Jesus. The imposition onto Jesus of the modern "superstar" category serves the same function, and it is quite revealing. Let us ask our modern skeptical questions of Jesus in our imagination, just as Judas does in his song beyond the grave; "I only want to know."

But has *Superstar*'s Jesus ever endorsed this view of himself? That he is God? We have been given no reason to think so. It is the inflated praise of his "half-witted fans" who have "go[ne] out of control" that Jesus is now being forced to answer for. In other places in the rock opera we receive the impression that the wild rhetoric of his followers is being attributed to Jesus, even though he did not start it. In a similar way, Congolese prophet Simon Kimbangu (twentieth century), jailed after his initial preaching, cringed at reports that some of his followers were proclaiming him the new "God of the blacks" or "Christ of the blacks." He had no such illusions about himself, but no protests of his would stem the tide.[142] And outsiders could be forgiven for assuming Kimbangu himself had started the rumors. With this remark of Caiaphas, that Jesus' own pamphlets make a claim of Godhood for him, are we dealing with the same thing? Are they spurious tracts never approved by Jesus himself? Could be.

Most likely, the mention of leaflets billing Jesus as Son of God is another pointedly anachronistic reference: Caiaphas is stepping out of historical sequence fully as much as Judas will in his last number ("If you'd come today . . ."). Caiaphas is asking if Jesus himself is responsible for the claims made for him in the yet-unwritten Gospels of Matthew, Mark, Luke, and John. It is clear that these documents do contain divine claims on Jesus' behalf, though scholars today usually regard such sayings as later Christian dogma read back by the gospel writers into the time of Jesus. So Caiaphas is asking, as the *Superstar* listener certainly does, "Do you think that you're who they [=the Church of later centuries] say you are?"

That's what you say-you say that I am

Jesus' reply seems, to say the least, equivocal. One could read it two ways: "So you say!" or "You said it!" It is like many of Jesus' frustrating answers that are really counter questions, tying up the inquirer in unintended implications, turning the tables and putting the questioner himself on the spot. In Mark 12:27–33, the questioner, seeking to embarrass Jesus, finds that he will damned if he does answer Jesus' counter question, damned if he doesn't. But this time, Caiaphas takes the bait. He takes Jesus' quizzical reply as a big Yes. Note that Pilate will hear pretty much the same reply to the same question and will take it first as an ambiguity ("That is not an answer!") and then, apparently, as a No ("This man is harmless, he's done no evil.").

Given the booby-trap character of Jesus' ambiguous replies, rather like the tricky oracles of the Delphic prophetess, one might expect to find that Caiaphas has trapped himself here: "Let the wicked fall into his own trap!" (Psalm 141:10). Has he? Yes indeed. Because Jesus' aim is to advance to his own death. He knows it has nothing to do with the utter misapprehensions of the Sanhedrin or Judas. But that doesn't matter. He is content for them to rationalize their plans with whatever schemes they choose. It is important to him only that he fulfill his mysterious destiny. Thus, though he doesn't want to accept the false charges as if true, neither does he want to derail the process. Thus the ambiguity.

The ambiguity of Jesus' reply is derived directly from the gospels. Matthew 26:64 and Luke 22:70 both render Jesus' reply as "You say that I am." John has completely rewritten the whole scene, as is his custom. But Matthew and Luke are following Mark here. Or at least they seem to be, until they get to this particular statement, because at this point most manuscripts of Mark 15:62 have "I am," a simple affirmation. Now why would Matthew and Luke tone down an unequivocal affirmation by Jesus of his own messiahship? And both of them independently? "Come on [Matthew and Luke,] this is not like you!" Our answer appears in only a few manuscripts of Mark which must reflect the original text of Mark 15:62, "You say so." This is what Matthew and Luke were reading in their copies of Mark. Some scribe later decided that Jesus ought to have offered a more ringing affirmation of his identity and changed it to what we now read in Mark. Such emendations of texts to make them conform more closely to emerging orthodox dogma was quite common.[143]

> **There you have it gentlemen—**
> **What more evidence do we need?**
> **Judas thank you for the victim—**
> **Stay awhile and you'll see it bleed!**

Annas has heard enough! Indeed, it is more than he could have hoped for, at least the way he hears it, according to his fondest wishes: a confession! Who needs more evidence? Really, who needs any evidence at all? Especially since they were all convinced before the trial even began. Maybe they mean that, having heard the confession for themselves, they can present an open and shut case to Pilate. In any case, Annas' statement comes directly from Mark 14:63, "And the high priest tore his mantle and said, 'Why do we still need witnesses? You have heard his blasphemy.'"

Next Annas turns to Judas to assure him that he has done his job well, inviting him to see the whole affair through to its end. He seems to mean that Judas is welcome to stay, having proved his worthiness to be part of the group in some sense, as if the betrayal of Jesus were some sort of fraternity initiation stunt. This is a surprise. None of the gospels intimates the presence of Judas at the trial before the Sanhedrin. It is, however, a perfectly natural inference, since the gospels all say that the party which came out to arrest Jesus took him to Caiaphas' residence, and there is no reason this number should not include Judas. Had the writers supposed that Judas promptly left the group to flee into the night, we might have expected them to have said so.

Does Judas take Annas up on his thoughtful invitation? Apparently we are meant to think he did. No more will be heard from him during the remainder of this scene, nor in the Herod and Pilate scenes. The next time we see Judas (singing the song "Judas' Death"), his first words will be, "My God, I saw him—he looked three quarters dead! And he was so bad I had to turn my head. You beat him so hard that he was bent and lame." And Judas is talking to the priests of the Sanhedrin. So he means he "saw the victim bleed." On the spot. And the gospels do have the goons of the high priest beat Jesus up on the spot: "And the guards received him with blows" (Mark 14:65).

It is striking that Annas himself refers to Jesus as a "victim," i.e., a sacrificial animal, the original denotation of the term before it came by extension to mean the one against whom a crime is committed. That he has an animal in mind is evident from the pronoun "it": "Stay a while; You'll see it bleed." Of course Annas does not mean to anticipate, much less to confess faith in, the later Christian theology that Jesus' death was an expiation for sins like that wrought by a slain sacrifice. We cannot rule out the use of irony here, much as in John 11:50, in which Caiaphas declares it better for Jesus to die to avert possible reprisals from Rome. And just as John recalls this prediction seven chapters later, once he gets further into the passion story (John 18:14), so does Tim Rice have Annas echo what Caiaphas had earlier said about Jesus' scapegoat death. But the victim terminology is new. It does foreshadow the eventual Christian teaching that is questioned by the chorus at the end: "What have you sacrificed?"

Now we have him! Now we have got him!
Take him to Pilate!

The crowd has waited impatiently during the sham trial, knowing it was all mere formality. Yet they all know how Jesus always managed to slip out of traps set for him by his enemies and interrogators before. Could anyone be sure he would not ride some technicality to freedom in this case too? "It's not over till it's over." But now, thankfully, it's over. Like politicians with a big lead in the polls who are nonetheless glued to the tube watching the election returns, the crowd has been optimistic but watchful lest the coveted triumph somehow elude them. And now it, and the hated false prophet Jesus, are in their grasp! All that remains, they think, is for Pilate to administer the coup de grace. But as we will see, Pilate, hardly eager to be manipulated by the people he rules, has a few ideas of his own. He will complicate the matter as much as he can to forestall the Sanhedrin, to find out exactly why they are afraid of Jesus, since the answer might be something he could use against them. Always suspicious of the Jewish leaders, who he knows must resent his power over them, he is not sure that a man who so worries them might not be advantageous for Rome to keep alive. He will not be an easy sell.

Peter's Denial

The action in this scene must be understood to be taking place simultaneously with the interrogation of Jesus. Peter has followed the arresting party back to Caiaphas' palace, though at a safe distance. He is still trying to prove Jesus' prediction of his denial untrue. He is outside in the high priest's courtyard trying to mix inconspicuously with the crowd, exchanging idle chit chat until one of them notices his distinctive Galilean accent. Galilean? Hey, that's too much of a coincidence! That troublemaker they've got inside is a Galilean. Say, you're not by any chance connected with that fellow, are you? Other eyes begin to focus on him, and Peter comes to the moment of truth—or falsehood. Will he deny his friendship with Jesus? Before, he could not imagine it. Or rather, he may have imagined something like Judas' deed, becoming a turncoat, turning against Jesus as an enemy. That temptation Peter would have resisted easily. But now he sees the temptation is more insidious than that. He sees that it is a question not of denying Jesus in the abstract, but rather whether he loves Jesus more than his own life ("If any man would come after me, let him deny himself and take up his cross and follow me. For whoever would save his life will lose it; and whoever loses his life for my sake and the gospel's will save it." Mark 8:34–35). Ironically, it is Peter's valiant determination to stick with his Lord through thick and thin, to prove Jesus' prediction wrong, that has led him into this blind alley where he must face a test far more difficult than he had imagined.

I think I've seen you somewhere-I remember
You were with that man they took away
I recognise your face

These are the words of an unnamed "maid by the fire," a fellow loiterer, a worker about the estate with no duties pending at the moment. She is left anonymous here, as in the gospel accounts, since she is a bit player, someone to elicit from Peter one of his denials. Her own anonymity, as a mere flunky of the Big Man, Caiaphas, is exactly what Peter had relied upon to protect him in this crowd. He hoped his own presence with Jesus would never be marked by any observer, since Jesus would presumably be the center of attention. Apparently, the maid has been part of the crowd that came to behold the arrest of Jesus. When else would she have had the opportunity to see Peter with Jesus? Not in the high priest's court yard, since Peter must have entered subsequent to Jesus. He had followed at a safe distance. Thus it is a bit surprising to hear her speak as an idle observer, apparently not even sure who the victim of the mob was: "that man." But then that's the way it is with mob hysteria. It doesn't matter who the lynch victim is! It's the sport of the thing!

You've got the wrong man lady I don't know him
And I wasn't where he was tonight-never near the place

Peter has decided: he might have denied himself to stand with Jesus, but he has instead opted to deny Jesus to save his own life. He dares not be connected with Jesus and then be handed over to share Jesus' condemnation. For the moment all remembrance of Jesus' haunting prophecy of the impossible has fled him. He has only short-term survival in view.

And yet even Peter's denial seems to give him away. "You've got the wrong man" implies there is such a culprit (an associate of Jesus) as she describes, only it is not Peter. But this is a strange way to answer her. She is not trying to locate a suspect for a known crime; she is only trying to place Peter—where has she seen him before? She asked "Who is he? Oh yes, I saw him in Gethsemane." He answers her: "You're looking for a man who accompanied Jesus? Well, it wasn't me!" She gives Peter the priority, while he gives priority to the mysterious companion of Jesus, thus implying the two are the same, even as he denies it.

"And I wasn't where he was tonight—never near the place." This is a strange way of saying that he was not a companion of that Jesus fellow, because Peter is making it sound like he knows just where the maid has in mind, as if he knows "where [Jesus] was tonight" even though, if he had not been with Jesus, he would not know where Jesus had been. He is pretty definite about "the place" even though the maid has not named it. Peter is protesting too much. His words are betraying not only Jesus but himself as well. He is giving away his own secret in the very moment he seeks to hide it!

That's strange for I am sure I saw you with him
You were right by his side and yet you denied—

These are the words of another bystander, a soldier who went on the raid to capture Jesus. He, too, was there. He seems to be simply taking up where the maid left off. They are said in the libretto to be different characters, and they are, but as Greimas says, they are sharing the same actantial role between them just as, in John's farewell discourses at the Last Supper, he makes all the disciples share the same actantial role. Various ones ask Jesus questions, but it scarcely matters which one asks which question. The important thing is that Jesus is questioned. So here: the important thing is not who provokes Peter to deny Jesus. The important thing is that Peter have someone provoke his denials.

The soldier merely shrugs off Peter's unbelievable denial with mockery: it is certainly odd if Peter really was not there, since the soldier is even more sure that Peter was there than the maid was. He simply asserts, "You were right by his side." And then the shameful irony of it, which exactly captures Peter's terrible reproach: even though you were one of his closest companions only a short time ago, here you are now denying you were even there!

I tell you I was never ever with him

Peter denies this. "In fact" he has never laid eyes on Jesus before in his life, so to speak, erasing his three years of association with him. Peter's lasting fame was the mere fact of his association with Jesus: shake the hand that shook the hand. He will be glad enough to make as much as he can of this fortuitous connection when it will be to his advantage to remind everyone of it, but for now, when it might stand to cost him his life, he will deny it on a stack of Bibles.

But I saw you too-it looked just like you

An old man who had gone along to see the outlaw Jesus run to ground also remembers now that he noticed Peter then. "It looked just like you" is sort of a "for the sake of argument" admission that Peter might be telling the truth. But then how to explain that whoever he had seen there looked just like Peter? Quite a coincidence, eh? Is that what you're asking us to believe?

I don't know him!

It's the Big Lie. Peter continues to stonewall, hoping he can manage to outlast their suspicions by sticking to his story. What he is really saying, and deep down he must know they realize this, is that he is by the act of saying these things severing his connection with Jesus. If they're worried about him, if they think he's as dangerous as the false messiah Jesus, he will set their minds at rest by denouncing Jesus. "Look, I'm on your side now! See? I'm one of you! That should satisfy you." This is pretty much the disgraceful position of Judas when he was playing footsie with the Sanhedrin, feeling his condemnation growing greater the farther he saw himself stepping into their camp. And now a frightened Peter has applied for admission to Jesus' lynch mob.

Peter—don't you know what you have said
You've gone and cut him dead

Only now do we see that Mary Magdalene, too, had made it this far. In fact, Mark and Luke do say that the women companions of Jesus were the only ones to stick with Jesus to the bitter end, even becoming eye witnesses of the crucifixion, unlike the terrified men. Perhaps they knew the Romans would never take them seriously as a threat and so felt freer than Peter to be identified as Jesus' disciples.

Mary has followed the whole exchange with interest—and with stunned disbelief. Can Peter really be saying these things? As if he had been hypnotized to say them, Mary tries to snap him out of it: did you hear what you just said? It is as if she expects him to be just as shocked as she was to hear it. And indeed, Peter was as shocked some hours before, when Jesus told him he would say these things. But time has caught up with him. He has played his terrible role to the letter.

To say "you've gone and done it" implies that someone has at last committed the act that hovered in dangerous but unlikely possibility. The act seems to have been feared and avoided since the potential doer of the act realized the danger, the magnitude of the act, and had stayed away from it—until now.

And what has Peter done? He has "cut [Jesus] dead." Here is the unkindest cut of all, the saddest cut of all, again. And what is so unkind about this sword blow? Mary implies that Jesus' last chance for escape somehow lay with Peter. By his failure Peter seems to have taken away the last remaining impediment to Jesus' death. No one will dare to come forward in his defense.

I had to do it don't you see?
Or else they'd go for me

What choice did Peter have?, he protests to Mary's accusation. His question is rhetorical: surely you didn't expect me to throw my life away like that, did you? Well, yes! Because Jesus had made things clear (at least in the gospels, though, admittedly, not in the lyrics so far) that this is precisely what Jesus had expected of them.

It's what he told us you would do-
I wonder how he knew . . .

Mary seems to be more mystified at how Jesus could have seen all this coming than genuinely reproachful or even angry with Peter. She seems resigned to what has happened. She does "see that's it's all over." Peter is right. There's nothing left to stand up for, no real reason to risk one's personal safety for a failed messiah. Their ideals are dying all around them. And yet how strange that he did seem to know what was ahead! Mary is beginning to realize that perhaps Jesus was as special as they thought, though maybe in a very different way than they thought.

Mary speaks as if the story is already over. She is already speaking as though Jesus is dead and gone. She can see what must happen next.

Pilate and Christ

**Who is this broken man cluttering up my hallway?
Who is this unfortunate?**

Jesus has been dropped off at Pilate's palace and left lying bruised and perhaps unconscious in custody of the Roman guard. The Sanhedrin and their hangers-on did not linger to wait for him. Why? "They themselves did not enter the Praetorium, so that they might not be defiled" (John 18:28b). What were they worried about? "You yourselves know how unlawful it is for a Jew to associate with or to visit anyone of another nation" (Acts 10:28a). Pilate is confused at first. There seems to be some street person, untidily deposited where ordinarily none would be allowed to lie. All Pilate sees is rubbish, scattered garbage. A street person lying astride the pavement. We can imagine that Luke's Rich Man character in 16:19–31 took as little notice of poor Lazarus silently festering outside his gate, never suspecting that in a few short hours their roles would be reversed. And Pilate is equally oblivious.

It is hard to miss the echo of Matthew 25:31–46, the Judgment of the Sheep and the Goats, whether Tim Rice had it in mind or not. There, too, we find the irony of people dismayed to discover that, when they had thought to see only street bums and vagrants, they were really seeing the incognito Son of Man. But the point of the irony here is that, face to face with the supposedly dangerous rebel Jesus, Pilate cannot even tell him from a common derelict. Later on he will express marvel over the apparent fear the Sanhedrinists feel for Jesus.

Someone Christ-King of the Jews

In a parody of the guard announcing the arrival of a visiting foreign potentate, the bored and sleepy soldier tells Pilate what little he can remember of the information given him by the priests who dropped Jesus there and left. The name is hard to recall because the man seems utterly unimportant. "Someone Christ, I can't remember exactly . . . and, oh yes, he's King of the Jews." It is as if the guard is a hospital orderly in a lunatic asylum for whom no wild-eyed delusion comes as much of a surprise anymore. "This here's Napoleon. Here's Elvis . . . and you're supposed to be . . .? Oh yes, Jesus."

"Someone Christ" or "Someone the messiah." This clever phrase anticipates what Pilate will later say (in the movie version). "You Jews produce messiahs by the sackful. Who is this Jesus? Why is he [any] different [from the rest of them]?" There are constant candidates for the job. Each has his fifteen minutes of fame, and then it's over. What was his name again?

> **Oh so this is Jesus Christ, I am really quite surprised**
> **You look so small-not a king at all**
> **We all know that you are news-but are you king? King of the Jews?**

Ah yes! Jesus the messiah! Why didn't you say so? In other words, Pilate had been informed of the momentary arrival of one Jesus, a man who would be king. Presumably Pilate has just now emerged from his palace in order to meet him. It just did not occur to him that this shabby pile of blood-stained rags might be the messianic boogey man. From the many rumors and reports Pilate has heard lately ("We all know that you are news"), he had expected something, someone, more impressive. Perhaps a bound Samson, a strapping fighter dragged in kicking and screaming.

When Pilate asks Jesus whether he is the king of the Jews, a paraphrase of "messiah," he is of course not considering the possibility that Jesus might be the messianic king destined to overthrow heathen Rome. How *could* he be, since there is no such character except in Jewish fantasies? No, he simply wants to know if Jesus himself is making the absurd claim. If he denies it, perhaps he is being railroaded, scapegoated by his enemies who find him dangerous for other reasons. On the other hand, if Jesus does think he is the destined Deliverer, then he is a seditionist advocating the expulsion of the Roman occupiers. And then he must die as an example to others, however evident it is that he poses no genuine threat.

That's what you say

Jesus returns the same ambiguous answer he gave to the Sanhedrin. He is noncommittal, evasive, throwing the ball back into the opponent's court. It is almost tantamount to the scene in Mark 8:27 where Jesus asks the disciples, "Who do you say that I am?" This section of *Superstar* parallels John 18:33, 37 ("Pilate said to him, 'So you are a king?' Jesus answered, 'You say that I am a king.'"), but it is based on the simpler version of Mark 15:2, "And Pilate asked him, 'Are you the King of the Jews?' And he answered him, 'You have said so.'"

What do you mean by that?
That is not an answer
You're deep in trouble friend—
Someone Christ-King of the Jews

Pilate is impatient. He is not interested in mystic allegories, double entendres from a fake oracle, inscrutable Zen koans. He wants to get to the bottom of things, and fast. This is no time to be coy, to play games. Jesus does not seem to realize the gravity, the urgency of the situation. So he'd best choose his words carefully. (Later, in a parallel scene, Pilate will offer the same advice: "You've got to be careful, you could be dead soon, could well be.") Repeating what the guard had called Jesus, "Someone Christ-King of the Jews," Pilate seems to be explaining why Jesus is in trouble: he is a peasant nobody making an absurd but dangerous claim. Better watch what you say!

How can someone in your state be so cool about your fate?
An amazing thing—this silent king

"In your state," of course, means "deep in trouble" as you are—and yet unperturbed? How can that be? Is he so half-witted that he doesn't realize it's not a game anymore? Or is he so heavenly-minded that he's out of touch with reality? We can detect that Pilate is already beginning to write off Jesus as a harmless eccentric. There is no threat here. The only question outstanding is why the Sanhedrin seems to think him dangerous.

Since you come from Galilee then you need not come to me
You're Herod's race! You're Herod's case!

Pilate suddenly thinks of a way to pass the buck: let Herod Antipas figure out what's going on here! Pilate is already trying to wash his hands of the whole business. So he appeals to a jurisdictional technicality. If Jesus is a Galilean, well, then, let's not presume to judge him here in Judea. We'll extradite him and let poor Antipas scratch his head over it. That's the ticket!

Presupposed here is that you know that Judea, the southern third of Palestine, was under direct Roman rule. It was governed by a Roman Procurator or Prefect, Pontius Pilate. But Galilee to the north was technically independent and under the nominal rule of Herod Antipas, a son of Herod the Great, the slaughterer of the innocents. His title was officially "Tetrarch" (ruler of a fourth of the territory), but he fancied himself "King Herod" like his famous ancestor. He ruled at the pleasure of Rome, and a few years later he fell from their grace.

Would Pilate need to extradite Jesus to Herod, according to Roman protocol? Not really, though he could, just as a courtesy, if he wanted. And Rice has cleverly made it so that Pilate did Herod this "favor" simply to be rid of a headache himself.

We do not read of any trial of Jesus before Herod Antipas in Matthew, Mark, or John. It appears only in Luke and in the Gospel of Peter. In Peter, it is actually Herod who condemns Jesus to death. In Luke, Herod decides to let him go, sending him back to Pilate with his compliments. What is the point of an inconclusive trial before Herod? The matter winds up back on Pilate's desk anyway. As Loisy saw,[144] Luke must have known of two contradictory traditions of Jesus' execution: one in which Jesus was condemned by Pilate, the other in which Jesus was executed at Herod's order. Since both were widely believed, though both could not be true at the same time, Luke decided to harmonize the two traditions. Thus he has Herod sitting in judgment over Jesus, yet not condemning him, since Pilate has to be retained from Mark's tradition as the one actually to order the execution. Thus Rice has left John's version of events aside and switched over to Luke for the moment. (And he does not need to have Jesus packed off all the way to Galilee, since, as in Luke, Herod Antipas happens to be close by in Jerusalem at the moment to observe the Passover.)

Ho-ho Sanna Hey Sanna Sanna Sanna Ho
Sanna Hey Sanna Ho and how

The chorus of praise and adulation that greeted Jesus' ears only days ago has now turned into a mocking taunt. The crowd is fickle.

Hey JC; JC please explain to me
You had everything where is it now?

Jesus' support had been a mile wide and an inch deep. Like a rock celebrity, he fell quickly from the height of his popularity. And those who had believed in him, naively as they now suppose, are taking out their own feelings of embarrassed self-reproach upon Jesus, the clay-footed idol. They are gloating over his fall to hide from themselves the mirror image fact of their own fall and disappointment. It was their own doing that they turned out to have "backed the [wrong] horse."

But what had been the turning point? What caused the crowd to seek him out in Gethsemane like a pack of blood hounds? Just as the turning point for Judas was Jesus' receiving the extravagant attentions of Mary Magdalene at Bethany, the crowd has seen enough as of that moment when, after the cleansing of the temple, Jesus had been thronged by a mob of the poor, the lame, lepers, and cripples, all clamoring for his help—and he told them to get lost! "Heal yourselves!" In Luke's scene of Jesus preaching back home in Galilee (Luke 4:16–30), everything is going just fine, the townspeople proud of a local boy made good—until Jesus purposely goads the crowd into a murderous frenzy! He remarks that they have no doubt heard the reports of his healing the sick in nearby Capernaum and will want him to heal a few of the old gang here at Nazareth. But, says Jesus, that's too bad. He plans to heal no one. "No doubt you will quote the proverb to me, 'Physician, heal yourself,'" here taken to mean "Heal your own townsfolk." And then the once-warm crown turns into an angry lynch mob. I'm betting that Tim Rice intended "Heal yourselves!" to be the seemingly heartless taunt that embittered the crowd against Jesus.

King Herod's Song

> **Jesus I am overjoyed to meet you face to face**
> **You've been getting quite a name all around the place**
> **Healing cripples, raising from the dead**
> **And now I understand you're God at least that's what you've said**

These lines are based directly on Luke 9:9: "Herod said, 'John I beheaded; but who is this about whom I hear such things?' And he sought to see him." Later on, at the trial before Herod, Luke picks up this hanging thread: "When Herod saw Jesus, he was very glad, for he had long desired to see him, because he had heard about him, and he was hoping to see some sign done by him"

(Luke 23:8). Hence Rice has Herod "overjoyed to meet" Jesus "face to face."

"You've been getting quite a name all around the place: healing cripples, raising from the dead." Yes, these are the miracles of Jesus Luke has Herod so intrigued by. But the last of these rumors, which Herod ascribes to Jesus' own propaganda machine, is not paralleled in Luke: "Now I understand you're God! At least that's what you've said!" This last, even in *Superstar*, is apparently something of a leap beyond the previous miracle reports. Miracles need imply no more that a prophet's identity, or that of a magician, for Jesus. But God! That's something quite different! And it is this which seems to account for Herod's unbridled ridicule in this song. "You're a joke! You're not the Lord! You're nothing but a fraud!"

Again, we are left asking if Rice intends that Jesus himself authored the rumors, including that of his own divinity, or if these are instead the wild exaggerations of his half-witted fans who've gone out of control. Annas and Caiaphas also held Jesus responsible for pamphlets hailing him as the Son of God. The throng of pushy lepers and demoniacs who rush Jesus after the temple incident also seem to have heard groundless rumors that Jesus could grant miraculous healings at will. It seems to me that, according to *Superstar*, we are to understand that Jesus has said and done none of the things for which his fans adore him and his foes hate him. All these reports, whether praising him or damning Jesus, are alike false witnesses and eventually get him "deep in trouble." And here Rice shows his familiarity, in a general way, with the scholarly consensus that the gospels obscure the real Jesus behind a smoke screen of miraculous exaggeration and dogma. As elsewhere, Rice has read such modern questions about Jesus back into the gospel story itself, as if to place his listeners on the scene, able and eager to have our questions settled once and for all. Herod is asking, in effect, "Is all that stuff we read about you in the gospels true?"

> **So you are the Christ you're the great Jesus Christ**
> **Prove to me that you're divine-change my water into wine**
> **That's all you need do and I'll know it's all true**
> **C'mon King of the Jews**

"The great Jesus Christ"—an anachronism, since Jesus was not known as "Jesus Christ," Jesus the Messiah, till after his death. But it is not clear Herod means "Christ" as a title at all. Rather, he seems to use it as a last name, as in Paul's letters, where any Jewish messianic connection has already faded away.

And yet Rice's main source, the Gospel of John, commits precisely the same anachronism. In John 17:3 Jesus, praying to his Father, refers to himself as "Jesus Christ" in the context of the gospel preaching the apostles are to do after his departure. It is very clear here that John is largely telling the story of Jesus in terms of his own later readers' beliefs and their historical standpoint. And Rice, as we have seen so often, is doing exactly the same thing, albeit for a much later (and more skeptical) audience.

The miracle Herod challenges Jesus to perform is, in accord with Rice's Johannine preference, drawn from John 2:1–11, where Jesus does mysteriously cause several large amphorae of water to change into wine. This miracle was one supposedly performed annually by the priests of Dionysus, according to ancient historians. It was not unlike the yearly miracle of Catholic priests who cause the dried-up blood of the martyr saint Jannarius to liquefy before the astonished flock. No doubt some petty priestcraft was involved to perform the carny trick. At any rate, John, who at other points borrows obvious Dionysus motifs and applies them to Jesus the True Vine, has here shown Jesus beating the rival savior at his own game. And Herod wants to see him do it.

It is as if Herod Antipas already knows the story of Jesus performing this miracle and only wants Jesus to "do here what you did in Capernaum." It is part of the rumor following "the great Jesus Christ." In other words, we see once more that Rice has Herod asking the listener's question: if only Jesus would do for us what the gospels say he did, then we, like the ancient disciples, could be satisfied as our more credulous ancestors were. We would "know it's all true," that the whole thing, the Christian gospel, is all true. John concludes the water-into-wine story with the note: "This, the first of his signs, Jesus did at Cana in Galilee, manifesting his glory; and his disciples believed in him." Herod, too, would believe in him if he could just do it again for his benefit.

"C'mon, King of the Jews!" Herod for the first time brings up the question of Jesus' messianic pretensions, the possibility that "the crowd [might] crown him king, which the Romans would ban." But, unlike Caiaphas, Herod cannot even take the prospect seriously—nor will Pilate, in an almost identical scene.

> **Jesus you just won't believe the hit you've made round here**
> **You are all we talk about the wonder of the year**
> **Oh what a pity if it's all a lie**
> **Still I'm sure that you can rock the cynics if you try**

So you are the Christ, the great Jesus Christ
Prove to me that you're no fool
Walk across my swimming pool
If you do that for me then I'll let you go free
C'mon King of the Jews

The first two lines here deftly convey the court of Herod Antipas, one of the first-century Jet Set, as a haunt of the idle rich enervated by ennui, looking for some new curiosity to provide conversational fodder for a while. Jesus, as it happens, has served them well, as Herod and his hangers-on welcome any latest morsel of sensational rumor concerning him and his exploits. And yet it has all been simple amusement. Caiaphas and Annas kept up with Jesus' activities out of growing concern and alarm. But with Antipas and his cronies it has been entirely different. Strictly entertainment. And to see Jesus in person, a command performance by the celebrated conjuror, would be the greatest treat of all! But once Herod sees the bedraggled figure before him, he cannot expect even so much from him. Show's over. "It was nice. But now it's gone." Thus Herod does not even mean to bluff Jesus into a miracle. The words suggesting this at face value are mockery pure and simple. Nor does he seriously mean to trade Jesus his freedom in return for one simple trick. He is merely taunting the poor sadsack, knowing there will be no miracle and no release.

Usually the phrase "you're no fool" or "I'm no fool" denotes that someone was shrewd or experienced enough not to miss a fortuitous opportunity when one comes along. So Herod means that Jesus ought to be able to see an unparalleled chance to escape his fate—all he need do is . . . perform a miracle! Surely nothing to make him work up a sweat, at least if the reports about him are anywhere near accurate. Notice the specific feat requested this time: "walk across my swimming pool." Mark, Matthew, and John all have Jesus walk on the surface of the Sea of Galilee (this miracle, like the water-into-wine, is a Johannine miracle, but not a Lukan one, despite this whole scene being cut broadly from Lukan fabric). It is a plausible speculation that an earlier version of the tale had Jesus simply walking *by* (the Greek word *epi* can mean either "by" or "upon") the water of Galilee, on the shore, and that the disciples' fear of seeing a ghost was due to the fact that Jesus had been killed, making this originally a resurrection appearance, another version of John 21:1–14. (Luke, who lacks the walking on the sea version, does have a story parallel to John 21:1–14, centering on the miraculous catch of fish, John

21:3, 5–7a, in Luke 5:1–11.)

Once more, Herod speaks as if he has read the walking on water story in the gospels and wants to see if there was anything to it. Only he sarcastically suggests his nearby swimming pool as a convenient substitute for the Sea of Galilee. This makes the whole thing come off as a simple party trick, as if Jesus were a professional magic act hired for a birthday party. And that's the whole point. When Herod sarcastically encourages Jesus, "Still I'm sure that you can rock the cynics if you try," the irony is doubled, since Herod is himself the greatest of these cynics. The whole scene is expanded from Luke's concise note that "Herod with his soldiers treated him with contempt and mocked him" (Luke 23:11).

> **I only ask things I'd ask any superstar**
> **What is it that you have got that puts you where you are?**
> **I am waiting yes I'm a captive fan**
> **I am dying to be shown that you are not just any man**

Jesus' reputation has preceded him to Herod's court because Jesus is the latest media darling, "the wonder of the year" (but not longer than that!), a superstar who, despite his meteoric rise, is destined sooner or later to decline and crash. "Top of the poll" one minute, stale news the next. A superstar is by definition a creature of a moment, surfing the wave of fickle popular enthusiasm until that wave breaks on the shore to be replaced by another. And now Jesus' star has fallen, been peeled off his dressing room door.

Herod says he is not picking on Jesus; he would ask the same questions of anyone like him. "You're a celebrity. You're more popular than me. So what makes you better than me?" Simply the fact that one enjoys the spotlight for a moment and the other does not—or does so no longer; witness the petty vengefulness of Elvis against the Beatles for eclipsing him in popular favor: he went to J. Edgar Hoover and volunteered to spy on the Fab Four! How appropriate that an off-Broadway revival of *Superstar* in the late Seventies had Herod made up to look like Elvis, the original "King," who refuses to yield his throne to Jesus, the new kid in town. And this is more appropriate still when one recalls Tim Rice's hope at one point to have John Lennon portray Jesus. Of all the depictions of Herod Antipas in the various incarnations of *Superstar*, the Elvis version is the only one that reflects, or even grasps, the meaning of the scene, the overall reference to the celebrity superstar misunderstanding of Jesus by his contemporaries (and ours). By contrast,

Tom O'Horgan, with his "give 'em the finger" aesthetic, costumed Herod in a gauzy crawfish costume, seemingly trying his best to distract the viewer from any hint of the significance of this rival "king."

But even more inexplicable was Norman Jewison's decision to cast the buffoonish Josh Mostel in the role of Herod Antipas for the film version. Here is a pot-bellied rich kid sitting on a barge (no swimming pool in sight, that's for sure!). The pasty-faced Jeff Neeley as Jesus looks on inertly as Mostel capers about in a poor imitation of Jackie Gleason doing the Hucklebuck and mumbles nasally the words of a song he seems to have forgotten has a tune. *Jesus Christ Superstar* suffered the same fate as the Jesus character himself: betrayal by his own supposed friends, in this case O'Horgan and Jewison. "The end is just a little harder when brought about by friends."

"I'm dying to be shown that you are not just any man." Readers must often ask themselves what it is that distinguishes certain writers (or directors!) lionized by the critical establishment as worthy of the honor. What objective criteria could the clique of judges at the Oscars possibly have for their god-like bestowals? Why, none at all, as Woody Allen pointed out in 1977 when he refused to appear to receive the honor for his film *Annie Hall*. And Herod only wants to know the same thing! What can Jesus have done to deserve his precious fifteen minutes of fame? The question implies that Herod can see nothing whatever in the insignificant figure before him that remotely suggests why such a fuss has been made over him. He is to all intents and purposes "just any man." We have all wondered the same thing when we scratch our heads at the terrific popularity of Whoopi Goldberg or Michael Bolton. Go figure.

It is worth noting that Herod finished his career when he yielded to the social-climbing desires of his second wife Herodias, the one, you remember, he took away from his half-brother. The woman he was already married to went home to daddy, King Aretas IV of Nabatea, who promptly marched on Herod and dealt him a handy defeat. Herod must have begun to wonder if Herodias was worth the trouble! Some years later he probably made up his mind on that question when Herodias pestered him into asking the Emperor Caligula for the traditional title of the Herodian monarchs Herod the Great and Archelaeus, which was none other than King of the Jews. Caligula judged that the mediocre Antipas had overstepped his bounds and not only turned him down, but sacked him as well! He must have rued the day he ever cast a lustful eye on Herodias.

So if you are the Christ yes the great Jesus Christ
Feed my household with this bread-
You can do it on your head
Or has something gone wrong? Why do you take so long?
C'mon King of the Jews

More of the same for the most part: another gospel miracle, which we pointedly have not seen during the course of *Superstar* (admittedly, perhaps, because the rock opera covers only the events of the passion, after the miracles are done). The point is, as before, the New Testament Christ, the Jesus of "your handouts," was supposed to be able to do these feats. Would the real, historical Jesus have been up to the challenge? And, again, the gospel miracle is being domesticated, trivialized: feed, not the hungry multitude of some thousands in the wilderness, but only Herod's household (who lacked for nothing) by multiplying a small bit of bread. Not for the sake of satisfying desperate hunger, but only for the sake of the prodigy.

And at this point we begin to notice something else. This notion of conjuring bread as a convenience, out of self-interest—have we not heard this before somewhere? Not in *Superstar*, to be sure, but rather in the temptation narratives of Matthew and Luke, where Jesus, emaciated from forty days of desert fasting and ripe for a paranormal vision (usually the goal of such shamanistic vision quests in the wilderness), beholds the approach of the devil who says something strikingly similar to Herod's last taunt, "If you are the Son of God, turn these stones to bread." "If you are the Christ . . . , feed my household with this bread." But there is no literal Satan to be seen in *Superstar*. Instead, we hear the Satanic voice as people usually do: in the words of fellow humans, including ourselves, who bid us compromise, sell out, take the path of least resistance. Mark casts Peter in the unwitting role of Satan in precisely the same fashion in Mark 8:31–33, when he prudentially advises Jesus to avoid the danger of the cross. Jesus turns on him with blistering words: "Out of my sight, Satan! You just can't see past common sense to the plan of God, can you?"

In traditional Christian terms, we might see Herod's challenge as a genuine temptation for Jesus, who would indeed have been able to perform the desired miracles and hold Herod to his promise and claim his freedom, escaping the cross. "Do you imagine I cannot appeal to my Father, and he will at once dispatch over a dozen angelic battalions to defend me?" (Matthew 26:53). But *Superstar* seems not to envision that possibility. Jesus' silence denotes rather his long-suffering, his enduring a lot of childish prattle unworthy of a response. (We will see more of this when he returns to Pilate's Praetorium.) It is Herod in his mockery who is taking himself seriously, no one else. The very next line makes Herod's self-delusion clear.

Hey! Aren't you scared of me Christ? Mr. Wonderful Christ!
You're a joke you're not the Lord-you are nothing but a fraud
Take him away-he's got nothing to say!
Get out you King of the Jews! Get out of my life!

The first and third line together anticipate the exchange between Pilate and Jesus to follow: "Why do you not speak when I have your life in my hands?"

"Mr. Wonderful Christ!" This sarcastic acclamation is equivalent to the very next words: "You're a joke! You're not the Lord! You're nothing but a fraud!" At last Herod is speaking plainly, without irony. But there is irony running through his words anyway, the ironic distance the reader can measure between what Herod thinks and what is actually true, just the opposite of what he thinks. For Jesus, in *Superstar*, is indeed the Lord, though not exactly God; he is the Christ, only Herod has it all wrong. He's altogether mistaken in his expectation that the messiah will be a wonder-working superman. At this point Rice echoes perfectly the traditional Christian view. The irony is that by his antics, Herod is only advancing the plan of God according to which Jesus must die an appointed death—for reasons known only to God. Herod (like Pilate and Caiaphas) is helping Jesus away from a path of false messiahship: the path of popularity and superstardom ("Woe unto you when all men speak well of you! For so their ancestors spoke of the false prophets!" Luke 6:26). Like so many angels ministering to him, these gentlemen extend pointing hands in the direction he must follow to true eternal fame, the way of the cross. With equal irony, it is Peter and the others, oblivious of the plan of God, who well-meaningly seek to dissuade Jesus from his marked-out path of destiny. As Martin Luther said, if it's really the gospel, it's the gospel even if Herod, Annas, and Pilate preach it, but if isn't, it doesn't make it the gospel just because Peter, James and John say so.

"Get out, you King of the Jews! Get out of my life!" Of course Herod means Jesus is to go out from his presence, and into Pilate's. Out of the frying pan into the fire! "Get out of my life," on the other hand, smacks of personal rejection by Herod, implying that, perhaps, Herod at some point had been positively interested in Jesus, based on the rumors. Thus his disappointment with Jesus once he sees him face to face is bitter. Jesus was once "in his life" in some way. And now Herod exclaims that he never wants to see Jesus again! It almost sounds like the rancor of a disappointed lover. If so, we must think of the ironic disappointment of the pair of disciples on their way home to Emmaus from Jerusalem where they had seen Jesus perish ignominiously: "We had hoped he was the one prophesied to set Israel free . . ." (Luke 24:21).

We cannot pass on without raising the possibility that Rice has purposely echoed the language of pietist evangelism in our own day. Lay evangelists buttonhole passersby or casual acquaintances with nosy questions like, "Why don't you ask Jesus to come into your life right now?" Herod, then, is turning down the invitation, and with a vengeance! "Get out of my life!"

Luke has Herod's troops give Jesus a beating once they have done simply ridiculing him. While Rice does not report this, what follows in both "Could We Start Again Please" (a song added for the Broadway version) and "Judas' Death" implies Jesus has been brutally beaten, since both songs start from the shocked reactions of the disciples at the sight of Jesus being led back from Herod's quarters to Pilate's. It is interesting to note that Judas' reaction is no different from that of Mary Magdalene and Peter.

Could We Start Again Please?

It was not Tim Rice, but rather Frank Corsaro (the Broadway director before they hired O'Horgan), who suggested this song, sensing the need to expand the original libretto and to inject a moment of tenderness after the initial encounter between Jesus and Pilate and the burlesque scene of the trial before Herod.

Mary Magdalene and Peter have, as in all the gospels, remained on hand to see what would happen next, unlike the rest of Jesus' men who decided to get while the getting was good. Peter had been unwavering in his protestations of loyalty to Jesus, though soon enough someone found his Achilles Heel. Mary has kept an even keel up to this point, keeping her cool while others, including Jesus, flew off the handle. But that, too, is on the point of changing.

I'd been living to see you
Dying to see you but it shouldn't be like this

The first line is apparently intended to refer to Mary's anxious anticipation over Jesus' fate since his arrest. She wanted to see him again, and to see that he was all right. She probably thought he'd escape in the final reel. She had been *living* for this moment; in other words, it was all that kept her going. She had by the same token been *dying* to see him, wasting away with the fever of anticipation, as it were. There is a double irony here. First, the equalizing of living and dying. The metaphors are interchangeable, but there is more to it. We are flirting here with the notions of Jesus' death and resurrection. Second, there is the irony of her long vigil and its horrifying reward. She has waited and waited, only to feast her eyes on a worse scene than she had beheld the last time she saw Jesus, under arrest in the Garden. "Don't you think it's rather funny?"

But a longer period of waiting seems implied in the first line. It sounds as if she has never seen Jesus, like Herod Antipas, but only heard the exciting reports and, like Herod, the actual sight of him took her aback. But this clearly does not fit Mary Magdalene, who has been with Jesus practically from the first. I wonder if we do not detect a hint of the post-canonical legend of Veronica, a woman of Jerusalem who grieved at seeing Jesus carrying his cross, beaten and bloodied, on his way to Golgotha and reached out with a washcloth to wipe his face of blood and sweat. When she looked at the cloth, it had picked up a miraculous image of his face. The whole thing is both an etymological tale explaining the Greek name Veronica (which actually means "She who bears away the victory") as if based on Latin and Greek and meaning "True [Latin *verus*] image [Greek *ikon*]" and an etiology supplying a pedigree for one of the many spurious "miraculous image of Jesus" relics, another of which is the infamous fourteenth-century Shroud of Turin. Here Mary Magdalene sees the battered Jesus from the roadside, like Veronica, and she expresses her tender-hearted concern that Jesus not suffer so.

This was unexpected
What should I do now
Could we start again please
I'd been very hopeful so far
Now for the first time I think we're going wrong

We catch echoes of Mary's earlier song "I Don't Know How to Love Him." There she was similarly at a loss to know what step to take next: "I never thought I'd come to this! What's it all about? . . . I'm the one who's always been so calm, so cool . . . running every show. He scares me so!" She contrasts her former cool command of any situation with her new sense of panic and bewilderment. Once she had remained placid in the face of Judas' accusation and the alarmism of the others. She was the only one with presence of mind to try to help Jesus relax and forget about the heavy weight of his destiny for the time being. Now she herself is every bit as concerned as Judas was then that Jesus has lost control of the course of events and will meet with disaster instead of destiny. Like Judas, she remembers all too well the way things were "when this whole thing began," and she only wishes they could turn back the clock and return to that auspicious beginning, this time alert to whatever wrong turn it was that brought them all to this sad pass.

> **Hurry up and tell me**
> **This is just a dream**
> **Or could we start again please**

So little can she abide the present turn of things that she can neither believe that it's really happening nor endure another moment of the nightmare. "Hurry up and tell me . . ." But if, horror of horrors, it should be reality, then let's stop the camera and take it from the top!

Whether Rice had it in mind or not, it is worth noting that Mary Magdalene's fanciful hope that none of it was really happening closely reflects the widespread view that Jesus did not die on the cross. It was only a dream, or strictly speaking either a hallucination sent by God to confuse Jesus' persecutors or else a case of mistaken identity.

As for "starting again," Darrell J. Doughty [167] has speculated whether this is exactly what happens in the Gospel of Mark. There, Jesus' public activity commences with his appearing at the shore of the Sea of Galilee to summon Peter, Andrew, James and John as his first disciples. And where does Mark's story end? Where it began: the Risen Jesus does not appear to anyone, but the mysterious young man at the empty tomb directs Mary Magdalene and her companions to tell the disciples to make for Galilee, where they will see Jesus. John 21 has the Risen Jesus appear to Peter, Andrew, James, and John as they are fishing in the Sea of Galilee. He calls to them from the shore, whereupon they return to the shore, and Jesus says to Peter "Follow thou me." It sounds remarkably like the initial seaside summoning by Jesus in the beginning of Mark. Perhaps Mark intended us to reach the end of his story, only to realize we were being led right back to the beginning because, in hindsight, the apparent beginning could now be seen to be the ending. That is, it was the Risen Christ who had approached the four fishermen as they struggled with their nets. That would certainly explain the otherwise strange fact that they drop everything and follow Jesus without a second thought: they already knew him, but had given him up for dead. Seeing him alive again was all they needed to take up again where they had left off. This would mean that the teaching of Jesus in the subsequent chapters is really to be understood as an extended period of post-resurrection teaching and revelation.

But so much of it? No problem: according to some noncanonical Gnostic gospels, Jesus remained on earth from eighteen months to eleven years teaching the disciples before ascending to heaven once and for all. But then are we to suppose that Mark means to say that all the same events, including the crucifixion, happen all over again? No; rather the point is that he is letting you know what he was doing all along: superimposing the later beliefs of Christians about Jesus, as well as the teaching that Christian prophets later attributed to him, onto the story of his historical career and crucifixion. John did the same in his gospel, as nearly all scholars agree. Could we start again, please? There are two layers of meaning through the whole gospel story, though you only realize this at the end.

> **I think you've made your point now**
> **You've even gone a bit too far to get the message home**
> **Before it gets too frightening**
> **We ought to call a halt**
> **So could we start again please**

This time it is Peter who seems in the grip of stunned disbelief. And he seems to believe even now that Jesus remains in control of events, instead of being their willing victim. As if it were in Jesus' power to turn suddenly toward them and say, "So, you've learned your lesson, eh? Then I guess we don't need to take this charade any further, do we?" As if the whole thing were a holodeck program on *Star Trek*.

Peter sounds like a frightened child who believes his parents can cancel reality with a snap of their omnipotent fingers. But at the same time he speaks to Jesus (perhaps apostrophaically, as if to Jesus even though he cannot hear: "Christ, I know you can't hear me, but . . .") almost condescendingly, patronizingly, as if to a potential leaper poised on a window ledge and threatening to jump. The police try to calm him down, soothe him, tell him he's made it plenty clear that he means business. He's made his point in spades. Now come on in! In a case like this, it seems the jumper had sent subtle signals to friends, family, coworkers, about how desperately unhappy, or unjustly treated, he had been, but nobody seemed to take him seriously. "Maybe this'll show 'em I mean it! They'll have to take me seriously after this!"

Peter seems to be trying, with kid gloves, to woo Jesus back off the ledge before it is too late and he loses his precarious grip on the windowsill. But what is it Peter thinks is Jesus' point? What message has he had to take such extreme measures to get across? He never says. Perhaps he does not know, but he dare not say so, lest he reveal that Jesus' worst fears had been right on target: no one had understood him. Then he would jump for sure, continue on to the cross, full speed ahead.

But I suspect Peter does have something specific in mind. My guess is that he is thinking back to the scene of the shouting match between Jesus and Judas. Jesus seemed to think Judas and the others were taking him for granted: "Think! while you still have me! Move! while you still see me! You'll be lost and you'll be so sorry when I'm gone!" Jesus came across as childish and petulant then, and so Peter speaks now, in patronizing tones, as one would speak to a petulant child who has decided to run away from home to prove to his parents that they should have taken him more seriously when they had the opportunity. Freud called it a childish revenge fantasy. As one will gladly suffer in order to take revenge on his loved ones who he thinks have neglected him, so does Peter imagine that Jesus is punishing them and saying "I told you so!" "Yes, yes, you were right! We admit it! Now come on back home, for God's sake!" But Peter understands as little now as he did then. He attributes to Jesus the only motive he can imagine, one on a level even lower than his own, because he cannot imagine any higher.

The last time we saw them together, Mary and Peter were at odds, Mary marveling equally at Peter's contemptible cowardice in denying Jesus and at Jesus' clairvoyant knowledge that Peter would do it. But now they are once again in complete agreement. The two of them and the chorus reprise all the lyrics of this song at this point, all saying the same things either one had said before.

Judas' Death

Judas, too, has seen the pathetic condition of Jesus after his cruel hazing at the hands of his enemies, though he has seen not the abuse of Jesus by Herod's troops. He is thinking rather of the blows delivered by the gloating Sanhedrinists and their guards. Though the scene was anticipated earlier ("Judas, thank you for the victim! Stay awhile; you'll see it bleed!"), Rice let it take place off stage. The beating in the high priest's house comes from Mark 14:65. It is reduced to a single slap in the face in John 18:22. In any case, the sight has jolted Judas back to reality. Just as Peter loathed himself for denying Jesus to fit inconspicuously into the courtyard crowd, so now Judas realizes the reproach implied in Annas' friendly, even collegial words to him—as a partner in this dreadful business.

He had earlier been disturbed by second thoughts that no concerns, however real, could justify his betraying his master. Now those doubts come rushing back in, the dam of rationalizations having collapsed in the meantime. Usually we do a bad thing and then begin rationalizing it to salve our conscience, the result being a deadening of conscience from here on in. But with Judas it is the reverse: his rationalizations were all used up before the fact, before the act, and now there is nothing left to protect him from the lurking truth.

The scene, on the whole, is based on Matthew 27:3–7, "Now when Judas, his betrayer, saw that he was condemned, he was sorry for what he had done and returned the thirty pieces of silver to the chief priests and the elders, saying, 'I have sinned in betraying innocent blood.' They said, 'What is that to us? See to it yourself.' And, throwing down the pieces of silver in the temple, he departed; and he went and hanged himself. But the chief priests, picking up the silver, said, 'It is not lawful to put them in the treasury, since they are blood money [i.e., bounty money].' So they took council and used the coins to buy the potter's field, to bury strangers in.'"

In *Superstar* all the emphasis is laid on Judas' self-recrimination. He does not throw down the money and leave. Thus in the movie the camera shows the spilled bag of silver coins at the foot of the tree where Judas hangs himself. And, needless, to say, this rewriting eliminates the part of the scene in Matthew where the priests piously scruple over what to do with the money. Here Matthew, who has freely composed the scene out of his imagination, has shown us the priests doing what Jesus had earlier condemned in the Pharisees: "You strain out a gnat and swallow a camel!" Despite the enormity of what they have just done in the judicial murder of Jesus ("innocent blood"—"What is that to us?"), they are careful now not to allocate the money in an irregular way. So what they wind up doing is to use it for charitable purpose, burial of those who had no loved ones to see to it. Burial of the indigent dead was considered one of the greatest of charitable acts in Judaism (as witness the Book of Tobit). This detail, omitted from the present scene, has transferred itself to the earlier scene where Judas is first offering his assistance to the Sanhedrin. When he is reluctant to accept the money they offer for his services, the priest shrug it off as misplaced moral concern: "Choose any charity, give to the poor." This anticipates what they themselves did with the money, in Matthew's version, when they received it back from Judas.

> **My God! I saw him-he looked three-quarters dead!**
> **And he was so bad I had to turn my head**
> **You beat him so hard that he was bent and lame**

Judas never expected anything like this! Though how could he not have? It just goes to show the extent to which he had hidden from himself the awful but obvious implications of what he was doing while he was doing it.

The description of Jesus as grotesquely beaten out of shape to such a degree that Judas cannot bear to see any more has probably been suggested by the Servant Song of Second Isaiah, from early times read by Christians as a prophecy of Jesus' suffering: "many were astonished at him; his appearance was so marred, beyond human semblance, and his form beyond that of the sons of men . . . He was despised and rejected by men; a man of sorrows and well-acquainted with grief; and, as one from whom men hide their faces [= "I had to turn my head"] he was despised, and we esteemed him not" (Isaiah 52:14; 53:3).

> **And I know who everybody's gonna blame**

Suddenly Judas' tune changes, though no doubt he is unconscious of it. His concern has shifted from Jesus (to whom Judas' heart genuinely goes out) to Judas himself and his reputation. We almost get the feeling that this is really the root of his distress, and yet on the whole the rock opera would not seem to support this reading of Judas. Generally speaking, Judas does what he does in good faith. His plaguing doubts, of which he could never quite get free, were prompted by his love for Jesus as well as by the instinctive feeling that somehow something else was going on in all this, that maybe he was somehow being manipulated, though by whom and for what reason, he could not imagine—though the realization is about to hit home.

Even here Judas is far from accepting responsibility for the disaster. Rather, his words imply that he will be unable to avoid becoming the scapegoat. And though his words make sense as spoken within his own historical context (there is nothing demonstrably anachronistic), anticipating the wrath of the other disciples, we cannot help picking up yet another hint of historical hindsight being retrojected onto Judas so that he speaks presciently of the future, our past. He seems to foresee his everlasting vilification as Judas "the Iscariot," the Betrayer. This is in keeping with what Tim Rice had said clearly about the narrative function of Judas: he represents the mystified perspective of the modern person for whom Jesus finally remains an enigma, asking the questions we ourselves must ask.

I don't believe he knows I acted for our good
I'd save him all this suffering if I could

Judas fears that Jesus must blame him, too. Jesus must view him as a traitor and a turncoat ("You liar, you Judas!"). And this, too, is a tragic misunderstanding. ("If you knew why I do it . . ." "I don't care why you do it! Save me your speeches; I don't want to know!") It might mitigate things if Jesus only knew Judas' motives were pure, albeit misguided. Before the fact, he had comforted himself with the rationalization that Jesus would understand ("Jesus wouldn't mind that I was here with you."), but now, in the cold light of dawn, he realizes how flimsy a self-deception that was.

Does Judas still believe he did the right thing? He says, after all, "I acted for our good." He doesn't exactly rue having made a big mistake so much as he regrets his motives will be misunderstood. He will have to take the blame. For what? Presumably for the vicious beating of Jesus ("all this suffering"). He must have known Jesus would be executed. That was a bitter pill to swallow, hence his agony in making the decision. But why all the cruelty leading up to it? Why not a clean death with dignity? Hence he seems to imply that the Sanhedrin should bear the blame for all the sadism.

Don't believe . . . our good . . . save him . . . if I could

Judas descends to muttering the same thing over and over. The ellipses indicate that he only begins repeating the same sentences, not being coherent enough to finish them, or that his voice keeps dropping so he finishes the sentences inaudibly. It sounds pedantic to mention this, except that the resulting string of sentence fragments may be read together as a new message, so to speak, contained within the original. Does Judas unwittingly admit, at least to himself, that the whole thing was a terrific blunder? Is he really saying, "I don't believe [it was for] our good [after all]; I'd save him [not merely from the excessive cruelty but from execution] if I could"?

Cut the confessions forget the excuses
I don't understand while you're filled with remorse
All that you've said has come true with a vengeance
The mob turned against him-you backed the right horse

Judas has been saying all this, really to himself, but ostensibly to the Sanhedrinists, to whose company he has returned. He was doing the same thing, you will recall, in the earlier song "Damned for All Time," when his words sought to convince the hearer of his innocent motives: the Sanhedrin scarcely needed convincing since his motives were irrelevant to them. He had really been trying to convince himself, to quiet his protesting conscience. But the priests and elders do hear it nonetheless, and, as before, one of them speaks, dismissing Judas' maudlin histrionics as not only immaterial but also as unbecoming for a hard-nosed man of decision like himself. After all, hadn't Judas tried to ingratiate himself with the Sanhedrin by claiming to be "one of the guys" like them? "Annas, you're a friend, a worldly man and wise! Caiaphas, my friend, I know you sympathize!" Well, if Judas was really a man of ruthless pragmatism, who "knew what must be done," whence this sudden sentimentality?

The priest, it is implied, is so hard-hearted, he doesn't really grasp what's ailing Judas, and says as much. To him it seems as if Judas is acting the way he might be expected to act had it all turned out some other way. He might be filled with self-pity and recrimination if, say, the crowd had rallied to support Jesus, prevented his arrest and rioted in the streets, bringing the Romans down not only on themselves but also on Caiaphas and company who would thus have proven themselves unable to keep order. In a case like that, all of them would be crying and moaning. But they won! Judas has been right in every detail, and the risk has proven worthwhile. The bold adventure had borne fruit. Just as Julius Caesar, by crossing the Rubicon against orders, irrevocably committing himself to the overthrow of Pompey, had taken a huge gamble ("The die is cast!"), so Judas had bet his whole stake on Pilate, though Jesus might have been thought to have better odds fresh out of the starting gate. But Judas had bet against the odds, his intuition sharper than the oddsmakers', and he had won big time! So why so downcast?

We can guess just what earlier words of Judas the priest has in mind when he refers to "all that you've said": he must mean Judas' soliloquy in "Heaven on their Minds": "Every word you say today gets twisted round some other way [tomorrow], and they'll hurt you when they think you've lied . . . They think they've found the new messiah, and they'll hurt you when they find they're wrong." The whole subsequent course of events has only demonstrated how right Judas was.

What you have done will be the saving of Israel
You'll be remembered forever for this

Caiaphas chimes in to encourage Judas in terms he thinks will probably mean more to him. He recalls all of Judas' earlier protestations of his idealistic motives, so he goes beyond the flattery of the previous, unnamed priest. Sure, Judas had been wise; his shrewd judgment had been vindicated by events. But, beyond this, his noble actions had proved out. He had saved Israel from certain destruction by the Romans who would have had no other choice but to crush the rebel Jesus movement if things had been allowed to continue as they were. (This observation is slightly inconsistent with the other priest's admission that Judas had been right in his assessment that Jesus' popular support was about to implode. Caiaphas still sees his own plan as the right one; thus, he understands Judas to have facilitated the preemptive strike he had thought necessary before Judas showed up offering his services.)

Caiaphas also rejects Judas' pessimism about how he will go down in history. It will not be as a villain at all. No, he will be memorialized as a national savior! Everyone will remember him as the man who narrowly forestalled disaster. Of course, he is wrong and Judas is right—again! Judas, not Caiaphas, has again "backed the right horse." Thus Caiaphas is again assuming the unwitting role of the oracle of irony. As he once pronounced

it better for a single man to suffer the wrath of Rome than for the whole
Jewish people to bear the brunt of it, a reference to the atoning death of Jesus
Caiaphas had made without even meaning to make it, so now he prophesies
better than he knows: Judas will be remembered forever for his role in the
drama, but as the blackest of villains.

Jesus Christ Superstar had received flack from the beginning from Jews
sensitive to the anti-Semitism of the traditional Christian portrayal of Jews
as villains and "Christ-killers." And they protested what they saw as the sad
tendency of *Superstar* to reinforce these stereotypes. Why must the Jewish
leaders come across as heartless, conniving villains? The issue was a delicate
one, since, while it is true Christians have for many centuries taken the
gospel picture of the Sanhedrin and the Pharisees as a license to blame and
persecute Jews, the vilification of Caiaphas and Annas in the gospels and
in *Superstar* hardly goes beyond the drubbing these two priestly aristocrats
receive in the Mishnah, the traditions of the scribes and rabbis themselves.
There they are called "the serpents of the house of Annas." Caiaphas bore the
blame for transferring the animal and money-changing market from outside
the temple to the Court of the Gentiles, the very thing Jesus himself was
protesting. Neither the gospels nor *Jesus Christ Superstar* are vilifying and
caricaturing Jews as a whole in their depiction of Annas and Caiaphas. In
fact, to the contrary, they are wholly in agreement with the traditional Jewish
opinion of these corrupt and high-handed priests. But then again, that's just
the problem: most listeners or viewers of the rock opera are ignorant of the
facts of the matter. But what are you going to do? As the story has come
down to us, Caiaphas and Annas play a rather crucial role in the plot. To
eliminate their involvement, or to try to portray them sympathetically, would
be confusing to the audience. If they were nice guys, what were they doing
involved in the plot to put Jesus out of the way? It was trouble enough to
make Judas into a somewhat sympathetic figure and yet retain some coherent
motivation for him.

One such attempt to whitewash the Sanhedrin may be found in the TV
miniseries *Jesus of Nazareth*, where not only is Judas depicted as incredibly
naive, but the Sanhedrin appear deeply reluctant that they cannot agree with
"our brother Jesus." In fact, the writers created a new character out of whole
cloth, Zerah, a kind of rogue Sanhedrinist, a wolf among the sheep, who
cleverly manipulates both Judas and the Sanhedrin into condemning Jesus.
It is all both highly implausible and painfully politically correct. It is a good

thing *Superstar* did not take this path. As with the whole issue of education in our degenerate era, the only alternatives seem to be remedial education for cultural literacy, or a further sorry spiral of "dumbing down," the systematic lowering of standards so as to reach students "where they are," i.e., in the slough of MTV-fostered ignorance.

In terms of *Superstar* and similar projects, our choices are to educate the public so that they do know some of the fine distinctions to be made within Jesus-era Judaism, or to distort the story in such a fashion that no one's feathers get ruffled. Which path did Tim Rice take? He took the former. But that was not the end of the matter. Since Norman Jewison directed the film version of *Superstar* in Israel, he had to be especially sensitive to Jewish objections. Many Israelis, after all, were understandably hesitant to have a Jesus movie made there at all. Jewison assured them the script would be reexamined with a view to eliminating anything liable to provoke offense. But, unwilling to look as if he had caved in to critics, Jewison eventually said he decided that nothing in the script really called for such a change.

In this he was stretching the truth. It wasn't that the script required correction that he failed to make. Rather, he fixed what wasn't broken even though he said he hadn't. In the lyrics now under discussion, the original libretto has, as quoted above, "What you have done will be the saving of Israel." Jewison changed this line (or had somebody change it) so that in the movie it comes out: "What you have done will be the saving of everyone." This is so clumsy a line, so inelegant and abrupt, that it can only be the result of ham-handed censorship. Think of the network TV presentation of, let's say, *American Graffiti*. There's a scene when one character tells another to "get your ass out of here." But that would shock the pious, so they changed it to the inane "get your act out of here." Presumably they were hoping the audience would confuse this gibberish with the familiar idiom "get your act together." But no one would ever write such a line of their own free will. It smacks of blatant bowdlerizing. And so does "What you have done will be the saving of everyone." And this is not the only ludicrous corruption of the text by Norman Jewison who, in his approach to this film, seems to have been much less concerned to safeguard the Mosaic Law than to implement Murphy's Law. Thanks to him, everything that could have gone wrong with the *Superstar* movie did.

And not only that you've been paid for your efforts

Pretty good wages for one little kiss

Caiaphas, having played to Judas' idealism, now tosses in another consolation for good measure: Judas ought to cheer up because he even made some money from the endeavor, not something every patriotic hero can claim. Icing on the cake. This might be thought in poor taste, or at least a stupid choice of tactics to cheer up Judas, who had after all refused to take money for the deed since he feared it would blur the clarity of his motives ("I haven't thought at all about my own reward . . . I don't want your blood money!"). But then we have to suspect that Caiaphas is bringing up the thirty pieces of silver precisely in order to mock the nobility of Judas' motives which he had praised only a moment before. Here he is letting the mask slip, letting Judas know that in the end Judas is nothing but a prostitute ("It's not that I object to her profession . . .") since he has been paid generously "for one little kiss." "A fee, nothing more." Just like the fees Mary Magdalene used to require from her customers.

> **Christ! I know you can't hear me**
> **But I only did what you wanted me to**
> **Christ! I'd sell out the nation**
> **For I have been saddled with the murder of you**
> **I have been spattered with innocent blood**
> **I shall be dragged through the slime and the mud**
> **I have been spattered with innocent blood**
> **I shall be dragged through the slime and the mud**

Judas speaks again, as in "Heaven on their Minds," by apostrophe as if to Christ. He still maintains his innocence. He protests that he deserves none of the blame he knows he will receive: he was only aiding in Jesus' plan, wasn't he? Remember, in his heated exchange with Jesus just before the arrest, Judas had begun to surmise that for some unfathomable reason, Jesus intended to do nothing to protect himself even though he was somehow already informed of Judas' intrigues with the Sanhedrin. Did Jesus actually *want* to be handed over to his executioners? "What if I just stayed here and ruined your ambition?" "You want me to do it!"

Judas was in pretty much the same position to Jesus as Jesus was to God: both knew there was a plan involving Jesus' death, though neither understood it. Had Judas asked Jesus why he felt he had to die, Jesus would have had no answer for himself, since he himself could not wrest one from his Father ("Why should I die?" "Show me there's a reason for your wanting me to die!")

Judas' regrets reach a new culmination. He still believes Jesus' death was a tragic necessity if Israel was to be spared terrible Roman reprisals, but now he decides, if he had it to do over again, he'd choose to save Jesus and let the nation fall to the wolves instead. He no longer concurs with Caiaphas' worldly wisdom that it would be better for one man to die in place of the whole nation. No, Judas says, he should have stayed loyal to Jesus and let the chips fall where they might.

And yet Judas' ultimate concern for his own reputation surfaces again. The burden he cannot bear is not so much the loss of Jesus and his responsibility in it, but rather the fact that his name will become a by-word for "blackguard" and "traitor" for all ages to come, not a pretty prospect. He dreads being "spattered with innocent blood." This line, drawn from Judas' hysterical confession to the priests in Matthew 27:4, "I have sinned in betraying innocent blood," adds a new implication. Whereas in the Matthean original Judas is frankly taking responsibility, in *Superstar* he is still disclaiming it. He is "spattered with innocent blood," i.e., he just happens to have the bad luck to be at the roadside when a horseman or a chariot passes, kicking up a wake of gutter mud to soil his garments. We are all familiar with the scene. He was too close when someone murdered someone else. Some of the flying blood hit him, and, sure enough, someone's going to think he got bloodied by committing the murder himself. But he didn't. Only an innocent by-stander, that's all. And this Judas sincerely does mean. His words a bit further on in the song make this apparent.

> I don't know how to love him.
> I don't know why he moves me
> He's a man-he's just a man
> He's not a king-he's just the same
> As anyone I know
> He scares me so
> When he's cold and dead will he let me be?
> Does he love me too? Does he care for me?

Judas reprises Mary Magdalene's song "I Don't Know How to Love Him" because he, like her, is a star-crossed and disappointed lover of Jesus. There is no hint of it being homosexual romantic love; it is the love of the disciple for the master. But Judas doesn't know what to do with the feelings he finds he still has. After all, nothing specific has happened to make him doubt his earlier assessment of the situation. He still thinks Jesus, if left alone, would have invited disaster. He still thinks Jesus was no king, no "new messiah." And yet he moves, even frightens, Judas. What is it about this man? Judas is echoing not only Mary but Herod Antipas as well: "What is it that you have got that puts you where you are?" "I'm dying to be shown that you are not just any man." But whereas Herod saw nothing remarkable about Jesus and so dismissed him, Judas, who also is unable to pinpoint anything superhuman about Jesus, nonetheless is unable to dismiss him—as much as he'd like to.

"Could We Start Again Please?" is, I suggested, something of a twin piece with this one in that both embody the reactions of disciples shocked to see the shameful treatment Jesus has received after his arrest. I also noted the parallels that make "Could We Start Again Please?" something of a sequel to Mary Magdalene's song, "I Don't Know How to Love Him." Here those judgments are vindicated; "Judas' Death" had already functioned as a parallel and a sequel to "I Don't Know How to Love Him," inasmuch as it reprised that song. So when a doublet of "Judas' Death" was subsequently introduced, it is no surprise that it, too, should have been an echo of "I Don't Know How to Love Him." The parallel is only further reinforced with the desperate words of Judas: "When he's cold and dead will he let me be?" In other words, will the haunting presence of Jesus make it impossible for Judas to "start again" on a new life?

And yet perhaps this omnipresent ghost of Jesus might hold out a positive hope. Since Judas still loves his master even after the betrayal, is it thinkable that his master's love for him might have survived the ordeal, too? Is Judas' love finally reciprocated after all? But this ray of hope is immediately extinguished by an enveloping darkness.

My mind is darkness now

At the start of the play Judas had announced "My mind is clearer now. At last I can see where we all soon will be." And he was, as the Sanhedrin priest assured him, right on the money. And yet now Judas is completely mystified. There was too much going on beneath the surface that he did not see, that he has not discovered until now, that made things go drastically wrong somehow.

My God I am sick I've been used
And you knew all the time
God! I'll never know why you chose me for your crime
For your foul bloody crime
You have murdered me! You have murdered me!

His mind was clouded in darkness, but he seems to see all too clearly! But perhaps the darkness is not that of confusion. Perhaps instead it is the darkness of a descending night in which all may nonetheless be clear by the cold light of the moon and the stars. And in the moonlight illumination, the dark truth becomes clear at last. Judas has been set up, manipulated to do the dirty work of God. We have here an echo of Mark 14:21, "the Son of Man goes as it is written of him, but woe to that man by whom he is handed over! Far better for that man never to have been born!"

Wait a second, protests the modern reader, little inclined to take everything the Bible says at face value. How is that fair? If Jesus was so sure it was going to happen, doesn't that mean it was predestined? And doesn't that mean God had a hit man picked already? If so, what choice did the poor dupe have? We might well ask Paul's rhetorical question of Romans 3:5, 7: "But if our wickedness serves to show the righteousness of God, what shall we say? That God is unjust to inflict wrath on us? . . . But if through my falsehood God's truthfulness abounds to his glory, why am I still being condemned as a sinner?" Good question, not that Paul has much of an answer to give. And it is the question of Judas, too. In fact, he asks it because we ask it. Again, he is the mouthpiece for the audience.

We must not miss the parallel between these five lines, short as they are, and Jesus' earlier song "Gethsemane (I Only Want to Say)." They are saying pretty much the same thing. Both rail against God as the master strategist against whom no mortal can hope to win. Both Judas and Jesus are bitter because of the mysterious plan God has trapped them into. And both plans involve the inevitable death of the two men. And each regards his death as apparently unnecessary and yet necessitated by the seemingly arbitrary Kismet of God. He has revealed only enough of the plan to Judas and to Jesus so that they may know their deaths are required, but not a bit of why it must be so. In short, as Rice himself put it, his Jesus is "as mixed up and as unaware as Judas."[168]

Poor old Judas
So long Judas

At this point Judas hitches the rope to the tree limb and ends it all, his neck snapping like a rotten branch like that from which he dangles. The brusque words of the choir seem to function as verbalizations of the senseless and cruel fate of Judas, as if the stones themselves had started to sing. And there is no compassion in their imaginary echoes. "Poor old Judas" sounds like the "too bad" muttered by passersby when they see a street bum has frozen to death over night. "Poor sad sack—but what could you expect?" And "So long, Judas" inevitably suggests "So long, sucker!" The mysterious providence of God seems to have cast him away as the mere tool to which it had reduced him.

Judas and Jesus have been paired and paralleled throughout the rock opera. That parallel has now been completed. Just as Jesus is shortly going to be suspended from the Roman cross, a tree fashioned into an execution stake, so has Judas now hanged himself from a tree made into a gallows. Let us wait and see which one of these men whose deaths were grist for the divine mill gets resurrected from the dead.

Trial Before Pilate

Having brought Jesus before Pilate, as all the New Testament gospels do, Rice then took a detour through Luke for the trial before Herod, then through Matthew for Judas' remorse and self-execution. Now he is back to John, and Jesus is back before Pilate. This interview between Pilate and Jesus is one of the places where the basically Johannine character of *Jesus Christ Superstar* is most evident. John's Gospel, more overtly novelistic than the others, takes off for blue skies at this point. Pilate's interrogation is much longer in this gospel, and it is this version that Rice has incorporated. Rice's redactional hand shows itself in the streamlining of the stiff, repetitive, and artificial quality of John's original account. He preserves most of the Johannine original, but he makes it sound like an actual conversation. We may be sure that if John based his account of the interrogation on any real facts at all, then the facts must have been something like this.

And so the king is once again my guest
And why is this? Was Herod unimpressed?

Pilate had meant to be finished with this matter. Like Gallio of Corinth (Acts 18:12–16), he was little inclined to be called in as an arbiter between Jewish factions on fine points of sectarian debate. In this he was unlike the later Roman potentate, the Christian Caesar Constantine, who took a keen layman's interest in theology and convened the Council of Nicea in 323 CE to settle the debate between the Christological theories of Arius and Athanasius. No, Pilate wanted to stay strictly on the sidelines, but he was not to be so lucky. Like Judas and Jesus himself, he has a key role in the unfolding drama that he cannot escape. And then again it may be that we are to think back to "Pilate's Dream," when Pilate foresaw all that has now begun to transpire. Perhaps he feels an eerie sense of *deja vue* and wants to avoid his destined fate: "And then I heard thousands of millions mentioning my name and leaving me the blame." What he had heard was the weekly chanting of the Nicene Creed, " . . . suffered under Pontius Pilate . . ." Like Judas, he does not much relish the idea of eternal infamy.

We turn to Rome to sentence Nazareth
We have no law to put a man to death
We need him crucified-it's all you have to do
We need him crucified-it's all you have to do

Caiaphas tries to get down to business. And he may be trying to answer Pilate's question. Why did Herod send him back? Simply because, Caiaphas says, under the terms of the Roman occupation, Jewish rulers lack the power of capital punishment, though otherwise they were self-governing. While this does seem to have been the case for the Sanhedrin, the ruling body for Jews in Judea, Herod Antipas, tetrarch of territories including Peroea and Jesus' native Galilee, manifestly did have the authority to execute criminals in his domain, as witness John the Baptist. We have the same problem as before. Once you mix Luke's Herodian trial into the Pilate story, you fall into a hopeless tangle. John's gospel did not have the problem since he lacked any Herodian involvement in the trial. For him the only players are Pilate and the Sanhedrin, and the latter had to obtain approval from the Roman procurator, which is what they are trying to do here.

If we look closely at John's text, we can see how Rice seized on a particular verse of John to use as a springboard for jumping over into Luke, bringing in Herod. John 18:31 has Pilate say to the Jewish elders, "Take him yourselves, and judge him by your own law." Again, in this attitude of secular impatience with Jewish theological debate, Pilate is just like Gallio. He wants to remand the prisoner to Jewish authorities, but which Jewish authorities? In John it is the Sanhedrin to whom he wants to hand the case back, not Herod Antipas. But, to harmonize John's account with Luke's, Rice has Pilate trying to pass the buck to a different Jewish authority: Herod. And just as in John Caiaphas swiftly bounces the ball back into Pilate's court ("It is not lawful for us to put any man to death" John 18:31), Luke has Herod do the same: "he [Herod] sent him back to Pilate" (Luke 23:11). Rice has substituted Herod's refusal for the Sanhedrin's. But, once he gets back to the Johannine sequence, he retains Caiaphas' protest that Jews have no authority to inflict capital punishment. This makes sense as the Sanhedrin's response to Pilate's attempt to hand the matter back to them, but it does not work well as a reply to Pilate as to why Herod would return Jesus to him. Call it redactional sleight of hand. This kind of thing is what scholars call a "redactional seam," a tell-tale "loose end" left untied and thereby calling attention to where the redactor (in this case, Tim Rice) has conflated two disparate sources.

"We need him crucified—it's all you have to do." Caiaphas sees no need for Pilate to take umbrage at their request: it's not much they're asking him to do, just accommodate them. Even as the procurator he has no right to second-guess the Sanhedrin's judgments. No one's asking him to retry the case. All they need is the go-ahead. Caiaphas expects Pilate to rubber stamp their verdict and to carry it out for them. Pilate needn't be irritated at the bother, since it is he, not them, who is making a federal case out of it (literally as well as figuratively).

> **Talk to me, Jesus Christ**
> **You have been brought here-manacled, beaten**
> **By your own people-do you have the first idea why you deserve it?**
> **Listen, King of the Jews**
> **Where is your kingdom?**
> **Look at me—am I a Jew?**

These lines are rather closely based on John 18:33–35, "Pilate entered the Praetorium again and called Jesus and said to him, 'Are you the King of the Jews?' Jesus answered, 'Do you say this of your own accord, or did others say it to you about me?' Pilate answered him, 'Am I a Jew? Your own nation and the chief priests have handed you over to me; what have you done?'"

Here we see Jesus answering Pilate's question by asking another in turn, the same way Jesus is elsewhere shown debating with his Jewish colleagues, classic rabbinical style. Jesus wants to know whether his supposed royal pretensions are of concern to the Roman administration, or whether Pilate is merely being put up to this interrogation by someone else, in which case (an implication Pilate is not likely to miss) he is being used and manipulated by those he supposedly rules. It may be that he is simply trying to raise this suspicion in Pilate's mind, "They're using you, you know. Do you intend to let them make a tool and a stooge of you? Who gives the orders here, you or them?" But that would only make sense as a tactic if Jesus were trying to divide his enemies and look for a chance to escape the both of them (as Paul does in Acts 23:6–10). And in John, as in *Superstar*, Jesus has no such intent. So he must mean something else, as if perhaps Jesus' reply to Pilate's question will be different depending on whether the question is genuinely Pilate's, or whether he is the mouthpiece for others. Perhaps Jesus would admit being King of the Jews, i.e., messiah, in one sense but not another. And in a moment he will indeed draw such a distinction. He is not claiming to be a king of the kind that "the Romans would ban," a political trouble maker.

Again Pilate shows his disdain for the sectarian infighting among the Jews. "Whose question do you *think* it is? Only Jews would be concerned with such niceties. Do I look like a Jew? Of course I'm asking you their question! You bet someone else put me up to asking the question. After all, it wasn't me who brought you up on charges; it was your own nation who indicted you. What did you do to outrage them so?"

Tim Rice has reversed the order of Pilate's questions, serious and sarcastic, so that the ironic "Am I a Jew?" serves a different, though no less rhetorical, purpose. Now it seems to underline the absurdity of any claim Jesus may be making to be monarch of the Jews. Where can this kingdom be? Let's see, it was the leaders of your people who chained you, beat you, and turned you over to me! Hardly loyal subjects! And here we are in the seat of power in Judea, and I am certainly not one of your subjects either. Jews don't rule here. I do, and I'm no Jew. The priests are Jews and yet they're not exactly obeying your orders either! What's left of this 'kingdom' you claim to rule?" I think Rice means this with the rhetorical question, "Where is your kingdom?" Pilate sure can't see it anywhere!

In John's original, Pilate asks no such question. Rice has inserted it to anticipate what Jesus will say next, to make it sound less arbitrary than it does in John, where Jesus suddenly says, out of the blue: "My kingdom is not of this world; if my kingdom were of this world, my servants would fight, that I might not be handed over to the Jews; but my kingdom is not from this world" (John 18:36). Rice's question "Where is your kingdom?" obviously assumes that "kingdom" means a realm, a piece of land ruled by Jesus. But the Revised Standard Version translators are certainly nearer the mark by rendering the word *basileia* in this verse "kingship," denoting kingly authority, the right to rule rather than the place that one rules. The same thing is in view in Luke 23:42, "Jesus, remember me when you come into your kingdom." Again, the RSV is right in translating *basileia* "kingly power."

Jesus, in John, seems to be saying that his reign is not that of a worldly potentate. Kings of that sort do not let themselves be taken captive so easily. Their retainers and bodyguards will fight to the death to prevent it. But his disciples did not defend him or, more to the point, they started to defend him but he told them to drop their weapons and run. Strange behavior if he had worldly ambitions. When he switches prepositions and describes his kingship as not merely "not *of* this world" (i.e., not a reign by military might and coercion), but also as not being "*from* this world," we have a claim that Jesus' authority has not been conferred on him by any earthly authority, as when Charlemagne received the crown of the Holy Roman Empire from the hand of the Pope. We have much the same claim here that Paul makes for his apostleship in Galatians 1:1, "Paul, an apostle-not from men nor through man, but through Jesus Christ and God the Father, who raised him from the dead."

John has already taken pains to demonstrate that Jesus neither sought nor accepted the acclamation of the crowds to become a revolutionary king on their behalf (John 6:15, "Perceiving then that they were about to come and take him by force to make him king, Jesus withdrew again to the hills by himself ").

I have got no kingdom in this world—I'm through, through, through

Talk to me, Jesus Christ

There may be a kingdom for me somewhere—if I only knew

These two statements, in answer to Pilate's question, "Where is your kingdom?," are punctuated by the crowd echoing Pilate's demand for Jesus to explain what he means by such riddles. Does he mean that he has abandoned hope in gaining a throne? That he is agreeing with Pilate's observation that the supposed King of the Jews' authority does not seem to extend beyond his own nose, since it is Jews who are turning him in to the real authority in Judea, the Roman procurator. It sounds like Jesus is agreeing with Pilate: all is lost, my plans have disintegrated. Is that what he means? And when Jesus elaborates, his words only become more ambiguous: does he now mean that there could be a throne for him somewhere else than this world? Where could that be?

In John Jesus was saying his reign was not of a worldly kind, not that it is located somewhere else, say, in outer space. Rather, it is of a completely different nature. Spiritual kingship, not spatial kingdom, is the issue. But Rice ingeniously transforms Jesus' answer into a despairing outcry. Pilate has hit a sore spot. "Can you show me now that I would not be killed in vain? . . . I'd have to know, if I die, what would be my reward?" Jesus has gone forth, ever since that prayer in Gethsemane, with an iron determination to continue in God's plan to the bitter end, but no less with an underlying despondency, knowing he will die without ever knowing why. John had Jesus answering Pilate from a lofty height, but, in Tim Rice's redaction, Jesus is made to mean, "Every door on earth is finally closed to me; my back's against the wall [against the cross, that is]. Maybe there's some kind of vindication waiting for me after death . . . Who knows?"

At this point in the disastrous movie version of *Superstar*, we have what would seem to be another blundering change, I would guess, by Norman Jewison, perhaps, this time, catering to tender Christian sensibilities. He has Jesus answer Pilate, "There may be a kingdom for me somewhere, if *you* only knew." While this would be a very good paraphrase of Jesus' answer in the Gospel of John, it completely misses, even reverses, the point Rice was making: Jesus was pursuing his appointed path, albeit a bit grudgingly, with no certain hope of reward. Jewison has returned us to the Johannine picture of Jesus as an Olympian godling who haughtily condescends to Pilate. John, followed obediently by Jewison, makes Jesus into an imitation of Apollonius of Tyana, who, in Philostratus' legend-laden hagiography, approaches his trial before the Pilate-like Domitian with nary a drop of perspiration, since he knows he is in no danger, but will vanish into thin air before Domitian can condemn him. He is just like Dionysus in Euripides' *Bacchae*, hauled before Pentheus, King of Thebes, who threatens to have him imprisoned and killed, thinking the incarnate god to be a mere trouble maker. Dionysus laughs him to scorn, knowing it is a bug threatening a lion. So with John's Jesus, whom Jewison here retrieves, pushing the carefully nuanced Jesus of Tim Rice off the stage.

Then you're a king?

In John 18:37a, Pilate, growing both impatient and confused, tries to cut through Jesus' sophistical fog: "So you are a king," as if to say, "Let me get this straight: so you're saying you *are* a king then? Is that what you're saying?" Rice's Pilate says the same. He just wants to get to the bottom of this thing, to find out what the wily Caiaphas, who seems a bit too eager to get this man up on a cross, is up to. Caiaphas is surprisingly tight-lipped with his explanations, as if there's something he's hiding. In fact, Pilate's curiosity and confusion stem from the fact that Caiaphas' taciturnity is reminiscent of God's keeping mum when Jesus asks for some explanations: "You're far too clear on where and how, but not so hot on why."

It's you who say I am
I look for truth and find that I get damned

Echoing his earlier question whether this accusation was Pilate's own concern or merely that of the Sanhedrin, Jesus now dismisses the whole matter as irrelevant, strictly beside the point. These lines come from John 18:37b, "You say that I am a king." Thus far, Jesus answers Pilate as he does in the other gospels: "You have said so" (Mark 15:2; Matthew 27:11; Luke 23:3). This is the same sort of ambiguous answer Jesus gave to the Sanhedrin. It is a tactic of evasion, trying to hide behind a smokescreen. And yet it is dangerous, too. It is like the non-directive counseling style of Carl Rogers in which the therapist simply repeats his patient's words back to him: the patient may read whatever he wishes into the repetitious words of the counselor. In the same way, Jesus' ambiguous replies, just noting the fact that his accusers charge him with claiming messiahship, allow the accusers to read whatever they will into his words. Thus Caiaphas took Jesus' words as a big "Yes," while Pilate takes them as a big "No."

But in John the answer of Jesus continues, multiplying the ambiguity. John frequently uses the technique of having Jesus, like the Oracle of Delphi, speak in double entendres, with his opponents slow on the uptake. Here is another instance. "You say that I am a king. For this I was born, and for this I came into the world, to bear witness to the truth. Everyone who is of the truth hears my voice" (John 18:37). If one reads these lines as poetic parallelism (common in the Bible), one would understand the words "For this was I born" as meaning the same thing as "For this I came into the world," and "You say that I am a king" as equivalent in meaning to "to bear witness to the truth." Thus Jesus' kingship is not a worldly power regime, but rather the kingship of the philosophers: the might and exaltation of the one who has "mastered" (i.e., understood) all things, including himself. Thus he sees past the errors and false priorities of the worldly man. He is superior to the worldly throng. In this respect the scene before us recalls the anecdote telling of the encounter between Alexander the Great and the Cynic philosopher Diogenes who lived with no possessions or permanent home, freed from all worldly cares. Alexander, the worldly ruler, exclaims that he is so impressed by Diogenes' uncompromising independence that "If I were not Alexander, I would be Diogenes!" The Johannine Jesus is telling Pilate that if he truly understood kingship, he would not be trying this king for sedition. Pilate seems to understand Jesus' point, but as a hard-nosed pragmatist he is impatient with all such talk. It is to him merely a lot of wheel-spinning. "What is truth?" An abstraction not worth making much of a fuss over. And nothing either to get killed for or to kill someone for. He is convinced that Jesus is a harmless dreamer.

Superstar follows up the brief saying "You say that I am a king"/"It's you that say I am" in a different direction and with a different implication than John's. "I look for truth and find that I get damned." Here is Rice's rendering of the lofty-sounding "For this was I born, and for this I came into the world: to bear witness to the truth." Rice's Jesus is speaking with bitter irony. All he did was to look for the truth, something one would not think a crime, and yet look how it ends up. What a world! He is scarcely less affronted than Judas was; like "poor old Judas," he has been played for a fool, his best intentions serving only to pave the path to hell.

One striking difference between the Johannine version and Rice's is that John has Jesus born with a knowledge of the truth and a mission to testify to it, while Rice properly sees this as more mythologizing. Only a god could be thought of as emerging from eternity with a truth to convey to mortals, a truth pre-packaged and decreed in heaven. If Jesus were a real human being, however, he must start out seeking the truth, and he may never quite succeed in finding it. Someone may cut short his quest by damning, condemning him.

But what is truth? Is truth unchanging law?
We both have truths-are mine the same as yours?

Pilate according to John is a man impatient with talk of truth, as we have seen. Rice's Pilate is essentially no different at this point, except that he elaborates his cynicism and skepticism. Is there really some universal standard of truth by which to accept some assertions and reject others? Such a truth is a really an ideological construct. It is not a truth at all, but rather a law against which Big Brother may declare all varying viewpoints "thought crime." Pilate is shrewd enough and has seen enough to anticipate Nietzsche's deconstruction of "truth" as ideology. Everyone has a so-called truth, a slant on things which advances one's own goals, and one campaigns for it as vociferously as one can. Jesus has his truth, Pilate has his. Neither is more valid than the other, because neither has any objective validity at all. What works is true enough for Pilate, the Roman procurator.

Perhaps ironically, and whether or not he knew it, Pilate has answered Jesus' implied question "Why am I condemned if all I did was to ask questions? To seek the truth for myself?" The answer is that certain people in power, like Caiaphas for instance, have an official party line that they ordain as the true one, and they can't afford to have anyone raise questions about it (as Jesus did when he disrupted the daily business of the temple in Jerusalem a few days before). In the real world, the scene of kingdoms that are of this world, to ask questions is to rock the boat. Questions such as Jesus is asking are not asked in the vacuum of pure theory as philosophers seem to think, says Pilate. They are asked in a real world, where a question topples a domino, and that domino knocks over another and another, and finally someone's dominion is shaken.

Crucify him!

This cry is attributed to the mob, presumably the same one that had turned on Jesus after he refused to heal the sick and deranged among them.

Their exclamation serves to bring us down from that airy realm of speculation that Pilate was (implicitly) talking about. We must leave the exchange of ideas between Pilate and his prisoner and get back to the real world in which people do get crucified for rocking the establishment's boat.

What do you mean? You'd crucify your king?

John's gospel continues: "After he had said this, he returned to the Jews and told them, 'I find no crime in him.'" His subsequent efforts to resist the demands of the Sanhedrin and the crowd probably proceed not so much from any zeal on behalf of Jesus as from a desire to push the issue and to try to get Caiaphas to disclose the real reason for his animosity to Jesus. In *Superstar* he asks pretty much the same probing questions and for the same purpose, and Rice makes clear the drift of Pilate's remarks by having him start off with a taunt. (In John's original, the taunt, "What? Shall I crucify your king?," comes in later, in John 19:15.) If he's the King of the Jews, why do they want him crucified? That's an odd way of showing loyalty to the crown! In other words, the claim of kingship by itself hardly accounts for their ire. After all, they might, as Jews, accept that claim. Since obviously they emphatically repudiate any such claim by Jesus, there must be some reason. They can't seriously expect Pilate to believe that they are all so loyal to Tiberius Caesar that the mere notion of someone challenging that regime would goad them into seeking the upstart's death! There must be some other issue that falsifies his messianic claim (if indeed he has made one, which Pilate is not convinced of either).

We have no king but Caesar!

Yes, Pilate was right: they are pretending to be the noblest Romans of them all. Do they mean to tell him that the messianic hope of the Jewish people is now anathema to them? Apparently so! They must be desperate. A close historical parallel to this scene would be the defection, about forty years later, of Josephus, hitherto a commander of Jewish patriots in the war against Rome. After he saw the way things were going, that their cause was doomed, Josephus decided he would cut his losses as best he could, and at least get out with his life. As it happened, he came away with much more than that. Taken by Roman soldiers to the camp of the Roman general Vespasian,

Josephus went on the offensive, hailing Vespasian himself as the one who would fulfill the messianic prophecies. God must have sent him, as he had once sent Nebuchadnezzar of Babylon, to punish Josephus' fellow Jews for their sins, real or imagined. God had once proclaimed Cyrus of Persia his Anointed One (messiah) in Isaiah 45:1, so why not Vespasian? To other Jews, this would have seemed the sickest of jokes, but Vespasian liked the sound of it, especially when events soon made him Caesar! Josephus was thenceforward guaranteed his own niche in the new order.

He's done no wrong—no not the slightest thing

It's not that Pilate denies that Jesus claims to be King of the Jews; it's just that he thinks Jesus poses no more threat than a mental patient who claims to be Napoleon. What's to worry about? He hasn't actually done anything wrong—at least nothing anyone will let Pilate in on. And if it's just some scheme of the Sanhedrin to silence a poor schmuck who dissented over some fine point in their legal code, then Pilate will have none of it.

We have no king but Caesar! Crucify him!

The crowd, presumably coached by the Sanhedrin members scattered among them, continue to play the "loyalty to Caesar" card. They are playing Pilate's own game with him, and they are going to win. Just as Pilate taunted them with disloyalty to their own king, Jesus, now the crowd taunts him with disloyalty to *his* king and master, Caesar! Does Pilate really want to be in the position of releasing a self-proclaimed "King of the Jews"? Especially one whom the Jews themselves have handed over as a treasonous criminal? That wouldn't look too good!

At this point Rice added new lyrics, not in the original libretto, more on the back-and-forth between Pilate and the crowd. It serves to clarify a few things.

> **Well this is new! Respect for Caesar!**
> **Till now this has been noticeably lacking**
> **Who is this Jesus-why is he different**
> **You Jews produce Messiahs by the sackful**

Pilate calls their bluff: if they really had such zeal for Caesar, it would have manifested itself before now. Before this any regard for the Roman regime has been conspicuous by its absence. And this was nowhere more clearly evidenced than in the constant appearance of new messiahs leading popular armies against Rome. "You Jews produce messiahs by the sackful," that is, like potatoes, a bumper crop of Christs. A national staple. Why is Jesus any different from them? That is, why doesn't the Jewish people support him against Rome? What is the missing piece of the puzzle? Pilate is putting his cards directly on the table now.

As a matter of historical accuracy it ought to be noted that the Sanhedrin never supported any of the popular messiahs. They reigned over domestic affairs strictly at the pleasure of Rome. The high priests were even chosen by Rome. They even collected taxes for the Romans, and these taxes were pretty exorbitant. So the priestly aristocracy was hated by the people, even though the people usually respected their office. The Pope's the Pope, after all, and if you're a Catholic, you're stuck with him until the next one replaces him. He's part of the package. Things had been this way for over four centuries, starting when Cyrus of Persia sent Ezra and Nehemiah, with imperial backing, to "reform" Judaism and carry out Persian policy. The priestly rulers were lapdogs of the foreign power and no one was deceived about it. So from time to time, when a popular messiah arose, his goals would include dispensing with the corrupt priesthood of Jerusalem and to replace it with a new set of clergy from the countryside whose zeal for the old ways would be their only qualification. In the tumultuous time of the war against Rome, already mentioned, messianic liberators occupied Jerusalem and did in fact execute the chief priests. Their worries had been fully justified. So Caiaphas and his ilk were never supporters of home-grown kings of the Jews. They were indeed loyal to Caesar and wouldn't want to see him go.

The crowds were another story, but then, as Judas had anticipated, these crowds eventually became disillusioned with Jesus and turned against him. Disappointed love turns readily into hate.

We need him crucified—it's all you have to do
We need him crucified—it's all you have to do

The crowd is adamant and has returned to its original simple demand. Why does Pilate insist on complicating what is essentially a very simple matter? Of course, the reason he's doing it is that he suspects there's something fishy going on here, that there is no capital crime here at all, and that the Sanhedrin knows it, but won't acknowledge it, else Pilate could not be expected to grant their request.

These lines, which we heard before, were originally those of Caiaphas. Now the whole crowd parrots them. This might denote Caiaphas' manipulating the crowd, prompting them to say what he wants said. In any case, we can identify Caiaphas and the crowd as sharing a single actantial role. They are just different people behind the same dramatic mask, that of "Jewish opponent of Jesus."

Talk to me Jesus Christ

Pilate turns to Jesus and says, in effect, "You're not being much help here, you know! It's your butt in the sling, after all!"

Look at your Jesus Christ-I'll agree he's mad
Ought to be locked up but that is not a reason to destroy him
He's a sad little man-not a king or God
Not a thief-I need a crime

(This stanza is a thinly veiled paraphrase of the one below, "I see no reason—I find no evil! This man is harmless, so why does he upset you? He's just misguided—thinks he's important." Of course, that one was the original. The new version is simply filler. To create it, Rice has treated his own original libretto as he has treated John's gospel elsewhere.)

Turning back to the crowd, Pilate seems next to try a different tactic, to appeal to their pity. For a moment he sounds as if he is actually trying to free Jesus, as if he himself cannot help feeling compassion for this pathetic figure, this "sad little man." As in Judas' earlier words to Jesus, "You sad, pathetic man" and "the saddest cut of all, someone had to turn you in," "sad" refers not to Jesus' subjective state of mind but rather to the sorry situation he is in.

But it may simply be that Pilate, unsentimental as ever, is just reasoning with the crowd. They can't expect him to use the Roman justice system as a blunt instrument. He can only execute Jesus for an honest-to-goodness criminal offense. If Jesus were a rebel king, Pilate would have no problem. If Jesus were a thief, Pilate could sentence him to the cross with no difficulty (remember the two thieves, "brigands" crucified on either side of him). These were in fact two of the four crimes requiring crucifixion, the other two being piracy and a slave running away from his master. And these are obviously out of the question.

"I need a crime!" This concise summation tells the crowd (and us) that Pilate is now willing to deal. He's not unwilling to execute someone the priests hate so much, but he can't just make something up. "I need a pretext! You'll have to come up with something better!"

Kill him—he says he's God-he's a blasphemer

The mob merely repeats one of the charges Pilate has already said he cannot take seriously. Even if he believed Jesus had made such eccentric claims, it hardly makes him any sort of threat—except maybe to himself, but whose business is that?

He'll conquer you and us and even Caesar
Crucify him. Crucify him

This appears to be intended as the real concern of the Sanhedrin and the crowd, the secret Pilate was asking for. They have no choice but to come clean, and their real concern is a shocker. Just as Pilate himself had a dream foretelling the future, including his own role in the events we are now witnessing, the crowd seems to be speaking with a preternatural vision of things to come, well beyond the horizon of their possible knowledge. This is what will happen, as the listener knows: Jesus will be remembered and even worshipped long after Judea has been swept off the map by Rome, long after the Roman Empire itself has bowed the knee to Jesus' name (Constantine would embrace Christianity himself, and after him Theodosius would make it the official creed of the empire). And Pilate's own name will escape utter historical oblivion solely because of the toe-hold it will gain in the story of this man.

It is at this point that Rice's retrospective anachronism technique is used most boldly, even more so than in the following song, "Superstar," since here it is Jesus' own contemporaries who speak as if from the distant future, not a disembodied spirit like the postmortem Judas. The gist of the crowd's urging is that Pilate must dispense with Jesus now, even in the absence of a legal excuse, because of what the result will be one day if he doesn't. The crowd is aware of a historical irony which actually became evident only long after the fact. It is as if Rice himself were among the crowd, a time-traveler trying to warn Pilate before it's too late.

It seems to me that what Rice has achieved here is an expose of the dogmatic logic that replaces ordinary narrative logic in what Todorov calls "the plot of predestination." The characters already know the butler did it. No narrative tension remains because there is no element of uncertainty. We had cause to observe the same phenomenon in the case of Jesus' passion predictions. In the real world, the events just would not have progressed as they do, as if Jesus and the disciples did not know what lay ahead of them—if they did know it beforehand! The characters are unconvincing masks for the author who is commenting to the reader through the characters as if the characters could not hear! Of course, they couldn't if the author made his comment to the reader outside the field of intra-narrative discourse. But if the author decides to speak to the reader through a character, telling some behind-the-scenes secret, then the characters are forced to "know too much," information that would completely change the direction of the story if, as characters, they knew to expect it.

It is as if the author of a historical novel about General Custer had a spy from Sitting Bull's camp sneak into Custer's tent and blab about the next day's plans. And then the spy remarks, "What an irony! The Great White Father's going to get his butt kicked this time!" Would Custer go ahead as if nothing had happened? Hardly. If it were a comedy, we could imagine the Indian spy turning to the camera and making his ironic remark as an aside to the audience, without Custer hearing him. But that's what makes it a comedy. The spy purposely destroys the audience's suspension of disbelief and reminds them not to take it seriously. It's only being played for laughs. In the same manner, Rice has the first-century crowd speak, not to Pilate, but to the audience in Rice's own voice. The idea is not to make *Superstar* into a comedy, but it is to make you stand back for a moment and recall that this is a Passion Play told from the perspective of a couple of thousand years later.

And what this forced disjunction of audience involvement reveals to us is that the gospel narrative itself has confused hindsight with foresight. Biblical scholars have repeatedly raised the question of why, given the gospel portrait of Jesus, anyone would have wanted to put him to death. The blasphemy charge would make sense only if one took the statements of Jesus in John's gospel (e.g., John 8:58: "Before Abraham was, I am.") at face value as authentic sayings of the historical Jesus. And this has become impossible, in view of the blatantly literary character of that gospel. In it Jesus is being used as a literary mouthpiece for the ideas of John. When he said that "the word was made flesh" (John 1:14), he correctly summed up the strategy of his whole gospel: the "word" of John's own teachings was embodied in the fictive character of the Johannine Jesus. Other than such instances of Christian writers putting Christian dogmas on the lips of Jesus, which is usually pretty blatant, most of the teaching attributed to Jesus sounds remarkably close to contemporary Rabbinical, Stoic, Cynic, and general Hellenistic ethics. Would this have upset anybody very much? Who'd want to crucify Leo Buscaglia or Deepak Chopra?

We are told that the pious Pharisee sect took great umbrage at Jesus mixing with sinners in order to persuade them to repent of their sins. Is this really likely? Christian scholars still say the problem was that Jesus preached a new gospel of the love of God, which Jews, fanatical legalists, found outrageous. This verges on anti-Semitic caricature. Christian readers see nothing amiss here, since they are reading the story not vis-à-vis what makes sense in terms of historical plausibilities, but rather through the lenses of traditional dogma. Since they "know" the real reason for Jesus being put to death was that God wanted him to die as an atoning sacrifice for human sin, they do not particularly care what must have been going on in the minds of those who condemned Jesus. Since they were just acting their assigned parts in the sacred drama, any other motivation is moot.

But without the refractive lenses of faith, the historian starts to wonder if indeed the whole story did not begin as precisely such an abstract myth of salvation and was later historicized, once later Christians wanted Jesus to have been a historical figure. They had to sketch in a believable historical-political background, including motives for the authorities' wanting to condemn Jesus. If the dots did not quite connect, the Christians could not see it, since the internal logic of the salvation myth was still uppermost in their minds. But once one insists, as any historian must, that the story justify its claim to be taken as history, the gaps begin to appear.

To take a more obvious case, look at the Nativity story of Matthew, as well as its parallels in the legendary lore of Moses, Zoroaster, Krishna, Augustus, and others. In all cases, some evil tyrant or priest somehow has an intuition that the birth of a special child will one day lead to the overthrow of the evil power. So the villain acts to nip it in the bud by seeking the child's death. But the child is always providentially preserved so he can grow up and fulfill his destiny. The basic prototype is probably the ancient myth of Uranos burying his children the Titans so none of them will grow up and challenge him for the throne. But his son Cronus manages to do just that. Then he in turn devours his children as soon as they emerge from the womb, except that baby Zeus is spirited away—and grows up to overthrow Cronus. In all these cases the father is alerted beforehand by a prophecy or an oracle, a direct supernatural revelation. This fits into an overt myth, but not so well into a historical account, as witness the shock with which Americans greeted the news that President Reagan was setting foreign policy according to the dictates of Nancy Reagan's astrologer. This was implausible in the real world, to put it mildly. But it works well enough in a Nativity legend when the Magi from the east get the news of Jesus' birth by star-gazing. And on the basis of this news flash from the beyond, Herod sets out to destroy the divine child.

When it comes to the story of the state execution of Jesus, we are supposed to be on the historical bedrock of the gospel story. Here, if we are really looking for history, we just cannot be content to accept theological dogma as the motivating force of events. We cannot accept the notion that the authorities crucified Jesus because the plan of salvation required them to do so. Is that what they thought they were doing? It is just conceivable that, as Hugh J. Schonfield suggested,[172] Jesus was doing what he did in order to fulfill the messianic prophecies of the Old Testament, but it is another thing entirely to picture the enemies of Jesus doing him in because otherwise prophecy will not come to pass, and that is pretty much what the gospels' passion narratives are saying.

In fictional tales, like "An Appointment in Samara" or Sophocles' *Oedipus*, a glimpse of tomorrow's destiny always results in (unsuccessful) attempts to cheat fate, and the fact that the crowd wants to avert the already known future by killing Jesus, unaware that it is his martyrdom that brings about that future, labels the whole thing as a fiction, too. It is based on the same retroactive irony we see, on the same subject, in 1 Corinthians 2:8, "None of the rulers of this age understood this; otherwise, they would never have crucified the Lord of glory." There is exactly the same attribution of supernatural foreknowledge, but not quite enough of it, to the villains. Just as in the Nativity legends.

There is neither historical nor literary verisimilitude in the gospel passion stories as they stand. In them, dogma has devoured the original facts of the matter or, alternatively, dogma has created the supposed facts of the matter.

In the latter case we ought to keep in mind Montaigne's warning to liars: it is very difficult to keep all one's lies straight. By having the crowd tell Pilate that the real reason to destroy Jesus is to avert what future history says will happen otherwise, Tim Rice is making baldly explicit what is implicit in the gospel accounts: dogma retrojected into the past is the real motivation for the characters' actions. And this betrays the story as a clumsy fiction rather than an historical report.

Behold the man-behold your shattered king

In the Gospel of John, this presentation of Jesus to the crowd ("'Behold, I am bringing him out to you so that you may know that I find no crime in him.' So Jesus came out, wearing the crown of thorns and the purple robe. Pilate said to them, 'Behold the man!'" John 19:5; "Behold your king!" John 19:14) follows the whip-scourging of Jesus, whereas in *Superstar* it precedes it. If we interpret this passage in John in light of Luke 23:14b-16 ("after examining him before you, behold, I did not find this man guilty of any of your charges against him; neither did Herod, for he sent him back to us. Behold, nothing deserving death has been done by him; I will therefore chastise him and release him.") we may guess that John means for Pilate to demonstrate his "not guilty" verdict by displaying that Jesus was dealt only a lesser punishment, and that will be quite sufficient. But since, according to Rice, the whipping has not yet transpired, what is the crowd to behold that they haven't already seen?

The occupational hazard of the literary critic is to demand more of a smooth connection from the text than the author may have bothered to put there. But still, we must take the text as it reads and allow it to speak for itself. And then one may hazard the guess that Pilate's point is to show the Jews the irony of their situation. Though they cannot seem to see it, "this broken man," "Someone Christ," is their true king, the only kind appropriate: the messiah of the pariahs. A triumphant Son of David would be all wrong. Caesar is the right kind of king for the Romans because they are the conquerors. But for the long-oppressed Jews? This "sad little man" is about right. "The King of the Jews" is like the chief representative sample of his kind, as if a man should be known as the King of the Pickpockets, or the King of the Hobos, the King of Rock and Roll. Thus the paradigm for the Jewish people would be this "shattered king." Don't they see? To repudiate this king, the only kind they could really have, is itself the act of sedition of which they accuse him! It means they are waiting for the kind of royal prince who will be able to slay Rome with the sword of his command. If that's the kind of messiah you insist on, then it is you who are no friend of Caesar.

We have no king but Caesar

The party line is unbending; as we will see, they mean to control the definition of the issue so that Pilate's own loyalty to Caesar will come into question the longer he refuses to punish this rebel king. And this will finally sway him.

You hypocrites-you hate us more than him

Here we might think of Mark Antony's speech, laden with irony: "Not that I loved Caesar less, but I loved Rome more!" Pilate might paraphrase this earlier Roman: "It's not that you love Rome more, but that you love Jesus less!"

We have no king but Caesar-crucify him

This is exactly the same phrase onto which Rice grafted the new lyrics. Now he repeats it in order to reproduce the original jumping-off point for the original continuation of the lyrics. This, by the way, is another standard "redactional seam," a telltale mark, this time, of a subsequent interpolation into an extant text, whether by the original author himself or by a later scribe. Once you return to the original wording, you have to reproduce the original linking phrase or another equivalent to it. See 1 Corinthians 12:31a, "But earnestly desire the higher gifts," which originally fed into 1 Corinthians 14:1b, "especially that you may prophesy." But a subsequent interpolator decided to splice in a still higher goal, namely love. So onto 1 Corinthians 12:31a he added a new continuation, the new 1 Corinthians 12:31b: "And I will show you a still more excellent way [i.e., than even the higher gifts]." This sentence adds a new spin and functions as a segue to the immortal love chapter, 1 Corinthians 13:1–13. Once it is completely installed, the interpolator has to go back and retrieve the original continuation of chapter 12, our present chapter 14. And to do this, he must supply a new socket joint like the one the chapter originally fit into, like lengthening an already composite extension cord by separating the original two segments and placing a third between them. It won't work unless the prongs of the original segments can plug into the same size socket they plugged into before. So the new socket into which chapter 14 will be plugged is almost exactly the same as chapter 12:31a. Chapter 14:1 reads, "Make love your aim, and earnestly desire the spiritual gifts, especially that you may prophesy." Another example would be 2 Corinthians 6:13, "In return—I speak as to children—widen your hearts also," the last verse before a subsequent interpolation. After the new section, chapter 6:14–7:1, the original continuation picks up, attached not to its original peg, but from another just as good: "Open your hearts to us . . ." (2 Corinthians 7:2).

I see no reason—I find no evil
This man is harmless so why does he upset you?
He's just misguided-thinks he's important
But to keep you vultures happy I shall flog him

Pilate is trying without success to show the crowd that they are just as misguided as Jesus, since they, too, imagine he's important. I think of a Telegraph Avenue restaurant with a flying saucer motif. Its proprietor billed himself as an extraterrestrial messiah. It was hard to believe he took himself seriously (if he did!), but even harder to fathom was that many fundamentalists took him seriously, too, only as the Antichrist. They thought the Great Beast of the Apocalypse was serving up burgers in Berkeley! Pilate implies the same thing: Get a hold of yourselves!

Thus Pilate judges Jesus as deserving of no punishment at all, but he is willing to go as far as a whipping if it will satisfy the arbitrary blood lust of the crowd. He ought to have known half-way measures would never do the trick. To the contrary, they are the beginning of the end, just as you know a repressive regime that makes a few concessions to a revolutionary movement is really capitulating, since it is signaling to the rebels that they have the regime right where they wanted it. Pilate is telling them that half a loaf is better than none, but what the crowd hears is that there's more where that came from.

Crucify him!

Even before the first stripe is cut into Jesus' flesh, the crowd is protesting. But they are not demanding Pilate recall the order and save Jesus from an undeserved flogging. Rather, they mean he mustn't be let off so lightly! This outcry allows us to gauge the futility of the act. Even before it happens, it is rejected: "No deal!"

[Thirty-nine lashes]

Why such an odd number? It was a specimen of the scribal practice of "building a hedge around the Torah," a protective buffer made of extensions of the literal commandments in order to keep people outside breaking distance of the Law. The same thinking led to the suppression of the divine Name. The Torah stipulated that the Name of the Deity not be "taken in vain"—whatever that meant. So, to play it safe, no one was permitted to utter the name at all (except that the high priest would pronounce it once a year on the Day of Atonement within the Inner Sanctum). It was a matter of playing it safe. In the same way, the Torah directed that criminals receive no more than forty lashes. Anything more would be what we call "cruel and unusual punishment." But then there's the possibility of losing count while flailing away. Gee, now was that number 26 or 27 . . . uh-oh! Should I start over? To avoid this, the scribes ruled that the whip-wielder should count only to 39 in case he skipped counting one blow. In 2 Corinthians 11:24 Paul reminisces, "Five times I have received at the hands of the Jews the forty lashes less one."

Though the libretto does not stipulate it, the recording has Pilate counting the whip lashes with a rising sense of tension, then finishing the count with an orgasmic sigh of release. He is a sadist, a stereotype of the depraved Roman.

Where are you from Jesus? What do you want Jesus? Tell me

Following as it does the flogging, Pilate's words suggest a desperation on Jesus' behalf, as if to say, "Don't make it even harder for yourself! Don't make me resort to even worse measures!" It is a familiar scenario from interrogation scenes in the movies. But in John, the question, "Where are you from?" (John 19:9) denotes a new sense of superstitious awe, a chill sent through him by something new the crowd adds to the accusations against Jesus: "We have a law, and by that law he ought to die, because he makes himself out to be the Son of God" (John 19:7). The moment is equivalent to that in Matthew's version when Pilate, about to pronounce sentence on Jesus, receives a hastily scribbled note from his wife. But in John's version, Pilate's superstitious panic is induced instead by the eerie report of the crowd, withheld from him until now.

Pilate's question, "Where are you from?" is a perfect Johannine straight-man set-up line, opening up the possibility that Jesus has a divine origin in a mysterious kingdom "not of this world." The question is more or less equivalent to Jesus' trick question to the hostile scribes in Mark 11:30, "The baptism John administered: was it from heaven or from men?" Or, again, in Galatians 1:1, "Paul, an apostle, not from men or through man, but through Jesus Christ and God the Father." In those cases it was a question of whether John the Baptist and the Apostle Paul had divine authorization and support for what they were doing. In John, the point is similar, but the focus has shifted to Jesus' own origin. Did he in some fashion come down from heaven?

But the news of Jesus' supposed claim to be God cannot be the motivation of Pilate's question in *Superstar*, since Pilate has already heard this revelation from the mob, at least in the additional lyrics ("Kill him! He says he's God!"), and he seemed unmoved at the time. He had even anticipated it: "He's . . . not a king or God."

You've got to be careful-you could be dead soon-could well be
Why do you not speak when I hold your life in my hands?
How can you stay quiet? I don't believe you understand

This last remark recalls a similar one made by Caiaphas at an earlier interrogation: "Jesus, you must realize the serious charges facing you."

In John, such words do follow Pilate's question, but not immediately. It seems that Jesus will not deign to answer Pilate, and the latter is surprised, given the circumstances: "Pilate therefore said to him, 'You will not speak to me? Do you not know that I have power to release you, and power to crucify you?'" (John 19:10). You'd best start coming up with some answers right now, mister.

You have nothing in your hands
Any power you have comes to you from far beyond
Everything is fixed and you can't change it

It is Pilate who is "a sad little man," who is sadly "misguided, thinks he's important," when he is really no more than an "innocent puppet."

These lines stray nary an inch from the Johannine original: "You would have no power over me unless it had been given you from above; therefore he who delivered me to you has the greater sin" (John 19:11). Who is deserving of this blame? At first we think of Judas ("The Son of Man goes as it is written of him, but woe to that man by whom he is delivered up."), but Judas did not hand Jesus over to Pilate. That was the deed of Caiaphas. At any rate, Jesus cuts Pilate down to size, disabusing him of his delusions of grandeur: he is only a flunky far down on the chain of command. He struts and swaggers like a bantam rooster, and it's in bad taste. In fact, that's what seems to prompt Jesus to break his silence: "Oh, really now!"

Tim Rice has focused the irony even more sharply. The gun Pilate thinks he has aimed straight at Jesus isn't even loaded. He has no power at all, whether to crucify or to release. All that has already been decided. It is not that Pilate cannot make his threat credible. Jesus doesn't need any threat from him; he's already resigned himself to an inevitable death. The joke is that Pilate does not even have the power *not* to kill him. "Everything [i.e., my death] is fixed and you can't change it."

You're a fool Jesus Christ-how can I help you?

This is a rhetorical question. He means Jesus has for some crazy reason made it impossible to receive any help from Pilate. It is thus Jesus, not Pilate, who condemns Jesus to death. And in this way, with an irony he does not understand himself, Pilate winds up acknowledging the truth of Jesus' strange words: Pilate is helpless to save Jesus, even if it is Jesus himself who has locked the controls and set the plane to crash. Jesus has dictated what Pilate can and cannot do. "Everything is fixed [—by Jesus' own death wish] and you can't change it"—[Jesus has seen to that].

Pilate! Crucify him!

So wrapped up is Pilate in this strange prisoner that the crowd must call out to pry him away from Jesus. And again they demand his death. Nothing less will satisfy them.

Remember Caesar—you have a duty
To keep the peace so crucify him! Remember Caesar

**—you'll be demoted, you'll be deported
Crucify him!**

As in John, where the crowd says, "If you release this man, you are no friend of Caesar; every one who would be king automatically ranges himself against Caesar" (John 19:12), the insinuation is clear. Pilate, as a loyal Roman, if that's what he is, must surely hold the policy, "No enemy of Caesar is a friend of mine." And by seeming to retain for himself the prerogative of deciding whether any particular "King of the Jews" deserves punishment, Pilate is almost making himself king and thus an enemy of Caesar. Isn't it enough that Jesus bills himself as King of the Jews? "What more evidence do we need?" Or maybe you think that's not a crime? Let's see what Tiberius Caesar has to say about that, why don't we?

Pilate is willing not to hold Jesus responsible for what other people make of him. But the crowd judges that possible distinction irrelevant. So what if he himself does not foment revolution? What happens if and when "his half-witted fans . . . go out of control"? The days of "no fighting, no armies, no riots, no slogans" will be gone, and it will be Pilate's fault! Fancy having to explain to Tiberius, "Well, sir, I guess I thought that this one was different somehow, I can't say why . . ." Better to lock the barn door before the horse escapes, eh? Let's not take any chances.

And if anything does go wrong, the blame will fall squarely on Pilate's shoulders. "You'll be demoted, you'll be deported." Which is exactly what would eventually happen. Only Jesus happened not to provide the occasion. Some years afterward, Pilate received word that some Samaritan, apparently making himself out to be the Taheb (the "Prophet like Moses" whose coming the Samaritans awaited in lieu of a Davidic messiah), had called a meeting on the slopes of Mount Gerizim, the ancient site of one of Joshua's shrines where he gave the law to Israel. A great Samaritan temple had been built there and was demolished by the Hasmonean kings. Samaritans believed that when the true Taheb arrived, he would prove himself by revealing the hiding place of the temple vessels, hidden away to escape destruction. This the Samaritan proposed to do. Pilate decided he'd rather be safe than sorry and so dispatched some troops there. Even though the rally was peaceful, the Samaritans unarmed, the Roman soldiers were directed to show no mercy. The resulting massacre was so abhorrent to Pilate's Roman master, once the surviving Samaritans lodged an official complaint about it, that Tiberius wasted no time calling Pilate to answer for his actions back in Rome. He never returned to Roman Palestine.

It is to just such an eventuality that the crowd points in order finally to intimidate him to carrying out their wishes. Recall how in the movies *Miracle on Thirty-Fourth Street* and *Inherit the Wind*, both trial judges are prevailed upon to be lenient in an unpopular case because elections are just around the corner. ("You're a regular Pontius Pilate the minute you start!")

What seems unaccountably strange is that Pilate should have been heedless of such factors later on, in the case of the Samaritan Taheb, if he had already learned prudential caution in the earlier case of Jesus the King of the Jews. This makes one start to wonder whether perhaps the Samaritan incident is factual and the Jesus incident a fictive rewriting of it by Christians who were casting about for any likely-sounding historical details to fill in the spare outlines of their earlier, more abstract, salvation myth.

> **Don't let me stop your great self-destruction**
> **Die if you want to you misguided martyr**
> **I wash my hands of your demolition**
> **Die if you want to you innocent puppet!**

Pilate has been fighting on two fronts, laboring under two different tensions. Jesus would not cooperate in Pilate's efforts to save him, thus making Pilate look foolish. And he was losing control of the situation; people were beginning to accuse him of being soft on Caesar's enemies. Together these two developments are enough to make Pilate throw in the towel. It's not worth this! I wash my hands of it!

He accuses Jesus of having a sick, masochistic martyr complex. We are driven to think of Judas' bitter and baffled words to Jesus at the Last Supper: "You want me to do it! What if I just stayed here and ruined your ambition?" And let's not forget the disgusted sarcasm of Brian of Nazareth's mother when she sees him up on the cross: "All right then—*be* crucified!"

Superstar

It is striking that in *Jesus Christ Superstar* there is no resurrection of Jesus. The only thing that even remotely suggests a resurrection is Jesus' vague guess that there might be some sort of kingdom prepared for him somewhere (contrast

John 14:1–3; Luke 22:29), but he doesn't seem too positive about it. And yet both Tom O'Horgan and Norman Jewison apparently felt squeamish leaving it out. So both anticipate it, O'Horgan by having Jesus as the cherry on the top of a great glittering ice cream Sundae, Jewison by having Jesus revealed in a cutaway as clean, blow-dried and wearing a laundered robe, while back in reality he is having the daylights flogged out of him. Plus, during the present song, "Superstar," Judas sees the Risen Jesus beckoning to him. This is in accord with Jewison's earlier direction of the scene in "Everything's Alright," where Jesus (Jeff Neeley), obviously acting against the grain of Rice's lyrics, is acted as calmly reasoning with the hotheaded Judas in a condescending manner suggesting Mr. Rogers or a Unitarian minister. Here, too, Jewison tries to force a Jesus-Judas reconciliation where Rice had left an open chasm. Rice expressed his view about the implications of the stage version: "I think O'Horgan's production hints more strongly at the resurrection than the record does ... The reaction of the crowd below [the cross]—going from hysteria to chaos to a beautiful sort of peace. O'Horgan is saying, 'This is not the end.'"[178]

In adding a resurrection where Rice had "forgotten" to provide one, Jewison and O'Horgan are following in the footsteps of Matthew, Luke, and John, while Rice is more like the earliest evangelist Mark. Mark had Mary Magdalene and the other women meet a mysterious young man at the empty tomb of Jesus. He told them Jesus had arisen but was on his way to Galilee, and he directed them to go tell this to Peter and the others, so they could meet him there. But the women are overwhelmed with superstitious terror and run away, saying nothing to anybody. The End! But the three other gospel writers, writing at a remove of some decades, when the resurrection legends had been more extensively embellished, decided that a good gospel just does not end so open-endedly. So all three cobbled together patchworks of originally disparate tales of resurrection appearances and supplemented the basic Markan outline with them. Later scribes felt the same way when it came their turn to hand-letter new copies of Mark, so some of them tacked such resurrection apocrypha onto the end of Mark. We have various manuscripts that end Mark some five different ways, though the earliest copies have the flight of the women as the grand denouement.

Every time I look at you I don't understand
Why you let the things you did get so out of hand

You'd have managed better if you'd had it planned

If Jesus does not rise from the dead, Judas does! The two characters are parallel through the whole length of the rock opera, each with somewhat similar attitudes, the main difference being that Judas is bitter over the baffling implosion of the Jesus movement, which seems to be Jesus' own doing, though for no apparent reason, while Jesus knows the plan a few yards farther than Judas can see. But Jesus is equally bitter, at God, since God is keeping Jesus in the dark in the same way Jesus is doing to Judas. But then Jesus does not particularly want to withhold his barely greater knowledge from Judas. It's just that nothing he could tell him would answer his questions. Jesus is, after all, nearly as baffled as Judas. "I could give you facts and figures; I could give you plans and forecasts, even tell you where I'm going [but what's the point?] If you knew the path we're riding, you'd understand it less than I." As Rice put it in an interview, "My lyrics tell the story of Christ the man, just as mixed up and unaware of exactly what he is—as mixed up and unaware as Judas."[179]

And now, at the end of the story, it appears that Judas has won the neck-and-neck race (just as in John 20:4, "They both ran, but the other disciple outran Peter and reached the tomb first."), though just by a nose. He died before Jesus and "rises" before him (if, that is, Jesus rises at all). What is the meaning of all this? It seems that Judas reappears after death instead of Jesus because to have Jesus rise, as the New Testament gospels do, is a way of finishing the story on a note of faith and affirmation. That is what floats to the surface after the shipwreck, so to speak. But this is no longer possible for the doubters of the present day, people like Rice and us. Thus it is not the voice of Jesus commanding the disciples to take the gospel to every nation that rings down the corridors of history, but rather the voice of puzzlement and doubt that is left echoing in our ears. The return of Judas is the eternal question mark of the modern age.

The point is not that Judas actually rises from the dead, as if he could stroll into Jerusalem and go back to his favorite bar and hang out. "Hey Jude! Long time, no see! Where ya been?" No, throughout the whole play Judas has functioned as the window for the modern listener onto the ancient and enigmatic story of Jesus. Judas is the focal character, and when he speaks he is voicing our own confusion. He is, as Rice has said: "a sort of common man," employed "to ask a whole series of questions, in a way, [to] sum up the attitude of the whole opera."[180] Like us, moderns whether Christians or not, Judas finds himself out of the loop and frustrated. Why can't it make sense? Even if it did all go according to plan, what was the plan? For centuries Christian theologians have debated numerous theories of the death of Jesus in order to try and make some kind of sense of how his death could be said to save us. In other words, even they cannot figure it out, but they are content to believe "it" (whatever "it" is), whether they can ultimately rationalize it or not. Bultmann eschewed all such attempts, claiming that to think you have to understand the mechanics of the atonement is tantamount to a Gnostic scheme of saving yourself by means of superior knowledge. I'd say that's making virtue of necessity. "It's a good thing that it doesn't make any sense! Yeah, that's the ticket!"

So when, here at the end of the play, we see Judas coming back on stage for an encore, we are not seeing one more event in the story. No, Judas' comments and questions are outside the story, asides to the reader by the author, albeit through the familiar voice of one of the characters. Again, our directors O'Horgan and Jewison lead us astray here. The both of them have Judas descend from the sky in phosphorescent finery and flanked by Motown angels, implying Judas has personally returned, somewhat in the manner of Jacob Marley, to have the last word. I love the staging, but it represents gross overinterpretation of Rice's libretto which simply attributes Judas' lyrics to the "Voice of Judas." This implies that the echoes of Judas' searching questions, unwilling to be lulled into silence by sentimental faith, will not die but continue to haunt us, since they are our own questions and doubts.

This means that "Judas" has at last slipped off his narrative disguise and speaks now simply for the modern listener. This is made explicit from the fact that he now speaks clearly, not from the perspective of the first century but from the twentieth. Paul Tillich said that when Jesus accepted his fate of crucifixion, all that was Jesus in him (his personal individuality) was sacrificed to that in him which was the Christ (his function as revealer), and he thus became the perfect lens through which God might be conveyed to history.[181] Early church fathers like Cyril of Jerusalem reasoned that the humanity of the incarnate Christ must have been "anhypostatic," meaning that there would never have been a human being called Jesus of Nazareth in the first place if God had not required a human vessel for the incarnation of his Son. We might, ironically, apply these theological perspectives to Judas in *Jesus Christ Superstar*.

Even in the New Testament, we would have had no Judas character except that the Christian tradition grew to feel uneasy at the idea of God himself directly handing over his Son to his torturers, and so they created "Judas Iscariot," Judas the Betrayer, to use as a kind of scapegoat for God. He never had any real historical existence. He was simply created to embody his narrative role. In precisely the same way, Tim Rice has rewritten, recreated the Judas character to embody the perspective of the audience. We are seeing the action through Judas' eyes, but it is equally true to say Judas is seeing things for our eyes. That is his only purpose in the rock opera. And now that the noose and the tree limb have driven his character off stage for good, what remains is the "Voice of Judas" echoing. That means his narrative function as poser of our questions to Jesus (and only rhetorically at that, since none of them ever gets answered!) has come out of hiding and into plain sight. All that seemed "Judas" in him has succumbed to his narrative function. The masquerade is over, and we finally see "face to face" (1 Corinthians 13:12): Judas is our own mirror.

In Bergman's *The Seventh Seal*, a superb dramatization of the Death of God theology of the early 1960's, the protagonist Antonius Block, a Swedish knight on his way home from the horrors of the Crusades, witnesses the devastation of the Black Plague which is sweeping Europe. One day Death comes for him, and the knight manages to buy some time by proposing a game of chess with the Grim Reaper. At one point the knight is sharing his torments of doubting God in the face of all he has seen. Knowing that his death will not be long in coming, he quips to the Reaper that soon all his doubts will be resolved. When Antonius Block dies, "You'll reveal your secrets at last!" Death looks at him quizzically: "And what makes you think I have any secrets to reveal?"

And, even so, after death nothing is clearer to Judas than it was before. He is still asking the same unrequited questions he asked earlier on, after the Last Supper when he marveled at both his own confusion and that of Jesus. He realized Jesus had something in mind, but it seemed to make no sense at all. What did you think you were doing? At times Jesus seemed to have things under control, passively manipulating those around him, at other times allowing events to overtake him and sweep him on towards death. And to what conceivable purpose? It is no clearer now than it was then. Nor has our retrospective knowledge of the events of two subsequent millennia made it any more intelligible. Seeing the big picture from a greater distance makes it all the more enigmatic.

Why'd you choose such a backward time and such a strange land?
If you'd come today you'd have reached a whole nation
Israel in 4 BC had no mass communication

Now Judas speaks to Jesus as if Jesus is present to hear so long after his death, and as if the choice of his time and place to be born had been up to him. But this does not imply that Judas has come to believe in Jesus as a divine spirit who entered history under conditions of his own choosing. The whole thing is a piece of dramatic apostrophe, the figure of speaking to one who is absent as though present, or to some abstraction as if it were a concrete person. We have seen it before in *Superstar*. Only this is a double apostrophe. Not only is Jesus not present as an individual; Judas addresses him not so much as a concrete individual but as a concretized generality. He is speaking not to the same Jesus of Nazareth Judas Iscariot would have been personally acquainted with, but rather to the "Christ" of Christianity, Christ as the concretization of Christianity. Perhaps "Christianity" was the word that was made flesh in the literary character Jesus of Nazareth, who may originally have been no more a historical personage than Judas. The point is, "If the gospel story is true in the way Christianity claims, then why would the incarnation have occurred so far off in time and space? Why should faith be required in matters no longer open to verification or even to understanding? Why should we as modern men and women feel guilty for not being able to believe in it anymore? Rice himself, as he heard the gospel stories through the years, had often pondered the question: "wouldn't it have been better for Christ to have come today? He could have the benefit . . . of mass communication—television and the print media—to teach his message."[182]

Why the reference to 4 B.C. (= B.C.E.) as the time Jesus chose to make his appearance? The traditional nomenclature B.C./A.D. was the innovation of the medieval monk Dionysius Exiguus (Dennis the Short), who divided history into pre-Christian and Christian eras. All the centuries before Jesus were counting down to his appearing (hence "Before Christ"), while all those since his birth were *Anno Domini* ("In the Year of Our Lord"). A.D. does not mean "After Death," as many people assume; this would imply a kind of "Leap Year" period of thirty or so years during the life of Jesus until the clock started ticking again at his death.

But as it happened, Dionysius was responsible for introducing some confusion of his own. Part of his reckoning was based on the implied chronology of biblical events. But he missed an important clue. In both Matthew and Luke (the only gospels with Nativity stories) Jesus is said to have been born before the death of Herod the Great, and we know that Herod the Great died in 4 B.C.E. Since Matthew has Herod the Great ascertain from the Magi that they saw the star signaling the birth of the infant King of the Jews two years before, this means Jesus could have been born any time between their first sighting of the star and their interview with Herod. Jesus might have been two years old when they caught up with him in Bethlehem. Thus Jesus must have been born as much as two years before Herod died in 4 B.C.E., anywhere between 4 and 6 B.C.E. Of course, this is only if you think Matthew's Nativity story has any solid factual basis, which seems highly unlikely. But it's the best we've got. (And, again, for Judas to refer to the date in terms of medieval Christian chronology as the listener would, reinforces the conclusion that Judas is now simply the doubting voice of modernity.)

What if Jesus had been born in modern times and lived in the age of mass media? The obvious answer is that nothing would have been different. If Judas, like today's TV evangelists, thinks it a shame Jesus had no access to mass media to get his message across, it is only because he hasn't read his McLuhan. The medium is the message, or in this case, the medium would be the gospel message, or would dictate the gospel message. That is why the Christian message has become in the hands of TV evangelists like Pat Robertson, Jim Bakker, Jerry Falwell, and Jimmy Swaggart a comical self-caricature, a superstitious get-saved-quick scheme pandering to the lowest intelligence and the basest instincts of the TV audience. Just as television talk shows finally gravitated to the most depraved side-show filth, just as tabloid journalism made all news no more than Yellow Journalism, TV religion early realized that only a certain kind of religion can grab the Nielsen ratings of salvation as well as the funds of the gullible. And so they "devour widows' houses and for a pretense make long prayers" (Matthew 23:4) in the name of him whose very denunciation they are incurring. These are "half-witted fans" of Jesus who have "go[ne] out of control," and this time the inflated claims they make for their Jesus are even more dangerous, not to mention more absurd.

To imagine that the mass media would have helped Jesus or furthered his project is exactly the wrong inference to draw from either *Jesus Christ Superstar* or from the New Testament gospels. It is to assume that Jesus was nothing but a media superstar after all, and that he "would get much higher" by going on TV. Would the Sermon on the Mount really lose all that much by being periodically interrupted by commercials? And if sayings like "Sell your possessions and give the proceeds to the poor" or "Turn the other cheek" did not test well with test market audiences, just cut them. Substitute a few more warm and fuzzy scenes of Jesus blessing the children and maybe give him a pet collie. Malcolm Muggeridge saw where it would lead. He said that if Jesus had come today, Satan's first temptation would be the offer of media coverage, and, if he knew what he was doing, Jesus would have turned him down.[183]

Don't you get me wrong-I only want to know

Judas means no mockery, nor does the modern doubter, who is no enemy of the cause of Christ but only doubts whether that cause has a thing to do with institutional religion. And this attitude we share not only with Judas ("I only want to know") but with Jesus ("I only want to say"), too. We see the justification for the demands he makes of his God in the Garden of Gethsemane—because we, too, have launched them, only to see them glance off the lead heavens and fall back into our hands.

Judas is dead, and yet his urgent curiosity echoes in our ears and in our voices. Thus Jesus' words before Pilate might as easily be Judas': "I look for truth and find that I get damned." I believe that this indignant lament sums up the deepest feelings of many of the unnumbered listeners who have found in *Jesus Christ Superstar* a word of spiritual encouragement and comfort. They, like Jesus, have perhaps learned the hard way that when establishment religion commands us to seek and to love the truth, what they meant was that we should learn to call their party-line dogma "the truth" and look no further. Naive, we did not realize this and instead embarked on a real search, in which our inherited faith was no help but only a hindrance. And when we found some truth, some fragment or some clue to it, we brought it home with rejoicing, expecting to hear the commendation, "Well done, thou good and faithful servant." What we heard instead was, "Depart from me, ye cursed; I never knew you!"

"If you'd come today you'd have reached a whole nation." And nothing would be different. And the greatest irony of all is that the creation and production of *Jesus Christ Superstar* itself is Jesus coming today, as Judas envisions, via mass communication. Remember the scene on the way to

Caiaphas' palace when Jesus is surrounded by hecklers who sound for all the world like TV reporters, intrusively sticking their mikes into the faces of the tragedy-struck, asking them to spill their feelings of shock and trauma for the delectation of the gore hounds in the viewing audience. That is what would happen if Jesus encountered the mass media.

And that is essentially what happened when Jesus came today in the form of *Superstar*. If his band of followers soon disintegrated into a dog-fight of warring factions and heretic-burning inquisitors, the same thing happened when numerous church groups and amateur theater groups spontaneously began to do their own local productions of the rock opera, simply working from the studio album and the libretto—and found themselves threatened with lawsuits by the music companies. If Jesus was hounded by rumors of blasphemy and heresy, so was *Superstar* the object of pulpit fulminations and Bible-quoting marchers. Fundamentalist preachers condemned Rice's Jesus with the same vehemence that Caiaphas did. When Judas warned Jesus to shun the innocent ministrations of Mary Magdalene lest his critics draw the wrong inferences, he might have been referring to all the plaster-saint pious who accused *Superstar* of making Jesus a Charles Manson with groupies. If Jesus declined Simon Zealotes' advice to trade the power of the simple word for the shining steel of violent spectacle, we would have done the same with Tom O'Horgan's stage and costume designs.

Jesus Christ, Jesus Christ
Who are you? What have you sacrificed?
Jesus Christ Superstar
Do you think that you're who they say you are?

These haunting questions can at last be heard as loaded in a way we might not have recognized till now. They presuppose the fact that Jesus has again become a media superstar after all. The church established in his name, though in dubious fidelity to his unknown cause, has become Jesus' new and highly effective PR firm (see the next stanza). But, like Dostoyevski's Grand Inquisitor, the church has lulled the masses into the very dogmatic slumber from which Jesus had tried to awaken them. Like Socrates before him, Jesus had dealt in disturbing questions, but the church took it upon itself to supply all the answers, and prepackaged ones at that. Jesus had loaded mankind's aching back with an Atlas-like burden of freedom, but the church called sweetly, "Come to me all ye that labor and are heavily laden, and I will give you rest. My load is easy, and my burden is light." Jesus rapidly became a figurehead, his supposed resurrection body actually a stuffed and taxidermied corpse. It stank of corruption, but all the incense of the church covered up the odor. That and all the bread and circuses of the liturgy.

The church, as the Inquisitor explained, rides high upon the horses of "Mystery, Miracle, and Authority." By promising the lepers whom Jesus turned away that the church will heal them, the church won their loyalty again. ("A trick or two with lepers and the whole town's on its feet.") They (we) will believe any dogma that Mother Church hands down. We have to simply believe them, because there is no way we will ever understand paradoxes like the three divine personae who are nonetheless one God. What is the sound of three gods in one person? Unable to crack the koan, we are told we must simply trust that this gibberish is a divine "Mystery." 'Nuff said. And anyone we may (and think we must) trust with our very souls has the strongest authority over us—because we think they do.

Notice that the questions use the "official" name of Jesus, "Jesus Christ," as if it were simply a first and last name. Any original messianic significance to the title "Christ," and especially any revolutionary reverberations it may once have unleashed, are safely forgotten. Indeed, we have seen this (intentional) anachronism throughout the rock opera. And he is still considered a superstar because the church has returned to the superficial view of Jesus it implies, a ship with sails filled by the mighty winds of fan-worship. Christianity has again become what Simon Zealotes saw it becoming: a personality cult centered about Jesus, just like the Elvis cult cynically promoted by commercial interests for the sake of selling their merchandise.

Beneath the heap of confused and confusing atonement theories and Christological doctrines, whatever original meaning the death of Jesus might have had is lost like a needle in a haystack. Whatever he sacrificed we can never know. But somehow it still occurs to us to wonder if Jesus was who "they," the church, say he is.

> **Tell me what you think about your friends at the top**
> **Who d'you think besides yourself's the pick of the crop?**
> **Buddah [sic] was he where it's at? Is he where you are?**
> **Could Mahomet move a mountain or was that just PR?**
> **Did you mean to die like that? Was that a mistake or**
> **Did you know your messy death would be a record-breaker?**
> **Don't you get me wrong-I only want to know**

This series of rhetorical, almost satirical, questions has one basic point: Jesus has entered the religious equivalent to the Rock and Roll Hall of Fame, the Valhalla of Superstars, among an elite company. They are those "at the top." The top of what? Why, at the "top of the poll." In life he had already eclipsed the fame of John the Baptist whose "baptism thing" was tantamount to the hula hoop craze or the Twist. But now he is hob-nobbing with the other platinum disk winners.

"Tell me what you think about" the others breathing the same rarefied atmosphere. Not general impressions, likes or dislikes among colleagues, but rather, what does Jesus think on the following specific points: Was Gotama the Buddha "where it's at?" Notice the particular phrase. Was he, like Jesus, a fashionable trend? Was he, too, a successful fad? Successful enough to ensure immortality among the icons of pop celebrity? Alongside Elvis? Rice thinks it's likely enough: "I'm not even sure that Jesus Christ is the biggest star of the superstars. After all, Buddha is probably as big a star in his own department, so to speak."[184]

And the Prophet Muhammad, of whom the proverb says, "If Muhammad won't come to the mountain, then the mountain will come to Muhammad"— is he within the charmed circle of the Saints and Bodhisattvas? You bet he is! Like Jesus, his historical figure was rapidly buried under an avalanche of miracle legends and second-hand sayings, in other words, a flood of PR. Did he deserve his fame, or was it just hype? Of course, this is just what is being asked concerning Jesus himself. The question, then, is really about Jesus, not Muhammad (or the Buddha): "If you strip away the myth from the man"— what will you see?

Despite all the talk in the gospels of Jesus obediently following the path of divine necessity, did Jesus really intend to die? Can we believe he really orchestrated his "messy death"? Or is this, as seems certain to New Testament scholars, a case of implausible spin-doctoring, damage-control? Or did Jesus decide it would be the best way to rocket to a superstardom from which he would never plummet, a record-breaking stunt no one would ever forget? "Would I be more noticed than I ever was before? Would the things I've said and done matter *any more*?" Interesting how this last sentence could be read two ways: "matter any more *than they would otherwise*," or "matter any *longer*." Again, "Will my words and deeds assume new prominence, be taken more seriously?" Or "Would my words and deeds perish with the passage of time? Will my name be remembered ten minutes after I'm dead?"

Jesus Christ, Jesus Christ
Who are you? What have you sacrificed?
Jesus Christ Superstar
Do you think you're what they say you are?

These questions, seconding the voice of Judas, descend from the heavenly choir. Or so it seems. But they really are the reverberations of the questions of the modern audience of *Superstar* and equally of the four gospels. And by now we can recognize them as the same questions asked Jesus by Judas, Caiaphas, Herod, and Pilate, all of whom have heard the rumors, "this talk of God." "Well, is it true?" The rock opera pointedly provides no answers, no more than Jesus did when his interrogators asked them of him.

The Crucifixion

God forgive them-they don't know what they're doing

This much is taken from Luke 23:34, "Father, forgive them; they know not what they do." The statement is a Lukan embellishment, as we can see not only from the absence of the line in all of the other gospels, but also from its tailor-made consistency with Luke's theme of Jesus' executioners acting oblivious of the fact that they were fulfilling messianic prophecy in their very actions of rejecting Jesus (see Acts 3:17; 13:27). Rice found this Lukan saying worth retaining, since central to his version of the passion is the notion that none of the characters quite understands what is going on, including the significance of their own actions.

Rice had at first considered having Jesus say at this point, "Father, forgive me, for I know not what I do." Just as the canonical version fits beautifully with Luke's redactional theology of the mitigating ignorance of Jesus' executioners, Rice's discarded draft version is wholly consistent with his own redactional theme of having Jesus follow God's strange plan grudgingly, not knowing the reason for his inevitable death. In fact, the draft version would have brought this theme to a neat and satisfying closure, with Jesus finally reconciling himself to the will of God, deciding that he can at last accept, like Job, whatever he receives from God, whether good or evil. It would also be implied that it may somehow have been Jesus' own fault that he did not understand the necessity for his death, i.e., "Forgive me for the fact that I don't know what I'm doing here." Perhaps if "we could start again, please," he would do things differently.

Who is my mother? Where is my mother?

These words perhaps reflect the confusion and pain of Jesus, that he cannot identify his mother's face in the crowd. But they are derived from John 19:26–27, "When Jesus saw his mother, and the disciple whom he loved standing near, he said to his mother, 'Woman, behold your son!' Then he said to the disciple, 'Behold your mother!' And from that hour the disciple took her to his own home."

My God My God why have you forgotten me?

Jesus knew it would come to this, but in the face of it, he can scarcely believe God had any plan except to abandon him. The passage of scripture that forms the basis of this line, Mark 15:34, "My God, my God, why have you forsaken me?" has been an embarrassment to pious readers throughout the centuries (which is no doubt why Luke and John already omitted it, substituting for it other, more pious words). It may mitigate this impression somewhat to remember that this line is the opening line of Psalm 22, a prayer for deliverance often repeated by those in great trouble. However, Mark gives no hint of this. He does not say Jesus was either quoting or fulfilling this scripture. In fact, the use of the unidentified Psalm quote is one of several hints that Mark had no genuine information about the death of Jesus: the whole scene is based on a skeleton of passages taken out of Psalm 22, as a close comparison of both texts will reveal.

I am thirsty [—O God! I'm thirsty!]
It is finished

This outcry of Jesus, feeling the agony of the cross comes directly from John 19:28–30, "After this, Jesus, knowing that all was now finished, said (to fulfill the scripture), 'I thirst.' A bowl full of vinegar stood there; so they put a sponge full of the vinegar on a lance and held it to his mouth. When Jesus had received the vinegar he said, 'It is finished;' and he bowed his head and gave up his spirit."

Father into your hands I commend my spirit

This line, a quotation of Psalm 31:5, comes from Luke 23:46. Luke substituted it for Mark's Psalm 22:1 quote, "My God, my God, why have you forsaken me?" In Luke's version Jesus sounds more Stoical and unperturbed. It allows Jesus to die in peace. And so he does here.

John Nineteen Forty-One

"Now in the place where he was crucified there was a garden, and in the garden a new tomb where no one had ever been laid. So because of the Jewish day of Preparation, as the tomb was close at hand, they laid Jesus there" (John 19:41–42).

NOTES

Chapter 1: The Aquarian Gospel of Jesus the Christ

1. Friedrich Schleiermacher, *The Christian Faith*. Trans. Hugh Ross McIntosh (Edinburgh: T&T Clark, 1956), pp. 59; Schleiermacher, *On Religion: Speeches to its Cultured Despisers*. Trans. John Oman (NY: Harper & Row Torchbooks, 1958), pp. 242–243.
2. Paul Tillich, *Dynamics of Faith* (NY: Harper & Row Torchbooks, 1958), p. 125.
3. E. Graham Waring, ed., *Deism and Natural Religion: A Sourcebook* (NY: Frederick Ungar, 1967).
4. Schleiermacher, *On Religion*, p. 242; Schleiermacher, *Christian Faith*, pp. 17, 47, 55, etc.
5. Jeremiah Zimmerman, *The God Juggernaut and Hinduism in India* (NY: Fleming H. Revell, 1914).
6. Nikos Kazantzakis, *The Last Temptation of Christ*. Trans. P.A. Bien (NY: Bantam Books, 1961), p. 2.
7. Robert Jay Lifton, *Boundaries: Psychological Man in Revolt* (NY: Vintage Books, 1970).
8. Thomas Oden, *Radical Obedience: The Ethics of Rudolf Bultmann* (Philadelphia: Westminster, 1964); James Gustafson, *Christ and the Moral Life* (Chicago: University of Chicago Press, 1979), p. 135; Joseph Fletcher, *Situation Ethics: The New Morality* (Philadelphia: Westminster Press, 1966), pp. 29–31.
9. Fletcher, *Situation Ethics*, pp. 57–68.
10. Benjamin B. Warfield, "The Real Problem of Inspiration" in Warfield,

The Inspiration and Authority of the Bible (Philadelphia: Presbyterian and Reformed Publishing Co., 1948), pp. 169–226.

11. Michael F. O'Keefe, "Regarding the Authenticity of The Aquarian Gospel (Defending Jesus' Book)." http://home.netcom.com/~mokeeffe/AGauthenticity.htm#one

12. Alfred Loisy, *The Gospel and the Church*. Trans. Christopher Home. Lives of Jesus Series (Philadelphia: Fortress Press, 1976), p. 166.

13. Paul Tillich, "Heal the Sick; Cast out the Demons," in Tillich, *The Eternal Now* (NY: Charles Scribner's Sons, 1963), p. 60.

14. Ibid., p. 63

15. Rod Blackhirst, "Fra Marino's Treasure: A Report on New Investigations into the Origins of the Gospel of Barnabas" *Journal of Higher Criticism* 11/2 (Fall 2005), pp. 55–66.

16. Hugh J. Schonfield, *The Lost "Book of the Nativity of John" A Study in Messianic Folklore and Christian Origins with a New Solution to the Virgin-Birth Problem* (Edinburgh: T&T Clark, 1929).

17. Oscar Cullmann, "Traces of an Ancient Baptismal Formula in the New Testament" in Cullmann, *Baptism in the New Testament*. Trans. J.K.S. Reid. Studies in Biblical Theology No. 1 (London: SCM Press, 1950), pp. 71–80.

18. Robert Eisler, *The Messiah Jesus and John the Baptist* (NY: Dial Press, 1931); S.G.F. Brandon, *The Fall of Jerusalem and the Christian Church. A Study of the Effects of the Jewish Overthrow of A.D. 70 on Christianity* (London: SPCK Press, 1957); Brandon, *Jesus and the Zealots: A Study of the Political Factor in Early Christianity* (Manchester: Manchester University Press, 1967).

19. Tillich, *Dynamics of Faith*, pp. 97–98; Tillich, *Systematic Theology Volume Two: Existence and the Christ* (Chicago: University of Chicago Press, 1957), p. 123.

20. John Dominic Crossan, *The Cross That Spoke: The Origins of the Passion Narrative* (NY: Harper & Row, 1988), pp. 117–142.

21. David Friedrich Strauss, *The Life of Jesus Critically Examined*. Trans. George Eliot. Lives of Jesus Series (Philadelphia: Fortress Press, 1972), pp. 221–222.

22. Paul Tillich, *Systematic Theology Volume Three: Life and the Spirit; History and the Kingdom of God* (Chicago: University of Chicago Press, 1963), p. 408.

23. John A.T. Robinson, "The 'Parable' of the Sheep and the Goats" in Robinson, *Twelve New Testament Studies*. Studies in Biblical Theology No. 14 (London: SCM Press, 62), pp. 76–93.

24. Paul Tillich, *Systematic Theology Volume Three: Life and the Spirit; History and the Kingdom of God* (Chicago: University of Chicago Press, 1963), p. 408.

25. George Eldon Ladd, "The Parable of the Sheep and the Goats in Recent Interpretation." In Richard N. Longenecker and Merrill C. Tenney, eds. (Grand Rapids: Zondervan, 1974), pp. 191-199.

Chapter 2: The Book of Mormon

1. Gershom G. Scholem, ed., *Zohar: The Book of Splendor, Basic Readings from the Kabbalah* (NY: Schocken Books, 1963).

2. Helena Petrovna Blavatsky, *The Secret Doctrine: The Synthesis of Science, Religion, and Philosophy*. Volume I. Cosmogenesis (Pasadena: Theosophical University Press, 1888, 1974), pp. xliii, 2, 27–34.

3. Lama Anagarika Govinda, "Introductory Foreword" to *The Tibetan Book of the Dead, or The After-Death Experiences on the Bardo Plane, according to Lama Kazi Dawa-Samdup's English Rendering*. Ed. W.Y. Evans-Wentz (NY: Oxford University Press, 1968), pp. liv–lv.

4. Bart D. Ehrman, *Forgery and Counterforgery: The Use of Literary Deceit in Early Christian Polemics* (NY: Oxford University Press, 2013).

5. James Barr, The Bible in the Modern World (NY: Harper & Row, 1973), p. 154.

6. Frank Kermode, *The Art of Telling: Essays on Fiction* (Cambridge: Harvard University Press, 1983), Chapter 8, "Institutional Control of Interpretation," pp. 168–184.

7. Clark H. Pinnock, B*iblical Revelation: The Foundation of Christian Theology* (Chicago: Moody Press, 1971), p. 94.

8. Gordon H. Fraser, *What Does the Book of Mormon Teach? An Examination of the Historical and Scientific Statements of the Book of Mormon* (Chicago: Moody Press, 1964).

9. Fraser, *What Does the Book of Mormon Teach?*, Chapter 19, "Who Did Write the Book of Mormon?" pp. 102–109. The title sounds strange to today's readers but is of a piece with contemporary works such as Poe's "MS. Found in a Bottle" and the anonymous *A Strange Manuscript Found in a Copper Cylinder* (NY: Harper & Brothers, 1888).

10. David Persuitte, *Joseph Smith and the Origins of the Book of Mormon*

(Jefferson, NC: McFarland & Company, 1991).

11. Geza Vermes, *Jesus the Jew: A Historian's Reading of the Gospels* (London: Fontana/Collins, 1977), pp. 139–140.

12. R. Clayton Brough, *The Lost Tribes of Israel: History, Doctrine, Prophecies, and Theories about Israel's Lost Ten Tribes* (Bountiful: Horizon Publishers, 1979), pp. 32–37.

13. Michael Barkun, *Religion and the Racist Right: The Origins of the Christian Identity Movement* (Chapel Hill: University of North Carolina Press, 1994), p 6. See also Jack Gratus, *The False Messiahs* (NY: Taplinger, 1975), pp. 179–185; H.L. Goudge, *The British Israel Theory* (London: A.R. Mowbray, 1933).

14. William Marrion Branham, *Twentieth Century Prophet: The Messenger to the Laodicean Church Age* (Jeffersonville, IN: Spoken Word Publications, nd.), pp. 68–69.

15. *Divine Principle* (NY: Holy Spirit Association for the Unification of World Christianity, 2nd ed., 1973), pp. 527–529.

16. Hugh J. Schonfield, *The Passover Plot: New Light on the History of Jesus* (NY: Bernard Geis Associates/Random House, 1965), pp. 215–227.

17. David Chandler, Book of Mormon Studies (http://www.mormonstudies.com). "Parallels," p. 4.

18. Rudolf Steiner, *The Fifth Gospel: From the Akashic Record*. Trans. A.R. Meuss (East Sussex: Rudolf Steiner Press, 1995).

19. Lord Dunsany, *The Complete Pegana: All the Tales Pertaining to the Fabulous Realm of Pegana*. Ed. S.T. Joshi (Oakland, CA: Chaosium, 1998).

20. Anne Read, *Edgar Cayce on Jesus and his Church* (NY: Paperback Library, 1971).

21. Translation of N.J. Dawood, *The Koran* (Baltimore: Penguin Books, 1956).

22. It is generally supposed that in his lifetime or soon after the Prophet Muhammad was not believed to have performed miracles, though later Muslim hagiography credited him with many. But we must ask if the accusations of magic do not imply that he did claim to perform miracles.

23. See, for instance, Merrill F. Unger, *New Testament Teaching on Tongues* (Grand Rapids: Kregel Publications, 1971), pp. 148–149.

24. "Moses" by itself is half an Egyptian name, meaning "—has begotten" or "Son of—," as in Ra*mses*, "Ra has begotten him," or Thut*mose*, "Thoth has begotten him." But "Mosiah," albeit a hybrid of Hebrew and Egyptian, would at least have the virtue of completing the fragmentary name as "Yahweh has begotten him."

25. Randel Helms, *Gospel Fictions* (Buffalo: Prometheus Books, 1989), p. 18.

26. Gershom Scholem, *On the Kabbalah and Its Symbolism*. Trans. Ralph Manheim (NY: Schocken Books, 1974), pp. 14–15.

27. "In their blindness they discounted more than *300 specific predictions* in their own sacred writings about this Messiah." Hal Lindsey and C.C. Carlson, *The Late Great Planet Earth* (NY: Bantam Books, 1976), p. 21. Authors' emphasis.

28. Richard Longenecker, *Biblical Exegesis in the Apostolic Period* (Grand Rapids: Eerdmans, 1975).

29. This is like insisting that Ma and Pa Kent came from Krypton.

30. Julius Wellhausen, *Prolegomena to the History of Israel*. Trans. J. Sutherland Black and Allan Menzies (Edinburgh: Adam & Charles Black, 1885).

31. Harry Emerson Fosdick, *A Guide to Understanding the Bible: The Development of Ideas within the Old and New Testaments* (NY: Harper & Brothers, 1938. 1956.) remains unsurpassed in comprehensiveness and clarity despite the progress of criticism beyond him at various points.

32. Easily accessible in any edition of *The Scofield Reference Bible*.

33. Fosdick, p. 210.

34. C.C. Dobson, *Did Our Lord Visit Britain as They Say in Cornwall and Somerset?* (Merrimac, Mass: Destiny Publishers, 1944).

35. William J. Samarin, *Tongues of Men and Angels: The Religious Language of Pentecostalism* (NY: Macmillan, 1972), pp. 25, 35, 130–138, 142.

36. Randel Helms, *Gospel Fictions* (Buffalo: Prometheus Books, 1988); Thomas L. Brodie, "Luke the Literary Interpreter: Luke-Acts as a Systematic Rewriting and Updating of the Elijah-Elisha Narrative in 1 and 2 Kings." Pontifical University of Saint Thomas Aquinas (Vatican, 1981); John Dominic Crossan, *The Cross That Spoke: The Origins of the Passion Narrative* (San Francisco: Harper & Row, 1988).

37. Both Luke-Acts and the Deuteronomic History are "hegemonic" co-optations of originally "counter-hegemonic" stories of various types, many concerning popular prophet figures on whom various peasant factions had placed their hopes. The stories themselves, despite redactional readjustments to defuse them, tend to depict Jesus, Elijah, Elisha, Micaiah ben-Imlah, etc., as champions of the downtrodden pious, representatives of traditional popular faith, over against their royal or hieratic oppressors (kings of Israel or Judah on the one hand, scribes and Pharisees on the other). But the stories are then tweaked and twisted to fortify the divine right of the new authorities who have replaced the old, to rule over the people anew. Elijah and Elisha

now appear in a text controlled by the priestly Exilic Community who will shortly dominate Judea once they return by Cyrus' decree. The dangerous prophet Jesus, on the run from Herod Antipas, crucified by Pontius Pilate, becomes the founder of the Church, an institution dispensing salvation to the baptized and with a corner on the market of dispensing the Holy Spirit. Jesus' disciples become "the apostles," ecclesiastical tyrants who can strike dead hapless welchers on their church pledges.

38. Graham Chapman, John Cleese, Terry Gilliam, Eric Idle, Terry Jones, and Michael Palin, *Monty Python's Life of Brian (of Nazareth)* (NY: Ace Books, 1979), pp. 76–77.

39. Tzvetan Todorov. *The Poetics of Prose*. Trans. Richard Howard (Ithaca: Cornell University Press, 1977), chapter 9, "The Quest of Narrative," pp. 132–135.

40. Vittorio Lanternari, *Religions of the Oppressed: A Study of Modern Messianic Cults*. Trans. Lisa Sergio (NY: New American Library, 1965), p. 27, 37, 38; Peter Worsley, *The Trumpet Shall Sound: A Study of "Cargo Cults" in Melanesia*. 2nd augmented ed. (NY: Schocken Books, 1968), pp. 112, 140.

41. Worsley, pp. 22, 137; Lanternari, pp. 53–54.

42. Jacques Derrida, *Writing and Difference*. Trans. Alan Bass (Chicago: University of Chicago Press, 1978), chapter one, "Force and Signification," esp. pp. 24–25. Just as Todorov alludes to the metaphysic of the eternal return, Derrida sees an implicit metaphysic in the Structuralist belief (which he rejects) in the simultaneity of the text, the inherent pattern, the reader's discovery of which provides and equals the meaning of the text. Structuralism mirrors Platonism: the structures are simultaneous, timeless forms that alone give meaning. Mobile-temporal elements of a text or myth or narrative are shifting, unstable, mere matter, like the lapping waters around the unmoving pillars of a pier.

43. Robert M. Fowler, *Let the Reader Understand: Reader-Response Criticism and the Gospel of Mark* (Minneapolis: Fortress Press, 1991), pp. 19–24.

44. Monika Hellwig, class lectures, Princeton Theological Seminary, Summer 1977.

45. Here we witness infinite regress: Paul's own conversion has similarly been rewritten by Acts' author from the conversions of Pentheus in Euripides' *The Bacchae* and of Heliodorus in 2 Maccabees.

46. I am afraid that we will have to suppose that such close matches of texts do denote borrowing by a King James reader of biblical texts. Once we begin to

hold open "possibilities" such as angels prophetically scanning the KJV and inspiring Mosiah, Nephi, Moroni, et. al., with these phrases and fragments, we have bidden scientific exegesis goodbye.

47. John W. Welch, "Benjamin's Speech: A Masterful Oration." In John W. Welch and Stephen D. Ricks, eds., *King Benjamin's Speech: "That Ye May Learn Wisdom."* (Provo: Foundation for Ancient Research and Mormon Studies, 1998), pp. 55–87. Welch, "Parallelism and Chiasmus in Benjamin's Speech." In Welch and Ricks, eds., *King Benjamin's Speech*, pp. 315–410.

48. Stephen D. Ricks, "Kingship, Coronation, and Covenant in Mosiah 1–6," pp. 233–275.

Chapter 3: The Gospel according to Thomas

1. Burnett Hillman Streeter, *The Four Gospels: A Study of Origins* (London: Macmillan, 1951); William Sanday, ed., *Studies in the Synoptic Problem* (Oxford at the Clarendon Press, 1911).

2. I tend to date Q very late because it already seems to regard converting Jews to Christianity as a lost cause ("Not even in Israel have I found such faith."), and it seems to quote 4 Ezra chapter one, which, unlike most, I do not chop off as a late Christian addition to the late first-century book. Valuable studies of Q include Adolf Harnack, *The Sayings of Jesus: The Second Source of St. Matthew and St. Luke*. Crown Theological Library Vol. XXIII. Trans. J.R. Wilkinson (London: Williams & Norgate: NY: G.P. Putnam's Sons, 1908); Richard A. Edwards, *A Theology of Q: Eschatology, Prophecy, and Wisdom* (Philadelphia: Fortress Press, 1976); John Kloppenborg, *The Formation of Q: Trajectories in Ancient Wisdom Collections* (Philadelphia: Fortress Press, 1987); John S. Kloppenborg, ed., *The Shape of Q: Signal Essays on the Sayings Gospel* (Minneapolis: Fortress Press, 1994); John S. Kloppenborg Verbin, *Excavating Q: The History and Setting of the Sayings Gospel* (Minneapolis: Fortress Press, 2000); Arland D. Jacobson, *The First Gospel: An Introduction to Q*. Foundations & Facets Reference Series (Sonoma: Polebridge Press, 1992); Burton L. Mack, *The Lost Gospel: The Book of Q and Christian Origins* (San Francisco: HarperSanFrancisco, 1993); Christopher M. Tuckett, *Q and the History of Early Christianity: Studies on Q* (Edinburgh: T&T Clark, 1996); Leif E. Vaage, *Galilean Upstarts: Jesus' First Followers according to Q* (Philadelphia: Trinity Press International, 1994); Ronald A. Piper, *Wisdom in*

the Q-tradition: The Aphoristic Teaching of Jesus. Society for the Study of the New Testament Monograph Series 61 (Cambridge: Cambridge University Press, 1989); Dale C. Allison, Jr., *The Jesus Tradition in Q* (Harrisburg: Trinity Press International, 1997); James M. Robinson, *Jesus according to the Earliest Witness* (Minneapolis: Fortress Press, 2007); Robinson, *The Sayings Gospel Q: Collected Essays.* (Leuven: Peeters, 2005).

3. Harry T. Fleddermann, *Mark and Q: A Study of the Overlap Texts.* Bibliotheca Ephemeridum Theologicarum Lovaniensium CXXII (Leuven: Leuven University Press / Uitgeverij Peeters, 1995).

4. Vincent Taylor, *Behind the Third Gospel: A Study of the Proto-Luke Hypothesis* (Oxford at the Clarendon Press, 1926).

5. Paul-Louis Couchoud, "Is Marcion's Gospel One of the Synoptics?" Trans. Joan Ferro. *Hibbert Journal* Vol. XXXIV, No. 2 (1936), pp. 265–277. Of course there are many other more or less viable Synoptic Problem theories. The mind boggles. Mine does, anyway.

6. David Trobisch, "Who Published the Christian Bible?" *Free Inquiry* (December 2007 / January 2008) 28/1, pp. 30–33; Stephan Hermann Huller, *Against Polycarp: An Investigation of Christianity before the Canon* (Selma: Institute for Higher-Critical Studies, 2008), Appendix: "Polycarp, Secret Mark, and our Gospels."

7. C.H. Dodd, *Historical Tradition in the Fourth Gospel* (NY: Oxford University Press, 1963); John A.T. Robinson, "The New Look on the Fourth Gospel," in Robinson, *Twelve New Testament Studies.* Studies in Biblical Theology No. 34 (London: SCM Press, 1962), pp. 94–106; John A.T. Robinson, *The Priority of John* (Oak Ridge: Meyer-Stone Books, 1987); Archibald M. Hunter, *According to John: The New Look at the Fourth Gospel* (Philadelphia: Westminster Press, 1968).

8. Rudolf Bultmann, *History of the Synoptic Tradition.* Trans. John Marsh (NY: Harper & Row, rev. ed., 1972), pp. 127–128; M. Eugene Boring, *Sayings of the Risen Jesus: Christian Prophecy in the Synoptic Tradition.* Society for New Testament Studies Monograph Series 46 (NY: Cambridge University Press, 1982).

9. Robert M. Grant and David Noel Freedman, *The Secret Sayings of Jesus: The Gnostic Gospel of Thomas* (Garden City: Doubleday Dolphin Books, 1960), p. 105; Ray Summers, *The Secret Sayings of the Living Jesus: Studies in the Coptic Gospel According to Thomas* (Waco: Word Books, 1968); H.E.W. Turner, "The Gospel of Thomas: its History, Transmission and Sources," in

Hugh Montefiore and H.E.W. Turner, *Thomas and the Evangelists*. Studies in Biblical Theology No. 35 (Naperville: Alec R. Allenson, 1962), p. 39.

10. Joachim Jeremias, *The Parables of Jesus*. Trans. S.H. Hooke (NY: Scribner's, 2nd rev. ed., 1972), e.g., pp. 79, 110, 176; Hugh Montefiore, "A Comparison of the Parables of the Gospel According to Thomas and the Synoptic Gospels," in Turner and Montefiore, *Thomas and the Evangelists*, pp. 40–78; Helmut Koester, *Ancient Christian Gospels: Their History and Development* (Philadelphia: Trinity Press International, 1990), pp. 84–85; Koester, *History and Literature of Early Christianity* (Philadelphia: Fortress Press, 1982), p. 52; Stephen J. Patterson, *The Gospel of Thomas and Jesus*. Foundations & Facets Reference Series (Sonoma: Polebridge Press, 1993), chapter 2, "A Question of Content: The Autonomy of the Thomas Tradition," pp. 17–93; Richard Valantasis, *The Gospel of Thomas*. New Testament Readings (London and NY: Routledge, 1997); Stevan L. Davies, *The Gospel of Thomas and Christian Wisdom* (NY: Seabury Press, 1983).

11. Joachim Jeremias shows this in some detail by demonstrating how Thomas' versions of many parables lack the redactional distinctives of the canonical versions. See his classic *The Parables of Jesus*. Trans. S.H. Hooke (NY: Charles Scribner's Sons, 2nd rev. ed., 1972). Helmut Koester and Stephen J. Patterson, "The Gospel of Thomas: Does It Contain Authentic Sayings of Jesus?" In *Bible Review* April 1990, pp. 28–29. Also see again Patterson's very impressive comparisons in his Chapter 2. And Koester, "Three Thomas Parables," in A.H. B. Logan and A.J.M. Wedderburn, eds., *The New Testament and Gnosis: Essays in Honor of Robert McL. Wilson* (Edinburgh: T&T Clark, 1983), pp. 195–203; Davies, *Gospel of Thomas and Christian Wisdom*, pp. 13–17.

12. This view, originating, I think, with Ernst Haenchen, is also to be found in April D. DeConik, *Recovering the Original Gospel of Thomas: A History of the Gospel and its Growth* (NY: T&T Clark, 2005); Risto Uro, "*Thomas* and oral gospel tradition," in Uro, ed., *Thomas at the Crossroads: Essays on the Gospel of Thomas*. Studies of the New Testament and Its World (Edinburgh: T&T Clark, 1998), pp. 8–32; Nicholas Perrin, *Thomas: The Other Gospel* (Louisville: Westminster / John Knox Press, 2007).

13. The whole discipline of Redaction Criticism grows out of such observations and comparisons. For a general introduction, see Norman Perrin, *What is Redaction Criticism?* (Philadelphia: Fortress Press, 1969). For a detailed summary of work in this discipline, see Joachim Rohde, *Recovering the Teaching of the Evangelists*. Trans. Dorothea M. Barton. New Testament

Library (Philadelphia: Westminster Press, 1969).

14. David Trobisch, *The First Edition of the New Testament* (NY: Oxford University Press, 2000).

15. Huller, "Polycarp, Secret Mark, and our Gospels."

16. *Thomas: The Other Gospel*, pp. 77–93; Perrin, *Thomas and Tatian: The Relationship between the* Gospel of Thomas *and the* Diatessaron. Society of Biblical Literature Academia Biblica No. 5 (Atlanta: Society of Biblical Literature, 2002), passim.

17. Patterson, Chapter 4, "A Time and a Place: The Date and Provenance of the Gospel of Thomas," pp. 113–120; Davies, pp. 16–17.

18. Davies, *Gospel of Thomas*, p. 81.

19. Giles Quispel, *Tatian and the Gospel of Thomas: Studies in the History of the Western Diatessaron* (Leiden: E.J. Brill, 1975), argues that Thomas and the Latin Diatessaron (as tentatively reconstructed) attest a pre-Synoptic tradition of Jesus-sayings that are pre-eschatological and sapiential in orientation.

20. James D.G. Dunn, *Unity and Diversity in the New Testament: An Inquiry into the Character of Earliest Christianity* (Philadelphia: Westminster Press, 1977), p. 286. April D. DeConick seconds his motion in *Recovering the Original Gospel of Thomas*, p. 46. Naturally, I must admit, Koester, Davies, Patterson and the rest might respond quite plausibly that while the sayings do reject and lampoon a prior eschatology, they represent Jesus' own repudiation of his contemporaries' futuristic expectation.

21. Ferdinand Christian Baur, *Paul, the Apostle of Jesus Christ: His Life and Work, His Epistles and Doctrine*. Trans. A. Menzies (London: Williams and Norgate, 1876); Walter Bauer, *Orthodoxy and Heresy in Earliest Christianity*, Robert Kraft and Gerhard Krodel, eds. Trans. by a team from the Philadelphia Seminar on Christian Origins (Philadelphia: Fortress Press, 1971); James M. Robinson and Helmut Koester, *Trajectories through Early Christianity* (Philadelphia: Fortress Press, 1971); Dunn, *Unity and Diversity in the New Testament*; John Charlot, *New Testament Disunity: Its Significance for Christianity Today* (NY: Dutton, 1970); Burton L. Mack, *A Myth of Innocence: Mark and Christian Origins* (Philadelphia: Fortress Press, 1991), Chapters 3 ("The Followers of Jesus") and 4 ("The Congregations of the Christ"), pp. 78–123; Robert M. Price, *Deconstructing Jesus* (Amherst: Prometheus Books, 2000).

22. Hans-Joachim Schoeps, *Jewish Christianity: Factional Disputes in the*

Early Church. Trans. R.A. Hare (Philadelphia: Fortress Press, 1969); Jean Danielou, *The Theology of Jewish Christianity*. Trans. John A. Baker. The Development of Christian Doctrine before the Council of Nicaea Volume One (Chicago: Henry Regnery Company, 1964); Richard N. Longenecker, *The Christology of Early Jewish Christianity*. Studies in Biblical Theology, Second Series 17 (Naperville: Alec R. Allenson, 1970); Ray A. Pritz, *Nazarene Jewish Christianity: From the End of the New Testament Period until Its Disappearance in the Fourth Century*. Studia Post-Biblica 37 (Jerusalem-Leiden: Magnes Press, Hebrew University / E.J. Brill, 1988).

23. Joachim Jeremias, *Jesus' Promise to the Nations*. Trans. S.H. Hooke. Franz Delitzsch Lectures for 1953. Studies in Biblical Theology 24 (London: SCM Press, rev. ed., 1967).

24. Danielou, Chapter Two, "Heterodox Jewish Christianity," pp. 55–85.

25. Keith Akers, *The Lost Religion of Jesus: Simple Living and Nonviolence in Early Christianity* (NY: Lantern Books, 2000).

26. Schoeps, *Jewish Christianity*, p. 67.

27. Rudolf Bultmann, *Theology of the New Testament*. Trans. Kendrick Grobel (NY: Scribner's, 1951, 1955), Chapter III, "The Kerygma of the Hellenistic Church aside from Paul," pp. 63–183; A.M. Hunter, *Paul and his Predecessors* (London: SCM Press, rev. ed. 1961); Marcel Simon, *St. Stephen and the Hellenists in the Primitive Church*. Haskell Lectures (London / NY / Toronto: Longmans, Green, 1958); Arthur Darby Nock, *Early Gentile Christianity and Its Hellenistic Background* (NY: Harper Torchbooks, 1964).

28. Rodney Stark, *The Rise of Christianity: A Sociologist Reconsiders History* (Princeton: Princeton University Press, 1996), Chapter 3, "The Mission to Jews: Why It Probably Succeeded," pp. 49–71.

29. Sam K. Williams, *Jesus' Death as Saving Event: The Background and Origin of a Concept*. Harvard Theological Review Harvard Dissertations in Religion 2 (Missoula: Scholars Press, 1975).

30. Schoeps, *Jewish Christianity*, pp. 42–46; Robert Eisenman, *James the Brother of Jesus: The Key to Unlocking the Secrets of Early Christianity and the Dead Sea Scrolls* (NY: Viking, 1996), Chapter 14, "The Stoning of James and the Stoning of Stephen," pp. 411–465.

31. Rudolf Bultmann, *Primitive Christianity in its Contemporary Setting*. Trans. Reginald H. Fuller (London: Thames and Hudson, 1956), pp. 162–174; Elaine Pagels, *The Gnostic Gospels* (NY: Random House, 1979); Hans Jonas, *The Gnostic Religion: The Message of the Alien God and the Beginnings of*

Christianity (Boston: Beacon Press, 2nd ed., 1963); Kurt Rudolph, *Gnosis: The History and Nature of Gnosticism*. Trans. P.W. Coxon, K.H. Kuhn, and Robert McLachlan Wilson (San Francisco: Harper & Row, 1983); Ioan P. Couliano, *The Tree of Gnosis: Gnostic Mythology from Early Christianity to Modern Nihilism*. Trans. Hillary S. Wiesner and Ioan P. Couliano (San Francisco: HarperSanFrancisco, 1992); Giovanni Filoramo, *A History of Gnosticism*. Trans. Anthony Alcock (Cambridge, MA: Basil Blackwell, 1990).

32. Edward J. Thomas, *The History of Buddhist Thought* (London: Routledge & Kegan Paul, 1953), pp. 40, 173–174.

33. Matti Moosa, *Extremist Shiites: The Ghulat Sects*. Contemporary Issues in the Middle East (Syracuse: Syracuse University Press, 1988), pp. 315, 359.

34. So I argue, adapting the thinking of Hermann Detering, in my book *The Amazing Colossal Apostle* (Salt Lake City: Signature Books, 2012).

35. Peter Robert Lamont Brown, *The Body and Society: Men, Women, and Sexual Renunciation in Early Christianity*. Lectures on the History of Religions, Sponsored by the American Council of Learned Societies. New Series, Number Thirteen (NY: Columbia University Press, 1988); Stevan L. Davies, *The Revolt of the Widows: The Social World of the Apocryphal Acts* (Carbondale: Southern Illinois University Press, 1980); Dennis Ronald MacDonald, *The Legend and the Apostle: The Battle for Paul in Story and Canon* (Philadelphia: Westminster Press, 1983).

36. MacDonald, pp. 81–85. For a treatment of the larger struggle between charismatic authority and institutional leadership in early Christianity, see Hans von Campenhausen, *Ecclesiastical Authority and Spiritual Power in the Church of the First Three Centuries* Trans. J.A. Baker (Stanford: Stanford University Press, 1969).

37. Wayne A. Meeks, "The Image of the Androgyne: Some Uses of a Symbol in Earliest Christianity," in Meeks, *In Search of the Early Christians: Selected Essays*, ed., Allen R. Hilton and H. Gregory Snyder (New Haven: Yale University Press, 2002), pp. 3–54.

38. Bruce J. Malina, *On the Genre and Message of Revelation: Star Visions and Sky Journeys* (Peabody: Hendrickson Publishers, 1995), p. 56, simply makes the 144, 000 the unfallen angels themselves, but in view of verse 4, I think they have to be glorified human saints.

39. Brown, p. 118.

40. Elaine Pagels, *Adam, Eve, and the Serpent* (NY: Random House, 1988).

41. Examples of this approach include Grant and Freedman, *Secret Sayings of*

Jesus (which almost reads as if the commentators were trying to make Thomas sound as bizarre and arcane as possible); Bertil Gärtner, *The Theology of the Gospel according to Thomas*. Trans. Eric J. Sharpe (NY: Harper & Brothers, 1961); Ray Summers, *The Secret Sayings of the Living Jesus* (Waco: Word Books, 1968).

42. Kendrick Grobel, "How Gnostic is the Gospel of Thomas?" *New Testament Studies* 8 (1962), pp. 367–373; W.C. van Unnik, *Newly Discovered Gnostic Writings: A Preliminary Study of the Nag Hammadi Find*. Trans. H.H. Hoskins. Studies in Biblical Theology No. 30 (London: SCM Press, 1960), pp. 56–57; Davies, *Gospel of Thomas and Christian Wisdom*, pp. 22–35.

43. For example, Richard Valantasis, *Gospel of Thomas*.

44. Jonathan Culler, *Structuralist Poetics: Structuralism, Linguistics, and the Study of Literature* (NY: Cornel University Press, 1976), Chapter 7, "Convention and Naturalization," pp. 131–160.

45. "The strange, the formal, the fictional, must be recuperated, or naturalized, brought within our ken, if we do not want to remain gaping before monumental inscriptions" (Culler, p. 134).

46. Gärtner, *Theology of the Gospel according to Thomas*, pp. 21–26.

47. Rudolf Bultmann, *The Gospel of John: A* Commentary. Trans. G.R. Beasley-Murray, R.W.N. Hoare, and J.K. Riches. (Philadelphia: Westminster Press, 1971), pp. 6–7; James M. Robinson, "On the *Gattung* of Mark (and John)." In David G. Buttrick, ed., *Jesus and Man's Hope*. Vo; I. A Perspective Book (Pittsburgh: Pittsburgh Theological Seminary, 1970), p. 112.

48. Davies, *Gospel of Thomas*, p. 19.

49. Davies, *Gospel of Thomas*, p. 31.

50. Davies, *Gospel of Thomas*, pp. 112–113.

51. S.R. Bhatt, *Studies in Ramanuja Vedanta* (New Delhi: Heritage Publishers, 1975), pp. 48–55; Ignaz Goldziher, *Introduction to Islamic Theology and Law*. Trans. Andras and Ruth Hamori (Princeton: Princeton University Press, 1981), pp. 220–222.

52. Davies, *Gospel of Thomas*, p. 39.

53. Davies, *Gospel of Thomas*, pp. 42–46.

54. Davies, *Gospel of Thomas*, pp. 48–49.

55. Adolf von Harnack, *What Is Christianity?* Trans. Thomas Bailey Saunders (NY: Harper & Row Torchbooks, 1957), p. 51.

56. Davies, *Gospel of Thomas*, p. 121.

57. Though Davies illuminates the Apocryphal Acts by showing their encratite

character in his *The Revolt of the Widows: The Social World of the Apocryphal Acts* (Carbondale: Southern Illinois University Press, 1980), he rejects any encratite coloring in Thomas (*The Gospel of Thomas and Christian Wisdom*, pp. 21–22). This seems very forced to me, as many of the sayings seem to make their best sense from that standpoint.

58. Davies, *Gospel of Thomas*, p. 74.

59. Howard M. Jackson, *The Lion Becomes Man: The Gnostic Leontomorphic Creator and the Platonic Tradition*. SBL Dissertation Series 81 (Atlanta: Scholars Press, 1985), pp. 5–7.

60. Jackson, p. 203.

61. James Breech, *The Silence of Jesus: The Authentic Voice of the Historical Man* (Philadelphia: Fortress Press, 1983), pp. 71–74.

62. Summers, p. 26.

63. Davies, *Gospel of Thomas*, p. 75.

64. Gerd Theissen, *The Miracle Stories of the Early Christian Tradition*. Trans. Francis McDonagh (Philadelphia: Fortress Press, 1983), p. 171.

65. Arlo J. Nau, *Peter in Matthew: Discipleship, Diplomacy, and Dispraise*. Good News Studies Volume 36. A Michael Glazier Book (Collegeville: Liturgical Press, 1992).

66. Gärtner, p. 123; Marco Frenschkowski, "The Enigma of the Three Words of Jesus in Gospel of Thomas Logion 13." *Journal of Higher Criticism* (Fall 1994) 1/1, pp. 73–84; *The Gospel according to Thomas* (Eugene: Messianic Brotherhood, 1981), p. 15.

67. Frenschkowski, p. 74.

68. Agehananda Bharati, *The Tantric Tradition* (Garden City: Doubleday Anchor Books, 1970), pp. 200, 228; Mircea Eliade, *Yoga: Immortality and Freedom*. Trans. Willard R. Trask. Bollingen Series LVI (Princeton: Princeton University Press, 2nd ed., 1969), Chapter Six, "Yoga and Tantrism," pp. 200–273.

69. From the Majjhima Nikaya. Trans. Christmas Humphreys. In Jack Kornfield, ed., *Teachings of the Buddha* (NY: Barnes & Noble, rev. ed., 1999), pp. 91–92.

70. F.F. Bruce, *Jesus and Christian Origins outside the New Testament* (Grand Rapids: Eerdmans, 1974), p. 122.

71. E. A. Wallis Budge, ed. and trans. *Coptic Apocrypha in the Dialect of Upper Egypt*, pp. 348–349.

72. Breech, 72–73.

73. Jonathan Z. Smith, "The Garments of Shame," in Smith, *Map Is Not Territory:*

Studies in the History of Religions (Chicago: University of Chicago Press, 1993), pp. 1–23.

74. Danielou, pp. 191–192; Harold R. Willoughby, *Pagan Regeneration: A Study of the Mystery Initiations in the Graeco-Roman World* (Chicago: University of Chicago Press, 1929), p. 167.

75. Jeremias, *Parables of Jesus*, pp. 151–152.

76. Christopher Rowland, *The Open Heaven: A Study of Apocalyptic in Judaism and Early Christianity* (NY: Crossroad, 1982).

77. George M. Lamsa, *Gospel Light: Comments on the Teachings of Jesus from Aramaic and Unchanged Eastern Customs* (Philadelphia: A.J. Holman, 1939), pp. 35–37.

78. Robinson, "On the *Gattung* of Mark (and John)," p. 112.

79. Mahaparinibbana Sutra, trans. T.W. Rhys-Davids, in Kornfield, p. 122.

80. Kahlil Gibran, *Jesus the Son of Man: His Words and Deeds as Told and Recorded by Those who Knew Him* (NY: Knopf, 1928), p. 154.

81. Davies, *Gospel of Thomas*, p. 73.

82. Fawn M. Brodie, *No Man Knows my History: The Life of Joseph Smith, the Mormon Prophet* (NY: Vintage Books, 2nd ed., 1995), Chapter II, "Treasures in the Earth," pp. 16–33; Roger I. Anderson, *Joseph Smith's New York Reputation Reexamined* (Salt Lake City: Signature Books, 1990); John L. Brooke, *The Refiner's Fire: The Making of Mormon Cosmology, 1644–1844* (NY: Cambridge University Press, 1994), Chapter 7, "Secret Combinations and Slippery Treasures in the Land of Zarahemla," pp. 149–183.

83. Bultmann, *History of the Synoptic Tradition*, p. 31.

84. Marvin Meyer and Richard Smith, eds., *Ancient Christian Magic: Coptic Texts of Ritual Power* (San Francisco: HarperSanFrancisco, 1994), pp. 33–34: "Come out, demon, since I bind you with unbreakable adamantine fetters, and I deliver you into the black chaos in perdition." From the Great Magical Papyrus of Paris; trans. Marvin Meyer.

85. Gerd Theissen, "The Wandering Radicals: Light Shed by the Sociology of Literature on the Early Transmission of Jesus Sayings," in Theissen, *Social Reality and the Early Christians: Theology, Ethics, and the World of the New Testament*. Trans. Margaret Kohl (Minneapolis: Fortress Press, 1992), pp. 33–59.

86. Gerd Theissen, "Legitimation and Subsistence: An Essay on the Sociology of Early Christian Missionaries," in Theissen, *The Social Setting of Pauline Christianity: Essays on Corinth*. Trans. and ed. John H. Schütz (Philadelphia:

Fortress Press, 1982), pp. 27–67.

87. Davies, *Gospel of Thomas*, p. 127.

88. Jeremias, *Parables of Jesus*, p. 201.

89. Jeremias, *Parables of Jesus*, p. 183.

90. Jeremias, *Parables of Jesus*, pp. 178–179.

91. Jeremias, *Parables of Jesus*, p. 65.

92. Jeremias, *Parables of Jesus*, p. 188.

93. Brown, p. 115; Gilles Quispel. "The Birth of the Child: Some Gnostic and Jewish Aspects," in Quispel and Gershom Scholem, *Jewish and Gnostic Man*. Eranos Lectures 3 (Dallas: Spring Publications, 1986), pp. 25–26.

94. David Friedrich Strauss, *The Life of Jesus for the People* (London: Williams and Norgate, 2nd ed., 1879), Vol. I., p.p. 272–273.

95. Elaine Pagels, *Adam, Eve, and the Serpent* (NY: Vintage Books, 1989), pp. 14–15.

96. Robert Winterhalter, *The Fifth Gospel: A Verse-By-Verse New Age Commentary on the Gospel of Thomas* (NY: HarperCollins, 1988).

97. Carl Michaelson, *The Witness of Radical Faith* (Nashville: Tidings, 1974), pp. 57–58.

98. Bernard Brandon Scott, *Hear Then the Parable: A Commentary on the Parables of Jesus* (Minneapolis: Fortress Press, 1989).

99. Solomon Schechter, *Some Aspects of Rabbinic Theology* (NY: Macmillan, 1910), Chapter XII., "The Zachuth of the Fathers. Imputed Righteousness and Imputed Sin," pp. 170–198.

100. Ismo Dunderberg, "Thomas' I-sayings and the Gospel of John," in Uro, ed., *Thomas at the Crossroads*, p. 63

101. Jeremias, *Parables of Jesus*, p. 134.

102. Davies, *Gospel of Thomas*, pp. 10–11.

103. Davies, *Gospel of Thomas*, p. 12.

104. Gärtner, p. 238.

105. Robert McLachan Wilson, *Studies in the Gospel of Thomas* (London: Mowbray, 1960), p. 93.

106. "Women Admitted to the Sangha," trans. Henry Clarke Warren, in Paul Carus, ed., *The Gospel of Buddha Compiled from Ancient Records* (La Salle: Open Court, 1917), pp. 92–93.

107. *Saddharma-Pundarika or The Lotus of the True Law*. Trans. H. Kern. Sacred Books of the East. Vol. XXI (1884; rpt. NY: Dover Books, 1963), pp. 252–253.

Chapter 4: The Necronomicon

1. H.A.R. Gibb, *Arabic Literature: An Introduction* (Oxford at the Clarendon Press, 1963), p. 2.

2. Saul Lieberman: "What is mysticism? Nonsense. But you see, ladies and gentlemen, nonsense is nonsense. But a history of nonsense is scholarship." Quoted by Irving Abrahamson, Highland Park, IL, in a now untraceable letter to a newspaper.

3. Margaret Alice Murray, *The Witch Cult in Western Europe* (Oxford at the Clarendon Press, 1921, 1967); Murray, *The God of the Witches* (Garden City: Doubleday Anchor Books, 1960).

4. Eric von Däniken, *Chariots of the Gods? Unsolved Mysteries of the Past.* Trans. Michael Heron (NY: Bantam Books, 1970).

5. Zecharia Sitchin, *The Twelfth Planet* (NY: Avon Books, 1978). This book is very erudite as well as fascinating.

6. Immanuel Velikovsy, *Worlds in Collision* (NY: Pocket Books, 1977).

7. Brian Lumley, *The Burrowers Beneath* (NY: DAW Books, 1974), p. 57.

8. Leo ("Levi") Dowling, *The Aquarian Gospel of Jesus the Christ: The Philosophic and Practical Basis of the Religion of the Aquarian Age of the World* (Santa Monica: DeVorss & Co., 1907, 1972).

9. I retain this nomenclature over the proposals of Dirk W. Mosig ("the Yog-Sothoth Cycle of Myth") and Lin Carter (the "Alhazredic Demonology"). The term "Cthulhu Mythos" does not seem particularly inadequate or misleading. Besides, it has the advantages of being more readily recognizable in general discussion, and of being less unwieldy than its two competitors. Both of these, like the mythical R'lyehian language, seem well-nigh impossible for human speech-organs to pronounce!

10. Fritz Leiber, "John Carter: Sword of Theosophy," in L. Sprague de Camp and George H. Scithers, eds., *The Conan Swordbook* (Baltimore: Mirage Press, 1969), pp. 101–109; Lin Carter, "The Magic of Atlantis," Introduction to Clark Ashton Smith, *Poseidonis*. Adult Fantasy Series (NY: Ballantine Books, 1973), pp. 3–5.

11. Montague Rhodes James, *The Apocryphal New Testament: Being the Apocryphal Gospels, Acts, Epistles, and Apocalypses with other Narratives and Fragments* (Oxford at the Clarendon Press, 1972), p. 1.

12. First-rate summaries of these developments may be found in Ronald E. Clements, *One Hundred Years of Old Testament Interpretation* (Philadel-

phia: Westminster Press, 1976); Stephen Neill, *The Interpretation of the New Testament, 1861–1961* (NY: Oxford University Press, 1966); and Albert Schweitzer, *The Quest of the Historical Jesus* (NY: Macmillan Company, 1950).

13. The principal discussion is to be found in David Friedrich Strauss, *The Life of Jesus Critically Examined* (Philadelphia: Fortress Press, 1972); Rudolf Bultmann, *The Gospel of John, a Commentary* (Philadelphia: Westminster Press, 1975); and J. Louis Martyn, *History & Theology in the Fourth Gospel* (Nashville: Abingdon, 1979).

14. To be completely accurate, there is some opposition to textual criticism, but this is mostly forthcoming only from the most extreme religious fundamentalists, e.g., ultra-right-wing Protestants (*Holy Bible-a New Eye Opener*, Junction City, Oregon: Eye Opener Publishers, n.d.) and hyper-orthodox Jews (this conflict figures into Chaim Potok's novel *The Promise*). From quite a different quarter comes the snobbish disdain for text-critical studies on the part of secular literary critics, as described by Fredson Bowers, *Textual and Literary Criticism*, Cambridge University Press, 1966).

15. Seyyed Hossein Nasr, *Ideals and Realities of Islam* (Boston: Beacon Press, 1975), p. 57.

16. Idries Shah, *The Secret Lore of Magic, Books of the Sorcerers* (NY: Citadel Press, 1970), pp. 75, 76.

17. H.P. Lovecraft, *History of the Necronomicon* (West Warwick: Necronomicon Press, 1984), p. 3. Lovecraft is in error when he places Wormius in the thirteenth century. The Danish physician and antiquarian's dates are 1588–1654, and his period of literary activity was 1636–1643. I owe this information to Richard L. Tierney.

18. See Stevan L. Davies, *The Revolt of the Widows: The Social World of the Apocryphal Acts* (Carbondale and Edwardsville: Southern University Press, 1980), p. 23; James Blish, *Black Easter, or Faust Aleph-Null* (NY: Dell Books, 1969), pp. 72–73.

19. This point has been well made by Wilfred Cantwell Smith in his essay "The Study of Religion and the Study of the Bible," in Willard G. Oxtoby (ed.), *Religious Diversity* (NY: Harper & Row, Publishers, 1976), pp. 41ff.

20. L. Sprague de Camp, *Al Azif* (Philadelphia: Owlswick Press, 1973), p. xi.

21. L. Sprague de Camp, *Al Azif* (Philadelphia: Owlswick Press, 1973), p. xi.

22. Richard Bell and W. Montgomery Watt, *Introduction to the Qur'an* (Edinburgh at the University Press, 1977), p. 77.

23. Ibid., p. 78.

24. H.A.R. Gibb, *Mohammedanism: An Historical Survey* (New York: New American Library, 1958), p. 36.

25. Lovecraft, *History of the Necronomicon*, p. 2.

26. Quoted in Shah, *Secret Lore*, p. 66.

27. Kurt Koch, *Between Christ and Satan* (Grand Rapids: Kregel Publications, 1979), pp. 134–135.

28. Tor Andrae, *Mohammed: The Man and His Faith* (NY: Harper & Row, Publishers, 1960), pp. 45–46.

29. Anton Szandor LaVey, *The Satanic Bible* (NY: Avon Books, 1969).

30. Charles G. Leland, *Aradia, or the Gospel of the Witches* (NY: Samuel Weiser, 1974).

31. For Wilson's suggestion, see his "The Return of the Lloigor" in August Derleth (ed.) *Tales of the Cthulhu Mythos* (Sauk City: Arkham House, 1969), p. 357; for the theories of Wetzel and Bannister see Lin Carter, "H.P. Lovecraft: The Books" in August Derleth (ed.), *The Shuttered Room & Other Pieces* (Sauk City: Arkham House, 1959), p. 226. For Lovecraft's hypothesis, see *Selected Letters* V, p. 418.

32. Lovecraft, *History of the Necronomicon*, p. 2.

33. S.T. Joshi, "Afterword," to Lovecraft's *History of the Necronomicon*.

34. R.H. Charles, *Eschatology, The Doctrine of a Future Life* (New York: Schocken Books, 1963).

35. Owen Davies, *Grimoires: A History of Magic Books* (NY: Oxford University Press, 2009).

36. M.R. James, *Old Testament Legends, Being Stories out of Some of the Less-Known Apocryphal Books of the Old Testament* (London: Longmans, Green and Co., 1913), "Solomon and the Demons," pp. 105–119.

37. *The Malleus Maleficarum of Heinrich Kramer and James Sprenger*. Trans. Montague Summers (NY: Dover Publications 1928, 1948, 1971).

38. https://en.wikipedia.org/wiki/Johann_Weyer; Lewis Spence, "Demonology," in Spence, *An Encyclopaedia of Occultism A Compendium of Information on the Occult Sciences, Occult Personalities, Psychic Science, Magic, Demonology, Spiritism, Mysticism and Metaphysics* (Secaucus: Citadel Press, 1960), p. 120.

39. E.g., *Phlegon's Book of Marvels*. Trans. William Hansen. Exeter Studies in History (Exeter: University of Exeter Press, 1996).

40. These texts are collected in James M. Robinson (ed.), *The Nag Ham-*

madi Library in English (New York: Harper & Row, Publishers, 1977). On Gnosticism in general, see Hans Jonas, *The Gnostic Religion* (Boston: Beacon Press, 1963); Elaine Pagels, *The Gnostic Gospels* (New York: Random House, 1979); and Rudolf Bultmann, *Primitive Christianity in its Contemporary Setting* (New York: New American Library, 1974), especially the chapter "Gnosticism," pp. 162–174.

41. Koch, *Between Christ and Satan*, p. 131.

42. This derivation is the suggestion of Baha'i scholars Paul and Karen Webb.

43. Quoted in H.P. Lovecraft, *The Case of Charles Dexter Ward* in his *At the Mountains of Madness and Other Novels* (Sauk City: Arkham House, 1964), p. 142.

44. For an excellent discussion of the Hermetic literature, see C.H. Dodd, *The Interpretation of the Fourth Gospel* (Cambridge at the University Press, 1953), especially Part I, Chapter 2, "The Higher Religion of Hellenism: the Hermetic Literature," pp. 10–53.

45. The title means "Shepherd of Mankind."

46. J. Everard, trans., *The Divine Pymander of Hermes Trismegistus* (NY: Societas Rosicruciana in America, 1953), pp. 9–10.

47. See Rudolf Bultmann and Karl Kundsin, *Form Criticism*. Trans. Frederick C. Grant (NY: Harper & Row, 1962).

48. Jack T. Sanders, *The New Testament Christological Hymns: Their Historical Religious Background*. Society for New Testament Studies Monograph Series 15 (Cambridge at the University Press, 1971), Part 1:" Formal Analysis of the Hymns," pp. 9–25; Ralph P. Martin, *Carmen Christi: Philippians ii.5–11 in Recent Interpretation and in the Setting of Early Christian Worship*. Society for New Testament Studies Monograph Series 4 (Cambridge at the University Press, 1965), Part I, Chapter II, "Philippians ii.5–11: Its Literary Form," pp. 24–41.

49. H.P. Lovecraft, *Fungi from Yuggoth*, in Lovecraft, *Collected Poems* (Sauk City: Arkham House, 1963), Stanza XXI, "Azathoth," p. 114.

50. Ibid., Stanza XXI, "Nyarlathotep," p. 124.

51. Lovecraft, "The Call of Cthulhu," in his *The Dunwich Horror and Others* (Sauk City: Arkham House, 1963), pp. 130–159.

52. An analogous process following the disappointment of the early Christian expectation of the soon return of Christ is traced by Martin Werner in *The Formation of Christian Doctrine* (Boston: Beacon Press, 1965). The sociological and psychological impact of this kind of thing on a religious

group (and it has happened to several) is explored by Leon Festinger, Henry W. Riecken, and Stanley Schachter in *When Prophecy Fails* (NY: Harper & Row, 1964).

53. Franklin E. Tillinghast, "Notes on a Newly-Discovered Commentary on the Necronomicon," *Anubis*, Vol. 1, No. 3, 1968, pp. 66–67.

54. Lovecraft, in *The Case of Charles Dexter Ward*, quotes a letter citing the "VII Booke" of the *Necronomicon*. Lin Carter refers to "Book IV" and to reference citations including "NEC. III, xvii." ("Zoth-Ommog," in Edward P. Berglund, ed., *The Disciples of Cthulhu* (New York: DAW Books, 1976), pp. 174, 175, and "III, 17" in his *Dreams From R'lyeh* (Sauk City: Arkham House, 1975), p. 3.

55. Quoted by Colin Wilson in *The Philosopher's Stone* (NY: Warner Books, 1974), p. 271.

56. Quoted by August Derleth in "The Keeper of the Key," in Derleth, *The Trail of Cthulhu* (Sauk City: Arkham House, 1962), p. 172.

57. H. P. Lovecraft, "The Call of Cthulhu," p. 145.

58. Quoted by H. P. Lovecraft in "The Dunwich Horror," in Lovecraft, *The Dunwich Horror and Others* (Sauk City: Arkham House, 1963), pp. 174–175.

59. The variant version is found in the passage as quoted in August Derleth in Lovecraft and Derleth, *The Lurker at the Threshold* (London: Victor Gollancz, 1968), pp. 109–110.

60. Quoted by Ramsey Campbell in "The Plain of Sound," in Campbell, *The Inhabitant of the Lake and Less Welcome Tenants* (Sauk City: Arkham House, 1964), p. 138.

61. Quoted by H. P. Lovecraft and E. Hoffmann Price in "Through the Gates of the Silver Key," in *At the Mountains of Madness and Other Novels*, p. 407.

62. Quoted by E. Hoffmann Price in "The Lord of Illusion," *Crypt of Cthulhu* #10, pp. 46–56.

63. Gershom Scholem, *Jewish Gnosticism, Merkabah Mysticism, and Talmudic Tradition* (New York: Jewish Theological Seminary of America, 1965). A somewhat different theory concerning the relation between the Barzai legend and Jewish mystical lore may be found in Robert Schwartz, "Pombo and 'The Other Gods,'" *Crypt of Cthulhu* #15, p. 21. Schwartz sees Barzai as a reflection of Judah ben Barzilai, twelfth-century commentator on the Kabbalistic text *Sepher Yetsirah*, who warned against the dangers involved in studying mystical wisdom. If this is in truth the origin of Barzai, then certainly the Barzai legend cannot have been in the mind of Alhazred since Judah ben Barzilai lived centuries after Alhazred.

64. "The Shi'a (Muslims) interpreted the Koran allegorically; hence they were called the People of Allegorical Interpretation (*ahl at-ta'wil*)." Sami Nasib Makarem, *The Druze Faith* (Delmar, NY: Caravan Books, 1974), p. 7. The name "Umr" or "Umar" or "Omar" means "speaker."

65. Quoted by Robert Bloch in "Fane of the Black Pharaoh" in Lin Carter (ed.), *Mysteries of the Worm* (NY: Zebra Books, 1981), p. 160.

66. Geo Widengren, *The Ascension of the Apostle and the Heavenly Book* (Uppsala: A. B. Lundequistaka Bokhandeln, 1950), p. 80.

67. Quoted by Clark Ashton Smith in "The Nameless Offspring," in Smith, *The Abominations of Yondo* (Sauk City: Arkham House, 1960), p. 3.

68. Quoted by H. P. Lovecraft in "The Festival," in Lovecraft, *Dagon and other Macabre Tales* (Sauk City: Arkham House, 1965), p. 195.

69. Quoted by Clark Ashton Smith in "The Return of the Sorcerer," in August Derleth, ed., *Tales of the Cthulhu Mythos* (Sauk City: Arkham House, 1969), p. 35.

70. Quoted by Brian Lumley in "Aunt Hester," in Lumley, *The Horror at Oakdeene & Others* (Sauk City: Arkham House, 1977), pp. 27–28.

71. Quoted by August Derleth in Lovecraft and Derleth, *The Lurker at the Threshold* (London: Victor Gollancz, 1968), pp. 110–111.

72. Lin Carter, "Zoth-Ommog," p. 181.

73. Quoted by R.C. Zaehner in *The Teachings of the Magi: A Compendium of Zoroastrian Beliefs* (NY: Oxford University Press, 196), p. 45.

74. Quoted by Lin Carter in *Dreams from R'lyeh*, p. 3.

75. This is another version of *Migu*, the Bhutanese name for the fabled Abominable Snowmen, as Lovecraft admits (*Selected Letters*, V, p. 356).

76. "Tcho-tcho" seems to derive from a Tatar-Tibetan word meaning "destroyer" or "fire-sorcerer." We find it in the twelfth-century hagiography of the Buddhist saint Milarepa. During an early period of occult studies, Milarepa invokes a hailstorm to destroy his villagers' crops. They jeer at him, taunting him as a "*Tcho,*" which W.Y. Evans-Wentz (*Tibet's Great Yogi Milarepa* [NY: Oxford University Press, 1974], p. 182) renders "destroyer," while Lobsang O. Lahlungpa (*The Life of Milarepa* [Boulder: Prajna Press, 1982], p. 142) translates it as "monster of evil." Milarepa's aunt rebukes him for his spiteful act with "cries of 'Cho! Cho!'" (Evans-Wentz, p. 229). Thanks to the learned Tani Jantsang for this information. There is also a village called Tchotchopola located in the Bassar Prefecture of the Kara Region of Togo in Africa.

77. Quoted by August Derleth in Lovecraft and Derleth, *The Lurker at the Threshold*, p. 112.

78. D.R. Ap-Thomas, *A Primer of Old Testament Textual Criticism*. Facet Books, Biblical Series-14 (Philadelphia: Fortress Press, 1966), p. 48.

79. See David Trobisch, *The First Edition of the New Testament* (NY: Oxford University Press, 2000), "The Notation of the *Nomina Sacra*, pp. 11–19.

80. Quoted by August Derleth in Lovecraft and Derleth, *The Lurker at the Threshold*, pp. 112–113.

81. Ibid., pp. 178–179.

82. Quoted by Derleth in *Lurker at the Threshold*, p. 179.

83. Quoted by Brian Lumley in *The Burrowers Beneath*, p. 57.

84. Quoted by Henry Kuttner in "The Salem Horror," in Derleth (ed.), *Tales of the Cthulhu Mythos*, pp. 253–254.

85. For the spelling "Vach" and "Viraj," see H. P. Blavatsky, *The Secret Doctrine*, Vol. 1 (Pasadena: Theosophical University Press, 1974), pp. 9, 89. I owe this reference to Tani Jantsang.

86. See H. P. Blavatsky, *Isis Unveiled*, Vol. II (Pasadena: Theosophical University Press, 1976), p. 276; Gershom Scholem, *Major Trends in Jewish Mysticism* (NY: Schocken Books, 1973), pp. 233, 245–246.

87. See Colin Wilson in *The Philosopher's Stone*, pp. 271, 273.

88. Quoted by Frank Belknap Long in "The Space-Eaters," in Long, *The Hounds of Tindalos* (NY: Jove Publications, 1978), p. 60. For some reason the quote has been omitted from the story as it appears in Derleth (ed.), *Tales of the Cthulhu Mythos*. May we suspect ecclesiastical censorship?

89. Quoted by Gerald Page in Mark Owings (ed.), *The Necronomicon: A Study* (Baltimore: Mirage Press, 1967), p. 5.

Chapter 5: Jesus Christ Superstar

1. Frank Kermode, "Institutional Control of Interpretation," chapter 8 of *The Art of Telling* (Cambridge: Harvard University Press, 1983), pp. 168–184.

2. "'Jesus Christ Superstar' Billed as Rock Opera," *New York Times*, October 31, 1971.

3. "Tom O'Horgan Superstar?" *America*, October 30, 1971, p. 352.

4. *Nation*, November 8, 1971, p. 444.

5. *Newsweek*, October 25, 1971, p. 243.

6. "Superchange, From Bach to O'Horgan," *Christianity Today*, September 11, 1971, pp. 42–43.

7. "Easter Show at the Music Hall," *Women's Wear Daily*, October 14, 1971, p. 240.

8. *Time*, October 25, 1971, p. 241.

9. *New York Times Theatre Reviews*, October 24, 1971.

10. *Christian Century*, November 6, 1971, p. 26.

11. *Wall Street Journal*, October 14, 1971.

12. Victor Shklovsky, "Art as Technique," in Lee T. Lemon and Marion J. Rice, (trans & eds.), *Russian Formalist Criticism, Four Essays*. Lincoln: University of Nebraska P, 1965, pp. 12–13; cf., Viktor Shklovsky, *Theory of Prose*. Trans. Benjamin Sher. (Elmwood Park, IL: Dalkey Archive Press, 1991), pp. 4–5.

13. Robert C. Tannehill, "The Disciples in Mark: The Function of a Narrative Role," *Journal of Religion* 57, 1977, pp. 394–395.

14. Tim Rice, in Molly Haskell, "J.C. Superstar Enterprises, Inc," *Saturday Review*, October 30, 1971, p. 66.

15. Don Cupitt, *Only Human* (London: SCM Press LTD, 1985), p. 204.

16. Bob Larson, *Rock and the Church* (Carol Stream: Creation House, 1971).

17. Jacob Needleman, *Lost Christianity: A Journey of Rediscovery to the Center of Christian Experience* (NY: Bantam Books, 1982), pp. 28–30.

18. Henry Chadwick, ed. and trans., *Lessing's Theological Writings*. A Library of Modern Religious Thought (Stanford: Stanford University Press, 1972), p. 43.

19. "Superstunt," *Saturday Review*, October 30, 1971.

20. Stanley Fish, *Is There a Text in This Class? The Authority of Interpretive Communities* (Cambridge: Harvard University Press, 1980); Wolfgang Iser, *The Implied Reader: Patterns of Communication in Prose Fiction from Bunyan to Beckett* (Baltimore: Johns Hopkins University Press, 1978); Iser, *The Act of Reading: A Theory of Aesthetic Response* (Baltimore: Johns Hopkins University Press, 1980; Umbert Eco, *The Open Work*. Trans. Anna Cancogni (Cambridge: Harvard University Press, 1989).

21. Rudolf Otto, *The Idea of the Holy*. Trans. John W. Harvey (NY: Oxford University Press, 1924).

22. Paul Tillich, *Systematic Theology. Volume I: Reason and Revelation; Being and God* (Chicago: University of Chicago Press, 1951), p. 109.

23. Carl Michaelson, *The Witness of Radical Faith* (Nashville: Tidings, 1974), chapter III, "Demythologizing and the Proclamation of Meaningful Faith," pp. 45–61.

24. Dietrich Bonhoeffer, *Letters and Papers from Prison*. Ed. Eberhard Bethge.

Trans. Reginald H. Fuller (NY: Macmillan, 1962), p. 167.

25. Max Scheler, *Problems of a Sociology of Knowledge*. Trans. Manfred S. Frings (London: Routledge & Kegan Paul, 1980), pp. 84–85.

26. Dietrich Bonhoeffer, *The Cost of Discipleship*. Trans. R.H. Fuller, rev. Irmgard Booth (NY: Macmillan, 1973), p. 46.

27. Robert North, *In Search of the Human Jesus*. Corpus Papers (NY: Corpus Publications, 1970).

28. Martin Kähler, *The So-Called Historical Jesus and the Historic Biblical Christ*. Trans. Carl Braaten. Seminar Editions (Philadelphia: Fortress Press, 1964.)

29. Tzvetan Todorov, *The Fantastic*. Trans. Richard Howard (Ithaca: Cornell University Press, 1993), p. 25.

30. Tim Rice quoted in Hubert Saal, "Pop Testament," *Newsweek*, November 16, 1970, p. 97.

31. Tim Rice, in Molly Haskell, "J.C. Superstar Enterprises, Inc," *Saturday Review*, October 30, 1971, p. 66.

32. Eric Hoffer, *The True Believer: Thoughts on the Nature of Mass Movements* (NY: Harper & Row, 1951).

33. "Alien Corn," *New Yorker*, October 23, 1971, p. 109.

34. Frans Neiyrinck, *Duality in Mark: Contributions to the Study of the Markan Redaction*. Bibliotheca Ephemeridum Theologicarum Lovaniensum XXXI (Leuven: Leuven University Press, 1972); Robert M. Fowler, *Let the Reader Understand: Reader-Response Criticism and the Gospel of Mark* (Minneapolis: Fortress Press, 1991).

35. *New York Post*, October 13, 1971, p. 240.

36. *Newsweek*, November 16, 1970, p. 96.

37. *Time*, October 25, 1971, p. 242.

38. Stephen Fuchs, *Rebellious Prophets: A Study of Messianic Movements in Indian Religion*, Publications of the Indian Branch of the Anthropos Institute No. 1 (NY: Asia Publishing House, 1965), p. 29.

39. Peter Worsley, *The Trumpet Shall Sound: A Study of "Cargo" Cults in Melanesia* (NY: Schocken Books, 2nd ed., 1968), pp. 250–251.

40. Fuchs, *Rebellious Prophets*, p. 175.

41. Talbot Mundy, *Old Ugly Face* (NY: D. Appleton-Century Company, 1940).

42. Masimo Introvigne, *The Unification Church*. Studies in Contemporary Religion (Salt Lake City: Signature Books, 2000), pp. 11, 65, n. 7.

43. J.K. Elliott, trans. & ed., *The Apocryphal New Testament* (NY: Oxford University Press, 1993), p. 256.

44. Reynold A. Nicholson, *Studies in Islamic Mysticism* (NY: Cambridge University Press, 1921, rpt., 1985), p. 63.

45. Ibid., p. 38.

46. Geza Vermes, *Jesus the Jew: A Historian's Reading of the Gospels* (London: Collins/Fontana, 1977), pp. 69–72.

47. Gershom G. Scholem, *Sabbati Sevi: The Mystical Messiah*. Trans. R.J. Zwi Werblowsky. Bollingen Series XCIII (Princeton: Princeton University Press, 1973).

48. Gershom G. Scholem, "Eighth Lecture: Sabbatianism and Mystical Heresy." In Scholem, *Major Trends in Jewish Mysticism* (NY: Schocken Books, 1961), pp. 287–324; Scholem, Redemption Through Sin" and "The Crypto-Jewish Srect of the Dönmeh (Sabbatians) in Turkey." In Scholem, *The Messianic Idea in Judaism and Other Essays on Jewish Spirituality.* (NY: Schocken Books, 1971), pp. 78–166; Arthur Mandel, *The Militant Messiah, or The Flight from the Ghetto: The Story of Jacob Frank and the Frankist Movement.* A Peter Bergman Book (Atlantic Highlands: Humanities Press, 1979; Bezalel Naor, *Post-Sabbatian Sabbatianism: Study of an Underground Messianic Messianic Movement* (Spring Valley: Orot, Inc., 1999).

49. Worsley, *The Trumpet Shall Sound*, pp. 116–117.

50. Fuchs, *Rebellious Prophets*, p. 29.

51. Worsley, *The Trumpet Shall Sound*, pp. 52–54, 107, 111, 139, 214.

52. Victor Turner, *The Ritual Process: Structure and Anti-Structure.* The Lewis Henry Morgan Lectures/1966 (Ithaca: Cornell University Press, 1977), Chapter 3: "Liminality and Communitas," pp. 94–130.

53. Worsley, *The Trumpet Shall Sound*, p. 87, cf. 155.

54. Roland Barthes, *Mythologies*. Trans. Annette Lavers (NY: Hill and Wang, 1972), p. 30.

55. Jorges Luis Borges, "Three Versions of Judas." In Borges, *Ficciones*. Trans. Anthony Kerrigan (NY: Franklin Library, 1985), pp. 151–157.

56. Gerd Theissen, *Sociology of Earliest Palestinian Christianity*. Trans. John Bowden (Philadelphia: Fortress Press, 1978; Richard A. Horsley, *Sociology and the Jesus Movement* (NY: Crossroad Publishing Company, 1990); Burton L. Mack, *The Lost Gospel: The Book of Q and Christian Origins* (San Francisco: HarperSanFrancisco, 1993)

57. Jane Howard, "The Groovy Christians," *Life*, May 14, 1971, p. 82.

58. Richard Watts, "The Passion with a Rock Beat," *New York Post*, October 13, 1971, 239.

59. Tim Rice, quoted in "A Reverent Rock Opera," *Life*, May 28, 1971, p. 24.

60. Graham Chapman, John Cleese, Terry Gilliam, Eric Idle, Terry Jones, Michael Palin, *Monty Python's The Life of Brian (of Nazareth)* (NY: Ace Books, 79), p. 124.

61. Rudolf Bultmann, *The Gospel of John: A Commentary*. Trans. G.R. Beasley-Murray, R.W.N. Hoare, and J.K. Riches (Philadelphia: Westminster, 1975), p. 252.

62. Tim Rice, quoted in Molly Haskell, *Saturday Review*, p. 66.

63. Gordon Clanton, *Christian Century*.

64. Wayne Booth, *The Rhetoric of Fiction* (Chicago: University of Chicago Press, 2nd ed., 1983), pp. 158–159.

65. Tim Rice, quoted in *Life*, "A Reverent Rock Opera," p. 24.

66. See Robert C. Gregg and Dennis E. Groh, *Early Arianism, A View of Salvation* (Philadelphia: Fortress Press, 1981).

67. See C.F. Burney, *The Poetry of Our Lord* (London: Oxford University Press, 1925).

68. Ellis Nassour, *Rock Opera: The Creation of Jesus Christ Superstar, from Record Album to Broadway Show and Motion Picture* (NY: E.P. Dutton, 1973), p. 46.

69. Ibid., p. 47.

70. Ibid., p. 37.

71. By Ms. Kiva Foster, a sharp-eyed student of mine.

72. *New Yorker*, p. 39.

73. Gordon Clanton, *Christian Century*, p. 26.

74. Peter L. Berger, *The Sacred Canopy: Elements of a Sociological Approach to Religion* (Garden City: Doubleday Anchor, 1969).

75. T.E. Hulme, *Speculations: Essays on Humanism and the Philosophy of Art* (London: Routledge and Kegan Paul, 1949), pp. 50–51, quoted in Dennis Nineham, *The Use and Abuse of the Bible: A Study of the Bible in an Age of Rapid Cultural Change* (NY: Barnes & Noble Books, 1976), p. 6.

76. Peter L. Berger and Thomas Luckmann, *The Social Construction of Reality: A Treatise in the Sociology of Knowledge* (Garden City: Doubleday Anchor, 1966, pp. 114–115.

77. Max Scheler, *Problems of the Sociology of Knowledge*. Trans. Manfred S. Frings (London: Routledge & Kegan Paul, 1980), pp. 84–85.

78. Ernst Troeltsh, *The Social Teaching of the Christian Churches*. Trans. Olive Wyon. Vol. 1 (NY: Harper & Brothers, 1960, pp 331–349.

79. Abraham Maslow, *Religions, Values, and Peak Experiences* (NY: Viking, 1974), pp. 23–29.

80. Max Weber, *The Theory of Social and Economic Organization*. Trans. A.M. Henderson and Talcott Parsons (NY: Free Press, 1947), pp. 363–386.

81. Anthony F.C. Wallace, *Religion: An Anthropological View* (NY: Random House, 1966), pp. 30–37.

82. Worsley, *The Trumpet Shall Sound*.

83. John G. Gager, *Kingdom and Community: The Social World of Early Christianity* (Englewood Cliffs: Prentice-Hall, 1975).

84. Nassour, *Rock Opera*, p. 228.

85. J. Ramsey Michaels, *John. A Good News Commentary* (NY HarperCollins, 1984), pp. xxvi, 193.

86. Ibid., pp. xxvi, 79, 129, 193, 295.

87. T.W. Manson, *Jesus the Servant Messiah* (Cambridge at the University Press,1961), pp. 15–16.

88. Manson, *Jesus the Servant Messiah*, pp. 18–19.

89. *Life of Brian*, p. 20.

90. Harvey Falk, *Jesus the Pharisee* (Paramus, Mahwah: Paulist Press, 1985). See also Hyam Maccoby, *Jesus the Pharisee* (London: SCM Press, 2003).

91. John Dominic Crossan, *Jesus: A Revolutionary Biography* (San Francisco: HarperSanFrancisco, 1995).

92. Barbara Thiering, *Jesus the Man: A New Interpretation from the Dead Sea Scrolls* (Corgi Books, 1993), Chapter Twenty: "Raising Lazarus," pp. 130–134.

93. Jürgen Moltmann, *Theology of Hope*. Trans. James W. Leitch (NY: Harper & Row, 1967).

94. *Nation*, November 8, 1971, p. 444.

95. At least this is my inference from what Bultmann says in Karl Jaspers and Rudolf Bultmann, *Myth and Christianity: An Inquiry into the Possibility of Religion without Myth* (NY: Noonday Press, 1958), pp. 68–71.

96. Michael Baigent, Richard Leigh, and Henry Lincoln, *Holy Blood, Holy Grail* (NY: Dell, 1982)

97. Loren R. Fisher, "'Can This Be the Son of David?'" In F. Thomas Trotter, ed., *Jesus and the Historian. Written in Honor of Ernest Cadman Colwell* (Philadelphia: Westminster Press, 1968), pp. 82–97.

98. The same identification already made by Robert Eisler in *The Messiah Jesus and John the Baptist* (NY: Dial Press, 1931), p. 254.

99. George Howard, *Hebrew Gospel of Matthew* (Macon: Mercer University

Press, 1995), p. 202.

100. Nassour, *Rock Opera*, p. 22.

101. Richard A. Horsley, *Jesus and the Spiral of Violence: Popular Jewish Resistance in Roman Palestine* (Minneapolis: Fortress Press, 1993); Horsley and John Hanson, *Bandits, Prophets, and Messiahs: Popular Movements at the Time of Jesus* (NY: Harper & Row, 1990).

102. E.J. Hobsbawm, *Primitive Rebels: Studies in Archaic Forms of Social Movements in the 19th and 20th Centuries* (NY: Norton, 1959.

103. Richard L. Tierney, "The Dragons of Mons Fractus." In Tierney, *The Scroll of Thoth: Simon Magus and the Great Old Ones* (Oakland: Chaosium, Inc., 1997), p. 282.

104. Hyam Maccoby, *Revolution in Judea: Jesus and the Jewish Resistance* (London: Ocean Books, 1973); S.G.F. Brandon, *Jesus and the Zealots: A Study of the Political Factor in Primitive Christianity* (NY: Scribners, 1967); Hugh J. Schonfield, *The Pentecost Revolution: The Story of the Jesus Party in Israel, A.D. 36–66* (London: MacDonald, 1974); A.J. Mattill, Jr., *Luke and the Last Things: A Perspective for the Understanding of Lukan Thought* (Dillsboro, NC: Western North Carolina Press, 1979, Section VIII, "'Fire Upon the Earth' (Luke 12:49): A Holy War?" pp. 208–235.

105. Eisler, *Messiah Jesus and John the Baptist*, pp. 252–253.

106. *Life of Brian*, p. 121.

107. Vermes, *Jesus the Jew*, pp. 139–140.

108. Kahlil Gibran, *Jesus the Son of Man* (NY: Alfred A. Knopf, 1926), p. 3.

109. Tzvetan Todorov, *The Poetics of Prose*. Trans. Richard Howard (Ithaca, NY: Cornell University Press, 1977), chapter 4, "Primitive Narrative," pp. 53–65; chapter 10, "The Secret of Narrative," pp. 143–178.

110. *New Republic*, November 6, 1971, p. 24.

111. Joachim Kahl, *The Misery of Christianity, or A Plea for Humanity without God*. Trans. N.D. Smith (Baltimore: Penguin Books, 1971).

112. Nassour, *Rock Opera*, p. 47.

113. Ibid., p. 41.

114. *Life of Brian*, pp. 56–58.

115. Alfred Loisy, *The Origins of the New Testament*. Trans. L.P. Jacks (London: Allen and Unwin, 1950), pp. 210–211.

116. *New York Times Theater Review*, Oct. 12. 1970, p. 140.

117. Malcolm Boyd, *Are You Running With Me, Jesus?* (NY: Avon Books, 1967), p. 20.

118. *Life of Brian*, pp. 123–124.

119. Ibid., pp. 26–29.

120. Fish, *Is There a Text in This Class?* pp. 28–29, 42.

121. "Jesus Christ Superstar: A Turning Point in Music," in Ray B. Browne, ed., *Popular Culture and the Expanding Consciousness* (NY: Wiley, 1973), p. 152.

122. Nassour, *Rock Opera*, p. 191.

123. Gordon Clanton, *Christian Century*, p. 25.

124. Frank Kermode, *The Genesis of Secrecy: On the Interpretation of Narrative*. The Charles Eliot Norton lectures 1977–1978 (Cambridge: Harvard University Press, 1979), pp. 84–89. Loisy had already suggested that Judas was a fictive embodiment of Jewish "Christ-rejectors" in *The Birth of the Christian Religion*. Trans. L.P. Jacks (London: George Allen & Unwin, 1948), p. 82. More recently, the case has been made at some length in Hyam Maccoby, *Judas Iscariot and the Myth of Jewish Evil* (NY: Free Press/Macmillan, 1992).

124. Bertil Gärtner, *Iscariot*. Trans. Victor I. Gruhn. Facet Books. Biblical Series 29 (Philadelphia: Fortress Press, 1971).

125. Brandon, *Jesus and the Zealots*, p. 204, n. 1.

126. Maccoby, *Judas Iscariot and the Myth of Jewish Evil*.

127. Hyam Maccoby, *The Sacred Executioner: Human Sacrifice and the Legacy of Guilt* (NY: Thames and Hudson, 1982.

128. Rene Girard, *Violence and the Sacred*. Trans. Patrick Gregory (Baltimore: Johns Hopkins University Press, 1979; *The Scapegoat*. Trans. Yvonne Freccero (Baltimore: Johns Hopkins University Press, 1989).

129. A.J. Greimas, *On Meaning: Selected Writings in Semiotic Theory*. Trans. Paul J. Perron and Frank H. Collins. Theory and History of Literature, Volume 38 (Minneapolis: University of Minnesota Press, 1987), Chapter 6, "Actants, Actors, and Figures," pp. 106–120.

130. Nassour, *Rock Opera*, p. 37.

131. John M. Allegro, *The Sacred Mushroom and the Cross* (NY: Bantam Books, 1971), pp. 100–101.

132. Samuel Sandmel, *A Jewish Understanding of the New Testament*. Augmented edition (NY: Ktav, 1974), pp. 159–160.

133. Burton L. Mack, *A Myth of Innocence: Mark and Christian Origins* (Philadelphia: Fortress Press, 1991), p. 55.

134. Henry J. Cadbury, *The Peril of Modernizing Jesus* (NY: Macmillan,1937), ChapterVI. "Purpose, Aim, and Motive in Jesus," pp. 120–153.

136. E.P. Sanders, *Paul, the Law and the Jewish People* (Minneapolis: Fortress Press, 1983).

137. Loisy, *Birth of the Christian Religion*, p. 82.

138. Ferdinand Christian Baur, *Paul, the Apostle of Jesus Christ: His Life and Works, His Epistles and Theology*. Two volumes in one. Trans. A. Menzies. (1875; rpt. Peabody: Hendrickson, 2003).

139. Thomas Whittaker, *The Origins of Christianity, With an Outline of Van Manen's Analysis of the Pauline Literature* (London: Watts, 4th ed., 1933; Hermann Detering, "The Dutch Radical Approach to the Pauline Epistles." *Journal of Higher Criticism* 3/2 (Fall 1996), pp. 163–193.

140. Loisy, *Birth of the Christian Religion*, p. 50.

141. Greimas, "Actants, Actors, and Figures."

142. Marie-Louise Martin, *Kimbangu: An African Prophet and his Church*. Trans. D.M. Moore (Grand Rapids: Eerdmans, 1975), Chapter 6, "The History of Simon Kimbangu's Movement after the Prophet's Arrest (1922–4), and the Rise of Ngunzism," pp. 65–78.

143. Bart D. Ehrman, *The Orthodox Corruption of Scripture* (NY: Oxford University Press, 1993).

144. Loisy, *Origins of the New Testament*, p. 167. More recently, see Joseph Tyson, "The Lukan Version of the Trial of Jesus." *Novum Testamentum* 17 (1975), p. 257; John Dominic Crossan, *The Cross That Spoke: The Origins of the Passion Narrative* (San Francisco: Harper & Row, 1988), p. 103.

145. Willi Marxsen, *The Resurrection of Jesus of Nazareth*. Trans. Margaret Kohl (Philadelphia: Fortress Press, 1970)

146. Alfred Loisy, *The Kingdom and the Church*. Trans. Christopher Home. Lives of Jesus Series (1903; rpt. Philadelphia: Fortress Press, 1976), p. 166.

147. Clifford Geertz, "Religion as a Cultural System." In Geertz, *The Interpretation of Cultures* (NY: Basic Books, 1973, pp. 87–125).

148. Berger, *The Sacred Canopy*, 1969, pp. 69–70.

149. Geertz, "Religion as a Cultural System," pp. 87–125.

150. Berger and Luckmann, *The Social Construction of Reality*, p. 25.

151. Ibid., p. 126.

152. *Doomsday Cult: A Study of Conversion, Proselytization, and Maintenance of Faith* (Englewood Cliffs: Prentice-Hall, Inc., 1966., pp. 208–209.

153. Mircea Eliade, *The Sacred and the Profane: The Nature of Religion* (NY: Harcourt, Brace & World, Inc., 1959), pp. 68–161.

154. Gager, *Kingdom and Community*, pp. 50–57.

155. Rudolf Bultmann, *The Gospel of John: A Commentary* (Philadelphia: Westminster Press, 1975), e.g, p. 261; see also Robert T. Fortna, *The Fourth Gospel and Its Predecessor: From Narrative Source to Present Gospel* (Minneapolis: Fortress Press, 1988), pp. 284–293.

156. Baha' ullah. *The Kitab-I-Iqan, The Book of Certitude*. Trans. Shoghi Effendi (Wilmette: Baha'i Publishing Trust, 1950), *passim*.

157. Scholem, *Messianic Idea in Judaism*, pp. 142–166.

158. Max Weber, *The Theory of Social and Economic Organization*. Trans. A.M. Henderson and Talcott Parsons (NY: Free Press, 1947), pp. 363–386.

159. Abraham Maslow, *Religions, Values, and Peak Experiences* (NY: Viking, 1974), pp. 23–29.

160. Stevan L. Davies, *The Revolt of the Widows: The Social World of the Apocryphal Acts* (Carbondale: Southern Illinois University Press: 1980), p. 36.

161. Fuchs, *Rebellious Prophets*, pp. 55.

162. Gerd Theissen, "The Wandering Radicals," in Theissen, *Social Reality and the Earliest Christians* (Minneapolis: Fortress Press, 1992), 33–59.

163. M. Eugene Boring, *Sayings of the Risen Jesus: Christian Prophecy in the Synoptic Tradition*. Society for New Testament Studies Monograph Series 46. (NY: Cambridge University Press, 1982).

164. Jonathan D. Spence, *God's Chinese Son: The Taiping Heavenly Kingdom of Hong Xiuquan* (W.W. Norton & Company, 1997), 147.

165. Fuchs, *Rebellious Prophets*, pp. 33, 154, 188, 197, 262; Worsley, pp. 24, 118.

166. Geza Vermes, *Jesus the Jew*, 139–140. See also Leibel Reznick, *The Mystery of Bar Kochba: An Historical and Theological Investigation of the Last King of the Jews* (Northvale, NJ: Jason Aronson Inc., 1996), pp. 130–131; 145–146.

167. Class instruction, Spring 1992.

168. Nassour, *Rock Opera*, p. 38.

169. *The Jewish War*, II, 183. Trans. G.A. Williamson (Baltimore: Penguin, 1959, 1978), p. 130–131.

170. *The Works of Philo*. Trans. C.D. Yonge (Peabody: Hendrickson Publishers, 1983).

171. *The Jewish War*, VI, 302, 21. Trans. G.A. Williamson (Baltimore: Penguin, 1959, 1978), pp. 349–350.

172. Hugh J. Schonfield, *The Passover Plot: New Light on the History of Jesus* (NY: Bernard Geiss Associates, 1965).

173. Paul Tillich, "The Theologian." In Tillich, *The Shaking of the Foundations* (NY: Scribners, 1948), pp. 118–129.

174. Joachim Jeremias, *The Parables of Jesus* (NY: Scribners, 2nd rev. ed., 1972), pp. 17–18); Archibald M. Hunter, *Interpreting the Parables* (Philadelphia: Westminster Press, 1960), Appendix 1, "The Problem of Mark 4:11–13," pp. 110–112). Both men also suggest that perhaps Mark has put the saying in the wrong place, and that originally it had nothing to say about the parables, which would be mighty handy.

175. Jonathan Culler, *Structuralist Poetics: Structuralism, Linguistics, and the Study of Literature* (Ithaca: Cornell University Press, 1975), Chapter 7, "Convention and Naturalization," pp. 131–160.

176. Albert Schweitzer, *The Quest of the Historical Jesus: A Critical Study of its Progress from Reimarus to Wrede.* Trans. W. Montgomery (1910; rpt. NY: Macmillan, 1950), p. 399.

177. Ibid., p. 403.

178. Nassour, *Rock Opera*, p. 210.

179. Ibid., p. 38.

180. Ibid., p. 22.

181. Paul Tillich, *Systematic Theology. Vol. II. Existence and the Christ* (Chicago: University of Chicago Press, 1957), p. 123.

182. Nassour, *Rock Opera*, p. 37.

183. Malcolm Muggeridge, *Christ and the Media.* London Lectures in Contemporary Christianity (London: Hodder & Stoughton, 1977).

184. Nassour, *Rock Opera*, p. 191.

ABOUT THE AUTHOR

Robert M. Price is a freethought advocate who has written on many subjects in many venues, and for many years. He has been at various times an agnostic, an exponent of Liberal Protestant theology, a non-theist, a secular humanist, a religious humanist, a Unitarian-Universalist wannabe, an unaffiliated Universalist, and a Fellow of the Jesus Seminar. Any way you cut it, his name is Legion. Not your typical atheist, Price continues to love the various great religions as endlessly fascinating creations/expressions of the human spirit. He loves theology, too. He hosts *The Bible Geek* and *The Human Bible* podcasts, and indeed the Bible is his main focus of interest. He is the author of numerous books, including *Jesus Christ Superstition*, *Beyond Born Again*, *Deconstructing Jesus*, and *Inerrant the Wind*. He is the founder and editor of the *Journal of Higher Criticism* and has debated William Lane Craig, Bart Ehrman, Craig Blomberg, and others. He lives in North Carolina.